To: Kimberly
With love,
Dad

Advocacy and Taxation in Canada

Advocacy & Taxation in Canada

Edited by David W. Chodikoff & James L. Horvath

Deloitte.

IRWIN LAW

Published in 2004 by

Irwin Law
347 Bay Street
Suite 501
Toronto, Ontario
M5H 2R7

www.irwinlaw.com

ISBN: 1-55221-093-6

Library and Archives Canada Cataloguing in Publication

Advocacy & taxation in Canada / edited by David W. Chodikoff and James L. Horvath.

Co-published by Deloitte.
Includes bibliographical references.
ISBN 1-55221-093-6

1. Tax courts—Canada. 2. Tax protests and appeals—Canada. 3. Taxation—Law and legislation—Canada. I. Chodikoff, David Wallen II. Horvath, James L. (James Leslie), 1947– III. Deloitte (Firm) IV. Title: Advocacy and taxation in Canada.

KE5717.A78 2004 343.7104 C2004-906043-0
KF6334.ZA2A38 2004

The publisher acknowledges the financial support of the Government of Canada through the Book Publishing Industry Development Program (BPIDP) for its publishing activities.

Printed and bound in Canada.

1 2 3 4 5 08 07 06 05 04

Contents

Foreword

A popular belief of many lawyers and lay persons is that taxation is a field for specialists only and generalists need not apply. This view is both correct and incorrect. Nowadays, it is inconceivable to be a part-time tax practitioner and be successful. The nature of tax law requires constant attention and commitment to a field in which developments are fast-moving and of significant importance. Thus, the opinion that taxation is a paradigm subject for specialization is correct in the sense that it demands full immersion in the subject.

But the specialist tag is incorrect unless one views taxation as a huge monolith unto itself, unrelated to other fields of law and commercial or human activity. The reality is that taxation, if not omnipresent, shows up in many areas of the law and of commerce and builds on these areas. In fact, these related fields have a considerable relevance to, and impact on taxation matters.

It is against that backdrop that I find this work on Advocacy and Taxation in Canada of particular interest and importance. The book's theme of advocacy and taxation illustrates both the pervasive nature of taxation and at the same time how the role of advocacy plays out in taxation issues and disputes.

I recall that one of Canada's most distinguished advocates, the late John Robinette, Q.C., stated that common sense was of central importance to advocacy. As usual, he was right. Of course, there are many other ingredients that are a part of what constitutes effective advocacy, both oral and written, and volumes have been written on the subject. This book adds considerable value to the literature on both advocacy and taxation.

More specifically, Part I of this book blends informative and insightful commentary on advocacy and taxation and cleverly combines a variety of topics on advocacy through the viewpoints of judges and practitioners. Special treatment is given to appellate advocacy in the first section of Part I and then to trial advocacy in the second section of Part I. This approach is appropriate because of the different considerations at play in the trial stage as compared to the appellate level. In appellate courts the role of legal arguments plays a more prominent role compared to that of fact determination at the trial level. Emphasis is also given to the importance of proper preparation, planning, and strategy along with helpful suggestions and pitfalls to avoid. The third section of Part I helpfully deals with special features of taxation litigation, namely, the role of experts and business valuation in tax disputes.

Part II deals with important and emerging substantive taxations issues such as interest deductibility, GAAR, aspects of international tax disputes, tax litigation in the new economy, Aboriginal tax issues, GST matters, indirect tax in the new economy, and derivatives.

As someone who has toiled in the appellate fields of taxation disputes for many years, I find this book to be a most valuable resource. The collection of authors includes eminent and talented jurists, practitioners from the public and private sectors, and academics, and this, along with their focus on present and future developments, makes for a most successful product. Indeed, the twenty-four chapters from the thirty contributors will be of great value to judges, practitioners, policy makers, students, and others who have an interest in taxation.

I wish to thank and congratulate all the authors for sharing their views and insights and for their efforts in joining this collaborative enterprise. It is without any doubt an outstanding contribution to the subject.

Lastly, I wish to commend the co-editors for their magnificent effort in nurturing this book from a concept to a reality. All of us who read or consult the book will be greatly edified and for that we sincerely thank all the contributors and editors.

Frank Iacobucci
Ottawa
August 2004

Preface

This book has been in the making for four years. In 2000, I commenced a tax litigation lunchtime speakers series at the Department of Justice, Ontario Regional Office in Toronto. The idea was pretty simple. I invited interesting and prominent people to visit at lunch and speak to the lawyers and staff of the Tax Law section. The guest, or sometimes guests, would be asked in advance to speak about an area of interest. The subject range was quite broad — the talk could be about advocacy before the Courts or on a topic related to tax law. The approach to the lunchtime engagement was determined by the speaker. Some events were formal — the speaker gave a speech typically followed by a question and answer session. Other events were less formal including roundtable discussions. However, there were two things that all of our guests had in common: first, each individual is a recognized leader in his or her chosen field; and second, each guest's work has some relationship to either advocacy and/or the field of taxation.

Over the course of two years, we had 16 speakers. In fact, it was at one of these events that Jim Horvath and I met. Subsequently, Jim appeared as a valuations expert in a tax case where I acted as lead trial counsel for the Minister of National Revenue.

At the end of 2002, I was getting ready for an assignment to the Federal Prosecution Service. Since I ran the speakers series, I knew that as a consequence of my departure the lunchtime speakers series would in all likelihood come to an end. I was discussing the program's fate with my friend and colleague, Harry Erlichman. I said to Harry that it was too bad we did not collect the wonderful thoughts and ideas conveyed at each of these lunchtime sessions and publish them in a book. Truly, some of our guests are brilliant. What a lost opportunity! After that conversation, Harry left my office. Within 15 minutes, he returned. He handed me a small piece of paper with a telephone number and name written on it. The name was Jeff Miller. Harry explained that Jeffrey of Irwin Law was the publisher of his book: *Tax Avoidance in Canada*. Harry said that I should give him a ring.

Immediately, I contacted Jeff. I pitched the idea for the book project. He responded positively. By the middle of January 2003, I was able to obtain the commitment from all of our speakers to participate in this project.

I realized fairly quickly that this book project was indeed a unique opportunity and I wanted to build upon it. My working relationship with Deloitte and Jim, in particular, led me to believe that I should discuss the broadening of the book's content and appeal with Jim.

By March 2003, Jim and I were working closely together to bring about a much-expanded original concept to fruition. Over the course of the next year and half that is what we attempted to do. And now our combined efforts are before you, the reader.

David W. Chodikoff

* * *

The book you are about to read is divided into two parts. The first part is further subdivided into three sections. Section One deals with appellate advocacy. The lead chapter is written by the Honourable Mr. Justice John I. Laskin of the Ontario Court of Appeal. An opinion that is shared by many across Canada is that Justice Laskin is the preeminent judicial educator on writing facta. We share his view. Moreover, we believe that you, the reader, will reach the same conclusion. An appeal from the Tax Court proceeds to the Federal Court of Canada. There are quite a few cases that are heard by this Court. That is why we are so pleased to have the contribution from the Honourable Mr. Justice Rothstein. As a veteran judge of the appellate court, Justice Rothstein is well placed to give guidance to both the young and experienced lawyers on advocacy in the Federal Court of Appeal. Rounding out the appellate advocacy section are chapters by William Innes and Harry Erlichman. Both writers offer very different and compelling perspectives on the litigation process at the appellate level.

Section Two of Part One starts off with a chapter written by two of Canada's leading civil litigators: Alan J. Lenczner and Peter H. Griffin. They offer strategic advice on preparing for trial. The chapter that follows is written by the Associate Chief Justice of the Tax Court of Canada, the

Honourable Mr. Justice Bowman. Entitled "Good Trial Practices in the Tax Court of Canada," Justice Bowman's chapter delivers a succinct, entertaining and pointed primer on how good counsel should prepare and conduct an appeal before the Tax Court of Canada.

Cliff Rand has been a successful tax litigator for over a decade. He knows what it takes to win a case before the Tax Court of Canada. He has won quite a few. In a delivery that is written in clean and direct language, Cliff's chapter outlines a basic approach to tax litigation from the appellant's perspective. The chapter that follows is written by David Chodikoff. Offering a Crown perspective, the chapter highlights many of the key Tax Court of Canada Rules that apply to the tax litigation process. It also gives the reader some important and practical tips on examination-in-chief, cross-examination and the presentation of argument before the Tax Court.

The next chapter is written by Ross Oake. It is a witness primer. Having testified many times as an RCMP officer, Ross knows a thing or two about preparing for the in-court experience. In sharing his views, he answers some of the fundamental issues in witness preparation. The last two chapters of Section Two deal with two different forms of tax litigation. Robert Goldstein takes the reader on a practical tour of a criminal tax prosecution. While Robert McMechan offers the reader insight into the conduct of a transfer-pricing case.

Section Three of Part One focuses upon experts and business valuations. It is common in civil tax disputes that experts are called to testify. And business valuation is a key area that necessitates the views of experts. This section commences with a superb analysis by Alan Schwartz and Edward Yanoshita on the current state of the law with respect to the use of expert witnesses in tax litigation. This is followed by two experts recounting their respective courtroom experiences. Jim Horvath and Steve Hacker provide an analysis of the expert's role in the Tax Court. This is followed by an American expert's perspective on the role of an expert in the Tax Court. Robert Pardo offers the reader a rare glimpse into the mind of a first time expert and the thoughts that such a person experiences. The last two chapters in this section deal with business valuation and problems of valuing intellectual property such as computer software. Howard Johnson delivers a fully understandable analysis of the litigious elements of business valuation. This is followed by a second chapter written by Jim Horvath and Steve Hacker. They examine the concepts, complexities and controversies surrounding the valuation of intellectual property.

Part Two of this book consists of eight chapters. All focus on substantive tax issues. The lead chapter is written by Professor David Duff. He provides an analysis of recent Supreme Court of Canada decisions on interest deductibility and the reasonable expectation of profit test. GAAR stands for the General Anti-Avoidance Rule. Professor Sandler presents a critical analysis of recent GAAR decisions by the Supreme Court of Canada. If you are involved in matters of international tax then it is likely that you have heard the term: Competent Authority. In their chapter, Sandra Goldberg and Gary Zed provide a framework for the understanding of the Competent Authority as a dispute resolution tool. Following the Goldberg/Zed chapter, Professor Cockfield discusses Tax Litigation in the New Economy. In their chapter, Lara Friedlander and Andrew Auerbach describe the fundamentals of income taxation of derivatives. By now everyone had heard of the Goods and Services Tax (GST). However, not everyone is familiar with or in fact understands the general principles of the GST. In their chapter, Blake Murray and Sean Aylward give the reader the basics of the GST. Following the Murray/Aylward chapter, Jim Vincze and Craig Robertson offer their collective cutting edge insights into the challenges for indirect tax in the new economy and the potential areas of tax litigation issues. The final chapter, written by Milan Legris, addresses tax issues of particular relevance to the Native community.

Whether you read some selected chapters or the entire book, we are sure that you will find the material both stimulating and informative.

David W. Chodikoff *James L. Horvath*

September 2004

Acknowledgments

We would like to thank and acknowledge the authors who made this book possible through their collaborative efforts, contributions, and suggestions. We also give special thanks to our enthusiastic supporting team: Joanne Tucciarone-Gentile, our book project coordinator; Tiffany Pegg, assistant book project coordinator, Kathryn Philpott, proof reader, and Steven Hacker for ensuring our continued progress through their diligent efforts at assisting Joanne and the two of us; Dr. Eric Myles, for his thorough and painstaking proof-reading and insightful editorial suggestions; Heather Raven of Irwin Law for production management; Wendy Dalkin for skillfully designing the dust jacket and book cover; and Jeffrey Miller for his encouragement and support for this project. Our thanks also go to our many friends and colleagues for their friendly advice, motivating comments, and encouragement throughout the project; your day-to-day comments have in many ways added to the richness of this book. To all of you, many, many thanks for your time and efforts.

Dedication

On Sunday, August 24, 2004, my aunt passed away. She died of cancer. It was not her first battle with this disease. Years earlier, my aunt fought and won against breast cancer. This time, it was different.

It is at times like these that you think about the "bigger picture." My eldest brother, Mark, and I spoke about our own lives and loss. You see-my father died of cancer at the age of 37. At age 32, my mother Beverley, was widowed and left to raise three boys aged 7, 9 and 13 by herself. Mark and I spoke about cancer on that Tuesday and how it changed all of our lives forever. We thought about how different life would have been had our father lived. But, this was not to be.

My mother, brothers (Mark and Richard) and I carried on after dad passed away. And over the years, we have all tried to make the most of our lives. We know how precious life is and what is truly important.

David Chodikoff

During the completion of this project, my thoughts were frequently with family members who have been touched by cancer. I dedicate this book to my father Eugene, brother Ed, and sister-in-law Julie, who are all currently undergoing treatment for cancer, and whose determination continue to inspire me, and to my mother Jeanette and sister Janet, who always lend their generous loving support. I also dedicate my efforts to the loving memory of my four wonderful grandparents, Paul and Elizabeth Horvath, George and Martha Szabo, two of whom also lived with cancer.

Jim Horvath

That is why we are so proud of the contributors to this project. Without hesitation every writer agreed immediately that the contributors' portion of the royalties would go to the Canadian Cancer Society. Everyone knows the consequences of cancer. You may die from it; you may survive it; but there is no doubt that it causes great pain and suffering for all those that come into contact with it. It is important that we all stand together as a community, united in the fight against this dreaded disease. This gesture on the part of the contributors is a reflection of their individual commitment to this fight.

On behalf of the contributors, and both of us, this book is dedicated most of all to those that continue their fight against cancer and those that survive the ravages of this disease.

David and Jim

Part One: Advocacy

Chapter 1

How to Write a Persuasive Factum: A Judge's View*

Hon. John I. Laskin

I begin with a caveat. I did not practise tax law, and in our court we hear very few tax appeals. So, this paper was not written for tax litigators. Instead, it is a general piece on factum writing. However, because the key principles of persuasive written advocacy embrace all areas of law, I hope that the tax bar will find my suggestions useful.

I have divided this paper into three parts. I begin with a discussion of how I use factums and what I look for in a factum. Next, I offer twelve suggestions on how to write a persuasive factum. Finally, I look at factums from the opposite perspective, by listing twelve things that I do not like to see in a factum.

A. THE USES AND QUALITIES OF A GOOD FACTUM

Effective advocacy today differs from what it was 25, 15 or even 10 years ago. One reason for the difference is the increased importance of written argument, of the factum.[1] In our court, the factum often influences the result more than oral argument. Even on motions in the trial court or on summary conviction appeals to a Superior Court, the factum is a powerful weapon

---

* I am indebted to my law clerk, Leigh Salsberg, for her excellent edit of this paper.

1 I discuss the reasons for the change in my earlier article "Forget the Windup and Make the Pitch," The Advocates' Society Journal, Vol. 18 No. 2, p. 3 (Summer, 1999).

in the advocate's arsenal. Moreover, if you work hard on your factum and produce a persuasive written argument, you will find preparation of your oral argument much easier.

The basic techniques of good written advocacy are the same whether you act for the Crown or a private litigant. But Crown factums may have to be written a little differently for at least two reasons. First, the court sometimes expects more from a Crown than from a private litigant. Second, the Crown is usually a respondent. Our factum rules are less friendly to respondents than to appellants (or applicants), especially in their requirements for dealing with the facts. Throughout this paper I will discuss some of the different considerations that apply to a respondent's factum.

Over the years legal writing has borne the brunt of much criticism. Will Rogers once remarked, "Whenever I read something I cannot understand, I know it was written by a lawyer." Yale law professor Fred Rodell commented, "There are two things wrong with almost all legal writing. One is its style. The other is its content."[2] I believe this criticism is overstated. On the whole, the factums that I see are well-written, sometimes exceptionally well-written.

Still, no matter how well we write, we can still improve our writing. I hope that this paper will inspire you to try to improve your writing; to realize that, though what you say is obviously important, so too is how you say it. Content cannot be divorced from language and style. Writing a factum is an exercise in persuasion. And language and style persuade. You must persuade the readers of your factum of the logic, the correctness, the fairness of your position. Turgid prose detracts from a strong legal point, from the clarity and persuasiveness of your logic.

Trying to write well is hard work. At least it is hard work for me. It does not come easily. Moreover, writing concisely is much harder than writing at length. Legal writing is difficult because what we write about is usually complicated. And all of us have time constraints — too much to do, and too little time in which to do it. But finding time to write well is worth it. You will better serve your clients and you will enhance your reputation as an advocate. Always remember Samuel Johnson's words: "What is written without effort is in general read without pleasure."[3]

To write well you have to think about your readers. This seems obvious, but many professional writers do not think about their readers when they

---

2 "Goodbye to Law Reviews," 23 Virginia L. Rev. 38 (1936).

3 Quoted in Paula LaRocque, *The Book on Writing* (Oak Park, Ill.: Marion Street Press Inc., 2003) at 86.

write. Their prose is writer-based, not reader-based. Moreover, writers tend not to be very good readers of their own writing. Often they are too immersed in what they are writing to realize that what seems perfectly clear to them is not as clear to their readers. So, you need to think about the readability of your factums.

In order to do that, you need to consider the audience for whom you are writing. The advocate's primary audience is the judge. Before you write your next factum, mentally trade places with the judge. If you were a judge, how would you use a factum? What would you want in a factum?

In our court my colleagues and I use factums in at least seven different ways:[4]

1. A factum gives appellate judges their first taste of the case. Judges read your factum when their minds are most open to persuasion. When I prepare for an appeal, a factum literally speaks to me first because I read each side's overview paragraph, if not the entire factum, before I read the trial judge's reasons or the charge to the jury. I want to know what counsel think the debate is about before I review what the trial judge did. Together, the two factums structure the debate for me. Because the factum speaks first, it can have a powerful influence on a judge's thinking. In most cases, by the time of oral argument a judge has at least a tentative opinion on the outcome. The message for counsel is obvious: do not squander this opportunity to persuade.
2. A good factum helps the court better prepare for the case. The factum signals what to read before the hearing. It should tell us the key pieces of evidence and the important case law.
3. The factum provides a roadmap of your oral argument. If you have written a clear, well-organized factum, we will be able to follow your oral argument more easily.
4. A good factum allows the court to engage you in a sophisticated oral argument. If your factum has effectively set out your basic position, your oral presentation can focus on filling out that position, answering the court's concerns and discussing the implications of your argument.
5. A judge will use a good factum to question opposing counsel on their arguments and to probe weaknesses in the other side's position.
6. A good factum is a ready resource for a judge giving a short oral decision. In our court, many of our decisions are given by an oral endorse-

4 David Lepofsky also discusses the uses of a factum in his excellent article, "The Unsung Art of Written Advocacy," The Advocates' Society Journal, vol. 23, No. 1, p. 10 (Summer, 2004).

ment immediately after argument. These endorsements frequently rely on the successful party's factum.

7. A factum not only speaks to a judge first, it often speaks last. When the court reserves judgment, the factum remains a "silent advocate" for your position. I often make heavy use of a good factum when I write reasons.

What does a judge want in a factum? Here is a list of seven qualities that I look for:

1. A factum that is clear. "I see but one rule: to be clear. If I am not clear, all my world crumbles to nothing."[5] The factum should be easy to read and understand. Readers should know what you are saying and where you are going. Clarity is a prized attribute of a good factum.
2. A factum that focuses on the controlling issue or issues and provides a simple statement of your position on each issue. Concentrate on the key questions the court has to decide. Do not clutter your factum with weak arguments.
3. A factum that simplifies the case. A judge can never know the case as well as you do. Uncomplicate it for us. Scale down the complexity that we have to deal with. Remember we have a lot to read and your case is only one of many on our plate. You need to distil, simplify and simplify some more. Simplicity is powerfully persuasive, a key to effective written advocacy.
4. A factum that takes a reasonable position. One of the best ways to persuade is to be (or seem to be) reasonable.
5. A factum that is fair. A judge looks for a factum that is fair to the factual record and the law. A factum should state your position persuasively without overstating it.
6. A factum that is concise. Conciseness is a relative term. Obviously some cases require longer factums than others. But conciseness adds to the persuasiveness of your written argument. Most factums are too long. Why? Time and fear are the main culprits. We don't take time to write a shorter factum, and we are afraid to leave anything out. Effective advocacy demands the courage of selection. You have to have the confidence to limit what you write. Resist the temptation to fill up the court's page limit in every case. A judge rarely complains that a factum is too short. Often, less is more.
7. A factum that is interesting. I know of no rule that requires lawyers to write dull factums. Lawyers are in the persuasion business. Try to write

---

5 Henri Stendahl, Reply to Balzac (1840), in *Bartlett's Familiar Quotations* (Fifteenth and 125th Anniversary Edition) at 453.

lively prose — prose that makes your case come alive for the court. Judges have a lot to read and short attention spans. Try to keep our attention by being interesting.

These, then, are my seven goals of a good factum. How do advocates go about writing a factum that achieves them? Here are my suggestions.

B. A DOZEN SUGGESTIONS FOR WRITING A GOOD FACTUM

1. Think and Plan Before You Write

Putting pen to paper to write your factum should come late in the writing process. Thinking comes first — whether at your desk, in the shower or walking your dog — because clear writing comes from clear thinking. Develop a theory of your case, and perhaps more important, an underlying theme. Ask yourself these two simple questions: "What is the case really about?" and "Why should I win?" The answer to these questions should give you your theory of the case and your theme. And that theory and that theme should permeate your entire factum.

Make sure that your theory and theme have a factual foundation. Jot down ideas about them and about the supporting facts. Then do some preparatory work before you write. Before I draft reasons for judgment, I prepare an outline, including headings and, under each heading, a list of points that I want to make. I believe strongly in the value of an outline. Something else may work better for you. But plan before you write.[6]

2. Write an Introduction or Overview

Whether the applicable factum rules call for it or not, write an introduction or overview.[7] Use the overview to tell the court in a nutshell what the case is all about and what your position is. In most cases, aim for a page or less.

The overview is probably the most important part of the factum. It reflects a fundamental principle of clear and persuasive writing: give the

---

6 See Bryan A. Garner, *The Winning Brief* (New York: Oxford University Press, 1999) Tip 1. Garner and his colleague Betty Flowers suggest breaking down the writing process into four steps, which they label "madman — architect — carpenter — judge." The "madman" jots down ideas and approaches to the case; the "architect" prepares an outline; the "carpenter" writes the first draft; and the "judge" improves and edits the draft.

7 In the Ontario Court of Appeal the factum rules now require both the appellant and the respondent to write a "concise overview statement." See Rules 61.11 and 61.12.

context before the details.[8] Why is this principle important? Cognitive psychologists tell us that we absorb and remember information better if we first know why it matters, how it is relevant. Moreover, because judges have short attention spans and a lot to read, advocates need to get to us and get to us quickly. A good overview helps you do so.

Thus, an overview turns the judge into a smart reader of the rest of your factum. The overview gives the judge a roadmap of what is to come. It lends predictability to the rest of your factum. It focuses the debate. When your spouse or partner (preferably not a lawyer!) asks you what case you are working on, your 30 second response is probably a good overview.

Your overview should contain at least these ingredients: a precise statement of the controlling issue or issues; enough facts to provide some context for these issues; your position on the issues; and if needed, a procedural history of the case. I will now elaborate on these ingredients.

In your overview, you should identify and characterize for the court the controlling issue or issues in the case. On appeal, rarely are there more than two or three key issues. Get to the heart of the case. Figure out the issue or issues that will decide the case then frame them in the best possible way. Remember that getting the right answer depends on asking the right question.

Frame the issue precisely, to make what follows clear to the judge. On a *Stinchcombe* motion, writing that the issue is whether the Crown breached its duty of disclosure is not nearly as helpful as writing that the issue is whether the Crown breached its duty of disclosure because it did not give the defence an internal audit report. Adding the "because" helps to define the issue more precisely.

The respondent need not accept the applicant's or the appellant's characterization of the issues. For example, on an appeal, the appellant may say that the issue is whether the trial judge erred in admitting evidence under s. 24(2) of the *Charter*. However, the respondent should take into account the standard of review and say that the issue is whether, in admitting the evidence, the trial judge exercised his or her discretion unreasonably.

The overview is where you should begin to persuade the judge that you have the fair and correct position. In your overview, you should put forward your basic theory of the case. You should also develop your underlying theme, even if you do not expressly state it. Typically, your theme will focus on the fairness and reasonableness of your position. For example, in most

8 See Stephen V. Armstrong and Timothy P. Terrell: *Thinking Like a Writer*, 2d ed. (New York: Practising Law Institute, 2003) at chapters 2, 3 and 7.

criminal appeals, the bottom-line question is whether the accused had a fair trial or whether the conviction was supported by the evidence. If you are acting for the Crown, your overview should support your position on these questions. Embellish your statement of the issues with enough facts to give them context and to bring out the fairness and reasonableness of your argument. If needed, include a brief procedural history of how the case got to the court.

The overview can serve another function for the respondent. This function arises out of our factum rules, which typically require the respondent to state which parts of the appellant's or applicant's statement of facts it accepts and which parts it does not. Of course, the appellant has put his or her own gloss on the facts. Although, as respondent's counsel, you may not "disagree" with the appellant's statement, you probably do not like its spin. You are then faced with the unpalatable choice of rewriting the facts or nit-picking with the appellant's statement, neither of which judges like. You can solve this dilemma by using the overview to get your spin across. (Alternatively, you can put some of the facts on which you rely in the argument section of your factum.)

Write your overview in everyday language. Get rid of the legal jargon. Appeal to the human being in the judge.

Finally, having written a good overview, make sure that you follow it. If you have identified two key issues in the case, make sure you discuss those two issues later in the factum, and frame them precisely as you did in the overview.

3. Write Point First (or Give the Context Before the Details)

Lawyers tend to begin with the details of their argument and build to their conclusion. In other words, they tend to write point last. Cognitive psychologists tell us that we have it backwards. We should begin with our conclusion, our point, or at least a context sentence or two. Why? Again, because readers will better remember and absorb the details when they first know the point of the details. So, write point first throughout your factum. Or, as I sometimes put it, write like a journalist, not like a mystery novelist.[9]

Point first writing is far clearer, far easier to follow and understand. It prevents the judge from notionally asking the advocate, "Why are you

---

9 Lawyers can learn from journalists. Journalists use the "lead" to grab their readers. See Tom Goldstein and Jethro K. Lieberman, *The Lawyer's Guide to Writing Well* (Berkeley: University of California Press, 1989) c. 8.

telling me this?" Readers never read passively. They are always looking for the context, trying to make sense of what they are reading. So you must give them that context. Point first writing is one of the most important ways that you can achieve clarity in your factums.[10]

In suggesting that lawyers tend to write point last, I do not suggest that they do not worry about clarity. They do. But they worry mainly about the substantive clarity of their arguments. To the reader, however, another kind of clarity is just as critical: cognitive clarity. It is cognitive clarity that comes from point first writing.[11]

Beginning with your conclusion or your point is important in the law section of your factum. Your conclusion or your point is your submission to the court. State what your submission is before you elaborate on it. And elaborate on it by setting out your argument, by applying the relevant law to the material facts. Do so even if the applicable factum rules do not expressly provide for argument. A concise argument is more helpful to the court than a bland statement of the law.

But where point first writing is especially important is in the facts section of your factum. It is in the statement of the facts that context really matters. Facts have no meaning apart from their context. So, when you are about to dump a lot of factual detail on the judge, begin with the point of the detail, or first give the context. Often all that is required is moving a sentence or two from the end of the paragraph to the beginning. For example, begin a paragraph with "The three hand writing experts each testified that Jones' signature on the tax return was a forgery" before you discuss the details of their expert evidence.

Headings are a form of point first writing. Use headings in both the facts and the law section. Here, I do not mean generic headings (introduction, facts, etc.) but case specific headings. Make your headings informative. In the facts section, try, for example, "The evidence showing the accused had a motive" or "The expert appraisal evidence." In the argument section, the question form of a heading can be effective: "Did the trial judge exercise his discretion unreasonably in admitting similar fact evidence?" or "Is the sentence demonstrably unfit?" The rhetorical form of a heading can also be effective: "The trial judge properly assessed the value of the property" or "The sentence imposed reflects no error in principle."

---

10 See Joseph M. Williams, *Style: Toward Clarity and Grace* (Chicago: University of Chicago Press, 1990) chapter 6. This is a superb book on professional writing. In it Williams stresses the importance of "point-early" documents.

11 Armstrong and Terrell, above note 8 at c. 2.

4. Make Your Organization Effective

Effective organization is another key to the clarity of your factum. Poor organization detracts from the clarity and persuasiveness of your writing. Where organization matters most is in stating the facts. You may not be able to change the facts, but you can control how they are presented.

I suggest that you let the issues drive your organization of the facts. Organize your telling of the facts around the issues in the case. An issue-driven organization makes your factum more coherent, more logical and easier to follow.

In stating the facts you are telling a story. Storytelling is an essential skill for advocates.[12] It is how you persuade. Judges know something of the law. They usually know little about the facts of your case. And the facts make your case interesting. But you have to decide what story to tell and how to tell it. Our natural instinct is to tell the story chronologically, but few stories actually begin at the beginning. A chronological telling can work, but usually the facts are more persuasive if they are organized around the issues in the case, or around your theme, or around topics that best bring out your side of the argument. Beware of telling the story witness by witness. This is a lazy telling of the story and almost always ineffective.

How you organize the facts also has a bearing on how concisely you write. Typically, you are presented with a mass of factual material. Your job is to distil and organize the mass. If you organize the facts around the issues, you will likely write a more concise factum than if you state the facts chronologically. If you do tell the story chronologically, edit ruthlessly.

No matter how you write the facts, you will be faced with a tension between thoroughness and conciseness. Everyone has a natural tendency to worry about leaving something out. But do not be afraid to be selective. Consider whether you need all the detail and whether the judge can really absorb it all. Make sure that every fact you include has a purpose. Cut out what you do not need.

This advice also applies to the respondent's factum. Consider whether you need to dispute every fact in the applicant's or appellant's factum with which you disagree. Some facts may be so unimportant that you can leave them alone. Focus on those facts that are critical to your position. Address your version of the facts in your overview, in a brief statement in the facts section, or in the argument section of your factum.

---

12 See Steven D. Stark, *Writing to Win* (New York: Doubleday, 2000) at 93 ff, on storytelling in writing the facts.

In the argument section, your organization should track the issues in the case. As applicant or appellant, begin with your strongest point unless you have a good reason for doing otherwise. One reason might be logical presentation. For example, if the court's jurisdiction is an issue in the case, you may wish to begin with that even though it is not your strongest point.

As respondent, you need not respond to the issues in the order that your opponent has listed them, though the court usually can follow your argument more easily if you do so. But, for example, if you believe one issue is decisive of the outcome, begin with it regardless of where it is found in your opponent's factum.

Some factums make the mistake of unnecessarily subdividing issues. These factums give the impression that the party's argument is more complex than it actually is. If you see such a factum, you can score points with the court by showing that your opponent's three issues are, in reality, only one issue. Always strive for simplicity. From the judge's perspective, the simpler the better.

Finally, you should not only organize your factum effectively, you should make your organization visible and explicit to the reader. An explicit organization is easier to follow. You can make your organization explicit and visible by using:

(i) **Headings.** For example, in the law part of your factum separate the issues and give each one a heading: first issue — Did Revenue Canada's seizure infringe the appellant's s. 8 rights . . . , second issue . . . etc.;
(ii) **Point first or context sentences.** For example, "This motion concerns the admissibility of business records seized from the taxpayer's home office." Identify the records and the seizure, then discuss them; and
(iii) **Internal roadmaps.** For example, "The Crown submits that the seizure of the records did not amount to a search under s. 8 of the *Charter* for three main reasons." List the reasons and then discuss each one. A word of caution: road-mapping is effective in moderation; do not overdo it.

Where appropriate, separate the disputed facts from the undisputed facts and admissions. This makes the judge's task easier.

5. Give Your Facts the Right Spin

Just as important as effectively organizing the facts is giving the facts the right spin. Judges want to do justice in each case they hear. They are highly influenced by their view of the equities of a case. Thus, the facts matter a lot, usually far more than the law. The facts section is the hardest part of the factum to write, but usually it is the most critical part. It is where most cases are won and lost. Indeed, I think precedent is overrated in our legal culture. It is the facts that persuade, not precedent. What judges believe to be a fair result usually turns on how they see the facts.[13]

In saying this, I do not suggest that judges do what they want to do regardless of the law. The facts must be anchored in a governing set of legal principles or standards. You must argue the facts in the context of these principles or standards. But these standards, whether statutory or judge-made, are often stated in broad terms: reasonable, relevant, material, in the interests of justice, etc. These broad standards give judges a lot of leeway to apply the facts to achieve a fair result. There is a lot of play in the joints.

Even on appeal, though we give deference to a trial judge's findings of fact and credibility, many facts are still in play. Even those that are the subject of findings can be put in a different light. The good appellate advocates recognize the critical importance of the facts to the outcome of an appeal.

As I said earlier, in setting out the facts, you are telling a story. Indeed, on one level a lawsuit is simply a clash of competing stories. The best advocates present the facts in a way that shows they have the better story. In their presentation of the facts, they show the justice or fairness of their position. In short, they show that their side has the moral high ground. You must be faithful to the record and you must apply the relevant legal principles. Within these parameters, how you characterize the facts is crucial to successful advocacy. If you set out the facts persuasively, often your argument on the law will be brief.

I add, however, this word of caution: Although you are trying to give your case the right spin, do not ignore facts unfavourable to your position. Manage bad facts, but do not avoid them. You can manage bad facts by explaining them, qualifying them with good facts or de-emphasizing them with your choice of language and sentence structure. Confronting the facts against you shows the court your candour and enhances your credibility. Managing bad facts is one of the hallmarks of a skilful advocate.

I end this section with one further point about storytelling. Telling your story coherently — making your account flow — increases its persuasiveness. When we think of making our prose flow better we immediately think of transitions. The English language is full of them: moreover, however, also, additionally, but, first, second, etc. In moderation, transitions can effectively increase the coherence of your writing.

---

13 Stark, above note 12, makes the same point. See pp. 67–71. See also Karl N. Llewellyn, *The Common Law Tradition: Deciding Appeals* (Boston: Little, Brown, 1960).

But other, more subtle techniques are perhaps even more effective. Organize your paragraphs around a single topic, concept, principle or idea. Emphasize this unifying idea by the wise repetition of it. At the sentence level, save your most important information for the beginning and end of each sentence: try to put new information at the end of a sentence, and link it up to the beginning of the next sentence.

These techniques cannot be learned overnight. They require constant practice. And a detailed discussion of them is beyond the scope of this paper. For those who would like to know more about them (and indeed more about all aspects of persuasive writing) I recommend three books: my favourite book on professional writing, Joseph Williams, *Style: Toward Clarity and Grace*[14]; and my two favourite books on legal writing, Stephen Armstrong and Timothy Terrell, *Thinking Like a Writer* (2d ed)[15], and Steven Stark, *Writing to Win.*[16]

6. Use Lists and Charts, and Quote Selectively From the Evidence and Case Law

You want to make your factum interesting. You want to give it a human dimension. You want to get the judge's attention. You want to make it easier for the judge to grasp what you are saying. How can you do all of these things? You have a variety of techniques available.

(i) **Use lists.** For example, if you are trying to support a trial judge's finding of fact, submit that the finding is supported by the evidence, which you then list as (a) (b) (c) or (i) (ii) (iii) or in bullet points. Lists stand out. They grab the judge's attention. They persuade.

If you do use a list, keep the list items parallel. The first word of each item in the list should begin with the same part of speech.[17]

(ii) **Use charts.** A chart can simplify complicated information and make it easier to absorb. Charts can be used effectively on an *Askov* motion to show chronology, on a sentencing hearing to show recent relevant decisions, in an identification case to summarize detailed evidence from eyewitnesses, or in a fraud case to show complicated corporate transactions. A chart often makes a busy judge's task easier. The judge will thank you for it.

14 See above note 10, especially the chapters on cohesion, emphasis and coherence.
15 See above note 8, especially chapters 8 and 9.
16 See above 12.
17 See LaRocque, above note 3, at 16–20.

(iii) **Use quotes from the evidence.** The odd pithy quote from a witness's evidence at trial humanizes your factum, makes it come alive and often has more force than your own words. This technique is effective as long as you do not overdo it.

(iv) **Use quotations from the case law.** A short quote from the case law can also be effective. But quote only if the exact words matter or the judge has said it better than you can. Otherwise paraphrase. The advantage of paraphrasing is that you can tailor the point to your case. You maintain control of your writing. If you do quote, make sure that you first give the context for the quotation. Tell the reader in a sentence what the quote is about. Giving the context increases the likelihood that the judge will actually read the quotation. Above all else keep the quotation short: MEGO — my eyes glaze over — is the common result of a long block quote.

7. Know the Role of Your Court

If you are writing a factum for the trial court then you want to give the court the ammunition it needs to make findings of fact and credibility in your favour. Set out the findings that you are asking the court to make. Also make sure that the remedy sought — by you or by the other side — is one that the trial court has jurisdiction to give.

If you are writing for an appeal court you have to be concerned about the standard of review. On appeal, the principle of deference comes into play. An appeal court does not ordinarily retry cases. It gives deference to the trial judge. Deference means at least three things.

First, appeal courts give deference to a trial judge's findings of fact and credibility, and will not interfere with them unless they are tainted by "palpable and overriding error." Inferences from primary facts and findings of mixed fact and law (which apply accepted law to the facts) also command deference on appeal.[18] Even where the case is tried on a written record, the principle of deference still applies. The old case law that said an appeal court is in as good a position as the trial judge to make findings on a written record no longer governs. Policy considerations now argue for deference, whether findings are based on oral evidence, written evidence or a combination of the two.[19]

---

18 *Housen v. Nikolaisen*, [2002] 2 S.C.R. 235; *Waxman v. Waxman*, [2004] O.J. No. 1765 (C.A.).

19 *Equity Waste Management of Canada Corp. v. Halton Hills (Town)* (1997), 35 O.R. (3d) 321 (C.A.); *Gottardo Properties (Dome) Inc. v. Toronto (City)* (1998), 162 D.L.R. (4th) 574 (Ont. C.A.).

The lesson for appellants is to think long and hard before trying to win an appeal by overturning findings of fact or credibility. For respondents often the most effective technique is to show that the trial decision rests on findings of fact and that these findings are supported by the evidence, which you then list.

Second, on appeal not every error made by the trial judge matters. The "who cares" principle comes into play. To get an appeal court to intervene you have to identify an important error that taints the trial judge's analysis, or the justice of the decision, or an error in the charge to the jury that could have affected the verdict.

Third, many decisions by the trial judge — especially in criminal law and family law — are discretionary: sentencing, rulings under s. 24(2) of the *Charter*, rulings on similar fact and *Corbett* applications, and spousal support awards all come to mind. Discretionary decisions command significant deference, making review even more difficult. Unless the trial judge has exercised his or her discretion unreasonably or erred in principle, an appeal court will not likely interfere.

Because the standard of review infuses almost all appeals, you often need to address it in your factum. You can do so in one of two ways. You can address it in a stand-alone section of your factum. Alternatively, you can simply incorporate it as part of your argument. You can write, for example: "The trial judge committed no error in principle and exercised her discretion reasonably in admitting the similar fact evidence. Therefore the court should not interfere with her ruling." This latter technique is more concise and often more effective.

8. Anticipate the Court's Concerns

In your factum, you will want to address the points raised against you. But the good factum writer will also anticipate the court's concerns. The two are not always the same.

You can deal with the court's concerns during oral argument, but you can also lay the groundwork for doing so in your factum. Again, notionally trade places with the judge and ask yourself what is likely to trouble the court about your position. Then try to provide an effective answer.

Some cases require you to think through the policy implications of your argument. Judges are concerned about the practical consequences of their decisions, about how what they say in your case may affect related cases or the interpretation of other provisions of the statutory regime in question. You can address these concerns by thinking and reading around your case and then showing that your position makes for sensible and coherent policy.

9. Be Fair

To be effective and credible, a factum must be fair. Any factum writer should heed this advice, but Crowns especially should do so. The court takes seriously the principle that the Crown's goal is not to win or lose, but to serve the public interest. Being fair furthers the public interest. To me, being fair has several components.

First, you must be candid with the court about both the record and the law. You must be fair to the factual record, managing but never ignoring unfavourable facts. And you must never misstate the law or applicable legal principles.

Second, you must face up to your difficulties and your weaknesses. You should concede a point where appropriate. I do not mean that you should concede your case away. But judges expect advocates to yield a point to which they have no meritorious answer. Moreover, the right concession is a disarming and persuasive technique. Not only is it less damaging for you to concede a weak point than for your opponent to use it against you, but it also makes your strong points seem even stronger. A concession also narrows the focus of the case, which judges like. And it enhances your credibility with the court.

Third, you must never overstate your position. Your persuasiveness as counsel depends on the court trusting you. To be trusted you have to be credible. Nothing will destroy your credibility as much as overstating your position or overreaching. Conversely, nothing will enhance your credibility as much as openly admitting the difficulties in your case.

Understatement is thus far more effective than overstatement. Use understatement to appeal to the judge's intelligence. Leave the judge a little bit to do.

Avoid conclusory superlatives in your factum. Not every argument of your opponent is frivolous and vexatious. Not every adverse ruling of the trial judge is a gross miscarriage of justice. Except in the rare case that calls for it, do not be dismissive of your opponent's position, much less the trial judge's reasons. You are better to state the case against you strongly and then answer it. Only then will you know whether you have a good argument.

Finally, you must avoid personal attacks on opposing counsel or an opposing counsel's factum. Personal attacks irritate judges. Take on your opponent's argument, not your opponent.

10. Take a Reasonable Position

In his book, *Overcoming Law*, Judge Richard Posner gives this simple piece of advice to litigators: the best arguments are those that reduce the costs of persuasion.[20] In other words, minimize the legal distance we must travel to agree with you and minimize our resistance to being moved. In practical terms, make the court as comfortable as you can with your position. Aim for a reasonable solution to the dispute.

I borrow a phrase from Cass Sunstein's path breaking book on decision making in the United States Supreme Court, *One Case at a Time*, when I say that most judges I know are "judicial minimalists" at heart.[21] Judicial minimalists like to decide "one case at a time." They worry about the unanticipated consequences of their decisions, about overly broad pronouncements that may come back to haunt them or their colleagues in future cases. They prefer to say no more than they have to in order to resolve the case in front of them. They wish to make few judicial errors — and those they do make, less damaging. Effective advocates can appeal to judicial minimalists by identifying the narrowest ground on which the court can decide in their favour. These advocates reduce the costs of persuasion. They take a reasonable position. Do not ask the court to write the next great *Charter* decision if you do not have to do so in order to win your case. Judges appreciate advocates who are reasonable with the court.

11. Use Active Verbs and Plain English

> "Verbs act. Verbs move. Verbs do. Verbs strike, soothe, grin, cry, exasperate, decline, fly, hurt, and heal. Verbs make writing go, and they matter more to our language than any other part of speech."[22]

I unreservedly endorse this view. Use strong, active verbs (and the active voice). The stronger the verb, the better the sentence.[23] Persuasive writing

---

20 (Cambridge, M.A.: Harvard University Press, 1995) at c. 24, "Rhetoric, Legal Advocacy and Legal Reasoning" at 500–501.

21 Cass R. Sunstein, *One Case at a Time: Judicial Minimalism on the Supreme Court* (Cambridge, MA: Harvard University, 1999).

22 Donald Hall, *Writing Well*, 4th ed. (Boston: Little, Brown, 1982) at 83.

23 As with any piece of advice there are always exceptions: Hamlet's words, "To be or not to be; that is the question . . . " is an obvious example. One "to be" phrase lawyers typically overuse is the sentence beginning with "there is" or "there are." Why write, "There are three Supreme Court of Canada cases that discuss this provision of the *Income Tax Act*," when you can write, "Three Supreme Court of Canada cases discuss this provision of the *Income Tax Act*."

does not come from a string of adjectives and adverbs. Indeed, the fewer of those the better. Vigorous verbs persuade.

Unfortunately many lawyers (and judges!) eschew active, vigorous verbs, replacing them with the verb "to be" (in all its forms) and with nominalizations and the passive voice. Nominalizations are abstract nouns, often characterized by words that end in "ion," and are preceded by a weak verb. The verb "to be," the passive voice and nominalizations have their place in good writing. But careful writers use them sparingly. Lawyers overuse them, perhaps thinking that they lend an aura of detachment and professionalism to their work. They are wrong. Be-verbs lack muscle. When you overuse them you weaken your writing.[24] Nominalizations and the passive voice create two difficulties for the writer: they are less forceful and, thus, less persuasive; and they are less concise.

Here is a simple example. "Revenue Canada investigated the taxpayer's financial dealings" (active verb — seven words in the sentence) in the hands of many lawyers becomes, "Revenue Canada conducted an *investigation of* the taxpayer's financial dealings" (nominalization — ten words), or worse still, "An *investigation of* the taxpayer's financial dealings *was conducted by* Revenue Canada" (nominalization and the passive voice — twelve words).

Thus, my simple advice: try to replace every "to be" verb with a more forceful verb; watch out for those "ion" words — see if you can change them into active verbs; and unless required for sentence flow or other good reason, get rid of the passive voice.

Do something else. Write your sentences in plain English. Replace any legal jargon with plain language and simple words. Think of your readers not as individuals with LL.B.s after their names, but as your well-informed next-door neighbours. Write factums that intelligent lay-readers can understand.

Instead of writing "Brown exited his vehicle and fled on foot," write "Brown left his car and ran." Do not imitate the anonymous authors of corporate annual reports who write "this equity account was not immune to the effects of the market's negative growth"; instead say simply "this fund lost money."[25]

I do not accept the argument that law and legal issues are too complex, too sophisticated for simplicity. John Kenneth Galbraith had it right when he wrote, "There are no important propositions that cannot be stated in

---

24 See Garner, above note 6, Tip 29.

25 These examples are taken from LaRocque, above note 3, at 24-31.

plain language . . . "[26] Simple words, short words, plain language will make your factums stronger and clearer. Dense, turgid prose that plagues much of legal writing is not just less persuasive, it risks being misunderstood. Always remember the words of one of the great writers of the twentieth century, Winston Churchill: "Short words are best and the old words when short are best of all."[27] Witness these words from a master of the craft: his famous speech to the House of Commons in 1940.

> We shall not flag or fail. We shall go on to the end. We shall fight in France, we shall fight on the seas and oceans, we shall fight with growing confidence and growing strength in the air, we shall defend our island, whatever the cost may be, we shall fight on the beaches, we shall fight on the landing grounds, we shall fight in the fields and in the streets, we shall fight in the hills; we shall never surrender.[28]

Simple words, short words, powerful message.

12. Edit Your Factum

Justice Brandeis once said, "there is no such thing as good writing — there is only good rewriting."[29] Not all lawyers take his observation to heart. Many factums are not properly edited; some look like first drafts. A decent edit can convert a mediocre factum into a very good factum. Editing also shows that you care about the reader. Of course, editing competes with the time pressures of getting your factum out. But, if you can, save time for editing.

You can edit for many different things, from grammar to punctuation to style. Do not try to edit for everything all at once. Instead, divide and conquer. Here are six editing suggestions.

(i) **Edit for conciseness.** This is my most important editing suggestion. Three main reasons for overly long factums are: unnecessary or repeated facts and evidentiary detail; wordy or unnecessary phrases; and nominalizations and the passive voice. Edit for all three. Ensure that every fact or evidence reference is necessary. Get rid of the ones you do not need.

---

26 Galbraith, "Writing, Typing and Economics," the Atlantic Monthly, March 1978. Quoted in Timothy Perrin, "Better Writing for Lawyers" (The Law Society of Upper Canada, 1990) at 154.

27 Quoted in *Bartlett's Familiar Quotations*, above note 5 at 622.

28 Churchill's speech on Dunkirk, House of Commons (June 4, 1940), quoted in Bartlett's, above note 5 at 620.

29 Quoted in Pierce, "The Legal Profession," 30 The Torch 5, 8 (1957).

Change or get rid of the wordy phrases that plague much legal writing. Change "at this point in time" to "now," "notwithstanding the fact that" to "although" and "in the event that" to "if." And cut out altogether phrases like "it is important to note that" or "it is urged at the outset that." Buy a little book titled *Edit Yourself* by Bruce Ross-Larson.[30] It contains a valuable list of words and phrases to cut or change. And, as I have already said, check each word ending in "ion" and every use of the passive voice.

It is easier to be long than short.[31] Always look to cut. No matter how concisely you think you have written, you can always make your factum shorter. Strive for brevity. All judges appreciate and remember the concise factum writers.

(ii) **Make sure your factum has enough white space.** The visual impact of your factum affects its readability and thus its persuasiveness. Avoid long dense paragraphs. They turn off your readers. Use generous margins, double spacing, headings and lists to give the appearance of a less dense document.[32]

(iii) **Edit what is not on the page.** Ordinarily we edit by looking at the words on the page. That is a necessary part of editing. But it is just as important to edit for what is not there: for example, to insert point first or context sentences, to add proper headings and to ensure that the structure of your factum is visible to the reader.

(iv) **Edit your sentences.** Lawyers like to qualify what they write by using subordinate clauses. If you need these clauses try to keep the core of your sentence — subject, verb, object — close together.[33] Also avoid long tangled sentences. Notice that I did not say avoid all long sentences and write only short ones. Good writing has a rhythm to it, a rhythm partly achieved by varying the length of your sentences. Still, longer sentences are harder to read. Try to keep the average length of your sentences to 20 words or less.[34] The grammar check on your computer will alert you to long sentences. If you do write long sentences, use a technique like parallelism to make them flow. And try the occasional short sentence (three or four words) for variation and emphasis.

---

30 (New York: W.W. Norton & Company Inc., 1996).

31 Samuel Butler, quoted in LaRocque, above note 3, at 14.

32 See Terri LeClercq, *Expert Legal Writing* (Austin: University of Texas Press, 1995) at 22–25.

33 Armstrong and Terrell, above note 8, at 232.

34 See Bryan A. Garner, *Legal Writing in Plain English* (Chicago: University of Chicago Press, 2001) at 19–21, LaRocque above note 3 at 14–15.

(v) **Read your draft factum aloud to yourself.** Sometimes your ear is a more reliable guide to an effective factum than your eye. You will sense the rhythm of good writing when you read your draft aloud. If your factum does not sound right, it probably needs fixing.

(vi) **Use the bottom drawer of your desk.** Put your draft away for a few days and then come back to it. The point here is to gain some distance between you and your writing. You will come back to your work more as a first-time reader and will see things that you would not have seen a few days earlier. Alternatively, have a colleague read your draft.

C. A DOZEN THINGS JUDGES DO NOT LIKE TO SEE IN A FACTUM

So far my paper has focused on what judges, or at least this judge, like to see in a factum. The flip side of the coin is what judges do not like to see in a factum. Here are twelve things — in no particular order — that I do not like to see in a factum.

1. **Respondents' factums that restate the facts.**
   Some respondents begin the facts part of the factum with something like "The Crown accepts the applicant's statement of the facts subject to the following clarifications and additions" but then go on to restate the facts in their entirety. A respondent should only restate the facts in the rare case where the applicant's statement is misleading or the respondent simply cannot live with the applicant's characterization of the facts. If that is the case then be candid — say you are restating the facts and say why you are doing so. Otherwise, comply with the factum rules that require you to state the facts you accept and the facts you disagree with, and to set out only any additional facts you rely on.[35]

2. **Respondents' factums that are not free standing.**
   Judges like to be able to read the respondent's factum as a stand-alone document. They do not like to be forced to flip back to the appellant's factum. So, if you are going to disagree with paragraph 9 of the appellant's statement of facts, do not say, "The respondent disagrees with paragraph 9 and says that . . . " Instead, summarize what the appellant says in paragraph 9 and then give your version.

35 See, for example, Ontario's Rules of Civil Procedure, Rule 61.12.

3. **Giving the court constitutional law 101.**
This is a common disease in *Charter* cases. You have to give judges credit for knowing a little law, especially the law that gets cited to them regularly. Resist the temptation to give the court a treatise on s. 8 of the *Charter*. Instead, go directly to the most relevant cases and principles.

4. **A long list of case citations.**
You do not need to overpower the court with a parade of learning or show the court that your research has left no stone unturned. Just give the court the principal authorities — usually not more than two or three — relevant to your case.

5. **A stream of consciousness statement of the facts.**
Factums that contain a long and detailed statement of the facts are hard to read and absorb. They are especially so when the presentation of the facts reflects no more than a continuous flow of counsel's thoughts. When you are about to throw a lot of factual detail at the judge, remember to do two things: organize the detail effectively and continually give the context for the detail. Use headings, internal roadmaps and context sentences.

6. **Long paragraphs.**
They are hard to read and hard to absorb. They turn off your readers. So watch the length of your paragraphs. No paragraph should be longer than a half a page. Most should be shorter than that.

7. **Convoluted long sentences.**
As I have said, long sentences can be hard to absorb. Convoluted long sentences can be next to impossible to absorb. If the sentence is convoluted, probably the writer has put too much distance between the subject and the verb. If you cannot keep the core together, try the simple but effective technique of breaking the longer sentence into two shorter ones.

8. **Repetition of "it is respectfully submitted."**
Use the phrase sparingly. It detracts from the flow and readability of your factum. Indeed, if you say it once at the beginning of your argument and once at the end that is more than enough.

9. **"Clearly," "certainly," "surely," "absolutely," and the like.**
If something is clear, you do not need to say it; if something is not clear, saying that it is will not make it so. These false intensifiers, as I like to call them, are best avoided. Use them rarely, if at all.

10. **The shotgun approach.**
Throwing as many arguments as you can think of at the court, hoping one will land, shows the court that you have not thought through your case. Focus on the core issues — usually not more than two or three — that will decide the case. Let the weak or minor points go.

11. **Generalizations.**
Generalities seldom persuade. And general principles seldom decide cases. It is the details, the specifics that persuade, that determine the result. Of course you must target the right amount of specificity. Too much detail can turn off your readers. But you will write more persuasively if you follow this simple principle: "show, don't tell."[36] Do not talk about the general duties of a tax auditor, but about the specific duties that apply to your case. Do not say, "Ms. Williams tried to sell her property but could not find a buyer" when you can say, "Ms. Williams listed her property with three different agents and each time reduced the price, but still did not get a single offer."

Similarly, where you can, prefer concrete language to abstract concepts. Paint word pictures. Describe people, places, things and actions so that your readers can see them. To do so you must give your readers concrete information. A good writer would not say, "The sunrise was strikingly beautiful," but instead, "The sun rose in a blaze of red and violet and gold."[37] In the discipline of law, which deals with ideas, principles and policies, abstraction is inevitable. And it is not necessarily bad. Law is replete with abstract words and phrases: relevance, reasonableness, interests of justice, free and democratic society, unconscionability, vulnerability and many, many more. At times the use of these abstract words is essential to the clarity of your arguments. But if you wish to engage your readers try not to stay too long on these high levels of abstraction.

Activate the judge's senses by examples, analogies, even the occasional simile or metaphor. Justice Oliver Wendell Holmes used a memorable metaphor to show that the right of free speech is not an absolute right: "The most stringent protection of free speech would not protect a man in shouting fire in a crowded theatre and causing panic."[38]

---

36 See Stark, above note 12 at 106.

37 LaRocque, above note 3, at 157, uses this simple example. See also Stark, above note 12, at 83–86; and Thomas S. Kane, The Oxford Essential Guide to Writing (Oxford: Oxford University Press, 2003) at 262–66.

38 *Schenck v. United States*, 249 U.S. 47 (1919).

12. **Over-defining names and terms.**
Corporate lawyers are fond of defining every term and name they use in a corporate document. They write: XYZ Limited (hereinafter "XYZ"); the amalgamation agreement date June 1, 2004 (herein "the amalgamation agreement"); John Smith ("Smith"). Avoid this practice. If the subsequent reference is obvious no definition is needed. For example, if there is only one XYZ Limited, do not define it. Just use XYZ. Save the definitions for when they are required for clarity. In a related vein, use ordinary names, not "applicant," "appellant" or "respondent," unless tactical reasons dictate otherwise.

D. CONCLUSION

Factum writing is not just a key component of the art of legal persuasion. It also puts the advocate's reputation and credibility on the line. Judges have long memories. They remember the good factum writers and they remember the bad. I hope that this paper helps all of you to write factums that are memorable for the right reasons.

Chapter Two

Advocacy in the Federal Court of Appeal*

Hon. Marshall E. Rothstein

A. INTRODUCTION

When he was at the Supreme Court of Canada, Bud Estey was asked what constituted good advocacy. He said: "There are three rules. Be clear, be brief, be gone." I guess I could leave it there. But my ego won't let me. So, I'll have more to say.

When I was preparing for this presentation, David Chodikoff advised me that I might provide some guidance as to whether the court expects counsel to go back to the *Duke of Westminster*[1] in each case or to get right to the point. Well, I would have thought that the answer to that question is obvious. We want counsel to get right to the point, unless, of course, we think counsel should tell us about the *Duke of Westminster.*

Do you remember who were the best teachers when you were in school? The best teachers were the ones who made the course seem simple. An advocate's job is to teach the judges about the case and why his or her position should be accepted. If the factum and argument are kept simple, linear, and logical, the advocate will be a good teacher.

---

* This chapter is based upon an oral presentation by Mr. Justice Rothstein in 2003 at the Department of Justice before members of the Tax Law Section, invited guests, and the members of the executive of the Tax Section of the Ontario Bar Association.

1 *Inland Revenue Commissioners v. Westminster (Duke of)*, [1936] A.C. 1 (H.L.).

I am going to deal with factums first and then oral argument. John Laskin, a highly-respected judge in the Ontario Court of Appeal, has written on the art of writing persuasive factums. His pointers are contained in a paper entitled "Forget the Wind Up and Make the Pitch: Some Suggestions for Writing More Persuasive Factums."[2] I rely heavily on his paper because it is, in my view, the most comprehensive and best work I have seen on written advocacy. I use it to help me write judgments, and you will find it instructive.

B. WHY IS A GOOD FACTUM IMPORTANT?

Why is a good factum important? I'll give you six reasons.

1. The Court schedules cases tightly. So counsel's time for oral argument is limited. I wish we provided more time because I hear better than I read. But we don't. So your opportunity for oral argument will be limited.
2. Some judges rely heavily on pre-hearing memoranda prepared by law clerks. All the law clerk sees is the factum.
3. The factum gives the judge an initial and perhaps lasting impression of your appeal.
4. There is no transcript of the oral argument on appeal. In taxation cases, we often reserve and when we write the judgment, we refer to the factums extensively.
5. Many judges operate on the theory that the factum that is the easiest to understand must be correct. We might be persuaded to the contrary in oral argument, but again an initial impression is formed on the basis of the factum.
6. You know that lawyers like to gossip. If you think lawyers are bad, wait until they become judges. Judges aren't concerned with chargeable hours, so they have more time to gossip. No one gossips more than judges. Just as we talk about who gave a good or a bad oral argument, we talk about who wrote a good or bad factum. Your credibility is affected by the quality of the factum.

So do not underestimate the importance of a good factum.

I'm going to cover six points in factum writing:

1. being concise;

---

2 The Advocates' Society Journal, Vol. 18 No. 2, p. 3 (Summer, 1999); also available online at www.ontariocourts.on.ca/court_of_appeal/speeches/forget.htm. Editor's note: Justice Rothstein did not have the opportunity to read in advance Justice Laskin's chapter for this book.

2. identifying the issue;
3. using point first style;
4. minimizing the facts;
5. when background is necessary; and
6. editing.

1. Being concise

Anyone can provide information. But your job is to persuade. Persuasion is affected by how you organize and present the information. Convoluted, lengthy or dense writing will detract from a strong argument. Judges don't like to read factums that are tedious and hard to understand. If it takes you thirty pages to explain a simple issue, you have a problem.

My point is that you have to force yourself to be concise all the time.

Writing concisely doesn't mean writing superficially. Concise means brief but comprehensive. You can be comprehensive at length. But the idea is to be comprehensive and brief. Therefore, writing concisely is harder than writing at length.

Thirty-three years ago I was an adviser on new consumer protection legislation in Manitoba, and I was asked to give a two minutes and twelve seconds presentation on a CBC morning program about the new law. I was up on the subject, and it took me less than an hour to write my first draft. It then took me eleven hours to get it down to two minutes and twelve seconds.

You have been intensely involved in the pleadings, discoveries and the trial. Your head is loaded with detail, but by the time the case gets to appeal, the issues are pretty narrow. You have to think hard about what it is you have to demonstrate and then question every sentence you have written. Ask yourself whether each sentence is absolutely essential.

The Federal Court Rules allow factums of up to 30 pages with 30 lines per page. In my experience, I would say that 3/4 of the factums that I read are 25 pages or longer. The 30-page limit isn't a mandatory length. It is the maximum length. When I grant intervener status, I specify that the intervener's factum is not to exceed five or sometimes seven pages. It is true the intervener doesn't have to set out the facts. But you would be surprised how meaningful and concise an argument of seven pages can be.

The first thing most judges do when they pick up a factum is to see how many pages they have to read. If the pages seem quite dense, then usually they count the number of lines on a page and if they see that a lawyer is meeting the 30 page and 30 line limit by using narrow margins and typeface that is so small that even an insect couldn't read it, they become resentful. You don't want resentful judges. So being concise is an element of strategy.

Judges never complain that a factum is too short. If you know the points you want to make, you should be able to do it in fewer pages without fear of leaving something out. Remember that the judges will be hearing seven or eight appeals in a week with two factums in each case, and more if there are interveners. At 30 pages per factum, the judges will be reading almost 500 factum pages that week. And they likely will have to re-read the factums. And they have to read the judgments appealed from as well, and sometimes portions of the record. So they may be reading close to 1,000 pages in a week of cases. I am not asking for your sympathy. However, the judges who are fortunate enough to be the recipient of a short, concise factum will consider it an act of mercy — and so will their law clerks; and it will give them confidence that you have thought carefully about what you have written, and that can only be positive for you in the appeal.

2. Identifying the issue

You are immersed in the case. You have done the research. You have read all the materials. You know the subtleties of the case. But the judges know nothing. They want to know what the appeal is about quickly. They want to know the key issue on which the appeal turns. So, before you begin writing, you have to figure out that issue.

I often wonder whether our Court Rules do a disservice to counsel and to judges by placing the issue section of the factum after the facts. I am sure many lawyers view this as an invitation to write extensively on the facts before even thinking about the issue. That is wrong. Think about the issue first. The rest will then fall into place.

Let me make the point by telling you about one of my less than stellar experiences. After about a year as a judge in the Trial Division of the Federal Court, I was sent to what we affectionately refer to as "dumb judges' school." In advance, we were told to submit a judgment we had written. I didn't know exactly why. Obviously I wanted to put my best foot forward. I had worked hard on a tax judgment about the replacement property rules under the *Income Tax Act*. It had received three out of four stars in one of the tax circulars. So I figured that others must have thought that this was a good judgment and I submitted it. At the "dumb judges' school," we met in groups of six. Each of us was given a judgment written by another member of the group, and we were asked to come back the next day and comment on it. When we came back the next day, all the judges said they had read the judgments given to them. And they were all the model of clarity and logical reasoning, and no improvements were suggested. All except the judge who read my judgment. He said he had read it at least five times and still didn't know what I was talking about.

What had I done? I wrote nine pages of facts, many of marginal significance to the issue. I then rambled into the issue, defining it in four different ways and doing a good deal of talking around it. I then wrote five pages of reasons before coming to my conclusion.

What the guy reading the judgment wanted to know was, what was the issue? He didn't want to wait until page 14 to discover it and then read four versions of it, none of which said quite the same thing.

I tell you this story to emphasize the importance of thinking carefully about the issue in advance before writing any part of the factum. Thinking precisely about the issue and writing it out in the clearest simplest form is hard work, but it will pay dividends. And when you are writing, refer back to the issue on each aspect of the factum and ensure that the issue has not been overtaken or overshadowed by other issues or unnecessary facts and arguments.

After that humiliating experience at "dumb judges' school," I tried to force myself to start each judgment out by stating the issue to be decided. I haven't always been successful, but I bet if I went back and ranked my judgments for clarity, the ones when I did state the issue up front would be the clearest.

I have referred to issue in the singular to make the point that usually in appeals there is one important issue. Some lawyers think that the appeal will be stronger if they are able to cite numerous errors committed by the trial judge. Wrong! Unless the trial judge is an idiot, if he erred, he will have done so on one point or maybe two. A multiplicity of issues suggests a lack of confidence in the major ground and a scattered, rather than a focussed, approach.

Let me put it to you this way. You don't see many appeal judgments that find numerous errors. The appeal judgment will usually be focussing on a key issue. If you identify the key issue in your material, chances are the judges will focus on the issue you state rather than going off on their own tangent and identifying an issue that will not be helpful to you.

Where you do have more than one point of appeal, make sure that you put the strongest one first. It is easier to write chronologically or just as a matter comes to mind. But if you haven't been able to decide what the strongest point is, you probably haven't put enough thought into the appeal. If your best issue is buried in the middle or at the end, the judge will implicitly give it less weight or may miss it altogether.

3. Using point first style

John Laskin says that point first writing is the most important suggestion for good factum writing. I agree. Point first writing means that you state your proposition first and then develop it. You may think that the judge needs to understand how an argument develops or that the judge will not appreciate the point until he or she is familiar with the relevant facts. Or that an anticipated conclusion will make the ultimate conclusion repetitive. Forget those concerns. Put the conclusion up front. There is a good reason for this.

No one, not even judges, reads every word. The experts say that we read by instantaneous prediction and confirmation. Think of this. If I put a random series of letters in front of you and then remove them and ask you to remember them, you would likely only remember a few letters. But if I gave you the sentence "If it isn't broken, don't fix it," you would remember as if you saw each and every letter. You didn't. Rather, you went through a process of prediction and confirmation. Point first writing provides prediction which is then confirmed by the details that follow. Point first writing is especially important in complex tax appeals where it is easy for non-experts, the judges, to get lost. So you keep the judges in familiar territory by telling them what to expect at the beginning and then developing it.

Point first style applies paragraph by paragraph. Don't quote from a statute or a case without first stating what proposition it is you are putting forward. Don't set out factual information without first saying what the information is intended to demonstrate. In court, I often have to ask counsel why they are citing a case or telling me about some fact. The same is true in a factum. Don't put the judges in the position of wondering why you are quoting the case or stating the fact. If you do, the judges will likely skim through what you have written, and it will have little or no impact on them.

An ancillary benefit of point first writing is that it will force you to restrict each paragraph to one main idea or topic. You know so much about the case and its various subtleties that it is easy to end up making two or three points in a paragraph. That will only confuse the judges. They don't know the case well enough to appreciate the subtleties in your argument and indeed, putting two or three points into a paragraph probably means that you haven't thought through the important point you want to make clearly enough.

A way of disciplining yourself to write in point first style is to use headings and subheadings to separate each point. Headings help a judge understand the order and organization of your factum. But make sure that the heading accurately reflects the point you are trying to make under it. As you choose a heading, you should be looking to see whether what is under the heading reflects the heading or whether there is more there that has to be taken out or moved. And when you are revising the factum, make sure to re-check the headings so that they still apply to what you are saying in substance.

If you come away with nothing else today, try to remember point first writing style.

4. Minimizing the facts

Some lawyers think that if you do not put down every fact in the facts section of the factum, the facts will not be able to be used in argument. Wrong! In the facts section, set out only those facts that are essential to give the judges a general understanding of the circumstances. And after you write the entire factum, go back and eliminate all the details that aren't needed for that general understanding.

In the argument section of the factum, however, the facts may be elaborated upon where they are important to make the point. If you elaborate in the facts section, you either have to do it all over again in the argument section or, in the argument section, you have to refer back to the facts section, which is very cumbersome. In the argument section, if you are trying to demonstrate that a business is active or that a bad debt deduction is unreasonable or that unrelated parties are or are not dealing with each other at arm's length, go into detail point-by-point. But do that in the argument section, not in the facts section of a factum.

Quoting from a transcript should be left to the argument section. Quoting can be effective but only if it is not overdone and if the quotation is relatively succinct and makes the point. And make sure that before quoting from the transcript, you state the point that you are trying to demonstrate with the quotation — point first writing again.

5. When background is necessary

Background is not necessary when the law is well-settled and when the issue is the application of the law to the facts. But tax appeals often involve the interpretation of a particular provision of the *Income Tax Act* ("Act") for the first time. In these circumstances, you will want to develop why your interpretation of the provision is the correct one. Therefore, it is helpful to the Court to be given some background of the statutory scheme, the reason why the statutory provision was brought into force, how it works, why your interpretation is consistent with the scheme and rationale of the Act and the negative implications of your opponent's interpretation.

That background will consist of legislative history, the wording before the present provision was introduced, statements made in Parliament or Parliamentary Committees, comments of authorities who have written about the provision in a textbook or in articles, perhaps the way a similar provision has been interpreted in the United Kingdom or even the United States. By the time the case comes to our Court, the provision in question will have been in effect for some period of years, so there will likely be some commentary on it. These references will be helpful.

When you are trying to advance a certain interpretation of the provision, you have to be very careful with your logic. Make sure you test your interpretation against the more extreme fact situations to ensure that your approach is solid. When you write the argument, only go as far as you have to. Rely on what has been written if it is ascertainable. It is inviting to draw analogies and examples, but they will likely just get you into trouble.

6. Editing: no amount is too much

If the three rules of real estate are location, location, location, the three rules of factum writing are edit, edit, and edit. Never file a factum that has not been revised and edited a number of times. Unless a judgment is very simple and straightforward, I find that it requires at least five to ten drafts, sometimes more. Not each draft constitutes a major revision, and you shouldn't be attempting to make major revisions at every redraft, but with today's technology, redrafting is a simple matter. Perhaps my view about editing is a reflection of not having to worry about charging a client or answering to a superior for all the time spent. Nonetheless, editing requires time and it must be done.

Part of redrafting will involve putting in the headings and rearranging the paragraphs or sentences to make sure that the flow is more logical and that context comes before details.

A factum with spelling and grammatical errors is an impediment to communicating a good, persuasive argument. It causes the judge to lose confidence in the substance of the argument. So proofread carefully and do not rely solely on computer spell checks or grammar programs.

It is also salutary to leave the draft for a day or two and then come back to it. You will have a fresh perspective and will be more readily able to pick up confusing language or gaps in the logic.

Also, it is advisable to read the draft aloud to yourself. You will be surprised at what you pick up when you do that. And have someone else read the draft. They will provide a more objective view and give you valuable suggestions.

And always look to cut. No matter how concisely you think you have written you can always make your factum more concise.

C. ORAL ARGUMENT

I will now turn to oral argument. Sometimes we see lawyers for taxpayers expressing righteous indignation at their client's shabby treatment by the Minister. And sometimes we see lawyers for the Minister expressing outrage at a blatant tax avoidance scheme.

John Laskin tells a story about Coulter Osborne, the former Associate Chief Justice of Ontario and now the Ontario Integrity Commissioner. He says he was on a panel with Coulter, where each side was arguing that they had the moral high ground in the case. But the panel didn't think much of either side's position. Osborne started his judgment out with the observation: "In this case, the moral high ground is largely unoccupied." When you argue orally, remember that judges by nature are sceptics. My point: righteous indignation is okay before a jury; it doesn't usually assist in an appeal.

By the time your appeal comes to court, the judges will have read the factums, the law clerks may have written pre-hearing memorandums; and the judges will have a preliminary view of what they think the decision should be. The judges will probably be looking to reinforce their preliminary view by getting confirmation of certain points from you in court.

Three things about reading the court: if hostile questions are asked, it's because the judge is trying to reinforce his or her preliminary view against you; if the judges are silent, it probably means they agree with you and wish you would sit down; and if they are not writing when you argue, you are not engaging them and you should move to the next point.

I told you that the three rules of factum writing are edit, edit and edit. The three rules of oral argument are preparation, preparation and preparation. Another way of putting it is that appeals are won in the library, not in the courtroom. You have to know the record backwards and the logic of your legal position thoroughly. The worst thing that can happen is to lose an appeal because you didn't bring something important from the record to the attention of the judges in answer to a question. The judges will not scour the record or necessarily read the cases that are relevant unless you point them out. So you must be prepared. And a by-product of being prepared is that if you tend to be nervous in court, thorough preparation is the best antidote.

I will give you seven brief points about oral argument.

1. Give the judges a road map

If you start your oral argument by telling the judges that you will be covering certain points, you will see them writing. That is always a good sign. You are giving them a road map. When you go to a concert, you want to see the program — what comes before the intermission, what comes after. It is always good to tell the judges in advance what points you will be making. And it is quick and simple. If you have five points, just give them to the judges in point form. Don't try to argue the points at that time. And then, in your argument, make sure that when you finish one point, you say so. And then expressly tell them that you are moving to the next point.

2. Give references

You will likely be referring to the record or a statute or case law in your argument. Some lawyers make glib references to authorities. That is unhelpful. If you are going to refer to a document or a case or a statute, take the judges step-by-step to where you are going, which book it is in, which tab number, and which page or paragraph number. When you quote, say exactly where in the paragraph you are starting. Don't paraphrase. That will just confuse. Don't skip words because you don't think they are important unless you tell the judges exactly what you are skipping. These are elementary points but if you follow them, you will keep the judges with you. You will minimize their frustration in trying to find out where you are. And you will instil their confidence that you know where you are going.

Now, as I told you about written argument, in oral argument, use point first style. Don't go to a reference in the record or a case or a statute without first telling the judges why you are going there and what the point is that you are intending to make by the reference. That kind of organized approach will give them confidence in your presentation.

3. Use a linear and explicit approach

A linear and explicit approach is one that starts at the beginning and explicitly deals with each step along the way. You would be surprised at how many lawyers dive right into the middle of an argument, use jargon or make implicit assumptions about what the judges understand. The judges will have read the material. They will have some familiarity with it, and you may sense from their comments as you go along that you can make assumptions about what they know. But otherwise you must be as explicit as possible as you make your legal argument about how one provision relates to another, or why a particular fact is significant. Don't assume the judges know. Take them to the relevant provisions of the Act or record, and explain to them why they are significant. Take it step-by-step and they will follow you. And as you do that, they will gain confidence in the logic and soundness of your approach.

4. Engage the judges

I recently had an appeal in which, when it came time for reply, the appellant's lawyer said he had no reply. I then said that I wanted to ask him some questions. He said "I have closed my case." I asked if he was refusing to answer questions. His reply was again "I have closed my case." I guess he must have forgotten this was an appeal and thought he was leading evidence in a criminal trial. He lost.

The point is that oral argument is your opportunity to engage the judges and satisfy their questions. If you are getting questions and you aren't answering directly and simply, you are missing the most important opportunity you have in oral argument — reinforcing what the judge already is thinking if it is favourable to you and changing the judge's mind if the questions are unfavourable. Sometimes the questions are just for information, but again, it is important to answer neutral questions simply and directly to give the judge the information he seeks. If you think the judge's hostile questions suggest he or she is getting off on a tangent, a polite but determined response to bring the judge back to the relevant point is required. If you have to disagree with a judge, do it with a clear explanation. It is not easy to tell a judge that he or she is wrong. So you have to be delicate. But you can't be bullied by a judge. And remember, there are three judges. Even if you can't convince the one asking the hostile question, your answer may be picked up by one of the other judges.

Three final points:

5. Time

Be conscious of the time. The judges will hold you to your allotted time even if they use up most of it asking useless questions.

6. Adjournments

Ask for an adjournment if you are caught off guard. Inexperienced counsel sometimes gets stampeded by the court. If you need time to consider an unexpected question, ask for a short adjournment. Now, you will only get one adjournment but if you think the answer is important and you need a few minutes to find something in the material or to organize your thoughts, then an adjournment can be useful.

7. Costs

Be prepared to argue costs at the end of your argument. The court may reserve, or the panel you get may not ask you to address costs, but for myself, if the decision is given from the Bench, or even if it is reserved, depending upon who my colleagues are, I will try to dispose of costs by a lump sum order. Party and party costs are not an exercise in accounting. They are a rough and ready award that partially compensates the winning party. When I read decisions of taxing officers that go on for 10 or 15 pages, assessing $2,000 or $3,000 in costs, I seriously question the resources that go into the determination. Counsel has to prepare a bill of costs, opposing counsel has to review it and make submissions. The court officer then has to read it and write reasons. Perhaps where costs are very large, there is justification for a more elaborate procedure. But when party and party costs are going to be $3,000, $5,000 or $10,000, I can't see the justification in the taxing process. So I have encouraged my colleagues to be prepared to make lump sum awards of costs and some of us are doing that now. And when we do that, we are not bound by the Tariff. The Tariff is unreasonably low. In a small case, we will likely be guided by the Tariff. But solicitor and client costs for an appeal can easily be $30,000 or more. And in those situations, a higher amount of party and party costs, either to the taxpayer or the Crown, is warranted. So be prepared to argue orally for costs.

D. CONCLUSION

Let me conclude with this thought. Some people have an innate ability on their feet. But, being good counsel is largely a question of experience and definitely one of preparation. Many of you today who are experienced counsel already know what I have told you. So consider this a refresher course. For those of you who are less experienced, you will go through a few rough times getting your feet wet and learning how to read the judges and how to roll with the rhythm of the courtroom. If I may say so, if you remember one or two of the things I have said today, your learning experience will be easier.

Chapter Three

Appellate Advocacy: A Practitioner's Viewpoint

William I. Innes[1]

A. INTRODUCTION

What is the most important element in appellate advocacy? Erudition? Logic? Psychology? As a young lawyer I would have chosen erudition. I soon learned however that knowing the statute and case law is not enough; judges have a troublesome habit of stretching the law if the result would be unreasonable or unfair. In the middle of my career I leaned in the direction of logic but soon discovered that logic by itself is not usually enough to sway an appellate panel. The common law tradition is not a Cartesian approach to problems; it is very much driven by the vagaries of human nature and reflects a practical attempt to arrive at a just outcome. I now believe that the most valuable skill in appellate advocacy is psychology.

When I use the term "psychology" I am not suggesting that an advocate can ignore erudition and logic. Quite the contrary. In appeals in tax matters nothing can replace a thorough knowledge of the workings of the

1 I would like to thank my colleague Leila Dabir for her careful and imaginative work in helping me compile this paper. In addition, I would like to thank The Hon. Mr. Justice Joseph T. Robertson of the New Brunswick Court of Appeal as well as David E. Spiro of Blake Cassels & Graydon LLP and David W. Chodikoff of the Department of Justice for their kindness in reviewing a draft and providing me with their comments.

statute and the case law. Tax appeals are notorious for the difficulty of the underlying subject matter. Moreover, where there are gaps in the legislation logic is indispensable in trying to arrive at a workable interpretation. Similarly, I am not using the term "psychology" to suggest that appellate advocacy is some form of hucksterism. What I am suggesting is that the good advocate tries to see the case through the eyes of his or her panel of judges. What issues will they regard as critical? What will trouble them about the decision under appeal? What arguments will interest them? Which will they simply discard?

Too many lawyers regard appellate advocacy as an advanced form of debating. Nothing could be farther from the truth. Appellate advocacy is at its best an intelligent, engaged conversation between the advocate and the bench. There is nothing new in this concept. More than two millennia ago the Greek grammarian Apollodorus wrote that the primary goal of advocacy is "to persuade the Judge and lead his mind to the conclusions desired by the speaker."[2] Robert F. Hanley put the same concept in a more modern context: "The advocate must be a psychologist. He must understand human nature, and he must know how his listeners think, their habits, desires and emotions."[3]

A good advocate uses psychology in selecting the arguments he or she can raise to persuade the bench of the merits of his or her position. Larding your factum or oral argument with obscure or unnecessary references may be a convincing display of erudition but it is rarely, if ever, persuasive. Pounding the table in mock (or actual) indignation may satisfy your sense of the dramatic but it usually just gets the bench annoyed. The essential difference between good advocacy and poor advocacy is the difference between talking with someone and talking at someone.

My goal is not to examine the technical rules governing appeals[4] but to provide some (I hope) helpful observations about the conduct of an appeal from the perspective of a practitioner. With that in mind, I have divided this paper into two parts: drafting the factum and oral advocacy.

---

2 Appollodorus: *Quintillian*, II. xv. 12.

3 Robert F. Hanley, "Brush Up Your Aristotle" (1986) *Litigation* 39.

4 Readers interested in such a treatment should consult John Sopinka and Mark A. Gelowitz, *The Conduct of an Appeal* 2d ed. (Toronto: Butterworths, 2000) which I find a valuable tool in appellate advocacy.

B. DRAFTING THE FACTUM

The Honourable Mr. Justice D. Gordon Blair of the Ontario Court of Appeal, in discussing the drafting of a factum, stated in his lecture on Appellate Advocacy on January 16, 1987:[5]

> One of my brothers (who shall be nameless) provided my text. He said, "If I had known, when practising law, how important factums were to members of this Court, I would have taken more care in preparing them."

He further stated:[6]

> . . . factums of high quality are required to assist the Court in dealing with its ever-expanding list. . . . It has been said that the trial is a search for truth and that the appeal is the search for error. The appellant's factum must answer basic questions: What is this case about? Why is it being appealed and, specifically, what errors are alleged? These become the issues in the appeal.
>
> The hallmarks of a good factum are selectively, clarity and economy of language. The factum must select the important issues raised by the case (rarely more than two or three) and rigorously discard all others. The issues must be clearly expressed and the facts and the law relevant to those issues clearly stated in the fewest possible words.
>
> . . . .
>
> If your factum is properly prepared you will create a favourable impression not only of your case but also of yourself.
>
> . . . we would not be human if individually we did not form a preliminary view based upon our preparation for the hearing. The counsel with the good factum enters the hearing with a great advantage . . . A good factum also stimulates questions from the Court and leads to a fuller discussion of the issues in the appeal. Counsel at the hearing is badly served by poorly prepared factum. If it is unrelated to his argument it can create confusion and even annoyance . . . A good factum is of invaluable assistance in the delivery of an oral argument . . . A factum should always be written with a view to its use in the preparation of a reserved judgment . . . Since much of the judge's work on reserved judgments is done at home it is as important at this stage as in the preparation of the appeal to have the factum supported by well-prepared appeal books and case books.

---

5 Alvin B. Rosenberg and Marvin J. Huberman, *Appellate Advocacy* (Toronto: Carswell, 1996) at 25.

6 *Ibid.* at 25–26.

The preparation of a factum is not some tedious preliminary step in the appeal process; it is an integral part of success in appellate advocacy. The factum is at least as important to the case as is the oral argument, probably more so. The factum is the court's first contact with your case. It provides the court with its first impression of the issues on the appeal and the facts. It provides the court with a road map during your oral argument and a written record of your position which becomes useful later on when preparing its decision.

The goal in drafting your factum should be to persuade the court to decide in your client's favour on the basis of the factum alone. As counsel for an appellant you will try to demonstrate that there has been an error and that error has caused an injustice to your client. The factum should be prepared with your audience in mind. Language can be used to illustrate, explain, and persuade. The job of the advocate is to do more than simply communicate the facts and law to the court: the objective is to convince the court that your position is the correct one.

1) Overview

Generally, it is good practice to start a factum with a one or two paragraph summary of the gist of the appeal. The overview should make the court want to keep reading. To accomplish this, the summary should be punchy but not argumentative or theatrical.

2) Statement of Facts

It is surprising to most young counsel to learn that many appeals are determined on the facts. The facts should be set out in a straightforward and chronological manner. If, however, any material facts are disputed, this should be clearly noted. It is imperative that the facts be accurate. If there is even a minor inaccuracy, this will cause the court to question everything else you say. While your opponent, on the other hand, may direct the court's attention to any inaccuracy in the facts set out in your factum, it is generally a mistake to quibble about the facts unless the point is directly relevant to the appeal.

All relevant facts, even those unfavourable to your case, should be included. This is an opportunity for you to bring unfavourable facts to the court's attention in a less harmful manner than opposing counsel will do in his or her factum. The facts should be set out fairly, in a manner that supports your position, but without being argumentative. The ideal effect is one where the recital of the facts is so well done that it suggests to the court, without any argument, how it should decide the issues.

A good deal of judgment is required in determining which facts are relevant and material. What is important is to get to the meat of the matter without boring your reader with unnecessary detail. If specific points of fact are necessary to advance particular arguments, it is often best to raise those points only in the argument rather than referring back to them or repeating them. As a rule of thumb, when trying to discard unnecessary factual material do not worry about omitting less important facts that support your position. You can always raise those in oral argument — often with very good results. Be very careful however about omitting facts that might tend to undermine your position. If you do and those facts are relevant and material, your opponent can make great mileage with them in his or her factum.

It is important to avoid the tendency to fill out a factum with unnecessary facts in the hope that their sheer volume will impress the bench. If, for example, you are dealing with a trading case, it is much more effective to state:

> "The appellant purchased and sold 16 pieces of real estate between 1992 and 1997," than it is to say, "On July 1, 1992 the appellant purchased 234 Wood Street which it then sold on April 15, 1994. On March 2, 1993 the appellant . . . , "etc.

Panels are impressed by cogency, not volume.

Respondent's counsel, in preparing his or her factum, should only add facts that are salient to the line of argument. He or she should not elaborate for the sake of elaboration.

While some facts may not be directly relevant, they can be important for the purpose of "colour," which is another aspect of the psychology of appellate practice. For example, in *Westar Mining Ltd. v. Her Majesty the Queen*,[7] the issue was whether business interruption insurance proceeds were income from the operation of a mine. On examination for discovery, counsel for the Respondent stated that the business "source" of the insurance proceeds was "filling a hole" caused by the loss of business income. The Federal Court of Appeal seized on this because it demonstrated that the Minister's argument was fundamentally implausible.[8]

---

7 92 D.T.C. 6358 (F.C.A.).

8 *Ibid.* at 6363.

> The artificiality of the Respondent's position is made manifest by several passages in the examination for discovery of the Crown's representative, of which the following is a fair example. Mr. Bowman and Mr. Lefebvre were, respectively, counsel for the taxpayer and the Crown.
>
> MR. BOWMAN: The Minister says this is income from a business.
>
> Q Is that right?
>
> A Yes.
>
> Q What is the business that the Minister says this is income from?
>
> A It's to fill holes.
>
> Q The Minister thinks the taxpayer is in the business of filling holes? The Plaintiff is in the business of making holes.
>
> MR. LEFEBVRE: We're arguing. I think we're arguing. We explained the position. In the course of its business, the Plaintiffs insure against the event, against the occurrence of certain risks. Now those risks occur, there's a loss of revenue that arises. The non-operation of the mine, of course, produces a loss of revenue which is filled under the insurance policy. In the absence of the insurance policy, there would have been no income. That filled the hole.
>
> The issue, therefore, is whether this is income derived from the operation of a mine, or whether it's income derived from the non-operation of a mine covered by the insurance policy.

Therefore, "colour" was fundamental to the taxpayer's success in the appeal.

3) The Issues

The next part of the factum sets out the issues. This is probably the most difficult area of the factum. Generally, if the case cannot be won on two or three major issues, then it is not likely that it can be won at all. Remember that when you are determining the number of issues to set out, you must keep in mind that judges lose patience with weak arguments. Feeble arguments do nothing more than cast doubt on the rest of your case, which may be perfectly solid. Do not leave to the Court the work of deciding which issues are important. Determine which issues are most important, concentrate your efforts on them, and make them clear and precise.

In preparing the order of the issues, place the strongest issue first. The material which a person reads or hears first will be more influential and more likely to be remembered.

4) Nature of the Argument

Ignore the dictum that factums should be restricted to concise statements of points of law, devoid of argumentation. The courts really do want to know the outline of your argument in advance. They do not, however, want a verbatim transcript of what you intend to say at the hearing. Consequently, there is a fine balance between outlining an argument and elaborating on an argument. A simple way to ensure that this balance is maintained is to remember that if it takes more than three sentences to make a point, you are probably going beyond the bounds of permissible argumentation for a factum.[9]

The next step is drafting the argument. For each issue, the appropriate cases and propositions should be set out under the appropriate headings. Do not include quotations unless they materially advance your argument. You can always refer to the book of authorities in argument if necessary. Lengthy and unnecessary quotations result in ponderous factums and break the line of argument.

Be selective. Do not include every case that supports your position in some way; citing a large number of cases will not help your cause. It may even harm it. Choose a few cases, which are very strong and omit the rest. Mr. Justice Morden, former Associate Chief of Ontario, in his lecture on the Partnership of the Bench and Bar, stated:[10]

> Discrimination has to be used in reference to cases. In *Lambert v. Lewis*, Lord Diplock said "The citation of a plethora of illustrative authorities apart from being time and cost consuming presents the danger of so blinding the court with case law that it has difficulty in seeing the wood of legal principle for the trees of paraphrase." One must assume that a jurist having the legal acumen of Lord Diplock would not be permanently blinded by the trees but possibly slowed down in isolating the relevant principle. In a recent case in our court, Chief Justice McKinnon in the course of his judgment said "Originally the court was asked to wade through a sea of cases. This was a metaphor because when a mass of cases is pushed at the court it often feels as though it is drowning."

---

9 It may also indicate that you have not yet conceptualized the issues in a succinct, cogent manner.

10 John W. Morden, "The Partnership of Bench and Bar," Law Society of Upper Canada, *Gazette*, September/December 1982, Vol. XVI, No. 3, at 46.

The above may be summarized by the simple phrase: less is more. This is an aphorism that advocates should never forget in practice as appellate judges tend to be quite familiar with most cases counsel cite (and have often participated in deciding them). As a pure practical matter, judges are not amused, to say the least, by hefty volumes of authorities when, in fact, only three or four cases are needed to support the proposition at issue.

In selecting the cases to cite, determine whether the law is settled on the proposition that you want to raise. If it is, then cite one or two cases. For example, the law in regard to reasonable expectation of profit has been settled by Supreme Court decisions in *Stewart v. Her Majesty the Queen*[11] and *Walls v. Her Majesty the Queen.*[12] Consequently, there would normally be no need to list more than these two cases when discussing reasonable expectation of profit. In rare cases where the proposition is novel and the jurisprudence is unsettled, multiple citations may be justified and required.[13]

Where there is damaging case law that you know your opponent will be raising confront it and attempt to distinguish it. The danger in not dealing with your opponent's authorities is illustrated by the decision of the Michigan Court of Appeal in *Denny v. Radar Industries:*[14]

> The appellant has attempted to distinguish the factual situation in this case from that in *Renfroe v. Higgins Rock Coating and Manufacturing Co., Inc.* (1969), 17 Mich. App. 259. He didn't. We couldn't. Affirmed. Costs to appeallee. All concurred.

After the argument and authorities for each issue are set out, you may wish to provide a short summary for the court, but it should generally be no longer than two or three sentences.

5) The Order Sought

The final part of the factum sets out the order or the judgement that you seek. State your request clearly. If you are asking for costs in the courts below, say so; failure to do so might be costly for your client.[15] Of course, if

11 2002 D.T.C. 6969.

12 2002 D.T.C. 6960.

13 A GAAR case would be a classic example of where it would be necessary to refer to a substantial number of authorities since the law in that area is very recent and in a state of flux. Even there, however, it would be overkill to refer to every GAAR case ever decided where the only issue was, for example, misuse of the Act or abuse of the provisions of the Act read as a whole.

14 28 Mich. App. 294, 294 (1970).

15 *Dupont Canada Inc. v. The Queen*, 2003 D.T.C. 5001 (F.C.A.); leave to appeal to the Supreme Court of Canada refused May 15, 2003.

you are representing the Respondent you will simply ask that the appeal be dismissed with costs throughout.

C. ORAL ADVOCACY

Oral argument is the most exciting and challenging aspect of appellate advocacy. This is your opportunity to have a dialogue with the court and to build on the solid foundation established by your factum. Oral argument provides you with the opportunity to deal with the court's concerns about your position.

1) Preparation

Preparation is essential if you want to be successful. You owe it to your client, the court, opposing counsel and yourself to be prepared when you enter the courtroom to argue an appeal.

You have to know your record on appeal and your transcripts almost by heart. You have to be able to refer quickly to exhibits and specific passages of transcript that come up during the course of argument. Moreover, you have to be able to respond to difficult questions by pointing out passages of transcript or exhibits that support your position.

If you are arguing a case without the benefit of a junior (a practice which I do not recommend), take great care in organizing your materials on the counsel table. The Record on Appeal, Transcripts, Books of Authorities, Factums should each be in separate piles so that you can reach them quickly in response to questions from the bench or when you need them to support your own argument. Fumbling through papers wastes time you cannot afford to waste and leaves a bad impression with the court.

2) Juniors

Juniors are very useful in assisting you with preparation. The role of a junior is to keep the materials organized and to be prepared to hand you a volume of transcript (preferably open to the correct page) or an exhibit on a moment's notice. As well, juniors can assist the advocate by taking notes of what is going on, while keeping an ear attuned to when an exhibit or piece of transcript may be needed. A junior should be made aware, however, that he or she should not leaf through the exhibits or transcripts during the hearing and should not inundate leading counsel with notes. If a junior has a suggestion, he or she should make a note in large print on a pad of paper and set the pad quietly on the counsel table next to leading counsel where he or she can glance at it during breaks in the argument. By the same token, leading counsel should always consult his or her junior before concluding the argument. This should be done not only out of courtesy but because junior counsel often have valuable and cogent points to add.

3) Technique

Whether you are acting for the Appellant or the Respondent, the technique is essentially the same. Your tone of voice should be conversational. The best approach is to engage in a dialogue with the court. Remember that you are not giving an oration, but are trying to persuade particular individuals to decide the appeal in favour of your client. With this in mind, your argument should be interesting and persuasive.

As you are presenting your argument the court will almost inevitably pose questions. If this occurs, do not interrupt the court with an answer until the court is finished. Too many counsel anticipate the entire question at the beginning of the question and then proceed to answer the question they anticipated rather than the one that was asked. This is quite irritating for the court.

When the court poses a question, it usually leads to something. In these situations, try to determine where the question is going. Remember that not all questions are hostile. Some questions are designed to set up a point in your favour. Welcome them as an opportunity to persuade.

It is imperative that you address the question when asked. The effect of not addressing the question immediately is that the court will be annoyed and tune out the rest of your argument. While it is important to address the question when asked, it does not need to be dealt with exhaustively. It may be sufficient to provide a brief response so that the court understands where you are going. You can then return to it later in greater detail. If you take this approach, you should pay close attention to the reaction of the court to determine whether the brief response you have provided is sufficient.[16] If the court appears dissatisfied, then deal with the question in the level of detail necessary.

4) Mannerisms

To be an effective advocate, avoid irritating personal mannerisms in court. These mannerisms can severely compromise your effectiveness. They are

16 Eye contact is important here. Indeed, it is always crucial to engage the court by making eye contact. Avoid, at all costs, being tied to a prepared text when making your argument which ensures that the court tunes you out.

at best distracting and at worst alienating. The following mannerisms run the risk of irritating the court and distracting attention from a good cause to a bad performance: chatting incessantly while opposing counsel is arguing or the court is asking opposing counsel a question; nodding affirmatively or dismissively; noisily pouring ice water; burying your head in your hands in utter disbelief — the list goes on. While some might suggest that courts should not be swayed by such personal matters the simple fact is the balance between victory and defeat in appeals is often extremely fine. Minor irritations can detract from your presentation and tip that fine balance against the interests of your client.

5) Role of Counsel for the Appellant

Generally, counsel for the Appellant has an uphill battle. Consequently, you should realize that you are an underdog and anticipate all of the reasons why a court might be reluctant to reverse the decision under appeal. As such, you should prepare yourself for questions that reflect that natural reluctance to reverse the trial court's decision.

Avoid appealing findings of fact if at all possible. Generally, courts are loathe to reverse findings of facts.[17] You should pursue such appeals only as a last resort and only if you have a strong chance of meeting the heavy onus which you must overcome in such appeals.

6) Role of Counsel for the Respondent

The role of the counsel for the Respondent is to defend the trial judge's position. Consequently, the basic position of the counsel for the Respondent should be that the trial judge's position is fundamentally sound even though counsel for the Appellant has raised some minor quibbles about the judgment under appeal.[18]

With this in mind, you should keep your eyes and ears finely tuned to the mood of the court. If counsel for the Appellant appears to have been

---

17 Although there are probably other examples, I am only aware of one tax case in which the Federal Court of Appeal reversed a finding of fact: *Rich v. The Queen*, 2003 D.T.C. 5115. In that case the taxpayer had very strong grounds for reversal. Nevertheless the panel split 2–1 with a strong dissenting opinion.

18 The most recent information (1995) suggests that the Crown is successful on 75% of appeals before the Federal Court of Appeal. B. Burns and I. MacGregor, 95 CR 33:3. Although we do not know precisely what percentage of those appeals involve the Crown as respondent it would certainly be the bulk of them since the Crown is successful in 65% of general procedure appeals under the *Income Tax Act*, R.S.C. 1985, c. 1 (5th Supp.): *Ibid.*

gaining headway on a point, then begin to anticipate how you can get the court back on course. To accomplish this, you should try to defuse the issue or demonstrate that it is not really material to the matters under appeal. For example, I was in an appeal where the trial court found that the transaction in question was a sham. My only real argument on appeal was that one of the participants, an elderly woman, had testified that transaction in question had in fact happened. The trial judge did not question her credibility, and she was not cross-examined on the point. I argued that the court could not sustain the judgment under appeal without concluding that this elderly woman was lying, a finding courts do not normally like to make. Counsel for the Respondent, Gordon Bourgard, devastated my argument by conceding, on behalf of the Crown, that the woman was telling the truth. She was, he argued, simply the unwitting tool of the other party to the transaction. That was enough for the court to dismiss my appeal.[19]

7) Replies

Do not reply unless it is necessary. Remember that you will invariably draw the court's attention back to the points made by Respondent's counsel referred to in the reply. As such, you should weigh whether it would be better not to reply and thereby avoid enhancing your opponent's argument by showing that you regard the issue as serious.

The function of a reply is to respond to a point raised by the Respondent, not to reiterate your own points. While the courts will normally allow a degree of latitude on this it is best not to abuse that latitude. An example of an effective reply would be:

> My learned friend suggested that there was no evidence that the software was available for use but *his own expert witness* testified that *he had used it* during the process of preparing his valuation.

An example of a bad reply would be:

> My learned friend cited *Stubart* but as I said in my opening . . .

The worst phrase you can hear from an appellate panel during the course of a reply is:

> Mr. (Miss) Smith, precisely what is this in reply to?

In making a reply, remember to make it brief. It should not take more than two or three sentences to make a point. If it does, then it is not worth

19 *Debeer v. The Queen*, 2001 D.T.C. 5385 (F.C.A.).

replying on the point. Generally, you should limit your replies to one to five points, preferably three points.

8) Interjections in the Course of Argument

Interjecting during your opponent's argument is a dangerous technique, which should only be used on rare occasions. Generally, you should confine interjections to serious misstatements of evidence. This means that you should not interject unless your factual point is significant and unambiguous. The purpose of interjections is to prevent the court from going down a long line of argument premised on a material factual error. You will have a chance to make your own points during your argument. Be very reluctant to antagonize the court by interrupting your opponent except in the most extreme circumstances.

D. CONCLUSION

The primary role of an advocate is to persuade the court. The three major elements of persuasion were identified by Aristotle:[20]

- Ethos — the element in which the speaker establishes his or her own character and credentials and hence his or her believability;
- Pathos — the element in which the speaker appeals to his listeners' emotions, so that they are disposed to decide in his favour; and
- Logos — the final element in which the speaker provides the logical reason why his or her side of the issue should prevail.

These principles still hold true.

You develop credibility with the court by means of accuracy, balance and courtesy. You lose credibility through sloppiness, bombast and evasion. You make the case real for the court by conveying a sense that real people are involved and rights are at stake. The Honourable Donald G.H. Bowman, Associate Chief Justice of the Tax Court of Canada always said that arguing a case involved painting a picture for the court. The final element emerges from a thorough understanding of the underlying legal issues and a logical, dispassionate analysis of how that law should apply to your fact situation.

---

20 Aristotle, *On Rhetoric*, translated by G. A. Kennedy (Toronto: Oxford University Press, 1991).

In the end, appellate advocacy is simply a form of interaction between people. The appellate advocate must master practical, common sense principles of persuasion. In assessing arguments, techniques and strategies, you must remember that the cardinal rule is to try to see the case through the eyes of your panel. As a corollary, you must always keep your ego in check; you are there to assist the court, not to dazzle the court with your rhetorical skills. If an advocate sticks to those fundamental rules, he or she will have a rewarding career before the courts of appeal.

Chapter Four

The Role of Ethos, Pathos, and Logos in Tax Appeals

Harry Erlichman

Bill Innes concludes his masterly summary of appellate advocacy by referring to its three major elements — ethos, pathos and logos, that is, the credibility of the speaker, the emotional context of the facts and the logic of the argument. These were identified by that ancient authority, Aristotle, who also tutored Alexander the Great, who motivated his troops to conquer the known world. How can they be applied in the context of the rules of the appellate courts and their current interpretative guidelines so as to conquer the known tax world?

By way of background, tax appeals are commenced in the Tax Court of Canada, which is a superior court of record. Where the amounts in issue total $12,000 or less or the loss determined is $24,000 or less, the appeals are usually heard under the court's Informal Procedure. All other appeals are heard under the General Procedure. An appeal from a judgment made under the Tax Court's General Procedure is heard by the Federal Court of Appeal under s.27 (1.1) of the *Federal Court Act*. Under s. 27(1.2) of the *Federal Court Act*, it hears appeals for judicial review of decisions of the Tax Court made under the Informal Procedure.

The Federal Court of Appeal may grant relief in an appeal under the Informal Procedure pursuant to s.27(1.3) of the *Federal Court Act*, if the Tax Court failed to observe a principle of natural justice, erred in law in making a decision, based its decision on an erroneous finding of fact made in a perverse or capricious manner or without regard for the material before it, or acted in any other way that was contrary to law.

All appeals from the Tax Court to the Federal Court of Appeal on questions of law heard under s.27 of the *Federal Court Act* are reviewed on the standard of correctness, regardless of the procedure under which the decision was made. This proposition was established in *Housen v. Nikolaisen*,[1] where a majority of the Supreme Court held that on a pure question of law an appellate court is free to replace the opinion of a trial judge with its own. This was applied by the Federal Court of Appeal in *The Queen v. Rhonda Ray*,[2] which case also confirmed that the Tax Court is owed no deference on the interpretation of the Act.

However, findings of fact are not to be reversed unless a trial judge made a palpable and overriding error. The Supreme Court in *Housen* stated that there should be a high level of appellate deference to factual inferences made by the trial judge. For questions of mixed fact and law, the standard of review will vary depending on whether a legal principle is readily extricable from the trial judge's interpretation of the evidence as a whole.

In the result, though credibility and logic are equally important at all levels, there may be less scope for an appeal to emotion at the Court of Appeal level than at the Tax Court, particularly with respect to obtaining crucial findings of fact. And though sympathetic facts are always to be preferred, the Court of Appeal judges do not see the witnesses and are less likely to be influenced by them. At the Supreme Court of Canada, however, there is ample scope for an appeal to emotion because that court must first be persuaded to give leave on a matter of national importance, and then determine which of various competing policy concerns should predominate. The framing of the issue on which leave is sought will bring into play pathos and logos because leave is granted in only a small minority of applications. These are considered by panels of three judges and the emotional or intellectual interest of at least one must be aroused. To achieve this result in a tax case is perhaps more difficult than one concerning criminal or family law.

Thus while at both appellate levels it is counsel's role to don Aristotle's robes and try to motivate the panel to find reasons to overturn or support the Tax Court's decision, it is at the Supreme Court that the fullest scope for emotional motivation is found.

Ethos relates to the credibility of counsel: can he or she be relied upon by the court to make a fair presentation within the context of the rules of court? At a basic level, ethos applies to the application of apparently mun-

1 [2002] 2 S.C.R. 23.

2 2004 FCA 1.

dane rules, such as those setting out the cover colour of different memorandums of fact and law. In the Supreme Court, Rule 42(1) sets out the colours for factums — beige for an appellant, green for a respondent, and blue for an intervener. Specific rules also govern the size of pages and typeface, i.e., Rule 21(3)(a), concerning the memorandum of argument, requires that it be printed in type no smaller than 12 print and no more than 12 characters per 2.5 cm. Rule 42(4) limits factums to 40 pages. Apart from limiting the natural loquaciousness of counsel, the purpose is to reduce the strain on the justices or their clerks who must read the volumes of materials filed. Following the rules also demonstrates that either the lawyer or the law clerk who prepared the appeal material cared enough to read them.

Similarly, in the Federal Court, Rule 70(4) limits the length of a memorandum of fact and law to 30 pages unless the court rules otherwise. Parties who try to evade this rule by using excessively small fonts risk being penalized in costs. Failure to follow the rules will adversely affect ethos and leave a bad impression with the court. Justices who have to read many pages in very small print the night before the hearing of an appeal may well not be receptive to the arguments of the counsel who imposed the hardship upon them.

The guides to the interpretation of the Tax Court Rules and Federal Court Rules are instructive.

S.4(1) of the Tax Court General Procedure Rules provides that the Tax Court rules "shall be liberally construed to secure the just, most expeditious and least expensive determination of every proceeding on its merits."

Similarly, s.3 of the Federal Court Rules, 1998,[3] requires that the Federal Court Rules be interpreted in a similar fashion.

Although the Rules of the Supreme Court of Canada[4] contain no similar statement of policy, their interpretation would undoubtedly follow the same guidelines.

With respect to the substance of an appeal, all arguments must be raised clearly in the memorandum. If not, the court may refuse to hear them. The credibility of counsel and their argument is reduced if a point said to be important is first raised only at the hearing of the appeal.

Credibility will also be affected by an overabundance of arguments. The strongest arguments must be raised first while the judges are still paying attention. Similarly, invoking the *Charter of Rights and Freedoms* may add drama to a presentation but also might indicate that the legal result

---

3 SOR/98-106, as am. S.C. 2007, c.8, ss.182(3), 183(2)(a).

4 SOR/2002-156.

sought is so bereft of merit as a matter of tax law that an extraordinary constitutional remedy must be claimed.

Ultimately, to preserve ethos, counsel must squarely address the weak points of her arguments and the strong points of her opponent's position.

Pathos is directed to emotions: where should the sympathies of the court lie? At its most blatant, a taxpayer dressed in black may sit quietly crying in the courtroom while her counsel slips in a reference to the recent death of her husband without insurance. For good measure, two small sniffling children could sit beside her. On the other hand, counsel for the Canada Revenue Agency could equate the amount of tax in issue to the cost of a new heart monitor for an emergency room or a new truck for soldiers on a United Nations peacekeeping mission.

A more appropriate resort to pathos concerns the on-going debate as to the role of equity in the interpretation of tax statutes — whether taxpayers are paying their fair share of the fiscal burden. This approach was formulated by Chief Justice Dickson in *Bronfman Trust*.[5] Note the telling use of "manipulating" and "patina of compliance."

> Assessment of taxpayer's transactions with an eye to commercial and economic realities, rather than juristic classification of form, may help to avoid the inequity of tax liability being dependent upon the taxpayer's sophistication at manipulating a sequence of events to achieve a patina of compliance with the apparent prerequisites for a tax deduction.

This passage echoed the concern raised by Mr. Justice Estey in the Supreme Court decision in *Stubart Investments Ltd. v. The Queen*[6] that the appropriate interpretative approach would "provide uniformity of the Act across the community, and at the same time, reduce the attraction of elaborate and intricate tax avoidance plans and reduce the rewards to those best able to afford the services of the tax technicians."

Chief Justice Dickson's concern over "inequity" and manipulation were qualified in the later decision of the Supreme Court in *Shell Canada Ltd. v. The Queen*,

> . . . absent a specific provision to the contrary, it is not the court's role to prevent taxpayers from relying on the sophisticated structure of their transactions . . . on the basis that it would be inequitable to those taxpayers who have not chosen to structure their transactions that way. . . .[7]

5 [1987] 1 S.C.R. 32 at 53.
6 84 D.T.C. 6305 at 6322.
7 99 D.T.C. 5669 at 5677.

However, in the shifting sands of our constantly developing tax jurisprudence, there is always a role for equity and a purposive approach in the interpretation of the Act, because as Mr. Justice Estey said in *Stubart*,

> Whatever the source or explanation, measures such as s.137 of the *Income Tax Act* are instructions from Parliament to the community on the individual member's liability for taxes, expressed in general terms. This instruction is, like the balance of the Act, introduced as well for the guidance of the courts in applying the scheme of the Act throughout the country. The courts may, of course, develop, in their interpretation of s. 137, doctrines such as the *bona fide* business purpose test; or a step-by-step transaction rule for the classification of taxpayer's activities which fall within the ban of such a general tax avoidance provision.
>
> In jurisdictions such as the United States and the United Kingdom, such doctrines have developed in the courts, usually in the guise of canons of construction of the statutes. These have included the business purpose test, step-by-step transactions analysis, substance over form, and expanded sham rules. Whether the development be by legislative measure or judicial action, *the result is a process of balancing the taxpayer's freedom to carry on his commercial and social affairs however he may choose, and the state interest in revenue, equity in the raising of the revenue, and economic planning.* [emphasis added][8]

When competing concerns are to be balanced, emotion may serve to tip the scales of justice one way or the other. Recently, the Supreme Court balanced tax policy and equity issues in *65302 British Columbia Ltd. v. The Queen*,[9] a case concerning the deductibility of fines and penalties under paragraph 18(1)(a) of the Act.

> Tax neutrality and equity are key objectives of our tax system. Tax neutrality is violated by tax concessions, since the purpose of such concessions is to influence people's behaviour through the tax system by providing incentives for engaging in certain types of behaviour. For example, a deduction for an RRSP or a charitable contribution is a tax concession. This is to be distinguished from deductions allowed for the purpose of gaining an accurate picture of a taxpayer's net income. One of the underlying premises of our tax system is that the state taxes only net, rather than gross, income because it is net income that measures a *taxpayer's ability to pay*. As has been pointed out, this results in business related

8 Above note 6 at 6321.

9 99 D.T.C. 5799 at 5811.

> fines being deductible: see Hogg and Magee, *supra*, at p.243. Moreover, Hogg and Magee, *supra*, note at p.40, "in a system that is generally related to ability to pay, the provisions that violate neutrality (tax concessions) tend also to violate equity by abandoning the criterion of ability to pay in favour of other policy objectives." [emphasis added]

Note the emotive use of the words "violate" and "abandoning" to emphasize the authors' concern.

Emotion and logic are also demonstrated in *Will-Kare Paving & Contracting Ltd. v. The Queen*[10] in which the Supreme Court was divided four to three on the question of whether an asphalt plant had been "acquired primarily for the purpose of manufacturing or processing goods for sale or lease." This in turn depended on whether the asphalt that was used by the owner of the plant to pave roads was a good for "sale" or was provided as a matter of commercial law pursuant to a contract for work and materials.

A dramatic illustration of an appeal to pathos is found in the dissenting reasons of Mr. Justice Binnie. He commences:

> The fundamental issue in this case is the interpretation of everyday words used by Parliament in the context of a tax regime based on self-assessment. In 1997, the last year for which precise statistics are available, 20,453,540 tax returns were filed with Revenue Canada. Most taxpayers are not (and likely have no desire to be) learned in the law. When confronted as here with the phrase "primarily in the manufacturing or processing of goods for sale or lease" under s.127(9) of the *Income Tax Act*, S.C. 1970-71-72, c. 63 ("Act"), he or she is entitled, in my opinion, to the benefit of the plain meaning of an everyday word like "sale." The taxpayer was denied that benefit by the Minister in this case. The millions of taxpayers who are not lawyers cannot be expected to reach for *Benjamin's Sale of Goods* to research the difference between a contract for the sale of goods and a contract for work and materials and to apply these distinctions in the assessment of their own income tax liability.[11]

Unfortunately, his appeal to pathos, as well as sarcasm, was found wanting by the majority of his colleagues, who presumably felt that the legal advisors of taxpayers who were concerned with whether an asphalt plant qualified for a s.s.127(5) investment tax credit, and fell into Class 8 or Class 39 of Schedule II of the Income Tax Regulations, could be expected to seek access to *Benjamin's Sale of Goods*. However, his approach is noteworthy to

---

10 [2000] 1 S.C.R. 915 [*Will-Kare Paving*].

11 *Ibid.* at para. 39.

demonstrate a subject of concern to members of the court that counsel might focus on: how would one of the twenty million taxpayers who file returns expect the Act to be interpreted? How would this huge, invisible jury of honest taxpayers apply the Act?

In another area of the reasons where both pathos and logos are employed, Mr. Justice Binnie, states:

> A major emphasis for the provision was on creating jobs. Asphalt plants create jobs irrespective of the form of the asphalt disposal contract.[12]

Clearly, it is important to demonstrate that the interpretation sought fulfills the policy behind the legislation.

Mr. Justice Binnie, also referred to the Supreme Court's decision in *Québec (Communauté Urbaine) v. Corp. Notre-Dame de Bon-Secours,*[13] saying that it

> . . . recognized that, while at one time tax legislation was arguably limited to raising funds to cover government expenses, "(i)n our time it has been recognized that such legislation serves other purposes and functions as a tool of economics and social policy. . .".[14]

It is therefore appropriate to emphasize how the interpretation being advanced will achieve the economic and social policy, such as the creation of jobs, which is the *raison d'être* of the tax regulation in issue. Under this approach, an interpretation that fails to fulfill the policy would be found wanting.

The majority decision of Mr. Justice Major also emphasized, that it was necessary to determine Parliament's intention in providing the incentive in issue.[15] In addition, he wrote:

> To apply a "plain meaning" interpretation of the concept of a sale in the case at bar would assume that the Act operates in a vacuum, oblivious to the legal characterization of the broader commercial relationships it affects. It is not a commercial code in addition to a taxation statute. Previous jurisprudence of this Court has assumed that reference must be given to the broader commercial law to give meaning to words that, outside of the Act, are well-defined. See *Continental Bank Leasing Corp. v. Canada,*

12 *Ibid.* at para. 61.

13 [1993] 3 S.C.R. 3.

14 *Will-Kare Paving,* above note 10, at para. 69.

15 *Ibid.* at paras. 27 and 28.

> [1998] 2 S.C.R. 298. See also P.W. Hogg, J.E. Magee and T. Cook, *Principles of Canadian Tax Law* (3rd ed. 1999), at p.2, where the authors note:
>
> > The *Income Tax Act* relies implicitly on the general law, especially the law of contract and property. . . Whether a person is an employee, independent contractor, partner, agent, beneficiary of a trust or shareholder of a corporation will usually have an effect on tax liability and will turn on concepts contained in the general law, usually provincial law.
>
> Referring to the boarder context of private commercial law in ascertaining the meaning to be ascribed to language used in the Act is also consistent with the modern purposive principle of statutory interpretation.[16]

The need to apply general law, usually commercial law, again emphasizes the need to employ ethos and logos to help direct the Court to the interpretative result desired, because of the appeal level competing policy concerns often need to be balanced. An appropriate balancing approach in commercial law is demonstrated in the recent decision of the Supreme Court in *H & R Block Canada Inc. v. National Trust Co.*[17] which though not a tax case, provides useful insights into what emotional and logical concerns will resonate with the court.

The case concerns the interpretation of the *Bulk Sales Act* of Ontario. Did the failure of a purchaser to comply with the requirements of that Act render it liable for the entire amount it paid to the vendor, or just the amount that would likely have been paid to creditors if the Act had been complied with?

The majority decision, written by Mr. Justice Bastarache, stated that in interpreting the *Bulk Sales Act* substance should govern over form.[18] As well, he observed:

> We must interpret the buyer's duty to account under s.16(2) in light of the rules of statutory interpretation and, in particular, of commercial realities. Accordingly, two factors have heightened importance: (i) predictability, since bright-line rules facilitate transactions and economic efficiency; and (ii) a sensible economic result, also to further economic efficiency. The actual text and case law drive that first of the factors; a purposive approach and policy consideration drive the second.[19]

---

16 *Ibid.* at paras. 31 and 32.
17 2003 SCC 66.
18 *Ibid.* at paras. 28 and 47.
19 *Ibid.* at paras. 28 and 47.

The court further considered to be of significance whether the unjust enrichment of creditors would occur i.e.: whether a creditor would be "the lucky recipient of a windfall."[20] As well, the majority decision referred to the need to accommodate modern commercial realities.

The dissenting opinion of Madam Justice Deschamps referred primarily to the object and spirit of the Act and the need for sanctions. She said: "If the Act had no teeth, it would serve no useful purpose."[21] In the context of some other provinces repealing their Acts, she expressed particular concern, that eliminating the consequences of violating the Act "would be an implicit repeal of the Act, and amount to a negation of the democratic institutional process."[22]

And she stated:

> when the Act is applied, there are financial consequences, which the parties anticipated. It is not the function of judges to substitute their judgment for the wills of the legislature or the parties simply to minimize the impact of commercial legislation that they believe to be cumbersome or unfair.[23]

It is therefore apparent that a "logical" conclusion may flow from an "emotional" concern with the results that will follow a particular interpretation. The concern voiced by Madam Justice Deschamps is of particular signifance to the interpretation of tax legislation, and the Supreme Court voiced a similar concern in *Ludco Enterprises v. The Queen*,

> Furthermore, when interpreting the *Income Tax Act* courts must be mindful of their role as distinct from that of Parliament. In the absence of clear statutory language, judicial innovation is undesirable.[24]

The General Anti-Avoidance Rule does provide clear statutory language stating that the courts should apply the Act with equity, and achieve fairness through the use of innovation.[25] Daniel Sandler's chapter in this volume on the General Anti-Avoidance Rule presents an unnecessarily gloomy forecast of the likely attitude of the Supreme Court to its interpretation. The language of s.245 speaks emphatically to emotion. e.g. "*bona fide* purposes," "misuse," "abuse." These words, as well as the remedies available in ss. 245(5) are "instructions from Parliament" in the words of

---

20 *Ibid.* at paras. 31 and 35.
21 *Ibid.* at para. 52.
22 *Ibid.* at para. 68.
23 *Ibid.* at para. 73.
24 2001 D.T.C. 5505 at 5512 [*Ludco*]. See also *65302 British Columbia Ltd. v. The Queen*, above note 9.

Mr. Justice Estey, direction to seek equity between taxpayers when applying the modern approach to statutory interpretation. The use of pathos to seize the moral high ground would therefore be appropriate. Mr. Justice Estey foresaw its need in *Stubart* commenting:

> Returning then to the issue of interpretation now before this Court, there are certain broad characteristics of tax statute construction which can be discerned in the authorities here and in similar jurisdictions abroad. The most obvious is the fact that in some jurisdictions, such as Canada and Australia, the legislature has responded to the need for overall regulation to forestall blatant practices designed to defeat the Revenue. These anti-tax avoidance provisions may reflect the rising importance and cost of government in the community, the concomitant higher rates of taxation in modern times, and hence the greater stake in the avoidance contests between the taxpayer and the state. The arrival of these provisions in the statute may also have heralded the extension of the *Income Tax Act* from a mere tool for the carving of the cost of government out of the community, to an instrument of economic and fiscal policy for the regulation of commerce and industry of the country through fiscal intervention of government.
>
> . . .
>
> . . . *the result is a process of balancing the taxpayer's freedom to carry on his commercial and social affairs however he may choose, and the state interest in revenue, equity in the raising of the revenue, and economic planning.*[26]

That there is continuing precedent for this approach is demonstrated in the decision of the Supreme Court in *Symes v. Canada*[27] which considered the applicability of the *Charter of Rights* to the deductibility of child care expenses under the *Income Tax Act.*

The tone of the debate between the majority and dissenting views of the court was set when Mr. Justice Iacobucci referred to the decision of Chief Justice Dickson in *Brooks v. Canada Safeway*,

> That those who bear children and benefit society as a whole thereby should not be economically or socially disadvantaged seems to bespeak the obvious. It is only women who bear children; no man can become pregnant . . . it is unfair to impose all of the costs of pregnancy upon one half of the population.[28]

---

25 See *Mathew et al. v. The Queen*, 2002 D.T.C. 1637 at 1695.

26 *Stubart*, above note 6 at 6321.

27 [1993] 4 S.C.R. 695.

28 [1989] 1 S.C.R. 1219 at 1243.

In dissent, L'Heureux-Dubé, J. maintained this policy concern,

> The tax system is . . . a powerful tool used to direct social and economic policy in Canada. The role that this "powerful tool" may play in the presentation of the attainment of substantive equity for women cannot be overlooked.[29]

Writing for the majority, Iacobucci, J differed only as to how fairness was to be measured or achieved.

> This Court was invited to use the Charter to rectify a disadvantage allegedly suffered by businesswomen vis à vis businessmen, and in the process, this Court was invited to ignore the effect of allowing a complete deduction on the rest of the system.[30]

Therefore, given the requisite statutory authorization, the courts are more then able to consider "fairness" and "substantive equity," topics that lend themselves to emotional context, when interpreting sections of the *Income Tax Act*. Indeed, even apart from the *Charter* or GAAR the courts have in recent decisions been concerned that the Act not be abused.

In *Ludco*,[31] the Supreme Court was concerned with whether borrowed money had been used for the purpose of earning income so that interest was deductible under paragraph 20(1)(c) of the Act. The court indicated that the sufficiency of the income expected or received was not a matter of concern, "absent a sham or window dressing or similar vitiating circumstances."

This caveat is necessary because following a single-minded focus on one policy concern, such as predictability, may lead to disastrous consequences, as illustrated by the Enron fiasco:

> Unobstructed by a compliant Arthur Andersen, the one-time big-time accounting firm, Fastow led the team that gave new meaning to the term aggressive accounting. An Enron employee described it this way. "Say you have a dog, but need to create a duck on the financial statements. Fortunately, there are specific accounting rules for what constitutes a duck: yellow feet, white covering, orange beak. So you take the dog and paint its feet yellow and its fur white and you paste an orange page beak on its nose, and then you say to your accountant, 'This is a duck! Don't you agree that it's a duck?' And the accountants say, 'Yes, according to the rules, this is a

29 *Symes* at 786.

30 *Symes* at 773.

31 Above note 24 at 5515.

> duck?' Everybody knows that it's a dog, not a duck, but that doesn't matter, because you've met the rules for calling it a duck."[32]

The concept of "window dressing or similar vitiating circumstances" provides scope to consider whether the receipt of income or other usual indicia of a genuine commercial transaction may be insufficient to demonstrate a right to a deduction under the Act when they are not truly reflective of commercial reality.

A recent example arose in the Tax Court in *McCoy v. The Queen*,[33] where Bowman, A.C.J., found that the full face value of promissory notes could not be taken into account in determining the cost of software for capital cost allowance purposes, because of the peculiar and complex agreements connected to the notes. He said that this conclusion was based "more on my commercial and common sense instincts than as a strictly logical or legal analysis. It is nonetheless a significant misgiving. . ."

References to "misgivings" and "commercial and common sense instincts" clearly call into play pathos that drives logos.

Similarly, in *Penner International Inc. v. Canada*,[34] the Federal Court of Appeal had to determine if diesel fuel purchased in Canada but consumed in the United States by commercial trucks transporting goods from Canada to the United States constituted goods "exported" from Canada for the purposes of obtaining a rebate of excise tax under the *Excise Tax Act*. Though the court was divided as to the outcome of the appeal, the need for the conduct to be in the ordinary course of commerce to qualify for the rebate was agreed upon by Rothstein, and Sexton JJ.A. Both quoted from the decision of the Supreme Court in *The King v. Carling Export Brewing and Malting Co. Ltd.*:

> I think there is a great deal to be said in favour of the view that "export" in the sense of the statute may be limited in such a way as to exclude export so entirely beyond the ordinary course of commerce. The considerations in favour of this view are so numerous and so obvious that they need not be dealt upon.[35]

Sexton, J.A., also referred to the negative policy decisions resulting from the majority's conclusion:

---

32 Bethany McLean and Peter Elkind, *The Smartest Guys in the Room: The Amazing Rise and Scandalous Fall of Enron* (New York: Portfolio/Viking Penguin, 2003) at 149.

33 2003 D.T.C. 660 at 685.

34 [2003] 2 F.C. 581.

35 [1930] S.C.R. 361.

> A pragmatic interpretation of the *Excise Tax Act* must be employed, such that consideration is given to the effects of a given interpretation. Statutes should be construed so as to avoid irrationality. When the issue is one of clarifying ambiguous wording, as it is here with regards to the vague definition of "export" in the *Excise Tax Act*, the absurdity of results can be a factor to consider in the interpretation of the wording.[36]

It should be noted, then, that if an argument can be made as to the absurd result flowing from an interpretation of ambiguous statutory language, there will be an expanded scope for pathos to assist the members of the court in agreeing with counsel's submissions. Of equal significance is the opportunity to explore the commerciality of the conduct or transaction which is said to result in the claimed tax treatment.

If commercial and common sense instincts point to a particular result, logic should more readily follow the same path.

While Aristotle's elements are not likely to lead counsel as far as they led Alexander the Great, they can still assist in the more modest triumphs of tax litigation.

36 *Penner*, above note 34 at 616.

Chapter Five

An Overview of Planning, Strategy and Tactics in the Trial Process

Alan J. Lenczner, Q.C. and Peter H. Griffin

Advocacy is the art of persuasion. That definition, accepted as wisdom for more than three centuries, is misleading in this modern era. A more appropriate definition states that: advocacy is foremost, knowledge of the facts and of the applicable principles of law, to which is applied the art of persuasion. Without a detailed exposition of the facts in a logical and cohesive sequence, oral, theatrical and presentational skills are mere shrouds. Equally, a convincing presentation of well-connected facts devoid of a theory that connects them to a sound principle of law is like an errant arrow that whizzes by its mark. Triers of fact are swayed by small incremental building blocks that fit comfortably together to form an attractive edifice built with as few difficult findings to make as possible. The young lawyer, armed with preparation, will defeat a more experienced adversary who has failed to do his or her homework.

The case must be won at trial. Counsel cannot rely on appeal. The Supreme Court of Canada in a number of recent decisions has accorded a very high degree of deference to the findings of fact and credibility made by trial judges or tribunal adjudicators.[1] Appeals are more and more limit-

1 See *Housen v. Nikolaisen*, [2002] 2 S.C.R. 235 at paras. 10–25; *K.L.B. v. British Columbia*, [2003] 2 S.C.R. 403 at para. 62; *M.B. v. British Columbia* [2003] 2 S.C.R. 477 at

ed to matters of correctness on a question of law; and/or they turn upon the court remedying procedural denials of the inferior tribunal that prevented a party from fairly presenting its case. Thus every effort must be made to enhance the probability of a successful verdict result at the trial.

A. PREPARATION — THE KEY TO SUCCESS

1) The Facts

Preparation for trial commences at your initial meeting with the client. Probably the facts are still fresh in his or her mind. Your duty is to obtain them at this time and to memorialize them in writing so that they are accurately preserved. These recollections will provide the foundation for the case and can be used at later dates to refresh the client's memory in preparation for discovery or for trial. What makes this task so critical is that the trial is generally several years distant. By then the client may well have forgotten many of the details. The guiding principle in preparing the initial account is to secure *every* relevant detail of the client's recollection. This meeting should not be hurried. If necessary, it should be continued and repeated in the next few weeks.

Once you have gained the trust and confidence of your client, you should advise them that you will be probing their story with scepticism in order to better allow you to assess the strengths and weaknesses in the case. At an early stage, there is no point in being a cheerleader for your client's position. Such an attitude will only mislead the client and will surprise and shock you when your adversary exposes the weaknesses in your case. At the outset, you should ask your client for every piece of documentation and other physical evidence that can support each statement made by him. You should also request the names, addresses, and telephone numbers of every key witness who can verify your client's story. There is no property in a witness. Those witnesses should be approached, at an early stage, by you, a law clerk or a junior lawyer skilled in interviewing witnesses or or, better still, a qualified investigator at an early stage to determine whether their evidence will support your client or whether their evidence presents some problems.

The case against your client should also be carefully examined. You must learn about the weaknesses in your case. Ask the client what they

---

para. 54; *Dr. Q v. College of Physicians and Surgeons of British Columbia*, [2003] 1 S.C.R. 226 at paras. 18–19.

think their adversary's explanation will be. Probe those explanations. Ask about documentation that the adversary will likely point to in support of its position. Review the witnesses likely to be called by the opposition and what they can be expected to say. If possible, have those witnesses also interviewed by your investigator. The more you know of your adversary's position, the more complete your knowledge, and the better the tactical decisions that you can make leading to trial.

Establish whether the client has made any statements relating to the subject matter of the dispute. Prior inconsistent statements can be used to great effect at the trial particularly where they are unknown to you and surface for the first time in the cross-examination. Many clients believe that only a written statement signed by them can be used against them. This is not so. Make it clear that you are searching for all of the client's oral remarks made to others, in particular, to persons investigating the case or to the opposing party in the lawsuit. If the statement is written, obtain a copy of the statement. It may contain admissions that are harmful to your position. If the client's premises were searched, review the search warrant. Was the warrant validly issued? Can it be quashed? Inquire, of your client, of the circumstances surrounding the search and what is known of what was removed. In a case involving wire tap evidence, determine whether there was a valid authorization. Obtain a transcript of the intercepted communications before committing your client to a definite position.

2) The Written Evidence

The next step is to obtain a full and complete copy of all the documentation that has a semblance of relevance to the issues in dispute. This documentation will emanate partially from your own client and partially from the adversary. When you receive production from your own client, review it sceptically. It is often the case that the client will withhold documentation that they believe to be harmful. Inevitably such documentation will be produced by the adversary, and the inference that can be drawn from such production from the adversary and a poor explanation by your client respecting the missing documentation is always unfavourable. Make sure that the client has preserved and produced to you all electronic documents. The prevalence of e-mail traffic both within a client and between the client and the adversary makes this a required — and potentially fertile — source of documentation. Likewise electronic calendars can be deleted over time. They must also be preserved.

Use the same critical eye to ensure that the adversary has also produced all documents that have a semblance of relevance.

Once you have all of the documentation, assemble it in chronological order. It is impossible for the lawyer, who is neither the author nor the recipient of the original documents, to fully understand their import without reading them in a chronological sequence. When reviewing the documents, make notes of supportive statements made by the adversary in writing. Those passages can be used to great effect at the trial. They constitute admissions or quasi-admissions. Such supportive statements place the adversary on the defensive and require explanation. With the same perspicacity, examine and note any unfortunate statements that your client has made from which the adversary will draw comfort.

Arrange a further interview with your client immediately upon the completion of the review of the documentation. The matters are fresh in your mind. You have identified statements and actions that might cast an unfavourable light on your client's position. Put those to your client, obtain their responses, and probe those responses. Do they provide a plausible explanation that can be buttressed by another piece of evidence that has not yet been brought forward or by another witness? Or will their explanation simply have to be taken on faith? If so, how will an objective third party judge view the client's credibility if you have trouble, even at this stage, with your own client's credibility respecting the explanation? Certainly a trial judge will have difficulty with it. This presages for you the need to work with the client to overcome the unfavourable impression.

3) The Evidence of Witnesses

Interview favourable and unfavourable witnesses. Favourable witnesses are far more willing to assist and to cooperate at a time that is closer to the factual events than years later when the trial occurs. By interviewing them at an early stage, you not only engage their cooperation, but you also capture in writing their precise recent recollection. Ensure that you provide a copy of your interview notes or a statement made from those notes to the witness. Ask them to make any changes necessary and to sign the statement, keep a copy and send one back to you.

By this procedure, you can be more assured that, when calling this witness at trial, they will review their statement and provide the evidence that you require. Absent receiving such a signed statement, you will be surprised at the reluctance and at the loss of memory of witnesses who once told you that they were very supportive of your client's position.

Hostile witnesses must also be interviewed. If they will meet with you or with your investigator, it means that you can develop a rapport with them and often establish a doubt in their mind whether their one-sided recollections ought not to be more balanced. At the very least, you will hear from the hostile witness' own mouth what they are likely to say at trial. This will assist you immeasurably in the preparation of your cross-examination of that witness and in thinking about other witnesses who might be called to contradict the version provided by the hostile witness. It also provides you with an early opportunity to assess the demeanour and credibility of the hostile witness, thus allowing you to develop an approach to cross-examination.

4) The Law

With the same thoroughness that you have assembled the facts and analyzed them, you must now research the law and understand the principles that may come into play in this particular dispute. A starting point is the pleading, or notice of reassessment or information if it is a criminal matter. Give this triggering document a generous reading, for it can be amended, embellished or amplified before trial or at trial. Do not look to limit the allegations being made by a narrow reading of the words. Having spoken to your client and having read all of the relevant documents, you should have a very good idea of the thrust of the allegations being made and deference likely to be put forward. Now turn your attention to the principles of law that are applicable. Researching the law can be painstaking in that far more reading is required than will ultimately be useful. However, by reading widely you will not only be sure not to have overlooked nuances, you will also have benefited by understanding the policy that underlies many of the decisions. When you have identified those authorities that set out the fundamental principles that are relevant, catalogue them with the authorities of the Supreme Court of Canada first, Court of Appeal decisions second, and trial court decisions third. A catalogue of decisions requires a short précis of the ratio and a brief description of the facts. By fulfilling this task, you will immediately identify whether your facts are comparable to those in the case that has been decided or are a wide departure therefrom. By expressing the ratio in your own words, you will force yourself to understand the principle in the case that you have read. If you have Supreme Court authorities that are thorough and that are on point, you can set to one side the lower court decisions. If, however, there are lower court decisions that are consistent with the decisions of the Supreme Court of Canada, but which address a wider fact situation, then these may be most useful in showing the breadth to which the ratio of the Supreme Court of Canada decisions is applied. It is especially useful to find such decisions of the court before which your case is being tried.

Take the decisions that you have garnered from your research and apply them critically to the allegations being made against your client and to the facts of your case as you have now understood them. You will be surprised how often attractive allegations of the opposite side, even if proved, do not lead to liability at law. If that is your situation, then you have a double-barrelled position, one that is strong at law, and a second that can defeat the opponent's case on the facts. If, on the other hand, research has shown that the application of the relevant principles depends upon which findings of fact are made, then it is incumbent upon you to marshal and shape your facts from that moment forward so that the trier of fact will make the determination that will lead to the application of the legal principles in favour of your client. From this point forward, you must never lose your focus on the relevant principles of law and the facts that need to be proved to support those principles of law. Every decision made hereafter has that focus and goal as its objective.

Periodic updates of the caselaw are important to ensure that there have not been new developments that will fundamentally affect preparation.

In similar fashion, it is never too early to begin to identify issues requiring expert evidence and to find the necessary expert. Early expert input helps guide both the pleading and discovery stages to ensure that the necessary evidence is available to support the expert conclusions that will be required. This is equally true whether one is looking at expert evidence on liability issues or upon damages.

B. STRATEGY AND TACTICS

The terms "strategy" and "tactics" must never be confused. They are quite separate ideas. You must always have an overall strategy or plan to ensure that the facts and legal principles that favour your case are brought out in full and in the best possible manner. The investigation, preparation and analysis already referred to form an integral part of the strategy. The balance of the strategy is executed at the trial. Tactics, on the other hand, represent enhancements that can be used with great effect to strengthen a portion of your case or to weaken your adversary's position. Tactics often are decisions that have to be made as a result of unexpected events.

1) The Opening

In a civil trial, the opportunity to present a full opening is invaluable in obtaining and exploiting the opportunity to begin to persuade the trial judge from the outset.

For their part, trial judges increasingly welcome a fulsome opening, especially in a complicated case.

Remember that before walking into the court room, a trial judge generally has had access to nothing more than the pleadings.

In opening a case for a plaintiff where there is a great deal of correspondence or other corporate documentation, make your opening a recitation of the key material facts and advise the court of the conclusions that you wish it to draw at the end of the case. Then file the brief of agreed documents as Exhibit 1 and walk the judge through the documents, reading passages from them and bridging the gaps between the documents with your own narrative. This tactic is also called "the second opening." It is very difficult for opposing counsel to object, as the reply is that you are drawing the judge's attention to portions of the exhibit brief that both counsel have agreed upon and that the judge has not yet had an opportunity to absorb. The tactical advantage of the second opening is that it validates what you said in your first opening and the judge can now see the evidence that supports each of the statements you made in your first opening. The judge sees it from contemporaneously written documents. It builds confidence in the judge that your theory of the case is correct. Then, when your client takes the stand and relates the facts, the judge will know *a priori* that what they are saying is supported by the documentation.

When opening for the defence, one has an equal opportunity to balance the case out before the evidence starts. While the traditional approach has been for a defendant to open at the beginning of the defence case, more and more in civil trials an opening by the defence immediately after the plaintiff's opening is crucial to laying one's perspective before the court.

A written outline of the opening statement is an invaluable tool to provide to the trial judge. It saves the trial judge the distraction of trying to keep track of your opening and allows him to concentrate on the opening itself.

2) Witnesses

The image that a witness projects is often as important as the substance of his or her testimony. The selection of witnesses can be vital to the success of the case. First impressions are critical. Open the case with a strong witness who will not be shredded on cross-examination. Try to garner as much empathy for your position as you can through the lead witness. Avoid complex or technical evidence in the initial stage of the examinations-in-chief. Get the story out first, then, if necessary, retrace your steps aided by documentation and explanations. End your case with a strong witness.

Sandwich the weaker, more vulnerable witnesses between the two pillars of your case. If your first strong witness was not involved throughout the entire chronology of the events, explain this to the trier of fact in your opening address and provide a rationale why that witness is being called first. Similarly, if the first witness to be called must lay a foundation or structure of an organization to better understand the factual evidence of other witnesses, explain this in the opening.

With every witness, address weak points in the testimony that will be exploited in the cross-examination. A witness is more able by an open-ended question to explain unfavourable evidence and to expand on favourable matters than in cross-examination. Owning up to one's weaknesses leaves a favourable impression with the trier of fact and takes much of the sting out of the cross-examination.

Do not call cumulative witnesses to the same fact. If a witness has established a fact and has not been shaken on cross-examination, leave well enough alone. The danger of calling additional witnesses is that they were often less involved in the totality of the facts, have less commitment to the lawsuit, and are less well prepared and do not know the documentation in depth. As a result, their evidence on the main point for which they were called might show an inconsistency with the former witness, which weakens the point. More importantly, however, they might readily agree with propositions in cross-examination on a host of other points, which you did not explore with them, for which they were not prepared, and which the cross-examiner can exploit to great advantage.

The only exception to this strategic direction is a circumstance where there may be conflicting evidence as to what occurred in a meeting or a discussion at which more than one participant from either side was present. In order to avoid an adverse inference being drawn it may be necessary to call the other witnesses to the events who are within at the very least the control or sphere of influence of the party you represent in order to avoid such adverse inference.

3) Documentary Evidence

Documents have increasing importance in modern day litigation. Indeed, everyday commerce is so well-documented that electronic communication is often the most reliable contemporaneous record of the events and of everyone's reaction to the events. In many trials, the content of the documents surpasses the oral evidence of the witnesses. Thus it is incumbent on the advocate to present the documentation that is necessary to the case in an easy to use, attractive format.

E-mails often cause the greatest difficulty. There may be several e-mails on a page. It is hard to distinguish one from the other. The time of the e-mail, the author and the recipient require effort to discern. Make sure that you isolate the e-mails in which you are interested and set them apart from other writings on the same page. Reproduce them, if necessary, on a separate page.

Provide an index at the front of the exhibit books identifying author, recipient and date. Place them in a chronological sequence so that the judge can easily retrieve them when writing a reserved judgment. Do not avoid including adverse or difficult correspondence and e-mails. If your opponent demonstrates that your exhibit brief is incomplete or one-sided, you have lost the entire effect that you were attempting to establish. Moreover, the judge loses confidence in you as counsel for seeking to hide contemporaneously existing but adverse communications. There will be less forgiveness in failing to present a complete brief of relevant documents than if a witness does not mention unfavourable facts in evidence-in-chief.

4) Demonstrative Evidence

Demonstrative evidence can be, if properly used, the most powerful tool of persuasion available to the trial lawyer. There are two types of demonstrative evidence:

(a) Real evidence — the actual object involved in the incident giving rise to the subject matter of the lawsuit; and
(b) Illustrative evidence — evidence that serves to explain or to illustrate testimony to the trier of fact so that they can better appreciate oral testimony. Diagrams, charts and models are examples of this form of demonstrative evidence.

If you wish to make use of illustrative evidence, do so sparingly. Ensure that the chart, bar graph or diagram that you intend to use with a witness will be entirely consistent with their evidence. Nothing is more aggravating to the trier of fact than having corrections made to chart during the course of the oral testimony.

Make sure that the depiction of the illustrative evidence is fairly balanced. Nothing is worse than the opponent demonstrating in cross-examination that if some apparently logical progression is continued, an absurd result is reached. Nothing is more hurtful to your client than opposing counsel demonstrating in cross-examination that the scale of the depiction is unfairly distorted. Since the purpose of illustrative evidence is to dramatize the oral evidence and to leave it in pictorial form before the trier of fact so that it can trigger a clear memory of the oral testimony, make sure that it is clear, understandable on its own, and unassailable as a piece of persuasive art.

If you are in the position of having to object to illustrative evidence, there are several grounds upon which to do so. First, it is not direct or testimonial evidence. It has no greater right to admissibility than does a self-serving written statement of a witness who is testifying. Second, its prejudicial effect may outweigh any illustrative assistance that it can provide to the trial judge. The objection in such a case is that the demonstrative evidence masks the nuances and weaknesses in the oral testimony and seeks to leave on the record, as an exhibit, the strong positive aspects of the oral testimony. The prejudice arises when on cross-examination, the nuances and weaknesses are exploited, but those are only to be found in the transcript record, and what the judge has in chambers is the illustrative chart that fails to capture the points made in cross-examination. Third, the witness has not prepared the chart and in any event, it is not an accurate representation or a fair depiction of the oral testimony.

The responding party may find that it is useful to recast the illustrative evidence based on the evidence that has come out at trial supportive of a different inference to be drawn. It is very powerful to take a piece of illustrative evidence and reflect in an amended version the effect upon its conclusions of different assumptions of underlying fact. Having the exhibit then marked as a lettered sub-exhibit of the original exhibit is very effective.

5) Expert Evidence

Expert evidence must be relevant. It must be necessary in that it is outside the experience and knowledge of the judge or jury. The question of its necessity must be assessed, in light of its potential to distort the fact-finding process. It must not be subject to an exclusionary role. It must be given by a properly qualified expert, that is, someone with special or peculiar knowledge gained through study or experience.[2]

2 *R. v. Mohan*, [1994] 2 S.C.R. 9.

The expert evidence must be reliable and essential in the sense that the trier of fact will be unable to come to a satisfactory conclusion without the assistance of the expert.[3]

Expert evidence is not admissible where it enters into the core judicial functions.[4] It approaches too closely the ultimate issue before the court.

Counsel must always remember that the expert is viewed by the court as providing independent assistance by way of objective unbiased opinion in relation to matters within his or her expertise. An expert should never assume, nor be encouraged to assume the role of an advocate.[5]

Accordingly, great care must be taken in the determination of what expert evidence, if any, will be of assistance in the case and in the review of the expert's opinions, both when notice is given by way of a report and when the evidence is delivered at trial.

Counsel who put the expert into the role of an advocate suffer a significant risk that the expert's evidence will not be compelling at trial. It is better to concede those points which should be conceded at the time that the report is prepared and the expert is in turn prepared for trial, rather than to attempt, through the expert, to "win" every point.

6) Pre-trial Review of Pleadings and Expert Reports

A trial occurs a long time after the pleadings were prepared.

Because the Rules of Practice allow significant latitude for amending pleadings, it is never too late to take a hard look at the pleadings.

It is important to make sure that every essential element is pleaded. From the point of view of the defence, those defences that are to be specifically pleaded must be clearly set out in the pleadings.

As your understanding of the case grows, so too your pleadings may need to mature. Timely motions to amend and even motions to amend at trial are appropriate in order to bring your pleading in line with the evidence as you have developed it and the theories of the case as they have evolved.

In the same manner, expert evidence may need to be supplemented by a supplementary report, to keep abreast of the development of the case.

---

3 *Ibid.*

4 *Pente v. Schneider* (1998), 42 O.R. (3d) 177 (C.A.).

5 *The "Ikarian Reefer"*, [1993] 2 E.G.L.R. 1983 (Q.B.D.) (Commercial Court); *Fellowes, McNeil v. Kansa General International Insurance Co.* (1988), 48 O.R. (3d) 456 (varied on other points as (2000), 138 O.A.C. 28 (C.A.)).

7) Trial Roadmaps

At the conclusion of the trial, you will be urging the trial judge to make certain findings of fact. The time to identify what those findings of fact are is at the latest during your preparation for trial.

These findings of fact inform:

(a) the witnesses whom you are going to call;
(b) the expert evidence that you will lead; and
(c) the documents that are material to the trial.

Accordingly, many counsel prepare a matrix of the findings of fact that are necessary and of the witnesses who will help deal with each.

This in turn informs your preparation of the examinations of witnesses, both in chief and in cross-examination.

8) Meet the Witnesses

There is no substitute for meeting your own witnesses prior to trial.

There is a great temptation to delegate that work to junior lawyers or clerks. This is a mistake.

You need to prepare witnesses personally. This allows you to develop a sense of how the witness will perform at trial and allows, as well, the development of a rapport between you and the witness. That rapport will assist the witness in giving evidence more comfortably and will develop confidence for a witness who has little or no experience in a courtroom.

There is also no substitute for careful discussion with the witnesses of the nature of the environment in which they find themselves and of the issues in the litigation that may bear upon their evidence. This sensitizes them to the issues in the case and creates context for their evidence, both in chief and cross-examination. A witness who does not understand the issues is not properly prepared.

9) Discovery Transcripts

It is essential to have an accurate and usable summary of the discovery transcripts and answers to undertakings.

Counsel need to be in a position to find a particular reference in the discovery transcripts quickly. This is especially important when a witness who has been discovered gives evidence inconsistent with the discovery transcript. There is nothing that creates more consternation for the witness (and annoying to the trial judge) than counsel leafing through transcripts looking for a reference that they know is somewhere but cannot find.

Likewise, a good summary allows you to quickly review the salient areas of discovery evidence to obtain the flavour of what has been said.

Ensure that the witness who has been discovered has their transcripts and has read them thoroughly.

They should be provided with their transcripts as soon as they are available after discovery and should be provided with specific instruction to review them and to alert you to anything that they feel needs to be corrected. Make the corrections promptly, so that there is no complaint that no correction was ever made when the witness attempts to correct an error when confronted with it in cross-examination at trial. Timely correction avoids effective cross-examination.

10) Tactics

Tactics involve the knowledge and use of procedural rules to advance your own case and to curtail the scope of your opponent's evidence. The sole objective of the utilization of the procedural rules is to limit the evidence that can be adduced against your case. Tactics can be used outside the courtroom and inside the courtroom. Outside the courtroom, every procedural advantage should be exploited to hem in the opponent. Inside the courtroom, greater discretion has to be displayed. If the trier of fact feels that you are making excessive, although proper, objections to the evidence that your opponent is seeking to adduce, with the result that your opponent is being hampered in getting the story out, you will lose much sympathy. Thus inside the courtroom, you must use tactical advantages sparingly. But use them you must — and should, where they lead to the exclusion of particularly harmful evidence.

Sound judgment is behind the use of every tactical advantage. You should ask yourself how the exploitation of a tactical advantage will appear to the judge. If you think it will annoy the judge or make it appear that you are trying to exclude particularly damaging evidence, do not use the tactic. If on the other hand, there is a sound rationale for using the tactic, then explain the rationale to the trial judge. A few examples of good and bad tactics, both inside and outside the courtroom, will best illustrate the points made.

If your opponent has given a number of undertakings at the examination for discovery but all or many of them were unfulfilled before trial, you have a choice whether to write to remind your opponent of the unfulfilled undertakings or to bring a motion to compel their fulfilment. If you think you know what the answers will be, you might choose to write opposing counsel reminding them that the undertakings remain unfulfilled and that you will take objection to the evidence on those subject matters being adduced at trial. If there is still no fulfillment of the undertakings, you can sensibly and reasonably take the position at trial that the evidence that opposing counsel is seeking to adduce with respect to those subject matters should not be permitted. You will be surprised how often a trial judge will not let the evidence in or will let it in and admonish opposing counsel in front of their client.

In addition, in cross-examination you can make great moment of the failure to answer the undertakings by asking the opposing client if they were given the transcript of the examination for discovery to review and why answers to the undertakings were never provided. No matter what answer is given, it will be defensive and destabilizing to the witness.

By way of further example, if your opponent provides you with an expert report that indicates that the expert has reviewed the pleadings, the productions and the examinations for discovery transcripts and then it states that he disbelieves your client's explanation in the examination for discovery and that in his opinion, your client is negligent, you should write a letter indicating that you will be objecting to the introduction of the expert report at trial and that your objections will consist of the following:

(a) the expert has not identified the assumptions of fact upon which the opinion is based;
(b) the expert has drawn conclusions of credibility that are not within his area of expertise; and
(c) the expert has addressed the ultimate issue rather than indicating in what particulars your client fell below the standard of practice.

When opposing counsel seeks to introduce the expert report at trial, you can rise to make your objection and present the letter that you have written some months before. The trial judge should refuse to receive the report. Should the expert be permitted to testify, however, the expert will be ordered to do it properly, i.e., state the assumptions on which the opinion is based, outline what are the standards practiced in the profession, and give particulars of how your client fell below those standards. It is highly probable that if opposing counsel and their expert have prepared a report that has been excluded, they will also be unprepared to deal with the testimony in a proper fashion. As a result, less will be adduced than otherwise. In any event, the expert will be less persuasive.

If your opponent puts in a brief of documents through their first witness that does not include some damaging documents because they have failed to ask you what additional documents you would like to have included in the brief of documents, once again you have a choice. Before trial you may send a letter insisting that additional documents being put in the brief, or you may choose to remain silent. Let them file their brief of documents. Tactically, it may be far more dramatic for you to raise the damaging documents in cross-examination for the first time. The witness may not be prepared for the questions. The documents assume a greater importance when isolated and highlighted in this way than if included in a brief of documents. Each of the damaging documents becomes a separate exhibit that carries equal weight to the one exhibit containing the rest of the documentation.

If your opponent should call a secondary and perhaps unnecessary witness to prove a small point, you may rest assured that that witness may well not have been fully prepared, expecting to testify only as to the point for which he was called. Knowing that they are a corporate officer, with management responsibility, you are not limited in your cross-examination to the one point to which the witness testified. Explore in cross-examination your client's theory. You will be pleasantly surprised how agreeable unprepared witnesses are to accepting your reasonable conclusions, with the use of leading questions.

11) The Closing

A written closing argument or outline of argument is becoming the norm in civil trials.

The written argument is of real assistance to a trial judge who can concentrate on the argument and need not attempt to keep an electronic or a written note of what is being said.

The argument should be readable and digestible. Dense paragraphs in single space format do not encourage a trial judge to read on.

What is essential is to have short factum-like paragraphs supported by references to the oral and documentary evidence. This assists the trial judge in essentially having a roadmap to the writing of a decision if they can be persuaded that your position is the right one.

Chapter Six

Good Trial Practices in the Tax Court of Canada

Hon. D.G.H. Bowman

The title of this chapter implies that there are a set of practices that if followed will improve your chances of winning — sort of a juridical version of *How to Win Friends and Influence People*, renamed as "How to Win Cases and Influence Judges." This is no doubt true to a point, but not entirely. The impossibility of formulating rules for all occasions results from four uncertainties that characterize all litigation — the court, the witnesses, the opposing counsel and the overall factual background as it develops. To these four uncertainties I would add a fifth: the uncertainty of the law as it evolves. These elements of uncertainty are not necessarily undesirable — they contribute greatly to the vibrancy and quality of our legal system and to its ability to respond to the changing needs of society. They do, however, demonstrate that there is only one invariable rule in litigation and that is to expect the unexpected and be ready to change your course at a moment's notice. One quality that distinguishes good counsel from mediocre counsel is flexibility — an ability to change direction in mid-course to meet and, if possible, take advantage of a new development.

What I am about to say about good trial practices may seem elementary or self-evident to experienced counsel. I am not, however, writing for the senior seasoned litigators. They probably won't be reading this anyway, and if they do they won't pay any attention to it. I am aiming at lawyers in the first few years of their practice who are venturing into the difficult and demanding field of tax litigation. There is certainly a subjective element on my part in describing practices of which I approve. Other judges might prefer other techniques.

A. THE PLEADINGS

The first step in an appeal is the preparation and filing of a notice of appeal. It is a document of singular importance. It should be drafted or at least approved by the counsel who will be arguing the case. A remarkable number of cases are lost because of sloppy drafting of the notice of appeal or, in the case of the Crown, the reply to the notice of appeal. The commonest errors are:

(a) omitting to plead material facts that are crucial to your case;
(b) pleading facts that are wrong; and
(c) admitting facts that should not be admitted.

There is another error that one sees occasionally in notices of appeal, and that is the making of allegations of bad faith or bias on the part of the revenue officials. Usually this sort of thing is found in notices of appeal prepared by unrepresented litigants, but occasionally lawyers who should know better are prevailed upon by their clients to do so. I have never known these personal attacks on assessors to do the slightest good, and in fact they are counterproductive because the court may assume that you are attacking the assessor because you have no grounds for attacking the assessment. If you have been retained after your client has prepared and filed the notice of appeal, look carefully at it and amend if necessary.

What is the essential point about the assessment that you wish to challenge? Focus on that, and after you have set out your facts, ask yourself, "If these facts are admitted or proved, must I necessarily win? Is there anything else that I need?" Remember, you are painting a picture, and the notice of appeal is the first impression the judge will have of the picture you want to portray. What sort of picture do you want to paint? If the facts are a little hazy and blurred around the edges, you may want to have the verbal pictures you are creating look a little like an impressionist painting, leaving you some room to manoeuvre. Or is your case so clear that your painting should be all sharp edges and straight lines, like Mondrian? I have seen pleadings where the drafter seems to have taken Jackson Pollock as a model.

What aspect of the judge's makeup are you aiming at — the brain, the heart or the solar plexus? Is the case one that must appeal to the judge's intellect, compassion or common sense? A failure to recognize this distinction can be fatal. I have seen cases lost where a lawyer has ignored the common sense strength of his case and concentrated solely on highly technical and arcane legal arguments.

What about the pleading of alternatives? There is a distinction between alternative facts and alternative propositions of law. Pleading alternative facts may be acceptable in a small group of cases but it is dangerous because if the alternative pleading is inconsistent with the facts that you want principally to establish, it detracts from your main point. A well known, if somewhat fanciful, example of this self-defeating kind of tactic is the statement by an accused, "I didn't shoot the deceased; in the alternative I didn't know the gun was loaded; in the further alternative, it was self-defence."

Alternative propositions of law are obviously acceptable, subject only to one proviso: too many alternative arguments weaken the overall strength of your case, and you end up looking like Leacock's Lord Ronald who jumped on his horse and rode madly off in all directions. As one senior tax litigator put it, "if I can't win on my strongest argument, what hope do I have of winning on my fifth strongest?"

I am not saying don't advance alternative arguments. I am simply cautioning against their excessive use. If you have an alternative argument, be sure it is a strong one. Judges are unimpressed with seeing a whole flotilla of trial balloons being launched.

Finally, I come to the *Charter*. The *Charter* is the supreme law of Canada and recourse to it should not be discouraged. Nonetheless, it should not be resorted to lightly. The use of the *Charter* in tax appeals has not been noticeably successful. To toss in a *Charter* argument every time you don't like something the Canada Revenue Agency ("CRA") has done detracts from whatever substantive merits your case may have. If you have an arguable case under the *Charter*, hit it for all it is worth. Don't treat it as an afterthought. Research, prepare and present your case thoroughly and meticulously. If it appears that you are not taking your *Charter* argument seriously, neither will the judge.

If you are drafting a reply to the notice of appeal it is imperative that the "assumptions" pleaded be accurate. The assumptions are supposed to be a full and accurate disclosure of the facts upon which an assessment is based. There is very little that will prejudice the Crown's case as much as a discovery that the Crown has either misstated the assumptions on which the Minister relied or has failed to disclose facts found or assumed by the Minister that support the taxpayer's case.

It is certainly open to the Crown to plead alternative reasons for upholding the assessment or alternative facts that are inconsistent with those assumed, provided the Crown assumes the onus of proving those facts. What is unacceptable is the pleading of inconsistent assumptions. The law that has grown up over the past half century with respect to the pleading of assumptions gives a considerable advantage to both parties. It gives the Crown the advantage of a reverse onus of proof and it gives the appellant the advantage of knowing precisely the case that must be met. The system works well if it is not abused. It is important that in responding to a taxpayer's appeal the Crown do so by forthrightly and robustly confronting the issues and not plead ambiguously.

One final point that I should have thought was obvious. Before you file or serve any pleading, show it to your client and get his or her approval. I have sometimes seen a party who is being cross-examined on a pleading deny ever having seen it. This casts doubt either on the witness' credibility or on the competence of counsel and the accuracy of the pleading.

The next question you will have to decide as counsel for the appellant is whether to file an answer to the reply. Answers are very seldom filed in the Tax Court. One reason for this is probably that the rules provide that an appellant who does not file an answer is deemed to deny the allegations in the reply. Nonetheless, I find answers very useful. They serve the function of more precisely joining issues on the facts that are in contention, and they give an appellant an opportunity of putting its own spin on the Crown's allegations.

The next step in the proceeding is the production of a list of documents. Section 81 and 82 of the rules provide for either partial or full disclosure of documents. Partial disclosure requires the party to list only those documents on which the party intends to reply at trial. The partial disclosure rule was based on a similar rule in the Federal Court rules which, as it happens, has since been removed, and the Federal Court has gone back to full disclosure consistent with the rule in all of the provincial courts. The rationale behind the partial disclosure rule is difficult to understand. Perhaps it reflects the somewhat jaundiced view of the drafter of the Federal Court rules that litigants will disclose only what supports their case in any event and, if challenged, will argue that the document that they neglected to disclose was irrelevant. If I were acting for either side I would always insist on full disclosure.

B. DISCOVERIES

If you are acting for a taxpayer, in almost every case it is useful to examine an officer of the Crown to determine:

(a) what facts the assessor had when the assessment was made;
(b) whether the assumptions pleaded by the Crown were in fact made;
(c) whether the assessor assumed any facts that were not pleaded that assist the taxpayer; and
(d) what facts alleged in the notice of appeal or the answer are admitted and, if any are denied, what the basis of the denial is.

Be sure to get the assessor's working papers, including the T-2020 and T-401 reports. Tax litigation is unique in the importance that is placed on what are called "assumptions." These are facts found or assumed by the assessor at the time the assessment was made, and the onus is upon the taxpayer to "demolish" those assumptions. I personally believe that too much time and effort is wasted on trying to chase down just what thoughts were going through the assessor's mind at the moment when the assessment was made. Lawyers' and judges' time would be more profitably spent in determining whether an assessment is right or wrong. Nonetheless, the peculiar role of assumptions in the procedure in tax cases is so deeply engrained that one cannot safely ignore them.

The questioning of the Crown's representative about departmental policies and interpretations has always seemed to me to be of marginal utility, but I am coming more to the view that it may be worthwhile. If you can find a departmental interpretation or practice that supports your position, it may assist in tipping the balance in your favour in a doubtful case.

Where an assessment is made under section 245, the general anti-avoidance rule, it is essential that you explore all aspects of departmental practice and policy, including all publications by the Department of Finance. Be sure to have the Crown representative state unequivocally what departmental policy or interpretation justifies the conclusion that there is an abuse or misuse that warrants the invoking of GAAR. We have certainly not heard the last word on what extraneous materials, if any, can be used in interpreting what is supposed to be plain and comprehensible legislative language, but until the Supreme Court of Canada pronounces definitively on this question, you should pursue it diligently on discovery.

If the Crown is to examine your client for discovery, you should examine or preferably cross-examine your client as thoroughly as you would if you were preparing him or her for cross-examination at trial. One frequent reason for cases being lost is sloppy preparation of witnesses. If you do not look behind the woodwork before trial, you can expect to be surprised at what may come out of it at trial.

Finally, before I move on to the trial itself, a word about expert witnesses. Experts can be dangerous. A good expert witness can win the case for you. A bad one can cause it to blow up in your face. Some cases obviously require expert witnesses — valuation cases or scientific research cases for example. Sometimes lawyers will try to bolster a weak case by calling an expert, and in my experience this seldom works. Judges tend to be wary of experts, particularly in areas which the judge believes is the court's domain. This is particularly true of accounting evidence. A good cross-examination can turn accounting evidence on its head. If you are uncertain whether to call an accounting expert, the better course is not to.

The cross-examination of an expert can be exhilarating or disastrous. Prepare your cross-examination meticulously — indeed, over-prepare. Identify the areas where you think the expert is on weak or shaky ground. Hit the witness hard on those points and then sit down. Be direct, precise and devastating. Vaguely meandering all over the expert report without any plan of attack is worse than useless. If you can shake the witness on two or three key points, it casts doubt on all of his or her evidence.

C. THE TRIAL

On the morning of trial let us assume you have done all the things you should have done to prepare, namely:

(a) you have subpoenaed your witnesses;
(b) you have cross-examined your own witnesses at least twice;
(c) you have your questions in chief written out and gone over them with your witnesses;
(d) you have anticipated what the other side's witnesses are going to say and have prepared a hard-hitting snappy cross-examination;
(e) you have your documents neatly indexed and in volumes, and either:
  (i) have an admission from the other side as to their admissibility or
  (ii) have served a notice to admit on the other side or
  (iii) are prepared to prove any disputed documents; and
(f) you have found out who the judge is and have read and analyzed all the cases decided by that judge on the point.

You come into court, and it turns out that at the last minute they switched judges on you. What do you do? You can collapse on the floor and be carried out at the same time asking for an adjournment or you can tough it out and change course. Suppose the new (or, for that matter, old) judge has consistently decided cases that are contrary to your client's position. Acknowledge that up front. At least the judge will be impressed that you have read his or her cases.

The first step is to stand up and introduce the case. An opening statement should be relatively brief, usually no more than half an hour, although this can vary depending on the nature and anticipated length of the case. It is helpful to have a written memorandum outlining the points you intend to cover, both factual and legal; but this is a matter of individual taste. There are pleaders, and there are readers. Pleaders prefer the spontaneity and freedom that results from oral presentation which gives full rein to their oratorical skills, unfettered by any written material. Readers want what they are going to say to be thought out in advance. Most good counsel hand in a written opening statement and then embellish on it somewhat.

Next, put in your documents. If there is an agreement on documents, as there usually is in tax cases, frequently the appellant and the Crown agree on a joint book of documents. Ideally you should put in three copies of the book of documents — one for the judge, one for the reporter and one to be marked as an exhibit. The last copy can be given to witnesses if they need to refer to documents during their testimony.

Next it is useful to take the judge through the pleadings and point out the facts that are admitted or denied. The judge should have done this already, but don't count on it. Moreover, it gives you a chance to put your own spin on the issues and to point out the particular assumptions that you propose to challenge and point out any omissions in the assumptions that are pleaded.

By this time the judge is probably getting bored or impatient, so call your first witness. This should go like clockwork. If a case is put in briskly and efficiently, with no gaps between questions and no hunting around for documents, a judge is more likely to take your case seriously.

If your witness has been properly prepared for cross-examination, he or she should be able to survive anything the other side chooses to throw. If facts come out in cross-examination that you didn't discover before trial, you have only yourself to blame.

Be careful of re-examination. You can lose your case with the wrong questions. If your witness has not been too badly mauled on cross-examination, it is better to stay in your chair. If you think you might be able to get the witness to improve on an answer that was given on cross-examination and you decide to ask the question again, you have a better than even chance that this whole thing will blow up in your face. The witness will conclude from the fact that you are asking a question that has already been asked that he or she gave the wrong answer the first time around and in confusion or desperation may jump in the wrong direction.

When you come to cross-examine the Crown's witness, ask yourself: What do I want to get from this witness? If the witness has said nothing to hurt you and has no information that will help you, then have the courage to ask no questions. It is dangerous to try to get from an adverse or possibly hostile witness information that could be elicited from a more friendly witness. Bear in mind that if you don't cross-examine you cannot ask the court to disbelieve the witness. The rule in *Browne v. Dunn*[1] is well known in the Tax Court and is often applied. The reason for its frequent application in this court is that in many appeals the Crown seeks to make its case out of an appellant's own mouth and it is unfair for Crown counsel to question the credibility of a witness in argument without having challenged the witness's testimony on cross-examination.

Cross-examination, whether of the Crown's witnesses or the appellant's, should be brief, snappy and to the point. The reason I am stating the obvious is that it doesn't seem obvious to quite a number of counsel who appear in our court. Frequently, it is a rambling repetition of the same questions that were asked in chief. Decide what you want to accomplish with the cross-examination. When you have achieved it, or determined that you won't achieve it, sit down. Two cardinal principles:

1) If you don't know the answer, don't ask the question.
2) If you get ninety per cent of what you want from a witness, sit down. The one question too many can be fatal.

Finally, if the Crown has called a CRA assessor, make sure that the witness's testimony is going in as evidence of the basis upon which the assessment was made and not as evidence of the truth of facts on which the assessor acted. After all, most assessments are based in greater or lesser degree on hearsay. Nonetheless, it is very useful to the court for an assessor to testify as to the basis of the assessment.

In cross-examining a CRA assessor, you may impress your client by attacking the witness' integrity or good faith, but you won't impress the judge.

Once the appellant's evidence is in and the Crown has called its witnesses, should you call rebuttal evidence? In most cases, if you haven't made your case in chief, you are not likely to do so in reply, and you may be subject to the objection that you are splitting your case.

A word about objections. Frequent objections on picayune points are irritating and counter-productive. If the evidence doesn't hurt you, let it go. All you do is call attention to it and give it an importance that it probably doesn't merit. This is particularly true of objections on the grounds of rel-

1 (1893), 6 R. 67 (H.L.).

evancy. They seldom succeed. After all, we don't have a jury, and judges are supposed to be able to separate relevant from irrelevant data.

After the *viva voce* and documentary evidence is in, it is usual to read in the portions of the examination for discovery upon which a party relies. There are several points to note here:

(a) Don't hand in the whole transcript. Photocopy the portions that you intend to read in and give them well in advance of the trial to the other side so that it can decide whatever it wants to ask that any other parts be read in, in which case it can photocopy the additional portions.
(b) Although you can ask questions on discovery that elicit hearsay answers, if you read any portion of the discovery in, it must be otherwise admissible. In other words, you can't put in inadmissible evidence through the discovery process.
(c) If you have the person in the witness stand who was examined on discovery, you should put the answers given on discovery to the witness and give him or her the opportunity of qualifying or explaining the answers. It is bad practice to lurk in the weeds until after the witness has left the stand and then read the evidence at the end of the trial. There are two schools of thought on this question: one that would prohibit you from reading it in at all if you could have put the discovery to the witness; and another that would let you do so, subject to allowing the witness to be recalled. The latter is perhaps the less stringent position but it could result in a penalty in costs.

After all the evidence is in, you are ready to start argument. Again, whether you use a written memorandum of argument or not is a matter of personal preference. I find written points of argument helpful. One practice that is very helpful is at least to hand in a memorandum of the findings of fact that you want the court to make. Bear in mind that cases are usually won or lost on the facts. A strong finding of fact in your client's favour is worth a dozen legal arguments however much they may be supported by authority. If the factual underpinning of your case is equivocal or unhelpful, legions of Supreme Court cases won't save you. Most judges prefer to base their decision on the facts. Therefore, spend time on the facts so as to give the judge the opportunity of making findings of fact that are favourable to you. If there are facts that are against you, don't ignore them but ask the judge to put them in the context of the evidence as a whole.

Dealing with questions of credibility is always a delicate matter. Some judges are more inclined to make adverse findings of credibility than others. If credibility is an issue, you can't duck it — you have to confront it squarely. If your client's case stands or falls on whether the judge believes the testimony of a witness, then be ready to invite the judge to make a finding. I have already mentioned *Browne v. Dunn*, and if the other side's cross-examination on the crucial point has been lacking or incompetent, don't hesitate to say so.

It is of consummate importance that you state the facts fairly, fully and accurately. Your credibility in the court is the most important piece of stock-in-trade that you have as a lawyer. If you lose it you will never get it back.

Once you have reviewed the facts and invited the court to make findings of fact in your favour, your job is largely done. Generally, you do have to refer to some authorities. Your book of authorities should contain the cases you intend to refer to as well as the statutory provisions as they apply to the years in question.

There are a number of observations that you may find helpful:

(a) You should try to find and refer to cases that have been decided by the judge before whom you are appearing. This elementary bit of psychology needs no elaboration.
(b) You should also refer to cases of judges that your judge has referred to. It should be obvious from the authorities that your judge has cited or not cited that he or she prefers some judges to others.
(c) Highlight the passages you intend to read in, but preface your reading of the passage by a brief description of the case and say what it stands for.
(d) Refer to cases that are against you and distinguish them if you can or invite the court not to follow them. Failure to cite adverse authorities is as bad as misstating the facts.
(e) Your research should encompass other jurisdictions. I do not regard punching a few words into a computer and having it spew forth a dozen cases as research.
(f) Don't swamp the court with a bunch of authorities that you do not intend to refer to. If you do not refer to them, neither will the judge.

A few final observations on arguing your case:

(a) Be brief. Make your point and move on to the next one. An intelligent judge does not need to have a point belaboured, and one who is not will not benefit by repetition.
(b) Listen carefully to questions from the bench and deal with them immediately. Don't do what some counsel do and say "I'm coming to that point shortly Your Honour," and then never get back to it.
(c) A question or observation from the bench can mean a number of things:

(i) The judge is against you and the question is a hostile one.
(ii) The judge is for you and has come up with an idea that he or she thinks may help you.
(iii) The judge genuinely is uncertain about a point and needs your assistance.
(iv) The judge is just showing off.

Distinguish between these four. If you fail to do so and if you ignore the judge's question or comment you do so at your peril. One error sometimes made by counsel is to assume that a question or observation by the judge indicates hostility when the judge is really only putting forward an alternative approach that helps counsel. Counsel who stubbornly argue against the suggestion made by the judge thereby risk losing the best chance of winning because ideas that a judge comes up with are often the best grounds on which you can win.

In other words, if a judge's observation is adverse to you, try to move him or her off that perch but deal with the problem right away. If the observation is helpful to your case, if it is sound, embrace it even though it is not an idea that you thought of. Be careful, though. Judges are as capable as anyone else of going off on a tangent. Don't be too quick to accept a judge's notion and reject your own. After all, you have been thinking about it a good deal longer than the judge. If the judge simply wants help, give it immediately or, if it is on a point of evidence or law that you can't answer immediately tell the judge you will look into it and answer the question after the first break.

Finally, what do you do when you encounter a difficult judge? Some judges are arrogant, rude, loquacious, opinionated or generally offensive. I suppose you have to tolerate this sort of thing to a point, particularly if you are fairly junior at the bar, but I am increasingly convinced that no counsel and indeed no one who appears in a court has to put up with offensive or abusive behaviour. I would hope that if I am ever guilty of that, counsel will tell me. It is hard to know what sort of advice to give that fits every occasion. I can only suggest that you be firm and stand your ground and not let yourself be bullied. And insist on making your case. No one can fault you for that. Remember, your obligation is to protect the rights of your client, and for this you sometimes need a fairly thick skin and a not too fragile ego.

Chapter Seven

Tax Court Litigation: Representing the Taxpayer

Clifford L. Rand

A. INTRODUCTION

Trial advocacy differs from appellate advocacy in one obvious respect. In both trial courts and appellate courts, lawyers base their legal argument on the facts of the case. Trial lawyers, however, must first establish those facts through the introduction of evidence consisting of documents and oral testimony. I will discuss the process and techniques by which taxpayer's counsel may adduce evidence in the Tax Court of Canada and then present their argument based on the evidence before the court. I will address these topics in the chronological order of a Tax Court case, which has three distinct phases: the pleadings phase; the discovery phase; and the trial phase. Before discussing the three phases, however, I will make a few general observations on the development of the taxpayer's litigation strategy.

B. THE TAXPAYER'S LITIGATION STRATEGY

The Tax Court process allows the taxpayer to seize and retain the initiative in the case, which in turn gives taxpayer's counsel the opportunity to develop and implement a comprehensive litigation strategy. The main goal of the litigation strategy, of course, is to win the case. The way to achieve this goal is to provide the judge with whatever is required by way of evidence and argument to grant judgment, and write persuasive reasons for judgment, in the taxpayer's favour. The strategy must be focussed entirely on the judge who will ultimately hear and decide the case.

The taxpayer's counsel may seize the initiative in a Tax Court case because the taxpayer must discharge the burden of proof in the case. Subsection 152(8) of the *Income Tax Act*[1] implies that the factual assumptions made by the Minister in issuing the reassessment are presumed to be true.[2] In order to win the case, the taxpayer must establish that the Minister's factual assumptions are inaccurate (in reality, prove a different set of facts) or establish that the reassessed tax liability does not flow from the Minister's assumptions.

Having to discharge the burden of proof can be a disadvantage, but it is rarely determinative in practice, and in any event, the disadvantage is outweighed by the benefit of the longstanding legal tradition that the party with the burden of proof is the first to present its case in court. Going first means that taxpayer's counsel will write the document that the judge reads first, providing the taxpayer's view of the facts and framing the legal issues. It also means that taxpayer's counsel will make the first opening statement at trial, introduce evidence first and present the argument first. It is like being in a chess match in which you get to play the white pieces, allowing you to make the first move of the game and, if you play the game well, to retain the initiative for the entire game. Having the burden of proof means that taxpayer's counsel gets to play offence and Crown's counsel must play defence. If all goes well, the Crown's case will be kept on the defensive throughout the trial.

Since the Crown does not have the initiative in a Tax Court case, Crown counsel are not in a position to devise a comprehensive litigation strategy. Their role is necessarily reactive and often consists mainly of trying to poke holes in the taxpayer's case as it unfolds. The Crown will cross-examine the taxpayer's witnesses but will call few if any witnesses of its own. Its cross-examination will be constrained by the fact that there is no requirement in

---

1 RSC 1985, c. 1 (5th Supp.), as amended, herein referred to as "the Act."

2 The origin of the rule that the taxpayer has the burden of proof appears to be the case of *Anderson Logging Company v. The King*, [1917–27] C.T.C. 198 (S.C.C.), aff'd, [1926] A.C. 140 (P.C.); see also *Johnston v. M.N.R.*, [1948] C.T.C. 195 (S.C.C.). The basis for the rule is that the taxpayer is normally the party in possession of the documents and information needed to show that the assessment is incorrect. In some cases, the onus is reversed, such as where the assessment was issued outside the normal reassessment period under paragraph 152(4)(a) of the *Act*, or where the Minister has assessed penalties under subsection 163(2) of the *Act*.

the Tax Court Rules[3] to provide the other side with one's list of witnesses. Accordingly the Crown may not know who some of the taxpayer's witnesses are, let alone what their testimony will be, until they are on the witness stand. Although the Crown may conduct an examination for discovery of the taxpayer, the answers given may provide little indication as to what the taxpayer will say during examination-in-chief at trial. As late as the trial phase, therefore, the nuances of the taxpayer's litigation strategy will often be a mystery to Crown counsel, as may be the main elements of the taxpayer's argument.

If the taxpayer's litigation strategy is designed to provide the judge with what is required to grant judgment in the taxpayer's favour and write persuasive reasons for judgment, the question for taxpayer's counsel is "What does the judge require?"[4] In order to answer this question, let us stop for a moment and consider the role of a Tax Court judge. It seems to me that all too often, the role forced upon a Tax Court judge is to sit in court all day, mostly in silence, and listen to witnesses who bend the truth to suit their interests and trial lawyers who spin arguments that reflect little in the way of thought or organization. Judges must sift through conflicting evidence, identify the relevant facts, and apply the correct legal principles to those facts. Tax Court judges face the additional burden of having to grapple day after day with the *Income Tax Act*, one of Parliament's most complex and prolix statutes. Finally, they have to look over their shoulders at the Federal Court of Appeal and the Supreme Court of Canada, which may criticize their rulings. If trial judges are therefore sometimes impatient, even ornery, it seems to me they have good reasons for being so.

The trial judges' goal is to dispense justice in the cases that are before them, in spite of all the obstacles and irritants. They must explain their decisions by writing reasons for judgment that describe how justice is served in those particular cases. The reasons for judgment are the judges' output in the cases and they will generally take great care in writing them. The reasons will be read by the parties, by tax professionals and by fellow judges including, quite possibly, appellate judges. The judges' reputation and respect in the legal community will depend on the persuasiveness of their reasons. What judges require in order to do their work, more than

---

3 SOR/90-688, as amended by SOR/92-41, SOR/93-96, SOR/95-113, SOR/96-144, SOR/96-503, SOR/99-209.

4 For the Tax Court judge's perspective of what is required, see Chapter 6 above, "Good Trial Practices In the Tax Court of Canada" by Associate Chief Justice D.G.H. Bowman of the Tax Court of Canada.

anything else, is a succinct, truthful and knowledgeable presentation and discussion by legal counsel of a case's facts, issues and legal principles. Taxpayer's counsel is an advocate for the taxpayer, but it does not aid the taxpayer's case for counsel to make a biased presentation of the facts, to frame the legal issues in a way that is unfair to the other side, or to make a one-sided legal argument. Extreme positions are of no help to the judge and therefore of no assistance to the taxpayer. The best way to help the taxpayer is to present an honest, fair and credible case.

Giving trial judges what they require seems simple enough, but is difficult in practice when the parties' positions have become polarized in the course of an already lengthy, and sometimes heated, dispute. The parties and their advisers usually believe they know all the facts. They are certain that the facts have been thoroughly tested over the years in which the dispute worked its way through the audit and administrative appeals process and their view of the facts may be deeply entrenched by the time legal counsel are retained to take the matter to Tax Court. Quite often, however, the relevant facts, issues and key argument may have become lost in a haze of acrimony. There will almost always be some facts in dispute that, on reflection, will have no relevance at all to the issues that must be addressed in court. Other facts that have been ignored by the parties may be helpful or even determinative in the case. The intense partisanship will often make it difficult for the parties to see the facts and issues from the neutral perspective of the trial judge, which of course makes it difficult to see what the judge will require to write persuasive reasons for judgment. It is our role as litigation counsel to determine what facts are truly relevant and then take a fresh look at those facts to see if they can withstand the intense scrutiny of a trial, when facts must be asserted under oath and witnesses are subjected to rigorous cross-examination. The only way to determine what is true or false is to carefully review all of the relevant documents and then engage in the role-playing exercise of cross-examining one's own client and other potential witnesses in the case.

It is not enough to avoid getting swept away by our client's partisanship. We must put aside partisanship altogether, if only for a period of time, which admittedly is not an easy thing for most litigators to do. Too often, we quickly become so invested in our client's view of the case that we summarily dismiss, even denigrate, most of the other side's points. To give judges what they require, however, we must look at all facets of our own case with a sharply critical eye and give full measure to the facts and argument that the other side is expected to present. The best way to understand the other side's case is to review with an open mind the correspondence between the taxpayer's advisers and the Canada Revenue Agency (the "CRA") at the audit and appeals stage and examine the CRA's internal reports, specifically the T20 Audit Report and T401 Appeals Report. In some cases, it is useful to make an access to information request,[5] but I have found that most documents may be obtained through the discovery process and, in particular, by asking probing questions of the CRA's auditor during examination for discovery and then asking for undertakings to produce the relevant documents in the CRA's possession. Also, most Crown lawyers are very forthright about how they see the matter and are glad to engage in a thorough discussion about the facts and issues of the case.

Counsel must resist any rush to judgment about the facts and issues. Instead, we must mull them over from every perspective and, better still, discuss them at length with colleagues. Throughout all three phases of the trial, we must sort out our weak arguments from our strong ones, untie the knots in the arguments and discard the blind alleys and red herrings that at one point seemed promising. It certainly helps to have a team of experienced tax lawyers working together on the matter and to assign to at least one member of the team the role of devil's advocate, to make the best possible case for the other side and to poke holes in the arguments that might be advanced on the taxpayer's behalf. It also helps to have a team dynamic in which people are free to express ideas that seem heretical at first glance. No idea is too unorthodox to be considered and the best ideas prevail, regardless of who thought of them. The process is psychologically difficult, since it requires normally combative litigators to temporarily languish in doubt, but the time spent in doubt is very well spent if it leads to a deeper understanding of the facts and issues of the case.

Once the other side's case has been explored in this fashion, it is time to shift one's perspective to that of the trial judge and ask the searching questions that the judge is likely to ask, such as: what are the truly relevant facts, as distinguished from the self-justifying assertions that each side is inclined to make? What are the legal issues in the case and how should the issues be framed so that they are fair to both sides? What legal principles ought to apply? What are the merits of the case from an average person's point of view, without reference to technical legal principles?

Having pondered and worked through these questions, and answered them truthfully, I am in a position to devise a litigation strategy that is built

---

5 *Access to Information Act.* R.S.C. 1985, c. A-1, s.1.

on a solid foundation, one that takes into account every conceivable rejoinder and objection, and that presents the case in a manner that is most helpful to the trial judge. The strategy will meld the facts, issues and legal principles in a way that represents a compelling case from the judge's perspective. The facts in support of the taxpayer's arguments are clearly identified, challenged and verified, and considerable thought is given at this stage to the persuasiveness of the evidence that is available to establish those facts. The relevant issues are framed in an impartial manner. The taxpayer's arguments are tried and tested, with every possible counterargument debated and answered. There is considerable instinct and judgment involved in the development of a winning litigation strategy for a particular case. Counsel's instinct and judgment are usually hard-earned, resulting from many "trials and errors" and, in particular, from having taken some approaches over the years that have failed outright and others that may have succeeded but make one very hesitant about trying them again.

The taxpayer's litigation strategy may be quite simple in simple cases. In a typical trading case (a capital gain versus income case), for example, the issue is whether the particular property that was bought and sold at a profit, such as a commercial real estate building, was acquired for resale or as a long-term investment. In order to write persuasive reasons for judgment in the taxpayer's favour, the trial judge will need to determine, based on the evidence, that the taxpayer intended to hold the property as a long-term investment, without even a secondary intention to sell it at a profit, and that the original intention was altered by unanticipated circumstances, such as a change in zoning regulations, the loss of a key tenant, or an unsolicited offer at an attractive price. If the facts of the case do not support what the trial judge would require to find in favour of the taxpayer, or if the taxpayer would not make a credible witness, then the taxpayer would be well advised to settle or even drop the case rather than waste a lot more of everyone's time and money. If the facts and evidence support the taxpayer's case, then the litigation strategy must focus on how best to present the taxpayer to the trial judge as a candid and honest person, what elements of the taxpayer's background should be brought out, and what other evidence is required to substantiate the taxpayer's testimony that the property was acquired as a long-term investment. Expert evidence, for example regarding the intricacies of the zoning process or the rental market at the relevant time, may be an important part of the taxpayer's case.

In more complex cases, the litigation strategy may have a dozen or more component parts that must come together as a coherent whole, like a carefully crafted mosaic for the trial judge to behold. A large number of material witnesses may be required to give the judge a complete picture of the facts. The testimony of one or more expert witnesses may also be necessary where the judge would need the assistance and opinion of a person with special knowledge or experience in a particular field. As in simple cases, however, the litigation strategy must be focussed on one goal: to give the judge the necessary facts and arguments to write persuasive reasons for judgment in the taxpayer's favour.

The taxpayer's litigation strategy must be well-developed before the start of the pleadings phase of the trial and will govern the drafting of the notice of appeal as well as the dozens of decisions to be made by taxpayer's counsel at each phase of the trial, such as those involving the selection of documents and witnesses, the nature of the testimony elicited from witnesses, whether any expert testimony is needed, and the manner in which the argument is presented. The strategy will rarely be static, however. It will usually evolve and be refined through all phases of the case as the discovery process brings new facts to light, as the evidence and argument are further developed and, in particular, as the judge begins to react to the evidence and argument at trial.

C. THE PLEADINGS PHASE

The pleadings in a Tax Court case consist of the taxpayer's notice of appeal, the Crown's reply, and the taxpayer's answer. The case begins with the filing of the taxpayer's notice of appeal, the formal requirements of which are set out in Form 21(1)(a) of the Tax Court Rules. Aside from providing basic information such as the taxpayer's name and the assessment under appeal, the form requires the notice of appeal to state the material facts relied on, the issues to be decided, the statutory provisions relied on, the reasons the taxpayer intends to rely on, and the relief sought.

The notice of appeal will normally be the first document read by the Tax Court judge assigned to the case. It provides taxpayer's counsel with the opportunity to set out the essential facts from the taxpayer's perspective and to frame the legal issues. It is through the careful drafting of the notice of appeal that taxpayer's counsel must seize the initiative in the case in the hope of retaining it throughout the trial.

Counsel should spare no effort in making a good first impression with the judge and in launching the case on the right track. The notice of appeal should be a pleasure for the judge to read, which means it should be well-written and concise. It should seldom be more than six or seven pages long, double-spaced, since a judge will want no more at this stage than a broad overview of the case. Although it is obviously written from the taxpayer's perspective, the notice of appeal should be assiduously fair to the Crown's position so that the judge will know from the outset that taxpayer's counsel may be relied upon to present the case in a balanced manner. Having read the notice of appeal, the judge should have a clear understanding in a nutshell of what the case is all about.

Prior to drafting the notice of appeal, taxpayer's counsel should have attained a thorough understanding of the facts, issues and legal argument from each party's perspective in the course of developing the litigation strategy.[6] They will then be in a position to set out the material facts that are supported by the available evidence and that will support the taxpayer's argument. Although subsection 51(2) of the Tax Court Rules allows the parties to make inconsistent allegations in their pleadings as long as they make it clear the allegations are being pleaded in the alternative, I cannot imagine making inconsistent factual allegations. Taxpayer's counsel should not put forward the facts of the case as though they were part of a judge's multiple-choice exam. One set of facts, the true facts, should be presented to the judge in a convincing manner.[7]

Some counsel seem afraid to leave any facts out of the notice of appeal and err on the side of including almost every factual detail that may come out at trial as well as the evidence that will be adduced to support the facts. This is a mistake. It detracts from the main elements of the taxpayer's case

---

6 This is obviously not possible when counsel is retained only shortly before the deadline for filing a notice of appeal. If insufficient time is available, then counsel will have to draft the notice of appeal in much more general terms, with the facts, issues and reasons set out with less precision than would be desirable. It is far better, however, to draft a very broadly worded notice of appeal and, if necessary, later file a more precisely worded amended notice of appeal, than to set out facts in the notice of appeal that are later determined to be inaccurate.

7 Pleading inconsistent conclusions to be drawn from the facts is another matter. There is no harm in admitting that we may be wrong about certain conclusions, provided of course that the case does not necessarily turn on them. For example, subsection 256(5.1) of the *Act* deems a corporation to be controlled "directly or indirectly in any manner whatever" by another corporation if that other corporation has any direct or indirect influence that, if exercised, would result in control in fact of the first corporation. However, the subsection contains a number of exceptions to the rule, including an exception for influence derived from a franchise agreement. A notice of appeal could state that the second corporation had no influence over the first that would result in control in fact and that, even if we are wrong and such influence is found to have existed, the influence was derived from a franchise agreement governing the manner in which the business of the first corporation was conducted, thus falling within the exception contained in subsection 256(5.1).

and risks confusing the judge about what the case is all about. The notice of appeal should usually make no reference to the evidence that may be presented at trial. It should provide only the basic facts that are needed to support the taxpayer's argument and to satisfy the judge's natural curiosity about the key details. In my earlier example of a typical trading case, the facts set out in the notice of appeal would be contained in a few short paragraphs that describe the nature and location of the property and the dates and prices at which the property was acquired and sold. I would then simply state that the taxpayer intended to hold the property for an extended period of time and describe the event or fact that led to its unanticipated sale. If, in another case, the issue is whether a corporation was entitled to claim the small business deduction, then the notice of appeal should briefly describe the shareholders and the taxpayer's business and state (i) that the taxpayer was a Canadian-controlled private corporation that was not associated with any other corporation, and (ii) that its income was from an "active business carried on in Canada" within the meaning of subsection 125(1) of the *Act*. Those facts are sufficient to establish the taxpayer's entitlement to the small business deduction. The notice of appeal should not add that the taxpayer was not controlled by a non-resident or that it did not carry on a "specified investment business" or "personal services business" within the meaning of subsection 125(7) of the *Act*, unless those were specified grounds on which the reassessment was based.

Counsel must resist the temptation to include any other extraneous material in the notice of appeal. For example, I have read some notices of appeal in which the material facts section included a list of the perceived wrongs committed by the CRA in the audit or appeals process. Including such information may be cathartic to the client and counsel, who finally get the opportunity to complain to a judge about the CRA's misdeeds, but the misdeeds have nothing to do with the merits of the taxpayer's appeal and rarely seem to be of much interest to the judge. The judge's function is not to condemn CRA officials for their conduct, even if such conduct occasionally deserves condemnation, but to write reasons for judgment that correctly apply the law to the material facts. Any diversions in the notice of appeal that interrupt the flow of the taxpayer's description of the material facts, issues and reasons will only distract the judge from the essential elements of the taxpayer's case. The result may be a loss of the prized initiative in the case as the judge gives up on making sense of the notice of appeal and looks to the reply for a roadmap on the facts and issues.

Another common error in the drafting of notices of appeal is to confuse "reasons" with "arguments." The reasons for the taxpayer's legal position may be given in a few short sentences, while the arguments in support of the reasons may require pages of text and include a detailed analysis of the statutory provisions and related case law. The notice of appeal must set out the taxpayer's reasons, but it is not the place to make the taxpayer's argument, quote provisions of the *Act* or cite case law. All of that must await the trial phase of the case.

If the taxpayer's counsel has submitted a well-drafted notice of appeal, the reply should add very little to the judge's understanding of the case, except perhaps to deny certain allegations of fact contained in the notice of appeal, or to add facts that are needed to support the Crown's argument. The formal requirements of the Crown's reply are set out in section 49 of the Tax Court Rules. The reply must state the facts that are admitted and denied, as well as those of which the Crown has no knowledge and which it puts in issue. The reply must also state the findings or assumptions of fact made by the Minister when making the assessment, which are simply the Crown's allegations of fact at the time. The reply must then describe the issues, list the statutory provisions relied on, provide the reasons the Crown intends to rely on, and state the relief sought.

When I receive the Crown's reply, I first mark up a copy of the notice of appeal by highlighting the facts that have been admitted in the reply and those that the taxpayer will need to prove at trial. I also read the Minister's findings and assumptions to see if there is anything new in them.[8] The Crown's description of the issues may hint at a change in the approach previously taken by the Minister at the audit or appeals stage, as may the basis or reasons given for the Crown's position.[9] If nothing else, reading the reply is an opportunity for taxpayer's counsel to consider whether we have missed something in our understanding of the case and, if so, to modify our litigation strategy.

---

8 The case law provides that the taxpayer must "demolish" the Minister's findings and assumptions that were made at the time of the reassessment: *Johnston v. M.N.R.*, [1948] C.T.C. 195 (S.C.C.). The word "demolish" suggests a very onerous undertaking. It is enough, however, for the taxpayer to make out a *prima facie* case, on a balance of probabilities, that the Minister's assumptions are incorrect. At that point, the onus shifts to the Minister to rebut the taxpayer's *prima facie* case: see *Hickman Motors Limited v. The Queen* (1997), 97 D.T.C. 5363 (S.C.C.), at paragraphs 93 and 94. Many cases are won without any major dispute regarding the facts, by showing that the reassessments do not flow as a matter of law from the Minister's findings and assumptions, even if they are true.

9 Subsections 152(5) and (9) of the *Act* allow the Minister to rely on a new basis or argument after the normal reassessment period has expired provided the Minister does not include in the taxpayer's income an amount that was not included during the normal reassessment period. See *Anchor Pointe Energy v. R.*, 2003 D.T.C. 5512 (F.C.A.).

Although the Tax Court Rules provide for the filing of an answer, I would file one only if there were something completely unexpected in the Crown's reply that cried out for a response. An answer is not strictly necessary since subsection 50(2) of the Tax Court Rules provides that the taxpayer is deemed to deny the allegations of fact made in the reply if no answer is delivered.

D. THE DISCOVERY PHASE

There are two parts to the discovery phase of a case: the discovery of documents and the oral examinations.

The discovery of documents may take place under Tax Court Rule 81 (partial disclosure) or Rule 82 (full disclosure). Rule 81 requires each party to file and serve a list of the documents that might be used in evidence to establish allegations of fact in the party's pleadings, or to rebut the other party's allegations of fact in its pleadings. In general, documents may not be referred to at trial unless they are included in the list or produced at the examination for discovery.[10] Most Tax Court cases proceed on the basis of the partial disclosure process set out in Rule 81, which initially allows each party to pick and choose from among the relevant documents in its possession. Although there is no requirement under Rule 81 to list documents that may be prejudicial to one's case, it generally makes sense to produce all the key documents regardless of whether they are helpful, since their existence will almost certainly be revealed in the course of the examination for discovery. As a rule, the examiner will ask the party under oath to describe all relevant documents that were not included in the party's list and produce those that seem of interest. This may lead to an adjournment of the examination, causing an unnecessary and costly delay in the case.

Rule 82 states that the parties may agree to file and serve (or, failing agreement, either party may apply to the court to require that the parties file and serve) a list of all documents "relating to any matter in question" between the parties and swear an affidavit that they have done so. It is rare, however, for either party to ask for full disclosure under Rule 82, since doing so is time-consuming and seldom worth the effort.[11]

---

10 Tax Court Rule 89.

11 In contrast, the full disclosure of documents is mandatory under the rules of many Canadian courts. See, for example, section 30.02 of the Ontario *Rules of Civil Procedure*, R.R.O. 1990, Reg. 194, as amended, which provides that the parties must disclose every document relating to any matter in issue.

Rule 92 provides that an examination for discovery may also be conducted, at the option of the examining party, by written questions and answers (often referred to as interrogatories).[12] I would be pleasantly surprised to have Crown counsel give up the right to conduct an oral examination of my client prior to trial, and instead ask a series of questions to be answered in writing. Unlike oral examinations in which the party being examined must answer the questions with little or no assistance from counsel, the answers to written questions are prepared with counsel's assistance.[13] It is also more difficult to follow up on answers to written questions with a new line of inquiry. More importantly, oral examinations provide counsel with an opportunity to hear the inflection in a witness's voice, or observe a witness's body language, which may suggest that an answer is not entirely truthful or complete. It is therefore difficult to see any rationale for choosing to conduct an examination by way of interrogatories, except in those rare cases in which the evidence would be of little or no importance to the outcome of the trial.

I always tell my clients that the Tax Court process is an open one and that the best way to win the case is to be entirely forthright concerning the facts and evidence. The adversarial nature of the trial process means that the relevant facts will eventually come out in any event, and it is in the taxpayer's best interest to lay the relevant facts on the table at the outset and focus on how to win the case on those facts, rather than waste energy trying to cover up unsupportive facts. I will of course be selective about the facts I choose to emphasize at trial and carefully consider the evidence to be adduced, but I will not pretend that unhelpful facts do not exist, since it is better to deal with such facts directly by explaining them to the judge in a forthright manner than to wait for Crown counsel to raise them.

Taxpayers are naturally reluctant to disclose documents they believe are prejudicial to their case, but they often misjudge what is truly prejudicial. If there are documents that are so prejudicial as to preordain a negative outcome, then the case should have been settled or abandoned long ago. Quite often, however, a taxpayer will whisper the existence of a document that, on inspection, is completely innocuous or utterly irrelevant to the issues in the case. For example, an accountant's tax planning memorandum that discusses the risk that a proposed transaction might not be viewed by the CRA as complying with a provision of the *Act* is irrelevant in determining whether that transaction did comply, unless improper tax

---

12 See also Tax Court Rules 113 to 118.

13 See *Montana Indian Band v. The Queen*, [2000] 1 F.C. 267 (T.D.).

avoidance were an issue in the case. Whether the tax plan succeeded or not is a matter for the judge to decide.

When I am first retained in a case, I ask my client to provide me with all of the documents and information that might be even remotely relevant in the case. As I develop the litigation strategy, I begin the process of deciding which documents to put in evidence under Rule 81 and am ready to produce all of the relevant documents should the Crown invoke Rule 82. My objective is to put into evidence those documents required to prove my client's allegations of fact and rebut those of the Crown, and only those documents. I may be tempted to include additional documents, but the inclusion of too many documents may only confuse or annoy the judge and is an indication that I have not sufficiently refined my litigation strategy.

At the taxpayer's examination for discovery, which is conducted under oath, the answers given must be responsive and truthful, but there is no obligation to provide answers that go beyond the scope of the questions asked or that reveal the taxpayer's litigation strategy. It is important for the taxpayer to understand that this is not the opportunity to tell the court the taxpayer's story, since the judge will never hear or read anything about the examination unless the Crown decides to put portions of the transcript into evidence. In other words, the examination is not an opportunity to win the case; at best it is an opportunity to avoid losing it. The taxpayer should therefore answer the questions truthfully and succinctly, but avoid elaborating beyond what is necessary to be truthful and responsive. The opportunity for taxpayers to tell their complete story, in their own words, will come at trial during their examination-in-chief.

The only way to prepare a client for an examination for discovery is to spend a considerable period of time in the role-playing exercise of asking all the questions that may be posed by Crown counsel and then discussing the answers given. There is, of course, more than one way to answer a question truthfully and the taxpayer must be made aware of how a particular answer, or even specific words used in an answer, may be perceived by a judge hearing the case. I will take the taxpayer through the documents on the parties' lists of documents, pausing to discuss the import of each document. I will also review and discuss the facts set out in the notice of appeal and reply. In role-playing for the examination, I will ask all the routine questions and also grill my client with the toughest possible questions. The preparation is time-consuming, but is well worth it if my client is prepared for any question that may be asked. At the end of the process, my client should understand the Crown's objectives in the examination and be ready to do a great job of answering all relevant questions. I am careful, however, not to script the taxpayer's answers. The preparation for an examination is not an exercise in determining how well the taxpayer memorizes the best possible answers. It is about making the taxpayer keenly aware of the adversarial nature of the litigation process and having the taxpayer tell the entire truth in a way that does not inadvertently harm the taxpayer's case.

I will always conduct an examination for discovery of the CRA's representative in the case. Although it is rare to get an answer out of the examination that may be usefully read into evidence at trial, I almost always learn something about the CRA's view of the facts and occasionally gain some valuable insights into how the Crown will argue its case at trial. I usually take the auditor through the Crown's list of assumptions in the reply and ask for the factual basis underlying those assumptions. I may also ask Crown counsel to explain the significance of certain assumptions so that I might better understand the argument that I will face at trial.

E. THE TRIAL PHASE

The trial phase of a Tax Court case may be divided into two parts: the preparation prior to the trial and the trial itself.

The pre-trial preparation begins as soon as it is clear, following the discovery phase, that the case is not likely to be settled prior to trial. The pre-trial work centres on drafting notes of argument and preparing witnesses, including any expert witnesses.

Drafting notes of argument is an essential part of our preparation for a Tax Court trial. The Tax Court Rules do not require the preparation of a factum, or memorandum of fact and law, but trial judges are always glad to receive a concise and informative document that sets out a party's legal argument. As a result, tax counsel have developed the practice of handing the judge a written argument, often called "notes of argument." The notes are really an informal factum designed to assist the judge in following counsel's oral argument. I hope that the judge will also refer to the notes after the trial is over, when writing the reasons for judgment.

I keep my notes of argument as short and simple as possible. Fifteen pages of text, double-spaced, should be long enough in an average case. I describe the main facts of the case, state the issues, and analyse the relevant statutory provisions in the context of the scheme of the Act as a whole. I also describe the facts and issues in the relevant case law and explain how the principles from those cases are applicable to the case before the court. Cases that seem to go against my argument are dealt with and, if possible, distinguished. I may include a description of the historical evolution of a statutory provision and, if its meaning is unclear, provide the legislative intent by quoting the Department of Finance's Technical Notes, speeches made in Parliament or its committees, and learned commentary. I wrap up my notes by driving home one consistent line of argument. I do not take the scattergun approach, used by some litigators, which involves advancing a number of often inconsistent arguments and inviting the judge to pick and choose from among them.[14] My objective is to draft notes of argument that are a pleasure for the judge to read, that persuasively convey my argument, and that provide exactly what the judge requires to write reasons for judgment in my client's favour.

The drafting and redrafting of my notes of argument, over the course of many weeks and months, is a fruitful way to develop my argument for trial. The redrafting process allows me to determine which facts are important and how best to integrate those facts into the many components of my argument. The drafting process also provides my litigation team with an opportunity to try out different arguments and helps us sort out the good arguments from the bad and refine the good ones. We may identify additional counterarguments at this stage and prepare answers to those counterarguments. As we all know, it is one thing to have the arguments nicely worked out in our own mind, but the act of writing them down and reading them, in particular reading them aloud, will reveal errors or weaknesses that would otherwise remain hidden until pointed out at trial by opposing counsel or the judge. In short, the notes of argument are the main vehicle by which our litigation strategy takes its final shape.

In a complex case, it is not unusual for me to go through ten or twenty drafts of the notes of argument. When I learn the name of the trial judge who will hear the case, ten days prior to the start of the trial, I make a point of reading the recent or important decisions of that judge. I try to get a sense of the judge's likes and dislikes and also examine how the judge has dealt with legal issues that are similar to those in my case. I may then tailor my notes of argument to some extent to suit the judge. For example, if the case involves the issue of whether parties are dealing with one another at arm's length, and the judge hearing the case has decided many recent cases on that issue, my notes would provide only a concise summary of the relevant legal tests. I would be sure to address in detail any particular aspects of the arm's length issue that have previously been of concern to the judge and that may be relevant to my case. I will continue to revise the

---

14 It is a bad sign when a judge indicates that counsel is using the scattergun approach. See *Hayes v. M.N.R.* (1989), 89 D.T.C. 334 (T.C.C.).

notes during the evidence portion of the trial, so that they are as current and complete as possible when handed to the judge prior to the start of oral argument. It is important to have an excellent draft of the notes of argument a few weeks prior to the start of a major trial, since those last weeks will be taken up with the preparation of witnesses and a number of other time-consuming tasks.

The testimony of well-prepared witnesses may be the deciding factor in the outcome of a case since judges say they often determine how they will decide a case by the time all the evidence is in. The preparation of witnesses usually begins with the expert witnesses, since their reports must be filed at least 30 days prior to the start of the trial. I may have interviewed potential expert witnesses long before this phase, preferably prior to the drafting of the notice of appeal, but they will likely be retained only after the discovery phase, once it seems clear that the case will not be settled prior to trial. After familiarizing the experts with the facts and issues of the case and discussing the nature of the evidence they will provide, I ask them for an outline of their expert report. I then review and discuss the outline and once it is on the right track, I ask them to write a draft report. I assist in making revisions to the draft report to ensure that the final report is written in a way that is most readable and informative for the trial judge. Depending on their area of expertise, some experts have a tendency to write a report that is so technical, or so rife with jargon or terms of art, that it is virtually incomprehensible to the lay reader. Working with the experts on their draft reports is also the best way to ensure that I fully understand the testimony they intend to give. Finally, several days prior to the start of the trial, I will take the experts through a dry-run of their examination-in-chief and engage in the role-playing exercise of asking them a series of difficult questions to ensure they are prepared for the Crown's cross-examination.

The preparation of my material witnesses will also take place a few days before the start of the trial, so that the points I discuss with them are still fresh in their minds when they take the stand. I make every effort to prepare my witnesses for both the examination-in-chief and cross-examination. As with the expert witnesses, the best way to prepare material witnesses is to spend a lot of time with them, reviewing the relevant documents and going over their testimony. I ask them questions as though they were on the witness stand, covering each topic they need to address and each document on which they may be questioned. My objective is to ensure that my witnesses are very comfortable with their testimony and are not taken by surprise in court. As in preparing for examinations for discovery, I also work with my witnesses to identify the best way of expressing their answers to various questions. Their answers must be entirely honest and accurately convey the meaning they intend to convey.

In preparing witnesses for their examination-in-chief, I encourage them to say what they need to say in their own words and above all, to speak candidly. I usually suggest that their story be told in chronological order, because that is the easiest way to recount events and have the judge understand them. I also tell my witnesses that they must take the initiative in presenting their evidence in court since I am not permitted to lead them to the correct answers and may ask them only neutral questions that prompt them to move through their testimony. It is mostly up to them to tell their story. My principal role is to ensure that the judge is following the questions and answers. I must gauge the judge's reaction to the witnesses' answers and if necessary, ask my witnesses to clarify or elaborate on certain parts of their testimony.

Similarly the witnesses will be mostly on their own during their cross-examination, since most Tax Court judges show little tolerance for objections unless a question is wholly irrelevant or improper. I take great care in preparing my witnesses for cross-examination, going over their answers with them and providing them with techniques for dealing with the Crown's thorniest questions and tactics, with a view to ensuring that they not only respond correctly to each question, but even turn some of the toughest questions to my client's advantage.

The most important thing about a witness's testimony is for the witness to tell the truth, not just because the witness is sworn to do so, but also because there is nothing more powerful and compelling in a courtroom than hearing a witness who speaks truthfully. Like the rest of us, judges tend to like people who tell the truth and dislike those who do not and I cannot expect to win the case if the judge considers my witnesses to be less than entirely truthful. It is difficult to tell the truth until one knows the truth, however, and it often takes considerable effort for the witness to get to the bottom of the facts so that the truth may be told. Occasionally the truth is wrapped up in a number of myths or falsehoods that have evolved over time and must be stripped away before the witness steps into the courtroom. Witnesses may also have a tendency to conveniently suppress facts that they think reflect badly on them or that are not particularly supportive of the case. These facts must be dredged up and dealt with in the course of preparation so that the witness will not shirk from discussing them openly at trial. My task is to confront and challenge my witnesses before they enter the courtroom so that their testimony will be entirely truthful and candid.

I also emphasize to my witnesses that, in the course of giving their testimony, they must stick to the facts rather than volunteer reasons and explanations for their actions or, even worse, argue the merits of the case from the witness stand, which many taxpayers in particular are inclined to do. Witnesses will seem defensive if they offer justifications or excuses for what they have said or done and the witness stand is not the proper place to argue one's case. The witness's role is to recount the facts and to do so, as much as possible, without editorial commentary. I assure my clients that once all the evidence is in, I will explain whatever needs to be explained and make a vigorous argument in the case.

My client is usually the first witness I call to the stand and is also the most important witness. If the judge likes my client, then the judge will be inclined to rule in my client's favour, and in a close case, the judge's high opinion of my client could mean the difference between victory and defeat. For this reason, I am always reluctant to proceed to Tax Court with an agreed statement of facts.[15] I prefer to have my clients testify and, in effect, personally ask the judge to grant them the relief they seek, rather than risk having the judge see them as just a name and social insurance number. It is also better to put a face on my corporate clients by calling a senior officer to the stand and demonstrating to the judge in the course of providing the evidence that my client is not some remote and impersonal entity, but consists of a dynamic group of hard-working, honest people who deserve the relief the corporation is seeking.

I also ensure that my clients are well-prepared regarding the facts of the case, adduce evidence in a way that is interesting for the judge to hear, and present themselves in court in a positive light. For example, in a typical trading case, it is relevant to discuss the taxpayer's dealings in other ventures. This provides me with an opportunity to discuss elements of the taxpayer's background in a way that brings out the taxpayer's decency and good character.

Often the first thing I need to do in preparing my clients for trial is to address their feelings of anger and resentment about the entire process. A judge will not take kindly to an individual who seems angry about being in the judge's courtroom, even if the reasons for that anger are well understood. Individuals may believe they have been unjustly singled out for reassessment by the CRA and then treated unfairly when the CRA's Appeals Division refused to overturn the reassessment. They feel as

---

15 I would be more inclined to file a partial agreed statement of facts, leaving a number of relevant facts to be established by my client's testimony.

though they have been victimized and are now involved in a struggle from which they cannot emerge unscathed. If they lose the case, they may suffer serious financial hardship. Even if they win, they will face significant legal costs after having suffered through years of uncertainty and heartache. They bemoan the fact they were reassessed when others, who seem guilty of far worse infractions, were not. They may view the Crown lawyer as their sworn enemy and may tend to react in a hostile manner to even innocuous questions. I tell my clients that, if they wish to win their case, they must put aside their anger and resentment while in the courtroom. They must carefully listen to the questions they are asked and then answer them fully and politely. They must not allow the Crown lawyer to make them angry or confused. Once they have overcome their anger, it is not unusual for taxpayers to enjoy their day in court and connect with the judge in a way that increases their chances of victory.

In the days prior to the start of the trial, taxpayer's counsel must focus on a number of matters other than the preparation of witnesses. Counsel must put together a book of documents and a book of authorities, prepare for cross-examinations of any Crown witnesses, and review read-ins from the transcripts of the examinations-for-discovery. Counsel's final task is to prepare an opening statement that sets out the evidence that will be adduced, describes the issues, and provides the judge with at least some indication of what the argument will be. The opening statement must capture the judge's attention and start the judge along the right course, but counsel must be careful not to promise the judge any evidence that cannot be delivered during the trial. I have found it useful to give the judge a written copy of my opening statement and may include as a schedule the main provisions of the Act to be interpreted in the case, so that the judge may get a head-start at considering the legal issues while hearing the evidence. All of these pre-trial tasks require careful attention to detail so that counsel are completely prepared and organized for the trial. Counsel will make a bad impression with the judge if, for example, they fumble through their examinations-in-chief while looking for missing pages in their book of documents. The objective is to be so well-prepared that the judge perceives counsel's presentation of the evidence and argument to be almost effortless.

When the trial begins, my goal is to launch my case with a riveting opening statement. I then call my witnesses to the stand and move at a steady pace through the evidence. I hope the taxpayer's testimony rings entirely true to the judge and that each subsequent witness helps to build an overwhelming case on the facts. If all goes according to plan, Crown counsel will score few if any points in the cross-examinations of my witnesses and the judge will begin to wonder why on earth the Minister ever reassessed the taxpayer. I then aim to seal the case with my argument by confirming the judge's view of the correct legal principles to apply to the facts and providing the judge with notes of argument that contain all the tools required to write persuasive reasons for judgment in my client's favour. Most cases, of course, will not proceed in this ideal fashion, but will be hard-fought contests with each side struggling to gain even the smallest advantage. In such cases, the side that ultimately prevails is often the one that is better prepared for every twist in the evidence and every turn in the argument.

The main benefit of being well-prepared and organized for trial is that counsel may focus most of their energy and attention on the judge, the only person in the courtroom whose views ultimately matter. If I am well-prepared for my examinations-in-chief and have a solid grasp of every aspect of my argument, I am in a much better position to watch and listen to the judge as the trial unfolds and make whatever adjustments are required to improve my client's chances of success. My goal is to try to figure out, at every moment of the trial, what the judge is thinking. Does the judge believe my witnesses? Does the judge perceive there is something missing from their testimony? Is the judge confused by one of my documents? Is there some point with which the judge disagrees in my argument? Is there anything more I need to say to get the judge on my side? Some judges will come right out and say what is unclear or troubling. More often, I have to interpret subtle indications, even the judge's body language, to identify any difficulties that the judge is having with my case.

I do my best to signal to the judge that I welcome the judge's active participation in the case and am very glad to have the judge ask questions of my witnesses and actively engage me in debate during oral argument. If there is one golden rule in encouraging the judge to participate actively, it is that counsel must never interrupt the judge when the judge is speaking. People interrupt each other all the time in casual conversation. We routinely nod our heads as people are speaking and then finish their sentences for them. Occasionally, we do so to express our disagreement with them. At other times, perhaps, it is because we are anxious to move the conversation along, or simply show that we agree with them and are on the same wavelength as they are on. Whatever our reasons may be, cutting someone off in mid-sentence is not an effective way to determine what that person is thinking. It may also make the person feel uncomfortable and reluctant to engage us in conversation. The best way to determine what judges are thinking is to listen very carefully and patiently to what they are saying, without any interruption whatsoever. Let judges take as much time as they need to articulate what is on their minds. If a judge stops in mid-sentence and is obviously thinking about some point, there may be a heavy silence in the courtroom. It is the judge's silence. Counsel must not break that silence.

If a judge communicates a concern about some aspect of my case through body language, such as a frown or grimace, then it is vital for me to determine its root cause. If I am in the middle of a witness' examination-in-chief and cannot readily identify the judge's concern, then I slow down and ask my witness to clarify and elaborate on the evidence that was just adduced. I linger on that evidence until the reason for the judge's concern becomes clear, either through other non-verbal clues, or because the judge finally verbalizes the concern. I may then have the witness address the matter directly, or perhaps have a subsequent witness clarify the point for the judge. Similarly, if a judge indicates through a glare that a particular document is confusing, I take the time to go over that document again with the witness and help the judge clear up the confusion.

I have seen counsel forge ahead with their case, like a runaway train, oblivious or indifferent to the judge's obvious confusion on a matter. Some may even treat the judge's interventions as hostile interruptions to the flow of their case, rather than an opportunity to get their case back on track. This sort of attitude reflects a misunderstanding about counsel's role in the courtroom. Our role is not to try and force our client's case down the judge's throat like a dose of bad-tasting medicine. Our role is to be at the judge's service and assist the judge to render judgment for our client.

Similarly, I have heard judges interrupt counsel's oral argument to ask about a particular matter and been told by counsel that they will get to that point later on in the argument. I can understand that some counsel are reluctant to have the judge's questions disturb the flow of the prepared argument, but if the judge is concerned enough to ask about a particular matter, then counsel is well-advised to deal with that point when the judge asks about it, rather than later on in the argument. It is therefore necessary to be well enough prepared and confident in our argument to make adjustments and deal with the issues in whatever order the judge wishes. Although demanding on counsel, the best scenario is for the judge to interrupt early in the argument and engage counsel in a vigorous debate that leads from one issue to the next in a manner that makes sense to the judge. In that scenario, counsel may help the judge navigate through the facts and issues, and even assist in untying the same intellectual knots that they had struggled to untie months earlier as they drafted and redrafted their notes of argument.

F. CONCLUSION

The key to success in tax litigation is preparation. From the start, taxpayer's counsel must work to identify the relevant facts and issues and develop a litigation strategy designed to win the case. Taxpayer's counsel must do so by examining the case from each side's perspective and, most importantly, from the judge's perspective. Taxpayer's counsel must ensure that all the evidence required to support the taxpayer's legal argument is before the court, and that the evidence is presented in a way that casts the taxpayer in a positive light. Throughout the trial phase, counsel's efforts must be directed to assisting the judge. Counsel must carefully watch and listen to the judge and commit themselves to identifying and responding to the judge's concerns. The result, one hopes, is that counsel will persuade the judge to see the case their client's way and write reasons for judgment in the taxpayer's favour.

Chapter Eight

The Good, the Bad and the Ugly: A Crown Perspective on Tax Court Litigation[1]

David W. Chodikoff

A. INTRODUCTION

Leaving aside the result of the process, tax litigation can either be efficient and effective (the "good"), dull and repetitious (the "bad"), or just plain confrontational and wasteful (the "ugly"). As lawyers practicing tax law, it is up to us to play our part in maintaining the "good" or, as I see it, the integrity of this litigation process. But how do we contribute to this worthwhile objective? This would seem to be a relatively easy and straightforward task. You must know and follow the *Rules* of the Tax Court of Canada[2]; you must know the law and all the facts concerning the issue or issues in your case

1 The views expressed in this chapter are my own and do not represent the opinions, views or positions of the Department of Justice and/or the Canada Revenue Agency (the "CRA"). I express my deep gratitude to John Shipley, General Counsel and Peter Kremer, General Counsel, of the Department of Justice. Both John and Peter reviewed earlier drafts of this chapter and provided me with constructive comments and valuable suggested revisions. I also want to thank Ian S. MacGregor, the Assistant Deputy Attorney General, Department of Justice. Ian provided me with his comments and helpful, suggested revisions.

2 *Tax Court of Canada Rules (General Procedure)* SOR/90-688, as amended by SOR/92-41, SOR/93-96, SOR/95-113, SOR/96-144, SOR/96-503, SOR/99-209 hereinafter the *Rules*.

that is before the Tax Court of Canada; and you should treat all parties with the same respect that you would expect in return.

The purpose of this chapter is to highlight and consider from the Crown's perspective some of the more important and interesting rules specifically, but not exclusively, in respect of the General Procedure appeals before the court.[3] This journey through the *Rules* is from the Crown's perspective, and to help you navigate with me, I have mapped out the process from file assignment to judgment. It is my hope that this discussion will help you become a more effective and efficient lawyer in the practice of tax litigation.

B. THE CROWN'S INITIAL INVOLVEMENT

The Tax Court of Canada sits in every province and territory in Canada. The tax litigation process commences with the taxpayer filing a Notice of Appeal with the Tax Court of Canada, at one of its several offices in Canada. Once filed, the Notice of Appeal is served upon the Minister of National Revenue and the Attorney General of Canada.

It has often been said that the Department of Justice is the largest "law firm" in the country employing nearly 2000 lawyers. There are justice offices located in Halifax, Montreal, Toronto, Ottawa, Winnipeg, Saskatoon, Calgary, Edmonton, Vancouver, Yellowknife, Whitehorse, and Nunavut. Across the country, there are approximately 275 Justice lawyers that work for the CRA.

Appeal files are typically assigned based on the taxpayer's selected geographic forum for the trial.[4] For example, if the taxpayer resides and files his or her appeal in Toronto, then the appeal will be assigned to the Tax Services Section of the Ontario Regional Office of the Department of Justice. Or, if the taxpayer files his or her appeal in Vancouver, then the appeal will likely be assigned to the Tax Services Section of the Vancouver Regional Office of the Department of Justice.

3 In addition to the discussion of the *General Procedure Rules*, I will also highlight key provisions of *Tax Court of Canada Rules (Informal Procedure)* pertaining to the conduct of the Informal Procedure Appeals, SOR/90-688, as amended by SOR/93-97, SOR/93-295, SOR/94-85, SOR/95-114, SOR/96-504, SOR/99-210.

4 See: "Tax Tales Conversations with Judges and Counsel" in *Report of Proceedings of the 54th Tax Conference*, 2002 Conference Report, Canadian Tax Foundation, September 29–October 1, 2002 at 33:10; the National Litigation Coordinator may direct the file to a specific regional office because the coordinator has the ability to look at counsels' expertise from a national perspective. Once assigned, the group head at the local office has control of the file.

Files are also assigned on the basis of complexity, the specialization of counsel and availability of resources. For example, if a Justice lawyer has acquired *Charter of Rights* or anti-avoidance experience, then the local group head will likely assign that type of work to the counsel with that specialized experience and skills. Of course, Justice human resources are finite, and management does its best to allocate these scarce resources in an effective manner.

There are two general observations I will make regarding the process of assignment of complex files. First, as one would expect, the more complex files are assigned to the more experienced lawyers in the various regional offices. Second, with respect to the large project files, typically more than one lawyer is assigned to the case. In these cases there will be a senior counsel on the file and possibly one or two other counsel.[5] In certain "mega projects," paralegals will be assigned to the file. The paralegals play a key role in the organization and control of documents. They also can have input on the development of the Crown's case.

C. THE CROWN'S FILE

Depending on the nature of the issues involved and the scope of review at the audit and objection stages, Justice counsel typically receive the file from the CRA already prepared for litigation to some degree. In the file there are a number of standard documents. In the case of an Informal Procedure appeal, a copy of the Reply to the Notice of Appeal that has been prepared by a CRA official will be attached to the file. This Informal Procedure Reply has been served on the opposing side and filed with the Registrar of the Tax Court of Canada.

If it is an appeal in the General Procedure, the Reply will be drafted by the Justice lawyer. At the drafting stage, there may be discussions between Justice counsel and CRA officials. These discussions are often wide-ranging. They may include anything from simply clarifying the information received from the taxpayer, to advising on appropriate legal positions or to other case development issues such as settlement discussions.

A first-time visitor to any Tax Section Justice Office may find some of the hallways and walls of these facilities stacked with dozens of banker boxes. It may even appear as "enhanced government fortifications," but

5 Large project files or "mega projects" refer to a large group of taxpayers that share the same issue or issues on appeal. These groups can range in the dozens to a thousand or more.

this is really not the case. However, Justice counsel do often receive a mountain of material from the CRA. Some of it is relevant. And for a short period of time, these documents remain in the halls until the material can be properly reviewed, sorted and catalogued.

All CRA files contain the Auditor's Report and the Report on Objection. More commonly referred to as the T20, the Auditor's Report summarizes the auditor's work and provides a detailed explanation for the basis of the assessment or reassessment. The file will also contain all of the original CRA working papers. These documents may include all correspondence to and from the taxpayer and/or his or her representatives; unaudited or audited financial statements; notes from meetings with the taxpayer and/or his or representatives; tax returns; cancelled cheques; receipts-where applicable; notes from telephone conversations with the taxpayer or his or her representative; communications by memoranda or letter to other branches of the CRA or any government department. Essentially, the CRA attempts to obtain from the taxpayer and other sources, all documents relevant to the assessment, reassessment or Notice of Determination of Loss. Sometimes the file will contain a permanent document folder. As the name suggests, this folder will hold original or certified copies of legal and/or other central documents.

In reviewing a taxpayer's Notice of Objection to an assessment, reassessment or Notice of Determination of Loss, CRA appeals officers will prepare a Report on Objection or Appeal. This report, more commonly referred to as the T401, is also in the CRA file that is initially provided to Justice counsel. In preparing this report, additional documentation may be uncovered which is then added to the file. Similar to an Audit Report, the appeals officer may also include memoranda in the file regarding correspondence with the taxpayer and/or his or her representatives. Armed with the documents and discussions with CRA officials, Justice counsel are now ready to prepare the Respondent's Reply to the Notice of Appeal.

D. THE PLEADINGS STAGE

Pleadings serve a number of important functions. They are the first steps in and create the basic roadmap for the tax litigation process. The pleadings should define with clarity, precision and brevity the question or questions in issue between the parties and the facts and argument in support of them as they relate to the assessment, reassessment or Notice of Determination of Loss in dispute. By defining the issues, this, in-turn, aides in the efficiency of the court process and is essential to procedural fairness. It serves to give fair notice to each side of the case of what is required to be made out at court and the relevant evidence that must be produced by either party at trial. In short, when the pleadings clearly and precisely define the question(s) in issue between the parties and the facts and argument(s) in support of them, the pre-trial and trial steps lead to journey's end, a settlement or a clear decision on the issue(s).

Subsection 44(1) of the *Rules* requires the respondent to file a Reply within sixty days after service of the Notice of Appeal, but the appellant can consent to, or the Court may order an extension of the sixty day period.[6] The sixty-day time limit is generally sufficient, but appeals involving complicated facts and/or issues, or multiple appeals sometimes require extra time for research or information collection. The consequence of failing to file a reply on time is a detour. Subsection 44(2) states that if the Reply is not filed within an applicable period as outlined in subsection 44(1), then the allegations of fact contained in the Notice of Appeal are presumed to be true for the purposes of the appeal. What this means in practice is that the Crown must call a case to rebut the factual allegations in the Notice of Appeal.

The Crown's reply or roadmap must be prepared according to subsection 49(1) of the *Rules*, which defines the required content of the Reply. Facts alleged in the Notice of Appeal must be admitted, denied, or the Minister has to state that he has no knowledge of such facts, to take issue with them.[7] The Reply must state the findings or assumptions of fact of the Minister and any other material fact. The issues to be decided by the court need to be articulated. The respondent must identify the statutory provisions relied on, the grounds the Minister relies on and finally, the relief sought. Subsection 49(2) states that the allegations of fact in the Notice of Appeal not denied in the Reply shall be deemed to be admitted unless it is pleaded that the respondent has no knowledge of the fact.

While the Crown's map is drawn from the Appellant's Notice of Appeal, the route is often far different than the Appellant has defined. The Tax Court judge will have the choice of which route to follow, although he or she will define a new route. The appellant can file an Answer to the Reply. Section 45 of the *Rules* provides that an Answer, if any, shall be filed and served within thirty days after service of the Reply. In my experience, Answers are not common. However, experienced counsel do use the Answer to restrict the debate, to highlight certain issues and to focus on weaknesses they perceive in the respondent's position. Counsel cannot use the Answer as a

6 *Rules*, above note 2.

7 Reference to "the Minister" means the Minister of National Revenue.

means of raising new issues not originally addressed in the Notice of Appeal. However, if the Reply raises new facts, then the appellant can address those new facts by admitting, denying or stating that the appellant has no knowledge and puts in issue those facts. Paragraph 50(1)(d) of the *Rules* also permits the appellant to raise facts material to the facts pleaded in the Reply which have not already been pleaded in the Notice of Appeal.

Sometimes, the maps are confusing. So, before you start your journey, clarification will be necessary so as not to lose your way. The *Rules* provide for the demand for particulars.[8] Particulars before pleading are to permit a party to plead with greater precision. Particulars for trial are necessary for greater clarity in defining the issues to be determined by the court.

As the process moves forward, it will sometimes become necessary to redefine or clarify the course. The *Rules* permit either party to amend a pleading. Sections 54 to 57 inclusive detail when an amendment may be made, how amendments are made, the service of an amended pleading and how a party may respond to an amended pleading. In my experience, amendments to pleadings often occur after the examinations for discovery where new or modified facts are heard for the first time.

E. THE DISCOVERY PROCESS

Now the map details are examined. Like a detailed city street map, the discovery process allows you to find out everything you need to know about the other party's case. The discovery process consists of two parts: the discovery of documents, and the oral or written examinations. To commence the first part of the process, both parties focus upon the filing of the List of Documents. Each party files a List of Documents either pursuant to sections 81 and 82 of the *Rules*. Section 81 provides for a partial disclosure of documents. Partial disclosure permits a party to disclose only those documents which might be used in proving its case or in rebutting the other party's case. An affidavit is not required. A partial List of Documents must be filed and served within 30 days of the close of pleadings. Generally speaking, both parties usually prefer to file by way of a partial List of Documents. For the most part, it is a simple and efficient procedure.

In more complex or fact driven cases, the parties may often use section 82 of the *Rules*. Section 82 provides for full disclosure. This form of disclosure can be obtained by agreement between the parties. Alternatively a party can seek a court order or can serve a Notice to Attend an examination

---

8 *Rules*, s. 52.

for discovery requiring production of all documents and things relating to any matter in issue in the proceeding that are in that person's possession, control or power and that are not privileged. A List of Documents made in compliance with section 82 must be verified by affidavit. Unlike the partial List of Documents (section 81) which must be filed and served within 30 days of the close of pleadings, there is no time set in section 82 for the filing of documents as this will be done by either agreement between the parties or an order of the Court. Of course, if the parties proceed by way of full disclosure (section 82), there may be future issues regarding the disclosure of documents that are withheld on the basis of relevancy to the matter in question, issues of privilege, confidentiality pursuant to section 241 of the *Income Tax Act*, and disclosure in respect of the protection afforded by sections 37 and 39 of the *Canada Evidence Act*.[9]

As you can see, there are a lot of potential issues lurking out there should the parties proceed by way of full disclosure. For example, from the Crown's perspective, full disclosure could involve extensive work preparing and searching for documents or dealing with issues of Cabinet confidentiality. The Section 82 "route" can therefore become a time-consuming, expensive approach to the disclosure of documents. In the "run of mill" type of tax cases, it is typically avoided by both parties.

Once the parties have delivered the List of Documents, each side is entitled to inspect and copy the documents listed.[10] Normally, both counsel exchange copies of the documents in their respective Lists. Subsection 85(2) provides that where a party is entitled to inspect the documents to which reference is made in the List of Documents, the other party on request and in advance payment of the cost of reproduction and delivery, deliver copies of the documents.[11]

There is no discovery procedure for Informal Procedure appeals.[12] It often happens that Justice counsel make every effort to get the appellant to produce all the relevant documents before the hearing date in order to determine if there is any basis for a resolution of the appeal before proceeding to trial. Sometimes such efforts are rewarded by a settlement of the appeal.

Informal Procedure appeals are often "trial by ambush" as new documents or information are often revealed to the Court and the Justice coun-

---

9 *Income Tax Act*, R.S.C. 1985, C.1 (5th Supp.) as amended; *Canada Evidence Act*, R.S.C. 1985, c. C-5, as amended.

10 *Rules*, s. 85.

11 *Ibid.*, subs. 85(2).

12 See above note 3.

sel for the very first time during the court hearing. Taxpayers and/or their representatives will often appear at court with a "just found" document. If the appellant could only just make the effort to produce all relevant documents — even in an Informal Procedure case — at the outset of the appeal process, then it might be possible to avoid the expense in time and money of a trial.

Once the Lists of Documents have been filed, both parties often schedule and hold oral examinations for discovery. Where the person to be examined is a party to the proceeding, subsection 103(1) of the *Rules* requires that a Notice to Attend be served on the party's counsel of record or where the party acts in person, served personally.[13] In the case of a cross-examination on an affidavit, a Notice to Attend is required to be served on the counsel for the party that filed the affidavit or where the party who filed the affidavit acts in person to be cross-examined, personally.[14] In the situation where the person to be examined is neither a party nor being examined on behalf of or in place of a party and resides in Canada, then that person will be served with a subpoena personally. When a subpoena is served on a person, witness fees and expenses calculated in accordance with the Tariff shall be paid or at least tendered at the same time.[15] In addition, section 104 of the *Rules* requires that the person to be examined be given not less than ten days notice of the time and place of the examination, unless the court directs otherwise. Finally, section 105 of the *Rules* requires the party being examined to bring all documents to the discovery unless the parties agree otherwise. In my experience, not all counsel comply with these rules, even though in law everyone is required to do just that. Generally, if the parties agree to a time, place and process, no one (read here . . . the Court) will interfere. However, if the parties cannot come to some agreement then the *Rules* are designed to enforce compliance.

Section 92 of the *Rules* permits, at the option of the examining party, an examination by written questions and answers. However, I have found that this form of examination is not very popular. It can be time-consuming and lacks a few of the particular advantages of an oral examination for discovery. Most importantly, an oral examination gives you the chance to assess the competence and credibility of a central witness.

One purpose of the discovery is to ascertain the opposing party's knowledge, information, recollection and belief as to the matters in issue.

13 *Rules*, subs. 103(1).
14 *Ibid.*, subs. 103(3).
15 *Ibid.*, subs. 103(5).

One of the key objectives for both parties is to find out if there are any "other" documents than those referred to in the Lists of Documents that are relevant. Both parties will want to devote ample time to thoroughly investigate the existence of any new documents. If such documents do exist, then counsel will want to learn how this new information impacts on the issues.

If you do not study the details of the map carefully, you may get lost or dead-ended. Planning a discovery requires creative thinking. With the advent of computer technology, everyone knows that government organizations and corporations communicate by electronic mail ("e-mail"). In some circumstances, counsel may ask on discovery for the hard copies of all e-mail communications. The fact is that such communication will probably be a very well-documented record of internal communication. This form of correspondence history could potentially be more informative than the few internal memoranda that are produced by either pen or computer and attached to the file and referred to in a List of Documents.

Pleadings should define the legal and factual issues. Sometimes they do not. The discovery process is an opportune time to clarify the facts and issues between the parties.

Some nominees are not properly or adequately prepared and do not know the answers to important and relevant questions asked on discovery. In accordance with subsection 95(2) of the *Rules*, a party can ask that the examination be adjourned so that the person being examined can be given some time to become better informed.

Resort to subsection 95(2) arises not infrequently where a financial officer, who may understand the tax dispute but not the underlying facts is examined in relation to a corporation's appeal. Subsection 95(2) is one available remedy. Another remedy is to require the production of another witness who is properly informed.

But what if the informed witness is no longer with the company? Third party examinations are possible. Section 99 of the *Rules* permits a party to seek leave from the court to examine for discovery any person who there is reason to believe has information relevant to a material issue in the appeal. Subsection 99(2) of the *Rules* stipulates a number of conditions that must be satisfied before such leave is granted by the Court.[16] But do not assume

16 The conditions include:

(i) [the Court must be satisfied that] the moving party has been unable to obtain information from other persons whom the moving party is entitled to examine for discovery, or from the person sought to be examined (*Rules*, para. 99(2)(a));

that because the witness is no longer in the employ of the company that he or she will be independent; this is not often the case.

At the discovery, counsel can cross-examine the witness unless the question is directed solely at the credibility of the witness.[17] The issues are whether and to what extent should counsel attempt to cross-examine at the examination for discovery. Cross-examination at discovery can help reinforce certain answers; it can also be used to focus the witness on areas requiring detailed testimony; and it can be employed to summarize evidence by way of leading questions. Obviously, counsel will want to avoid creating a transcript that is all "lawyer speak" as opposed to a witness' answers. No matter what side you represent, a useful transcript that helps your case at trial is what is most desired.

Often counsel for the appellant will try and answer on their client's behalf or even go so far as to coach their witness. Counsel should object as this is an abuse of process. Section 97 of the *Rules* states that questions must be answered by the person being questioned but, where there is no objection, the question can be answered by counsel and the answer shall be deemed to be the answer of the person being examined unless, before the conclusion of the examination the person repudiates, contradicts or qualifies the answer. In the event that after the discovery the party that has been examined discovers that the answer to a question on the examination was incorrect, incomplete or no longer correct or complete, then the party must provide the information in writing to every other party in accordance with subsection 98(1) of the *Rules*. In a situation where information is provided in accordance with subsection 98(1) of the *Rules*, subsection 98(2) permits the adverse party to require that this information be verified by affidavit or be subject to further examination for discovery and the written response may be treated at the trial as if it formed part of the original examination of the person examined. Failure to comply with subsection 98(1) or a requirement under paragraph 98(2)(a) and the information subsequently discovered is favourable to that party's case, the presiding judge can decide whether to deny or permit the introduction of that information into evidence. If the information is not favourable to the party's case, the court may give such direction as is just.[18]

(ii) the issue of fairness to both parties (*Rules*, para. 99(2)(b)); and

(iii) the examination will not unduly delay the commencement of the hearing of the proceeding, cut all unreasonable expenses for other parties; or result in unfairness to the person the moving party seeks to examine (*Rules*, para. 99(2)(c)).

17 *Rules*, para. 95(1)(b).

18 *Rules*, para. 98(3)(b).

Section 107 of the *Rules* requires all objections to questions on discovery to be supported by brief reasons on the record. The question may be answered with the objector's consent. Where it is answered, a ruling must be obtained from the court before the evidence is used at the hearing. Pursuant to subsection 107(3), a party can bring a motion to obtain a ruling on the propriety of a question that is objected to and not answered.[19]

Following the examinations for discovery, prudent counsel will review and reassess the strengths and weaknesses of his or her case. After this review, one of the purposes of discovery may be achieved, i.e., settlement. If the parties fail to resolve the appeal then both parties continue the pre-trial process by fulfilling the undertakings given at the examinations for discovery. Usually, the parties agree to give each other 30 days to fulfill undertakings.

At trial the parties can read into evidence as part of their case portions of the discovery transcript, including answers to undertakings.[20] A party can also make use of the discovery transcript to cross-examine a trial witness who has testified at discovery.[21] The Tax Court of Canada Practice Note No. 8 requires counsel who intend to read in portions of the discovery transcript to give four (4) days notice to the opposing side and to identify the passage which that party intends to read in at the trial.[22] The notice requirement also applies to the adverse party. It must provide two days notice before the hearing of the passages upon which it intends to rely upon as qualifying or explaining the passages cited by the opposing party.

F. THE STATUS HEARING

The Tax Court directs the traffic and helps to direct the parties in their journey to the Court. The Status Hearing is one of the Tax Court's most effective case management tools. The Court will issue a Notice of Hearing where an appeal has not been set down for hearing or terminated within 6 months after the Reply filing date. Paragraph 125(5)(a) requires the appellant to show cause why the appeal should not be dismissed for delay. If a Reply has not

19 *Ibid.*, ss. 107, 108, 110 and 172.4. If an examination for discovery really breaks down and becomes abusive, the person being examined or a party present or represented at the examination may adjourn the examination and seek the court's direction and assistance. In this context, the court has many powers including the ability to find a person guilty of contempt of court.

20 This does not extend to third party examinations.

21 *Rules*, s. 100.

22 Tax Court of Canada Practice Note Number 8, amended July 19, 2001.

been filed, paragraph 125(5)(b) permits the Court to allow the appeal or direct that the appeal be heard on the basis that the facts alleged in the Notice of Appeal are presumed to be true. This presumption is rebuttable.

The Status Hearing procedure serves as an accelerant to the litigation process. The procedure allows the court to establish realistic and reasonable deadlines for completing the filing of Lists of Documents, discoveries, undertakings and the setting of dates for trial. The court can further manage an appeal by ordering a pre-hearing conference where an appeal has been set down for a hearing.[23]

G. THE PRE-HEARING CONFERENCE

A pre-trial conference can be requested by the parties or directed by the Court.[24] In every appeal that is expected to take more than two (2) days, a judge will determine whether a pre-hearing conference is necessary.[25] If a pre-hearing conference is scheduled another judge, who will not be the trial judge will be assigned.

Counsel are expected to be well-prepared. The parties should be prepared to present to the judge a brief that explains the theory of the party's case. The pre-hearing judge can play a very persuasive role, even though he or she cannot hear the appeal. To encourage frank and open discussion, statements made at the pre-hearing are confidential.[26]

While the judge cannot fetter the trial judge's discretion, he or she can give directions considered advisable or necessary for the conduct of the trial, including a memorandum signed by counsel setting out the results of the conference.[27]

Pre-hearing meetings encourage agreement on such things as an Agreed Statement of Facts, a Joint Book of Documents, alleviating the requirement of formal proof of the documents and, in appropriate cases, settlement of some or all of the issues. Often the journey is abandoned at this stage.

---

23 *Rules*, s. 126.

24 For an interesting discussion the uses of a pre-hearing conference see: J.E. Swystyn, "Pre-trial Conference Can Help Simply Issues and Expedite Settlement" (1993) 2:1 Tax Litigation 63.

25 Tax Court of Canada, Practice Note Number 11, November 30, 1998.

26 *Rules*, s. 128.

27 *Ibid.*, subs. 127(1).

H. REQUEST TO ADMIT

Section 130 of the *Rules*, which deals with a Request to Admit Fact or Documents is very useful. By utilizing the Rule, either party can conveniently prove a fact or document without the necessity of calling evidence or impose cost sanctions on the recalcitrant opponent.[28] When one party serves a Request to Admit, the opposing party must either admit the fact or document or expose himself or herself to a cost sanction. If no response is given to the Request to Admit, then for the purposes of the appeal that party is deemed to have admitted the truth of the facts or authenticity of the documents.[29]

I. THE HEARING

1) Just Before the Trial Starts

The taxpayer is in the best position to explain the facts supporting his or her filing position or his or her position on appeal. Accordingly, the taxpayer bears the onus of disproving the facts and assumptions upon which the assessment is founded.[30] The appellant will therefore adduce evidence first at trial, with limited exceptions.

Subsection 135(2) of the *Rules* provides that unless the judge directs otherwise, the appellant presents evidence first, then the respondent, and the appellant, if necessary, may call rebuttal evidence. The respondent will call its case first in appeals where the sole issue concerns the imposition of civil penalties or the reopening of statute-barred years.[31]

The presentation of argument follows the same order as the presentation of evidence.[32] Where the appellant is self-represented in Informal Procedure appeals, the court will often ask the respondent to argue first. The rationale for this approach is simple: it gives the unrepresented non-lawyer a better understanding of the Crown's case.

---

28 Generally, the admissions obtained are in respect to non-controversial facts or documents.

29 In accordance with s. 131, the opposing party must respond to the Request to Admit within fifteen (15) days by serving on the opposing side a response to the Request to Admit. This response can range from the admission of the fact or document to a denial of the truth of a fact or the authenticity of a document or a refusal to admit the truth of a fact or the authenticity of a document along with the reasons for refusal.

30 See *Anderson Logging Company v. The King*, [1917–1927] C.T.C. (S.C.C.), aff'd [1926] A.C. 140 (P.C.); *Johnston v. M.N.R.*, [1948] C.T.C. 195 (S.C.C.).

31 Subsection 163(2) of the *Income Tax Act*; subsection 152(4) of the *Income Tax Act*.

32 *Rules*, subs. 135(3).

In any General Procedure appeal, counsel can make an opening statement. Subsection 135(1) of the *Rules* states that a party can open his or her case by making a short statement giving a concise outline of the facts that the party proposes to prove and of the applicable law. Appellant's counsel should make an opening statement in cases involving complicated issues of fact or law. The advantage is the Appellant's since he or she has the first opportunity to characterize the facts and issues.

Respondent's counsel does not, as a general rule, make opening statements. On some occasions judges will invite the respondent's counsel to reply or to add to the appellant's opening remarks.

Before the trial commences, either party can seek to have witnesses excluded from the courtroom.[33] The request for an order excluding witnesses is almost invariably granted. However, the Order will not extend to the appellant or its nominee, expert witnesses and/or a representative of the CRA, because the parties are entitled to have a knowledgeable person advise them during the course of the trial.

Attendance of witnesses may be compelled pursuant to subpoenas issued under subsection 141(1) of the *Rules*. The subpoena may require the person to produce at the hearing the documents in the person's possession, control or power relating to the matters in question in the appeal. The subpoena must be served on the witness personally and at the same time, the witness fees and expenses must be paid. In the event that the witness who is properly served with a subpoena fails to attend, the judge has the power to issue a warrant for arrest of the witness. The witness will then be arrested and brought before the court to show cause why he should not be held in contempt.

2) Evidence at Trial

Unless the court orders otherwise, witnesses shall be examined orally in court and the examination may consist of direct-examination, cross-examination and re-examination.[34] Tax Court judges also have the power, indeed the responsibility, to exercise reasonable control over the mode of questioning so as to protect the witness from undue harassment or embarrassment. A judge will disallow a question that is vexatious or irrelevant.

While the focus of this chapter is on procedural rules, the balance of the chapter is directed to rules connected with advocacy.

---

33 *Ibid.*, subs. 133(1).

34 *Ibid.*, subs. 144(1).

3) Direct-Examination

Direct-examinations call on the lawyer to make basic facts understandable to a judge who is unfamiliar with them. Direct-examinations are considered by many advocates to be the hardest exercise to properly conduct.[35] Why? Because the advocate must paint a clear focused picture of his or her client's version of the facts while at the same time deal with objections and other interruptions that may detract from the storytelling process.

Planning is key to an effective direct-examination. What do you want from a witness? Why call the witness at all? What significant evidence does the witness have to offer? How does the witness' evidence relate to the theory of the case?

- Start an examination on a strong point and end with a bang.
- Ask short questions. The judge is not there to listen to counsel but to hear the evidence of the witness.
- Ask one question at a time.
- Keep the examination simple. Counsel should not bury his or her head in his or her trial notes but rather should display an interest in the witness' answers.
- Use headlines or headings such as: "now I am going to discuss your employment income for the 1995 taxation year." This helps to create an organized structure and flow to the examination.
- Try to be precise in the use of language and avoid the superfluous such as: "if it pleases the court, or please tell the court."
- Vary rhythm, pace, tone and volume of voice to keep the judge actively listening to what is being said by the witness.
- Deal with potentially adverse evidence and attempt to have the witness explain it away.
- Use the opportunity to cast the adverse evidence in the most favourable light and minimize the sting of cross-examination on this evidence.

---

35 For further reading on the subject of direct-examinations (as well as other trial techniques), see the following publications: S. Lubet, *Modern Trial Advocacy: Canadian Edition*, S. Block & C. Tape, eds. (Notre Dame: National Institute for Trial Advocacy, 1995); J. Sopinka et al., *The Trial of an Action* (Toronto: Butterworths, 1998); R.B. White, *The Art of Trial* (Aurora: Canada Law Book, 1993); G. Adair, *On Trial: Advocacy Skills, Law and Practice* (Markham: Butterworths, 2004); Bryan Finlay, Q.C., "Examination in Chief of the Lay Witness" in OBA Institute 1994, *Civil Litigation: Winning With Witnesses, Practical Tips, Tactics and Techniques* (January 27 to 29, 1994); J. Olah, *The Art and Science of Advocacy* (Toronto: Carswell, 1990-looseleaf); T.A. Mauet, *Fundamentals of Trial Techniques* (Toronto: Little, Brown & Co., 1995); W.B. Williston and R.J. Rolls, *The Conduct of a Action* (Toronto: Butterworths, 1982).

- Demonstrate to the judge that counsel is straightforward about the evidentiary strengths and weaknesses of your client's appeal.

4) Cross-Examination

In many tax appeals, the respondent does not call a case. So, counsel for the appellant may not even get the opportunity to cross-examine.[36] On those occasions where the Respondent calls evidence, it is often the auditor who raised the assessment or reassessment in dispute who will testify.

Counsel will wish to benefit from the discovery in conducting a cross-examination of a CRA officer. The useful admission of fact obtained on discovery cannot be evaded at trial. The witness must either admit the facts previously admitted or expose him/herself to a contradiction on inconsistent statement. In short, the prudent counsel will receive no less than he or she received on discovery. The rules demand that counsel who intends to impeach the credibility of the witness give the witness the opportunity to explain the apparent contradiction. Subsection 100(2) of the *Rules* states that contradictory answers cannot read in as evidence unless counsel first cross-examined the witness. This rule is the codification of the common law rule established in *Browne v. Dunn*.[37] It is an issue of fair play and fair dealing with witnesses.[38]

Most advocates would agree that there are several objectives of a cross-examination: to bolster one's own case, to destroy one's opponent's case and to impeach the credibility of the witness.[39] The cross-examiner first must decide if it is even necessary or worthwhile to cross-examine a wit-

---

36 However, s. 146 permits the taxpayer to compel attendance of employees of the CRA through a notice to counsel. As an employee of the adverse party, he or she may be called as part of the taxpayer's case but cross-examined at large. Also, the Court can draw an adverse inference if an important witness is not called to give evidence. Consequently, this is a real issue that counsel will be forced to wrestle with from time to time.

37 *Browne v. Dunn* (1893), 6 R. 67 (H.L.).

38 *Ibid.*, at pp 70–71.

39 For further reading on the subject of cross-examination see: R. E. Salhany, Q.C., *Cross-Examination: The Art of the Advocate*, 2d ed. (Toronto: Butterworths, 1999); J. Porter, *Cross-Examination Techniques* (Toronto: Law Society of Upper Canada, 1989); J. N. Iannuzzi, *Cross-Examination: The Mosaic Art* (Toronto: Prentice Hall, 1982); B. Finlay & T.A. Cromwell, *Witness Preparation Manual* (Toronto: Canada Law book, 1991); R.F. Reid & R.E. Holland, *Advocacy: Views from the Bench* (Aurora: Canada Law Book, 1984); W.B. Williston & R.J. Rolls, *The Conduct of an Action* (Toronto: Butterworths, 1982)); A.W. Bryant "The Adversary's Witness: Cross-Examination and Proof of Prior Inconsistent Statements" (1984) 62 Can. Bar Rev. 43; and M.A. Dombroff, *Direct and Cross-Examination* (New York: John Wiley & Sons, 1985).

ness. Restraint should be exercised and the temptation to cross-examine resisted if the witness has not harmed an essential part of one's own case or not significantly advanced the appellant's case. The reality is that every advocate thinks that he or she can get "something useful" from a witness, but in truth, this is not always the case.

An effective cross-examination begins with in-depth preparation and mastery of a number of fundamental principles:

- Be brief.
- Keep questions short.
- The language should be simple and clear.
- At all times the cross-examiner should be in control of the witness.
- A key to maintaining control is to use leading questions.
- Try to avoid asking a witness a question that you do not already know the answer to.
- Do not ask a question that will cause you to lose control over the witness.
- Never argue with a witness. You will lose momentum and possibly control of your cross-examination not to mention that you could embarrass yourself.

Throughout the cross-examination, the key is to control the witness and that is achieved by the way in which you pose your questions:

- Resist the temptation to repeat testimony by the witness in examination-in-chief.
- Refrain from self-congratulatory, over excitement-questioning — in other words, once you have obtained a "good answer," do not ask the same question again — hoping to obtain an even "better" answer — but only getting a worse answer than before.
- Counsel must know when to end the cross-examination.
- Avoid the urge to ask one question too many.
- Always question a witness on a subject that will demonstrate the witness' bias. By so doing, you will provide the presiding judge with a basis for rejecting the witness' evidence.
- Try to keep a witness off-balance. What this means is that if a witness is uneasy on the stand, he or she will likely be unable to arrest control of the examination from the examiner. Furthermore, by keeping the witness off-balance, the questioner may be able to elicit information from the witness that he or she otherwise might not be prepared to give the questioner but for this state of uneasiness.

Each witness is different. An effective cross-examiner understands psychology and uses this understanding to direct the manner of his or her cross-examination. For example, if the cross-examiner is satisfied the witness is truthful, questions are asked to evoke the relevant information. On the other hand, if the witness is lying, an aggressive and pointed cross-examination may well be appropriate to highlight the dishonesty. Most witnesses intend to tell the truth but are coloured by their self-interest or are forgetful, nervous or otherwise prevented from giving accurate evidence. The approach to these witnesses must be flexible depending on the reason for the inaccurate evidence.

5) Re-Examination

Re-examination is limited to matters that were dealt with in cross-examination and that could not have been reasonably anticipated in your direct-examination of the witness. It can, however, serve a number of useful purposes including obtaining an explanation from a witness on some contentious point or points raised in cross-examination; correcting misstatements or errors; and/or qualifying adverse facts drawn out during cross-examination. While counsel cannot split his or her own case, the courts have ruled that counsel can bring out relevant matters in re-examination or a matter that counsel failed to elicit in cross-examination.[40]

The decision to re-examine is made very quickly. Remember that counsel has no obligation to re-examine even though Tax Court justices will often ask — out of polite habit, I suspect — if counsel would like to re-examine the witness. Ultimately, the decision to re-examine, calls for counsel to weigh the pros and cons of proceeding. It is possible that if counsel fail to re-examine after a particularly damaging or revealing cross-examination, he or she may lose the chance to minimize the damage from the cross-examination. However, if counsel proceeds with a re-examination and conducts a poor one, he or she could invite a recross-examination or simply boost the effectiveness and weight of the opponent's cross-examination. Generally speaking, if the cross-examination has not damaged your case or raised an issue that must be addressed, either limit the re-examination or better yet, refrain from conducting one at all.

---

40 *R. v. Kozody*, (1957) 117 C.C.C. 315 (Ont. C.A.); *R. v. Wood* (1986), 28 C.C.C. (3d) 65 at 82 (Ont. C.A.); *Robillard v. R.*, [1978] 2 S.C.R. 728 at 732 [Que.].

6) Recross-Examination

Subsection 144(1) of the *Rules* is silent on the subject of recross-examination. However, in some cases, where re-examination elicits new matters, the Court, as a consequence of its discretionary powers, will permit counsel to recross-examine. In keeping with its more informal approach to the conduct of a trial, this is commonly permitted by the Court.

7) Dealing with Documents

Subsection 143(1) of the *Rules* permits the Court before or at the hearing to take evidence of a particular fact in a manner and subject to such conditions as the Court specifies and in particular that evidence shall be given: (i) by affidavit; (ii) by statement made under oath or affirmation; (iii) by the production of documents or of entries in books or copies; or (iv) where a fact is of common knowledge, either generally or in a particular place, by the production of a newspaper which contains the statement of fact.

There are a number of pre-trial procedures that allow counsel to deal with the admissibility of documents.[41] For example, at the examination for discovery, a party can be questioned as to the authenticity of a document and asked other questions necessary to establish the foundation for the admission of the document at trial. Another approach is to resort to the use of the Request to Admit.[42] Still further at the pre-hearing conference, the presiding judge can make an advance ruling on the admissibility of evidence.[43] Finally, both parties may agree on a joint book of documents. In the alternative, counsel may agree on submitting separate books of documents. They may also agree on what documents that will cause the issue of admissibility to be raised at trial.

As a practical matter in court, counsel establish the foundation for the admission of the document by showing the document to the witness and having him or her identify it. Of course, the document must be relevant, and once it is authenticated and identified, the foundation for the admission of the document is complete. It can then be offered into evidence by counsel. Typically, counsel will ask the judge to mark the document "A-1" or "R-1 (i.e. "Appellant's Exhibit 1" or "Respondent's Exhibit 1"). Subject to

---

41 On Documentary Evidence, see: J.D. Ewart, *Documentary Evidence in Canada* (Toronto: Carswell, 1984); also G.S. Lester, "The Rules of Evidence Governing Cross-Examination Based on Documents: A Practical Guide" (Sept. 1996) 18:3, Advocates' Quarterly, 261.

42 *Rules*, s 130.

43 *Ibid.*, subs. 12(1)(c).

the rules of law, once the exhibit has been admitted into evidence, it can be used by any witness.

Where opposing counsel objects to the introduction of the document as an exhibit, you should respond by clearly stating why the document has been tendered as evidence to the court. Generally, Tax Court Justices do not like to disallow documents into evidence. Tax Court judges often prefer to allow the document into evidence and then determine what weight, if any, should be given to this evidence.

A few final words about documents. There are certain documents that are subject to special rules that are detailed in the *Canada Evidence Act*.[44] The *Income Tax Act* has certain provisions that deal with the proof of documents.[45]

8) Expert Witnesses

It seems that there are more experts testifying in tax appeals than ever before. The use of an expert witness in a tax appeal is a subject all unto itself.[46] If counsel has decided to call upon an expert to testify at trial, you must be concerned with section 7 of the *Informal Procedure Rules*[47] or section 145 of the Rules.

In accordance with section 7 of the *Informal Procedure Rules*, and expert report must be filed and served 10 days before the hearing. If counsel fails to abide by this rule, then the expert can only testify with leave of the judge.[48] In General Procedure appeals, subsection 145(2) of the Rules requires that the expert set out a full statement of the proposed evidence in

---

44 See: ss. 24, 25, 26, 28, 29 and 30 *Canada Evidence Act*, R.S.C. 1985 c. C-5, as amended.

45 Section 244 and s. 231.5(1) *Income Tax Act*, R.S.C. 1985, c. 1 (5th Supp.), as amended.

46 See, for example: in this book, Alan M. Schwartz and Edward T. Yanoshita's chapter entitled "The Use of Expert Witnesses in Tax Litigation"; also M.G. Quigley, "Dealing with Expert Evidence in Tax Cases" (1993) 41:6 Canadian Tax Journal, 1071; I.A. Blue, "Cross-Examining the Expert" (1986–1987) 7 Advocates' Quarterly 13; J.A. Epp, "Avoiding Rookie Mistakes When Using Experts in Canadian Courts" (1982) 14 Advocates Quarterly 185; M.D. Smitiuch "Expert Evidence: Setting the Stage for Expert Testimony at Trial" (2000) Advocates' Quarterly 397; M.A. Dombroff, *Expert Witness in Civil Trials* (Rochester, N.Y.: The Lawyers Co-op, 1984); Robert L Habush, *Art of Advocacy: Cross-Examination of Non-Medical Experts* (New York; Matthew Bender, 1985); R.B. White, *Art of Using Expert Evidence* (Toronto: Canada Law Book, 1997)); K.M. Matthews, *The Expert: A Practitioners Guide* (Toronto: Carswell, 1995) (Looseleaf); M. Freiman & M. Berenblut, *The Litigator's Guide to Expert Witnesses* (Aurora: Canada Law Book 1997); A.W. Mewett, *Witnesses* (Toronto: Carswell, 1991) (looseleaf); and G.D. Cudmore, *Civil Evidence Handbook* (Toronto: Carswell, 1997) (looseleaf).

47 See above note 3.

48 *Informal Procedure Rules*, s. 7, above note 3.

chief in an affidavit, of which the original must be filed with the Court; a copy of this affidavit must be served on all other parties not less than 30 days before the commencement of the hearing.

If counsel decide to file an expert rebuttal report, subsection 145(3) requires this report to be filed and served on all other parties not less than 15 days before the commencement of the hearing.

Before leaving the subject of expert witness' at trial, there are some basic points of advocacy particular to the expert witness that I would like to share with you. In direct-examination, counsel must establish that the witness is an expert in the area in which the opinion is sought in order for the opinion to be admissible.[49] The Court must first accept the witness' qualifications as an expert before the witness can give opinion evidence. This procedure is straightforward. Counsel calls the witness to the stand and the witness is sworn. Counsel then introduces the witness' qualifications usually by tendering the curriculum vitae. The witness' lawyer will then, by leading questions, take the witness through the résumé identifying the qualifications. Once all of the qualifications are identified and detailed, the lawyer will then tender to the Court the witness as an expert witness, qualified to give opinion evidence in a specified area. The opposing counsel can at this point cross-examine the expert on his or her qualifications prior to the Court's ruling on the witness' expertise. In many cases, the opposing side does not cross-examine; this is ultimately a case-by-case tactical and practical decision. Once the court accepts the witness as an expert, then counsel can proceed with the direct-examination.

The direct-examination of an expert witness requires much more preparation than most lay witnesses. Counsel's objective should be to persuade the trier-of-fact that the expert is eminently qualified to give expert evidence, has employed an appropriate methodology, has approached his assignment in an objective fashion and has given his testimony in a forthrightly manner.

Before counsel can proceed with the cross-examination of the expert witness, counsel simply must prepare by taking all the following steps: start with obtaining an understanding of the area of expertise involved in the appeal; learn all that you can about the expert including reputation, writings and credentials; find out as much as possible about the expert's prior court experience as an expert; and if you have retained your own expert, get that person to help you prepare your questions for cross-examination. All of these measures should help counsel build a solid foundation for an effective cross-examination of the expert witness.

---

49 *R. v. Mohan*, [1994] 2 S.C.R. 9; *R. v. Marquard*, [1993] 4 S.C.R. 223.

9) Argument

After all the evidence has been adduced, all that remains is argument. Subsection 135(3) of the *Rules* stipulates that the parties shall be heard in argument in the order in which they adduced their evidence.

As a practical matter, if you are relying upon several cases you should have them bound, tabbed and indexed. In addition, if it is a complex case, it is useful to provide the court with a written outline of the argument. Even in shorter trials, I suggest that counsel prepare a point or bullet form outline. If counsel prepares a written argument, avoid merely reading from it. The last thing a lawyer should do at this stage of the trial is bore the judge. Finally, sometimes judges of the Tax Court engage counsel in argument. This can provide a final opportunity for he or she to convince the court of the correctness of the client's position.

J. JUDGMENT

In Informal Procedure appeals, the court will render judgment within 90 days of the hearing unless there are exceptional circumstances.[50] The Court is required to give reasons for judgment but they do not need to be in writing.

In General Procedure appeals, subsection 63(1) of the Rules states that where a reply has not been filed within 60 days, the appellant may apply on a motion for judgment.[51] Section 64 states that the respondent can move to have an appeal dismissed for delay where the appellant failed to prosecute the appeal with due dispatch.[52] Finally, subsection 167(2) states that a judgment shall be dated the day it is signed and that is the date pronouncement of the judgment.[53]

K. COSTS

In Informal Procedure appeals pursuant to section 18.26 of the *Tax Court of Canada Act*, if the appellant is more than 50 per cent successful, then the Court may award costs to the appellant.[54] The respondent cannot receive

50 Section 18.22, *Tax Court of Canada Act.*
51 *Rules*, subs. 63(1).
52 *Ibid.*, s. 64.
53 *Ibid.*, s. 167.
54 Section 18.26, *Tax Court of Canada Act.*

costs. In General Procedure appeals, section 147 of the *Rules* leaves costs in the court's discretion.[55]

L. CONCLUSION

We all strive to be better at what we do. As lawyers specializing in the area of tax litigation, the starting point should be the knowledge of the rules and law. It has been my intention and hope that my tour of the *Rules* will help you achieve the goal of good practices before the Court. Have a good journey!

55 *Rules*, s. 147.

Chapter Nine

Witnesses: Preparing For Court And the Court Experience

L. Ross Oake

A. INTRODUCTION

My purpose in writing this chapter is to share with the reader information that will assist in preparing witnesses. It is based mainly on hundreds of hours of personal experience on the witness stand, thousands of hours of interviewing and preparing witnesses with and without counsel and observing witnesses on the stand, as well as interviews with judges, former judges and counsel. While this chapter deals with the lay witness, much of what is contained herein can also apply to the expert witness as well.

Whether expert or lay, it is the *credible* witness that all counsel strive to present to the court. Credibility is a very important element in weighing the testimony of any witness. His Honour, Brian D. Williston, a Provincial Court Judge from the Province of Nova Scotia, has stated that:

> The trier of fact in a criminal case may believe all the evidence, a part of the evidence, or none of the evidence given by a witness. Some of the factors that are considered in weighing the evidence and judging credibility are the following:
>
> 1. The interest the witness has in the outcome of the case; whether he is biased and in such circumstances is giving a prejudiced account.

2. Whether the witness has been discussing the case with others and has gradually built up an account of what he believes is true but is more the result of rationalizing what took place, rather than what the witness personally observed.
3. The attitude of the witness when testifying: whether he answers frankly or gives the impression that he is hesitant and attempting to conceal information.
4. Whether there are any discrepancies between what the witness states in court and what he may have said at an earlier time.
5. Whether there are any discrepancies between what the witness stated during direct examination and what that same witness said during cross-examination.
6. Whether the testimony given by the witness is confirmed or contradicted by the testimony of other witnesses or evidence.[1]

I have worked with counsel who have neither taken the time nor seen the need to meet with and prepare witnesses before appearing in court. Sadly, in some of those cases, the evidence was presented in a way that was detrimental to their case. This was mainly due to the fact that the witness was nervous, lacked a rapport with counsel or did not clearly understand his/her role. Coupled with these facts, it was also clear that counsel neither understood the witness nor what the witness had to offer, making this situation a recipe for disaster.

Conversely, I have had the pleasure of working with counsel who have taken the time to meet and prepare witnesses, and they tend to have a high success rate at trial.

Except for the time involved, there is absolutely no downside to meeting, interviewing and preparing a witness. There are lots of opportunities for failure by not doing so. In my opinion, it is not just an option — it is a must — that is, to meet and prepare the witness. It is also a wise investment of time.

B. ROLE OF COUNSEL — PREPARING THE WITNESS

Most experienced counsel and judges will tell you that it is often the simple things that can throw off your most meticulously prepared case. Mr.

1 B.D. Williston, "Basic principles of Evidence," in J.E. Pink & D.C. Perrier, eds., *From Crime to Punishment, An Introduction to the Criminal Law System*, 5th ed. (Toronto: Carswell, 2003) 215 at 229–230.

Justice Leonard T. Montgomery stated in an interview that in his nearly thirty years experience on the bench . . .

> It is the simple things of familiarity and lack of preparation that throws off witnesses. Lawyers take it for granted that witnesses will not react to the strangeness of the experience. The Court Room is a very strange environment to most and the whole concept of being the centre of attention can be very intimidating.[2]

Preparing your case for presentation in court can be tricky business. It is extremely important to know how the evidence of each witness fits with the other evidence being presented. The order of witnesses is also important to present the evidence in a logical manner. This needs to be planned in advance with built-in flexibility depending on availability and performance.

> To place a witness's story in context and to assess the probabilities, counsel must know as much of the factual context of the case as possible, including all the other evidence likely to be adduced. Witness preparation conducted without this knowledge is conducted in a vacuum for the witness and the lawyer.[3]

It is not always possible to call each witness in the exact order you have planned, especially with out of town witnesses and court scheduling. The performance of one witness may make it prudent to rearrange the order of appearances.

Some observers have written that counsel's role in witness preparation is that of the director preparing the cast for a performance. While I agree that counsel should know how all the evidence fits together and the order in which it is best presented, the big difference is that the performer's role is scripted and that should never be the case in preparing a witness. The evidence must be in the words of the witness, not those of counsel.

Coaching witnesses how to behave and how to answer questions is one thing, but coaching them as to what to say can, at the very least, be very dangerous. It is worth repeating that it is important that the words be those of the witness.

> The lay witness should be informed that it is the substance of his testimony rather than the exact language which is important, unless (as in a case of slander) the exact slanderous language is vital. He should understand

---

2 Interview, September 2003.

3 B. Finlay & T.A. Cromwell, *Witness Preparation Manual*, 2d ed., Aurora, Ontario: (Canada Law Book Inc., 1999) at 6.

> the aim of the examiner, the purport of the question and the nature of the answer which each of the questions seeks to elicit. He will be not only a more intelligent and cooperative witness but also a more effective one if he uses his own language and knows what he is talking about.[4]

It can be very rewarding when opposing counsel asks witnesses that you have prepared what advice you gave them during your pre-trial meeting and they reply "to stick to the facts and tell the truth."

Effective witness preparation will greatly reduce the stress levels of the witness and counsel. Building rapport is one of the most important steps in interviewing and it certainly extends to the preparation and examination of witnesses. If you show enough interest to spend time helping the witnesses feel at ease by getting to know them and their evidence a little better, you will be rewarded with a much better quality of witness. It is human nature to try to help people you like, trust and respect. If you have evoked even one of those emotions in a witness, you will be ahead of the game.

Building rapport is such an important part of successfully gaining the cooperation of witnesses (yet overlooked by most) that I have devoted a section of this chapter on building rapport and the reasons for it.

Take the time to familiarize the witness with the process and the setting in which they will be testifying. Most litigators find themselves in court on a daily basis and are very comfortable there. Some forget that for many people, it is a first time experience and a scary one. If you do not have the time, have someone else take him or her to the court to see the set up and understand the function of the various participants.

I recall a witness who had not used a microphone before being on the witness stand in a large courtroom that was equipped with activated microphones and speakers. No one thought of the need to tell him that he would be using a microphone. The witness became so preoccupied with the sound of his voice on the speakers that he was not paying attention to what he was saying, but rather the sound of it. To add to everyone's stress level, he continuously bumped into the microphone with his head and hands, each time apologizing to the microphone.

In your preparation meeting, ask the types and style of questions you will ask in court. This will familiarize the witness with the types of questions to expect and the kind of answers that is expected of him or her. Examination-in-chief will quite often preclude counsel from asking leading

---

4 H.S. Bodin, *Civil Litigation and Trial Techniques* (New York: Practising Law Institute, 1976 ed.) at 185 ff.

questions, as a result it is asked in a manner that may be confusing to the witness. Give them some examples of how you will ask your questions in chief and the reason for it. Often stating the obvious is lost on a witness. The witness will appreciate knowing the kinds of answers that will be most helpful to the court. Here is the opportunity to practice with the witness the order in which his or her evidence will be presented. Try not to change the order of the evidence if at all possible; some witnesses have very good memories but do not like surprises.

I recall assisting the Crown as instructing officer through an eleven-week judge and jury trial on a very complex fraud case in which I was the lead investigator. The Crown counsel, now the Honourable Mr. Justice David Doherty of the Ontario Court of Appeal, had been successful in having me exempted from the witness exclusion order, although I was a key witness for the Crown. We spent hundreds of hours preparing witnesses together prior to and during the trial. The night before my evidence we went through the areas we would cover during the next two or three days in great detail. We were ready. After asking me my position with the RCMP, he threw in the following question: "How old are you?" I couldn't remember! While it did afford some comic relief for the jury, it threw me off my evidence for a few seconds, because it was not what I was expecting. If this happens to an experienced witness, you can imagine the effect on one new to the experience.

The majority of people have an unrealistic fear of cross-examination. This is a result no doubt of the courtroom dramas played out on television and in movie theatres. I have been cross-examined by many of the top legal counsel in Canada and the United States, and I have always found it to be a lot less intimidating than I had expected. There is no secret. The key is to know your facts, listen carefully to every question, understand the question and tell the truth. The witness should be directed to let you do the battling with opposing counsel and that his or her job is to listen carefully, be respectful of opposing counsel, be fair and only answer what is asked. No matter how much a witness grows to dislike opposing counsel or the other party, it should be impressed upon him or her not to be argumentative and to answer the questions honestly and fairly. Drama and sarcastic remarks can undermine what otherwise would be valuable testimony.

The witness should understand the role of each of the participants, including the court reporter and the clerk. An understanding of the process and individual roles is important, because some witnesses think that counsel who called them is acting as their lawyer. Explain to the witness that you will do everything in your power to ensure that the evidence is presented by the rules, however, opposing counsel have a lot of leeway on cross-examination. It is important the witness knows that you have another opportunity to ask further questions in re-direct. It will give your witness some sense of comfort when opposing counsel has asked questions that require answers that puts his or her evidence in a different light than intended, if he or she knows you can ask further questions to rectify this.

Witnesses are often flustered when the judge questions them. They automatically think that they have not explained things well enough or that the judge does not believe them. It is more intimidating than questions from counsel. An explanation by counsel to the witness in advance that the judge has the right and may ask questions for the purpose of clarification and that he or she is to answer the question in the same manner as other questions, will assist to allay those fears.

While you may have been supplied with a statement or summary of the anticipated evidence of a witness, now is the time to find out if this is *all* the evidence this witness has to offer on the subject. In my experience, I have found that some investigators and counsel fail to gather all the relevant facts from a witness once they have acquired what they needed and/or wanted to hear. In fact, most witnesses will hold something back. This may be for any number of reasons, not the least of which is they did not have the proper rapport with the person interviewing them to tell all. I have experienced the effect of finding out during cross-examination that the witness has much more relevant evidence than the investigator and counsel bothered to canvass in pre-trial meetings.

Some witnesses are difficult to prepare because they are reluctant to volunteer anything. That is why building a rapport and spending the time will assist. Some witnesses are too verbose and take the opportunity to give their views on sundry irrelevant issues. It is important to explain to the witness that they are to answer only the questions asked of them and not to elaborate. If further clarification is needed, counsel will ask for it.

C. WITNESSES AND DOCUMENTS

This section does not deal with the legal issues of production of documents and the use of documents to refresh a witness' memory but instead the practical use of a document during the preparation stages and in court.

I have met and worked with very few counsel who like working with documents in a court case, especially numerous documents.

Most of the cases I have been involved in have involved numerous documents, generally introduced through witnesses. The pre-trial meeting is the opportunity to review any documents or other exhibits that you are relying on the witness to identify, to answer questions about or explain.

I have worked with counsel who have had to ask me during examination of the witness in court what it is we are asking the witness about a certain document and why. While some counsel can manage to be effective this way, it is rare.

Documents should be organized in a manner that introduces the evidence in an orderly fashion. If it is the witness' documents they will be most helpful in pre-trial in assisting you with this. During examination in court, the witness should be given the document before you start asking questions about it. Before you get to any contentious issues on a document, ask a few easy questions, such as: Do you recognize the document? What are the date, the addressee, the signatory and the file/reference? In addition to identifying the document for the record, it gives the witness an opportunity to become re-acquainted with the document and to get used to the feeling of answering questions in this setting.

As a cross-examination tactic, it may be feasible to ask questions about a document without showing the witness the document first. However, if the witness is well-prepared he or she may be more inclined to ask to see the document before answering such questions.

There is often a need to call witnesses for the express purpose of identifying documents. In this case, it is not so important to spend a lot of time with this witness. For example, in a stock market manipulation case, there may be reams of documents from brokerage houses that only need to be identified as records kept in the usual course of business and may only be needed to support analysis completed by your expert witness. However, be sure to find out if this witness has any knowledge of the relevant issues to your case or the other parties. Otherwise what you thought might be a few questions to introduce a few documents may turn into important ammunition for cross-examination.

D. WHAT YOU NEED TO KNOW ABOUT THE WITNESS

1) Previous Testimony

If your witness has testified before, know what the case was about and how this witness fared. If you are calling an expert witness, be sure to canvass if they have given evidence before as an expert on this topic. If so, read a copy of the transcript. I once experienced a witness who did not divulge, nor was he asked, that he had testified at another hearing where he had admitted lying under oath, but "only a little lie!" Unfortunately, this came out during cross-examination as opposing counsel had done his homework and was able to successfully argue that this witness was not credible, and that he just didn't *tell* lies, but *had categories* for them. The trial judge agreed and did not rely on his evidence to reach a verdict. During the preparation stage, it is imperative that you discuss any discrepancies in your witness' evidence and the reasons for it.

2) Alliances with the Accused or Opposing Parties

Be sure you canvass the relationship between the witness and the person or persons he/she will be offering testimony against. In one jury trial I was involved in, with eight accused, the Crown was introducing wire tap evidence by way of consent of one of the parties to the intercepted conversations. This co-accused, turned witness, gave his consent to the admissibility of the intercepted conversations while testifying in chief; withdrew this consent during effective cross- examination with respect to one of the accused; and, gave the consent back again during effective re-direct. He explained the reason for doing this is that he had a special relationship with the one accused and did not want to hurt him. Thankfully, the Crown was not relying on this witness' credibility but instead on the content of the intercepted conversations.

3) Articles or Quotes

Find out if they have written any articles or books on the topic or have been quoted in any publication. Be sure you are not taking a different position on the same/similar set of facts. It would be more than just embarrassing to have opposing counsel bring this out during cross-examination.

4) Oath or Affirmation

Find out now if this witness wishes to give evidence under oath or by affirmation. Dealing with this in advance and letting the court clerk know may avoid an embarrassing situation and save you and the witness considerable stress. The judge and the court clerk will appreciate your efforts in advance as well. Obviously, the impact of giving false testimony in any case should be discussed and understood by the witness.

5) How to Address the Court

Very few people know the various levels of court and the proper way to address the judge. Many judges understand this and will settle for anything respectable. However, everyone will be a lot happier and therefore give you a better result if the witness knows how to properly address the court.

E. ON BEING A WITNESS — THINGS YOU SHOULD SUGGEST TO YOUR WITNESS

As counsel know, testifying in court is a stressful experience. It is expected that your witness will be nervous when taking the witness stand. It is normal and shows that your witness cares about how he/she will perform. The following suggestions should help your witness reduce his/her stress level.

1) Know Your Facts

Whether you are an expert witness, investigator, eyewitness or otherwise, know your facts. Know what it is you are expected to tell the court and know it well.

2) Meet with Counsel

If you have been requested to meet with counsel before appearing in court, make the time to do so. If you have not been requested to meet with counsel you should make the request of counsel yourself. Meeting with the person who will be asking you questions in court and getting an understanding of their style of questioning and the subject matter will be most helpful to all parties.

3) Get Familiar with the Setting

If it is your first time in court, visit the court beforehand and understand what goes on and the roles played by the participants in the proceedings. On the day you testify, you will be the centre of attention as you enter the courtroom. Seeing the setting in advance will help to make you feel more comfortable.

4) Mentally and Physically Prepared

Be well rested, sober and appropriately dressed. Appearing in court otherwise will erode your credibility and add to your stress level. While it is not a fashion show, it is important to dress appropriately in suitable, simple business attire. Leave the gum and candy in your pocket/purse. A judge and/or jury will size you up in mere seconds, so it is important to make the right first impression. Remember "you don't get a second chance to make a first impression."

If you are tired or hung over or under the influence of alcohol or drugs, your task will be much greater. Listening is not easy. Witnesses are often careless listeners because they are distracted by what's going on in a strange environment. It is very important to listen to the question carefully and answer that question only. Do not try to anticipate where the questions are leading; this takes a lot of effort and experience. Just listen to the question and answer it honestly to the best of your ability.

If counsel raises an objection during your answer, stop talking. The judge will rule on the objection and will give you direction to answer or not answer the question. Do not insist on finishing your answer despite the objection, as that will erode your credibility.

5) Did You Discuss Your Evidence with Anyone?

I do not remember an occasion when I have not been asked this by opposing counsel. It is a trick question! It is generally asked in a way that attempts to make you think that there is something wrong with discussing your evidence with someone. Of course there is *nothing wrong* with discussing your evidence with counsel in preparation for testifying. Indeed, it is prudent to do so.

6) Don't Guess

Do not be embarrassed to admit that you do not know something, if that is the truth. You are not expected to know everything. It is perfectly okay to say "I don't know" if in fact that is the truth. If you do not understand the question, say so. But do not use it as a stall if you do understand. This only serves to irritate the judge and the jury and/or weakens your credibility.

7) Who is my lawyer?

You are a witness for the court. The lawyer who called you is not there to represent you. He or she should make every effort to ensure your evidence is presented in the proper manner.

8) Don't be Argumentative

Answer the questions in a thoughtful, concise and fair manner. Do not spar with counsel; leave the battling to the lawyers. No matter how much you like or dislike the other party or opposing counsel, you will be much more credible if you follow this advice. It is the job of opposing counsel to try to discredit your evidence, accept this and stick to the facts and the truth. Do not try to "stick it to them"; you will only diminish the weight/impact of your evidence.

9) The Multiple Part Question

Lawyers like to ask questions that are compound and then attempt to get you to answer yes or no. Do not be forced into a yes or no answer, if it requires further explanation, provide it. For example, the question may be as follows: Isn't it true that you were present when Mr. Smith attended at the Toronto Dominion bank machine at 24 Main Street on May 24, 2002 and used Mr. Brown's debit card to withdraw $300.00 in cash? Assuming you were present on one occasion when Mr. Smith took money from a bank machine, be sure you know the answers to the several questions embedded here, such as; Do you remember the name of the bank? Do you know the address of the bank? Do you remember the exact date? Do you know it was Mr. Brown's debit card? Could it have been a credit card? Do you know how much cash he took out?

If a compound question requires different answers and you can remember the various parts of the question then give your answer that way. If you cannot remember all the parts of the complete question, ask to have it repeated.

10) Speak Normally!

I have seen experienced police officers who when not on the witness stand, appear to be able to speak in plain language; however, when they take the stand, they sound like robots. Here is an example: The simple facts are that the police officer was walking along the sidewalk on Bloor Street, westbound around 5:30 p.m. on July 20, 2003 when he saw two men running out of the variety store wearing masks and carrying hand guns. When the officer was asked by counsel to explain what he saw on the witness stand, he stated: "At approximately 1730 hundred hours on the 20th day of July, 2003 I was proceeding on foot, westward along the side walk on Bloor Street. I observed two male persons proceeding by foot in an accelerated manner from the variety store. Their faces were incomprehensible because of a woolen material over them. They were brandishing what looked like a weapon . . . ." Use plain language that everyone can understand. If there is specific terminology you must use to explain technical issues, explain them in plain language as well.

F. BUILDING RAPPORT

Rapport is defined as harmony, conformity, accord, having a level of comfort and trust, and being on the same wavelength. Rapport is established by successful communication on a number of different levels.

1) Communication

Communication is the key to building rapport. Communication has been defined as: "you have only communicated when someone attaches some significance to what you have said or done." The meaning of the communication is reflected in the response that you get. You have mis-communicated when someone attaches the wrong significance to what you have said or done. I am sure we can all think of times when someone has not understood what we meant by a statement or question or gesture.

Much has been written on the various means by which we communicate and what that supposedly means. A little knowledge in this area can be dangerous. In this section, I will only deal with a few of the basics and what you can learn from it and how you can apply it to being a better communicator and therefore better at building rapport.

2) Non-verbal Communication

Some state that more than fifty percent of what we communicate is non-verbal. Therefore, if we are not paying attention to the non-verbal, we are missing more than half of what is being "said."

Sigmund Freud once wrote: "He that has eyes to see and ears to hear may convince himself that no mortal can keep a secret. If his lips are silent, he chatters with his fingertips; betrayal oozes out of him at every pore."

One of the attributes of a good interviewer is being an excellent listener. An excellent listener is perceptive to the subject's behaviour at all levels of communication.

Non-verbal communication is often more reliable than verbal because it is spontaneous. In most cases we have no control over what happens to our body physiologically when we tell a lie or avoid telling the truth. I believe the theory that we are born with the basic value that telling the truth is the morally right thing to do. However, we have all learned that lying successfully may assist in avoiding punishment. We learn that at a very early stage in our childhood.

This conflict between the two creates anxiety and tension. This anxiety and tension causes us to physically react involuntarily. Some times it is hard to read those reactions, sometimes impossible. However, the better the rapport you have, the better you will be able to read the signs. Drawing conclusions from those signs can be dangerous; rather, they should be a guide to let you know that there is some degree of discomfort with the topic/question. It may mean that the person does not feel comfortable with the topic in the forum. It may mean they don't want to talk about it. It may mean you haven't asked the right question. It may mean you need to probe this area a little more. Be careful, it may mean that in their culture it is impolite to look a person in the eye.

The best way is to observe the person in normal circumstances, notice how the person reacts to questions that are non-threatening, such as, "Which way do you come in to the office each day?" or "How old are you?"

If you take the time to build rapport with your witness, especially if it is a reluctant one, by understanding how they communicate at all levels you may have a witness who may even want to help you.

3) Establishing Rapport with a Witness

One of the most successful and impressive lawyers I experienced in cross-examination was Mr. Justice David Humphrey when he was acting as defense counsel. He took the time to build rapport with the witness and approached the witness with respect, empathy and with a firm understanding of the facts. Most witnesses liked him as a result of this and wanted to help him if possible. He was very good at reading the witness' body language and picking up on how that witness was communicating. His success rate of having a Crown witness try and help his client, the accused, was well-known.

Building rapport will assist in extracting information that is more likely than not to be the truth from a witness, or at least better enable you to be able to detect deception.

Here are some rapport building suggestions that work.

1. Be genuine and act as the person you are as opposed to stereotyping yourself and the person you are interviewing in a role. While you may be in a perceived position of power, remember the best use of power is not having used it.

2. Be a good listener at all levels and show an interest in what the person is saying. One of the best ways to destroy rapport is to appear not to be listening to the person who is talking to you. Just think about what happens if you are telling a story and someone walks into the room and attracts your audience's attention. Unless you are overly disciplined and have an unusual focus, you will stop talking because you feel no one is listening.
3. Be aware of your body language. Remember, we are always communicating. I have seen many experienced investigators spend too much time and effort trying to improve their ability to read the body language of an interviewee, rather than pay attention to their own. For example, always look at the person when they are talking. I once saw counsel reading his mail while the witness he had called was being cross-examined with great enthusiasm. While this counsel may have been quite capable of multitasking, the witness got the impression that he didn't care, which destroyed the rapport they had developed during pre trial interviews and examination-in-chief. This became quite apparent during re-direct when counsel was trying to repair the damage done by effective cross-examination.
4. Do not downgrade the importance of what someone is saying. They are saying it because they feel it is important. While you may not appreciate the relevance of it at the time, it may become important later in assessing whether this is a witness you want to present or rely on.
5. Rather than interpreting what the person is saying and run the risk of being wrong, paraphrase what you feel you have heard and ask for clarification or confirmation. This demonstrates to the person that you are listening and want to clearly understand what they are saying.
6. When you ask a question, listen to the answer. We all remember occasions when someone has asked "how is business? or "how are you?" and the answer is "terrible" and the reply to that is; "that's good." One of the reasons we remember it is because it left us with the feeling that this person really does not care. This will tend to destroy any rapport you have begun to build.
7. Do not ignore the person's emotions. A lot of witnesses have experienced very emotional events and become very upset when talking about it. It does not mean you have to stop the questioning because someone starts to cry, but offering them some kind words of understanding and a tissue will enhance your rapport with this person.
8. Trying to impress with your vocabulary is a sure way to ensure that you will not have a good rapport with the person you are interviewing. The

majority of witnesses you will encounter will not have the same level of vocabulary as counsel. Whenever possible speak at the same level.

9. Mirroring the physical actions of the person you are interviewing is a very effective way to build rapport. This needs to be done subtly of course. You need to get into the same mode/position as the person you are interviewing and then lead the way back to where you would like them to be.

By practicing some of the skills that have proven to be effective in interviewing, especially building rapport, witness preparation will be a much more enjoyable and successful experience.

Chapter Ten

Anatomy of a Tax Prosecution: A Practical Guide[1]

Robert Goldstein

A. INTRODUCTION

You've just walked into the office, coffee in one hand and briefcase in another when your assistant informs you that a new file has crossed your desk and a new client is sitting in your office. No problem. You're the firm's top litigator. You're a highly trained (and compensated) professional that can handle any problem. Or at least that's what the firm's website says.

After settling in, your new client tells you his story.[2] *He says he is under criminal investigation by the Revenue Canada!*[3] *You choke back your first reaction,*

---

1 The opinions expressed in this paper are solely those of the author and do not in any way reflect the views of the Department of Justice. Special thanks to Ian MacGregor, Assistant Deputy Attorney General, Tax Law Services, and Jim Talbot, Senior Investigator, Canada Revenue Agency, for their valuable input and review.

2 This paper uses the facts in *R. v. Jarvis* (2002), 169 C.C.C. (3d) 1 (S.C.C.) [*Jarvis*] as a reasonably typical fact pattern in a tax evasion case.

3 The official name for Revenue Canada is the Canada Revenue Agency ("CRA") The Agency has had many iterations of its name over the years. It was previously referred to as the Canada Customs and Revenue Agency ("CCRA") and prior to that as the Department of National Revenue. From time to time Revenue Canada was an official name but it is now a colloquial name. All references below are to the official name. The author has no financial interest in any company that has a contract to develop new names for Revenue Canada, but wishes that he did.

which is "can they do that?" and listen carefully. It seems your new client, a farmer named Jarvis, was married to a now-deceased local artist of some repute. After Mrs. Jarvis died, Mr. Jarvis continued to sell her paintings. Somewhere along the line, Mr. Jarvis tells you, he and his accountant received calls from a Revenue Canada auditor, and they had some meetings where the auditor, a supervisor, and the accountant were present. Mr. Jarvis just assumed he was being audited. Then, one day, a bunch of investigators swooped down on his farm, his accountant's office, and who knows where else and executed search warrants. Now, Mr. Jarvis thinks that they are going to charge him with something, and he wants to know a few things, such as what he should do (if anything) before the charges are laid, if he is charged, what the process involves, and if he is convicted, what could happen to him.

After listening, making notes, and asking a few questions that are designed to show that you are engaged with the process but hide the fact that you have no clue what to do, you tell your new client to leave the documents that he has brought, as you need to review them. You don't tell him that is a cover for the fact that since you're not a criminal lawyer you're going to have to call someone who knows something about this area of the law.

This chapter is designed to guide you through the process of a typical criminal tax evasion trial (with reference to GST evasion and GST refund fraud), especially if you are not a criminal lawyer. This is not a comprehensive treatise on advocacy in criminal cases. Rather, it touches on some of the aspects of criminal proceedings that are unique to criminal tax evasion proceedings.

There are a few important things that any counsel dealing with a criminal tax matter should keep in mind. First, tax evasion cases rarely involve technical tax issues. They are usually frauds where the victim is the government. This is even more so when the offence is tax refund or GST fraud. Technical or substantive tax issues rarely emerge during tax evasion prosecutions. These are basically criminal cases with a few unique twists. Having said that, complete ignorance of the *Income Tax Act* and accounting principles won't exactly help — counsel should at least know, for example, the difference between a deductible expense and a shareholder loan. You need to know something about income tax and something about accounting, but you don't need a Chartered Accountant designation or a Master's of Business Administration. If significant technical issues arise you may need to retain tax counsel or an accountant to help you work through them.

Second, counsel defending tax evasion cases possess a supreme strategic advantage: nobody likes the CRA. Indeed, if there is one thing that the courts are generally on the lookout to curb, it is the overweening power of a large bureaucratic organization that can use intrusive powers against ordinary people and suck up their money like a giant vacuum — after all, judges pay taxes, too. This was exactly the effect of the Supreme Court of Canada's decision in *Jarvis.*

Third, there is another important strategic advantage possessed by counsel representing persons under investigation: the investigative process is a target-rich environment. CRA usually uses search warrants to seize documents from banks, accountants, businesses, and even personal residences. Since charges are rarely laid simultaneously with the execution of warrants, there are usually applications to retain the documents. The regime for the issuance of search warrants and the retention of things seized is full of opportunities for aggressive counsel intent on defending the rights of a client. Long and complex investigations can breed potential *Charter* issues.

Fourth, it is important to bear in mind the nature of CRA. Like many other government agencies, it is both a law enforcement body and a regulatory authority.[4] As a regulator, CRA possesses the power to make its own rules, and the power to administer them and fulfill its legislative mandate.[5] But as a law enforcement body, CRA is more circumscribed in its powers. The Supreme Court's decision in *R. v. Jarvis* has clarified that CRA, and regulators like it, are not generally entitled to use their compulsory powers where the predominant purpose of their investigations is the gathering of evidence for criminal liability.

For many years a fierce battle was waged in the courts about the exact nature of CRA's powers of audit and investigation, and where the line should be drawn, if at all. The line was decisively drawn in *Jarvis,* and it was not drawn in CRA's favour. So by all means guide your client through the process with the confidence to know that CRA is not invincible in the courts. But at the same time bear in mind that CRA has not been left entirely toothless. Legitimate investigations that uncover criminal breaches of the *Income Tax Act* or the *Excise Tax Act*[6] will not lightly be overturned by the courts. As well, the Investigations Unit is generally a highly professional and very sophisticated organization. So if you are going to handle your client's problems with confidence, then you should know not only about the arrows in your quiver, but the arrows in theirs as well.

---

4 Such bodies are often referred to as "governments in miniature" since they make their own rules and then enforce them. They have both criminal and civil powers. Classic examples of such bodies include securities commissions and competition authorities.

5 For example, CRA's policy regarding the investigation of tax evasion is contained in Information Circular IC73-10R3, dated February 13, 1987.

6 *Income Tax Act*, R.S.C. 1985, c. 1 (5th Supp.); *Excise Tax Act*, R.S.C. 1985, c. E-13.

B. WHEN SHOULD COUNSEL GET INVOLVED?

1) How do you know your client is under investigation and what can you do about it?

As you learn more about the facts, you discover that a CRA auditor contacted your client. The auditor was interested in your client's taxes, and in the estate of your client's deceased wife. After playing some "telephone tag," there was a meeting between Mr. Jarvis, his accountant, and two CRA auditors. Your client admits to you that he isn't all that fussy about his record-keeping. He also tells you that he has been particularly careless since the death of his wife. Still, the auditors borrowed some records, and obtained banking information on the basis of authorizations signed by your client. After a period of time with some contact between the accountant and the auditor, but with virtually no information provided by CRA, a posse of investigators suddenly descended on the farm and the accountant's office and seized numerous files. Mr. Jarvis had had only a vague idea that the file might have been transferred to something called "special investigations" but the implications did not sink in until the day the search warrants were executed.

"White collar" offences, especially sophisticated frauds, are unlike most other crimes — sometimes you know a crime has occurred, sometimes you don't. Indeed, if the "white collar" or financial crime in question is well-planned and executed, no one may ever know about it. In contrast, if a bank is robbed or a murder committed, everyone knows that a crime has occurred. In the regulatory context, where there is a violation of a statute (such as an oil spill engaging the provisions of the *Fisheries Act* or the *Canada Shipping Act*) there is an obvious possibility of criminal charges. Income tax evasion is essentially a fraud where the government is the victim and often the victim does not even know that a crime has taken place. Since Canada has a large economy and a large and complex tax system that requires self-reporting of income and deductions, CRA depends on a system of random audits to enforce compliance. The Supreme Court of Canada has recognized that such audits are crucial to maintaining the integrity of the system.[7]

Can you prevent a referral from Audit to Investigations? If your client is under audit, he or she will know since it is his or her own books and records that CRA will want to see. Your client will also likely know that he

---

7 *R. v. McKinley Transport* (1990), 55 C.C.C. (3d) 530 at 540 (S.C.C.); *Thomson Newspapers v. Director of Investigation and Research* (1990), 54 C.C.C. (3d) 417 (S.C.C.).

or she is under investigation. Generally speaking, the taxpayer is notified when a file is accepted for full-scale criminal investigation, although there is no statutory requirement to inform a taxpayer that a file has gone from Audit to Investigations. As well, although most investigations are the result of referrals from Audit, others are the result of informant leads that are directed to Investigations, referrals from other government departments or the police, or they are generated by Investigations itself as a result of criminal or other activity that it becomes aware of through its own sources.

It is important to remember that there is no obligation on an auditor to refer a file to Investigations. Indeed, it is rare that a referral is accepted by Investigations for full-scale criminal investigation. Of those that are fully investigated, not all are referred to the Department of Justice for prosecution, and not all that are referred to the Department of Justice result in criminal charges. For example, in 2002-03 Investigations referred 374 cases of suspected tax, GST, and customs evasion to the Department of Justice. That number, 374 referrals, must be seen in the context of thousands of routine audits that CRA conducts every year.[8]

Thus, there is usually great value in your client cooperating with the audit process, particularly if your goal is to prevent a referral to Investigations, and, ultimately, charges. Cooperation is wise in any event because the auditor can always compel production of documents and answers to questions, as well as re-assess returns, if there is no cooperation.[9] The auditor can also be a valuable source of information. A cooperative relationship with an auditor may give your client the opportunity to explain what might otherwise look like a suspicious transaction. Furthermore, the auditor is under no obligation to refer a file to Investigations. There usually is no reason to give him or her an incentive to do so.

The CRA has a voluntary disclosure policy. If your client makes a disclosure to CRA that he or she has failed to pay all taxes necessary, or has taken ineligible deductions, then CRA may waive relief from penalties and criminal investigation. Taxpayers may not, however, take advantage of the policy if they do so with knowledge that an audit, investigation, or other enforcement action is underway. In other words, since you became involved after Mr. Jarvis had been audited and investigated, it is too late to take advantage of the policy and make a voluntary disclosure.[10]

---

8 CCRA Annual Report to Parliament, found on the CRA Website at www.ccra-adrc.gc.ca.

9 *Income Tax Act*, s. 232.1(1), s. 232.2(1); *Excise Tax Act*, s. 288(1), s. 289(1).

10 Information Circular IC 00-1R, dated September 30, 2002.

2) Should you advise your client to cooperate with the investigation or attack it?

Once CRA's inquiry turns from Audit to Investigation you will have to make a strategic decision as to your best course of action. How to proceed is a question of fact and judgment and depends on the situation. Should you co-operate and provide information and documents in an attempt to convince CRA that there has been no fraud? Or should you advise your client to exercise his or her right to remain silent and not lead CRA to places they might not otherwise go? And what is your client's goal? Is it to prevent charges being laid against your client? Or is it simply to minimize the amount of tax payable as the result of a reassessment? In order to properly advise your client and make tactical decisions, you need information. You need to know what evidence is possessed by CRA. In other words, what do they have on your client?

Every search warrant must be supported by a sworn Information to Obtain a Search Warrant.[11] CRA's theory can be found in the Informations to Obtain that were filed when the warrants were issued. The Information to Obtain should set out:

- A description of the alleged offences;
- A description of the manner in which the investigator believes that the offences were committed;
- The places where the investigator believes that evidence will be found;
- The reasons why the investigator needs the seized evidence;
- The basis for the investigator's belief.

CRA Informations to Obtain and Search Warrants tend to be very lengthy and detailed in comparison to routine Informations to Obtain sworn by most police officers. They tend to set out the genesis of the investigation as well as the evidence obtained thus far in the investigation that support the allegations. After reviewing the Information to Obtain you will know quite a bit about the investigation.

You can, and should, request that the investigator send you copies of the Informations to Obtain. If he or she refuses, you can usually obtain

11 *Criminal Code*, s. 487, s. 487.01. Although the *Income Tax Act* and the *Excise Tax Act* contain a search warrant provisions, CRA typically resorts to *Criminal Code* warrants. The use of a *Criminal Code* warrant to seize evidence in respect of an offence under any Act of Parliament is lawful: *R. v. Multiform Manufacturing* (1990), 58 C.C.C. (3d) 257 (S.C.C.).

them from the court office where the warrants were issued, unless a sealing order has been made.

Along with the Information to Obtain, another piece of useful information is the inventory of seized documents and the Report to Justice. Every time a search warrant is issued, the officer who executed the warrant must file a report with a justice of the peace. The report must indicate what occurred, and what, if anything, was seized.[12] Typically, the investigator will prepare inventory reports of documents seized and attach them as part of the Report to Justice. These reports, along with the Information to Obtain, will give you the information as to the nature of Revenue's accusations, and whether there sufficient evidence exists to validate those accusations.

A further, important source of information is the audit file. The audit file should contain a copy of the referral memorandum, which will explain why the file was referred to Investigations. Your client also has the right to make a request for the file under the *Privacy Act*.[13]

3) How do you attack the investigation?

Investigators pursuing financial crime face several hurdles. As a result, a CRA investigation is a target-rich environment for defence counsel. It is during the period that the investigators are still gathering evidence and analyzing it that the investigation is vulnerable to attack. There are several opportunities to aggressively attack an investigation. As noted, tax evasion is basically a type of fraud and tax evasion investigations are therefore like fraud investigations — investigators need time to analyze the documents and prepare a referral to the Department of Justice if there is a recommendation to lay charges. As well, investigators frequently need to execute fresh search warrants on new locations as a result of information they glean from the execution of earlier search warrants. In routine cases police officers typically lay charges at the same time or shortly after the execution of search warrants. In criminal tax investigations the results of the warrants have to be analyzed over a period of months before it can be determined whether charges can even be laid.

One significant problem faced by CRA, and one that is not well-known, is that investigators frequently have great difficulty in obtaining financial records from banks. Any criminal investigation involving money will involve banks. Banks are large, disparate organizations and they frequently have information relating to a single customer in several different places. As

---

12 *Criminal Code*, s. 490.

13 *Privacy Act*, R.S.C. 1985, c. P-21, s. 12.

well, most Canadian banks have subcontracted the storage of information and documents. Moreover, banks frequently take the position that customer information is not under their "control" and therefore that they cannot produce it. The result for CRA: a major headache consuming time and resources. The result for your client: an opportunity to litigate, if necessary.

Another problem is that the scheme for the retention of seized evidence in s. 490 of the *Criminal Code* is, as the Supreme Court of Canada has called it, "a confusing statutory process."[14] Prior to the laying of charges, an investigator may retain seized evidence for up to three months from the date of seizure without any kind of formal order. After three months, a justice of the peace may grant one or more periods of further retention up to one year after the search warrant was executed if no charges are laid (laying charges obviates the need for a retention order). After one year, if CRA is still not in a position to lay charges, the investigator must apply to a Superior Court judge for a period of further retention.[15]

Every time CRA applies for a period of further retention, notice must be given to the person from whom the item was seized. That person has a right to be present and make submissions to the justice of the peace. If documents were seized directly from your client, and many times they are, obviously you can be there to attack the retention process. At the one-year mark, the burden on CRA becomes especially heavy, since it must be shown that the documents are required "due to the complex nature of the investigation."[16] The courts have interpreted this requirement to mean that granting more than one year should not be automatic. Furthermore, "complexity" is not to be equated with volume: a large case is not necessarily a complex case.[17] Some of the factors that the courts have examined in determining whether to grant an extension beyond one year include "the assistance of experts to help decipher documents seized; a need to interview witnesses in and beyond Canada; a combination of complexity with unique time consuming issues; the absence of 'feet dragging,' delay or procrastination; and, an absence of prejudice." Other factors have been held to include "the training and experience of those involved in the investigation; the time dedicated to the investigation by such persons; and, the need for

---

14 *R. v. Raponi*, 2004 SCC 50.

15 *Criminal Code*, s. 490(3). Section 490 does not apply to copies of books and records obtained from financial institutions pursuant to a search warrant: *Canada Evidence Act*, s. 29(7).

16 *Criminal Code*, s. 490(3)(a).

17 *Re Bromley et. al.*, an unreported case of the British Columbia Supreme Court, January 31, 2002.

further investigation or inquiry as a consequence of information derived or received as a result of earlier enquiries."[18]

The warrants themselves can also be attacked by way of a *certiorari* application if they were issued by a justice of the peace or provincial court judge. If the warrants were issued by a judge of the superior court, then a "Wilson application" can be brought before a superior court judge to review the warrant.[19] There are many legal attacks that can be made on the warrants, but the basic arguments are that there was no basis upon which the issuing justice could have issued the warrants, that the warrants did not describe the information sought with enough particularity, or that the warrants were too broad.[20]

In the past, some counsel have attacked the investigation at every turn so as to divert resources from the investigation itself and frustrate the laying of charges, and then, after the one-year period, argued to a superior court judge that CRA did not deserve more time because it did not devote enough resources to the file. Obviously such an approach would be particularly cynical and ethically questionable.

4) Can you negotiate with Investigations before a referral to the Department of Justice?

Procedurally, CRA refers possible prosecution matters to the Department of Justice for a decision prior to the laying of charges. Although you may attempt to negotiate with CRA prior to a referral, it is highly unlikely that CRA will agree to refrain from referring on the basis of, for example, the payment of a larger civil penalty. Negotiation at this stage is extremely difficult unless your client is part of a larger fraudulent scheme. If that is the case, you may attempt to negotiate a cooperation agreement that includes a promise not to lay charges in exchange for information and testimony.

Having said that, however, there may be all sorts of opportunities to legitimately influence the investigative process. You may wish to draw the investigator's attention to facts of which he or she was not aware that point away from *mens rea*. You obviously have the right to be present if your client is interviewed. You can provide documents to CRA that had not previously been seized that might show that your client's tax liability is lower than previously thought. You can interview the same witnesses that CRA

18 *Minister of National Revenue v. Welford* (1996), 18 O.T.C. 388 (Gen. Div.).

19 *R. v. Wilson* (1983), 9 C.C.C. (3d) 97 (S.C.C.); *R. v. Budd* (2000), 150 C.C.C. (3d) 108 (Ont. C.A.).

20 *R. v. Church of Scientology (No. 6)* (1987), 31 C.C.C. (3d) 449 (Ont. C.A.).

interviewed. Of course, by taking these steps you run the risk that CRA will see your involvement as trying to complicate the process, hinder the investigation, or just meddle, but you do have the right to intercede with CRA on behalf of your client.

5) Can you stop a referral to the Department of Justice?

Once a referral has been made to the Department of Justice, decisions as to the laying, withdrawal, and prosecution of charges are out of the hands of CRA and within the discretion of counsel for the Attorney General of Canada. Unlike the discretionary decisions of an investigative agency, the discretionary decisions of the Attorney General are generally not subject to review by the courts.[21] Obviously it is in your client's interest to prevent a referral, if possible.

Prior to referral it is CRA policy to inform the taxpayer that the matter is going to be referred to the Department of Justice and to permit the taxpayer to make submissions to CRA. This is potentially an important opportunity to prevent a referral. There may be important information of which CRA is not aware that could tip the scales against a referral. For example, if your client is suffering from advanced cancer, then you might be able to convince CRA that it would be unduly harsh to lay charges. Or, if your client is a small player in a larger tax fraud, an offer of cooperation might persuade CRA to classify your client as a cooperating witness rather than an accused person. Alternatively, your client could be presented as someone like Mr. Jarvis — an elderly gentleman in poor health devastated by the loss of his wife and not much interested in taxes or accounting. The situation in which Mr. Jarvis found himself — where he did not learn about the referral to Investigations until the search warrants were executed — is extremely rare, as CRA usually notifies the taxpayer that the matter has been accepted for full-scale criminal investigation.

C. WHO HAS BEEN CHARGED AND WHAT HAVE THEY BEEN CHARGED WITH?

It turns out that Mr. Jarvis has been charged with offences contrary to s. 239(1)(a) (making a false statement in a return), s. 239(1)(d) (tax evasion) of the Income Tax Act, *and s. 327(1)(c) of the* Excise Tax Act *(GST evasion). These charges arise both in relation to his personal taxes, and in his capacity as*

---

21 *R. v. Power* (1994), 89 C.C.C. (3d) 1 (S.C.C.).

the executor of his wife's estate. The Excise Tax Act *charges relate to GST he charged on Mrs. Jarvis's paintings that he sold. According to CRA, it turns out that he charged the GST, but never remitted the taxes.*

1) Who can be charged?

Charges under the *Income Tax Act* and the *Excise Tax Act* can be laid against individuals, corporations, or individuals as directors and/or officers of corporations. In fact, there are a number of different ways that individuals and corporations can be charged. Obviously individual taxpayers can be charged in their personal capacity for taxes that they have allegedly evaded on their personal income tax returns. Individuals can be charged under s. 242 of the *Income Tax Act* as officers and/or directors of corporations that have committed offences where that director or officer has essentially caused or acquiesced in the corporate offence. Directors and officers can be liable for such corporate delicts as failing to remit source deductions, making false statements in a return, or actual evasion by the corporation. Tax preparers who have knowingly prepared returns containing material misrepresentations (such as false deductions) on behalf of their clients and promoters of fraudulent tax shelter schemes can be charged in relation to the total tax loss suffered by CRA.[22]

Obviously corporations can be charged criminally. Corporations are not capable, however, of thinking and acting independently of the person or persons that guide them. Since *mens rea* is obviously an essential element of any criminal offence, and a corporation is incapable of forming the requisite mental intention to commit a crime, the courts will look to the "directing mind" of the company to determine whether criminal liability ought to be imposed on the corporation. Where the "directing mind" can be sufficiently identified with the actions of the company, a conviction can be registered. This theory of corporate criminal liability is called the "identification" theory, and was set out by the Supreme Court of Canada in *Canadian Dredge and Dock*. Of course, the theory also works in reverse, in the sense that officers and directors can be found liable for the criminal behaviour of corporations. One of the key factors in determining whether criminal liability can be visited on the corporation is whether the corporation has received a benefit from the acts of its employees. In circumstances where the corporation has been the victim of a fraud and has received no benefit

---

22 Individual taxpayers or investors are usually re-assessed but rarely charged in those situations.

there is no basis to impose criminal liability. Mr. Justice Estey for the Court stated the test this way:

> Where the directing mind conceives and designs a plan and then executes it whereby the corporation is intentionally defrauded, and when this is the substantial part of the regular activities of the directing mind in his office, then it is unrealistic in the extreme to consider that the manager is the directing mind of the corporation. His entire energies are, in such a case, directed to the destruction of the undertaking of the corporation. When he crosses that line he ceases to be the directing mind and the doctrine of identification ceases to operate. The same reasoning and terminology can be applied to the concept of benefits.
>
> Where the criminal act is totally in fraud of the corporate employer and where the act is intended to and does result in benefit exclusively to the employee-manager, the employee-directing mind, from the outset of the design and execution of the criminal plan, ceases to be a directing mind of the corporation and consequently his acts could not be attributed to the corporation under the identification doctrine. This might be true as well on the American approach through respondeat superior. Whether this is so or not, in my view, the identification doctrine only operates where the Crown demonstrates that the action taken by the directing mind (a) was within the field of operation assigned to him; (b) was not totally in fraud of the corporation, and (c) was by design or result partly for the benefit of the company.[23]

The Court clearly distinguished between cases where the corporation had been the victim of a fraud, and cases where the corporation, while perhaps victimized itself, had also received a benefit, such as in a tax evasion case where the corporation reported lower sales as a result of employee theft. In *Canadian Dredge and Dock* the accused corporation had benefited from the criminal bid-rigging scheme. Thus, in a tax evasion case a significant question might be "who is the directing mind?" In many tax evasion cases the issue will not arise, because much of the time the "directing mind" of the corporation is the owner/operator. In such circumstances identifying the corporation's liability with its "alter ego" is not difficult. There are, however, times where the tax evasion has been carried out by the corporation without the participation or knowledge of the owner/operator or the board of directors. For example, in *R. v. Forges du Lac Inc.* the Quebec Court of Appeal found that the corporation could be guilty of tax eva-

23 *R. v. Canadian Dredge & Dock Co.* (1985) 19 C.C.C. (3d) 1 (S.C.C.) at 37–38.

sion where the wife of the owner/operator (who handled all of the financial, banking, and accounting aspects of the business) had misappropriated funds without the husband's knowledge.[24] Since the corporation had received a benefit (lower taxes) notwithstanding that it had also been defrauded, it was found guilty.

Who can be a directing mind? In *R. v. Safety-Kleen Canada Inc.* Mr. Justice Doherty for the Ontario Court of Appeal found that a court had to determine whether "the discretion conferred on an employee amounts to an express or implied delegation of executive authority to design and supervise the implementation of corporate policy rather than simply carry out such policy."[25] An employee might have extensive responsibility and discretion, but can not be considered a directing mind without the power to design and supervise corporate policy.

2) What types of charges can be laid?

Most tax-related charges fall into four basic categories: tax evasion, GST evasion, tax refund fraud, and GST refund fraud. Most tax evasion is accomplished by making false statements on a return, although some cases also involve a total failure to file.[26] The number of ways to commit tax and GST fraud is limited only by the ingenuity of people willing to commit them. In general however, offenders fall into two categories: those who commit tax or GST evasion in relation to their own personal or business affairs in order to reduce their own personal tax liability; and those who commit tax or GST fraud in order to generate refunds (or fees for promoting phoney tax shelters or preparing false tax returns) and thereby enrich themselves (and/or their clients or investors) at the expense of Canadian taxpayers. Examples of the former include fraudulently using shareholder loan accounts to hide income, or deducting purely personal expenses as business expenses. Examples of the latter include the creation of false documents to fraudulently obtain GST and tax refunds, or the promotion of fraudulent tax shelters.

All of these offences are "hybrid" or "crown option" offences, meaning that they can be prosecuted on summary conviction, or, at the election of the Attorney General of Canada, by indictment. The *Federal Prosecution Ser-*

---

24 *R. v. Forges du Lac Inc.* (1997), 117 C.C.C. (3d) 71 (Que. C.A.).

25 *R. v. Safety-Kleen Canada Inc.* (1997), 114 C.C.C. (3d) 214 at 220 (Ont. C.A.).

26 More minor offences, such as failure to file or comply with a requirement, are captured by s. 238(1) of the *Income Tax Act* and s. 326(1) of the *Excise Tax Act*, and are straight summary conviction offences.

vice Deskbook, the guiding policy document for federal prosecutors, lays out a series of criteria upon which Crown counsel determine whether a charge should be prosecuted summarily or by indictment.[27] Chapter 19.3.1 of the *FPS Deskbook* provides that tax evasion cases will only be prosecuted on indictment in one of two circumstances: either where the alleged evader has committed a previous evasion offence, or where the amount of tax evaded exceeds $250,000.00 and at least one major aggravating factor is present, such as whether there have been damages to a third party, a highly sophisticated scheme has been used, or the accused has had a previous conviction for a similar offence.

Counsel should also bear in mind that any set of facts that support a conviction under s. 239 of the *Income Tax Act* and s. 327 of the *Excise Tax Act* can usually also support a conviction under s. 380 of the *Criminal Code*,[28] the general fraud provision, and that s. 380 carries a maximum penalty of ten years.[29] The courts have upheld the use of *Criminal Code* charges by Crown counsel for income tax offences.[30]

3) What are the elements of the offences?

The elements of the offences of tax evasion and fraud have much in common. One of the best statements of the elements of the offence of fraud was set out by Mr. Justice Dickson (as he then was) in *R. v. Olan, Hudson, and Hartnett*:

> Courts, for good reason, have been loath to attempt anything in the nature of an exhaustive definition of "defraud" but one may safely say, upon the authorities, that two elements are essential, "dishonesty" and "deprivation." To succeed, the Crown must establish dishonest deprivation.
>
> Using the assets of the corporation for personal purposes rather than bona fide for the benefit of the corporation can constitute dishonesty in a case of alleged fraud by directors of a corporation. This proposition finds full support in *Cox and Paton*.

---

27 The *FPS Deskbook* is available online at http://canada.justice.gc.ca/en/dept/pub/fps/index.html.

28 *Criminal Code*, R.S.C. 1985, c. C-46.

29 Bill C-13 (*An Act To Amend the Criminal Code*, S.C. 2001 c. 41) has amended s. 380(1)(a) to increase the penalty to 14 years. At the time of the writing of this paper Bill C-13 had received Royal Assent but not yet been proclaimed in force.

30 *R. v. Corr* (1990), 58 C.C.C. (3d) 53 (Ont. C.A.); *R. v. White and Sennet* (1997), 114 C.C.C. (3d) 225 (Ont. C.A.).

> The element of deprivation is satisfied on proof of detriment, prejudice, or risk of prejudice to the economic interests of the victim. It is not essential that there be actual economic loss as the outcome of the fraud.[31]

Of course, for the Crown to succeed on a charge of tax evasion, dishonesty need not be proved, although where the evasion is accomplished by filing a return with false or misleading statements that element is obviously satisfied. Indeed, virtually all tax evasion encompasses the elements of dishonesty and deprivation. The only exception is where the evasion is accomplished simply by failing to file a return and remit taxes. All that is required for a conviction under s. 239(1)(d) of the *Income Tax Act* is a "wilful evasion" and it may be accomplished in any manner. No dishonest scheme or artifice is necessary.[32]

The one significant difference between the elements of the offences of fraud and tax evasion is the presence of actual loss. The Crown need not prove any actual loss in a fraud case; all that is required is that the fraudsman place the victim at risk of deprivation. In both GST refund fraud and tax evasion cases, however, the Crown is required to prove an actual loss, so that a fine may be imposed — both offences carry minimum fine provisions. The Crown need not prove any actual amount during the trial portion of the case in order for a conviction to be registered. On sentencing, however, an actual amount must be ascertained so that the court can impose a fine, since the fine must be expressed as a percentage of the actual loss.

D. WHAT ARE THE INVESTIGATIVE ISSUES?

Was the audit and subsequent investigation of Mr. Jarvis carried on in a manner that violated Mr. Jarvis's rights, generally under s. 7 or 8 (but possibly also 10(b)) of the Charter?[33] *If violations have occurred, your job will be to attempt to have any evidence obtained as a result of those violations excluded from the trial where you think that remedy is warranted. This part of your analysis forms a crucial aspect of your trial strategy. CRA charges are sometimes dismissed at the stage of pre-trial motions, precisely because defence counsel have been able to*

31 *R. v. Olan, Hudson, and Hartnett* (1978), 41 C.C.C. (2d) 145 (S.C.C.) at 150–51.

32 *R. v. Pavely* (1976), 30 C.C.C. (2d) 483 (Sask.C.A.).

33 Section 7 protects the right to life, liberty, and security of the person. In the criminal context it takes on many manifestations, but the main concern here is the right against self-incrimination: *R. v. Hebert* (1990), 57 C.C.C. (3d) 1 (S.C.C.); *R. v. White* (1999), 135 C.C.C. (3d) 257 (S.C.C.). Section 8 deals with the right against search and seizure; s. 10(b) deals with the right to counsel.

show that a Charter *violation occurred. But in order to do that, you need to know what happened during the investigation. And for that you need disclosure.*

1) Do you have all the disclosure you need?

Once the charges have been laid, you should receive all of the information you require through the disclosure process.[34] If the investigation was the result of a referral from audit, the entire audit file including the referral, working papers, notes and memoranda should be disclosed to you. If you do not receive the entire file, you have an obligation as counsel to write to the Crown to request further disclosure. You certainly want to have any internal CRA communications between the auditor or the auditor's supervisor, and any person in CRA regarding the file. Since the investigation may have been generated as the result of informant information, a referral from a police investigation, or the investigation of another taxpayer, you must be informed as to the genesis of the investigation. Be aware, however, that there is generally very little that can be done with that information unless your client's rights were engaged. If the investigation (or audit) was commenced as the result of an informant's tip, that information is privileged and not subject to disclosure.[35] It is irrelevant whether the informant has asked for protection.[36] Likewise, public interest privilege may protect investigative techniques, although this consideration probably carries somewhat less force with CRA than it does with police forces that engage in undercover activities, surveillance, and wiretapping.[37]

You cannot use ambush disclosure tactics: you cannot lie in wait until the trial to complain about disclosure if you knew or should have known that there was other material. You have an obligation to pursue meaningful disclosure in a responsible way.[38]

2) How did this file get to Investigations?

In fact, the disclosure has revealed a great deal about the process of referral from Audit to Investigations. It turns out that the auditor did a great deal of work on the file. It almost seems that she was doing an investigation herself. She visited

34 *R. v. Stinchcombe* (1991), 68 C.C.C. (3d) 1 (S.C.C.) [*Stinchcombe*].

35 *R. v. Liepert* (1997), 112 C.C.C. (3d) 385 (S.C.C.).

36 *R. v. Thomas* (1998), 124 C.C.C. (3d) 178 (Ont. Ct. Gen. Div.).

37 *R. v.Thomas, ibid; R. v. Richards* (1997), 115 C.C.C. (3d) 377 (Ont. C.A.).

38 *R. v. Dixon* (1997), 122 C.C.C. (3d) 1 (S.C.C.); *R. v. Girimonte* (1997), 121 C.C.C. (3d) 33 (Ont. C.A.).

art galleries to see whether your client had sold art and not reported the income. She obtained copies of bank statements and checked them against known sales of art. When she was satisfied that there was significant unreported income, she consulted her boss and then filled out a form that referred the file to Investigations. Although Investigations accepted the file, and began to look at the issue from the point of view of laying criminal charges, it does not appear that Investigations did much other than look at the audit file and then obtain search warrants.

You should also be alive to the fact that referrals from Audit are by no means the only manner in which matters make their way to Investigations. Files are frequently generated as a result of information received from informants, referrals from police agencies, or other tax or GST frauds uncovered in the course of unrelated taxpayers. But most CRA criminal investigations are the result of referrals from auditors.

3) What did the auditor do?

The Audit branch of CRA has virtually unlimited powers to obtain information from taxpayers. Auditors can demand copies of any documents in order to determine a person's tax liability, enter the premises of any business and demand to see books and records, and require persons to answer questions.[39] Where a business is carried on in a dwelling house, an auditor can also enter, with judicial authorization, and obtain documents.[40]

And, of course, the audit branch has two important "hammers" to obtain compliance: first, failure to comply with a requirement or a demand from CRA can result in a charge under s. 238(1) of the *Income Tax Act*. Section 238(1) creates a strict liability offence that includes failure to comply with a requirement or demand, and carries a maximum fine of $1000.00 or six months imprisonment or both.[41] The second "hammer" that the audit branch has is the power to reassess any return. If a taxpayer refuses to hand over information to support a particular deduction or income figure, then an auditor can certainly reassess on the basis of the information already in his or her possession. There are, therefore, powerful incentives for a taxpayer to comply with demands from audit. These powerful incen-

39 *Income Tax Act*, s. 231.2(1)(a); 231.1(1)(c); s. 231.1(1)(d).

40 *Income Tax Act*, s. 231.1(2).

41 *R. v. Merkle*, [1979] C.T.C. 519 (Alta. C.A.). A strict liability offence is one where intention is not an essential element: the Crown need not prove *mens rea*. It is sufficient merely to prove that the act was done to obtain a conviction. The accused may only avoid criminal liability through a defence of "due diligence": *R. v. Sault Ste. Marie*, [1978] 2 S.C.R. 1299.

tives lay at the heart of the Supreme Court's reasoning in *Jarvis*, and influenced the decision that the audit powers could not be used for a criminal investigation.

As you examine the audit file in preparation for trial, you need to understand what the auditor did and, crucially, when she did it. Did the auditor go beyond merely satisfying herself that there was unreported income, and become an investigator? When did she become suspicious? In other words, what was the "predominant purpose" of her inquiries, did it change over time, and if it did change when did it change?[42] If she began to conduct her own investigation, the predominant purpose of which was to determine criminal liability rather than civil liability, then a violation of s. 7 or s. 8 of the *Charter* may have occurred. In *Jarvis* the Supreme Court laid down the list of factors that a court ought to look at in order to determine the "predominant purpose" of the inquiry:

> In this connection, the trial judge will look at all factors, including but not limited to such questions as:
>
> a. Did the authorities have reasonable grounds to lay charges? Does it appear from the record that a decision to proceed with a criminal investigation could have been made?
> b. Was the general conduct of the authorities such that it was consistent with the pursuit of a criminal investigation?
> c. Had the auditor transferred his or her files and materials to the investigators?
> d. Was the conduct of the auditor such that he or she was effectively acting as an agent for the investigators?
> e. Does it appear that the investigators intended to use the auditor as their agent in the collection of evidence?
> f. Is the evidence sought relevant to taxpayer liability generally? Or, as is the case with evidence as to the taxpayer's mens rea, is the evidence relevant only to the taxpayer's penal liability?
>
> Are there any other circumstances or factors that can lead the trial judge to the conclusion that the compliance audit had in reality become a criminal investigation?[43]

This is where those crucial communications, memoranda, and working papers will play a role. Was there communication between the auditor,

42 *Jarvis*, above note 2 at 39.
43 *Ibid.* at 41.

or the auditor's supervisor, and Investigations? Was there direction by Investigations to the auditor or audit team or merely advice sought? Was there a discussion of the timing and content of the referral such that the auditor really should have transferred the file to Investigations earlier?

As well, did the auditor obtain answers from your client that could be considered incriminatory? If so, at what point in the process did that occur? If the questions were asked and answered during the course of a *bona fide* audit, your client's statements could well be used against him, as they would not be considered to be "conscriptive": in other words, although the statements were compelled they were not created during the course of an "antagonistic" relationship with the government and therefore are not considered to be a violation of the right against self-incrimination. No criminal warning or caution is necessary if the questions were asked purely for the purpose of determining tax liability. If, however, the auditor had crossed the line and begun a criminal investigation, then any questions asked are *prima facie* in violation of the right against self-incrimination and therefore a violation of s. 7 of the *Charter*.[44]

Likewise, did the auditor obtain documents from your client or any third party? Of so, at what point in the process did that occur? Once again, if the documents were obtained in the course of a *bona fide* audit, then no violation of s. 8 has occurred. If, however, the auditor (or investigator) has gone beyond merely auditing and begun a criminal investigation, then there may well have been a violation of the right against search and seizure.

As noted earlier in this paper, where audit powers under s. 231.1(1) and/or 231.2(1) of the *Income Tax Act* (or the equivalent *Excise Tax Act* sections) are used to further an inquiry into the taxpayer's potential criminal liability, the result is a violation of section 7 and/or 8 of the *Charter*, which can in turn result in the exclusion of evidence at trial, and an acquittal entered due to lack of evidence.[45]

You should also be alert to information and documents obtained from arms-length third parties during the course of the audit or investigation. Where search warrants have been executed at locations under the control of third parties, you must be in a position to show that your client had a reasonable expectation of privacy in the place searched in order to raise a *Charter* argument.[46] If your client cannot show that he or she had a reason-

44 *R. v. White*, above note 33; *R. v. Stillman* (1997), 113 C.C.C. (3d) 321 (S.C.C.); *R. v. Fitzpatrick* (1995), 102 C.C.C. (3d) 144 (S.C.C.).

45 *R. v. Collins* (1987), 33 C.C.C. (3d) 1 (S.C.C.); *R. v. Stillman, ibid.*

46 *R. v. Pugliese* (1992), 71 C.C.C. (3d) 295 (Ont. C.A.); *R. v. Edwards* (1996), 104 C.C.C. (3d) 136 (S.C.C.); *R. v. Belnavis and Lawrence* (1997), 188 C.C.C. (3d) 405 (S.C.C.).

able expectation of privacy in the place searched, and, therefore, standing to raise a *Charter* issue, there is precious little that can be done to oppose the introduction at trial of the evidence. If, however, the evidence was derived from a breach of your client's rights (so-called "derivative evidence") and would not have been discovered but for the breach, that evidence could well be excluded from the trial. If the evidence has been obtained through a breach of your client's right to silence, or otherwise "conscripted" from your client, the courts will be particularly alert to deal with those violations.[47] You therefore need to be able to trace the origin of each piece of evidence against your client.

One of the more interesting issues arising from *Jarvis* is the interplay between that case and the "standing" cases. In *Jarvis*, the Court stated that audit powers are simply not available for the purpose of a criminal investigation, and information obtained using those powers may not be used to advance a criminal investigation:

> Likewise, no written documents may be inspected or examined, except by way of judicial warrant under s. 231.3 of the ITA or s. 487 of the Criminal Code, and no documents may be required, from the taxpayer or any third party for the purpose of advancing the criminal investigation. CRA officials conducting inquiries, the predominant purpose of which is the determination of penal liability, do not have the benefit of the ss. 231.1(1) and 231.2(1) requirement powers.[48]

Thus, it is very clear that audit powers are not available to criminal investigators. If an auditor or investigator were to use the requirement power to obtain documents from an arms-length third party during the course of an inquiry that the courts subsequently determine had crossed the line from audit to a criminal investigation, it would amount to a warrantless search. Notwithstanding that the search would have been warrantless, the standing cases hold that if the taxpayer could not show a reasonable expectation of privacy in the place searched, he or she would have no basis to seek the exclusion of the evidence pursuant to s. 24(2) of the *Charter*. The interplay between *Jarvis* and the standing cases has not been worked out.[49] This issue will undoubtedly be the subject of much litigation in the future.

---

47 *R. v. Stillman*, above note 44; *R. v. Burlingham* (1995), 97 C.C.C. (3d) 385 (S.C.C.).

48 *Jarvis*, above note 2, at 42–43.

49 *R. v. Pugliese*; *R. v. Edwards*; *R. v. Belnavis and Lawrence*, above note 46.

4) What did Investigations do?

Your examination of the evidence is not, of course, limited to the audit file but must also encompass any information obtained by the CRA from all sources. The investigation may have been generated on the basis of something other than a random audit. There may have been an informant's tip, a referral from a police officer, or the audit of a third party. Indeed, the audit itself may not have been random.

Investigations has two main tools: search warrants and witness interviews. If search warrants were executed, as they frequently are in CRA investigations, you must examine them for facial validity. You must also examine the Informations to Obtain search warrants, to determine whether they disclosed reasonable and probable grounds to believe that an offence had occurred, and that there were reasonable and probable grounds to believe that there was evidence in the place to be searched.[50] The Information to Obtain must also describe the things to be searched for with reasonable particularity.[51] If the warrant was issued pursuant to s. 487.01 of the *Criminal Code*, the so-called "general warrant" provision, then you must be satisfied that the requirements of that section have been met. For the most part, CRA warrants are issued under s. 487.01 to obtain banking information where the investigator does not know the precise location of the documents.

You must also compare the assertions in the Informations to Obtain with the information that was known to Investigations. Are there any misleading statements in the Informations to Obtain? Is there any contradictory information in the investigative files that was not pointed out to the justice that issued the warrants? Is there important information that the issuing justice should have known that was left out of the Information to Obtain?

The test for reviewing an Information to Obtain a Search Warrant was set out by the Supreme Court in *Garofoli*:

> The reviewing judge does not substitute his or her view for that of the authorizing judge. If, based on the record which was before the authorizing judge as amplified on the review, the reviewing judge concludes that the authorizing judge could have granted the authorization, then he or she should not interfere. In this process, the existence of fraud, non-disclosure, misleading evidence and new evidence are all relevant, but,

---

50 *Criminal Code*, s. 487.

51 *Re Church of Scientology No. 6*, above note 20.

> rather than being a prerequisite to review, their sole impact is to determine whether there continues to be any basis for the decision of the authorizing judge.[52]

The scope of the review is obviously quite narrow. Even if the investigator has told outright lies in the search information or perpetrated a fraud on the court, that is still only one factor to be considered by the reviewing judge.[53] The lies, fraud, and misleading disclosure are to be excised from the search information. The reviewing judge then determines whether there remains enough information in the search information, after being "amplified" on the review, upon which a justice could have issued the warrant.[54] Cross-examination of the affiant is only available with leave of the reviewing judge, as a basis for cross-examination must be shown.[55]

The search warrant review process is the place to bring together your analysis of the audit with the examination of the Informations to Obtain. Remember those incriminating statements that your client made to the auditor? Did they find their way into the search information and form part of the investigator's reasonable and probable grounds? If you can show that the "predominant purpose" of the audit had changed from a focus on tax liability to a focus on criminal liability at the time the statements were made, then they should be excised from the warrant. The same analysis is applied to documents provided by your client to the auditor. Were they obtained after the "predominant purpose" of the audit changed to a criminal investigation? If so, the information gleaned from those documents that supports the issuance of the warrant should also be excised from the search information.

Another important question in your examination of the actions taken by an investigator or an auditor is whether their own rules were followed. The failure of an investigator or auditor to follow procedure or policy does not, in and of itself, give rise to a breach of the *Charter*. Likewise, following procedure or policy does not insulate the investigation or audit from committing a *Charter* breach in that procedures could, in and of themselves, be

---

52 *R. v. Garofoli* (1990), 60 C.C.C. (3d) 161 (S.C.C.) at 188. The Court subsequently confirmed that the test also applies to search warrants: *R. v. Grant* (1993), 84 C.C.C. (3d) 173 (S.C.C.) at 195.

53 *R. v. Bisson* (1994), 94 C.C.C. (3d) 94 (S.C.C.).

54 *R. v. Grant*, above note 52; *Garofoli*, above note 52; in *R. v. Araujo* (2000), 149 C.C.C. (3d) 149 (S.C.C.) the Court held that the wiretap affidavit could be "amplified" to correct errors made in good faith.

55 *Garofoli*, *ibid.*

the problem.[56] It is true, however, that the good or bad faith of an auditor or investigator can be measured, to at least some degree, by diligence in following procedure or policy. The issue of how and when the predominant purpose of the CRA inquiry became criminal liability may well be determined by reference to the viva voce evidence of investigators and auditors. Their credibility will be at issue. As counsel, you need to understand what the procedures were, whether they were followed, and, if not, why not. You will need disclosure of internal policies and perhaps the relevant sections of the Investigations Manual (formerly called the Tax Operations Manual). At the end of the day, you will have to assess the evidence to determine whether CRA's failure (or not) to follow their own procedures has had an impact on your client's *Charter* rights.

5) Has Investigations acted properly?

Like criminal investigators everywhere, individual members of CRA Investigations may occasionally cross the line from good, aggressive interviewing to threats and intimidation, notwithstanding that Investigations is a highly professional organization and such behaviour is exceedingly rare. As counsel, however, you must be on the lookout for it. Did an investigator threaten a third-party witness with an audit if he failed to cooperate? Or was the witness threatened with charges against him or herself? Such threats, if they occurred, would have an impact on the credibility of any such witness, as well as the credibility of the investigator that made them. Your responsibility is not only to examine witness statements, but also to interview third party witnesses if you think it is fruitful. It may be trite to say that "there is no property in a witness" but it is also absolutely true that you can interview anyone that the investigators have interviewed, including the auditors or investigators themselves. They need not agree to an interview, but there is nothing improper whatsoever in requesting one.

A somewhat more common issue than the rogue investigator is the cooperating co-accused. Where multiple parties are charged, it is not uncommon for one of the parties to try and negotiate a favourable resolution with the Crown that contemplates assistance in exchange for a benefit (such as reduced charges or a lower penalty). If you are not negotiating the resolution then the other guy might be. While these situations will rarely

56 For example see *R. v. Chusid* (2001), 57 O.R. (3d) 20 (Sup. Ct.) at para. 68, where Mr. Justice Beaulieu stated "I agree with defence counsel's characterization of Revenue Canada's former policy with respect to banking records as 'a recipe for Charter violations'."

give rise to a violation of your client's *Charter* rights, you must still be aware that they can arise and can affect your trial strategy, particularly on the pre-trial motions that will determine the evidence that is admitted against your client. This issue is dealt with in more detail later, under the heading "should you attempt to negotiate a guilty plea?"

6) Is there a section 241 issue?

Section 241 of the *Income Tax Act* prohibits the unauthorized disclosure of "taxpayer information" except in accordance with the scheme of that section. "Taxpayer information" is defined in s. 241(10) to mean information relating to one or more taxpayers "obtained by or on behalf of the Minister for the purposes of this Act" or prepared from information obtained by or on behalf of the Minister. The unauthorized disclosure of taxpayer information is a criminal offence. Subsection 241(3) does, however, permit communication of taxpayer information where criminal proceedings have been instituted under an Act of Parliament, or in proceedings related to the administration or enforcement of the *Income Tax Act* or related federal or provincial legislation. Counsel should certainly be aware that during the course of an audit or investigation investigators may have disclosed taxpayer information improperly, for example to a third party. If improper disclosure of taxpayer information contrary to s. 241 does occur, it can form part of the basis of an application to stay proceedings on the grounds that an abuse of process has occurred.

On the other hand, s. 241 issues are exceedingly rare. Although the general prohibition is quite strict on its face, subsection 241(3) has been interpreted to permit the release of taxpayer information in circumstances where there is a connection (even if somewhat distant) to the administration or enforcement of the *Income Tax Act*.[57] For the most part, s. 241 issues arise in the context of the improper release of taxpayer information by CRA employees for corrupt purposes — such as the sale of social insurance numbers.

E. WHAT ARE THE SUBSTANTIVE ISSUES?

1) What is the Crown's theory of the case?

Apparently the Crown believes that Mr. Jarvis is a serial tax evader. The theory is not complicated: Mr. Jarvis made money by selling his wife's art and simply

57 *Slattery v. Doane Raymond Ltd.* (1993), 106 D.L.R. (4th) 212 (S.C.C.).

failed to report the income and pay tax on it, either personally or by filing a tax return for his wife's estate. Your initial plan had been to characterize Mr. Jarvis' sactions as purely inadvertent, and, therefore, lacking in the necessary mens rea *to commit the offence. Unfortunately, it turns out that Mr. Jarvis not only failed to report the income, but that he also charged GST for the art and then failed to remit the tax. This will give a huge boost to the Crown's theory that the failure to report and remit was part of an overall scheme of evasion, rather than a purely inadvertent act by an elderly and unwell gentleman.*

The basis of the Crown's case should be obvious from the very beginning, and, if the Crown has properly prepared its material, all of its decisions and actions should conform to its theory of the case, including the manner in which disclosure has been prepared and disseminated. Your real work begins when you get the disclosure, go about trying to understand the Crown's theory, and look for the flaws in the theory or material which might undermine that theory. As well, you must formulate your own theory of the case, and guide your own decisions by it, including how you attack the Crown's case, cross-examine the Crown's witnesses, and seek to characterize the Crown's documentary evidence. Disclosure will also help you decide how to advise your client regarding a possible guilty plea.

2) What is the evidence against my client?

In a typical criminal tax or GST fraud case the evidence against your client is usually the mass of documents that the Crown has collected (whether by seizure or otherwise). There will, of course, be live witnesses to identify and enter the documents, and perhaps expert evidence, but these cases are generally document-intensive. Thus, preparation usually involves an extensive period of time reviewing documents.

In most tax evasion cases, the Crown seeks to show that the income reported on the taxpayer's returns is inconsistent with the income actually earned. Thus, banking evidence is obviously crucial. Many tax evasion cases have ended in a guilty plea when defence counsel have reviewed the disclosure material and found that very significant amounts of funds had been deposited to the taxpayer's bank accounts in comparison to the amounts reported on his or her tax returns.

Accounting evidence is also crucial. The Crown routinely seeks to admit documents generated by the taxpayer's accountants, including working papers. Where the taxpayer under investigation is the principal behind a successful company, the characterization of income taken from the company is obviously important for tax purposes — how the income was treated and how the accountants dealt with it will yield important evidence where, for example, your client insists that the funds should be characterized as a repayment of a shareholder's loan rather than income.

In Mr. Jarvis's case, the key documents would likely be the banking evidence showing that the proceeds of the sales of Mrs. Jarvis's paintings were deposited into the account of Mr. Jarvis or the estate of Mrs. Jarvis. The crucial third party records would be the cheques written by the galleries that bought the art, and any other documents generated by the sales. If Mr. Jarvis gave them invoices, and charged GST, then those documents would also be crucial and would obviously go directly to his state of mind.

3) Are there solicitor-client privilege issues?

Documents from lawyers may also play a crucial role. The flow of funds through a lawyer's trust account may tell CRA investigators a great deal about the beneficial owner of funds. As well, corporate minute books, which are typically kept in law offices and updated by law clerks, reveal information about the relationship between the taxpayer under investigation and his or her corporate alter ego. Mortgage documents, sales contracts, shareholder's agreements, and even tax planning documents may all be important to the Crown's case and may all have been seized from a law firm. Interestingly, many people (and many lawyers) labour under the illusion that law firm trust accounts are privileged. They are not.[58] As well, the mere fact that documents are kept in a lawyer's office does not make them privileged.[59] The only documents to which privilege may attach are those that reflect the giving or receiving of legal advice. A lawyer's dockets and bill, which may tend to reveal solicitor-client communications, are *prima facie* privileged, although the Crown may rebut the presumption.[60]

Anyone defending a tax case where there are law firm documents involved should also be aware of the possibility that privilege might be vitiated due to the criminal/fraud exception to solicitor-client privilege. Communications between a lawyer and a client made with a view to facilitating a crime are not privileged, even if the lawyer acted in good faith and had no idea that the client was using him or her to perpetrate an offence.[61]

---

58 *Re Ontario Securities Commission and Greymac Credit Corp.* (1983), 41 O.R. (2d) 328 (Div. Ct.); *R. v. Serfaty*, [2004] O.J. No. 1952 (S.C.J.). Although trust account records are not privileged, they may contain some privileged information.

59 *Ventouris v. Mountain; The Italia Express*, [1991] 3 All E.R. 472 (C.A.); *Upjohn Co. v. United States*, 449 U.S. 383 (1981).

60 *Maranda v. Richer* (2003), 178 C.C.C. (3d) 321 (S.C.C.).

61 *Descoteaux v. Mierzwinski* (1982), 70 C.C.C. (2d) 385 (S.C.C); *R. v. Serfaty*, *supra*.

4) How does the Crown plan to introduce the evidence?

Since tax evasion cases (as well as GST evasion and GST fraud cases) are overwhelmingly documentary in nature, counsel will have to be very familiar with the rules of evidence pertaining to the introduction of documents at a criminal trial. Although the most common method of introducing a document is by a s. 29 *Canada Evidence Act* affidavit (for Canadian financial institutions) or a s. 30 *Canada Evidence Act* affidavit (for business records), there are actually numerous ways in which a document can be introduced, either to prove that the document exists or was made, or to prove the truth of the contents. Indeed, the Crown may well seek to introduce a document in order to prove that it is false in a material respect, such as a financial statement filed with a tax return. GST and tax refund frauds are obviously perpetrated primarily by means of false documents.

Where a document is an original, it may be received in evidence as a piece of real evidence or simply by virtue of s. 30(1) of the *Canada Evidence Act* with no affidavits required to authenticate it.[62] Where a person can give oral evidence that a document was made in the usual and ordinary course of business, even if that person has no knowledge of the particular contents of the document, then the document is admissible.[63] Section 30 itself is extremely wide, and can encompass virtually any type of document made for any purpose, and not only a "business" purpose in the sense of an undertaking for profit.[64] Documents can also be admitted under the "principled approach" to the hearsay rule, where there is no hearsay exception that readily fits to admit them into evidence.[65] As well, documents can be introduced to show that they were generated in furtherance of a conspiracy.[66]

Having said all that about documents, it is a rare tax case (except where the accused simply evaded taxes by failing to file) where the Crown is able to prove the case solely on the basis of documents. Obviously testimony will be crucial — particularly employees, accounts, bankers, and possibly lawyers. In the case of poor Mr. Jarvis, the art gallery owners to whom Mrs. Jarvis's paintings were sold would be the obvious witnesses for the Crown.

---

62 *R. v. Wilcox* (2000), 152 C.C.C. (3d) 157 (N.S.C.A.); *R. v. Cloutier* (1979), 48 C.C.C. (2d) 1 (S.C.C.).

63 *R. v. Martin* (1997), 8 C.R. (4th) 246 (Sask. C.A.); *R. v. Grimba and Wilder* (1977), 38 C.C.C. (2d) 469 (Ont. Co. Ct.).

64 *Canada (Minister of Citizenship and Immigration) v. Oberlander*, [1999] 1 F.C. 88 (F.C.T.D.).

65 *R. v. Khan* (1990), 59 C.C.C. (3d) 92 (S.C.C.); *R. v. Smith* (1992), 75 C.C.C. (3d) 257 (S.C.C.); *R. v. Lukacko* (2002), 164 C.C.C. (3d) 550 (Ont. C.A.).

66 *R. v. Lukacko, ibid.*

They could give evidence with regard to the purchase of Mrs. Jarvis's art, the amounts paid, and the invoices (if any) issued by Mr. Jarvis.

5) Should you attack the continuity of the documentary evidence?

"Continuity" refers to whether the physical evidence presented in court (including the documentary evidence) is the same evidence that was actually used in an alleged crime. In a murder case, for example, the jury must be satisfied that the murder weapon that is presented in court is the same weapon that was actually used in the murder. Usually proof of continuity involves showing an unbroken chain of possession from the seizing officer to the exhibits officer to the officer presenting the evidence in court. The principle is no different when it comes to documents.

The continuity of the physical (including documentary) evidence is a matter of weight for the trier of fact rather than a matter of admissibility for the trial judge.[67] The Crown need not "prove" continuity, although it is certainly open to the defence to attack continuity, particularly where there is an allegation that documents or other physical evidence has been tampered with or distorted in some manner. As a practical matter, however, defence counsel do not usually contest the continuity of the documents in a tax case. To force the Crown to show the chain of continuity of hundreds of documents will unreasonably lengthen a trial, and may accomplish no more than annoying the judge (and/or jury) and prejudicing them against your client.

6) Are there offshore aspects to this case?

Rare is the large and sophisticated tax fraud that does not have an aspect involving a tax haven of some kind. Tax havens are jurisdictions where it is illegal for banks (and usually professionals, such as lawyers and accountants) to disclose any information about a customer or a customer's affairs. Essentially, all aspects of the banking relationship are set up to prevent interested foreign authorities (especially tax authorities) from obtaining information. A sunny Caribbean isle is the perfect place to hide money that the taxman might like to get his or her hands on. Since most of the tax havens remain places with no taxation and no tax treaties, the element of

---

67 *R. v. Parsons* (1977), 37 C.C.C. (2d) 497 (Ont. C.A.); affirmed without reference to this point, *Charette v. The Queen* (1980), 51 C.C.C. (2d) 350 (S.C.C.); *R. v. DeGraaf* (1981), 60 C.C.C. (2d) 315 (B.C.C.A.).

dual criminality necessary before mutual legal assistance can be extended is usually missing. For example, even though Canada has a mutual legal assistance treaty with the Bahamas, the treaty limits assistance by the Bahamas to offences that carry a term of imprisonment in the Bahamas of one year or more. The Bahamas has no income tax and therefore no offence of tax evasion, and can therefore refuse cooperation where the Canadian offence under investigation is an income tax offence.[68]

After a great deal of pressure was applied by the major Western countries, including Canada, most of the tax havens eliminated the most egregious practices associated with large-scale money laundering, especially laundering of the proceeds of drug crime.[69] Bank secrecy laws remain in place in most offshore jurisdictions, however, and it remains very difficult for Canadian tax authorities to obtain information from banks in those places. Although there may be legitimate reasons to bank offshore, there is really no doubt that the primary reason remains the avoidance or evasion of tax or the laundering of proceeds of crime. Where there is evidence that your client has engaged in offshore transactions or used a bank in a tax haven, this will raise a very large red flag to Investigations.

If the Crown does manage to obtain documents from a tax haven, it must still file the necessary affidavits or find some other way of introducing those documents, in the same manner as any other documents that the Crown seeks to introduce.

7) Is there a substantive defence? Are there technical tax issues that can be raised?

Mr. Jarvis claims that he never intended to evade the payment of taxes. He's just very sloppy with his records and does not really understand tax and accounting. His accountant and his children all say that the farm's records were always disorganized, but that the situation has become much worse since the death of Mrs. Jarvis.

As noted above, tax evasion cases rarely engage technical tax issues. Having said that, there may still be technical defences available to your client.

---

68 Treaty Between the Government of Canada and the Government of the Commonwealth of the Bahamas on Mutual Legal Assistance in Criminal Matters, CTS 1999/8, in force December 2, 1999.

69 *Annual Report of the Financial Action Task Force*, on the website of the Organization for Economic Cooperation and Development (OECD): http://www.oecd.org/fatf/pdf/AR2001_en.pdf.

Indeed, there may well be technical aspects of the taxes owed that can be exploited by the defence. For example, CRA in calculating the taxes may not know about all legitimate deductions available to a taxpayer. Did CRA figure the costs of canvases and paints into the profits allegedly made on the sale of Mrs. Jarvis' paintings? What about fuel used to drive Mr. Jarvis' old pickup around selling the paintings? And what about the old pickup itself — surely a part of the depreciation was due to all those sales calls? Your preparation for a criminal tax trial should, therefore, include consultation with tax counsel.

Many different defences have been tried over the years, and some have been more successful than others. Heaping blame on the spouse is popular ("I thought she was filing the tax returns"), especially when the spouse actually works in the business. Blaming the accountant is also popular ("I just left everything to my accountant"). Mr. Jarvis' defence ("I'm just a dumb, disorganized, old farmer") goes to his state of mind, and, if believed, could result in an acquittal.

Another popular defence is to argue that CRA misunderstood the corporate or commercial transactions in question. For example, where CRA has found that a tax shelter is really just a criminal tax fraud, the defence may well be that the shelter really exists and that CRA just did not understand how it worked. Another example is the use or misuse of shareholder loan accounts. Since tax evasion frequently takes place in the context of a private business, the taxpayer will argue that the funds taken out of the business are really the return of shareholder loans, and that CRA mischaracterized the funds as income. Whether these defences work or not is obviously fact-specific.

F. HOW DO YOU PREPARE FOR AND CONDUCT THE TRIAL?

1) Do you try and negotiate a guilty plea?

Obviously every case is fact-specific as to whether a guilty plea should be negotiated, and many factors will be considered when entering into resolution discussions with Crown counsel. Is there a viable *Charter* motion? Is the Crown's case extremely strong or are there weaknesses? Will my client have to testify to explain his actions and how convincing will he be? If there is a co-accused, should a resolution that includes co-operation and testimony be pursued? If jail is a realistic possibility after trial, should a resolution that contemplates only a fine be pursued? If a corporation has been charged as well as your client, is the Crown willing to accept a plea from the corporation in exchange for dropping the charges against your client in his personal capacity? In the case of Mr. Jarvis, can his age and ill-health be used to persuade the Crown to accept a resolution that includes lesser amounts of tax to pay and no jail time?

One complicating factor of which counsel must be aware is that federal prosecutors have no ability to negotiate civil and criminal resolutions together. In other words, prosecutors are precluded from using the threat of instituting, prolonging, or in any way conducting criminal proceedings in order to obtain a civil result. Such actions could be considered an abuse of process. Thus, if you want to wrap up the criminal and civil proceedings together, you must deal separately with the CRA appeals officer and the Department of Justice. Obviously, however, any resolution that you obtain in the criminal proceedings will influence the civil proceedings. For example, if you are able to negotiate a guilty plea to a lesser amount of tax evaded, that will have an impact on the amount of tax imposed in the Tax Court or in any negotiated proceeding with the Appeals Division of CRA.

Clearly a key factor in determining whether a guilty plea should be negotiated is the simple fact that your client might not have the resources to go to trial. If the Crown chooses to proceed by indictment, then there is the additional cost associated with a preliminary inquiry. It is rare for a person charged with tax evasion to receive legal aid, so most people are on their own when it comes to mounting a defence. This is a cost-benefit calculation that only your client can make.

2) What mode of trial should you choose?

Where Crown counsel chooses to proceed by summary conviction, the mode of trial is by provincial court judge. However, where the Crown chooses to proceed by indictment, then choice as to the mode of trial is up to you and your client. Obviously the answer will depend on the particular facts of the situation. As noted, your client may have the resources for a trial but not a trial and a preliminary inquiry. Alternatively, your client may have the appropriate resources, but you may feel that there might be some tactical advantage in trial before a provincial court judge. For example, many tax evasion cases are a "work in progress." The investigation may not be complete when the charges are laid. CRA may have been forced to lay charges, however, where retention orders for seized documents were about to expire. A provincial court judge trial at an early opportunity may well force the Crown to trial before the prosecution case is fully ready.

A preliminary inquiry, where the resources exist to fund one, is usually very fruitful for the defence — you get a look at the Crown's case, and have a chance to explore the evidence of the Crown's witnesses. It can also give you the opportunity to build a record for your *Charter* motion. As well, where major flaws in the Crown's case are exposed, it might provide an incentive for Crown counsel to offer better terms for a future guilty plea.

A preliminary inquiry also has certain disadvantages for the defence. Getting discovery of the Crown's case, also means that the Crown gets to discover yours as well, in the sense that your cross-examination questions will probably give Crown counsel a pretty good idea of your trial strategy, likely defence, and possible *Charter* motions. The Crown will also get a chance to discover its own case, get an idea of the strength and weaknesses of its witnesses, and generally fine-tune the evidence for trial.

One of the key questions in electing your mode of trial is whether you anticipate that your client will testify. Clearly your evaluation of whether he or she is likely to do better with a jury or a trial judge sitting alone will have an important impact on that decision. Although no two cases are alike, it is fairly clear that juries are often less sympathetic persons to charged with tax evasion than many other accused persons. Few things will annoy twelve average taxpayers more than seeing an accused person in the stand explaining how it is that he can drive a luxury car, eat at expensive restaurants, and take fancy vacations yet still claim that he does not make enough money to pay taxes. Again, this is one of those areas where it is a question of fact, judgment, and experience in determining what is best for your client.

3) Do you bring *Charter* motions?

Since tax cases are document-intensive, if you take away the Crown's documents there is usually not much evidence left for the prosecution. And since document-intensive cases usually involve searches and seizures, there are opportunities to bring motions under s. 8 of the *Charter*. As noted earlier, the *Jarvis* issue in particular is a fruitful area for examination by defence counsel where there has been a referral from Audit to Investigations. If a *Charter* violation can be proven it is virtually always in the interests of the defence to bring an application to exclude the seized evidence, since it will very likely totally undermine the prosecution's case. That is why motions to exclude the evidence are typically brought in criminal tax cases. As is discussed later in this paper, a successful motion to exclude evidence can also have a significant impact on subsequent civil proceedings.

Another fruitful area for defence counsel is a motion to stay proceedings under s. 11(b) of the *Charter* for unreasonable delay. Routine criminal tax cases tend to be vastly more complex than most other routine criminal cases, and disclosure in routine criminal tax cases tends to be vastly more voluminous than in other routine criminal cases. Complex cases take more time — disclosure takes more time to complete, defence counsel need more time to study the disclosure, and the court needs more time to accommodate the case. Complexity and volume breed delay which is why motions to stay the proceedings for unreasonable delay are typically brought in a criminal tax case. The courts do recognize that tax cases are complex and require more time than routine cases, so delay motions are not necessarily sure-fire winners.[70]

Many defence counsel bring delay motions on the mistaken assumption that it is cost-free, in the sense that if the motion is dismissed the accused is no worse off. This is sometimes a tactical error. A delay motion usually requires calling evidence of prejudice which in turn usually requires calling the accused, which means that Crown counsel can cross-examine. Most accused tax evaders are not elderly gentleman farmers like Mr. Jarvis. They tend to receive less sympathy. Where the client does not do well in cross-examination, is found not to be credible by the trial judge and the motion is dismissed, or the trial judge simply forms an unhelpful impression of the client, there may well be negative consequences for defence counsel's trial strategy. The approach to plea, election, and calling a defence may all have to be re-evaluated in light of the evidentiary findings on the delay motion.

4) Do you bring disclosure or third party records applications?

There are two ways for a defence counsel to obtain material that is relevant to the defence and not otherwise available from sources available to defence counsel (such as a private investigator or cooperative third parties): through the disclosure process (the *Stinchcombe* process[71]), or through a third-party records application (the *O'Connor* process[72]).

It is obviously the Crown's duty to make disclosure to the defence of all material that is relevant — relevant being defined to mean, it could be of "some use."[73] Crown and defence counsel frequently take a different view

---

70 *R. v. Morin* (1992), 71 C.C.C. (3d) 1 (S.C.C.); *R. v. White and Sennett* (1997), 114 C.C.C. (3d) 225 (Ont. C.A.).

71 Above note 34.

72 *R. v. O'Connor* (1997), 103 C.C.C. (3d) 1 (S.C.C.). It is also possible to obtain information through Access to Information and Privacy requests. Those extra-judicial methods are not covered in this paper, although they are a legitimate means to pursue information.

73 *Stinchecombe*, above note 34; *R. v. Egger* (1993), 82 C.C.C. (3d) 193 (S.C.C.) at 204.

of whether material is relevant. Where defence counsel becomes aware that there is material in the Crown's possession that is relevant to a fact in issue but not yet disclosed, it is counsel's responsibility to request the material. It is then up to Crown counsel to either disclose the material, indicate why it will not be disclosed, or claim that it is not in the Crown's possession. The Crown need not disclose material that "is beyond the control of the prosecution."[74] This is a point that is frequently litigated in the course of tax prosecutions. Many government departments hold information relevant to a taxpayer, or to third parties that have dealt with the taxpayer, and defence counsel may want some of that material for cross-examination purposes. Alternatively, the taxpayer may have been investigated by a different law enforcement agency (for example, there may have been a proceeds of crime investigation run by the RCMP). Crown counsel has no obligation to seek out that material, or even to disclose it — a third party records application must be brought.[75]

Where the Crown has the material but refuses to make disclosure (presumably on the basis of a legal principle, such as informant privilege), then counsel must make a disclosure application, either to the trial judge, or to a superior court judge. For example, where the Crown has elected to proceed by indictment, and the matter is at the stage of a preliminary inquiry, a disclosure application must be made to a judge of the superior court since the preliminary inquiry judge has no *Charter* jurisdiction and disclosure is a *Charter* right. The judge will then make his or her decision based on the principles set out in *Stinchecombe*. As noted, the threshold is low. The applicant need only show that the material is of "some use."

Where the Crown claims that the material is not in its possession, the defence must serve a subpoena on the third party and make the appropriate application, again, either to the trial judge or to the superior court. The procedure for a third party records application (that does not involve sexual therapy records) is set out in *R. v. O'Connor*. The burden is on the party seeking the material. The threshold is higher than in the disclosure process. First, the applicant must show that the material is "likely relevant." If that is achieved, the judge then examines the material to determine whether it should be disclosed, balancing the accused person's right to make full answer and defence against the third party's privacy interests.

---

74 *Stinchecombe*, *ibid.*; *R. v. Chaplin* (1995), 96 C.C.C. (3d) 225 (S.C.C.) at 223.

75 *R. v. Gingras* (1992), 71 C.C.C. (3d) 53 (Alta. C.A.).

5) How do you attack the Crown's documentary and testimonial evidence?

Once a criminal tax trial actually starts, the same principles that apply to an ordinary criminal trial will also apply, with a few twists:

(a) *This is a document-intensive case*: As noted, criminal tax cases tend to have many documents. In the case of poor Mr. Jarvis, the Crown must prove that he sold art. That will require sales slips, credit card slips, cancelled cheques, bank statements, the sales journal (if he kept one) and possibly excerpts from the purchase journals of the galleries to which he sold the art. The Crown will have to show that he actually received the money for the art that was sold. This will also require cancelled cheques, bank statements, and the sales journal (again, if he kept one). Next, the Crown will need to prove *mens rea*. For that, accounting working papers, correspondence, and perhaps legal documents will be necessary. Then, of course, the Crown must prove that there was an amount of tax evaded. This will require calculations and either an affidavit or a live witness to show how the numbers were crunched. Your job as counsel is to prevent the admission of these documents, show that the Crown has not construed them correctly, or show that there were legitimate deductions.

(b) *There are probably offshore elements to the case*: Again, as noted, a very large red flag goes up when CRA sees transactions involving a tax haven — especially when there is frequent travel to a particular tax haven. A large red flag will probably go up with the jury as well. Most average taxpayers don't bank in the Caribbean and would not be likely to believe that anyone needs to, unless they are hiding money. The jury might believe that one trip to the Cayman Islands was a beach vacation. But three or four? Your best strategy might simply be to try and convince a judge that the prejudicial effect of the offshore elements to the case might outweigh the probative value and that the Crown should not be permitted to refer to them. Alternatively, you might argue that offshore transactions can be legitimate. At the end of the day, you should count yourself lucky that Mr. Jarvis never thought to bank offshore.

(c) *The witnesses are generally more sophisticated and professional than in typical criminal cases*: The Crown's witnesses in a tax trial are generally the accountants, the lawyers, the bankers, and perhaps third parties with whom the taxpayer has done business. In the case of Mr. Jarvis, the Crown would be likely to call Mr. Jarvis's accountant and perhaps his banker. The accountant would obviously testify that he received no instructions from Mr. Jarvis to include sales of art in Mr. Jarvis's return. The Crown would certainly call the gallery owners who purchased art from Mr. Jarvis.

(d) *There will be financial and banking analysis*: Usually the investigator will create an analysis of the flows of money and correlate it with the banking documents. The purpose will be to show that funds have ended up with Mr. Jarvis, and are therefore "taxable in his hands." The investigator will correlate all those pieces of paper representing financial transactions by putting them in a comprehensive and comprehensible package.

(e) *The Crown will try to make your client look bad*: In many tax cases this is not particularly difficult. The Crown will certainly do its best to make sure, in a casual and non-prejudicial way, that the judge or jury knows that your client happens to drive a Mercedes and live in a mansion, but reports no income. The rules of evidence generally do not permit the introduction of evidence where the prejudicial effect outweighs the probative value — but the taxpayer's lifestyle is often a relevant piece of evidence, especially if the Crown's case is based on a "net worth" assessment. However, it may also be only tangentially relevant. In that case, defence counsel would do well to bring the issue to the judge's attention so that the Crown is not permitted to entirely prejudice the defence in front of the jury. In this case, since Mr. Jarvis appeared to live quite simply, the Crown probably won't gain much traction from the issue.

6) Do you call a defence? Do you call your client?

As with running the trial itself, these questions are a matter of fact and judgment. There may be cases where you may wish to call third parties such as lawyers and/or accountants to explain how the client arranged his or her tax affairs, and why. You may also want to call your client. Doing so is always a risk. Many factors will come into play, including your perception of whether your client will be believed, the exposure to cross-examination and your judgment of how your client will fare, and whether it is better to have a judge or a jury listen to your client's evidence (as noted earlier, your decision as to mode of trial will also be influenced by whether or not you have to call your client). In the case of Mr. Jarvis, he might be a good client to call if you think that his age and obvious distraction at the death of his wife is likely to engender sympathy, particularly if you think that your judge or jury is already pre-disposed against CRA (remember that supreme strategic advantage). On the other hand, calling Mr. Jarvis could be dangerous if you think that he is unlikely to remain consistent and will be unable to explain his actions.

G. WHAT ARE THE CONSEQUENCES OF A CONVICTION? AN ACQUITTAL?

Things did not turn out all that well at trial for Mr. Jarvis. He was convicted of all the charges against him. Now he wants to know what can happen to him. Will he go to jail or just pay a fine? Or both? What can be done to keep him out of jail? And how will a criminal conviction affect his civil tax problems?

1) Can the *Kienapple* rule be applied?

It is a basic common law rule that multiple convictions cannot be entered for the same transaction.[76] This issue frequently arises in the context of charges under s. 239(1)(a) and s. 239(1)(d) of the *Income Tax Act*, where a misleading statement is made in a tax return such that the result is that tax is evaded. For example, if the reported income is deliberately understated or the deductions overstated, an offence contrary to s. 239(1)(a), then the natural and obvious result is that tax is wilfully evaded, an offence contrary to s. 239(1)(d). Although the elements of the two offences are distinct, they are often based on the same factual transaction, depending on the particular factual circumstances. In that situation, the court is required to enter a stay of proceedings on one of the alternative charges. Since s. 239(1)(d) is broader than s. 239(1)(a), it is certainly possible, however, that the *Kienapple* rule won't be applied.[77]

In this case, since Mr. Jarvis filed returns that were not only misleading in a material respect, but also evidence of an intention to wilfully evade taxes, you might have a good argument that a stay of proceedings should be entered on either the s. 239(1)(a) or the s. 239(1)(d) charges that have been laid in respect of each particular return. The rule obviously applies to *Excise Tax Act* charges as well.

---

76 *R. v. Kienapple* (1974), 15 C.C.C. (2d) 524 (S.C.C.); *R. v. Prince* (1986), 30 C.C.C. (3d) 35 (S.C.C.).

77 *R. v. Kidd* (1974), 21 C.C.C. (2d) 492 (Ont. H.C.).

2) What penalties is your client exposed to?

A conviction under the *Income Tax Act* or the *Excise Tax Act* exposes a taxpayer to a wide range of penalties or combination of penalties. Both the *Income Tax Act* and the *Excise Tax Act* provide for the imposition of mandatory fines and the possibility of imprisonment. Under both statutes, on summary conviction a court may impose fines between fifty and two hundred percent of the tax (or GST) sought to be evaded (or GST not remitted or GST refunds obtained fraudulently), as well as up to six months imprisonment per count. If convictions are registered after a trial by indictment, upon conviction the fine rises to between one and two hundred percent of the tax (or GST) sought to be evaded (or GST not remitted or GST refunds obtained fraudulently) as well as up to five years imprisonment per count.

If the Crown has laid *Criminal Code* fraud charges, as is frequently done in large and sophisticated tax evasion cases, there is no mandatory fine but the maximum term of imprisonment per count is ten years for a conviction under s. 380 of the *Code*. Recently Parliament increased the maximum penalty for fraud from ten to fourteen years in prison, and, for the first time, enumerated aggravating factors that a sentencing court may take into account and mitigating factors that may not be taken into account. For example, Parliament has recognized that since serious frauds are often committed by persons in a position of trust (and therefore able to use their good reputation in the community to further the fraud) evidence of previous good character may not be used as a mitigating factor on sentence.[78] Notwithstanding that the *Criminal Code* has no mandatory fine provision, large frauds usually attract significant fines or restitution orders.

One significant problem that Mr. Jarvis will face is the fact that he collected Goods and Services Tax and failed to remit it to the government. The *Excise Tax Act* deems those funds to be held in trust. The *Income Tax Act* deems source deductions (such as taxes deducted from employee payrolls, employment insurance premiums, and Canada Pension Plan contributions) also to be held in trust. The courts consider the failure to remit these funds to be a breach of trust, and breaches of trust are significant aggravating factors. Breaches of trust usually lead to jail sentences, and frequently to penitentiary sentences.

Section 731(1)(b) of the *Criminal Code* provides that a court may impose probation along with either a fine or imprisonment for less than two years, although not all three at the same time.

---

78 Bill C-13, above note 29, s. 380.1(2).

3) Has the tax been properly calculated?

If a conviction is registered, the court has no discretion with regard to the fact that a fine must be imposed. A fine is mandatory. The only discretion allowed to the court is the amount of the fine within the applicable range.

Although the Crown need only prove that an amount of tax was evaded (or sought to be evaded) to obtain a conviction under either s. 239(1)(a) or s. 239(1)(d) of the *Income Tax Act* (or the *Excise Tax Act*), even if it is only one dollar, the amount of tax actually evaded (or sought to be evaded) must eventually be calculated and proven for the benefit of the trial judge. The judge needs a number. That number is important so that the appropriate quantum of fine is applied.

Many defence counsel who conduct tax evasion trials do not question the Crown's tax calculations and overall numbers. This is often a tactical error. When the Crown wishes to prove a particular amount, it is required to call evidence, usually in the form of an affidavit from a CRA employee who has taken the information supplied by he investigator and simply calculated the taxes owed. Usually this consists of simply plugging the numbers supplied into a computer program and pressing a button.

Since the tax calculations are only as good as the numbers that were supplied, you can sometimes cross-examine the investigator as to the basis of the calculations in an effective way that deflates the amount of tax evaded. For example, did the "tax calculator" include the amount of paint that Mrs. Jarvis used in her paintings? How about the cost of canvases, marketing, and gasoline to take the paintings to galleries? This is one of those areas where criminal counsel is well-advised to consult with tax litigation counsel, or even retain tax litigation counsel to conduct the cross-examination.

4) Can you keep your client out of jail?

Maybe. Obviously the likelihood of a jail sentence is higher the more serious and sophisticated the offence. A large, sophisticated tax fraud is likely to attract a significant jail sentence.[79] For a more mundane offender the real question is whether a jail sentence will be imposed at all. Tax evaders of the lesser sort tend to attract either fines only or fines and conditional

79 For example: in *R v. Lawrence*, [1994] B.C.J. No. 355 (S.C.), 7 year sentences were imposed for a $17 million Scientific Research Tax Credit ("SRTC") fraud; in *R. v. Wilder*, 2004 BCSC 644 the principal player in a $36 million tax fraud received 9 years and a $5 million restitution order; in *R. v. Bellfield and Minchella*, 2003 DTC. 5659, the principal players received sentences of 7 and 10 years in addition to fines of $1 million in a large tax shelter fraud totalling over $100 million.

sentences. Tax evaders are often ideal candidates for a conditional sentence: They are usually first offenders, they usually are educated and have jobs, and they rarely are detained prior to trial, so they are able to continue working. They are also non-violent, and since they rarely breach their bail conditions (and are usually on bail for a long time, given the amount of time it takes to bring these kinds of cases to trial) they can usually point to a track record of complying with court orders. Under those circumstances, many tax evaders can satisfy the factors set out in *Proulx* for the imposition of a conditional sentence.[80]

5) The endgame: how do criminal tax proceedings affect civil tax proceedings?

Losing a criminal tax trial will prove to be very, very expensive for Mr. Jarvis. Not only is it possible that he will go to jail, but in addition to a hefty criminal fine he will face a harsh result in the Tax Court: Payment of the tax, payment of gross negligence penalties amounting to 150 percent of the tax, and interest on the tax evaded. And that is before even the mention of the cruellest penalty of all: your legal fees. Like many tax evaders, Mr. Jarvis may end up paying not only the tax he owed, but with interest, fines, and penalties he could pay triple or quadruple the actual amount evaded. And, he might still go to jail.

One of the most important questions for any counsel engaged in the defence of a client who has difficulties with CRA is the interplay between the criminal and civil tax proceedings. What happens in the criminal courts will have a significant impact on what occurs in the Tax Court. Bear in mind that the whole system is designed to make tax evasion very, very expensive. And it certainly can be.

Tax Court proceedings may be stayed while awaiting the outcome of criminal proceedings, since the outcome of the criminal proceedings will have a profound impact on the civil proceedings. If your client is convicted of an offence contrary to s. 239 of the *Income Tax Act* then it is almost impossible to win a civil tax proceeding based on the same facts. In other words, issue estoppel operates and the Tax Court will not find for your client where the Minister need only prove facts on a balance of probabilities after your client has been convicted beyond a reasonable doubt on the same facts. At the same time, an acquittal in a criminal proceeding does not in any way guarantee a successful result in the Tax Court — the Crown may not have the evidence to win a case beyond a reasonable doubt, but

80 *R. v. Proulx* (2000), 140 C.C.C. (3d) 149 (S.C.C.).

may well have enough to meet the balance of probabilities threshold in civil matters.[81] Where a guilty plea has been entered, as opposed to a finding after trial by a judge or a jury, there may be some room to argue that circumstances other than guilt beyond a reasonable doubt motivated the plea, and that issue estoppel should not fully apply.[82]

Of course, courts can give as well as take away. The Tax Court has jurisdiction to exclude evidence under s. 24(2) of the *Charter*, although, as in a criminal case, it is not required to do so. The exclusion of evidence is not automatic and the remedy will only be granted where "a flagrant and egregious violation of the appellant's rights" has taken place. Where that remedy is not sufficient to vindicate the taxpayer's rights, the Tax Court may also vacate assessments pursuant to s. 24(1) of the *Charter*.[83]

Where a criminal court makes a finding that evidence was obtained against your client in violation of the *Charter* and excludes the evidence under s. 24(2), that finding is not binding on the Tax Court but will obviously have a very persuasive effect. Thus, a favourable *Charter* ruling in the criminal proceeding will assist enormously in the Tax Court. Some *Charter* rulings, however, will only apply in a criminal context. A stay of criminal proceedings based on unreasonable delay under s. 11(b) of the *Charter* will not be binding on the Tax Court.

As noted, the Tax Court may also vacate assessments as a general s. 24(1) remedy. A finding by a criminal court that there has been an abuse of process that is so shocking that it rises to the level of the "clearest of cases" will obviously merit considerable deference by the Tax Court.[84]

Obviously, therefore, when counsel conduct proceedings in criminal courts, they must give very serious consideration as to how those proceedings will affect the client's subsequent position with the Appeals Division, and ultimately with the Tax Court. An unfavourable result will certainly not help your client's civil position, will be very expensive, and might still result in a criminal conviction and a term of imprisonment. On the other hand, while a favourable result in a criminal proceeding will not necessarily guarantee a favourable civil result, it will certainly be very helpful to your client's position.

---

81 *R. v. Van Rooy*, [1989] 1 F.C. 489 (C.A.).

82 *Hagon v. Her Majesty the Queen* (1999), 99 DTC 336 (T.C.C.).

83 *Her Majesty the Queen v. O'Niell Motors Limited*, [1998] 4 F.C. 180 (C.A.); *Donovan v. Her Majesty the Queen*, [2000] 4 F.C. 373 (C.A.).

84 *R. v. O'Connor*, above note 72; *R. v. Regan* (2002), 161 C.C.C. (3d) 97 (S.C.C.).

Chapter Eleven

The Litigation of a Transfer-Pricing Case[1]

Robert McMechan

A. INTRODUCTION

Although transfer-pricing provisions were introduced in Canadian tax legislation over 60 years ago, there are very few reported court cases involving transfer pricing.[2] This seems likely to change, given the number of transfer-pricing cases decided by the US Tax Court and the enormous growth in the International Tax Directorate of the Canada Revenue Agency (CRA) over the last several years.[3] This chapter offers a "bare bones" overview of the elements in a Tax Court appeal, where possible, put in a transfer-pricing context.

1 First published by the Canadian Tax Foundation in Report of Proceedings of the Fifty-Fourth Tax Conference, 2002 Conference Report (Toronto: Canadian Tax Foundation, 2003) and updated in 2004 for *Taxation and Advocacy in Canada*.

2 François Vincent, *Transfer Pricing in Canada: A Legal Perspective* (Toronto: Carswell, 2002).

3 See "Canada Customs and Revenue Agency—Taxing International Transactions of Canadian Residents," in Canada, *Report of the Auditor General to the House of Commons* (Ottawa: Public Works and Government Services, December 2002), chapter 4.

B. PLEADINGS

1) *Tax Court of Canada Rules (General Procedure)*

The *Tax Court of Canada Rules (General Procedure)*[4] provide that appeals are to be instituted by filing a notice of appeal. General Procedure Rule 48 of stipulates that every notice of appeal shall be in Form 21(1)(a).[5]

2) Contents and Function of Pleadings[6]

See the Federal Court of Appeal's Reasons for Judgment in *Smithkline Beecham Animal Health Inc. v. The Queen*,[7] partially reproduced below, for an example of the contents of a notice of appeal in a transfer-pricing case. This case was settled before trial in the Tax Court upon the basis that Revenue Canada's "CUP" (comparable uncontrolled price) adjustment of $67 million under now-repealed subsection 69(2) of the *Income Tax Act* was reduced to $51.5 million. Costs of $3.2 million for expert witnesses and document management were also paid to the Crown. The judgment was signed by Judge Bonner on December 16, 2003.

The following additional (non-transfer pricing) cases help to delineate the function of pleadings and provide guidelines for the contents of a notice of appeal.

a) *Lubrizol Corp. v. Imperial Oil Ltd.*[8]

Pleadings have a valuable function. The court expects parties to adhere to the rules of pleadings so that each side will know the case and the other is required to meet when it comes to trial. It may be said that it is the facts as pleaded and the issues defined in the pleadings that determine the relevancy of evidence, whether oral or documentary; and if the latter, whether a document must be produced before trial. That is why objections to pleadings are not merely technical or formal matters.

---

4 *Tax Court of Canada Rules (General Procedure)*, PC 1990-2121, SOR/90-688 (1990) vol. 124, no. 22 *Canada Gazette Part II* 4376-4476, as amended.

5 Form 21(1)(a) is reproduced in the appendix to this paper.

6 The case annotations in this paper are a selection from chapter 4 of *Tax Court Practice* by Robert McMechan and Gordon Bourgard, (Toronto: Carswell) (looseleaf), and are reproduced here with the permission of Carswell, a division of Thomson Canada Limited, Toronto, Ontario.

7 2002 F.C.A. 229; [2002] 4 C.T.C. 93 (F.C.A.).

8 [1996] 3 F.C. 40; 197 N.R. 241 (C.A.).

b) *Zelinski v. The Queen*[9]

A pleading must set forth a concise statement of the material facts upon which a party relies. Material facts are those that, if established at trial, will tend to show that the party pleading is entitled to the relief sought. The requirement for material facts has four elements:

1) every pleading must state facts, not conclusions of law;
2) it must not include immaterial facts;
3) it must state facts and not the evidence by which they are to be proved; and
4) it must state facts concisely in summary form.

c) *Archer v. M.N.R.*[10]

The court quoted the following passage from Holmested and Watson, *Ontario Civil Procedure*, vol. 2:[11]

> Pleadings are responsive written statements of position by the parties, with respect to the subject matter of the action, designed to define what are the issues in the case. This issue definition aids efficiency, since the parties and the court need not worry about matters which are agreed upon. More importantly, the information exchange provided by pleadings is essential to procedural fairness. The right to participate in the proceeding and to be heard are of limited value unless the party knows the case alleged against him so that he can marshal the relevant evidence and argument to meet it.

C. AMENDMENTS TO PLEADINGS

1) *Tax Court of Canada Rules (General Procedure)*

The need for amendments can be a result of the discovery of an omission in a pleading, the discovery of new facts after a pleading is filed, or a development in the law that affects the positions originally pleaded. Rule 54 governs amendments to pleadings:

> A pleading may be amended by the party filing it, at any time before the close of pleadings, and thereafter either on filing the consent of all other parties, or with leave of the Court, and the Court in granting leave may impose such terms as are just.

---

9 [2002] 1 C.T.C. 2422; 2002 D.T.C. 1204 (T.C.C.).
10 [1989] 2 C.T.C. 2300,at 2304; 89 D.T.C. 571 at 574 (T.C.C.).
11 (Toronto: Carswell, 1984) at paragraph 25(6).

2) Tax Court Ruling in *SmithKline Beecham Animal Health Inc. v. The Queen*[12]

The Tax Court ruled on an application by the Crown in the *SmithKline* case, for an amendment to permit the pleading of an alternative statutory basis for defending assessments of Part XIII tax.[13] The following extract from the Tax Court's decision sets out principles relevant to amending pleadings and the effect of subsection 152(9) of the *Income Tax Act* on the Crown's raising of alternative arguments for upholding an assessment after the limitation period for reassessing has expired. Bonner T.C.J. stated:

> [9] Counsel for the Respondent submits that the amendments are required for the purpose of determining one of the real questions in controversy, namely, whether the alleged overpayment by the Appellant to the affiliated corporations for cimetidine results in liability for Part XIII tax. Counsel points out that the Respondent does not seek to appeal the existing assessments by asserting a claim for more tax than already assessed. Rather, the objective is to ensure that it is open to the Respondent to defend the existing assessments by relying on statutory provisions which, when applied to material facts already pleaded, will support the assessments of Part XIII tax, either in whole or in part. Counsel relied on the general rule governing amendments as stated by the Federal Court of Appeal in *Canderel*[14] as follows:
>
> > [W]hile it is impossible to enumerate all the factors that a judge must take into consideration in determining whether it is just, in a given case, to authorize an amendment, the general rule is that an amendment should be allowed at any stage of an action for the purpose of determining the real questions in controversy between the parties. Provided, notably, that the allowance would not result in an injustice to the other party not capable of being compensated by an award of costs and that it would serve the interests of justice. . . .
>
> [14] In my view *Continental Bank*[15] was never authority for the proposition that the Minister is, when defending an appeal from an assessment after the expiry of the subsection 152(4) period, confined within a concep-

12 2000 D.T.C. 1526; [2000] 1 C.T.C. 2552 (T.C.C.).

13 *Income Tax Act*, RSC 1985, c. 1 (5th Supp.), as amended.

14 *The Queen v. Canderel Limited*, 93 D.T.C. 5357 at 5360; [1993] 2 C.T.C. 213 at 217 (F.C.A.).

15 *The Queen v. Continental Bank of Canada*, 98 D.T.C. 6501; [1998] 4 C.T.C. 77 (S.C.C.).

tual prison called "basis of assessment" comprising only the facts and statutory provisions relied upon by the assessor. In my view *Continental Bank* is an application of the long standing rule governing litigation in appellate courts which rule prevents litigants from raising points on appeal which were not pleaded and argued in the trial court.[16] Appellate courts cannot be expected to deal with a new issue on appeal resting on an evidentiary record which is deficient by reason of the failure to plead and direct evidence to that issue. Here the Respondent seeks leave to amend well before the commencement of the trial. The situation is in no way analogous to *Continental Bank*. . . .

[16] It is long settled law that the validity of an assessment depends on the application of the statute to the facts and not on the assessor's analysis. It is, I believe, unlikely that it was the intention of the Court in *Continental Bank* (*supra*) to overrule decisions such as *Minden*[17] and *Riendeau*[18] without referring to them. Accordingly, I am of the opinion that nothing said in *Continental Bank* (*supra*) can apply to prevent the Minister from relying on section 245 in the present case.

[17] In any event, I disagree with the Appellant's argument which essentially asserts that subsection 152(9) of the Act is inapplicable because the Minister is attempting by amendment to change the basis of assessment at a time when it is too late to do so by reason of subsection 152(4). When subsection 152(4) is read in the new statutory context which includes subsection 152(9), it is evident that it cannot be said that the legislature intended that the advancing of arguments in support of an existing assessment can constitute the exercise of the power to reassess. Section 152 differentiates between assessment and reassessment on the one hand and the appeal process on the other. What the Respondent seeks is an amendment to the Reply which will permit him to do precisely what the plain language of subsection 152(9) permits, namely, advance an alternative argument in support of the Part XIII assessment. He seeks to argue in the alternative that the existing assessment of tax is supported by provisions of the Act other than those relied upon by the assessor and this he is entitled to do.

[18] I turn next to the question whether leave to amend should be granted under section 54 of the *Tax Court of Canada Rules (General Procedure)*. A valuable summary of the law on this point may be found in the decision of the Federal Court of Appeal in *Canderel* (*supra*) at pages 5360

---

16 *The "Tasmania"* (1890), 15 App. Cas. 223 at 225 (H.L.).

17 *M.N.R. v. Minden*, 62 D.T.C. 1044 at 1050; [1962] C.T.C. 79 at 89 (Ex. Ct.).

18 *Riendeau v. The Queen*, 91 D.T.C. 5416 at 5417; [1991] 2 C.T.C. 64 at 65 (F.C.A.).

and 5361. It is not necessary to repeat it. The Appellant argues that it would suffer prejudice if the amendment is allowed. This argument is focused on the fact that a finding that the Appellant was under a duty to withhold based on section 245 and not on subsection 56(2) would change the identity of the primary non-resident taxpayer and person from whom the Appellant has a right of recovery of under subsection 215(6). In my view, the Appellant is not prejudiced. Allowing the amendment now will do nothing more than place the parties in the same position as if the Respondent had adequately raised section 245 in the first place. Counsel for the Appellant did not suggest that the discovery process would have to be reopened if leave to amend is granted. Nothing in the material suggests that the amendment sought would delay the expeditious trial of the matter. Failure to permit the amendment would have the effect of preventing the Court from considering a possibly relevant provision of the Act when deciding the case on its merits. If the assessment is upheld on the basis of section 245 the judgment will not change the identity of the person primarily liable for the Part XIII tax. Rather, it will identify the person, if there is one, who has been liable all along. . . .

[20] Finally, the Appellant argues that the amendment ought not to be allowed because the assessor made an informed decision not to use subsection 245(2). This circumstance has no bearing on the question whether the amendment ought to be allowed.

[21] An order will therefore issue permitting the amendment. The Appellant shall have costs of this application in any event of the cause.

3) The Federal Court of Appeal's Decision in *SmithKline Beecham Animal Health Inc. v. The Queen*[19]

The Federal Court of Appeal upheld the Tax Court's decision to permit the amendment sought, on the basis that the amendment was authorized as an alternative argument for upholding an assessment, within the meaning of s. 152(9) of the *Income Tax Act*. Sharlow J.A. stated:

> [1] We are all of the view that the Tax Court Judge was correct in characterizing the proposed amendment to the Crown's pleadings as a new argument in support of the assessment, and that subsection 152(9) of the *Income Tax Act* permitted the argument to be made.

The Supreme Court of Canada refused leave to appeal this decision.

---

19 2000 D.T.C. 6141 at 6142; [2000] 2 C.T.C. 329 at 329–30 (F.C.A.), leave to appeal denied [2000] S.C.C.A. no. 170.

4) Cases Regarding Amendments to Pleadings

Several further cases are helpful in understanding when amendments will be permitted by the Court if the opposing party refuses to consent to amendments.[20]

a) *Canderel Ltd. v. Canada*[21]

The general rule is that amendments to pleadings should be allowed for the purpose of determining the real question in controversy between the parties, provided that the allowance does not result in an injustice to the other party not capable of being compensated by an award of costs and that it serves the interests of justice. The question to be asked is whether, if the amendment is allowed, the other party will be in the same position as if the applicant had pleaded correctly in the first instance. However, the courts and the parties have a legitimate expectation in litigation coming to an end, and a late amendment raising a new issue may be seen as frustrating the course of justice. In the case of amendments sought at the end of a trial, there is a clear difference between allowing amendments that clarify the issues in dispute and allowing those that permit a distinct defence to be raised for the first time. Although leave to amend may be sought at any stage, the nearer the end of the trial a motion to amend is made, the more difficult it will be for the applicant to get through both the hurdles of injustice to the other party and the interests of justice. Factors to be considered include the timeliness of the motion; the extent to which the proposed amendments will delay the expeditious trial of the matter; the extent to which the original position of one party has led the other to follow a course of action that it would be difficult to alter; and whether the amendments sought will facilitate the court's consideration of the true substance of the dispute on the merits.

b) *Villeneuve v. The Queen* (1999)[22]

The court permitted the respondent to amend the reply to the notice of appeal to add an allegation of material fact concerning convictions of the appellant for conspiracy to smuggle liquor into Canada and unlawful possession of currency. The question of whether smuggling constituted a source of income to the appellant was held to be clearly relevant to the question of whether he disclosed his income from all sources in his returns of

20 See further case annotations regarding Rule 54 of the *General Procedure Rules* in chapter 4 of *Tax Court Practice*, above note 6.

21 [1993] 2 C.T.C. 213; 93 D.T.C. 5357 (F.C.A.).

22 [2000] 1 C.T.C. 2171; 2000 D.T.C. 1447 (T.C.C.).

income. The respondent was simply defending the Minister's net worth assessments by pleading a material fact that, if established, would tend to demonstrate that the assessments were well-founded. The amendment was therefore required in order to determine the real question in controversy.

D. LISTS OF DOCUMENTS

1) *Tax Court of Canada Rules (General Procedure)*

After the time specified in the *General Procedure Rules* for filing pleadings has closed, the parties to a tax appeal are obliged to file and exchange lists of documents. In a transfer-pricing context, this will almost invariably involve "full disclosure" of documents under Rule 82, as opposed to "partial" or "self-serving" disclosure of documents under Rule 81. Rule 82 provides as follows:

> 82.(1) The parties may agree or, in the absence of agreement, either party may apply to the Court for a judgment directing that each party shall file and serve on each other party a list of all the documents which are or have been in that party's possession, control or power relating to any matter in question between or among them in the appeal.
>
> (2) Where a list of documents is produced in compliance with this section, the list shall describe, in separate schedules, all documents relating to any matter in issue in the appeal,
>
> (a) that are in the party's possession, control or power and that the party does not object to producing,
>
> (b) that are or were in the party's possession, control or power and for which the party claims privilege, and the grounds for the claim, and
>
> (c) that were formerly in the party's possession, control or power, but are no longer in the party's possession, control or power, whether or not privilege is claimed for them, together with a statement of when and how the party lost possession or control of, or power over them and their present location.
>
> (3) A list of documents filed and served under this section shall be in Form 82(3).
>
> (4) A list of documents made in compliance with this section shall be verified by affidavit (Forms 82(4)A and 82(4)B),
>
> (a) if the party is an individual, by the party unless that person is under disability in which case the affidavit shall be made by that person's tutor, curator, litigation guardian or committee,

(b) if the party is a corporation or any body or group of persons empowered by law to sue or to be sued, either in its own name or in the name of any officer or other person, by any member or officer of such corporation, body or group, and
(c) if the party is the Crown, by any departmental or other officer of the Crown nominated by the Deputy Attorney General of Canada.

(5) The affidavit shall contain a statement that the party has never had possession, control or power of any document relating to any matter in issue in the proceeding other than those included in the list.

(6) The Court may direct a party to attend and be cross-examined on an affidavit delivered under this section.

2) Tax Court's Ruling in *SmithKline Beecham Animal Health Inc. v. The Queen*[23]

Judge Hamlyn reviewed the jurisprudence governing full disclosure of documents under General Procedure Rule 82 and ordered further production, where the Crown brought a motion in the Tax Court alleging insufficiency in the Appellant's list of documents:

> [15] Regarding relevancy of documents, from *Owen Holdings Ltd. v. R.*, [1997] 3 C.T.C. 351 (F.C.A.), at page 361:
>
> > [R]elevancy exists where the document sought may lead the party seeking discovery to a train of inquiry which may directly or indirectly advance its case or damage that of its adversary.
>
> [16] Regarding access to documents in a non-related, non-identical proceeding, in *AGT Ltd. v. Canada*, [1997] 2 C.T.C. 275 (F.C.A.), at page 284:
>
> > The fact that the documents in issue were prepared for another forum, namely providing CRTC with information required under a rate setting process, does not prevent the Minister from having access to them since they are relevant to the potential tax liability of the taxpayer.
>
> [17] Regarding confidentiality orders in relation to documents made in other Courts on consent. From *Miller (ED) Sales & Rentals Ltd. v. Caterpillar Tractor Co. et al. (no. 1)*, September 8, 1988, 90 A.R. 323, the Alberta Court of Appeal has concluded, at page 330, Laycraft, C.J.A., said:

---

23 (1998), 98 D.T.C. 1929; [1998] 4 C.T.C. 2331 (T.C.C.).

> I am unable to agree that a party can prevent production of a relevant document, otherwise subject to production, in a Canadian court by its own action (or inaction) in another jurisdiction.

[18] From *The Promex Group Inc. and The Queen*, [98 DTC 1588], 95-1950(IT)G, (T.C.C.), Judge Bowman of this Court has said at paragraph [55]:

> I find it somewhat absurd that a party to a proceeding in the Tax Court of Canada can refuse to produce relevant documents because it has, as a result of its own motion and on consent in another court, caused those documents to be covered by a confidentiality order—particularly long after the action in which the order was made has been dismissed.

Conclusion

[19] In relation to document production and in respect of the matter in question, the scope is broad, the relevancy threshold is low. . . .

Costs

[23] The ultimate reason for a costs award is the transparency of the relevancy issue in view of the jurisprudence and the threshold test of relevancy at the stage of document production.

[24] The relevance of the Dyson Report to the issues under appeal becomes clear from both a reading of the Reasons for Judgment of Justice Strayer of the Federal Court Trial Division in *Smith, Kline & French Laboratories Ltd.*,[24] and from the affidavit of Mr. Truckle. In the case of *Smith, Kline & French Laboratories Ltd.* (*supra*) it is clear that Justice Strayer regarded the Dyson report as having significant value in the determination of the costs, profits, and most importantly the differentiation between competing prices for cimetidine. From the affidavit of Mr. Truckle comes the evidence of the notes made by Wayne Voege as to the table of contents of the Dyson Report. Such descriptions in the table of contents as "comparison of actual cost to open market price of raw cimetidine" or "open market cost of raw cimetidine" were recorded by Mr. Voege during his inspection of documents at the offices of Gowling, Strathy & Henderson in Ottawa.

[25] From the Appellant's statement as to the issues in this appeal included "whether the amount paid by the Appellant to the Affiliates was

---

24 *Smith, Kline & French Laboratories Ltd. v. A.G. Can.* (1985), 24 D.L.R (4th) 321 (F.C.T.D.).

reasonable in the circumstances had they been dealing at arm's length," [it] is clear to me that the Dyson Report has real relevance in the determination of what price was, or would have been, reasonable in arm's length circumstances.

[26] The jurisprudence for section 82 of the Rules is clear that the test for relevance has a low threshold as to what documents are required to be listed. On the basis of the evidence before me it is obvious that the Dyson Report was, and is, relevant to issues under appeal. The Appellant should have at the very least listed the document in compliance with section 82 of the Rules. Had the Appellant an issue with its production, it should have listed it under paragraph 82(2)(b), and claimed privilege against its production.

E. EXAMINATION FOR DISCOVERY

1) *Tax Court of Canada Rules (General Procedure)*

Following the exchange of lists of documents, the parties to a transfer-pricing appeal normally conduct oral examinations for discovery in order to obtain admissions of fact and to find out as much as possible about the other party's case before trial. General Procedure Rules 92 and 95 govern examinations for discovery:

General
92. An examination for discovery may take the form of an oral examination or, at the option of the examining party, an examination by written questions and answers, but the examining party is not entitled to subject a person to both forms of examination except with leave of the Court.

Scope of Examination
95.(1) A person examined for discovery shall answer, to the best of that person's knowledge, information and belief, any proper question relating to any matter in issue in the proceeding or to any matter made discoverable by subsection (3) and no question may be objected to on the ground that,

(a) the information sought is evidence or hearsay,
(b) the question constitutes cross-examination, unless the question is directed solely to the credibility of the witness, or
(c) the question constitutes cross-examination on the affidavit of documents of the party being examined.

(2) Prior to the examination for discovery, the person to be examined shall make all reasonable inquiries regarding the matters in issue from all of the party's officers, servants, agents and employees, past or present,

either within or outside Canada and, if necessary, the person being examined for discovery may be required to become better informed and for that purpose the examination may be adjourned.

(3) A party may on an examination for discovery obtain disclosure of the findings, opinions and conclusions of an expert engaged by or on behalf of the party being examined that relate to a matter in issue in the proceeding including the expert's name and address, but the party being examined need not disclose the information or the name and address of the expert where,

(a) the findings, opinions and conclusions of the expert relating to any matter in issue in the appeal were made or formed in preparation for contemplated or pending litigation and for no other purpose, and
(b) the party being examined undertakes not to call the expert as a witness at the hearing.

(4) A party may on an examination for discovery obtain disclosure of the names and addresses of persons who might reasonably be expected to have knowledge of transactions or occurrences in issue in the proceeding, unless the Court orders otherwise.

2) Judge Bonner's Ruling on Refusal No. 28 in *SmithKline Beecham Animal Health Inc. v. The Queen*[25]

A ruling from Judge Bonner of the Tax Court outlines principles applicable at examination for discovery:

I will deal with refusal number 28.

This is an application by the respondent to compel the appellant to answer question 5003: what kind of markup would Franklin earn on a third party contract like that, that is to say a contract whereby Franklin was to produce a chemical other than cimetidine for a client that is not a member of the SmithKline Group of Companies.

The respondent argues that it is open to it to inquire into a document that is tab 6582 produced in the course of the discovery process. What the respondent, by its question seeks to determine is what mark-up Franklin would charge to an arm's length client.

The appellant objects. Appellant's counsel argues that the assessments in issue are CUP based assessments. CUP, which means comparative uncontrolled pricing, was what the Minister relied on as the basis of

25 September 2, 1999, court file no. 95-1077(IT)G (T.C.C.) [unreported].

reassessment. And, according to the appellant, the Minister did not rely on any sort of cost-plus analysis in making the assessment in issue. . . .

As I read the pleadings, the central fact in dispute is the amount that it would have been reasonable for the appellant to have paid or agreed to pay for cimetidine in the circumstances in which the chemical was purchased. That is the issue of fact and the respondent is not, in my view, confined in seeking to establish that fact, and in seeking to rebut the appellant's assertion that the amount is no less than the amount which the appellant in fact paid, or agreed to pay, to methodology adopted by the Minister in arriving at the figures which he used on assessment.

The principle which is to be applied is to be found in a passage in the Reasons for Judgment of the late Judge Christie in *Shell Canada Limited v. Her Majesty the Queen* at page 2213 where Judge Christie quotes from Holmested & Watson's work on the Ontario Civil Procedure as follows:

> It is a cardinal rule that discovery is limited by the pleadings. Discovery must be relevant to the issues as they appear on the record . . .

And the cases there are cited.

> . . . The party examining has no right to go beyond the case as pleaded and to interrogate concerning a case which he has not attempted to make by his pleadings. But "everything is relevant upon discovery which may directly or indirectly aid the party seeking discovery to maintain his case or to combat that of his adversary": . . .

And the case is cited as authority for that provision.

> . . . While clearly irrelevant matters may not be inquired into, relevancy must be determined by the pleadings construed with fair latitude: ibid. The court should not be called upon to conduct a minute investigation as to the relevance of each question and where the questions are broadly related to the issues raised, they should be answered.

On that principle, as I see it, the question in dispute is relevant to the issues raised by the pleadings in this case. The respondent is not, in my view, seeking to allow the Minister to appeal from his assessment or to advance a different basis of assessment where the respondent is seeking in this case to look into facts pertaining to the reasonableness in the circumstances of the price paid or agreed to be paid by the appellant.

Accordingly, I will order that the question be answered.

3) Reasons for Judgment of Federal Court of Appeal in *Smithkline Beecham Animal Health Inc. v. The Queen*[26]

The Federal Court of Appeal also outlined principles applicable at examination for discovery in an appeal from the Tax Court's refusal to require the Crown to produce information at discovery regarding the profitability of third parties. This decision is important because, *inter alia*, it refers to OECD transfer-pricing methodologies and sets out factors that are potentially relevant in the application of the comparable uncontrolled price (CUP) method. Sharlow J.A. stated:

> [1] This appeal raises the issue of scope of pre-trial discovery under the *Tax Court of Canada Rules (General Procedure)*, SOR/90-688a, as amended. The appellant Smithkline appeals the decision of the Tax Court, reported as *Smithkline Beecham Animal Health Inc. v. Canada*, 2001 D.T.C. 192, [2001] 2 C.T.C. 2086, [2001] T.C.J. No. 86 (T.C.C.), dismissing Smithkline's application to compel the Crown to disclose certain information in preparation for an appeal of assessments under Part I and Part XIII of the Income Tax Act, R.S.C. 1985, c. 1 (5th Supp.), as amended and predecessor statutes.
>
> [2] Smithkline is a manufacturer of pharmaceutical products. During the period relevant to this appeal, 1981 to 1986, Smithkline manufactured a drug named Tagamet, the active ingredient of which is cimetidine. During those years, Smithkline bought cimetidine from related corporations outside Canada. All of the assessments under appeal are based on the Crown's allegation that the price paid by Smithkline for cimetidine during that period was $66,982,990 more than would have been reasonable in the circumstances if SmithKline and its suppliers had been dealing at arm's length. . . .
>
> [5] Broadly speaking, Smithkline wishes to compel the production of documents and answers to questions asked in the examination for discovery of the Crown's nominee about the profitability of pharmaceutical manufacturers who are not parties to this appeal. Its entitlement to that information depends primarily on the pleadings. The relevant provisions in the pleadings read as follows:
>
> > *Notice of Appeal*[27]
> >
> > 9. During the relevant period, in the course of carrying on its business, the Appellant acquired SmithKline cimetidine from

26 Above note 7.

27 An Amended Notice of Appeal in appeal no. 95-1077(IT)G was filed in the Tax Court on November 13, 2002.

two corporations (hereinafter "Affiliates") resident outside Canada with whom the Appellant did not deal at arm's length as that phrase is used in subsection 69(2) of the Income Tax Act. The SmithKline cimetidine purchased by the Appellant during the relevant period was manufactured by the Affiliates in their respective dedicated manufacturing facilities i.e. no other products were produced in those facilities. . . .

22. During the reassessed period, in the case of each purchase of SmithKline cimetidine to which the Minister has purported to apply subsection 69(2) of the Income Tax Act in determining the amounts of the aforesaid reassessments, the amount that the Appellant paid or agreed to pay as price for SmithKline cimetidine was reasonable in the circumstances.

23. In the case of each purchase referred to in paragraph 22 *supra*, the price for SmithKline cimetidine that it would have been reasonable for the Appellant to have paid or agreed to pay a vendor in the same circumstances, had the vendor and the Appellant been dealing at arm's length, as that phrase is used in subsection 69(2) of the *Income Tax Act*, is no less than the amount that the Appellant in fact paid or agreed to pay to the Affiliates.

Amended Reply to Notice of Appeal[28]

9. In answer to paragraph 9 of the Notice of Appeal, he admits only that, during the relevant period, the Appellant acquired cimetidine from two corporations (the "Affiliates") resident outside Canada with which the Appellant did not deal at arm's length. He further says that: (a) the Appellant paid or agreed to pay to the Affiliates amounts for the cimetidine that were greater than the amounts that would have been reasonable in the circumstances if the Appellant and the Affiliates had been dealing at arm's length . . .

20. In answer to paragraphs 22 and 23 of the Notice of Appeal, he says that the Minister has applied subsection 69(2) of the *Income Tax Act* and denies that the amounts the Appellant paid or agreed to pay to the Affiliates for cimetidine, set out below, as the cost of goods sold, were reasonable in the circumstances. He says that the amounts that would have been reason-

---

28 A Reply to the Amended Notice of Appeal in appeal no. 95-1077(IT)G was filed in the Tax Court on December 12, 2002.

able in the circumstances if the Affiliates and the Appellant had been dealing at arm's length are set out below and he consequently disallowed amounts in excess thereof:

Year	Amount claimed as cost of goods sold	Reasonable amount	Difference	Amount disallowed (includes inventory adjustment)
1981	$28,601,108	$17,875,693	$10,725,415	$ 5,388,389
1982	$22,950,979	$ 9,818,953	$13,132,026	$13,803,842
1983	$21,869,720	$ 6,560,777	$15,308,943	$14,778,753
1984	$ 9,439,808	$ 2,241,133	$ 7,198,675	$ 9,731,626
1985	$13,642,098	$ 2,113,850	$11,528,248	$11,796,197
1986	$10,658,489	$ 1,568,806	$ 9,089,683	$ 6,421,868
1987	*	*		$ 5,062,315
		$66,982,990	$66,982,990	

* No transfer-pricing issue.

21. In assessing the Appellant under Part I of the *Income Tax Act*, the Minister, in addition to the facts stated in paragraph 20 hereof, made inter alia, the following assumptions of fact . . . [f] The Appellant paid or agreed to pay amounts aggregating $66,982,990 in excess of the price that would have been reasonable in the circumstances if the Appellant and the Affiliates had been dealing at arm's length during the relevant period. . . .

25. The Respondent respectfully submits that: (a) the amounts assessed under Part I of the *Income Tax Act* reflect that the amounts payable by the Appellant to the Affiliates for cimetidine were greater than the amounts that would have been reasonable in the circumstances if the Appellant and the Affiliates had been dealing at arm's length, within the meaning of subsection 69(2) of the *Income Tax Act* . . .

[6] To explain the significance of these pleadings, both parties rely on the 1979 OECD Guidelines (*Transfer Pricing and Multinational Enterprises: Report of the OECD Committee on Fiscal Affairs* (Paris: Organisation for Economic Co-operation and Development, 1979); there is at least one later edition of the OECD Guidelines, but in terms of the broad propositions to be considered in this case, the differences between the editions may be disregarded).

[7] The OECD Guidelines are referred to in Information Circular 87-2, *International Transfer Pricing and Other International Transactions*, dated February 2, 1987, which is intended to advise taxpayers about international transfer pricing issues. Information Circular 87-2 was cancelled on September 27, 1999 and replaced by Information Circular 87-2R, *International Transfer Pricing*, which also refers to OECD Guidelines.

[8] It appears to be common ground that the OECD Guidelines inform or should inform the interpretation and application of subsection 69(2) of the *Income Tax Act*. The OECD Guidelines state the principles for determining international transfer prices and, where possible, the agreement among OECD members with respect to the practices to be followed. According to the OECD Guidelines, there are a number of methods for determining an arm's length price in the context of international transactions. The method that is said to be in principle the most appropriate and in theory the easiest is the comparable uncontrolled price method, or "CUP" method. In general, the CUP method requires a direct reference to prices in comparable transactions between enterprises that are independent of each other.

[9] The OECD Guidelines also describe a number of other pricing methods that could be used in situations where the CUP method cannot be used. For example, the CUP method cannot be used if reliable information as to comparability cannot be obtained, or the available comparisons result in too many unquantifiable differences.

[10] The basis for the assessments under appeal is the Crown's determination of the "arm's length price" for cimetidine, using the CUP method. The comparator transactions are purchases of cimetidine by three manufacturers of generic pharmaceutical products, F.S. Horner Ltd., Apotex Ltd. and Novopharm Ltd.

[11] Following the close of pleadings, both parties produced lists of documents and copies of the documents themselves. The parties have also conducted examinations for discovery. The Crown's nominee for examination for discovery is Tim Truckle. The main session of the examination was completed on February 23, 1999, subject to the usual reservations as to questions arising from undertakings, advisements and refusals. . . .

[19] Counsel for the Crown objected to . . . questions on the basis that Revenue Canada had not made any comparisons between the profitability or profit margins of Smithkline and other pharmaceutical companies, and that the questions did not arise out of any answers given in the examination for discovery or in subsequent correspondence relating to the examination for discovery. . . .

[22] The *Tax Court of Canada Rules (General Procedure)* contain extensive and detailed rules for pre-trial disclosure of documents and oral examinations for discovery. The main provisions relating to the issues in this appeal read as follows. [Rule 82 is quoted at page 199 above; Rules 92 and 95.1 are quoted at page 202 above.]

[23] There are numerous additional rules that apply if material provided under these rules needs to be corrected or supplemented, or if there is a question about the accuracy or completeness of the material provided.

[24] The scope and application of these rules quoted above depend upon the meaning of the phrases "relating to any matter in question between . . . them in the appeal" and "relating to any matter in issue in the proceeding." In *Compagnie Financiere et Commerciale du Pacifique v. Peruvian Guano Company* (1882), 11 Q.B.D. 55 (C.A.), Brett, L.J. said this about the meaning of the phrase "a document relating to any matter in question in the action" (at page 63):

> It seems to me that every document relates to the matters in question in the action, which not only would be evidence upon any issue, but also which, it is reasonable to suppose, contains information which may—not which must—either directly or indirectly enable the party requiring the affidavit either to advance his own case or to damage the case of his adversary. I have put in the words "either directly or indirectly," because, as it seems to me, a document can properly be said to contain information which may enable the party requiring the affidavit either to advance his own case or to damage the case of his adversary, if it is a document which may fairly lead him to a train of inquiry, which may have either of these two consequences. . . .

[29] The cases . . . establish that the question of whether a document or question "relates to" an issue in the case depends upon a reasonable interpretation of the pleadings, see particularly: *Compagnie Financiere, supra; Boxer v. Reesor* [(1983), 43 B.C.L.R. 352 (S.C.)]; and *The Queen v. Special Risks Holdings Inc.*, [1983] 2 F.C. 743, 46 N.R. 361, [1983] C.T.C. 36, 83 D.T.C. 5046 (F.C.A.).

[30] In this case, the Tax Court Judge cited *R. v. Stinchcombe*, [1991] 3 S.C.R. 326 as the basis of his understanding of the test of relevance at the pre-trial discovery stage. This appears at paragraph 10 of his reasons:

> On discovery the examining party may seek information and admissions which will assist it not only to defeat its opponent's case but also to advance the case which it seeks to put forward.

[31] In my view, this statement of the test is substantially the same as the "train of inquiry" test and thus is correct. It remains only to consider the argument of Smithkline that the test has not been correctly applied in this case.

[32] In this regard, it must be recalled that the Crown, based on the OECD Guidelines, has chosen to employ the CUP method for determining an arm's length price for cimetidine. However, the OECD Guidelines also describe alternative pricing methods that the Crown has chosen not to employ. The choice of method depends upon finding appropriate comparators, which in turn depends upon analysis of points of difference and similarity between the structure, operations and activities of Smithkline and the various candidates for comparison (in this case, potentially all other Canadian pharmaceutical manufacturers). That might, at least in theory, include such things as profit margins and profitability.

[33] At the commencement of the pre-trial discovery process, Smithkline might have had a basis for attempting to discover information in the possession of the Crown that could lead to a train of inquiry that would explain why and how the CUP method was used in this case, or that would discredit either the use of the CUP method or the manner in which it was used, including the choice of comparator. In theory, such information might be subject to disclosure even if the Crown undertook not to use it at trial, because such an undertaking would not derogate from the fact that the information might have proven to be of assistance to Smithkline in strengthening its own case or weakening that of the Crown.

[34] However, in this case, the examinations for discovery took quite a different course, with the result that it is not necessary to reach any conclusions as to whether information about the profitability or profit margins of other pharmaceutical manufacturers is discoverable in pre-trial proceedings on the basis of a liberal reading of the pleadings. Nor is it necessary to deal with the arguments of the Crown that the degree of relevance associated with the requested information is so marginal that it would not justify the extraordinary effort it would require for the Crown to assemble and present it, or that section 241 of the *Income Tax Act* obliges the Crown to keep the information confidential despite Smithkline's entitlement to pre-trial discovery.

[35] Prior to the commencement of the examination for discovery, Smithkline must have been aware of the theoretical connection between subsection 69(2) of the *Income Tax Act* and the many factual problems that may arise when trying to compare enterprises and their transactions. If information about the relative profit margins and profitability of potentially compara-

ble pharmaceutical manufacturers was ever in the Crown's possession (and there is a factual dispute on that question), the door to its discoverability closed on February 23, 1999 when counsel for Smithkline completed the examination for discovery of Mr. Truckle without asking for it.

[36] The door could have been reopened in one of two ways. First, it could have been reopened with leave of the Tax Court in a motion under subsection 93(1) of the *Tax Court of Canada Rules (General Procedure)*. The hurdle faced by Smithkline in a motion to reopen an examination for discovery is well illustrated by the following comments of Prothonotary Hargrave in *McLeod Lake Indian Band v. Chingee* (1998), 149 F.T.R. 113 (T.D.), dealing with a similar provision of the *Federal Court Rules, 1998*. He said this at paragraph 18 (emphasis added):

> To require Harry Chingee, whose discovery has been concluded, to answer further questions, the Plaintiffs must establish a special reason to do so. Here I have in mind Rule 235 which provides that "Except with the leave of the Court, a party may examine for discovery any adverse party only once." This rule is a watering down of what was, until 1990, Rule 465(19) which required special reason in an exceptional case in order to obtain further discovery. The present form of the rule, however, ought not to be interpreted so as to easily allow further discovery, once an examination has been concluded, for *discovery must, at some point, come to an end*. In the present instance I would deny further discovery because the material on which counsel wishes to examine was available at the time of the discovery of Harry Chingee and, with diligence, might have been [put] to him at that time.

[37] Second, the door could have been reopened in the context of a question arising out of information provided after February 23, 1999 to fulfill an undertaking, to correct or clarify a previous answer, to answer a question taken under advisement, or to answer a question to which an objection had been made.

[38] Counsel for Smithkline argues that the Crown, in its various letters after February 23, 1999 culminating in the October 20, 2000 letter, opened the door by implicitly suggesting a comparison between the profit margins and profitability of Smithkline and other companies. I do not interpret the Crown's comments in those letters as suggested by counsel for Smithkline. The Tax Court Judge correctly held that those comments address Smithkline's own circumstances and nothing more.

[39] In my view, the Tax Court Judge was correct to refuse the motion to require the Crown to respond to the questions referred to above. I would dismiss this appeal with costs.

F. EXPERT WITNESSES

1) *Tax Court of Canada Rules (General Procedure)*

Transfer-pricing appeals will generally not be conducted without parties adducing expert evidence. Rule 145 governs the introduction of expert evidence at trial:

145.(1) In this section, "affidavit" includes,

(a) a solemn declaration made under section 41 of the *Canada Evidence Act*,

(b) a statement in writing signed by the proposed witness and accompanied by a certificate of counsel that counsel is satisfied that it represents evidence that the proposed witness is prepared to give in the matter, or

(c) a statement in writing in any other form authorized by direction of the Court in a particular case and for special reasons.

(2) Unless otherwise directed by the Court, no evidence in chief of an expert witness shall be received at the hearing in respect of an issue unless,

(a) the issue has been defined by the pleadings or by written agreement of the parties stating the issues,

(b) a full statement of the proposed evidence in chief of the witness has been set out in an affidavit, the original of which has been filed and a copy of which has been served on all other parties, not less than thirty days before the commencement of the hearing, and

(c) the witness is available at the hearing for cross-examination.

(3) Unless otherwise directed by the Court, no evidence of an expert witness shall be led in rebuttal of any evidence tendered in writing under paragraph (2)(b) unless the rebuttal evidence has been reduced to writing in accordance with this section, and the original filed and a copy served on all the other parties not less than fifteen days before the commencement of the hearing.

(4) Subject to compliance with subsection (2), evidence in chief of an expert witness may be given at the hearing by,

(a) reading the whole or part of the affidavit into evidence by the witness, unless the Court, with the consent of the parties, permits it to be taken as read, and

(b) if the party calling the witness so elects, the verbal testimony of the witness,

  (i) explaining or demonstrating what is in the affidavit or the part that has been given in evidence, and

  (ii) in respect of other matters by special leave of the Court, upon such terms as may be just.

(5) A witness shall not be cross-examined before the hearing on an affidavit filed under subsection (2) without leave of the Court, and if such leave is granted, the witness shall not be cross-examined at the hearing without leave of the Court but the witness may, with leave of the Court, be produced for re-examination and shall be produced for examination by the Court, if the Court so requires.

(6) An affidavit filed under subsection (2) shall not become part of the evidence at the hearing unless given in evidence under subsection (4).

2) Cases Regarding Testimony by Expert Witnesses

There is a wide body of jurisprudence concerning the admissibility and weight of expert opinion evidence.

a) *D.D. v. The Queen*[29]

A basic tenet of our law is that a witness may not give opinion evidence but may testify only to facts within his or her knowledge, observation, and experience. However, since the fourteenth century, common law courts have recognized that certain exceptional issues require the application of special knowledge that lies outside the experience of the trier of fact. Expert opinion evidence became admissible as an exception to the rule against opinion evidence in those cases where it was necessary to provide "a ready-made inference which the judge and jury, due to the technical nature of the facts, are unable to formulate." Expert opinions are sometimes derived from academic literature and out-of-court interviews, which material is unsworn and is not available for cross-examination. Expert evidence is time-consuming and expensive. Modern litigation has introduced a proliferation of expert opinions of questionable value. The significance of the costs to the parties and the resulting strain upon judicial resources cannot

29 [2000] 2 S.C.R. 275; 191 D.L.R. (4th) 60.

be overstated. When the door to the admission of expert evidence is opened too widely, a trial has the tendency to degenerate into a contest of experts, with the trier of fact acting as referee in deciding which expert's evidence to accept. It is not enough that an expert's opinion will be helpful for it to meet the requirement of necessity. The expert's opinion should be admitted in evidence only where a wrong conclusion is likely to be reached without expert evidence or where access to important information will be lost unless it is obtained from experts.

b) *R. v. J.-L.J*[30]

The trial judge must be a gatekeeper when presented with expert evidence. The trial judge should scrutinize its admissibility at the time it is proffered, and not allow it too easy an entry on the basis that frailties go to weight rather than to admissibility. The court in *R. v. Mohan* (discussed below) established criteria against which the admissibility of expert evidence must be judged. The threshold requirement is that ordinary people would be unlikely to form the correct opinion about the subject if unassisted by persons with special knowledge. Novel scientific theory or technique may be admissible if it meets the reliable foundation test. The closer an opinion comes to the ultimate issue the more it should be scrutinized. The expert must be properly qualified, and the expert's evidence must be relevant when tested on a cost-benefit basis. But before any weight at all can be given to an expert's opinion, the facts upon which the opinion is based must be found to exist.

c) *R. v. Warsing*[31]

In many cases, the evidence of experts depends on the hypotheses or assumptions that they are asked to make. The value of the opinion depends on the validity of the assumptions, but that relates to weight, not to admissibility. The more the expert relies on facts not in evidence, the less the weight to be given to the opinion. Self-reported facts raise questions of weight.

d) *R. v. Mohan*[32]

Admission of expert evidence depends on the application of the following criteria: (1) relevance; (2) necessity in assisting the trier of fact; (3) the absence of any exclusionary rule; and (4) a properly qualified expert. Evidence may be logically relevant and hence *prima facie* admissible, yet still

---

30 [2000] 2 S.C.R. 600; 37 C.R. (5th) 203.

31 21 C.R. (5th) 75; [1998] 3 S.C.R. 579 (S.C.C.).

32 [1994] 2 S.C.R. 9; 89 C.C.C. (3d) 402.

be excluded if its probative value is overborne by its prejudicial effect, if it involves an amount of time that is not commensurate with its value or if it is misleading in that its effect is out of proportion to its reliability. For the evidence to be necessary, it must provide information that is outside the experience or knowledge of the trier of fact so that the trier would be unlikely to form a correct judgment about the evidence without the assistance of someone with special knowledge. The expert evidence must not fall afoul of some rule of evidence separate and apart from the opinion rule. Finally, the evidence must be given by a witness who is shown to have acquired special or peculiar knowledge through study or experience. Expert evidence that advances a novel scientific theory, technique, or approaches and an opinion on an ultimate issue is subjected to special scrutiny.

e) *R. v. B.(R.H.)*[33]

The fundamental requirement for expert evidence is that it assist the trier of fact on a technical or scientific matter. Expert evidence on matters of fact should not be excluded simply because it suggests answers to issues that are at the core of the dispute before the court. Experts may rely on hearsay in giving their opinion, but the judge must then assess the weight to be given to the opinion.

f) *R. v. Marquard*[34]

The only requirement for the admission of expert opinion is that the witness possesses special knowledge and experience going beyond that of the trier of fact. Deficiencies go to weight, not to admissibility. Admissibility does not depend on how the skill was acquired as long as the court is satisfied the witness has sufficient experience.

g) *R. v. Seaboyer*[35]

The opinion evidence rule is less a rule of exclusion than a means of setting certain conditions for the reception of evidence that might otherwise be unreliable. Provided that the witness can be shown to be qualified to give the opinion, and provided that the opinion is relevant and does not trench unduly on the judge's or the jury's ultimate task, it may be received. Considerable discretion rests with the trial judge in weighing the proper considerations.

---

33 [1994] 1 S.C.R. 656; 89 C.C.C. (3d) 193.

34 [1993] 4 S.C.R. 223; 25 C.R. (4th) 85.

35 [1992] 7 C.R. (4th) 117; 6 C.R.R. (2d) 35 (S.C.C.).

h) *R. v. Lavallee*[36]

As long as there is some admissible evidence to establish the foundation for the expert's opinion, it cannot be completely ignored. The more the expert relies on facts not proved in evidence, the less the weight given to the opinion. Sopinka J, concurring, said at 365 (C.C.C.):

> Where, however, the information upon which an expert forms his or her opinion comes from the mouth of a party to the litigation, or from any other source that is inherently suspect, a court ought to require independent proof of that information. The lack of such proof will . . . have a direct effect on the weight to be given to the opinion, perhaps to the vanishing point.

i) *Saint John (City) v. Irving Oil Co.*[37]

The fact that a real estate appraiser had based his opinion of value on calculations made from unrecorded interviews with numerous persons who had been parties to comparable sales, none of whom had been called to testify, did not render the opinion inadmissible. It was not the direct facts of each of the comparable transactions that were at issue, but rather the value of the opinion. The nature of the source upon which such an opinion is based cannot have any effect on its admissibility. Any frailties that may be alleged concerning the information upon which the opinion was founded are relevant only in assessing the weight to be attached to that opinion.

3) Testimony of Expert in *Cudd Pressure Control Inc. v. The Queen*[38]

The following extract from a trial transcript is an example of expert opinion evidence given in a transfer-pricing case. The expert testified about the necessity for the identification of a sufficient number of transactions, in comparable circumstances, before the CUP method can be applied, and about the necessity for comparables to be chosen from the same level of the relevant industry as the transaction under scrutiny:

> *Examination in chief:*
>
> Q. Miss Holgate, when did you first become a Chartered Accountant.

---

36 [1990] 1 S.C.R. 852; 55 C.C.C. (3d) 97.

37 [1966] S.C.R. 581; 58 D.L.R. (2d) 404 (S.C.C.).

38 *Cudd Pressure Control Inc. v. The Queen*, "Response to Application for Leave To Appeal in the Supreme Court of Canada Before the Honourable Judge A.A. Sarchuk, on Monday, the 18th Day of November, 1993"; court file no. 91-2257 (IT) (T.C.C.) [unreported].

MR. WARD: I would be prepared to admit that Miss Holgate is qualified as an expert for the purposes of giving evidence.

HIS HONOUR: Very well.

Cross-examination

Q. Well, we've heard from the Cudd representatives and we've heard from other people in the industry that everybody seems to know that it's available.

A. Sorry, what is available?

Q. That these comparable "arm's-length" rent values are available in this industry.

A. The fact that the equipment is available for rent does not prove that there has been a sufficient number of transactions in comparable circumstances on which to rely. If there were to be a publicly available base of information such as that, I would concur that, yes, it would become a viable option.

Q. Well, you read the testimony of the representatives of Cudd, who testified that at least that company has, in the ordinary course of its business, often leased its equipment on a stand-by basis at the price set out in the rate book?

HIS HONOUR: Mr. Ward, they didn't lease their equipment. They were providing a service, part of which was a stand-by charge for those days when they didn't have their staff there, and to say there was a lease, I think, is incorrect, with respect.

MR. WARD: I agree. There was no lease document. There was an agreement to pay for the presence of the equipment on the site.

HIS HONOUR: As part of their overall service contract.

MR. WARD: In the course of their service contract.

THE WITNESS: And I would have to say that does not appear to me to be a comparable circumstance.

By Mr. Ward
Q. What's different about that?

A. In the first case they would have to look at the level of the industry. I would suggest here we're looking at two geographic segments, branches of the same entity, so we're looking at a single entity operating in two places.

Now, the Canadian branch deals with customers and the U.S. branch deals with customers, but I would suggest that a transaction between a U.S. branch and its customer is not necessarily comparable to a transaction between the U.S. branch and the Cudd branch.

Although we're assuming a hypothetical situation, I think we are all aware that it's not an "end use" customer. If there is a distinction to be made between the level and the market, it should be a level between a service industry and a sub-contractor service industry, [rather] than dealing with an ultimate customer.

So I find it inappropriate to compare transactions per se between a service industry and an ultimate customer, to a service industry and another service industry.[39]

G. TRIAL

A decision of the Tax Court in *Glaxo Smithkline Inc. v. The Queen* deals with the effect at trial of failing to comply with a requirement made by the Minister under section 231.6 of the *Income Tax Act* for the provision of foreign-based information and documents.[40] The Minister had sought, *inter alia*, the production of comparative data on the chemical ranitidine hydrochloride produced by Glaxochem (PTE) Ltd. in Singapore, in relation to ranitidine hydrochloride produced from other sources/suppliers.

No application had been made to have the requirement varied or set aside under s. 231.6(4), and only one document had been produced to the Minister pursuant to the requirement. The evidence before the Court on a motion brought by the Crown to exclude any other foreign-based information or document covered by the requirement at trial established that there were at least two hundred documents (and perhaps many more) that would be affected by an exclusion order under s. 231.6(8) of the Act.

Judge Bowie noted that since the requirement was written by the Minister, and the consequences of non-compliance by the taxpayer are far-reaching, it should be read *contra proferentem*. Judge Bowie also found that the effect of an order under s. 231.6(8) might in some circumstances

39 This extract is from transcript page 141, lines 24–25; page 142, lines 1–5; page 191, lines 15–25; page 192, lines 1–25 and page 193, lines 1–19, before the Honourable Judge A.A. Sarchuk, November 18, 1993; Tax Court of Canada file no. 91-2257 (IT).

40 *Glaxo Smithkline Inc. v. The Queen*, [2003] 4 C.T.C. 2916 (T.C.C.).

infringe a taxpayer's right to a fair hearing. This could occur, for example, if the Crown chose to put into evidence one document which was the subject of the order, whereas there was another document subject to the order which contradicted or qualified the first document. Having regard to the jurisprudence involving remedies which are available under paragraph 2(e) of the *Canadian Bill of Rights* where a person would otherwise be deprived of the right to a fair hearing, Judge Bowie concluded that all that was needed in order to prevent injustice was that the trial judge have the power to permit the taxpayer to proffer evidence in rebuttal that would otherwise be excluded by subsection 231.6(8) of the Act.

The conduct of transfer-pricing trials before the Tax Court is governed by General Procedure Rules 133 through 146.[41] However, the most conspicuous trial involving transfer pricing in recent times does not owe its existence to a tax assessment. *Ford Motor Company of Canada, Limited v. OMER*[42] was an action under s. 190 of the *Canada Business Corporations Act*[43] and s. 185 of the *Business Corporations Act* (Ontario)[44] brought in the Superior Court of Justice of Ontario. This case involved expert transfer-pricing opinion evidence during 49 days of trial dealing with issues concerning the valuation of shares and the oppression of minority shareholders. Mr. Justice Cumming released Reasons for Decision on January 22, 2004, in which he found that the operating results of Ford Canada over 1985–1995 were not consistent with arm's length results and that the profit split method utilized by one of the transfer pricing experts provided adjusted results that were more reasonable than reported results. Under that method $3.06 billion would be added to the profits of Ford Canada for the period 1985–1995 and also deducted from the profits of Ford U.S. Justice Cumming also accepted the expert opinion of a second transfer-pricing expert using different methodologies which showed that Ford Canada's profits were understated by $2.573 billion.[45]

H. CONCLUSION

Given the fact-intensive nature of transfer-pricing disputes, the sizeable number of documents that can be involved, and the large amounts of

---

41 See the text of these rules and related annotations in *Tax Court Practice*, above note 6.

42 *Ford Motor Company of Canada, Limited v. OMER*, [2000] O.J. no. 1480 (Sup. Ct.); [1999] O.J. No. 1263 (Gen. Div.).

43 R.S.C. 1985, c. C-44, as amended.

44 R.S.O. 1990, c. B.16, as amended.

45 *Ford Motor Company*, above note 42.

money that are in issue, transfer-pricing litigation is likely to be both expensive and time-consuming. Nevertheless, the enormous importance of transfer-pricing to the Canadian tax base and to the profits of multinational corporations suggests that there is likely to be a lot more of it.[46]

46 The transfer-pricing appeals in the Tax Court at this time are *GlaxoSmithKline Inc. v. The Queen*, court file no. 98-712(IT)G; *Hoffman-LaRoche Limited v. The Queen*, court file no. 2000-935(IT)G; *Pacific Ammonia v. The Queen*, court file no. 2002-81(IT)G; *Attila Dogan Design & Construction Ltd. v. The Queen*, court file no. 2002-3833(IT)G; *Attila Dogan Design & Construction Ltd. v. The Queen*, court file no. 2002-3836(IT)G; *BMO Nesbitt Burns Inc. as successor to Burns Fry Limited v. The Queen*, court file no. 2002-3137(IT)G; *Norand Data Systems v Her Majesty the Queen*, court file no. 2003-3525(IT)G; and *Canada Safeway v. The Queen*, 2003-2925(IT)G.

APPENDIX

General Procedure Form 21(1)(a)

Notice of Appeal—General Procedure

TAX COURT OF CANADA

BETWEEN:

[name], Appellant,

and

HER MAJESTY THE QUEEN, Respondent

NOTICE OF APPEAL

(a) In the case of an individual state home address in full and in the case of a corporation state address in full of principal place of business in the province in which the appeal is being instituted,
(b) Identify the assessment(s) under appeal: include date of assessment(s) and if the appeal is under the *Income Tax Act* include taxation year(s) or if the appeal is under the *Excise Tax Act* include the period to which the assessment(s) relate(s),
(c) Relate the material facts relied on,
(d) Specify the issues to be decided,
(e) Refer to the statutory provisions relied on,
(f) Set forth the reasons the appellant intends to rely on,
(g) Indicate the relief sought, and
(h) Date of notice.

____

(Signature)

Address for service, telephone number, fax number if any, of appellant's counsel or, if appellant is appearing in person, state telephone number.

Chapter Twelve

The Use of Expert Witnesses in Tax Litigation*

Alan M. Schwartz and Edward T. Yanoshita

A. INTRODUCTION

> But at the end of the day, the expert's role is limited to providing the court with a set of prescription glasses through which technical information may be viewed before being analyzed and weighed by the trial judge. Undoubtedly, each opposing expert witness will attempt to ensure that its focal specifications are adopted by the court. However, it is the prerogative of the trial judge to prefer one prescription over another.[1]

The use of expert witnesses in tax litigation has become almost routine. At common law, expert evidence is admissible in cases where the subject-matter of the inquiry is such that "ordinary people are unlikely to form a correct judgment about it, if unassisted by persons with special knowledge."[2]

In such cases, expert witnesses are permitted to state their opinion on the subject matter, of which they have specialized knowledge, in order to

---

* The authors wish to express their appreciation to Robert S. Harrison, an experienced cross-examiner of expert witnesses, for his thoughtful suggestions. Any inaccuracies remain the responsibility of the authors.

1 Robertson, J.A. in *RIS-Christie Ltd. v. The Queen*, 99 D.T.C. 5087 (F.C.A.), at 5089.

2 *R. v. J.- L.J.*, [2000] 2 S.C.R. 600, 37 C.R. (5th) 203, at p. 627 citing Sopinka, J. in *R. v. Mohan*, [1994] 2 S.C.R. 9, 18 O.R. (3d) 160n, 114 D.L.R. (4th) 419.

assist the judge and jury in correctly interpreting the facts before them.[3] The role of the expert witness has been described by Dickson J. (as he then was) in an often quoted passage in *R. v. Abbey*:[4]

> Witnesses testify as to facts. The judge or jury draws inferences from the facts. "In the law of evidence 'opinion' means any inference from observed fact, and the law on the subject derives from the general rule that witnesses must speak only to that which was directly observed by them" (*Cross on Evidence*, at p. 442). Where it is possible to separate fact from inference the witness may only testify as to fact. It is not always possible, however, to do so and the "law makes allowances for these borderline cases by permitting witnesses to state their opinion with regard to matters not calling for special knowledge whenever it would be virtually impossible for them to separate their inferences from the facts on which those inferences are based" (*ibid.*).
>
> With respect to matters calling for special knowledge, an expert in the field may draw inferences and state his opinion. An expert's function is precisely this: to provide the judge and jury with a ready-made inference which the judge and jury, due to the technical nature of the facts, are unable to formulate. "An expert's opinion is admissible to furnish the court with scientific information which is likely to be outside the experience and knowledge of a judge or jury. If on the proven facts a judge or jury can form their own conclusions without help, then the opinion of the expert is unnecessary" (Turner (1974), 60 Crim. App. R. 80, at p. 83, per Lawton L.J.).

Whether a judge or jury can form their own conclusions without the aid of experts is a question of fact in each case.[5] Courts have expressed concern about the dangers of allowing expert evidence into the courtroom without safeguards:

> The primary danger arising from the admission of any opinion evidence is that the province of the jury might be usurped by that of the witness. This danger is especially prevalent in cases of expert opinion evidence. Faced with an expert's impressive credentials and mastery of scientific jargon, jurors are more likely to abdicate their role as fact-finders and simply attorn to the opinion of the expert in their desire to reach a just result.[6]

---

3 John Sopinka, Sidney N. Lederman and Alan W. Bryant, *The Law of Evidence in Canada*, 2d ed., (Markham: Butterworths, 1999) at 622.

4 *R. v. Abbey*, [1982] 2 S.C.R. 24 at 42.

5 *The Law of Evidence*, above note 3, 617.

6 *D.D. v. The Queen*, [2002] 2 S.C.R. 275, at 300, per Major J.

Therefore, to safeguard the judicial process, the trial judge has taken on the role of "gatekeeper"[7] ensuring that expert evidence which may "distort the fact-finding process"[8] is excluded and that the threshold for the admissibility of expert evidence is met. The need for the trial judge to vigilantly perform this gatekeeper role is particularly acute in today's litigation environment where experts seem to testify in every case, thereby creating the risk in some circumstances that the trial will degenerate into a contest of experts, with the judge or jury merely acting as referee in deciding which expert to accept.[9]

The nature of the subject-matter requiring expert assistance during the course of litigation has been described by Sopinka J. as being in a "state of continual flux."[10] In tax litigation,[11] some of the matters that have been the focus of expert evidence include accounting,[12] appraisal,[13] valuation,[14] for-

7 *R. v. J.-L.J.*, above note 2, at 630.

8 *Ibid.*

9 *D.D. v. The Queen*, above note 6, at 301.

10 *The Law of Evidence*, above note 3, 617.

11 Robert McMechan, *Tax Court Practice*, vol. 2, looseleaf (Toronto: Carswell), chapter 17.

12 *Canderel Ltd. V. The Queen*, [1998] 2 C.T.C. 35 (S.C.C.); *Times Motors Ltd. v. MNR*, [1969] C.T.C. 190, 69 D.T.C. 5149 (S.C.C.); *Argus Holdings Ltd. v. The Queen* (2000), [2001] 1 C.T.C. 115, 2000 D.T.C. 6681 (F.C.A.); *Buck Consultants Ltd. v. The Queen* (1999), [2001] 1 C.T.C. 93, 2000 D.T.C. 6015 (F.C.A.), leave to appeal refused (Sept. 21, 2000), Doc. No. 27707 (S.C.C.); *Northwood Pulp and Timber Ltd. v. The Queen*, [1999] 1 C.T.C. 53, 98 D.T.C. 6640 (F.C.A.); *The Queen v. Foothills Pipe Lines (Yukon) Ltd.*, [1990] 2 C.T.C. 448, 90 D.T.C. 6607 (F.C.A.); *The Queen v. Cyprus Anvil Mining Corp.*, [1990] 1 C.T.C. 153, 90 D.T.C. 6063 (F.C.A.); *Royal Trust Co. v. The Queen* (2000), [2001] 3 C.T.C. 2268, 2001 D.T.C. 52 (T.C.C.); *The Queen v. Consumers' Gas Co. Ltd.*, [1987] 1 C.T.C. 79, 87 D.T.C. 5008 (F.C.A.); *Ticketnet Corporation v. The Queen*, [1999] 3 C.T.C. 564, 99 D.T.C. 5409 (F.C.T.D.); *E.C.E. Group Ltd. v. MNR*, [1992] 2 C.T.C. 2376, 92 D.T.C. 2019 (T.C.C.).

13 *The Queen v. Zelinski (sub. nom. Whent v. The Queen)* (1999), [2000] 1 C.T.C. 329, 2000 DTC 6001 (F.C.A.); *Global Communications Ltd. v. The Queen*, [1999] 3 C.T.C. 537, 99 D.T.C. 5377 (F.C.A.); *Connor v. The Queen*, [1979] C.T.C. 365, 79 D.T.C. 5256 (F.C.A.); *Hallatt v. The Queen* (2000), [2001] 1 C.T.C. 2626, 2001 D.T.C. 128 (T.C.C.); *Aikman v. The Queen*, [2000] 2 C.T.C. 2211, 2000 D.T.C. 1874 (T.C.C.), appeal dismissed [2002] 2 C.T.C. 147, 2002 D.T.C. 6874 (F.C.A.); *Cote v. The Queen* (1998), [1999] 3 C.T.C. 2373, 99 D.T.C. 72 (Fr.) (T.C.C.), appeal dismissed (2000), [2001] 4 C.T.C. 54, 2000 D.T.C. 6615 (Fr.) (F.C.A.); *Western Securities Ltd. v. The Queen*, 97 D.T.C. 977 (T.C.C.); *Bibby v. The Queen*, [1983] C.T.C. 121, 83 D.T.C. 5148 (F.C.T.D.); *Dubbel Wear Holdings Ltd. v. MNR*, [1981] C.T.C. 2348, 81 D.T.C. 351 (T.R.B.).

14 *U.S.M. Canada Ltd. v. The Queen*, [1996] 2 C.T.C. 2289, 96 D.T.C. 192 (T.C.C.); *Taylor Estate v. MNR*, [1990] 2 C.T.C. 2304, 90 D.T.C. 1777 (T.C.C.); *Hallatt v. The Queen*, [2001] 1 C.T.C. 2626, 2001 D.T.C. 128 (T.C.C.).

eign law,[15] reasonable expectation of profit,[16] highest and best use,[17] and native rights.[18]

The starting point for assessing a taxpayer's liability for tax in respect of income from a business or property is a determination of the taxpayer's profit from that business or property.[19] The meaning of profit was discussed comprehensively in the Supreme Court of Canada decision in *Symes v. Canada*.[20] The Court stated that the determination of profit was a question of law, which made it appropriate to consider "well accepted principles of business practice"[21] or "well accepted principles of commercial trading"[22] rather than more fiscally conservative "generally accepted accounting principles."

However in subsequent cases, *Toronto College Park Limited v. The Queen*[23] and *Canderel v. The Queen*,[24] the Supreme Court of Canada stated that generally accepted accounting principles ("GAAP") should form the foundation for well-accepted business practices. Certain sections of the *Income Tax Act* impose liability for tax based on GAAP. For example, the tax on large corporations is based on the carrying value of assets determined in accordance with GAAP.[25]

Frequently, experts retained to express opinions on GAAP are practitioners in accounting firms who also sit on The Accounting Standards Board of the Canadian Institute of Chartered Accountants ("CICA"). Given their dual role, these experts can have considerable credibility in the courts. The Accounting Standards Board issues Recommendations from time to time with respect to accounting practice. The Recommendations are published in the CICA Handbook and are accompanied by interpretive Accounting Guidelines.

---

15 *Minet Inc. v. The Queen*, [1998] 3 C.T.C. 352, 98 D.T.C. 6364 (F.C.A.); *The Queen v. The Capital Life Insurance Co.*, [1986] 1 C.T.C. 388, 86 D.T.C. 6164 (F.C.A.); *Cadillac Fairview Corp. v. The Queen*, [1996] 2 C.T.C. 2197 (T.C.C.); *Madigane v. MNR*, [1989] 1 C.T.C. 2103, 89 D.T.C. 37 (T.C.C.).

16 *Ludmer v. MNR* (2001), [2002] 1 C.T.C. 95, 2001 S.C.C. 62 (S.C.C.); *Timmins v. The Queen*, [1996] 3 C.T.C. 175, 96 D.T.C. 6378 (F.C.T.D.).

17 *Ung v. MNR*, [1987] 1 C.T.C. 2246, 87 D.T.C. 176 (T.C.C.), *Frith v. MNR*, 91 D.T.C. 1160.

18 *Benoit v. The Queen*, 2003 D.T.C. 5366, 2003 FCA 236.

19 Subsection 9(1) of the *Income Tax Act*, R.S.C. 1985, c. 1 (5th Supp.), as amended (herein referred to as "the Act"). Unless otherwise stated, statutory references are to the Act.

20 *Symes v. Canada*, [1993] 4 S.C.R. 695.

21 *Ibid*, above note 20, at 713.

22 *Ibid.*

23 *Toronto College Park Limited v. The Queen*, 98 D.T.C. 6088 (S.C.C.).

24 *Canderel v. The Queen*, 98 D.T.C. 6100 (S.C.C.).

25 Subsection 181(3).

Sometimes expert evidence is required to determine the proper accounting treatment for a matter which is not dealt with in the CICA Handbook.

The Canada Revenue Agency ("CRA") often finds it difficult to retain practitioners in private practice because a determination of the issues being litigated may adversely affect the interests of their other clients. Accordingly, the CRA often retains experts from university faculties.

Valuation issues can range from the value of a particular parcel of real estate on certain critical dates such as death to more sophisticated questions as to the value of shares of a corporation. The latter may require a determination of minority or holding company discounts.

B. ADMISSIBILITY

Manifestly, the use of expert witnesses can be a key element in tax appeals. An understanding of the rules being applied by the courts to determine the admissibility of expert evidence is therefore fundamental. (It should be noted in passing that tax appeals are tried by a judge without a jury.)

The criteria for the admissibility of expert opinion evidence were reviewed by the Supreme Court of Canada in *R. v. Mohan*.[26] In *Mohan*, as in several other leading cases on the admissibility of expert evidence,[27] experts were called to provide psychiatric or psychological testimony. Some subjects are without question beyond the understanding of the ordinary person, for example nuclear physics; however other subjects are less obviously so, particularly in the area of human behaviour, which might well be considered within the realm of knowledge of the judge or jury. Wilson, J. stated the issue in *R. v. Lavallee*:[28]

> The long standing recognition that psychiatric or psychological testimony also falls within the realm of expert evidence is predicated on a realization that in some circumstances the average person may not have sufficient knowledge of or experience within human behaviour to draw an appropriate inference from the facts before him or her.

In *Lavallee*, the Supreme Court of Canada determined that expert evidence was required to assist the court on the subject of battered women syndrome. The Supreme Court held that the subject was surrounded by so many myths that it was beyond the scope of understanding of the average

---

26 *R. v. Mohan*, [1994] 2 S.C.R. 9, 18 O.R. (3d) 160n, 114 D.L.R. (4th) 419.

27 See *R. v. Lavallee*, [1990] 1 S.C.R. 852, at 870.

28 *Ibid*, at p. 111 cited in *The Law of Evidence*, above note 3, 617.

juror and required the opinion of experts in the field to assist the jury in its assessment of the evidence.

The criteria for the admissibility of expert evidence outlined by the Supreme Court in *Mohan* are:[29]

1. the evidence must be relevant to some issue in the case;
2. the evidence must be necessary to assist the trier of fact;
3. the evidence must not violate an exclusionary rule; and
4. the witness must be a properly qualified expert.

To those criteria, the Court also added a "cost benefit analysis: that is whether its value is worth its costs." The Court felt that evidence otherwise logically relevant could be excluded if its probative value is overborne by its prejudicial effect, if it involves an inordinate amount of time not commensurate with its value or if it is misleading in the sense that its effect on the trier of fact, particularly a jury, is out of proportion to its reliability.

We will attempt to review these criteria separately as they relate to tax litigation. However, these criteria for admissibility are interdependent and their application may overlap in the context of admitting or excluding expert evidence in a particular case.[30] This is best illustrated in the case of *Mathew v. The Queen*.[31]

In *Mathew*, Mr. Richard Taylor, a chartered accountant and business valuator prepared an expert's report where he expressed his opinion that a profit-oriented business person acting reasonably would not enter into the subject transactions in the absence of or excluding tax considerations. Mr. Taylor also stated that the monetary returns provided by the tax deduction greatly exceeded the potential returns to be generated from the real estate portfolio.

Mr. Taylor based his opinion on hypotheticals as well as on certain assumptions. His hypotheticals came from certain documents including the transcript of the testimony of other witnesses in another case involving substantially similar facts and transactions and the transcript of the examination for discovery of the taxpayer Mathew and others in the subject case.

The issue in the *Mathew* case was whether the transactions entered into contravened the general anti-avoidance rule in the *Income Tax Act*.

---

29 *The Law of Evidence*, above note 3, 618.

30 *Ibid.*

31 *Mathew et al. v. The Queen*, 2002 D.T.C. 1637 (T.C.C.), aff'd 2003 D.T.C. 371 (F.C.A.). See [2001] 4 C.T.C. 2101, 2001 D.T.C. 742 (T.C.C.) for the reasons of Dussault, T.C.C.J.in support of an order concerning the admissibility of an expert report filed with the court.

Fundamental to that determination is whether the transaction was entered into primarily for a purpose other than tax savings. Clearly the opinion being proffered was relevant to the central issue in the case.

However, Dussault, T.C.C.J. relying on the Mohan criteria refused to admit Mr. Taylor's report in evidence. Firstly, he found that there had been a failure to clearly state the hypothetical facts and assumptions relied on. The Court felt that the opinion was based on Mr. Taylor's own findings of fact which were unknown to the Court. The Court said that the admission of the expert evidence would as a result of the extreme difficulty in determining what assumptions were actually relied on and how accurate they were as well as which ones were not considered, leave the court wondering when assessing the weight to be attached to that evidence.

Moreover, the Court found and Mr. Taylor admitted that he did not possess any special knowledge and experience going beyond that of the trier of fact.

The Court observed that Mr. Taylor founded his analysis on assumptions he made based on his review of transcripts from another case and from the examination of discovery of the taxpayer Mathew and others which were not necessarily before the Court. The Court stated that Mr. Taylor has heard a different trial, a trial of his own making.

The Court was particularly concerned that in admitting Mr. Taylor's report and testimony based on conclusions of fact stemming from the OSFC trial, there would be a danger that the Court might use that evidence to decide the present appeal.

1) The Evidence Must be Relevant to Some Issue in the Case

Relevancy is the threshold requirement for the admissibility of evidence and is a matter to be decided by a judge as a question of law.[32] The evidence must be "logically probative of a fact in issue."[33] A concern of the courts is the introduction of otherwise irrelevant evidence "through the mouths of experts."[34] The "aura of reliability"[35] surrounding an expert who offers evidence that may not be relevant to the matter in issue could inappropriately influence a trier of fact.

---

32 Sopinka, J. in *Mohan*, above note 26, at 10.

33 Mark J. Freiman and Mark L. Berenblut, *The Litigator's Guide to Expert Witnesses* (Toronto: Canada Law Book Inc., 1997) at 5.

34 *The Law of Evidence*, above note 3, at 618.

35 *Ibid.*

2) The Evidence Must be Necessary to Assist the Trier of Fact

Major, J. in *R. v. D.(D.)*,[36] stated:

> Mere relevance or "helpfulness" is not enough. The evidence must also be necessary.

The condition of necessity requires that the expert evidence to be introduced at trial must provide information "which is likely to be outside the experience and knowledge of a judge or jury"[37] and that that information is necessary to enable the trier of fact to "appreciate the matters in issue due to their technical nature."[38] Further, mere helpfulness is too low a standard to warrant accepting the dangers inherent in the admission of expert evidence.[39] The reasons for this are:[40]

(a) expert evidence is time consuming and expensive;
(b) expert evidence frequently reflects an interpretation of academic literature or is based on information from people who may not testify. This means that the trier of fact has to somehow decide whether the expert is reliable; and
(c) there is always the risk that the province of the jury might be usurped by the expert witness so that the jury abdicates its role and simply attorns to the opinion of the expert.

Our courts have consistently held that questions of law are for the judge to decide, and in some cases, expert evidence has been rejected on this basis.

In *Oligny v. The Queen*, the Tax Court of Canada stated that "it is the responsibility of the judge, not of an expert, to interpret the Act (*Income Tax Act*)."[41] Accordingly, in several tax cases, expert evidence has been excluded on this basis. *Oligny* involved the determination of eligibility for clergy residence deduction under paragraph 8(1)(c). The court in *Oligny* followed the approach of the Ontario Court of Appeal in *R. v. Century 21 Ramos Realty Inc.*:[42]

> With respect, we do not believe that the witness Claerhout should have been permitted to give an opinion as to when the appropriation occurred.

---

36 *D.D. v. The Queen*, above note 6, at paras. 46–47 cited in *R. v. Derose*, [2003] 1 C.T.C. 378 (Alta. Prov. Ct.), at 405, a case involving taxpayer net worth assessments.

37 Sopinka, J. in *Mohan*, above note 26, at 23, quoting Dickson, J. in *R. v. Abbey*, above note 4.

38 *Ibid.*

39 Major, J. in *D.D.*, above note 6.

40 *Ibid*, at paras. 53–56 (S.C.R.), cited in *Derose*, above note 36.

41 *Oligny v. The Queen*, [1996] 2 C.T.C. 2666, 96 D.T.C. 1744 (T.C.C.), at 1746 (D.T.C.).

> It was a question of law for the judge as to what constitutes an appropriation. It was for the judge to determine, in compliance with the legal definition, if and when an appropriation took place. This was not something on which an expert witness could give evidence.
>
> The *Income Tax Act* does not define the word "appropriate." It is, however, a common English word.

In *R. v. Silvestri*, a case involving a taxpayer's purported reliance on tax advisors, the Ontario Superior Court upheld the trial judge's decision to refuse to allow the taxpayer to call an expert to offer an opinion as to "what section of the Act was applicable with respect to the transaction."[43]

It should be noted, however, that expert evidence will not be excluded just because it relates to an ultimate question of law which the judge must decide. Indeed, such expert evidence may be necessary.

In *Telecomsyst Services Inc. v. R.*,[44] a case involving taxpayer eligibility for investment tax credits in respect of scientific research and experimental development pursuant to subsection 127(5) et seq. and section 127.1 of the Act, Dussault, T.C.C.J., writing for the court, suggested that in high technology fields, the necessity for expert evidence becomes "increasingly obvious." He said:

> If the question whether a taxpayer's activities constitute eligible scientific research and experimental development activities within the meaning of section 2900 of the Regulations is ultimately one of law, one may easily conceive that it is nevertheless necessary to have an expert's assistance in order to explain the context, nature and importance of the activities in specialized fields in which the judge clearly has very limited knowledge. Generally speaking, it may be said that this necessity becomes increasingly obvious as the activities become increasingly numerous and complex.

In other similarly scientific and technical areas, the Tax Court of Canada has considered it necessary to rely on expert evidence in reaching its decisions. In *Resman Holdings Ltd. et al. v. The Queen*[45] and *Wheeler v. The Queen*,[46] two cases involving oil and gas well drilling and exploration and

---

42 *R. v. Century 21 Ramos Realty Inc.*, [1987] 1 C.T.C. 340, 87 D.T.C. 5158 (Ont. C.A.), at 5164 (D.T.C.).

43 *R. v. Silvestri*, 2001 D.T.C. 5595, [2002] 1 C.T.C. 183 (Ont. S.C.J.), at 5597 (D.T.C.).

44 *Telecomsyst Services Inc. v. R.*, [1997] 1 C.T.C. 2256 at 2262, 97 D.T.C. 684 (T.C.C.) at 687.

45 *Resman Holdings Ltd. et al. v. The Queen*, 98 D.T.C. 1999 (T.C.C.), varied 2000 D.T.C. 6350 (F.C.A.), leave to appeal denied [2000] S.C.C.A No. 404.

46 *Wheeler v. The Queen*, 2 C.T.C. 2960, 97 D.T.C. 1156 (T.C.C.).

claims for Canadian Exploration Expenses ("CEE"), the trial courts preferred the expert evidence of the taxpayers over the Crown's experts in deciding for the taxpayer.

Even in a less scientific subject area, namely determinations of taxpayer net worth assessments, Allen J. in *R. v. Derose*,[47] stated the necessity for expert evidence, in some cases, to assist the trier of fact:

> In my view, the application of net worth assessments are generally technical in nature. In many circumstances, ordinary persons would be unlikely to form a correct judgment without the assistance of persons with specialized knowledge. There may be prosecutions where ordinary persons would be likely to form a correct judgment without expert assistance; this is not such a case.

In *Donohue St-Felicien Inc. v. The Queen*,[48] the court allowed expert evidence as to how the word "roadway" should be interpreted in the context of the logging industry. The Minister objected to the taxpayer's expert evidence in this regard, arguing that it was the court's responsibility not that of the expert witness to define the meaning of the word "roadway" in the Act (Reg. 4600(2)(h)) for the purpose of eligibility for investment tax credit. The court took counsel's objection "under advisement,"[49] but decided that the expert's evidence was required to assist the court in determining whether the word "roadway" had a "special meaning for people in that industry." The court stated that this was "a factor which could have a bearing on the scope of these words"[50] but cautioned that the evidence was admitted only to assist the court in making its decision.[51]

3) The Evidence Must Not Violate an Exclusionary Rule

Expert evidence that might otherwise be admissible, having satisfied the criteria of relevance and necessity, may still be excluded if it offends any of the general exclusionary rules of evidence.

For example, expert evidence designed to suggest that the accused had a disposition or propensity to commit the crime charged is inadmissible since it violates the "exclusionary character rule."[52] The Crown is prevented

47 *R. v. Derose*, above note 36, at 405.
48 *Donohue St-Felicien Inc. v. The Queen*, 98 D.T.C. 1757 (Fr.), [1998] 4 C.T.C. 2704.
49 *Ibid*, at 2707.
50 *Ibid.*
51 *Ibid.*
52 *The Law of Evidence*, above note 3, 622.

from adducing evidence of the accused's disposition unless the accused has placed his or her character in issue.[53]

Another common law rule excludes evidence presented to affirm the truthfulness of another witness.[54] This is the rule against oath-helping. A party is prohibited from bolstering the credibility of its own witness.[55] For example, polygraph tests are inadmissible since they are considered to offend this rule.[56]

Expert evidence will be rejected if, on careful analysis, it constitutes an inherently inadmissible opinion on human conduct. In *Mathew*, the Crown's expert had concluded that "a profit oriented business person acting reasonably would not enter into the transactions, as described herein, in the absence of or excluding tax considerations." Dussault, T.C.C.J. seized upon this aspect of the expert's evidence and said:

> However, I would add that I agree with counsel for the Appellants that Mr. Taylor's conclusion that a "a profit oriented business person acting reasonably would not enter into the transactions, as described herein, in the absence of or excluding tax considerations" relates to how a reasonable person would behave and would seem to be contrary to the *Adam*[57] case, supra. In that case the Supreme Court of Canada, at p. 458, referred to *Phipson on Evidence*, 8th ed., p. 385, in stating the following:
>
> > [n]either experts nor ordinary witnesses may give their opinions upon matters of legal or moral obligation, or general human nature, or the manner in which other persons would probably act or be influenced.[58]

4) The Witness Must be a Properly Qualified Expert

Since it is the role of the expert to provide information necessary for the court's understanding of scientific or technical issues,[59] the expert witness must be shown to have acquired special or peculiar knowledge in the subject matter[60] through study or experience.

53 *Mohan*, above note 26, at 11.
54 *The Litigator's Guide to Expert Witnesses*, above note 33, at 11.
55 *The Law of Evidence*, above note 3, at 631.
56 See *R. v. Beland*, [1987] 2 S.C.R. 398 and *R. v. Phillion*, [1978] 1 S.C.R. 18.
57 *Adam v. Campbell*, [1950] 3 D.L.R. 449 (S.C.C.).
58 *Mathew*, above note 31, at 748 D.T.C..
59 *The Law of Evidence*, above note 3, 622.
60 *Mohan*, above note 26 at 25.

How the expert acquired the knowledge is not of prime importance. In *Telecomyst*,[61] Dussault, T.C.C.J. observed that "on numerous occasions, our courts have reiterated the principle that it is knowledge and expertise in a field that count, not the manner in which that knowledge and expertise have been acquired," citing McLachlin, J. in *Marquard*[62] who in turn relied on the remarks of Sopinka, Lederman and Bryant:[63]

> The admissibility of such [expert] evidence does not depend upon the means by which that skill was acquired. As long as the court is satisfied that the witness is sufficiently experienced in the subject-matter at issue, the court will not be concerned with whether his or her skill was derived from specific studies or by practical training, although that may affect the weight to be given to the evidence.

This broad leeway to be given regarding the source of an expert's expertise has been recognized in Canadian tax cases. In *Resman*, the trial court judge preferred the evidence given by the expert on behalf of the taxpayer on the basis that this expert had significant practical experience as opposed to the witnesses who appeared for Revenue Canada who had no such experience in the field of drilling and exploration.[64]

5) Impeaching an Expert's Qualifications

It is common for opposing counsel to seek to impeach an expert on the basis of his or her qualifications. An objection on the basis that the proposed expert witness is not qualified to give opinion evidence at all should be made immediately after the witness has stated his or her qualifications and has been tendered as an expert and before the witness has given substantive evidence.[65] If the objection is not raised at this stage, then any subsequent objection to the expert's qualifications usually will only go to the weight, rather than to the admissibility[66] of the evidence. Failure by counsel to object to an expert's qualifications before giving evidence is only a bar to a subsequent objection so long as the expert stays within his or her purported area of expertise.[67] Notwithstanding this general principle, even if

61 *Telecomyst*, above note 44.
62 *R. v. Marquard*, [1993] 4 S.C.R. 223 at 243.
63 *The Law of Evidence* in Canada, above note 3, at 536–37.
64 *Resman*, above note 45. See also *Mathew*, above note 31, quoting McLachlin, J. in *Marquard*, above note 62. See also *Wheeler*, above note 46, at para. 24.
65 *The Litigator's Guide to Expert Witnesses*, above note 33, 12.
66 *Ibid.*
67 *The Law of Evidence*, above note 3, at 624.

an expert has been qualified to give opinion evidence, if it is subsequently shown that the expert does not have the expertise to testify on the subject area in question, then it is immaterial that no preliminary challenge of the expert's qualifications was made and the evidence must be disregarded.[68] If opposing counsel advises the court when the witness is tendered that he or she is prepared to concede that the expert is qualified, counsel should nevertheless take the court through the expert's curriculum vitae to reinforce the expert's expertise.

It is not often that opposing counsel will be successful in a preliminary challenge to the expert's qualifications[69] such that the witness will be prevented from testifying. Accordingly, it is frequently a good idea to save cross-examination on an expert's qualifications until after the expert has testified in chief. It can be very effective to point out particular shortcomings in an expert's qualifications during the main cross-examination.

The successful cross-examination of an expert can be challenging. Sometimes, it may not be possible to uncover any obvious flaws in the opposing expert's report. In such cases, one approach for opposing counsel may be to attempt to demonstrate that to a significant degree the expert's testimony is compatible with the conclusions of opposing counsel's own expert.[70] Another tactic might be for opposing counsel to seek the concession on cross-examination that opposing counsel's expert is also qualified, and that in the particular field at issue, there exist genuine areas of disagreement amongst experts.

Commentators caution that "to engage an expert in cross-examination, and then lose, is a major setback to your case."[71] Care should be taken in engaging the expert in a technical discussion on the subject matter of his expertise since this can sometimes be "fatal to a successful cross-examination."[72] Some suggestions for cross-examining an expert include:[73]

(a) Do not start off by attacking an expert's ultimate conclusions head on. First, go after such things as assumptions, methodology and data limitations.
(b) Perhaps try to demonstrate that the expert has branched out into an area in which he or she has no real expertise.

---

68 *Ibid*, citing *R. v. Marquard*, above note 62, at 243–44.
69 *The Litigator's Guide to Expert Witnesses*, above, note 33, at 12.
70 *Ibid.* at 20.
71 Ian A. Blue, *ibid.*
72 Roger E. Salhany, *Cross-Examination, The Art of the Advocate*, (Toronto: Butterworths, 1991) at 123.
73 Ian A. Blue, above note 33, at 19.

(c) Try to confront the expert with contradictory views that have been expressed in writing by recognized experts on the subject. Confronting an expert with his or her own prior contradictory views can be pure gold.

With respect to the assumptions relied on by the experts, courts are reluctant to admit expert evidence where the expert's assumptions of fact are not clearly stated or are based on evidence that may never go before the Court. As noted above in *Mathew*, the Court refused to admit the expert testimony because of lack of specific articulation of the assumptions and the relevance of testimony from another hearing. Dussault, T.C.C.J. said:

> If there is one well settled rule of law it is that a judge cannot take cognizance of facts coming directly to his attention in the course of another proceeding to decide on the fate of a proceeding in which those facts were not entered in evidence.[74]

C. ADMISSIBILITY VERSUS WEIGHT

It is a common plea for counsel to urge that whatever frailties there may be in the expert evidence that is being tendered, the evidence should be admitted and any weaknesses dealt with only as a matter of weight.

In this context, the Supreme Court of Canada in *R. v. J.-L.J.*[75] reiterated the importance of the judge's "gatekeeper" function with respect to admissibility of expert evidence, cautioning against allowing expert evidence "too easy an entry" into the trial proceedings.

> The admissibility of expert evidence should be scrutinized at the time it is proffered, and not allowed too easy an entry on the basis that all the frailties could go at the end of the day to weight rather than admissibility.

In fulfilling its "gatekeeper function," the trial judge in *Mathew* was careful to exclude the evidence of an expert because of the tainted nature of the facts forming the basis of his report. The Crown in that case had argued that even if their expert's report was "flawed" and "overreaching", the expert should still be permitted to give verbal testimony on business valuations, his area of expertise. The judge refused, agreeing with the taxpayer's counsel that the expert could not "disabuse himself"[76] from the questionable facts contained in his expert report.

---

74 *Ibid*, Dussault, T.C.C.J. citing *Pompa c. R.*, 94 D.T.C. 6630 (Fr.) at 6632; [1995] 1 C.T.C. 466 (F.C.A.) at 469 (C.T.C.).

75 *R. v. J.-L.J.*, above note 2, at 613.

76 Mathew, above note 31, at 747.

Similarly, in *Hallatt v. The Queen*,[77] the court refused to receive a valuation report introduced by one expert valuator that had been prepared by another expert valuator who had left the firm and was unable to testify.[78] In *Haslam v. The Queen*,[79] a case involving valuation of a vacant property, the court would not allow the expert's evidence on the basis that the expert had not done all research himself but had relied on others and had not verified some of the facts he was given:

> Although I am most impressed with Mr. Fraser's evidence, it is flawed by the fact that he himself did not do all of the research, having relied on others in his office and by the fact that on certain matters he failed to verify some of the facts he was given to check their accuracy.

The result in *Haslam* may be open to question. Other courts have recognized the right of the parties to "put forward the most complete evidentiary record consistent with the rules of evidence"[80] available to them. As the court stated in *Derose*, a case involving expert witnesses providing taxpayer net worth methodologies, "an expert frequently refers to hearsay information."[81]

Expert evidence is frequently admitted as an exception to the general rule prohibiting witnesses from testifying on matters that are not factually based or within their personal knowledge.[82] The determination of the weight to be given to such expert evidence, which is often based in part on hearsay circumstances is the function of the court.

The Supreme Court of Canada in Abbey appeared to say that *all* of the foundational evidence of an expert's report must be proved or else the opinion is valueless.[83] Dickson, J. (as he then was) was commenting on the hearsay element of a psychiatrist's opinion based on information told to the psychiatrist by the accused:

> Before any weight can be given to an expert's opinion, the facts upon which the opinion is based must be found to exist.

---

77 *Hallatt v. The Queen*, [2001] 1 C.T.C. 2626, 2001 D.T.C. 128 (T.C.C.).

78 *Ibid.* at 130. However, since the evidence was the basis of the appellant's case, rather than dismiss the appeal completely, the judge allowed the expert's oral testimony to be admitted.

79 *Haslam v. The Queen*, [1988] 1 C.T.C. 153, 88 D.T.C. 6081, at 6087 (D.T.C.).

80 *Ibid.*

81 *Derose*, above note 36, at 406.

82 *The Litigator's Guide to Expert Witnesses*, above note 33, at 4.

83 *The Law of Evidence*, above note 3, at 645.

In *Lavallee*, Wilson, J. interpreted *Abbey* as standing for the following propositions:[84]

1. An expert opinion is admissible if relevant, even if it is based on second-hand evidence.
2. This second-hand evidence (hearsay) is admissible to show the facts on which the expert opinion is based, not as evidence going to the existence of those facts.
3. Where psychiatric expert evidence is based on hearsay evidence, the problem is the weight to be attributed to the opinion.
4. Before any weight can be given to an expert's opinion, the facts upon which the opinion is based must be found to exist.

In separate reasons for judgment in *Lavallee*, Sopinka, J. also addressed the possibility of expert evidence being admissible but being entitled to little weight, "perhaps to the vanishing point." He suggested that this situation would be a rarity and that it would be unlikely that an expert's evidence would be based entirely upon information of a hearsay nature. He suggested that second-hand, even third-hand information obtained from sources with "strong circumstantial guarantees of trustworthiness" (such as the information a physician obtains through colleagues) that is relied on by the expert in his or her area of expertise,[85] should be worthy of the court's consideration. Sopinka, J. stated the matter as follows:

> The resolution of the contradiction inherent in *Abbey*, and the answer to the criticism *Abbey* has drawn, is to be found in the practical distinction between evidence that an expert obtains and acts upon within the scope of his or her expertise (as in *City of Saint John*) and evidence that an expert obtains from a party to the litigation touching a matter directly in issue (as in *Abbey*).[86]

In most cases, an expert's opinion will be based on some combination of admitted facts or facts sought to be proven, and on facts considered possibly suspect. In these situations, the issue before the court is purely one of weight. Specifically, Sopinka, J. said:

---

84 *Ibid.* at 646 citing *Lavallee*, above note 27, at 898.

85 *Saint John (City) v. Irving Oil Co.*, [1966] S.C.R. 581, 58 D.L.R. (2d) 404 cited by Sopinka, J. in *Lavallee*. In *Saint John*, the opinion of a real estate appraiser regarding property valuations was admissible even though his opinion was based on persons who had been parties to comparable real estate sales and who had not been called to testify.

86 *Lavallee*, above note 27, at 899.

> Where an expert's opinion is based in part upon suspect information and in part upon either admitted facts or facts sought to be proved, the matter is purely one of weight.[87]

Where the evidence of the expert witness is not based on facts in place for the tax years under appeal, the court will "not place much weight on the expert evidence."[88]

In *Misik v. M.N.R.*,[89] the taxpayer was permitted to introduce the expert evidence of an agronomist, who was an expert in farm economics, to provide data regarding profitability of farming operations similar to the taxpayer's. The judge ruled that the expert's opinion was to be given little weight on the question of profitability in the taxation years in question.[90] The court held that the information upon which the expert had based his opinion was "mostly of a hearsay nature provided by the appellant," mostly from memory, and inherently unreliable.[91]

D. THE HYPOTHETICAL QUESTION

As discussed in the previous section, the courts have recognized that the expert's evidence is not necessarily based on the expert's personal knowledge of the facts of the case:

> It is important to recognize that when an expert gives testimony, it is in the nature of an opinion as to the possibility or probability that this or that happened or did not happen. He is not saying that something, in fact, happened unless he was there and saw it with his own eyes. What he is saying is that based on his training, expertise and any experiments performed, it is "likely," "possible," or "probable" that a certain thing has happened or will happen in the future.[92]

Therefore, it has become common practice for an expert to render an opinion based on a set of hypothetical facts. It is very important to establish the basis of the expert's opinion. An expert should state the facts or assumptions upon which his or her opinion is based.[93] If the expert lacks personal knowledge of the matters in issue and is called to provide an opin-

87 *Ibid*, at 900.
88 *Ferster v. R.*, [2003] 2 C.T.C. 2232, 2003 D.T.C. 473 (T.C.C.) at 479.
89 *Misik v. M.N.R*, [1993] 1 C.T.C. 2360, 93 D.T.C. 172 (T.C.C.).
90 *Ibid*, at 182.
91 *Ibid*.
92 *Cross Examination*, above note 72, at 124.
93 *The Law of Evidence*, above note 3, at 624.

ion on certain disputed facts, that opinion may only be elicited through the use of the hypothetical question.[94]

As noted above in *Mathew*, Dussault, T.C.C.J., confirmed the duty of the expert witness to state any hypothetical facts or assumptions of fact upon which their opinion is based:[95]

> Although I recognize that the nature of the source upon which an expert opinion is based cannot affect the admissibility of the opinion itself, as stated by the Supreme Court of Canada in the *Saint John* case, I am of the opinion that that source, regardless of its nature, has to be clearly stated.

The hypothetical fact situation put to the expert witness should be clear, uncontradictory and proved at trial.[96] The hypothetical question should be kept simple and only contain the essential premises so as not to mislead or unnecessarily confuse a jury or be used by a litigant to state its theory through the mouth of its expert.[97]

> If the trier of fact ultimately rejects the factual premises on which the opinion was based then, of course, the expert's opinion must be rejected as well.[98]

Without the use of the hypothetical question, the expert might be placed in the position of having to weigh evidence or assess the truthfulness of other witnesses in order to arrive at his or her opinion. This is not the proper role or responsibility of the expert witness.[99] There is a danger that the trier of fact, in particular a jury, may be influenced in their thinking by an expert opinion based on the expert's version of the facts. When some of the facts are either rejected or unproven, the trial judge must give careful directions to the jury to discern the factual basis of the expert opinion.[100]

Hence the compelling necessity, as expressed by the trial judge in *Mathew*, for the expert to be given "clear, unambiguous and uncontradict-

---

94 *Ibid.* at 625.

95 *Mathew*, above note 31, at 747.

96 *The Law of Evidence*, above note 3, citing *Lindala v. Canadian Copper Co.* (1920), 47 O.L.R. 28, 51 D.L.R. 565 (C.A.); 2 Wigmore, *Evidence* (Chadbourn rev., 1979) s. 682, at 947–56.

97 *Ibid*, citing *R. v. Ryan* (1993), 80 C.C.C. (3d) 514 (B.C.C.A.); *D.D.*, above note 6.

98 *Ibid*, citing *R. v. Lake* (1996), 153 N.S.R. (2d) 44, 450 A.P.R. 44, 49 C.R. (4th) 224 (C.A.); *R. v. Kelly* (1990), 41 O.A.C. 32 at 37, 59 C.C.C. (3d) 497 at 504 (C.A.); 2 Wigmore, *Evidence*, above note 96.

99 *Ibid.*

100 *Ibid.*, citing *R. v. Millar* (1989), 33 O.A.C. 165, 49 C.C.C. (3d) 193, 71 C.R. (3d) 78 at 105–7 (C.A.).

ed"[101] hypothetical facts on which to offer an opinion, unless it can be based on facts proven in the case at bar.

As Wilson, J. noted in *Lavallee*, before any weight can be given to an expert's opinion, the facts upon which the opinion is based must be found to exist. Thus, counsel in seeking to diminish the importance of an expert's report should attempt to prove facts contrary to those assumed in the hypothetical question. Similarly, an effective cross-examination can be made by obtaining a concession from the expert witness that the opinion would be different — perhaps even the opposite — if the facts assumed by the expert were not true.

E. THE ULTIMATE ISSUE

Historically, expert evidence going to the ultimate issue was excluded because of the concern that the function of the trier of fact would be usurped, but this rule is no longer strictly followed.[102] The Supreme Court of Canada in *Mohan* has made it clear that the rule which excluded expert evidence in respect of the ultimate issue is "no longer of general application" but the concerns underlying the rule remain and the criteria of relevance and necessity must be strictly applied in admitting such evidence.[103]

According to the authors, the law can be summarized as follows:

> In the final analysis, the closer the expert's testimony approaches an opinion on the ultimate issue, the stricter the courts will apply the requirements of reliability and necessity before admitting the evidence.[104]

In tax cases, the evidence presented by experts often may go directly to the ultimate issue being decided by the courts, as in the valuation cases above. The issue was also addressed by Allen J. in *Derose*,[105] involving taxpayer's net worth assessments, where he stated:

> The use of Mr. Smith's [the taxpayer's expert] evidence must be carefully considered so that he does not usurp the functions of the court. Some of his evidence does go to the core of the dispute.

101 *Mathew*, above note 31, at 748.
102 *Mohan*, above note 26, at 11.
103 *Ibid.*
104 *The Law of Evidence*, above note 3, at 641.
105 *Derose*, above note 36, at 406.

More often, expert evidence will now be rejected as being superfluous, rather than going to the "ultimate issue"; the court determining that it is able to reach its decision without the assistance of the expert.[106]

In *Placer Dome Inc.*[107] Bell, T.C.C.J. permitted a witness[108] to give evidence of a prior opinion that he had rendered to the taxpayer. The opinion, namely whether subsection 55(2) of the *Income Tax Act* applied to a dividend received by the taxpayer in the course of disposing of its shares of Falconbridge, was the same issue to be decided by the court. It is noted that the witness was not giving expert evidence but was giving evidence as to the scope of the review the witness had conducted in order to determine whether the dividend had a tax or other purpose.

F. THE EXPERT WITNESS SHOULD BE OBJECTIVE

As many commentators have pointed out, expert witnesses, unlike most other witnesses in a trial, are often specifically sought out, interviewed and paid for by the litigants.[109] This undoubtedly creates tension in litigation between the duty of the expert to "not assume the role of an advocate"[110] and the "partisan affiliation [of the expert] with one side of the case."[111] At least one commentator has expressed a cynical viewpoint of experts in contemporary litigation, commenting that experts are "chosen not for their wisdom or sagacity but for their willingness to say in the simplest, clearest, least tentative way what a particular side wants said."[112]

Canadian courts have supported the proposition that expert witnesses must provide objective unbiased opinion in relation to matters within their expertise. The leading case cited with approval in Canadian courts[113] is

106 *Ibid*, see also *Mathew*, above note 31.

107 *Placer Dome Inc. v. The Queen*, 96 D.T.C. 1787, aff'd 96 D.T.C. 6562 (F.C.A.).

108 The witness happens to be one of the authors of this chapter.

109 *The Litigator's Guide to Expert Witnesses*, above, note 33, at 15.

110 See *The Law of Evidence*, above note 3, at 624.

111 *The Litigator's Guide to Expert Witnesses*, above, note 33, at 15.

112 Professor Krouser, "Are Expert Witnesses Whores? Reflections on Objectivity in Scholarship and Expert Witnessing" (Winter 1984), 6 *The Public Historian* 5, quoted in W. Ian C. Binnie, "Preparing the Expert Witness," in Expert Evidence, Law Society of Upper Canada, Department of Continuing Legal Education, November 18, 1995 at p. B-1, cited in *The Litigator's Guide to Expert Witnesses*, above, note 33, at 15.

113 *Jacobsen v. Sveen*, [2000] A.J. No. 365 (Q.B.); *Kozak v. Funk*, [1995] S.J. No. 569, appeal allowed on other grounds [1998] 5 W.W.R. 232 (Sask. C.A.); *Perricone v. Baldassara*, [1994] O.J. No. 2199 (OGen. Div.), which were all motor vehicle accident cases; *Kirby Lowbed Services Ltd. v. Bank of Nova Scotia*, [2003] B.C.J. No. 917 (S.C.), a business valuation case.

"*Ikarian Reefer*,"[114] an English decision, in which Cresswell J. commented that expert witness evidence should be *and should be seen to be* the independent product of the expert, uninfluenced as to form or content. He summarized the duties and responsibilities of an expert witness as follows (paraphrased in *Perricone*[115]):

> 1. Expert evidence presented to the court should be and should be seen to be the independent product of the expert uninfluenced as to form or content by the exigencies of litigation.
> 2. An expert should provide independent assistance to the court by objective unbiased opinion in relation to matters within his or her expertise. An expert witness should never assume a role of advocate.
> 3. An expert should state the facts or assumptions on which the opinion is based and should not omit to consider material facts which detract from that opinion.
> 4. An expert should make it clear when a particular question or issue falls outside of the expert's expertise.
> 5. If an expert's opinion is not properly researched because insufficient data is available, this must be stated with an indication that the opinion is no more than a provisional one.

Macdonald J., in *Perricone*, cautioned that if an expert rendering evidence assumes the role of an advocate, they risk losing their status as an expert witness:

> If the person rendering the evidence assumes the role of advocate, he or she can no longer be viewed as an expert in the legally correct sense; instead, he or she must be viewed as advocating the case of a party with the attendant diminishment in the credibility of the report.[116]

In a recent tax case, *Whent v. The Queen*,[117] the issue was the fair market value of art donated by the taxpayers to public art galleries. Donald Robinson of Kinsman Robinson Galleries was called as an expert witness to give evidence on the fair market value of works of art by the Canadian

---

114 *National Justice Compania Naviera SA v. Prudential Assurance Co. Ltd. ("Ikarian Reefer")*, [1993] 2 Lloyd's Rep. 68, at 81, rev'd on other grounds [1995] 1 Lloyd's Rep. 455 (C.A.), in which the appeal court endorsed Cresswell J.'s "admirable resume of the duties and responsibilities of expert witnesses."

115 *Perricone*, above note 113, at para. 21.

116 *Ibid*, at para. 22.

117 *Ken A. Whent v. The Queen*, 96 D.T.C., 1594, [1996] 3 C.T.C. 254, aff'd *sub nom. The Queen v. Zelinski et al* 2001 D.T.C. 6001 [2001] 1 C.T.C. 321 (F.C.A.).

artist Norval Morrisseau. Mogan T.C.C.J. placed very little reliance upon Mr. Robinson's appraised value on the basis that "he ha[d] a hopeless conflict of interest in trying to be objective about the quality of value of Morrisseau's works when he [was] currently the exclusive distributor of Morrisseau's new works in Ontario."

Another issue in tax cases is whether an expert witness in the employ of one of the parties in the appeal should be disqualified from providing expert evidence on behalf of that party, on the grounds of bias.

In tax cases, some judges have held that the mere fact that an expert witness was in the employ of the CRA was insufficient reason for their evidence to be inadmissible for reason of lack of objectivity:

> If a person who is otherwise qualified as an expert happens to be employed by the party who calls him or her, this is not a basis for excluding that person's evidence. If there is any ground for believing that their evidence may be tainted by bias or lack of independence, this is something that can be explored on cross examination.[118]

In *Hallatt*, a case involving the valuation of corporate shares, Bowman T.C.C.J. (as he then was) agreed with the reasoning of Bowie T.C.C.J. in *Gilvesy Enterprises Inc. v. The Queen*,[119] in which he refused to reject the evidence of an expert in the employ of Revenue Canada stating that:

> [I]t is the integrity, training, experience and judgment of the witness that will ultimately determine the value of the evidence, not the type of contractual relationship shared by the witness and the party for whom the evidence is led.[120]

In *Gilvesy*, a case involving business valuation and allowable business investment losses, Bowie T.C.C.J. went as far as stating, "I reject the suggestion that bias, even at a subconscious level, is a factor that should diminish its probative value."[121] However, in his final analysis, he rejected the Crown's expert evidence on the basis of being too limited, and influenced "whether consciously or not," by hindsight that rendered the opinion "highly theoretical."

---

118 Hallatt, above note 77, at 129 (D.T.C.).

119 *Gilvesy Enterprises Inc. v. The Queen*, [1997] 1 C.T.C. 2410, 97 D.T.C. 811.

120 *Ibid.* at 815.

121 *Ibid.*

The cases of *Friedman v. MNR*[122] and *Frith v. MNR*,[123] are two cases involving the Ministers' expert witnesses who had previously acted for the Minister as appraisers during the negotiations with the taxpayer. In Friedman, the court held that an employee of the Minister could qualify as an expert, but in the case at bar, the expert had "disqualified himself" as an expert witness by "admitting to having attempted to negotiate a fair market value of the subject property with the appellants."[124]

In *Frith*, however, Mogan T.C.C.J. disagreed with many of the statements in *Friedman* suggesting that it would be common practice, and the most cost-effective practice, for parties to retain as expert witnesses the appraisers involved in the failed negotiations leading up to the litigation.

> The attendance of a qualified appraiser at such a meeting [negotiation] does not, in itself, affect the appraiser's objectivity or expertise.[125]

If a qualified appraiser has, through the negotiation process, permitted himself to become an advocate for his client and has abandoned his professional objectivity, the other party can be expected to bring that out in cross-examination.[126] Mogan T.C.C.J. suggested that, in such an instance, a court would not likely attach much weight to the opinion of such an appraiser. He comments that if the parties were required to retain "fresh" experts for the litigation resulting from failed negotiations, this would result in significant and unnecessary added costs.

Mogan T.C.C.J. distinguished *Friedman*, stating that in that case the qualified appraiser had taken on a much broader role than advisor, and in fact had attempted to negotiate the settlement himself. In this regard, he cautioned that a qualified appraiser should attend negotiations only as an advisor and not as principal negotiator in order to retain their objectivity.

Bowman T.C.C.J. (as he then was), in *Hallatt*, acknowledged that opposing experts will most often have opposing views. In commenting on the major differences in valuation that can arise from the choice of comparables, he commented that the duty of the court is to ultimately make its own decision based on the assistance of the often opposing views of the experts. He quoted from his earlier decision in *Western Securities Limited v. The Queen*, 97 D.T.C. 977 at 979:

---

122 *Friedman v. MNR*, 78 D.T.C. 1599.

123 *Frith v. MNR*, 91 D.T.C. 1160.

124 *Friedman*, above note 122, at 1602.

125 *Frith*, above note 123, at 1169.

126 *Ibid.*

> It frequently happens that the judge determines a value somewhere between the opposing positions of the experts, not because of any desire to reach a Solomic compromise, but because of a recognition that the positions adopted by the experts represent the polarized extreme ends of value.[127]

The duty of the Court to make its own decision was articulated in the *Bibby* case.[128] The issue was the fair market value of certain land on December 31, 1977. Each party called expert evidence on the question of value but Walsh, J. in deciding not to accept the opinion of either expert, made the following statement:

> While it has frequently been held that a Court should not, after considering all the expert and other evidence merely adopt a figure somewhere between the figure sought by the contending parties, it has also been held that the Court may, when it does not find the evidence of any expert completely satisfying or conclusive, nor any comparable especially apt, form its own opinion of valuation, provided this is always based on the careful consideration of all the conflicting evidence. The figure so arrived at need not be that suggested by any expert or contended for by the parties.

Given that the expert can be perceived as a "hired gun" of one of the parties, it is very important to note how the courts measure and value an expert's evidence. An important insight into this analysis may be found in the commentary of Bowman T.C.C.J. (as he then was), in *Hallatt*, where he stated, "the expert's conclusion is frequently of less importance than the reasoning that lies beneath the conclusion."[129]

In cases where critical facts are in dispute, it is not unusual for the Department of Justice to request an order excluding witnesses from the hearing until they are called to give evidence. Courts have been reluctant to exclude expert witnesses because they are often necessary to assist counsel in interpreting and appreciating the evidence.

G. PRIVILEGE OF EXPERT WORKING PAPERS

In the course of retaining an expert during the litigation process, there will typically be numerous documents resulting. These documents can gener-

---

127 *Hallatt*, above note 77, at 134 (D.T.C.).

128 *Bibby v. R. (sub nom. Bibby Estate v. The Queen)* [1983] C.T.C. 121, 83 D.T.C. 5148 at 5157 (F.C.T.D.).

129 *Ibid.*

ally be referred to as the expert's "working papers" and typically would consist of:[130]

1. the expert's communications with the lawyers;
2. the expert's communications with the clients;
3. the expert's communications with other experts associated with the case;
4. preparatory materials used in connection with the expert's report; and
5. draft reports including opinions and conclusions.

Copies of these materials may be in the possession of the expert, the lawyer or the client. These materials, if required to be disclosed to the opposing counsel, "could cause unnecessary or damaging complications in discovery or cross-examination of the expert at trial."[131]

The Supreme Court of Canada has recognized solicitor-client privilege to be "more than a rule of evidence" and arguably has elevated it to a fundamental right.[132] Whether solicitor-client (or litigation) privilege is waived when an expert witness takes the stand at trial has been the subject of a long-standing debate.

From one perspective, it is argued that privilege should be absolute; that a client should be in a legal position to instruct his lawyer to examine all aspects of the matter at issue without apprehension that "full and frank" examination of such facts may somehow become available to opposing counsel and be used against the client.[133] The contrary viewpoint argues that in the interests of full disclosure in the adversary process, the privilege protecting expert working papers must be "truncated."[134] The law regarding the extent to which experts' working papers are protected by privilege remains unsettled and appears to be dependent on the jurisdiction in which the proceedings are taking place.[135]

In Ontario, in *Bell Canada v. Olympia & York Developments Ltd.*,[136] the High Court of Justice held that there was no waiver of privilege with

---

130 J. Douglas Wilson, "Privilege in Experts' Working Papers," [1997] C.B.R. 346, 350.

131 *Ibid*, 349.

132 See "Privilege in Experts' Working Papers," above note 130, at 377; *Law of Evidence*, above note 3, at 739, citing *Solosky v. Canada*, [1980] 1 S.C.R. 821 at 836; *Descoteaux v. Mierzwinski*, [1982] 1 S.C.R. 860, 141 D.L.R. (3d) 590.

133 "Privilege in Experts' Working Papers," above note 130, citing *Solosky*, above note 132, at 834.

134 *Ibid.* at 382.

135 *Ibid.*

136 *Bell Canada v. Olympia & York Developments Ltd.* (1989), 68 O.R. (2d) 103, 33 C.L.R. 258 (H.C.J.).

respect to documents disclosed to an expert even when that witness testified at trial. Eberle, J. took the position that the expert witness testifying was no different than if the client had taken the stand[137] and it was just as if confidential communications had taken place between the client and the lawyer, and therefore disclosure was not required.

The contrary viewpoint seems to have been adopted in British Columbia. In *Vancouver Community College v. Phillips Barratt*,[138] the court held that where an expert's report is placed in evidence or where the expert testifies, there is a waiver of the privilege that would previously have protected the expert's working papers from production:[139]

> So long as the expert remains in the role of a confidential advisor, there are sound reasons for maintaining privilege over documents in his possession. Once he becomes a witness, however, his role is substantially changed. His opinions and their foundation are no longer private advice for the party who retained him. He offers his professional opinion for the assistance of the court in its search for the truth. The witness is no longer in the camp of a partisan. He testifies in an objective way to assist the court in understanding scientific, technical or complex matters within the scope of his professional expertise. He is presented to the court as truthful, reliable, knowledgeable and qualified.
>
> . . . It seems to me that in holding out the witness's opinion as trustworthy, the party calling him impliedly waives any privilege that previously protected the expert's papers from production.

This viewpoint has found support in the Federal Court. In *Jesionowski v. Gorecki*,[140] Reed, J. held that privilege in expert working papers is lost once the expert takes the stand at trial. She noted the useful description drawn by an author[141] between solicitor-client privilege and litigation privilege. The author observed that the interest that underlies solicitor-client privilege is that of all citizens to have full and ready access to legal advice. If an individual cannot confide in a solicitor knowing that what is said will not be revealed, it will be difficult, if not impossible, for that individual to have proper candid legal advice.

---

137 *The Law of Evidence*, above note 3, at 762.

138 *Vancouver Community College v. Phillips Barratt* (1987), 20 B.C.L.R. (2d) 289 at 296–97, 27 C.L.R. 11 (S.C.).

139 *Ibid*, see also *Henderson v. Lodge* (1993), 16 C.P.C. (3d) 276 (B.C.S.C.).

140 *Jesionowski v. Gorecki*, [1993] 1 F.C.R. 36 (T.D.).

141 Sharpe, "Claiming Privilege in the Discovery Process," Special Lectures of the Law Society of Upper Canada, 1984 (Don Mills, Ont.: De Boo, 1984) at 164–65.

Litigation privilege, on the other hand, is geared directly to the process of litigation. Litigation privilege is based upon the need for a protected area to facilitate investigation and preparation of a case for trial by the adversarial advocate.

Reed, J. then said that the need for a protected area to facilitate a lawyer's investigation and preparation of a case does not extend to the information provided to an expert if the expert is called to the stand. She further stated that while the operation of the adversarial trial process requires protection of counsel's work product, it does not require protection of an expert witness's work product. Reed, J. further noted that expert witnesses are different than other witnesses. If the expert has given a contrary opinion in the past on the same facts or if there is evidence that his opinion has been changed or gerrymandered in response to counsel's suggestions, then the credibility of that opinion is significantly undercut.[142] Reed, J. concluded as follows:

> The witness is being put forward because of his particular expertise, to assist the court in coming to a conclusion and this imposes obligations of disclosure on him that may not exist for other witnesses. The *Vancouver Community College* case implicitly states that the search for truth with respect to the evidence being given by this category of witness outweighs any interest that might be served in protecting drafts or working papers of the witness.[143]

This part of the decision, however, was *obiter*, since the documents were ultimately not requested for production, and Reed J., in the final analysis, held that the expert's report was not necessary to enable the court to reach a decision.

Other courts have taken a middle ground. In *Highland Fisheries Ltd. v. Lynk Electric Ltd.*,[144] the court held that privilege was waived where the expert testified, but this waiver extended only to the expert's report and material related to the factual basis of the opinions expressed, but not to the expert's preliminary report.

Similarly, in Ontario, in *Piche v. Lecours Lumber Co.*,[145] the court held that privilege can be waived in respect of those facts or premises in the expert's file on which the expert's opinion was based.[146] The court stated

142 *Jesionowski*, above note 140, at 46.

143 *Ibid.* at 46.

144 *Highland Fisheries Ltd. v. Lynk Electric Ltd.* (1989), 63 D.L.R. (4th) 93 (N.S.S.C.T.D.).

145 *Piche v. Lecours Lumber Co.* (1993), 13 O.R. (3d) 193 (Gen. Div.).

146 *The Law of Evidence*, above note 3, at 762.

that, as a general rule, if facts are supplied that are not found in other evidence, or if certain assumptions are asked to be made in the instructing documents, the privilege claimed for those facts or assumptions should be considered waived.[147] Confidential communications which are outside this scope are not waived.

Such an approach is espoused by the authors of *The Law of Evidence*,[148] namely, that "confidential communications which are not the foundation of the expert opinion are not waived," but they caution that this may lead to a questionable practice among solicitors to destroy preliminary materials to avoid their disclosure. The latter concern was not shared by the Honourable W. David Griffiths who, with reference to an expert's draft material and preliminary reports, stated in a lecture that he knew of "no reason, legal or ethical, why the expert may not destroy his or her early draft."[149]

H. PROCEDURAL RULES AND COSTS

Income tax appeals of federal tax assessments and penalties arising from the *Income Tax Act* or Part IX of the *Excise Tax Act* (relating to the Goods and Services Tax) are heard before the Tax Court of Canada. Trials before the Tax Court of Canada are referred to as hearings and may proceed under either the General Procedure or Informal Procedure.

There are different rules regarding expert witnesses and costs in the general and informal procedures. We will first deal with the General and then the Informal Procedure.

I. GENERAL PROCEDURE

Rule 145 of the *Tax Court of Canada Rules (General Procedure)* governs the introduction of expert evidence at trial. It requires a statement by the proposed witness of the evidence that the proposed witness is prepared to give. Unless otherwise directed by the court, (a) such statement must be served on the other parties not less than 30 days before the commencement of the hearing and (b) the witness must be available for cross-examination. A similar rule applies in respect of evidence of an expert witness to be led in rebuttal except that the time requirement is not less than 15 days before the

147 *Ibid.*

148 *Ibid.*

149 *The Litigator's Guide to Expert Witnesses*, above note 33, at 34.

commencement of the hearing. The statements filed with the Court do not become part of the evidence unless they are given at the hearing.

The Tax Court of Canada has held that compliance with Rule 145 is fundamental to the principle of procedural fairness which is embodied in the rule. The party being challenged by the expert must be given sufficient time to prepare their case accordingly,[150] hence the requirement for a "full statement of the proposed evidence" to be served on all opposing parties no less than 30 days prior to the hearing (para. 145(2)(b)). Dussault T.C.C.J., in *Oligny*,[151] in rejecting a report by the taxpayer's expert, commented:

> I decided to reject Dr. Wilson's testimony because not only was his report submitted before the hearing not made in affidavit, not signed and not accompanied by the certificate of counsel required by paragraph 145(1)(b) of the Rules, but also, and this element is more important, because it did not constitute under paragraph 145(2)(b) of the Rules "a full statement of the proposed evidence in chief" that the expert intended to establish. It seems obvious to me that Dr. Wilson's testimony at the hearing went beyond what was contained in his report. Compliance by a party with the provisions of section 145 of the Rules is fundamental in order to avoid the effect of surprise and to enable the other party to prepare adequately for the cross-examination of the expert whose report is adduced.

As pointed out in *Mathew*, Dussault T.C.C.J. found that the Crown's expert could not "disabuse himself" of the inadmissible evidence contained in his report and would not permit the expert to testify even on limited matters that were within his area of expertise such as market rates of return. The prejudice to the taxpayer outweighed any need to allow the expert evidence. Dussault T.C.C.J. said:

> The 30 days' notice ensures that the other party can prepare his case accordingly.
>
> Because neither the exact opinion Mr. Taylor would be asked to give on limited matters nor the hypothetical facts which he would have to assume are precisely known at this point and because counsel for the Appellants could not and cannot receive advance notice thereof so as to be able to obtain a rebuttal opinion if necessary, I am convinced that the prejudice that would be suffered outweighs the necessity of Mr. Taylor's evidence.[152]

---

150 *Mathew*, above note 31, at 749 (D.T.C.).
151 *Oligny*, above note 41, at 1746 (D.T.C.).
152 *Mathew*, above note 31, at 749 (D.T.C.).

The *Federal Court Rules*[153] contain an equivalent provision in subsection 279(b) except that the Federal Court Rule requires service of a statement of the expert witness at least 60 days before the commencement of the trial.

In an interesting case heard before the Federal Court Trial Division, *Harris v. The Queen*,[154] a taxpayer brought a class action suit against the Crown and the Minister of National Revenue. The taxpayer claimed breach of fiduciary duty by the Minister, alleging that an advance tax ruling that was not made public on a timely basis conferred a preferential benefit on one taxpayer and denied other taxpayers in a similar situation the same benefit.

In *Harris*, Dawson, J. allowed certain expert evidence where the requirements of subsection 279(b) had *not* been met, exercising the court's discretion under the provision to permit expert evidence to be adduced that has not complied with the Rules. Dawson, J. commented that "departure from the rule will, however, be exceptional"[155] and stated the goals of procedural fairness implicit in the rules.

> Sub-part (b) of the rule is designed to avoid trial by ambush and will not be departed from unless the court is fully satisfied that the opposing party will not be prejudiced.[156]

In the circumstances of that case, he was satisfied that the information contained in the expert evidence had previously been disclosed in an earlier Auditor General Report, and that the disclosure requirement in Rule 279 had substantially been complied with. The defendants had not been "taken by surprise."[157]

In *Rosenblat v. The Queen*,[158] Collier, J. was prepared to make an order allowing the evidence of an expert witness as to U.S. law relating to the escrow of securities even though the affidavit was filed a few days late. Collier, J. commented that it was his practice to overlook a technical breach of the rules of practice where there was no prejudice to the other party which could not be compensated by costs.

Another interesting aspect of the expert evidence in the *Harris* case was the court's acceptance of evidence with respect to the "operation of govern-

---

153 *Federal Court Rules*, SOR/98-106.

154 *Harris v. The Queen*, [2002] 1 C.T.C. 243.

155 *Ibid.* at 253 (C.T.C.).

156 *Ibid.*

157 *Ibid.* at 254 (C.T.C.).

158 *Rosenblat v. The Queen*, 75 D.T.C. 5274 (T.C.C.).

ment departments and Revenue Canada in particular."[159] However, Dawson, J. was careful to point out that the expert's reports were admitted only in "the narrow area in which the witnesses were proffered as experts" and not as experts on domestic law, as that evidence would certainly have been inadmissible.

Similarly, in *Eco-Zone Engineering Ltd. v. Grand Falls-Windsor (Town)*,[160] a case involving whether a low bidder's tender price was to be inclusive of the Goods and Services Tax ("GST"), the court allowed experts to explain how the GST worked in practice, the "mechanics" of the GST. The admissibility of this expert evidence was challenged by counsel but the Newfoundland Court of Appeal held that this part of the expert evidence was not opinion evidence but more in the nature of a factual description and therefore not subject to the rules of admissibility governing expert evidence.

> I would place such evidence within the factual matrix which may be considered in interpreting the contract. While the source of information is an expert, it is not opinion evidence and it is not the evidence to which the rules of admissibility of expert evidence are directed.[161]

As noted, Rule 145 requires that an expert witness be available to the court for cross-examination in order for their evidence to be admissible. This enables counsel for the other party to question the expert on the factual basis of his evidence to determine its reliability. Without testimony from the author, the court will generally not assign any probative value to the evidence.[162] Also, where a report has been authored by more than one expert, both experts must be available to provide testimony, otherwise the qualifications of all the experts cannot be confirmed by the court rendering the evidence inadmissible.[163]

J. INFORMAL PROCEDURE

A taxpayer pursuant to section 18 of the *Tax Court of Canada Act* can elect to have the case heard under the Informal Procedure in certain circumstances. These circumstances are:

---

159 *Harris*, above note 154.

160 *Eco-Zone Engineering Ltd. v. Grand Falls-Windsor (Town)*, 2000 NFCA 21, [2000] G.S.T.C. 106.

161 *Ibid.*, at para. 14.

162 See *Taylor Estate v. MNR*, [1990] 2 C.T.C. 2304, 90 D.T.C. 1777 (T.C.C.), at 1781 (D.T.C.).

163 *Ibid.*

1. federal tax and penalties excluding interest for one year are $12,000 or less;[164]
2. the amount of the loss determined under subsection 152(1.1) of the Act is $24,000 or less;[165]
3. the only subject matter is interest.[166]

Otherwise or where ordered by the court, the appeal will proceed under the General Procedure.

Note that most GST appeals are heard under the Informal Procedure since the *Tax Court of Canada Act* does not impose restrictions on the dollar amount in question as it does for income tax appeals. The Informal Procedure offers a speedier, less costly appeal process[167] for the taxpayer. Similar rules apply regarding the use of expert evidence but in keeping with the intent of offering a simplified procedure, the rules are somewhat relaxed. Under the *Tax Court of Canada Rules (Informal Procedure)*[168] and the *Tax Court of Canada Rules of Procedure respecting the Excise Tax Act,*[169] Rule 7 (identical in both) governs the use of expert witnesses.

> 7. Expert Witnesses —
> (1) A party who intends to call an expert witness at the hearing of an appeal shall, not less than 10 days before the commencement of the hearing, file at the Registry and serve on the other parties a report, signed by the expert, setting out the expert's name, address and qualifications and the substance of the expert's testimony.
> (2) An expert witness may not testify, except with leave of the presiding judge, if subsection (1) has not been satisfied.

The period for filing and serving of the expert's report is shortened to not less than 10 days before the hearing compared to 30 days under the General Procedure, however the intent of the notice period is still the same. The filing is required to provide the opposing party the time to review the expert's report and prepare for cross-examination of the person who prepared the report.

---

164 *Tax Court of Canada Act*, R.S.C. 1985, c. T-2, as amended, para. 18(1)(a).
165 *Ibid*,para. 18(1)(b).
166 *Ibid*,para. 18(2).
167 See David Sherman's Analysis (306) of Tax Court appeals, Analysis/Commentary available online at http://www.taxnetpro.com.
168 *Tax Court of Canada Rules (Informal Procedure)*, SOR/90-688, as amended.
169 *Tax Court of Canada Rules of Procedure respecting the Excise Tax Act*, SOR/92-42, as amended.

Notwithstanding the requirements of Rule 7(1), the court in *Sundquist v. The Queen*[170] applied a broad reading of the provision in the spirit of the "informal" nature of the proceedings and allowed the taxpayer's expert evidence. The case was a GST appeal concerning a New Housing Rebate on a home which the taxpayer had built. The taxpayer had called an expert to provide opinion evidence as to the value of the house. Bowie T.C.C.J. was critical of the expert's report referring to it as a "bare-bones" report containing only a "cryptic" description of the expert's qualifications.[171] However, the judge commented on the "marked contrast" between the requirements of the Informal Procedure and the General Procedure. The Informal Procedure requires that the report contain the "substance of the expert's testimony" (Rule 7(1)) whereas the General Procedure requires the report to contain "a full statement of the proposed evidence-in-chief of the witness" (Rule 145(2)(b)). Although the report in *Sundquist* would not satisfy the requirements of the General Procedure Rules, it was held to meet the "substance" requirement of the Informal Procedure Rules. Bowie, T.C.C.J. remarked on the intent of the Informal Procedure as a speedier, and less costly appeal process to the taxpayer.

> The Informal Procedure in this court, however, is designed to permit the resolution of disputes with minimum delay and minimum cost.
>
> . . . It would not serve the purpose for which the Informal Procedure exists to require that the appellant incur, in a case like this, the expense of having a witness prepare a more complete report of the kind that the General Procedure s. 145 require.[172]

K. DISCLOSURE RULES

The requirements for the disclosure of expert findings on examination for discovery are contained in Rule 95 of the *Tax Court of Canada Rules (General Procedure)*. Under the Informal Procedure there are no "discoveries," in keeping with the desire to minimize legal costs and the length of the proceedings.

The uncertainty in the law remains concerning privilege in expert's working papers discussed earlier in the chapter.

Under Rule 95(3) a party may on an examination for discovery obtain disclosure of the findings, opinions and conclusions of an expert engaged

---

170 *Sundquist v. The Queen*, [1996] G.S.T.C. 26, 4 G.T.C. 3102.

171 *Ibid*, at para. 5.

172 *Ibid*, at para. 9.

by the party being examined and that relate to a matter in issue in the proceeding but the party being examined need not disclose the information or even the name of the witness where the findings, opinions and conclusions of the witness were made in preparation for contemplated or pending litigation and no other purpose, and the party being examined undertakes not to call the expert as a witness at the hearing.

L. COURT-APPOINTED EXPERTS

In some jurisdictions, the rules of the court permit the use of court-appointed experts.[173] The issue is, of course, the concern surrounding the objectivity of expert witnesses retained by one or the other of the parties in the litigation. In these jurisdictions, independent expert witnesses can be called by the court to offer "independent technical evidence" when it is considered necessary.

Neither The *Tax Court of Canada Rules* or the *Federal Court Rules* contain such provisions. The Tax Court of Canada takes the position of allowing each side to call its own expert witnesses, anticipating an adversarial situation, and will assess the weight to be given to expert evidence in reaching its decisions.

M. COSTS

Expert's fees can be a substantial component of the costs in tax litigation.[174] Generally, the *Tax Court of Canada Rules* permit the successful party to recover the fees paid to an expert under the category of disbursements. Costs under the General Procedure are dealt with in Rule 147 to 152 and determined according to the Tariffs set out in Schedule II to the Rules. Costs under the Informal Procedure are dealt with in Rule 10 to 14 and determined according to the Tariffs set out in Schedule 13 of the Rules. Under the Rules, the Court has complete discretion as to costs.

In order for an expert's fees to be recovered, it must be shown that that the disbursement was incurred as a necessary and proper expenditure of

---

173 Ontario, *Rules of Civil Procedure*, R.R.O. 1990, Reg. 194, r. 52.03; Alberta *Rules of Court*, r. 218(1); the *Supreme Court Rules of the Northwest Territories*, r. 230; Nova Scotia *Civil Procedure Rules*, r. 23, Prince Edward Island *Civil Procedure Rules*, r. 23; Newfoundland *Rules of the Supreme Court*, 1986, r. 35, referenced in *The Law of Evidence*, above note 3, at 667.

174 Robert W. McMechan, "The Valuator as an Expert Witness and Managing the Tax Dispute Resolution Process," 95 C.M.C. 18, 18:14.

the party's case.[175] In *Leung v. MNR*,[176] the appellant's expert witness fees were allowed because the appellants had provided the Minister with an "itemization of the hours and the hourly rates." However the court denied recovery of costs incurred by an associate and a secretary of the expert. The court held that there was no corroborative information linking the work of those individuals with the expert's preparation for trial and therefore would not allow those expenses.[177]

Numerous cases are reported in McMechan, *Tax Court Practice*,[178] Vol. 1, where the court disallowed claims for expert fees on the basis that the witnesses had not been recognized as experts by the court.[179] In other cases, the expert's fees claimed were ground down to a "reasonable" amount by the court where the expert had used some of the research time claimed to refresh her knowledge.[180] The Federal Court, Trial Division has held that if a party chooses to hire a "Cadillac" of experts, the unsuccessful opposing party will not have to compensate for extravagant fees but will only have to pay reasonable fees.[181]

One important consideration to note is that the courts have allowed the cost of an expert witness who was *not* called to testify. Failure to call a witness has, in many cases, resulted in a negative inference against the party not calling the witness.[182] However, other cases have held that there could be many reasons for a party not to call a witness, and not necessarily that the information being withheld was detrimental to their case.[183]

In *RMM Canadian Enterprises v. The Queen*,[184] Bowman, T.C.C.J. (as he then was), allowed costs for a U.S. tax expert who was available but not called to testify. This decision was followed in *Comsense Inc. v. The Queen*.[185]

---

175 *Ibid.*

176 *Leung v. MNR*, [1993] 2 C.T.C. 2103, 93 D.T.C. 795 (T.C.C.).

177 *Ibid*, at 802 (D.T.C.).

178 McMechan, *Tax Court Practice*, above note 11,at 2.4-360.

179 See *Hassanali Estate v. The Queen*, [1998] 2 C.T.C. 3055 (T.C.C.); *Canwest Capital Inc. v. The Queen*, (unreported), Doc. No. 94-503 (IT)G (T.C.C.); *Bastone v. Canada* (unreported), Doc. No. 91-2346 (IT)G (T.C.C.).

180 See *L.& M. Wood Products (1985) Ltd. v. The Queen*, [1998] 2 C.T.C. 2701, 98 D.T.C. 1410.

181 *Apotex Inc. v. Syntex Pharmaceuticals International Ltd.*, (1999) 2 C.P.R. (4th) 368, 176 F.T.R. 142 (F.C.T.D.).

182 See *DeGeer v. The Queen (1999)*, 2000 D.T.C. 1749 (T.C.C.); *Huneault v. The Queen*, [1998] 3 C.T.C. 2788, 98 D.T.C. 1488 (Fr.) (T.C.C.); *Nelson v. The Queen*, [1998] 1 C.T.C. 2008, 97 D.T.C. 1253 (T.C.C.).

183 *Jolivet v. The Queen*, [2000] 1 S.C.R. 751, 33 C.R. (5th) 1; *Alemu v. The Queen*, [1999] 2 C.T.C. 2245, 99 D.T.C. 714 (T.C.C.).

184 *RMM Canadian Enterprises v. The Queen*, [1997] T.C.J. No. 445.

185 *Comsense Inc. v. The Queen*, [2000] 3 C.T.C. 2790, 2000 D.T.C. 2345 (T.C.C.).

In that case, an expert was retained and an expert report was filed and served, however, the other party subsequently chose to withdraw their appeals. Nevertheless, Tanasychuk, T.O., considering the decision in *RMM Canadian Enterprises*, allowed the respondent's expert fees.

N. CONCLUSION

Opinion evidence is becoming an ever important part of a tax case. The principal areas for expert witnesses are in the area of the proper accounting treatment and the valuation of properties. Accounting treatment can involve the sophisticated distinction between Canadian and U.S. GAAP and the proper accounting treatment for a matter not set out in the CICA Handbook. Valuation matters can range from the value of real estate to more abstruse principles of minority and holding company discounts. As business becomes more global and companies engage in transactions that transcend Canadian borders, evidence as to foreign law becomes more prevalent in Canadian tax cases. Special issues arise that relate to the credibility and independence of the experts called on behalf of CRA who are also employees of CRA. Care in tax cases must be given to evidence that goes to the ultimate issue to ensure that the expert is not usurping the function of the Court. Otherwise, the role and rules regarding expert witnesses is not much different than that found in civil litigation.

APPENDIX

Tax Court of Canada — General Procedure Rules

145 . Expert Witnesses —

(1) In this section, "affidavit" includes,

(a) a solemn declaration made under section 41 of the Canada Evidence Act,

(b) a statement in writing signed by the proposed witness and accompanied by a certificate of counsel that counsel is satisfied that it represents evidence that the proposed witness is prepared to give in the matter, or

(c) a statement in writing in any other form authorized by direction of the court in a particular case and for special reasons.

(2) Unless otherwise directed by the court, no evidence in chief of an expert witness shall be received at the hearing in respect of an issue unless,

(a) the issue has been defined by the pleadings or by written agreement of the parties stating the issues,

(b) a full statement of the proposed evidence in chief of the witness has been set out in an affidavit, the original of which has been filed and a copy of which has been served on all other parties, not less than thirty days before the commencement of the hearing; and

(c) the witness is available at the hearing for cross-examination.

(3) Unless otherwise directed by the court, no evidence of an expert witness shall be led in rebuttal of any evidence tendered in writing under paragraph (2)(b) unless the rebuttal evidence has been reduced to writing in accordance with this section and the original filed and a copy served on all the other parties not less than fifteen days before the commencement of the hearing.

(4) Subject to compliance with subsection (2), evidence in chief of an expert witness may be given at the hearing by,

(a) reading the whole or part of the affidavit into evidence by the witness, unless the court, with the consent of the parties, permits it to be taken as read, and

(b) if the party calling the witness so elects, the verbal testimony of the witness,

(i) explaining or demonstrating what is in the affidavit or the part that has been given in evidence, and
(ii) in respect of other matters by special leave of the court, upon such terms as may be just.

(5) A witness shall not be cross-examined before the hearing on an affidavit filed under subsection (2) without leave of the court, and if such leave is granted, the witness shall not be cross-examined at the hearing without leave of the court but the witness may, with leave of the court, be produced for re-examination and shall be produced for examination by the court, if the court so requires.

(6) An affidavit filed under subsection (2) shall not become part of the evidence at the hearing unless given in evidence under subsection (4). [SOR/95-113, s. 9]

95. Scope of Examination —

(1) A person examined for discovery shall answer, to the best of that person's knowledge, information and belief, any proper question relating to any matter in issue in the proceeding or to any matter made discoverable by subsection (3) and no question may be objected to on the ground that,
(a) the information sought is evidence or hearsay,
(b) the question constitutes cross-examination, unless the question is directed solely to the credibility of the witness, or
(c) the question constitutes cross-examination on the affidavit of documents of the party being examined.

(2) Prior to the examination for discovery, the person to be examined shall make all reasonable inquiries regarding the matters in issue from all of the party's officers, servants, agents and employees, past or present, either within or outside Canada and, if necessary, the person being examined for discovery may be required to become better informed and for that purpose the examination may be adjourned.

(3) A party may on an examination for discovery obtain disclosure of the findings, opinions and conclusions of an expert engaged by or on behalf of the party being examined that relate to a matter in issue in the proceeding including the expert's name and address, but the party being examined need not disclose the information or the name and address of the expert where,

(a) the findings, opinions and conclusions of the expert relating to any matter in issue in the appeal were made or formed in preparation for contemplated or pending litigation and for no other purpose, and
(b) the party being examined undertakes not to call the expert as a witness at the hearing.

(4) A party may on an examination for discovery obtain disclosure of the names and addresses of persons who might reasonably be expected to have knowledge of transactions or occurrences in issue in the proceeding, unless the court orders otherwise [SOR/93-96, s. 13].

Chapter Thirteen

Reflections on the Expert's Role in the Tax Court of Canada*

James L. Horvath and Steven A. Hacker

A. INTRODUCTION

One of the highlights of any professional's career is the opportunity to testify in court at a trial or other legal proceeding as an expert in their field. The experience can be both useful to the court, and personally and professionally rewarding. Professional reputations, however, can also be tarnished by an actual or perceived poor performance in the witness box. This paper draws on personal experiences from court appearances, discussions with colleagues, and reported judgments involving other experts (mainly in the field of business valuation and real estate appraisal), and presents our reflections on the role of experts in court and the process of providing expert testimony. The paper includes a look at some of the unique issues faced by expert witnesses and factors key to a successful expert witness experience.

The role of experts appearing in courts such as the Tax Court of Canada is to serve as a friend of the court, providing expertise in their field of

* The authors wish to thank their colleagues John Anderson, CA, PhD, Steven Blau LLB, BCL, Stu Douglas, FCA, CFE, D. Alan Jones, FCBV, and Michael Shaen, LLB, LLM for their review of and suggestions for this paper.

practice. The expert witness must be objective, and not be aligned with either of the parties to a dispute, despite typically being retained by only one of the parties. The expert witness is called upon to substantiate or explain factual evidence and/or to provide opinion evidence relevant to the matter being tried. The ability to offer their opinion in court sets the expert witness apart from other witnesses, however, the degree to which an expert opinion is accepted by the court, rests upon the expert's credibility. Credibility is a function of a number of characteristics and factors (examined in this paper), some of which are based on the quality of the expert's court testimony and demeanour, and others on the strength of the expert's written report, and the depth of his or her relevant experience and expertise.

For most professionals, appearing as an expert witness occurs only occasionally, even for those such as Business Valuators whose core professional activity often involves providing opinions in a dispute context. This is largely because over ninety percent of disputes are resolved either before proceeding to court, or before the court proceedings are completed. For the authors of this paper, as business valuators and appraisers who are engaged full time in providing written opinions of value, often in a context of litigation, the chance to orally present and defend an opinion in an adversarial setting is an occasional and special occurrence.

B. EXPERT TESTIMONY IS THE CLIMAX OF THE LITIGATION SUPPORT DRAMA

We tend to view the providing of expert testimony in court as the climax of the litigation support drama. This may be difficult to imagine, given that the few courtroom films or TV dramas involving experts tend to deal with criminal, family law or class action matters involving medical experts such as coroners, toxicologists, pathologists, psychiatrists, social workers and so on, as opposed to tax accountants, business valuators, or appraisers. It is useful to consider the role played by an expert in providing litigation support from the time of retainer, leading up to expert testimony, and through to the denouement of providing assistance to counsel post-testimony. In our experience, the expert provides critical support to counsel at all stages of the litigation, starting from the initial meeting of counsel, their client, and the expert.

The expert's first significant role is in assessing the viability or merits of the case. For example, a software expert may provide a preliminary technical analysis of the subject software. An expert such as a business valuator would, in turn, provide preliminary analysis on the reasonability and risks associated with a business plan, or even a very preliminary valuation analysis. Such analysis may be important to counsel in determining litigation strategy.

Once retained, the expert begins a detailed critical analysis of all the available documentation. This process results in a detailed information request, which the counsel can incorporate into a list of productions requested from the other party to the dispute. Depending on the nature of the dispute, this review of documents may include examination of the pleadings, all material in the document brief including agreements, articles of incorporation, minutes, discovery transcripts, other expert reports, including those of experts in other disciplines. For the sake of completeness of our investigation, and to maximize the opportunity to provide thorough pre-trial assistance, we often try to review all accessible portions of the file in addition to relying on counsel to provide what he or she thinks is appropriate for our purposes.

The expert will often be hampered by a lack of evidence, either because of a non-cooperative party, or due to items not documented or retained. In such cases, the expert may have to make significant assumptions, leading to a more qualified opinion.

The expert report, discussed in more detail below, forms the basis of the courtroom testimony. Once the report is completed, the expert may be involved in the examination for discovery process (either by being examined, or assisting by submitting suggested questions, attending discoveries, reviewing answers to undertakings and transcripts). The expert will also typically be involved in analyzing and critiquing reports by experts retained by opposing parties, reconciling differences between expert reports (e.g. by assessing other experts' methodology, assumptions, scope of review, factual foundations, conclusions), and in some cases preparing a written critique or rebuttal to be formally filed as evidence.

Other forms of pre-trial assistance which we have provided in the past include identifying and evaluating potential expert witnesses in other disciplines (e.g., computer software developers and function point analysts, machinery and equipment appraisers, and third party industry experts), attending at pre-trials, court conference meetings, mediation and arbitration hearings, evaluating settlement offers, and on occasion, advising counsel and their client on various financial and valuation principles and concepts and their applicability to the matter at hand (e.g., valuation methodologies, valuation discounts and premiums, use of hindsight data).

During the trial, in addition to providing expert testimony, the expert often provides input to counsel on cross-examination questions for the opposing side's experts, and on closing arguments. After the trial, in what could be termed the denouement, there is still scope for expert involvement, for example in assessing the reasons for judgment, and possibly assisting with evaluating the potential for launching an appeal.

C. ROLE OF THE EXPERT IN COURT

The role of the expert is to:

- provide the court with technical assistance in establishing facts;
- explain technical matters that are outside the domain of knowledge of the judge or an ordinary person; and
- present an opinion or conclusion, based on the facts, and the expert's knowledge and experience.

Accordingly, for the expert evidence to be admissible, it must be shown that the expert is sufficiently qualified and impartial. Such qualities will be discussed below.

The court may hear opinion evidence from a number of experts, but is not bound to give equal weight to each. For example, in cases with more than one expert witness, it is not uncommon for the court to reject all expert advice, and form its own opinion of value, rejecting either extreme positions or even a middle ground. In such judgments, it is sometimes the case that the judge believes there is fault in an expert's analysis such as exclusion of relevant facts, unreasonable assumptions, and lack of objectivity, to name a few. The following reasons for judgment are illustrative.

Connor v. R.[1] dealt with the appeal of an income tax case involving the valuation of shares of a private company. The Trial Judge accepted some of the evidence, but he rejected the methods used by the experts to arrive at their valuations. The appellant attacked the valuation by the Trial Judge, who used his own method to value the shares. In relation to the experts' testimony, the Trial Judge found that "both parties took, and maintained throughout, extreme positions which were entirely disassociated from reality." In the reasons for judgment dismissing the appeal, Urie, J. wrote:

> It is trite to say the Trial Judge is the trier of fact and he is thus entitled to accept or reject, in whole or in part, any of the evidence adduced before him. In this case he accepted some of the evidence but he rejected in all cases the methods, at least in part, whereby the experts arrived at their valuations. He

1 79 D.T.C. 5256 (F.C.A.).

> was entitled to do so and unless it can be said thereafter he proceeded on a wrong principle or that he made a palpable error in reaching his own conclusions as to value, we ought not to interfere with his findings.[2]

Bibby v. R.,[3] a case dealing with real estate valuation, included the testimony of several experts. The judgment noted that there was a significant difference in the comparable properties on which the respective valuation opinions were based. It was noted by Walsh, J. that:

> While it has frequently been held that a Court should not, after considering all the expert and other evidence merely adopt a figure somewhere between the figure sought by the contending parties, it has also been held that the Court may, when it does not find the evidence of any expert completely satisfying or conclusive, nor any comparable especially apt, form its own opinion of valuation, provided this is always based on the careful consideration of all the conflicting evidence. The figure so arrived need not be that suggested by any expert or contended for by the parties.[4]

In some cases, despite the considerable expertise and skill of the expert, and the use of acceptable methods in the circumstances, the court prefers a common sense or common person approach. This was evident in the judgment of Bowman, J. in *Hallatt v. R.*, where one expert's report was accepted (after making some adjustments), on the basis that "it results in a figure that is more consistent with my common sense and idea of reality."[5] We have long been supporters of this view and have generally placed more weight on actual market evidence over notional marketplace characteristics that are often assumed to exist.

Practice Tip

Experts should not excessively rely on esoteric or overly theoretical methods and analyses. Judges often prefer or place more weight on relevant actual market evidence, and comprehensible valuation techniques.

In the cost hearing in *Brown v. The Queen, Reasons for Costs*, Rip, J. succinctly summarized the role of the expert valuator and expert valuation report as follows:

2 *Ibid.*, at para 4.

3 3 D.T.C. 5148 (F.C.T.D.).

4 *Ibid.*, at para. 32. This finding has been subsequently referred to in numerous other judgments.

5 2001 D.T.C. 128 (T.C.C.), at para. 52. This theme is also apparent in judgments in which actual transactions are selected over an expert's theoretical or hypothetical findings.

> Valuation reports should serve to assist a trial judge to determine the proper valuation. A valuator should not advance his client's position. Once the author of a valuation report is effectively examined and cross-examined the strengths and weaknesses of the report are highlighted; the puffery and hyperbole hopefully disappear and the judge can appreciate the quality of the valuation and give the valuation its due weight. . . . taken together, the reports — and the testimony of their authors, and their examinations in chief and cross-examinations — did help me to develop guidelines to serve as the basis of the valuation.[6]

Although the expert witness is an unbiased and objective party to the court proceeding, both expert and counsel should be aware of how to

- appropriately qualify one's own expert;
- how to leverage the expert's testimony;
- how to introduce critical evidence;
- manage the cross-examination;
- maximize the opportunities afforded by the reply; and
- effectively cross-examine and challenge opposing experts.

D. STEPPING TO THE PLATE: QUALIFYING AS AN EXPERT WITNESS, AND OTHER POTENTIAL ROADBLOCKS TO TESTIFYING

Qualification as an expert is the prerequisite to giving evidence. The qualification process establishes the expert's credentials, and is a critical stage in the development of the judge's perception of the expert's credibility. The qualification process, which involves an in-depth analysis of the expert's past experience and credentials, underlines the importance of a well-documented and organized curriculum vita. It is typical for an expert to be questioned on the nature and details of past assignments (particularly those closely related to the matter at hand), and education. An expert who has a professional designation or is a member of a professional association should expect to explain the requirements to attain the designation or membership, requirements for continuing education (including proof that the requirements have been adhered to). Industry knowledge and experience with the specific market will also be challenged.

The expert should expect that opposing counsel has reviewed all articles, speeches, or books authored by the expert, and any written judgments involv-

6 2002 D.T.C. 1925 at para. 17 (T.C.C.) aff'd 2003 D.T.C. 5298 (F.C.A.).

ing the expert's previous testimony, and may attempt to challenge the opposing expert either in the qualification or cross-examination stage of testimony. We find that it is important that counsel be very familiar with their expert's background to maximize the credibility building aspect of expert witness qualification. It is therefore one of the most significant elements of the preparation process that counsel and expert undertake. The demonstration of the expert's qualifications should be in a manner that emphasizes qualifications that are relevant to the specific circumstances of the case, in order to avoid a perception that he or she is opining on an area outside his or her expertise.

There are many instances in which experts have been either prevented from testifying or have had less weight given to their evidence, because of lack of appropriate qualifications, or issues related to authorship of expert report, lack of independence, and lack of experience in or exposure to the specific circumstances of the matters being opined on. The following cases deal with issues relating to qualifications, independence, experience, and other obstacles to testifying.

1) Authorship

It is not unusual for an expert witness to utilize a team of staff in the completion of an expert report, for example to do research and complete analysis. In our practice, valuation reports are generally a team effort, in which a senior professional is generally the leader and plays a significant role, and the opinion expressed in the valuation report signed by the senior professional is his or hers. Similarly, it is important for the author of the expert opinion to contribute the judgment applied, and the assumptions made,[7] and participate in the selection of relevant methodology, among other items. On cross-examination, opposing counsel may seek to discredit the expert, by attempting to minimize the role of the witness in the preparation of the report. On this subject, in a mock trial presented by the Canadian Institute of Chartered Business Valuators (CICBV) at its November 1984 conference, Clayton Schulz, CA, CBV stated:

> . . . we all use staff. It's very critical to ensure that you know precisely what your staff did; and it's very critical that you be able to say what they did and whether or not the opinion is yours or theirs. Of course, if the opinion is theirs, then you've got some difficulty.[8]

---

7 In some instances, certain assumptions are made at the request of counsel. The expert must ensure that the assumptions made do not compromise his or her integrity, or the overall reasonableness or consistency of their findings.

8 *Journal of Business Valuation*, (1985), at 175.

Delegation of research and analysis tasks is permissible, provided that the testifying expert has reviewed and discussed the work, accepts the findings, and incorporates it into the expert opinion.

The issue of authorship arose in *Hallatt*. In that case, the author of the appellant's expert report, had switched employers, and the terms of her new employment prevented her from providing expert evidence in court. The appellant called as an expert, another valuator with the original author's employment, who sought to introduce the original report. Bowman J. wrote, "One expert of course cannot put in another's report."[9] Instead of simply disallowing the appellant from rebutting the Minister's valuation, the judge resolved the matter of appellant valuation evidence by allowing the alternate valuator to express his opinion orally, and then adjourning the hearing to allow the respondent time to prepare a cross-examination. Similarly, in *McCoy v. The Queen*, a case in which the co-author of this paper gave expert testimony for the Respondent, the expert opinion of the Appellant's business valuator was found by the Court to be "essentially a commentary"[10] on the report of another author, who was not called as an expert witness. The Judge acknowledged the strong qualifications of the valuator, but stated that his testimony concerning the methodology used by the other author was not sufficient to give the other report "the sort of evidentiary weight or value necessary to establish in this court the conclusions expressed in the report. One expert cannot put in another expert's report and make it evidence: *Hallatt*." The Judge concluded that it may well be that the methodology used by the author "conforms to traditionally accepted standards but if the underlying premises, assumptions and selection of facts cannot be tested the conclusions can be given no weight."[11]

> *Practice Tip*
>
> *Over the past thirty years, we have seen numerous cases where senior valuators have used essentially the same valuation methodology but have come up with dramatically different opinions of value. It is always useful to isolate the sources of such differences (e.g., facts considered or ignored, assumptions made, professional judgment, etc.)* For example, in one case, the four valuators involved all used similar methodology, but the opinion of value varied dramatically, from \$3 million to \$8 million to \$17 million, and to \$19 million. (The out-of-court settlement price was \$17 million).

9 *Hallatt*, above note 5 at para. 11.

10 2003 D.T.C. (T.C.C.) 660, at para. 46.

11 *Ibid.*, at para. 49.

2) The Importance of Professional Association Membership

In evaluating qualifications of a potential expert witness, the tax court has on several occasions considered whether membership in a professional association for the respective discipline was a necessary prerequisite to qualification as an expert. In the case of valuation experts, it seems clear that in this era, such a professional designation is required. In *Schaefer Brothers Inc. v. Minister of National Revenue,* a case dealing with a business valuation related to an expropriation, the Board considered an objection raised regarding the testimony of a business valuator who was not a member of an association of valuators. Tremblay, C.G.A. ruled against accepting the valuator's testimony, commenting:

> The witness who testified as an appraiser was not a member of an association of appraisers even if he was a member of an association of accountants. He had not attended courses in valuation. However, he made 100 valuation reports in two years.
>
> The Board thinks it is useful to repeat what it said in the case of *Les Meubles de Maskinonge Inc. et al. v. M.N.R.*, (1978) C.T.C. 2285, 78 D.T.C. 1235. There is no reason in 1978 that one can testify as appraisal expert without being member of an association of appraisers. The policy of the Board during the former years by accepting as expert, a person who was not member of an association of appraisers, was only a temporary policy. It is the Board's opinion that to give an expert opinion there is a presumption: only the members of an appropriate professional association are qualified to testify in court.
>
> Because of the evolution of the appraisal science in Canada during the last seven years and the incorporation of appropriate associations, an appraisal report must be given in court by a member of an association of appraisers. It would be exceptional and on a strong evidence of a very great experience that this rule should be infringed.[12]

This case was also cited in *Trepanier v. Minister of National Revenue,*[13] where it was found similarly: "With rare exceptions, anyone who represents himself as an expert in valuation should be a member of a professional corporation of valuators. If an exception is to be made, it must be shown, for example, that the individual not only has a great deal of experience but has also worked in the property field for a number of years."[14]

---

12 *Schaefer Brothers Inc. v. Minister of National Revenue,* 79 D.T.C. 288 (T.A.B.) at paras. 65–88.

13 79 D.T.C. 924 (T.R.B.).

14 *Ibid.* at para. 26.

Professional associations and designations exist for various valuation disciplines, and other areas of expertise; however, the courts frequently rely on the expertise of individuals whose unique knowledge or experience does not lend itself to such credentials. In two recent tax cases dealing with the value of ownership interests in software (i.e., taxpayer investments in software tax shelters), *Brown*[15] and *McCoy*,[16] experts in the area of the specific kind of software being addressed by the court provided expert testimony based on the strength of their qualifications gained through their career training and experience. For example, in *McCoy*, Robert Pardo, a successful and recognized Commodity Trading Advisor, developer of software similar to the subject of the case, and published author on the subject matter, testified as to the software's viability, profitability, marketability, and development methodology.[17]

The need for academic or professional qualifications was dealt with in *Rice v. Sockett*.[18] In this case involving litigation relating to the construction of a silo, expert evidence was heard from two witnesses whose respective experience was in cement construction and general concrete construction. In considering whether the witnesses should be considered as expert witnesses, the Court noted the following:

> Dr. John D. Lawson, in *The Law of Expert and Opinion Evidence*, 2nd ed., p. 74 lays down as rule 22: "Mechanics, artisans and workmen are experts as to matters of technical skill in their trades, and their opinions in such cases are admissible," citing numerous authorities and illustrations. "The derivation of the term 'expert' implies that he is one who by experience has acquired special or peculiar knowledge of the subject of which he undertakes to testify, and it does not matter whether such knowledge has been acquired by study of scientific works or by practical observation. Hence, one who is an old hunter, and has thus had much experience in the use of firearms, may be as well qualified to testify as to the appearance which a gun recently fired would present as a highly-educated and skilled gunsmith": *State v. Davis* (1899), 33 S.E. Repr. 449, 55 So. Car. 339, cited in *Words and Phrases Judicially Defined*, vol. 3, p. 2595.[19]

15 Above note 6.

16 Above note 10.

17 Mr. Pardo's reflections on his experiences as an expert witness in *McCoy* are found in Chapter 14 of this publication.

18 [1912] O.J. No. 49, 27 O.L.R. 410 (Div. Ct.).

19 *Ibid.* at paras. 21–22.

In *R. v. Kinnie,*[20] an appeal case relating to a conviction of impaired driving, the British Columbia Court of Appeal found that a witness with a Ph.D. in biology, who had completed related research and had experience in administering breathalyzer tests, was not qualified to testify as an expert in the case because he lacked specific experience in the drug impairment that was the subject of the appeal.

The above examples underline the importance of qualifications that are both strong, and sufficiently relevant to the issue at hand.

3) Independence of Expert Witness

The issue of whether the expert is independent of their client, unbiased and objective is frequently argued when expert testimony is to be heard. Except in the instance when the expert is either jointly retained, or retained by the court, the expert witness is paid by one of the parties to the dispute. In tax litigation, the appellant's expert witness (or others in the expert's firm) sometimes has a historical professional relationship with the taxpayer as auditor, accountant and/or tax advisor. Along with the in-depth knowledge of the business that comes with the historical relationship comes the potential for attack from opposing counsel, and the perception of bias by the judge. Experts acting for the Canada Revenue Agency ("CRA") are frequently CRA employees, and have been alleged in court to be biased by virtue of their employment.

Working for a large multinational accounting firm, we have often been retained to act for clients of the firm. We do not perceive this to be a compromise of the expert's independence or a barrier to testifying in court, provided the expert is not influenced by the opinions of the client, partners, or other business considerations, and provided the relevant professional standards regarding the provision of services to clients are observed. The provision of valuation services to audit clients of chartered accounting firms is now governed by strict guidelines such as the Sarbanes-Oxley legislation in the US, and equivalent regulations in Canada. Similarly, depending on the facts and circumstances, an appraiser or business valuator who is an employee of the CRA should not be precluded from testifying for reasons of their employment.

The question of partiality was addressed in the judgment of *Gilvesy Enterprises Inc. v. R.*[21] In this case, the respondent's expert business valuator was an employee of Revenue Canada. Counsel for the appellant did not

20 [1989] B.C.J. No. 2021, 40 B.C.L.R. (2d) 369.

21 97 D.T.C. 811 (T.C.C.).

challenge the valuator's qualifications, but instead challenged the probative value of her opinion, based in part, on her employment status. Bowie J. wrote in his reasons for judgment:

> Bias in favour of the party for whom the evidence is given, and who, therefore pays the witness, is always a potential cause for concern in evaluating opinion evidence. In the absence of specific evidence going to the issue, there is no reason to believe that the potential for bias is any greater cause for concern in the case of evidence given by an employee of a litigating government or corporation than in the case of a self-employed consultant who bills by the hour or by the day. In either case it is the integrity, training, experience and judgment of the witness that will ultimately determine the value of the evidence, not the type of contractual relationship shared by the witness and the party for whom the evidence is led.[22]

The judge observed no reason to doubt the integrity or sincerity of the expert witness in giving her evidence, and concluded: "I reject the suggestion that bias, even at a subconscious level, is a factor that should diminish its probative value."[23] In *Laycock v. R.*, the decision was reached to admit the expert evidence of a Department of National Revenue senior appraiser, "but that careful consideration would be given to the question of possible bias, either conscious or unconscious."[24] The judge found the testimony of the expert to be completely frank, honest and objective and fair, but noted the difficulty of evaluating unconscious bias, about which he concluded: "I can only say that in nothing that he said or did and in nothing in his attitude did I find any indication that it might exist."[25]

The issue of the subconscious bias of an expert employed by the government was addressed in *Attridge (E.J.) v. Canada*. In this case, a real estate appraiser, employed by the Minister of National Revenue gave expert testimony. Muldoon J. cited an instance where the witness, whose testimony he described as candid and truthfully forthright, was less than evenhanded in her professional conclusions:

> The disparity of the sums is hardly worth mentioning; but the underlying, perhaps unconscious, please-my-patron bias is worth mentioning. Once

---

22 *Ibid.*, at para. 18.

23 *Ibid.* Similar rulings regarding the credibility of expert evidence provided by CRA employees can be found in *Groeneveld v. Minister of National Revenue*, 90 D.T.C. 1121 (T.C.C.); *Bay Centre Apartments Ltd. v. Minister of National Revenue*, 81 D.T.C. 4891 (T.R.B.); and *Laycock v. R.*, 78 D.T.C. 6349 (F.C.T.D.).

24 *Laycock, ibid.* at para. 25.

25 *Ibid.*

> recognized, such bias is admittedly hard for the Court to quantify in a report which aims at quantifications of values in place some 16 years before the defendant's employee undertook her task of appraisal, on her employer's behalf.[26]

He noted that there were other more significant aspects of the expert's work which "erroneously support her employer's posture in this litigation . . . The Court is not convinced that such aspects of her work were deliberately configured. Nevertheless, they are evinced through Ms. Crumb's candid testimony."[27] In this case, the Court found fault with the conclusions and opinions of all the experts.

The influence of an expert for the appellant's relationship with the taxpayer was addressed in *Majean Investment Co. v. R.*,[28] in which case the evidence of the appellant's business valuation expert was favoured, and the fact that the expert had a forty year history with the appellant's business as their auditor was a strength, as opposed to a potential detraction: "Mr. Parrot, on the other hand, has been associated with McGrath Canada for 40 years as their auditor and, as such, had an intimate knowledge of the company and its operations and he expressed himself clearly, such that his evidence showed a depth of analysis, not only on facts but on experience that was founded in his many years of private chartered accountancy practice, including other business valuations and opinions tendered in other clients' tax matters."[29]

A different finding obtained in *Chinneck v. Chinneck*,[30] a family law case. The chartered accountant of the subject business gave valuation evidence for the husband. This ongoing relationship with the subject business, and the social relationship of the accountant and the husband was noted by the Judge.[31] The Judge observed that the accountant's evidence "lacked conviction and appeared symptomatic of advocacy on behalf of the respondent"[32] and subsequently stated: "Mr. McNeil, in a very human context, given his ongoing interest, appears to have crossed the line of objectivity and entered the area of advocacy."[33]

---

26 91 D.T.C. 5161.

27 *Ibid.*

28 94 D.T.C. 1247 (T.C.C.).

29 *Ibid* at para. 43.

30 [1995] O.J. No. 2786 (Gen. Div.).

31 *Ibid.* at para. 93.

32 *Ibid.*

33 *Ibid.*

The reasons for judgment also addressed the lack of independence of another valuations expert witness, who was described by the judge as "not a good witness,"[34] and who was strongly criticized:

> When he left the witness stand, he literally fled from the courtroom as one attempting to put a very unpleasant experience behind them. That is understandable in that his credibility was for the purposes of this litigation destroyed. He left the overwhelming conclusion that if he were asked to do an appraisal for a certain purpose that you could rely upon the opinion as to value reflecting the desire of the particular request.[35]

Although the Court's perception of bias may only be formed once the expert has completed testimony, an underlying bias contained in the expert's report will significantly influence the impression and can undo an otherwise strong performance in the witness box.

4) Reliance on Third Party Experts

Business valuations often involve discussions with industry participants (e.g., competitors, regulators, purchasers/vendors of similar businesses). In such instances, it is permissible for the expert witness to refer to the discussions in his report. In some cases however, the business valuator or other expert needs to rely on the expertise and opinions of third parties in technical matters. As discussed above, the courts permit the use of hearsay evidence by an expert witness. We have frequently incorporated the findings of software developers/engineers, equipment appraisers, real estate appraisers, and third party industry experts, to name a few disciplines and experts. In such situations, it is critical that the reputation and qualifications of the third party expert are carefully evaluated and determined to be suitable for qualification in court as an expert witness, and that the third party expert is made aware that they need to be available to testify in court, if necessary. In *McCoy*,[36] several futures trading software industry participants were interviewed in the process of selecting Mr. Robert Pardo, the expert whose findings we relied on in our own expert report. We also relied on the findings of a software developer in our expert report.

Several cases have underlined the importance of the proper use of third party expertise. In *Petro-Canada v. Her Majesty the Queen*,[37] a case

34 *Ibid.*

35 *Ibid.*

36 Above note 10.

37 2003 D.T.C. 94 (T.C.C.).

involving the value of seismic data, the CRA valuator made reference to matters of judgment obtained from third party individuals who had been involved in advising others on the value of seismic data. These individuals were not called at trial as expert witnesses, and the court had no opportunity to evaluate their qualifications and competence, nor were they subject to cross-examination. Bowie J. wrote in his reasons for judgment:

> Opinion witnesses, at least in civil proceedings, have a certain latitude to base their opinions upon information that they have gathered outside the courtroom, and which is not formally proved. It becomes part of the general body of knowledge that contributes to the expertise of the witness. No such latitude is available in respect of matters of judgment or opinion, however. The reason that certain witnesses may express opinions is because they possess knowledge and expertise acquired through study and experience that will assist the Court. They may consult recognized texts and reference materials in formulating and in defending their opinions, but they may not simply reiterate the opinions of others, with or without attribution.[38]

The evidence of the CRA valuator was found by the court to be pervaded by the opinions of third parties "to such an extent, and so inextricably, as to destroy any probative value that it might otherwise have."[39]

In *Harry Taylor Estate v. Minister of National Revenue*,[40] a matter involving the valuation of shares, a valuator, in determining the break-up value of the business, relied on information provided by employees of the business: "the market value of the moveable and immoveable property had been determined on the basis of information provided by persons in the firm and then determined also what was buildings and what was land on the basis of the municipal assessment."[41] The court found that this statement was not admissible evidence, and no probative value was assigned to that part of the valuator's report:

> A statement of this kind is not admissible evidence and for this reason I cannot assign any probative value to this feature of the report. An expert is permitted to complete his valuation on the basis of a valuation prepared by another expert when among the property to be valued by him is property that he does not have the requisite skill to value. Moreover, for a val-

---

38 *Ibid.* at para. 104. See also *City of Saint John v. Irving Oil Co. Ltd.*, [1996] S.C.R. 581 at 592.

39 *Ibid.*

40 90 D.T.C. 1777 (T.C.C.).

> uation prepared by a second expert to be admitted as evidence, the qualifications of the second expert must be clearly established to the satisfaction of the Court and also the author of the report be at least accessible to the other party so that it may examine or cross-examine him in order to determine whether his expert opinion is correct. Absent testimony from the author, the Court cannot assign any probative value to this valuation.[42]

Similarly, an adjustment made by a valuator expert witness regarding excessive wages paid to arm's length parties, made on the basis of the opinion of another "expert" (whose qualifications were not identified in evidence) was criticized by the court in *Taylor* as a "purely gratuitous statement . . . . A claim of this kind without supporting evidence cannot be accepted seriously as one of the factors determining the value of the business."[43]

E. CRITIQUING THE OPPOSING EXPERT

The expert is usually requested to critique an opposing expert's report. This can be done in a verbal or informal memorandum form, for the use of counsel in cross-examining the opposing witness, or more typically, in a formal written rebuttal, which is then entered as evidence. According to s. 145(3) of the *Tax Court of Canada Rules (General Procedure)*,[44] such rebuttal evidence must be reduced to writing, and a copy must be served on all the other parties not less than fifteen days before the commencement of the hearing.

In addition to the rules of procedure of the court in which the testimony is being heard, care must be taken to ensure that written rebuttal evidence is prepared in a form that is in compliance with the relevant professional practice standards governing the expert's discipline or professional body, if applicable.

The Canadian Institute of Chartered Business Valuators, the professional body of Chartered Business Valuators has recently adopted reporting standards and recommendations concerning the preparation by its members of what it refers to as Limited Critique Reports. The standard, No. 410, specifies information that, as a minimum, must be contained in a Limited Critique Report, which includes many of the items that must be contained in a Valuation Report. Standards were also adopted concerning the scope

41 *Ibid.* at para. 36.

42 *Ibid.*

43 *Ibid.*

44 SOR/90-688, as amended by SOR/92-41, SOR/93-96, SOR/95-113, SOR/96-144, SOR/96-503, SOR/99-209.

of work required for Limited Critique Reports, (CICBV Standard No. 420), and file documentation standards (CICBV Standard No. 430). In addition, in preparing rebuttal evidence, care should be taken to adhere to rules of ethical conduct dealing with relations with fellow members of the profession. Like many such bodies, the CICBV has a "golden rule" relating to courtesy and consideration[45] that requires its members to treat other members with due professional courtesy and consideration.

An expert's alleged non-adherence to the rules of conduct and professional practice in any aspect of the engagement can be the subject of questioning or referred to during cross-examination. The well-prepared, credible expert must be adequately knowledgeable of the rules of the relevant professional body.

In some matters, parties to a dispute hire more than one expert in a particular discipline, in which case counsel will typically have each expert critique the other's reports to strengthen the presentation.

F. PREPARATION

> *Practice Tip*
>
> *"The wheels of justice move slowly. Don't rely on your memory. Review your report and ancillary documents before the hearing."*
>
> – Steven Blau, LLB, BCL

Obviously, the expert witness must be thoroughly prepared to present his or her evidence in court, and be cross-examined. No matter what the strength of the expert's written report, it can be undone by a lack of suitable preparation for oral testimony. The question then is what constitutes suitable preparation?

Based on our experience, an expert's preparation should not be done in isolation but instead with the active involvement of counsel. The expert should expect that counsel will spend time reviewing the actual questions that will be asked during the qualification process, the examination in chief, and in particular, the type of questions that could be anticipated in cross-examination. The preparation stage is the time for counsel and expert to share their thoughts on the strengths and weaknesses of their case (and that of their opponents), and the strategy for addressing potential problem areas or issues, if they have not already done so. For example, if the expert

45 CICBV Code of Ethics, Rule 107/301.

has identified an aspect of the written expert report that will likely be attacked by opposing counsel, counsel can anticipate this and plan for an effective re-direct examination.

We have found the preparation phase to be a useful forum for ensuring that counsel fully understands the expert report, and the foundation on which the opinion rests (i.e., the assumptions made, the documents and other items of information reviewed, the methodology and the basis for its selection, among other report details).

Preparation of the expert should also include a detailed review of documents and commentary referred to in the expert's written report (i.e., all items included in the scope of review), as well as pleadings, discovery transcripts, opposing experts' reports. The expert should at this time ensure that the working paper files are organized, and that the copy of the report that will be brought to the courtroom is suitably cross-referenced or annotated. The qualification process should not be overlooked in the preparation phase. The lawyer should be fully familiar with the qualifications and experience of the expert. In turn, the expert should be prepared to succinctly summarize their qualifications, experience and achievements, in order to maximize the opportunities to impress the court during the qualification phase.

During cross-examination, the expert will typically be asked for an analysis of the impact on the conclusion of varying assumptions, hypothetical facts, or of factual information not previously known at the time the written report was prepared. To the extent possible, preparation should include anticipation of such questions, and how they will be answered.

There is no rule-of-thumb for the amount of time required to adequately prepare for the giving of oral expert testimony. In fact, given the tendency for many cases to settle just prior to commencement of trial, experts are sometimes instructed to delay preparation and lawyers are unavailable to meet with the witness, if settlement discussions are underway. We have often been consulted on the eve of trial on the valuation implications of specific settlement alternatives (e.g., the fair market value of a stream of future settlement payments, compared to the fair market value determination that is the subject of the case). Preparation is further challenged by the tendency for the trial to be scheduled months or years after the submission of the expert's original written report.

G. PRACTICAL TIPS FOR SUCCESS ON THE STAND

Based on our own experiences, and some reported cases involving expert witnesses, the following are a selection of tips to assist the expert preparing to testify. It should be pointed out that success while on the stand is not easily gauged. For one thing, not all cases are reported, and many cases settle in the midst of the trial. Also, in some reported cases, expert witnesses are not identified by name. Moreover, a successful court appearance does not necessarily coincide with a favourable outcome for the expert's client. For many business valuators, testifying in court is not something they enjoy, and we have known some to say that the best outcome of a court appearance is emerging with their good reputation intact.

1) Before Trial

1. *Prepare your report with the full expectation that the matter will go to trial.* Anything in your written report is open for cross-examination, and you should be able to answer questions like "How do you know that such and such is the case?", "On what do you base ____?", or "Why did you not use the ____ method of valuation?" As evidenced by the judgment in *Fraser Inc. v. Aitken*,[46] the court's perception of a business valuator's credibility will be influenced by its perception of how thorough the expert's review of data was, the extent to which employees, customers and competitors or other industry participants were interviewed, the expert's understanding of the business and industry, and the consistency of the expert's conclusion with the evidence of the case.

2. *The expert report and methodology or approach adopted should be both consistent with the facts and other evidence, and consistent with the expert's other published reports, articles and other publications, and if not, the expert should be prepared to explain why.* The expert's credibility can be adversely affected if it can be shown by opposing counsel that an earlier report or other publication written by the expert, involving similar circumstances, contradicts the position or approach currently adopted. It is not unusual for counsel and their expert witness to complete a search and analysis of published decisions and valuation reports involving the opposing expert or quotes from articles and other publications for purposes of cross-examination. The well-prepared expert should be ready to be confronted with their past, and be able to reconcile the differences, for example due to differing facts and circumstances, or quotations that are taken out of context. In some cases, it may be that the expert's opinion of the treatment of a certain issue

46 [1988] O.J. No. 1962 (1988), 41 B.L.R. 87 (H.C.J.), additional reasons at (1989) 33 C.P.C. (2d) 49 (Ont. H.C.J.).

advocated in a previous case or publication has changed over time, in which case the change should be readily acknowledged, rather than having a potentially sensitive issue being dragged on and emphasized before the judge.

One tax case in which an expert's past came back to haunt them was *Riendeau c. R.*,[47] a case involving real estate appraisal expert evidence. On cross-examination one of the real estate appraisers was questioned about an appraisal that he had prepared for a neighbouring farm. The reasons for judgment included references to that other appraisal, and the judge appears to have used the earlier appraisal as a basis for rejecting the expert's conclusion on the subject property, and for supporting the findings of other appraisal experts involved in the case.

In an Ontario civil court matter involving a number of issues, including the valuation of shares of a private company by several business valuators, *Morris Waxman et al v. Chester Waxman et al*,[48] one business valuator was criticized by an opposing expert for not using the capital asset pricing model in the determination of a capitalization rate used in the valuation. On cross-examination however, it was put to the opposing expert that in a textbook he had co-written, the use of capital asset pricing model was judged to be inappropriate in the valuation of private companies.[49]

3. *Ensure that you are aware of the relevant rules of procedure and evidence, such as required timing for submission of reports, rebuttals, replies, and access to working paper files.*

   This is a critical part of the pleadings, discovery and trial preparation process for the expert along with his or her counsel. Time frames and deadlines are rigidly adhered to as stipulated in the court's procedural rules. Potential experts seeking to provide litigation-related support need to make themselves aware of the schedules and practices in each jurisdiction.

4. *Ensure that you are aware of the appropriate rules of conduct and conventions for the court you will be testifying in*, for example, how to address the judge, whether to gesture on entering or leaving the witness box or the courtroom. Some experts consider it useful to see the courtroom in

---

47 [1995] CarswellNat 2078, 96 D.T.C. 1442 (T.C.C.).

48 [2002] O.J. No. 2528, (2002), 25 B.L.R. (3d) 1 (S.C.J.), varied, [2004] O.J. No. 1765 (C.A.).

49 *Ibid.*, at para. 1554.

advance of the trial so that they are more comfortable when they testify. As well, you should be aware of the rules governing whom you can/cannot talk to during mid-testimony recesses, and whether or not you can bring any notes or analyses with you to the witness box.

5. *Be aware of the relevant facts of the case, and the relevant legislation.* The expert should be cognizant of any legislation relevant to the case (e.g., income tax, securities law, zoning laws related to real estate matters, intellectual property protection laws related to patent or trademark valuations, etc.).

2) In the Witness Box

1. *Be fully prepared to have your suitability as an expert witness challenged by opposing counsel.* Undermining credibility is a core cross-examination tactic — be it related to qualifications, previous opinions and/or publications, or otherwise participation in your field of professional expertise. Adequate steps should be taken to prepare for those likely challenges.

2. *Carefully listen to the question and only answer what has been asked.* Do not anticipate questions, and particularly during cross-examination, do not volunteer information that has not been asked for. It is important not to guess where opposing counsel is trying to go with a line of questioning, or to disrupt your counsel's line of questioning by jumping ahead.

3. *Ensure that you understand the question, and if necessary ask for it to be rephrased, repeated or clarified.* Experts should strive to answer only the question being asked. Accordingly, the expert should ensure that the question is understood, and should not be afraid to request that the question be repeated, rephrased or otherwise clarified.

4. *Take your time. Think about what is being asked, and how you will respond, before you actually respond.* Do not risk providing an incorrect response by rushing into an answer. It should be remembered that in the transcripts that will undoubtedly be reviewed by the judge, no matter how long you take to develop a response, your reply will appear on the very next line of the transcript, as though the response was given immediately. A rushed response may unwittingly result in an answer that is inconsistent with your report, examination-in-chief, etc. If you are asked to refer to a specific document or passage, do not hesitate to take the necessary time to re-read or reacquaint yourself with it.

5. *Speak clearly, slowly, confidently, and with sufficient volume.* In addition to helping the judge, this will assist the court reporter and avoid disruptive transcribing delays. Avoid lengthy sentences, jargon, and provide organized responses.

6. *Make reference to, or quote from, your written report in your responses.* It is important to assist the court by providing references to your report in responses to questions from counsel. If the judge is reviewing the transcript of the expert testimony, responses that are referenced to, or quoted from, the written expert report, will help focus the judge's assessment of the written report and testimony.

7. *Request the opportunity to elaborate on your responses, if necessary.* Opposing counsel may attempt to force you to limit your answer to a specific question to "yes" or "no." Similarly, opposing counsel may attempt to cut short a response by the expert. In some situations however, a full explanation by the expert may be warranted, in which case the expert should make clear the need to provide an explanation to the court. Any argument about whether or not such elaboration is permissible should be done by counsel alone, and not the expert witness. If elaboration is not permitted during cross-examination, counsel has the opportunity to allow the expert to revisit the response during re-direct examination.

8. *Face the judge when giving responses.* He or she is the one who will be considering all the evidence and making the judgment.

9. *Be prepared to explain technical concepts in layman's terms.* For example, a fundamental topic such as the use of and determination of a capitalization rate or discount rate will be unfamiliar to some judges. An appearance of arrogance or of talking down to the court should be avoided. Key terminology and core concepts should therefore be thought through as part of pre-trial preparation, on the assumption they may require "layman's clarification."

10. *Work with counsel to allow a description of your valuation methodology to be put before the court.* "De-mystifying" the review, and value allocation methods used, will result in a presentation that is both less intimidating and more illuminating.

11. *Do not be argumentative, hostile or emotional.* This type of behaviour detracts from the court's perception of your objectivity, independence, and is frequently cited in judgments. An expert does not have to win on every issue, and should not risk their credibility (or that of their

client) trying to win a point that can't be won, or not conceding when arguing a lost cause. A rigid appearance should be avoided at all costs. In many situations, the court will place more reliance on the evidence of the expert who appears flexible, and able to alter their conclusions based on changes in assumptions or facts.

In the reasons for judgment of *Inmet Mining Corp. v. Homestake Canada Inc.*,[50] a case involving the value of a mining business, and the testimony of both geological experts and business valuators, it was noted that a geological expert for the defendant did not have all the data, and had done no statistical analysis like the plaintiff's experts. The expert's credibility was hurt by his statement that he would not have changed his mind if he had had all the data, even though he had not seen it. The judge noted: "This statement struck me as strange and somewhat partisan coming from an expert witness."[51]

In *Majean*, although the court found that both experts were credible witnesses, one of the experts was cited as being "unwilling to recognize new variations, as presented, that would significantly affect his valuation."[52] The court concluded, "the degree of reliance I place in the report of the expert for the respondent is minimal; fundamentals were there but the ability to accept and assimilate new information was absent."[53]

When giving expert testimony, remember your client is focused on winning. Emotions may therefore be running very high. Your task as an expert is to attempt to remain above the fray — independent and objective, and not swayed by one party's preferred outcome.

12. *Maintain a thick skin in the face of courtroom antics.* Although you are supposedly giving evidence as a friend of the court, it is not unusual for opposing counsel to insult or seriously challenge your reputation. To our surprise, judges seem to lend a deaf ear to such courtroom antics or tactics, and seldom come to the assistance of the expert.

13. *Do not guess.* If you do not remember something, take the time to go through your report. If you do not know the answer to a question, admit that you do not recall or do not know.

---

50 [2002] B.C.J. No. 42, 2002 BCSC 61.

51 *Ibid.*, at para. 150.

52 *Majean*, above note 28 at para. 42.

53 *Ibid.*, at para. 44.

14. *Stay in your field of expertise.* The expert should not guess or speculate on matters that are outside the field of expertise, e.g., matters of law, real estate or equipment appraisal, environmental science, software, etc., in order to maintain your credibility and the perception of objectivity and independence. If your conclusion relies on such expertise, your report should incorporate the findings of such other experts, who are made available to the court to provide their own testimony.

15. *Become "synchronized" with your counsel.* Successful expert witness testimony — and in turn successful litigation outcomes — are dependent on a symbiotic relationship between counsel and expert: the witness needs to understand the cadence of questions, the level of detail to be shared, and ultimately how to respond to hostile cross-examination. In turn, counsel needs to recognize the expert's strengths and weaknesses (in everything from qualifications to reporting style) and prepare the witness accordingly. The courtroom is a lawyer's familiar arena. To get the most from his or her expert, counsel must fully prepare the expert to become comfortable in that setting.

H. VALUATION IS AN ART *AND* A SCIENCE

In closing, we note that judges and valuation authorities have sometimes opined that valuation is an art, not a science.[54] In our view, valuation is both an art, and a science. Although it is the case that there is a significant element of judgment applied in forming an opinion of value, and valuation is not a rigidly applied discipline governed by dogmatic principles, it is our view that a valuation opinion can be regarded as a hypothesis, with the conclusion supported by the application of appropriate, widely accepted theories and methodologies, supported by facts and other empirical evidence such as comparable market transactions, statistics and established trends. The valuation hypothesis often requires testing and verification reconciliation using alternate methods, approaches, assumptions, and reconciliation, much in the way a scientific experiment is conducted. The well-prepared and competent valuation expert witness is the one who can support matters of judgment with such objective technical support, capable of explanation to the court in layman's terms.

---

54 For example, *Taylor*, above note 40 at para. 10; *Majean*, above note 28 at para. 45 (quoting *Ample Investments Ltd. v. Minister of National Revenue*, [1990] 2 C.T.C. 2217 (T.C.C.), at 2220), *Attridge*, above note 26 at para. 80.

I. BIBLIOGRAPHY

In preparing this paper, we reviewed many published articles and court decisions on the general subject of the role of the expert witness. The following are some of the sources we found particularly relevant to the subject of the role of the expert witness in the Tax Court of Canada:

Barsalou, P. W., "Preparing and Arguing a Tax Appeal: Practical Tips" (1997) 45:2 Canadian Tax Journal 223.

McMechan, R. W., "Valuator as Expert Witness" (1995) 95 CMC 18.

Quigley, M. G., "Expert Evidence in Tax Cases" (1993) 43:6 Canadian Tax Journal 1071.

Carr, F. C. & Reilly, R. F., "Expert Testimony Procedures Related to Intellectual Property Controversies" (2003) 9: 1 Business Valuation Digest, 1.

In addition, the *Valuation Law Review*, published by the Canadian Institute of Chartered Business Valuators, summarizes taxation, family, and corporate/commercial court decisions with a business valuation context.

Chapter Fourteen

The First Time Experience as an Expert: An American Perspective

Robert Pardo

A. INTRODUCTION

When I was first asked to contribute this chapter, I was quite honoured *and* a bit overwhelmed. I kept asking myself, "How on earth can I make such a topic useful, helpful, and *interesting*?" To say the least, it does appear to be a rather dry topic!

As I thought about this question more deeply, an answer began to form. What would I have liked to see before I undertook this very daunting task? And mind you, those who know me don't think of me as one who is lacking in self-confidence! Furthermore, I suspect, given my limited experience in this rarified legal domain — that of being an expert witness in the Canadian Tax Court — I was given tremendous support by my clients. In addition, having read the expert witness reports that were part of the material I needed to review for my preparation was also a great confidence builder. They were so amateurish and weak that I still have a hard time believing that anyone actually had the gall to offer these documents as "expert testimonials."

So, all that being said in preparation, I will make my best effort to produce the type of guidelines from which I would have benefited. This will best unfold if looked at in chronological order of my encounter. But before I get into this chronologically, I feel that a few preparatory comments are in order.

B. BASIC PREMISE

I think it best at the outset to emphasize the two most important and valuable attitudinal qualities that will most contribute to a successful expert "outcome."

The first essential attitude necessary to be an effective expert witness is best characterized by that quintessential Boy Scouts of America motto: "*Be Prepared*!"

Perhaps a more appropriate way of phrasing this would be "Say or write nothing that you cannot defend against the most vigorous possible onslaught," and the flip-side of this expression might be "Be prepared to defend *everything*." And by everything I mean just that — everything. It is easy to pay attention to the thorough defence and presentation in detail of the "big" statements — however, it is equally important to be just as thorough and to be able to defend the so-called "small" points.

This was never brought home so clearly to me, my client, and the client's lawyers as when the appellant's counsel attempted to completely exclude my expert witness report over my use of one word for which I was not expertly qualified to "use" (due to legal implications of the word unknown to me) in the manner in which I did in my report. More on this later. However, it does highlight, loudly *and* clearly, the need to be very thorough and to be able to *defend everything*.

The second essential quality that I believe most contributes to expert witness success is honesty, especially self-honesty.

One might ask, "Well of course I will be honest, after all, I am being asked to be an expert witness in a trial, for God's sake! How can I be anything *but* honest?"

I am not suggesting that one undertaking such a project such as expert witnessing would be *intentionally* or *consciously* dishonest. Rather, it is more of an issue of not "biting off more than one can thoroughly chew!" Also, it is a question of whether one's expertise is really sufficient to do what is needed. I believe these considerations fall more under the category of self honesty, of really knowing one's limits, and, of really understanding what is needed and clearly seeing that one can or *cannot* provide what is necessary.

C. MY BACKGROUND

I don't want to spend much time here, but there is one thing that is very important to take away from this that I think is not unique to me.

I have spent my professional career engaged in various aspects of the futures industry. For the last twenty years, I have been an entrepreneur and chief executive (and some would probably say a rather autocratic one at that!). I was a software pioneer throughout the 1980s providing technical analysis and trading model development software to the trading public (Pardo Corporation). From there, I engaged in extensive large-scale consulting projects with major firms such as Goldman Sachs, Daiwa Securities of America, and Transworld Oil (Pardo Group Limited). Along the way, John Wiley & Sons published my book *The Design, Testing and Optimization of Trading Systems*, which, I am pleased to be able to say, is widely considered the definitive book on the topic. These consulting projects organically led to my current occupation as a Commodity Trading Advisor (CTA) where I have enjoyed some success in the difficult world of futures trading (Pardo Capital Limited).[1]

1
1) Barclay Managed Funds Report, 4th Quarter 2003, #1 Top 20 CTA Performers Past Three Years and #7 Top 20 CTA Performers 2003;
2) Futures, October 2003 — #1 July's Top CTA, More than $10 Million under Management;
3) Barclay Managed Funds Report, 3rd Quarter 2003, #2 Top 20 CTA Performers Past Three Years;
4) Futures, May 2003 — #1 February's Top CTA, More than $10 Million under Management;
5) Barclay Managed Funds Report, 2nd Quarter 2003, #6 Top 20 CTA Performers Past Three Years;
6) Futures, March 2003 — #2 Top CTAs of 2002, Programs Managing More than $10 Million;
7) Barclay Managed Funds Report, 4th Quarter 2002, #4 Top 20 CTA Performers Past Three Years and #3 Top 20 CTA Performers 2002;
8) Barclay Managed Funds Report, 3rd Quarter 2002, #9 Top 20 CTA Performers Past Three Years and #7 Top 20 CTA Performers 2002;
9) Futures, October 2002 "Bob Pardo: Perfecting a Model" in Trader Profile;
10) Futures, June 2002 — #3 March's Top CTAs, Less than $10 Million under Management;
11) Futures 2002 Sourcebook, #1 2001 Top CTAs Under $10 Million;
12) Futures, February 2001 — #3 November's Top CTAs, Less than $10 Million under Management;
13) MAR, January 2001, Trading Advisor Reviews — Pardo Capital, Ltd: It's Simple: Big wins, small losses;
14) Futures, November 2000 — #5 August's Top CTAs, Less than $10 Million under Management;
15) Commodity Traders Consumer Report, March 1997, Commodity Expert in the Spotlight — Bob Pardo.

All that being said, for those of you who are not familiar with the futures arena, no one cares how "expert" one is if one's products don't produce. And in futures trading, "produce" is equal to the "greatest possible consistent profit." Futures trading is a zero-sum game. For every dollar of profit earned there is a corresponding dollar of loss.

The point of all this is not to just brag. Rather, the point is to indicate the extent and range of my credentials. More importantly, the cultures of my varied professional work experience, did not prepare me for the humility (not a common characteristic of futures traders, I might add!) and thoroughness needed to be an effective expert witness. When I produced software, what mattered was that it worked as advertised, quickly and free of bugs. When I consulted, either I was asked for my opinion, which was usually offered without demonstration or proof, or my staff created a product that worked as designed. As a CTA, all that matters is that our trading accounts produce consistent profit.

The long and the short of it is that — for better or for worse — I am not a person who is accustomed to being questioned nor am I a person who is often asked to defend his opinions. Rather, I am the person from whom people have bought opinions in one form or another for many years. Nothing in my extensive and varied professional background — other than the various forms of expertise with which it has endowed me — prepared me for the extensive and sometimes exhaustive questioning and careful and methodical communication required to be an expert witness.

And, I make a point of this, because, although I am in a rather unique industry, I don't think my career preparation is that much different than that of any other expert. For, in truth, all of us who are asked to be expert witnesses are, by definition, experts in our domain. However, I will make one proviso to this that I think true. There appear to be those who make a living at being expert witnesses.

This is relevant in two ways. The first would perhaps account for what I considered to be the very shabby quality of the expert witness reports that our opposition presented. These reports were packed full of irrelevant material which was included, I presume, to make the report seem authoritative, and perhaps even daunting, through its ponderousness! In addition, they seemed to possess a certain quality that indicated that one should simply take their word for it — without the burden of proof — because the authors were "experts!"

The second point is that those who are "expert" or professional expert witnesses — who earn their fees and produce a good quality report — know the ropes. They are the more formidable opponent because they know the intricacies and the "ins" and "outs" of what is allowed and necessary to make a strong legal and evidentiary case in their reports.

The point is that one should be prudent and never underestimate one's opponent in the legal arena. This is the approach I take to all of my ventures, and it was the approach I took in preparing my expert report. In addition, in the tax court case for which I was hired to prepare an opinion, the subject matter of my expert report touched on some still lively and debated practical and philosophical points in my profession. Being cognizant of this pushed me to spare no expense in making as solid a case as I was able. I saw that my expert report touched on areas that are highly relevant to my main occupation as a Commodity Trading Advisor.

D. DEADLINES

While this may seem a bit silly, one thing important to remember is that a deadline for an expert witness report is a *dead* line. If your expert witness report is not filed with the court when it is due, your client will have no expert witness report to file.

E. PRELIMINARY INTERVIEW

My expert witness project began with a phone call from out of the blue, as one might say. I am a Commodity Trading Advisor (asset manager trading in the futures markets) by profession and not a professional expert witness, so more the surprise.

I was contacted by a senior consultant working for Deloitte and asked "Have you ever been an expert witness?" "*No.*" "Did I know what it entailed?" "*To a rather limited degree, yes.*" "Would I be interested in doing some work in this area?" "*Yes, if you think I am capable, I would be, it sounded interesting.*" It turns out, they had been looking for someone with my sort of highly specialized expertise and had learned of me through my book *Design, Testing and Optimization of Trading Systems* and to some extent by reputation.

I was intrigued by doing something like this that would require me to dig into my area of expertise and to present this information in terms that would be both irrefutable *and* understandable and accessible by and to a non-expert. I was also a bit uncomfortable in that I really had little idea of what this would entail beyond the writing of the report, the outlines of which were *very* clear to me.

My contact was very effective in helping me see what was involved with a project of this sort. He helped me to see — *for myself and to my own satis-*

faction — that with some help, support, and guidance, this project was within my professional capabilities. Perhaps most importantly to me, he stressed that his firm was experienced in this area and would do all that was needed to provide any support or information I would need to complete this project successfully. This proved very important because without their guidance and support, my expert witness report would not have turned out as well as it did.

My contact also helped me to see exactly what type of evidentiary material and what sort of logical argument would be needed to accomplish our purpose in this expert report. He also stated very clearly what they needed from me to complete their report. My expert witness report was presented as a supporting document in their expert witness report.

After clearing this hurdle, I had a couple of phone calls with two senior lawyers from the Department of Justice (Canada). They represented the end client, the Canada Revenue Agency ("CRA"). The lawyers were interested in my background and experience. In hindsight, I see that this was less about a determination of my expertise (this determination, from my point of view, had already been made to their satisfaction by the people at Deloitte) but more a matter of the suitability of my character and how they felt that would "play" in court as an expert witness.

I personally found all of the people with whom I was to ultimately work very agreeable and people with whom I both felt comfortable working with and *for*. And both of these, I feel, are very important considerations. For, just like in any project, to do one's best, one needs to feel comfortable working with respectful and capable peers and one needs to feel that one is working on a worthwhile cause. I felt that both of these needs were more than met and my subsequent experiences proved my first impressions to be accurate.

After the determination was made that I was to be hired for the job and that I was comfortable with the time schedule and financial arrangements, there was of course a need to work out the contract details, disclosures, and other procedural details. This all went very quickly and smoothly.

F. CULTURE

A question was raised as to whether I felt any impact as an American working in Canada (a foreign country) with Canadians ("foreigners!")

Well I am not really sure how Canadians feel about Americans, but I have had dealings with Canadians before and was perfectly comfortable working with Canadians again. With a common language and cultural heritage as well as similar contemporary cultures, I never felt there was any impact of a negative kind on our working relationship.

There was one cultural "difference" that I thought I did note between Americans and Canadians and that was that I felt a distinct warmth and friendliness on the part of the Canadians that was more "pronounced" and noticeable than it is in my "homeland!" As an American, I would *like* to think that it has to do with that noted American "reserve!" I also don't know if it was just a "sampling error" or whether this is true of Canadians nationwide! But, in any case, the impact of this noted "Canadian friendliness" was to make my project that much more enjoyable and easy.

One thing that did eventually emerge regarding national or regional differences was that some of the lawyers felt that my Chicago accent (in my typical American egocentrism, I was somewhat amused by this!) might prove to be "too much" and hence an impediment in my testimony. Fortunately for me (since there would be little that I could do about that!) the opinion prevailed that instead of an impediment, my Chicago accent would prove to be an asset in that — I am supposing here — it lent me greater credibility due to my "authenticity" as a *native* Chicago futures (Chicago has long held a position of global leadership as a futures trading centre) expert!

Another issue, not necessarily directly related to national concerns, was my natural tendency to speak a bit rapidly, especially by Canadian standards. This was further compounded, I think, by my accent, and by the complexity of the material upon which I was giving testimony. There was something that I could do about that! I made every effort to slow down my rate of speech when testifying, under cross, and *especially* when speaking directly to the judge.

According to my recollection of events, I was a *great success* in this effort! However, according to what I gathered from the Justice lawyers, I enjoyed *some limited* success in this regard, and they just gave up further efforts to modulate my speech! However, as they say, all is well that ends well, and rather than make it appear that my lawyers were remiss (for they were never anything but impeccable in my opinion) it really wasn't all *that bad*!

Another "cultural" difference that I believe was noteworthy was the affability, cordiality, and generally respectful and friendly attitude of the lawyers towards each other and towards me and the other witnesses. Perhaps this can be credited to the general tendency for Canadians to be a bit more friendly and relaxed than their American counterparts. In any case, my professional experience in this area is a bit limited (however, I do have a number of friends who are lawyers) so I don't know how relevant it is.

However, if this amicable environment prevails in all Canadian courts, this is worthy of note in my opinion. It makes the job a lot easier, as in less intimidating and threatening. However, the "flip side" of this is that it was also a bit disarming. So, when the opposing counsel "came at me" in a more aggressive manner (which is how I am assuming is more typically the case in American courts) I was a bit surprised and fortunately, for me, my "native American aggressiveness" surfaced and saved the day for me.

G. PREPARING THE REPORT

1) Planning

The next stage was relatively brief but I felt it was essential to the success of our project. We spent the time necessary so that I was comfortable knowing exactly what needed to be accomplished by, and therefore included in, my report. We also worked out a time schedule for completion of the project in accordance with the various legal deadlines.

This all went very smoothly largely due to the fact that I had the good fortune to work with very capable people and this greatly facilitated the necessary communications and information exchange.

There were three stages to this process. The first, as indicated, I had to arrive at a clear understanding of what the lawyers needed to prove their case. The second was for me to examine some of the main evidence that I needed to evaluate and to make an initial assessment as to how this did or did not fit into our plan of attack. Once my initial assessment of this evidence was completed, the third stage involved further discussions about to how to integrate these findings into the report.

After all of this was done, I then put together a very detailed outline of my report which was circulated among the relevant parties. Information was exchanged back and forth, and integrated into the final draft of my outline. Once this outline met with everyone's approval, it was time to get to work.

2) Content

There is one primary focus regarding the presentation of the content of your expert witness report — it will be read by a judge. If your report loses the judge, you have lost your "expert" battle. Period.

Under the category of "accessible" two major areas come to mind. First, very technical and sometimes difficult material should be presented in "lay terms" which are as easy to understand as possible. Second, the information should be organized and it should be "layered,"or formatted, so as to allow the reader to follow the main logic and conclusions of your argument without the evidence "bogging things down" or interfering with its natural flow.

a) The "Lay Presentation" of Technical Information

This dimension of "accessibility" is of paramount importance. The judge who will be reading your report will be an intelligent and highly professional individual. Beyond this, it is also the duty of the judge to understand your report.

Be mindful that your expert report will be crystal clear to you no matter what type of and how much jargon you use because you are so intimately familiar with the material and its jargon.

However, to the judge, who very likely knows little if anything about your area of expertise, the great majority of the "buzz words" and technical terminology that are oh so familiar and common place to you and your associates will most likely sound as foreign as *ancient Greek*.

Does this mean one is not to use technical terms in an expert report? No, it does not. However, it does mean that every technical term to be used must be clearly defined, patiently, completely and, as much as possible, *in lay terminology*!

By extension, this also means that technical terms must be introduced in their order of appearance. In other words, if *new* technical terms that are yet to be used are built upon or are defined in terms of *other* and *previous* technical terms, then be sure that these other terms are defined *prior* to the new technical terms that are yet *to be defined*.

I think the easiest way to clearly explain and provide a model of how to best approach this type of structure comes from the structure of geometry. Recall that geometry begins by stating its axioms — its fundamental and unprovable assumptions — and definitions. These axioms and definitions, since unproveable by definition in geometry, are kept to a minimum. In turn, they are then used as the foundation and the basic building blocks upon which all further theorems and more complex statements of geometric principles are built.

In my limited experience, an expert witness report that closely follows this pattern with will turn out to be a very sound and defensible document. As well, a report patterned in this manner will be well-organized both in logical argument and informational structure and its central argument will therefore be straightforward and easy to follow.

Another stylistic principal that will facilitate accessibility is to use technical terms more lightly — or with less *density* — than you would if speaking with a technical peer. Looking back to the "geometric model" will shed some light here as well. Remember, technical terms are essentially a form of "short hand." Just like a more advanced — and, by definition, more complex — theorem in geometry will be built upon a number of previously demonstrated theorems, technical terms build upon and use previously defined technical terms. Of course, all words are defined in terms of other words. However, this is developed to a much greater extent in technical language. It is always helpful to remember that the purpose of technical terminology is to make possible and to facilitate the efficient communication of sometimes highly complex concepts *in as few words as possible.*

Now, of course, it is *fine to speak with a plethora of technical language,* as long as one is speaking with a peer who is equally *fluent* and *facile* in the language of this technical domain. However, in all likelihood, the readers of your expert report will not be your peers in your field of expertise; why else would they need you?

If one keeps in mind the "shorthand" purpose of technical language, it will then come as no surprise that keeping its usage to a minimum will facilitate and promote efficient communication with those unfamiliar with the technical language of a particular realm of expertise.

It is an important rule of thumb to follow that one can only use technical terms after the term has been adequately defined in lay terminology. Also, remember that, although it will take more words, it is best again to keep the more technical discussions in lay terminology as much as feasible.

I would like to go a bit further in defence of clear language. Bertrand Russell — one of the greatest English philosophers and mathematicians of the 20th century — is one of my favourite writers and philosophers and is known for the clarity and accessibility of his writing style. He is also known for his ability to present highly technical material, for example, the Theory of Relativity, in a clear, concise and style accessible to the intelligent lay person. Russell's contention was that if one could not explain a complex and technical topic to an intelligent child or lay person, then one *did not truly understand the topic oneself!* Based upon my experience, I tend to agree with Russell's contention.

I cite this not simply as an interesting philosophical contention or a comment on writing style by a brilliant stylist, but as a sound rule of thumb and guidance for the writer of technical material, the expert witness included. I would offer for your consideration the idea that if you cannot explain your domain of expertise clearly and easily to an intelligent lay person(s) —

read here the judge and your client — then perhaps you are not as *expert* as you think! The bottom line here is that if your expert report remains unintelligible to the parties who require your expertise, it is *your fault* not theirs. *And* — and this is a very important "and" — if you are not willing to create an expert witness report that will conform to this stylistic approach, perhaps you should decline the expert witness job.

b) Formatting and Organization

As in most things, first impressions matter. The more professional, attractive, and accessible the appearance and formatting of the expert report, the better the initial impression. And, if the expert report — by some odd coincidence — just happens to contain sound information, its excellent appearance and organization will certainly provide additional support for the equally excellent content. In short, the more striking the appearance of your report, the greater its potential impact.

The primary reason one employs good formatting is to make the document inviting, appealing, easy to follow, easy to quickly locate information, and most of all, accessible.

Good formatting should include:

- A pleasant, easy to read and large enough type-face;
- Use of different type styles for body text, quotations, definitions, etc.;
- The break up blocks of text with ample spacing and frequent headings, sub-heads, etc., preferably in a second colour;
- An easy to follow numbering system for the heads, sub-heads, etc.;
- Clear demarcations for footnotes; and
- A complete and easy to follow table of contents.

To anyone who has any experience presenting complex and technical information, the absolutely essential need for excellent organization of such material is obvious. Since this is being written for the "beginner" expert witness, it is impossible, in my opinion, to overemphasize the necessity of excellent organization.

What does good organization mean beyond "first things first" and following the rules of logical argument fastidiously? In the case of an expert witness report, there seem to be two other things that are important.

The first is that the organization of one's report. Like any good and logical presentation the organization should reflect the logic and order of your argument. Nothing obscures the best reasoned argument so thoroughly as presenting it in a disorganized manner which requires the reader to think *overly much* so as to just *follow* the argument. In contrast, an elegant and logically organized argument is put together, presented, and developed in a way that helps the reader follow and remember it with as little effort as possible. This is never as valuable as when attempting to persuade a very busy judge of the efficacy of your argument. This is never as true as when the judge is not an expert in your area of expertise and testimony.

The second important dimension to organization is the clear separation in the main body text and in the flow of the central argument of the argument, conclusions and sub-conclusions from the secondary, supporting arguments and blocks of evidence. This is particularly important when the necessary evidence is very detailed, lengthy and difficult.

Various mechanisms can be used to facilitate this separation: 1) the judicious use of footnotes both concise and somewhat lengthy, and 2) presenting very extensive bodies of detail and information in appendices.

Footnotes are best kept reasonably brief so as to avoid unnecessary page flipping and skipping around in the document. Of course, definitions, references, and citations are typically relegated to footnotes. Definitions of terms or ideas that are essential to understanding the main argument are best when in the text itself. Supporting evidence that is not directly essential or central to the argument may also be a candidate for a footnote where such evidence can be provided in a short block of no more than one or two paragraphs and there is a desire to keep the information more accessible than it would be in an appendix.

Longer pieces of information that may be essential for evidentiary purposes but are more peripheral to the central argument are best directed to an appendix. Secondary arguments, extensive quotations and their associated commentaries, and large blocks of evidentiary data fall into this category.

There is another useful guideline to follow in determining the appropriateness of appendix material. Multi-page supporting material that is detailed, complex, and very technical often only needs to be read where a reader remains unconvinced of the main argument and the evidence presented in support of it. Reference as "For Further Reading" should be made to such an appendix in the main body of the expert report.

An appendix is also a good location for tables of numbers and data as well as for graphic elements that are more complex and require some consideration or additional text commentary to grasp their complete message.

In closing this section, there is another important dimension to organization and formatting that is worthy of mention. During court testimony, the judge and the opposing legal parties will all refer to the expert report. When I was on the witness stand under examination by the appellant's counsel and needed to explain and elaborate upon complex points to the presiding judge — who was following my oral testimony in my written testimony — I was certainly glad that my expert report was well-organized and professionally formatted.

Consider what type of impression "jumping hither and yon" and "hunting and pecking" in an unformatted mass of undifferentiated text with poor logical flow would create for opposing counsel — "Why don't we try to boost their confidence a bit more!" And, consider the possible reaction of the judge to such a report — annoyance, frustration, perhaps contempt, and even insult, because of the lack of professionalism and consideration for his needs and time.

As a consequence, I feel that it is absolutely essential to present an expert witness report that is well-organized and that meets all standards of professionalism in formatting.

3) Editing

All forms of written communication usually benefit from a good editor and someone who is a good sounding board. An expert report is no exception. And, for the less experienced expert witness, an editor with knowledge of, and experience with, previous expert witness reports can be indispensable.

In my case, my report was circulated to all parties to the project and their input and feedback were integrated into the final report. There were not a lot of changes, but I would say that this process did result in some very good changes, deletions, and minor modifications.

This also has the "side benefit" of making the report a bit of a group effort, with the benefit of the insights, perspective and expertise of a diverse group of people above and beyond that of the expert alone. It also provides some comfort to the author of the report that the client is getting what they need.

All in all, I feel that this input is very valuable to a project of this sort. It lends additional perspective, it provides a greater assurance of its comprehensibility by a lay audience, and it tends to eliminate potential rough edges that may have cropped up.

H. TRIAL PREPARATION

The next big step after the completion of the report was my trial preparation. This entailed my spending a day with one of the lawyers from Justice. The lawyer I worked with was very patient and very thorough — almost painfully so at times! Yet, in hindsight, this thoroughness really paid off.

This preparation covered three main areas: 1) what to expect in just a human way, 2) how I was to comport myself, and 3) a detailed run through of how the evidence was to be presented.

1) The Human Perspective

This covered things like what the courtroom was like, who, and how many people, would be in the court, how long I would have to testify, and a bit about what to expect from the judge. While far from essential, this information was helpful in setting me at ease regarding my testimony.

I was also able to ask any and all questions that I had — and I have been known to have a few! This too went to create a greater sense of ease and comfort regarding my testimony.

2) My Composure

This is pretty much as you would expect it to be: be respectful of the judge, be patient, communicate clearly and directly, answer all questions honestly and directly, speak slowly and clearly, and project well.

However, there are a couple of other things worthy of mention.

First, say nothing more than is necessary, especially if saying more might get one into areas that could prove to be difficult or which might work to the disadvantage of the expert witness process.

Next, be sure to say *all* that *is* necessary even if this becomes rather intricate and takes a bit of time. It is important to remember to be sure to state the information in a clear and comprehensive manner so as to leave no doubt as to its accuracy, truth and conclusiveness. The judge will listen and appreciate this and it will also enhance your image as an expert, hence also enhancing the impact of your testimony and your expert report.

The last item of note was something that I was not specifically prepared for by counsel, but was prepared for by life experience. And that is to speak up in one's defence if one feels that one is being misrepresented or maligned by opposing counsel.

There was one point during my cross-examination where the opposing counsel was trying to pull — what felt like to me — a "Perry Mason" and get me to stumble over a matter of some importance. While he was doing this, he would not let me get a word in edgewise. I generally don't take well to this type of treatment and I was none too thrilled at this attempted "railroading" by the opposing counsel, so before the lawyers for Justice could intervene, I spoke up and set the matter straight to my satisfaction. After that the lawyer from Justice very clearly objected to my treatment by opposing counsel, and that further worked in our favour. So, even though the lawyers from Justice handled this quite well and professionally, I think it is an important point to take matters into your own hands — within reason — if it looks as if things are getting a bit out of control.

I am not and do not propose doing the lawyers job nor grandstanding, but one does need to ask oneself what type of expert lets himself be manipulated to his disadvantage in his area expertise. If you are manipulated, you do not look expert and it does nothing for your credibility or report. Further, such behaviour by opposing counsel builds their case and their confidence and, if left uncorrected will most likely invite more of the same as the case unfolds.

Hold your ground, budding expert witness.

3) The Detailed Run Through

This comprised a review of the way counsel would direct me in the presentation of my evidence. It was very helpful in two ways. First, it was a confidence-building practice of what I was to actually do during my testimony. Second, it allowed us time to examine and discuss this material with an eye towards refining and perfecting the presentation of the evidence in court. This also proved helpful in that it did lead to its intended objective.

This detailed run-through produced the following results:

- greater confidence in me and my ability to present the material;
- an enhancement of the lawyer's grasp of and facility with the material; and
- a refinement of the presentation of the material to an even higher level of clarity and quality.

I. THE TRIAL

The trial or courtroom experience actually has four components: 1) expert support, 2) testimony, 3) cross-examination, and 4) re-examination.

However, before I get into that, I would like to share a few general impressions that might prove helpful in understanding the courtroom experience.

The court itself was pleasant and unimposing. I would guess that it was approximately eighty by eighty feet in size, attractively furnished with light wood furniture and the bench. Seating for the judge, witness and lawyers was arranged in a diamond with the judge directly across and elevated from the witness, lawyers for the government to the right (facing the bench) and lawyer for the appellant to the left. Supporting personnel were seated at tables behind the lawyers' bench. There was seating in the rear of the courtroom for observers and there were a few in attendance. Also, there was a dramatic high-rise view of the city which served as a backdrop to the proceedings.

As I have indicated previously, lawyers on both sides were unfailingly friendly, cordial, courteous, and professional. So were the court personnel with whom I had contact.

Perhaps most importantly, was the judge. In my case, the judge was an older gentleman, very sharp, friendly, interested, courteous, and professional. Not that it would have mattered to me, but I did sense that this judge's friendliness would brook neither nonsense nor the wasting of his time (given that, perhaps it was a good thing that I spoke relatively rapidly!). I also sensed that the judge would make every effort to comprehend what I was presenting. All in all, I took a personal liking to this judge which made it even easier for me to do my utmost to present the material in a comprehensible and accessible way.

1) Expert Support

This was ongoing throughout my presence in the court room. Whenever I heard evidence or testimony occurring upon which I could meaningfully comment, I brought this additional evidence, insight or comment to the attention of the government lawyers. I learned that sometimes what I thought was meaningful was not all that useful in the eyes of the government lawyers and conversely sometimes what I thought was not all that meaningful in my eyes was to the government lawyers. Hence, I came to the conclusion that I would point out anything that seemed relevant and let them decide what to do with the information.

This support also took the form of responding to questions that the lawyers posed as a result of proceedings in the trial.

Consequently, it became clear to me that it was prudent to pay attention to everything that was going on in court while I was present.

2) Testimony

Of course, as useful as ongoing expert support can be, the prime directive of the expert witness is to provide persuasive, understandable and conclusive evidence in support of his conclusions.

Towards that end, it is essential to present one's testimony in an organized way. It is also important to make every effort to communicate effectively and efficiently and with enthusiasm, earnestness and directness. It is perhaps equally important to avoid becoming anxious or jittery for this will directly undermine one's credibility.

It is also important to remain calm and implacable. At the beginning of my testimony, the appellant's counsel attempted to completely bar my testimony based upon what was essentially a technicality regarding the way I used a word in my conclusion. Fortunately, the government's attorneys were able to see through this ploy and convinced the judge to allow my testimony.

However, I must confess that when this first occurred, a broad range of emotions rushed through me, none of which would have been constructive to reveal. I made every effort to keep a good "poker face" and show no emotion and await the outcome as calmly as possible. I believe that I was relatively effective in so doing. I mention this because, while in my case, similar events were few and far between, they can and will happen because this is part of the approach any good lawyer will use in an attempt to "rattle" the witness. And I suspect the frequency and intensity of such attempts are likely in increase in proportion to 1) how important your testimony is, 2) how rattled one became by the first attack, and 3) the frequency of attackable errors in your testimony.

Effective oral communication calls for speaking clearly, projecting so that the judge and all counsel can clearly hear what you are saying (Is there anything more annoying than someone mumbling in a soft voice and having to ask repeatedly "What did you say?") explaining one's concepts in an understandable vocabulary, and presenting one's material in a complete and logical form.

One's attitude in court is also important. Clearly, the best attitude that one can bring to this effort is one of extreme patience, alertness and helpfulness. Remember, the judge will most likely not be an expert in your area, so, consequently, no question from the judge is a *stupid question*! In contrast, questions from the judge are most likely a good indication of interest and that he is closely following your testimony. As long as the questions are not "What did you say?" or things which are indications that one's presentation or information is weak in some area or another!

It is also important to pay attention to how the judge is responding to your testimony. Of course, the worst that can happen is that you put the judge to sleep with a boring testimony in a monotonous voice! An equally poor outcome would be indications that the judge is suspicious or mistrustful of you or your testimony.

It is also important that you reply to the judge's questions with honesty, frankness, openness and appropriate replies.

In short, it is best to do everything that you can to help the judge completely understand your testimony and to trust you. Anything that works counter to this end is to be avoided.

In order to communicate effectively and to build confidence in your testimony, you should, within reason, take all the time necessary to express yourself clearly and completely. Your expert testimony is an important part of this trial and the judge wants to understand the information you present. Hence, make every effort to be thorough. By doing this, you are making the judge's already difficult job just a bit easier.

Also, do not overreach. "I don't know the answer to that question, Your Honour, but I will be happy to look into it," is an acceptable answer if it is the correct and honest answer. It would be far more damaging to one's credibility to present questionable answers to legitimate questions.

3) The Cross-Examination

The purpose of the cross-examination by opposing counsel is to find some way to weaken or discredit your expert testimony. Consequently, one should be prepared to defend one's testimony with vigour, passion, calmness and precision. The cross-examination is perhaps the best place for a good poker face!

I would have to say that there were not too many surprises in my cross-examination. One place that was a bit of a surprise was the extent of familiarity with my area of expertise the "crossing" lawyer was able to demonstrate. This was a bit of a surprise in that our lawyers did not anticipate this degree of in-depth effort. Yet, this being said, the primary thrust of the cross-examination was an attempt to undermine my approach to the analysis of the information and to weaken my credentials by making them look more commonplace than in fact they were.

In my case, the cross-examination was relatively ineffective because of the completeness and thoroughness of my expert report, my preparation for the trial experience and the vigilance of the lawyers for the government.

The essential elements that will enable the expert witness to weather his or her cross-examination are 1) a sound report, 2) a sound and credible testimony, and 3) a calm, confident, helpful and implacable attitude. If any of these elements are missing, one may have a rougher cross-examination than desired!

4) The Re-examination

After the cross-examination, the government lawyers had an opportunity to re-examine. This was brief and rather uneventful in my case. The government lawyers used the re-examination mostly to offer some rebuttal to some minor issues that were raised during my cross-examination. If memory serves, I believe they also used it to seek further clarification regarding my testimony on issues that were also raised during the cross-examination.

J. CONCLUSION

Above and beyond the financial rewards I received, I personally found my experience as an expert witness to be very interesting, educational and rewarding in a number of ways.

For an expert to function successfully as an expert witness in a well executed and complex case is, in fact, quite a challenge. It is a test of not only one's expertise and command thereof, but also of one's character, one's communication skills, and perhaps first and foremost to those not familiar with the legal domain, one's ability to function calmly and efficiently under fire.

The only thing that the potential expert witness can do to confront the issues effectively, and the many potential unknowns, is to prepare, prepare, and prepare more. Know your material, know yourself, and *believe* in yourself and in the "crew" with whom you are working. And if you cannot do all of these things, then my best advice is, don't take on an expert witness assignment.

Chapter Fifteen

The Litigious Elements of Business Valuation

Howard E. Johnson

A. INTRODUCTION

This chapter deals with the valuation of business interests as it relates to income taxation in Canada. The discussion focuses on the determination of the fair market value of the shares of a privately-held Canadian company. This includes situations where the business interest in question represents 100% of the equity (i.e., "en bloc" value), a controlling interest, or a non-controlling (i.e., "minority") interest in the business.

The objectives of this chapter are twofold:

- first, to familiarize the reader with business valuation methodology, and
- second, to highlight some of the elements of a business valuation that might successfully be challenged by counsel in an income tax litigation matter.

The valuation of any business, or interest therein, is a complex task that, by its nature, involves some degree of subjectivity. Every valuation is unique in certain respects. It is not possible to address the myriad of issues that sometimes arise within the confines of a single chapter. For those who are interested in a more in-depth discussion of business valuation, there are many published texts that are available. For reasons that are self-evident, I am partial to the following:

- I. Campbell & H.E. Johnson, *The Valuation of Business Interests* (Toronto, Canadian Institute of Chartered Accountants, 2001); and
- I. Campbell, H.E. Johnson & H.C. Nobes, *Canada Valuation Service* (Toronto, Carswell Publishing, 1984), loose-leaf periodical.

This chapter begins with a discussion of certain general issues surrounding the determination of the fair market value of the shares of a privately-held Canadian company for income tax purposes. It then addresses various methodologies commonly used to determine the fair market value of the shares of a privately-held company "en bloc." This is followed by a discussion of how the rates of return and valuation multiples that are used in business valuation are determined. The chapter concludes with a discussion of minority discounts that sometimes are applied when valuing a non-controlling interest in a privately-held company.

Within each section I have included a discussion of some of the more common challenges and shortcomings in the application of the various business valuation concepts, and the issues that might be contested in the context of income tax litigation. Certain cases dealing with the various issues are mentioned. It is important to note that the relevance of any given particular argument and the applicability of case law are dependent on the fact-specific circumstances of the valuation at hand.

Much of the discussion in this chapter is technical in nature. However, I believe that a sound understanding of the underlying technical elements of business valuation is fundamental to effective litigation.

B. DETERMINING VALUE FOR INCOME TAX PURPOSES

1) The Definition of Value

The value term typically adopted when determining the value of a business interest for income tax purposes is fair market value. Fair market value usually is defined as "*the highest price available in an open and unrestricted market between informed and prudent parties acting at arm's length and under no compulsion to act, expressed in terms of cash.*"

For income tax purposes the fair market value of a business interest normally is determined on an intrinsic (or "stand-alone") basis, without consideration of the synergies, economies of scale, or other advantages that might be perceived to exist by one or more corporate or public purchasers (so called "special purchasers"). This is because, in the absence of an open market transaction, it normally is difficult to quantify the additional value that might be perceived by a particular (often hypothetical) purchaser of a given business. Furthermore, even if such additional value can be meaningfully quantified, it normally is speculative as to whether a purchaser can be negotiated into a position of paying for some or all of that premium.

Historically the Canada Revenue Agency ("CRA") normally has accepted valuations that are prepared on an intrinsic basis. That said, there might be circumstances where a special purchaser price should be considered, and where sufficient information is available to meaningfully quantify a special purchaser premium. For example, in certain industries, obvious synergistic purchasers do exist, and the disclosure surrounding recent open market transactions in those industries is sufficient to permit a meaningful analysis of the synergistic component of the purchase price. Unless qualified to the contrary, the definition of fair market value in Canada may include a premium due to the existence of so-called "special purchasers."

There are several cases that have addressed the issue of special purchasers. Most decisions have held that the premium that a special purchaser might pay should not be considered when determining fair market value.[1] However, some decisions have ruled in favour of considering a special purchaser premium.[2] Therefore, where fair market value is not qualified to exclude special purchasers (and possibly even where it has been) counsel should consider whether the circumstances justify the argument of a special purchaser premium. Depending on the situation, the impact of a special purchaser on the valuation conclusion could be substantial.

2) The Valuation Date

In most income tax cases, fair market value is determined in a notional context. That is, an actual transaction has not taken place at the valuation date. In this regard, it is important to determine the appropriate valuation date because it establishes the information base that can be considered when determining fair market value. The fair market value of a business interest can fluctuate significantly over time based on factors such as prevailing economic and industry conditions and the outlook for a given business at a particular point in time. It generally is accepted that hindsight is not admissible in the determination of the value of a particular business interest at a given point in time.[3] However, the use of hindsight has some-

1 See, for example, *National System of Baking of Alberta Ltd. v. The Queen*, [1978] C.T.C. 30, 32 D.T.C. 6018, (F.C.T.D.), aff'd [1980] C.T.C. 237, 34, D.T.C. 6178 (F.C.A.).

2 See, for example, *Lakehouse Enterprises Ltd. and Lakehouse Holdings Ltd. v. The Minister of National Revenue*, 1983 D.T.C. 388 (T.R.B.).

3 See, for example, *National System of Baking of Alberta Ltd. v. The Queen*, [1978] C.T.C. 30, 32 D.T.C. 6018, (F.C.T.D.), aff'd [1980] C.T.C. 237, 34, D.T.C. 6178 (F.C.A.).

times been allowed for the limited purpose of assessing the reasonableness of certain assumptions made at a particular valuation date.[4]

One challenge sometimes encountered by valuation experts in notional valuations for income tax purposes arises when the value of a business interest must be determined at a date that is many years past. Often in such cases, individuals having detailed knowledge of the business' operations at the valuation date are no longer accessible, or they simply cannot recall what their knowledge base and expectations were at that time. In addition, many companies do not retain all of their documentation for long periods of time (e.g., detailed forecasts of previous years). In some cases, the valuation conclusions are qualified where the valuation expert believes that all of the necessary information could not be obtained. Such qualifications sometimes impair the usefulness of the valuation report and the credibility of its conclusions.

Therefore, when reviewing a business valuation report, counsel should carefully consider the information base that was relied upon by the valuation expert when developing the value conclusions. Where the valuation date is long passed and the challenges of information availability were encountered, counsel may be able to argue that the credibility of the valuation report is diminished. The credibility of the value conclusions may also be suspect where undue reliance was placed on hindsight information.

3) Goodwill

An issue sometimes encountered in business valuations prepared for income tax purposes is in determining the nature of the "goodwill" that exists. This is particularly the case for smaller businesses, especially those businesses that rely on the continued active involvement of the owner.

In the context of business valuation, goodwill is represented by the difference between the "value" of the shares of a business and the value of its underlying net tangible assets (see discussion under "Valuation Methodologies"). As a simple example, assume that the "value" of the shares of a business was determined to be $5 million, and that the value of its underlying net tangible assets was $2 million. It follows that the difference of $3 million would be attributed to goodwill (or other intangible assets, or a combination of these things). However, whether or not the goodwill component forms part of fair market value for income tax purposes depends on

4 See, for example, *Cyprus Anvil Mining Corp. v. Dickson et al.* (1983), 20 B.L.R. 21, 40 B.C.L.R. 180 (S.C.); rev'd (1986), 8 B.C.L.R. (2d) 145 (C.A.).

what that goodwill is attributable to. That is, whether it represents commercial goodwill, individual goodwill, or personal goodwill.

Commercial goodwill includes such things as a business' brand names, market presence, favourable location, and so on. These are things that a purchaser normally expects to inherit when it acquires a business. Therefore, a purchaser normally is prepared to pay for the commercial goodwill of a particular business. Hence, commercial goodwill forms part of fair market value.

Individual goodwill is defined as the goodwill attributed to one or more individuals (often the business owner) due to his/her knowledge, abilities, reputation, and so on. A business may enjoy increased earnings because of the characteristics of those persons having individual goodwill. However, these characteristics would be detrimental to the business if the particular individual(s) left the company and competed with the business. Therefore, the issue arises as to whether the value attributed to individual goodwill rests in the business (and therefore forms part of its fair market value), or whether the value of individual goodwill is embedded in the individual(s) possessing those characteristics (sometimes termed "value to owner"), in which case, the fair market value of the business would exclude such goodwill.

In the context of an open market transaction, a prudent purchaser will only pay for individual goodwill where that component of value will remain with the business following the transaction. This normally is accomplished through deal structuring, whereby the purchaser requires the individual vendor(s) possessing individual goodwill characteristics to enter into a non-competition agreement and/or a management contract concurrent with the transaction. In addition, a purchaser often will structure a portion of the purchase price such that payment is contingent upon the achievement of certain prospective operating results of the acquired business (a so-called "earn-out arrangement"). Hence, in open market transactions, individual goodwill often forms part of the price paid. It follows that when determining the fair market value of a business for income tax purposes, individual goodwill normally should be included, consistent with the "highest price available" component of fair market value. Stated differently, reasonable "commercial terms" normally should be assumed in a fair market value determination.

However, a notional valuation must consider that the definition of fair market value assumes a cash transaction (where the vendor assumes no risk), whereas the form(s) of consideration used to pay for individual goodwill often transfers some or all of the risk from the purchaser to the vendor. As such, the cash-equivalent value of the individual goodwill component of the purchase price may be less than its face value. In the context of a notional valuation, recognition of the risk associated with payment for individual goodwill normally is done by adjusting (increasing) the required rate of return to recognize the risk of a business' reliance on one or more key individuals. Any such "individual goodwill risk premium" factored into the rate of return inherently is subjective, and often is challenged in the context of income tax litigation.

Personal goodwill also is attributed to an individual's knowledge, abilities, reputation, and so on. However, unlike individual goodwill, the value of personal goodwill is lost to a business as soon as the individual possessing personal goodwill departs the business for any reason (including death, retirement, and so on). In an open market transaction a purchaser will not pay for the personal goodwill component of value. Hence, personal goodwill is excluded from fair market value. The courts generally have confirmed this view.[5]

The distinction between individual goodwill and personal goodwill often is a gray area. In many companies that rely on the reputation and abilities of their owner(s), some customers will depart when the owner is no longer involved, whereas other customers may remain with the business so long as their needs can be satisfied by other individuals within the company. Therefore, in a notional valuation the valuation expert should perform a rigorous analysis to determine what portion of goodwill should form part of fair market value. Such analysis usually is subjective, and hence it often is challenged in the context of income tax litigation.

When faced with a situation where individual and/or personal goodwill may have a significant influence on the valuation conclusion, counsel should consider the procedures the valuation expert undertook to assess this element of value. This should include consideration of the nature and extent of the work that the valuation expert undertook when determining the form and quantum of goodwill, including the depth of the customer analysis that was undertaken, and whether the valuation expert interviewed key customers to directly ascertain the likelihood that they would continue to deal with the business following the departure of the owner. Where the valuation expert cannot demonstrate that a thorough and objective analysis was undertaken, counsel might be in a position to successfully argue that the conclusion of fair market value is suspect.

5 See, for example, *W.H. Crandall v. M.N.R.*, [1974] C.T.C. 2289, 28 D.T.C. 1204 (T.R.B.).

C. VALUATION METHODOLOGIES

When determining which valuation methodology(ies) should be adopted to determine the fair market value of a privately-held business, an assessment must first be made as to whether the business is a going concern. For businesses that are not a going concern, a liquidation approach normally is adopted. Liquidation calculations can be complex, and are beyond the scope of this chapter.

For a business that is a going concern (which usually is the case), valuation methodologies may include:

- capitalization of earnings;
- capitalization of discretionary cash flow;
- multiple of EBIT or EBIT-DA;
- discounted cash flow;
- comparable public companies;
- comparable transactions; and
- adjusted net book value.

The balance of this section outlines the mechanics of each of these valuation methodologies, including hypothetical examples for illustrative purposes. For each methodology, some of the common challenges and shortcomings in their application are addressed.

1) Capitalization of Earnings Methodology

The capitalization of earnings methodology involves dividing estimated normalized maintainable (after-tax) net income by a capitalization rate (or alternatively, multiplying estimated normalized maintainable net income by an earnings multiple). Adjustments are then made for the interest bearing debt (and equivalents) outstanding, and any redundant (i.e., "non-operating") assets that may exist.

In most cases, normalized maintainable net income is estimated based on a review of a business' historical operating results. In this regard, actual operating results as reported for the most recent fiscal years ended are adjusted to eliminate unusual and non-recurring items, and to "normalize" remuneration and other payments made to shareholders and other related parties. Normalized maintainable net income should reflect the income that an arm's length buyer would expect to generate from the business on a go-forward basis (without consideration of synergies, which should be assessed separately, if applicable), on the assumption that arms' length managers are retained to run the business.

Normalized maintainable net income usually is determined on an "unlevered" basis. That is, before consideration of interest expense on outstanding debt. This is because the ability to utilize debt to finance a business (in lieu of equity) is a financing decision, which is distinct from the operations of the business itself. The value of a business' operations typically is independent of the way its operations are financed.

An illustration of what a schedule of normalized net income might look like for a hypothetical business ("Company X") is as follows:

Company X Schedule of Normalized Net Income			
	2001	2002	2003
Income before taxes as reported	$185,000	$195,000	$190,000
Add back:			
Actual shareholder-manager remuneration	$550,000	$300,000	$600,000
Non-recurring expense		$242,000	
Interest expense	$133,000	$148,000	$114,000
Deduct:			
Market rate shareholder-manager remuneration	-$150,000	-$150,000	-$150,000
Normalized earnings before interest and taxes	$718,000	$735,000	$754,000
Deduct: Income taxes	-$287,200	-$294,000	-$301,600
Normalized net income (unlevered)	$430,800	$441,000	$452,400

Normalized maintainable net income is divided by a capitalization rate to determine the capitalized earnings of a business. Where unlevered net income is used as the base by which business value is determined, the capitalization rate represents a "weighted average cost of capital," which reflects the after-tax cost of debt and equity financing. The determination of capitalization rates is addressed in the section entitled "Rates of Return and Valuation Multiples."

Redundant assets are then added to capitalized earnings. Redundant assets are those that can be removed from the business without impairing its ongoing operations or its ability to generate earnings as anticipated. Examples of redundant assets include marketable securities, vacant land, advances to related parties, and so on, where these things can be readily removed from the business. Redundant assets represent a source of additional value to the shareholders of a business. In most cases, the value ascribed to redundant assets is based on their net realizable value, being their market value less disposition costs and income taxes. Where redundant assets exist, it is important to ensure that any revenues and expenses associated with those redundant assets are removed when calculating normalized net income, in order to avoid double counting.

Capitalized earnings plus redundant assets represent the "enterprise value" (or "firm value") of a business. That is, the total value of a business' operations, including its debt and equity components. In order to determine the fair market value of the equity (i.e., shares) of the business, it is necessary to deduct interest-bearing debt outstanding at the valuation date. This is because interest-bearing debt has a prior claim on the underlying assets and cash flows of a business. The equity value of a business is represented by the residual. Therefore, while the "enterprise value" of a business usually is not affected by how a business is financed, the equity value of a business is. In the context of business valuation, interest-bearing debt normally includes such things as term debt, mortgages, capitalized leases, and operating lines of credit. Interest bearing debt also includes "equivalent" amounts, such as advances from shareholders and other related parties, whether or not these things are interest bearing. In most cases, any cash on hand is applied to reduce the amount of interest bearing debt (or equivalents) outstanding.

Continuing the example above, assume that normalized maintainable (after-tax) net income for Company X is estimated at $450,000, and that a capitalization rate of 10% is believed to be appropriate. Further assume that Company X has redundant assets of $100,000, and interest bearing debt of $800,000. The "en bloc" fair market value of the shares of Company X would be calculated as follows:

Company X
Determination of En Bloc Fair Market Value of Shares
Capitalization of Earnings Methodology

Normalized net income	$450,000
Divided by capitalization rate	10%
Equals: capitalized income	$4,500,000
Add: redundant assets	$100,000
Equals: enterprise value	$4,600,000
Less: debt outstanding	-$800,000
Equals: en bloc fair market value of equity	$3,800,000

The two principal variables underlying the capitalization of earnings methodology are the maintainable earnings base and the capitalization rate. The determination of both these things inherently is subjective. A reasonable estimate of the earnings base and the capitalization rate requires a sound understanding of the business and the industry in which it operates, as well as an objective assessment of the risks and opportunities faced by a particular business.

It is important to recognize that the earnings base and the capitalization rate applied thereto are interrelated. The more optimistic the assumed maintainable earnings base, the greater the risk in achieving (or maintaining) same, and hence the greater the required rate of return. In the example of Company X, the amount of capitalized earnings was calculated as $4.5 million, arrived at by dividing estimated maintainable earnings of $450,000 by a capitalization rate of 10%. The same $4.5 million of capitalized earnings could have been arrived at by assuming maintainable earnings of $500,000 with an 11.1% capitalization rate, or maintainable earnings of $400,000 with an 8.9% capitalization rate, or an infinite number of other combinations. The point is that the capitalization rate and the earnings base to which it is applied are interrelated. Hence the value of a business cannot be changed by altering one of these underlying components in isolation.

While the capitalization of earnings methodology historically has been popular and has often been accepted by the courts[6] (and continues to be popular in the context of public equity market analysis), it suffers from significant shortcomings. Most notably, net income for accounting purposes may be significantly different than the cash flow generated by a business. In modern corporate finance, the economic value of a business is a function of its ability to generate cash flow for its stakeholders. Therefore, the capitalization of discretionary cash flow methodology (discussed below) generally is preferred. In addition, the maintainable earnings base used in a capitalization of earnings methodology normally is determined through an analysis of historical operating results, which may not be reflective of a company's prospective earnings ability. This is particularly the case where a business is experiencing strong growth, or where it has undergone significant changes in the past few years. In many cases, valuation reports adopt a "weighting" of historical (adjusted) operating results as a mechanical exercise, without assessing whether such results are indicative of a company's future earnings ability.

Therefore, when reviewing a business valuation developed on a capitalized earnings basis, counsel normally should first assess whether the valuation expert's determination of maintainable earnings is well-founded. Common shortcomings in this regard are where the valuation expert:

- adopts the most current (adjusted) operating results, which do not reflect the cyclical nature of the given business;

---

6 See, for example, *Domglas Inc. v. Jarislowsky et al.* (1981), 13 B.L.R. 135 (Que. S.C.), aff'd (1982), 138 D.L.R. (3d) 521 (Que. C.A.).

- does not adjust historical operating results for unusual or non-recurring items, or alternatively, makes adjustments for certain historical revenues or expenditures that are not truly unusual or that are recurring; and
- adopts historical operating results that are not reflective of prospective results due to fundamental changes in the business or the industry in which it operates (e.g., due to a major business expansion or changes in the regulatory environment).

Common shortcomings in developing the capitalization rate are addressed in the section entitled "Rates of Return and Valuation Multiples."

2) Capitalization of Discretionary Cash Flow Methodology

The capitalization of discretionary cash flow methodology generally is preferred to the capitalization of earnings methodology. This is because the former is based on a company's ability to generate prospective discretionary cash flow as opposed to accounting earnings. Discretionary cash flow represents cash that is available to the providers of capital to a business, and that can be:

- withdrawn from the business in the form of dividends, excess remuneration, and so on, to provide a return on investment;
- reinvested in the business, thereby creating growth opportunities in excess of what would otherwise be the case;
- applied against outstanding interest bearing debt, thereby increasing the equity value component of enterprise value; or
- retained in the business as a "redundant asset," thereby increasing the "enterprise value" (and in turn the equity value) of the business.

The mechanics of the capitalization of discretionary cash flow methodology are similar to the capitalization of earnings methodology, except that normalized maintainable (after-tax) discretionary cash flows are used as the "base" in lieu of normalized maintainable (after-tax) net income. Discretionary cash flow normally is calculated as normalized maintainable earnings before interest, taxes, depreciation and amortization ("EBIT-DA"), less income taxes, and sustaining capital reinvestment (net of the related income tax shield).

Pursuant to the capitalization of discretionary cash flow methodology, depreciation expense and amortization expense (being non-cash expenditures) are not deducted. Rather, an estimate is made of sustaining capital expenditures, which represents the cost of fixed assets that must be acquired, each year on average, in order to maintain the operations of the business at the levels indicated. Capital expenditures give rise to capital cost allowance ("CCA") for income tax purposes. Therefore, the present value of the income tax savings on CCA is deducted from sustaining capital expenditure requirements. Further, in the context of the capitalization of discretionary cash flow methodology, an adjustment is made to account for the present value of the CCA tax shield on the undepreciated capital cost of existing assets owned by the business.

Referring to the previous example, assume normalized earnings before interest and taxes ("EBIT") of Company X is estimated at $750,000, and that Company X has annual depreciation and amortization expense of $100,000. It follows that Company X's normalized maintainable EBIT-DA would be calculated as $850,000 (being $750,000 EBIT plus $100,000 of depreciation and amortization). Further assume that annual sustaining capital reinvestment for Company X is estimated at $120,000 and that the present value of the CCA tax shield on that capital reinvestment is $30,000.[7] Assume that the present value of Company X's CCA tax shield on its existing assets is $150,000.[8] As before, assume that income taxes are 40%, a capitalization rate of 10% is considered appropriate, and that Company X has redundant assets of $100,000 and interest bearing debt outstanding of $800,000. The en bloc fair market value of Company X's shares determined pursuant to the capitalization of discretionary cash flow methodology would be as follows:

Company X Determination of the En Bloc Fair Market Value of Shares Captitalization of Discretionary Cash Flow Methodology		
Normalized maintainable EBIT	$750,000	
Add back: depreciation and amortization	$100,000	
Equals: normalized maintainable EBIT-DA		$850,000
Less: income taxes		-$340,000
Equals: net cash flow from operations		$510,000
Less: sustaining capital reinvestment	-$120,000	
Add: CCA tax shield thereon	$30,000	
Net sustaining capital reinvestment		-$90,000
Normalized maintainable discretionary cash flow		$420,000
Capitalization rate		10%
Capitalized cash flow		$4,200,000
Add: present value of existing CCA tax shield		$150,000
Add: redundant assets		$100,000
Equals: enterprise value		$4,450,000
Less: interest bearing debt outstanding		-$800,000
Equals: en bloc fair market value of shares		$3,650,000

7 The formula for determining the CCA tax shield on capital additions is:

[Cost × CCA Rate × Tax Rate] ÷ [Cost of Capital + CCA Rate].

For those assets subject to the "half-year rule," the above formula is further multiplied by

[1 + (0.5 × cost of capital)] ÷ [1 + cost of capital].

8 The formula for determining the present value of the CCA tax shield on existing assets is:

Note that the en bloc fair market value of Company X's shares determined pursuant to the capitalization of discretionary cash flow methodology is less than what was calculated pursuant to the capitalization of earnings methodology. This is because, in this example, Company X's sustaining capital reinvestment exceeds its depreciation expense for accounting purposes. The capitalization of discretionary cash flow methodology provides a better measure of true economic value compared to the capitalization of earnings methodology.

The principal determinants of value pursuant to the capitalization of discretionary cash flow valuation methodology are the estimated maintainable discretionary cash flow and the capitalization rate. Both of these factors are subjective and inter-related. A reasonable estimate of the discretionary cash flow base and the capitalization rate requires a sound understanding of the business and the industry in which it operates, as well as an objective assessment of the risks and opportunities faced by a particular business. Counsel should assess the manner and the degree to which the valuation expert considered these factors. Again, valuation reports sometimes adopt a mechanical approach when developing maintainable discretionary cash flow based on historical operating results, without considering whether such results are reflective of prospective cash flow. Many of the possible arguments in respect of the development of maintainable earnings under the capitalization of earnings methodology apply to the development of maintainable discretionary cash flow under the capitalization of discretionary cash flow methodology.

One additional common shortfall in the determination of the discretionary cash flow base is the estimation of a reasonable figure for sustaining capital reinvestment. This should reflect a long-term average amount of fixed asset additions required to maintain the operations of the business. In many cases, sustaining capital reinvestment is overestimated or underestimated due to overemphasis on capital spending in the most recent fiscal years, which may not be indicative of a company's capital spending needs over the long term. Counsel should assess the manner in which the valuation expert developed estimated sustaining capital expenditures to determine whether it was done on a reasonable and objective basis.

3) Multiple of EBIT and Multiple of EBIT-DA Methodologies

The "multiple of EBIT" and "multiple of EBIT-DA" valuation methodologies are simplifications of the capitalization of earnings and capitalization of discretionary cash flow methodologies, respectively.

[Undepreciated capital cost × CCA rate × tax rate] ÷ [cost of capital + CCA rate].

The mechanics of these methodologies are fairly straightforward. An estimate is made of normalized maintainable EBIT (or EBIT-DA), to which a valuation multiple is applied. The valuation multiple represents the inverse of a pre-tax rate of return (and in the case of EBIT-DA, pre sustaining capital as well). The determination of multiples is addressed under the section "Rates of Return and Valuation Multiples." As before, redundant assets are added, and outstanding interest bearing debt is deducted, in order to determine the "en bloc" fair market value of the shares of a business.

In the example of Company X, assume that maintainable EBIT is estimated at $750,000, and that a multiple of 6X is considered appropriate (which represents a pre-tax rate of return on total capital of 16.7%). Again, assume that redundant assets are $100,000 and interest bearing debt is $800,000. The determination of Company X's en bloc equity value pursuant to the multiple of EBIT methodology would be as follows:

Company X Determination of En Bloc Fair Market Value of Shares Multiple of EBIT Methodology	
Normalized maintainable EBIT	$750,000
EBIT multiple	6×
Capitalized EBIT	$4,500,000
Add: redundant assets	$100,000
Equals: enterprise value	$4,600,000
Deduct: interest bearing debt	-$800,000
Equals: en bloc equity value	$3,800,000

While the multiple of EBIT methodology and the multiple of EBIT-DA methodology may appear attractive due to their simplicity, their application can be hazardous. Similar to the capitalization of earnings methodology, the multiple of EBIT methodology does not consider important differences between capital spending and depreciation. The multiple of EBIT-DA methodology ignores capital spending requirements in their entirety, except to the extent that they may be reflected in the EBIT-DA multiple that is adopted.

As a result, the multiple of EBIT and multiple of EBIT-DA methodologies normally are adopted only for the purpose of a preliminary indication of value, or as a test of reasonableness on the valuation conclusions pursuant to a preferred valuation approach (such as the capitalization of discretionary cash flow methodology or the discounted cash flow methodology). While multiples of EBIT and EBIT-DA often are referred to in the context of transaction analysis (see "Comparable Transactions" below), this normally is because such earnings bases often are the only ones publicly disclosed. In most cases, corporate acquirers primarily are interested in the prospective discretionary cash flows to be generated following the acquisition of a particular business.

For the reasons explained above, counsel often can successfully challenge the multiple of EBIT or EBIT-DA methodology as unsound (at least as a primary basis for determining value), particularly in the valuation of capital-intensive industries. In addition, the valuation expert's determination of maintainable EBIT or maintainable EBIT-DA may suffer from some of the same shortcomings as the estimate of maintainable earnings under the capitalization of earnings methodology, discussed above.

4) Discounted Cash Flow

The discounted cash flow methodology generally is the preferred methodology for determining the en bloc fair market value for the shares of a business. The courts have increasingly recognized the validity of the discounted cash flow methodology in recent years.[9]

The discounted cash flow methodology involves forecasting the discretionary cash flow of a business for each year over the next several years (normally 3 to 5). Annual discretionary cash flows are discounted to present value at a discount rate considered appropriate to reflect the risks involved in achieving the projections. An estimate is then made of the value of the business following the forecast period. This is termed the "terminal value" (or "residual value") of the business. Terminal value normally is calculated in a manner similar to the capitalization of discretionary cash flow methodology — i.e., assuming a point estimate of maintainable discretionary cash flow beyond the forecast period, multiplied by a "terminal value multiple" (or divided by a capitalization rate). This calculation assumes that, following the forecast period, the business will continue to generate discretionary cash flow at a constant rate over the long term. The terminal value component is then discounted to present value. Adjustments are made to account for the present value of the CCA tax shield on existing capital assets, as well as redundant assets and interest bearing debt outstanding.

Recall that discretionary cash flow normally is calculated as EBIT-DA less income taxes, less capital investment requirements (net of the related CCA tax shield). However, when calculating discretionary cash flow pur-

9 See, for example, *Cyprus Anvil Mining Corp. v. Dickson et al.* (1983), 20 B.L.R. 21, 40 B.C.L.R. 180 (S.C.), rev'd (1986), 8 B.C.L.R. (2d) 145 (C.A.).

suant to a discounted cash flow methodology, it is important for the valuation expert to take into account all cash flows that must be incurred or realized in order to meet the projections. For example, pursuant to the discounted cash flow methodology, capital investment requirements not only include sustaining capital, but also incremental capital spending required to achieve sales growth, generate operating efficiencies, and so on, that form part of the projections. Furthermore, where a business expects to grow its sales, it normally requires additional working capital (i.e., accounts receivable, inventories, and so on). To the extent that a business requires incremental working capital to support its' growth, that represents a cash outflow, and must be deducted when calculating discretionary cash flow.

As an example of the discounted cash flow valuation methodology, assume that Company X expects that its EBIT-DA will increase from its current level of $850,000 in 2003 to $1,100,000 by 2006, and will remain at that level beyond that time. In order to achieve this growth, Company X must acquire additional capital equipment (i.e., in excess of the $120,000 annual sustaining capital assumed in the capitalization of discretionary cash flow methodology), and support its sales growth with incremental working capital. Assume that a discount rate of 13%, and a "terminal value

Company X
Determination of Fair Market Value of Shares
Discounted Cash Flow Methodology

		2004	2005	2006	Beyond
EBIT-DA		$900,000	$1,000,000	$1,100,000	$1,100,000
Less: income taxes		-$360,000	-$400,000	-$440,000	-$440,000
Net operating cash flow		$540,000	$600,000	$660,000	$660,000
Capital investment		-$400,000	-$250,000	-$150,000	-$150,000
Less: tax shield thereon		$100,000	$62,500	$37,500	$37,500
Less: working capital		-$40,000	-$80,000	-$80,000	0
Discretionary cash flow		$200,000	$332,500	$467,500	$547,500
Terminal value multiple					10×
Terminal value					$5,475,000
Present value at	13%	$176,991	$260,396	$324,000	$3,794,449
Valuation:					
Sum of present value				$4,555,838	
Add: present value of existing CCA tax shield				$150,000	
Add: redundant assets				$100,000	
Equals: enterprise value				$4,805,838	
Less: interest bearing debt outstanding				-$800,000	
En bloc fair market value of shares				$4,005,838	

multiple" of 10X are considered appropriate. These rates of return are explained in the section entitled "Rates of Return and Valuation Multiples." Consistent with previous examples, assume an income tax rate of 40%, and that Company X has redundant assets of $100,000, interest bearing debt outstanding of $800,000, and that the present value of the CCA tax shield on its existing assets is $150,000.

Note in this example the discounted cash flow methodology results in a higher en bloc fair market value for the shares of Company X than what was determined pursuant to the capitalization of discretionary cash flow methodology. This is due to the assumptions relating to Company X's near term growth in EBIT-DA. Also note that a substantial portion of the overall value conclusion rests in the "terminal value" component. This is not unusual in the discounted cash flow methodology, particularly where considerable capital expenditures and working capital must be invested in the earlier years in order to realize the assumed growth.

While the discounted cash flow methodology is conceptually sound, counsel often can challenge a business valuation developed pursuant to a discounted cash flow methodology on one or more of the following bases:

- the reasonableness of the projections. Fundamental to a credible value conclusion are financial projections that are founded on reasonable, internally consistent assumptions. In some cases, the valuation expert relies on so-called "hockey stick" projections that are premised on aggressive sales growth assumptions or cost savings that are not realistically attainable. Counsel should assess the nature and extent of the work that the valuation expert undertook to scrutinize the financial projections in order to satisfy themselves as to their reasonableness. An objective assessment of financial projections normally requires that the valuation expert develop a sound understanding of the business itself and the industry in which it operates. The scope of review section of the valuation report should set out the procedures that the valuation expert undertook in this regard;
- inadequate costs. While the sales growth forecasts set out in the cash flow projections may be plausible, the costs associated with achieving that growth sometimes are not adequately considered. For example, sales growth often necessitates additional capital spending or other fixed costs to support expansion. A common oversight in financial projections is the failure to consider the incremental investment required in terms of working capital to finance growth in sales. Failure to consider the cost of growth can significantly influence (overstate) the valuation conclusion. Counsel can perform simple calculations on the projections, such

as profit margins by year, to assess the degree to which the projections inherently assume the ability of the business to "leverage" its cost structure. If significant operating leverage is embedded in the financial projections, counsel should endeavour to challenge the valuation expert as to how they satisfied themselves as to the reasonableness of such implicit assumptions;

- technical errors. Because discounted cash flow calculations sometimes are complex, they generally are more prone to include technical valuation errors as opposed to other valuation methodologies. One of the more common technical errors is the inconsistency between the discount rate adopted and the basis by which the projected cash flows have been developed. For example, where inflation is included in the cash flow projections, inflation also should be reflected in the discount rate, and vice-versa. While technical errors of this nature may not be self-evident, counsel might be able to detect them through a careful assessment of the internal consistency of the assumptions made throughout the valuation report; and
- the terminal value calculation. In most discounted cash flow valuations, the terminal value component represents the majority of the "enterprise value" conclusion. However, the terminal value calculation sometimes is premised on assumptions in terms of discretionary cash flows and growth rates that may not be sustainable over the long term. Counsel sometimes can effectively challenge the terminal value calculation by making the court aware of the degree to which the valuation conclusion is influenced by the terminal value component, and the sensitivity of changes in terminal value maintainable cash flows and terminal value multiples to the overall value conclusion.

5) Comparable Public Companies

The comparable public companies methodology (sometimes referred to as the "guideline public companies method") involves identifying public companies whose operations are similar to the privately-held business being valued. The observed public equity market valuation multiples are applied to the earnings or cash flow base of the privately-held company to determine the value of its shares. Common public equity market multiples include:

- equity value (i.e., market capitalization) to net income (or sometimes equity value to net book value); and
- enterprise value (i.e., market capitalization plus interest bearing debt) to EBIT-DA or EBIT.

For example, assume that an analysis of publicly-held companies operating in the same industry as Company X traded at an average multiple of 6.5X trailing EBIT. Recall that Company X's normalized EBIT for its 2003 fiscal year was determined to be $754,000. As before, assume that Company X has $100,000 of redundant assets and $800,000 of debt outstanding. It follows that the value of the shares of Company X based on the comparable public companies methodology (using a multiple of trailing EBIT) would be determined as follows:

Company X Determination of Fair Market Value of Shares Comparable Public Companies Methodology	
Normalized trailing EBIT of Company X in 2003	$754,000
Public equity market EBIT multiple	6.5×
Capitalized earnings	$4,901,000
Add: redundant assets	$100,000
Equals: enterprise value	$5,001,000
Deduct: interest bearing debt	-$800,000
Equals: en bloc fair market value of shares	$4,201,000

As evidenced from the above illustration, the mechanics of the comparable public companies methodology are substantially similar to the multiple of EBIT methodology (or multiple of EBIT-DA methodology, or capitalization of earnings methodology, depending on the earnings base selected).

The comparable public companies methodology is popular in the United States due to guidelines published by the tax authorities in that country, which normally require that comparable public companies be considered in the course of a notional valuation. However, in both Canada and the United States, the application of so-called "comparable" public company multiples is fraught with difficulties. This is because it rarely is possible to find a publicly held company whose operations are substantially similar to the privately-held business being valued so as to provide a meaningful basis of comparison. Important differences usually exist in terms of business size, product offerings, markets served, and so on, all of which can have an important influence on value. Furthermore, even if so called "comparable" public companies can be found, there are important differences between the value of the shares of a privately-held business determined "en bloc," and the prices observed in the public equity markets for small lots of freely traded shares of publicly-held companies. Consequently, reliance on comparable public company multiples as a principal valuation methodology can result in misleading conclusions. The courts sometimes have criticized reliance on public equity market prices, particularly where trading in that stock is irregular or thin.[10]

As a practical matter, the comparable public companies methodology generally is restricted to large private companies (and public companies) where meaningful comparables are available. Even where adopted in such cases, the comparable public companies methodology normally is used as a secondary methodology to test the conclusions derived pursuant to a cash flow based methodology (such as the capitalization of discretionary cash flow or discounted cash flow methodology).

In a litigation context, where the comparable public companies methodology has been used to determine the value of a privately-held business, counsel can often successfully challenge the validity and/or application of the methodology. Specific areas of contention include:

- the quality of comparables. It is not uncommon for a valuation report that has adopted the comparable public companies methodology to set out a lengthy list of public companies purported to be "comparable" to the subject (private) company simply because they operate in the same industry. As noted above, important differences usually exist between any two companies in terms of size, product offerings, market coverage, and so on, such that the validity of each so-called "comparable" can be brought into question;
- differing accounting policies. Even where reasonable comparables can be found, companies often have different accounting policies in terms of inventory costing, depreciation, and so on, that affect their reported operating results. Therefore, to provide a meaningful basis for comparison, the financial results of the "comparable" public company must be restated to reflect the accounting policies of the privately-held company, assuming that sufficient information exists to make such calculations. Valuation experts often fail to make such adjustments;
- use of an average or median figure. The multiples adopted from a list of "comparables" often represent an average or median figure. In many cases, public company multiples in a given industry fall within a wide range due to the fact-specific circumstances of each business. In these cases, counsel can raise the issue of how an average or median figure from such a wide range can produce a meaningful result; and
- application of a "control premium." In some cases, a notional valuation performed pursuant to the comparable public companies methodology

10 See, for example, *Smeenk v. Dexleigh Corp.*, 1990 CarswellOnt 130, 72 D.L.R. (4th) 609, 49 B.L.R. 1, 74 O.R. (2d) 385 (H.C.).

includes an adjustment for a so-called "control premium." Such an adjustment normally is made on the assumption that public company shares trade at prices that reflect "minority discounts" and that an adjustment is necessary in order to eliminate the inherent minority discount embedded in the trading price (see discussion under "Minority Discounts"). Counsel can challenge the application of a control premium on the basis that its determination is subjective. Further, it is debatable whether public company share prices actually reflect a minority discount at all.

In light of the foregoing, counsel should be prepared to vigorously contest the adoption of the comparable public companies methodology as a primary basis for establishing the fair market value of a privately-held business.

6) Comparable Transactions

The comparable transactions methodology is premised on identifying open market transactions involving companies (public or private) whose operations are similar to those of the private company being valued. The valuation multiples observed from those transactions are applied to the earnings or cash flow base of the private company to determine the value of its shares. Popular comparable transaction multiples include enterprise value to EBIT or EBIT-DA, and equity value to net income (or sometimes adjusted net book value). The mechanics of the comparable transactions methodology are similar to the comparable public companies methodology, previously illustrated.

Comparable transactions sometimes are of interest to the courts because such they represent prices actually paid for similar business interests.[11] In addition, "sell-side" investment bankers often refer to multiples observed in comparable company transactions when negotiating price in open market transactions.

However, reliance on comparable transactions when determining the fair market value of the shares of a particular privately-held company is fraught with challenges. As noted above, there usually is an issue with respect to the level of comparability between any two companies due to differences in size, product offerings, markets served, and so on.

In addition, there can be important differences between the determination of price in an open market transaction and fair market value deter-

11 See, for example, *John A. Carruthers v. M.N.R.*, [1982] C.T.C. 5, [1983] 2 F.C. 350, 82 D.T.C. 6009 (Fed. T.D.).

mined in a notional market context. The price paid for a particular business is influenced by such things as the number of interested purchasers at a given point in time, the effectiveness of marketing the business for sale, the negotiating abilities of the purchaser and vendor (and their respective advisors), and other factors. These "market imperfections" are assumed not to exist pursuant to the standard definition of fair market value.

Furthermore, prices observed in open market transactions may incorporate an element of synergies or strategic advantage that is perceived by the purchaser. This is inconsistent with the definition of fair market value where it is determined on an intrinsic basis.

Many open market transactions are not conducted on cash terms, and other forms of consideration (such as share exchanges, earn-outs, management contracts, and so on) may be used. Attempting to convert a non-cash deal to a cash equivalent amount, consistent with the definition of fair market value, often requires subjective adjustments.

Finally, the disclosure accompanying an open market transaction often is limited, particularly where one or both of the companies involved in the transaction were privately-held. As a result, it generally is not possible to know whether other important elements of a particular deal influenced the stated price that was paid. Because of its limitations, the comparable transaction methodology normally is used as a secondary methodology, as a test of the value conclusions derived at pursuant to a cash flow based approach.

From a litigation standpoint, where the comparable transaction methodology has been adopted to value the shares of a particular privately-held company, counsel often can successfully challenge its use on the bases of:

- many of the same arguments used in respect of the comparable public companies methodology. This includes the quality of comparison between any two particular companies, and the use of an average or median multiple computed from a wide range of figures;
- the non-cash terms observed in various "comparable" transactions. It often is not meaningful to compare a non-cash deal with the "cash equivalent" aspect of fair market value. Further, determining the cash equivalent value of non-cash forms of consideration often is subjective;
- the inclusion of synergies. Prices observed in open market transactions often include an element of purchaser-perceived synergies or strategic advantage, which component of value cannot be readily segregated, and which is inconsistent with the definition of intrinsic fair market value;
- the computation of valuation multiples. Where a company has experienced an abnormal year, its reported operating results (e.g., EBIT-DA, EBIT, and so on) may not be reflective of its prospective operating

results (i.e., they may be higher or lower). This fact likely was known by the purchaser pursuant to its due diligence investigation. However, sufficient information usually is not available to a valuation expert to make the necessary adjustments to "normalize" trailing operating results. Hence, the computed multiples of enterprise value to EBIT-DA, EBIT, and so on, become distorted; and
- insufficient information. In most transactions, important details that may have had a significant influence on the price that ultimately was paid generally are not disclosed, and therefore the valuation expert likely did not take such factors into account.

In light of the foregoing, counsel should be prepared to vigorously contest the adoption of the comparable transactions methodology as a primary basis for establishing the fair market value of a privately-held business.

7) Adjusted Net Book Value Methodology

The adjusted net book value methodology (sometimes referred to as "tangible asset backing") involves adjusting the reported shareholders equity of a business to reflect the fair market value of its underlying assets and liabilities, as opposed to their book values. In this regard, non-identifiable intangible assets (e.g., goodwill and deferred charges) are reduced to nil, while tangible assets (e.g., property and equipment) and identifiable intangible assets (e.g., patents) are increased (decreased) where their market values exceed (are less than) their net book values.

The adjusted net book value methodology is most commonly used for businesses with no active operations (e.g., holding companies), and where it is believed that a business has no transferable goodwill. It is also used when comparing the underlying net tangible assets of a business to the fair market value of its shares determined pursuant to a cash flow based methodology (or other valuation methodology) in order to calculate the amount of goodwill embedded in the latter.

As an example, assume that Company X had a net book value for accounting purposes of $1.5 million. Further assume that Company X's assets included deferred charges of $50,000, and that it owns fixed assets with a book value of $600,000, but with a fair market value of $800,000. The fair market value of all other assets and liabilities approximate their net book values. The adjusted net book value of Company X would be determined as follows:

Company X Determination of Adjusted Net Book Value	
Shareholders equity as reported	$1,500,000
Deduct: deferred charges	-$50,000
Add: fair market value of fixed assets	$800,000
Deduct: book value of fixed assets	-$600,000
Adjusted net book value	$1,650,000

The value conclusions for the shares of Company X determined pursuant to a cash flow based methodology would be compared to its adjusted net book value. An analysis of the implied quantum of goodwill may provide some insight as to the reasonableness of the value conclusions otherwise determined.

In the context of litigation, where it is used as a primary valuation methodology to ascribe value to the shares of an operating business, counsel can sometimes challenge the adoption of the adjusted net book value methodology on the basis that:

- the assumption that no transferable goodwill exists may not be appropriate, depending on the nature of the business. In this regard, counsel should establish what procedures the valuation expert undertook to satisfy themselves as to the conclusion that no transferable goodwill exists (see discussion under "Determining Value for Income Tax Purposes"); and
- purchasers generally are interested primarily with the cash flow generating ability of a business as opposed to its underlying net assets. Adjusted net book value does not take into account the income-producing capability of a business.

Finally, whether the adjusted net book value methodology is adopted as a primary valuation methodology or for purposes of calculating goodwill, it often is criticized on the basis that adjustments made to account for the fair market value of underlying tangible and identifiable intangible assets usually are subjective. In this regard, where large adjustments are made to a business' assets and liabilities to arrive at adjusted net book value, counsel should determine what procedures the valuation expert undertook to justify such adjustments.

8) Conclusion — Valuation Methodologies

In summary, the preferred valuation methodologies generally are the discounted cash flow methodology (where meaningful projections exist) and the capitalization of discretionary cash flow methodology. The results from these valuation methodologies normally should be tested with reference to one or more 'secondary' methodologies, such as a multiple of EBIT (EBITDA), comparable transactions, and so on. In addition, it usually is helpful to calculate the adjusted net book value of a privately-held company, and to compare that figure to the valuation of the business determined pursuant to a cash flow based approach to assess the amount of goodwill embedded in the value conclusion.

Every valuation methodology is subject to underlying assumptions (both implicit and explicit). The reasonableness and internally consistency of these assumptions is fundamental to developing a meaningful valuation conclusion.

D. RATES OF RETURN AND VALUATION MULTIPLES

1) Overview

Rates of return and valuation multiples often have been regarded as the "mysterious black box" of business valuation. While there always is some element of subjectivity in their determination, the key issues are whether the rates of return and valuation multiples adopted in a fact-specific situation have been developed based on a thorough and objective assessment of the pertinent facts, and whether they have been applied in a way that is conceptually correct and internally consistent.

This section defines the various types of multiples and rates of return, and then addresses how they are developed and applied. It also examines some of the bases for contesting valuation multiples and rates of return in the context of income tax litigation involving the valuation of a privately-held company.

2) Definitions

It is important to understand the different terms commonly found in valuation reports when discussing rates of return. This includes discount rates, capitalization rates, and valuation multiples. These things are all interrelated, but they are not interchangeable.

A discount rate is the rate of return required by a purchaser in order to place capital at risk in exchange for the prospective discretionary cash flows to be generated by a business, given the nature of the business, the industry in which it operates, and general economic conditions. A discount rate is used in the discounted cash flow valuation methodology to determine the present value of the forecast discretionary cash flows.

A capitalization rate is determined by deducting the growth rate from the discount rate. In this context, the growth rate normally refers to inflation plus real growth (i.e., growth in excess of inflation — see discussion that follows). A capitalization rate is used in a capitalization of discretionary cash flow methodology (or capitalization of earnings methodology), and when determining the "terminal value" component of the discounted cash flow methodology.

A valuation multiple is simply the inverse of the capitalization rate (not the discount rate). Valuation multiples often are converted to a pre-tax basis, and applied to figures such as EBIT or EBIT-DA, as opposed to after-tax earnings or cash flows. Valuation multiples are most often used in the multiple of EBIT or EBIT-DA methodology, as well as the comparable public companies methodology and the comparable transactions methodology.

The relationships between discount rates, capitalization rates, and valuation multiples can be demonstrated with reference to the previous examples pertaining to the valuation of the shares of Company X. Assume that an appropriate (after-tax) discount rate for Company X was believed to be 13% (the derivation of which is discussed below). Recall that 13% was the discount rate adopted when determining the fair market value of the shares of Company X pursuant to the discounted cash flow methodology previously illustrated.

If we assume that a long term rate of growth for Company X of 3% was anticipated (including inflation and real growth), its (after tax) capitalization rate would be calculated as 10% (being 13% less 3%). Recall that a 10% capitalization rate was adopted when determining the fair market value of the shares of Company X pursuant to the capitalization of discretionary cash flow methodology (and the capitalization of earnings methodology).

Given the capitalization rate of 10%, the equivalent after-tax multiple for Company X would be calculated as 10X (being 1/10%). This is the multiple that was adopted when determining the terminal value component of the shares of Company X pursuant to the discounted cash flow methodology.

Given Company X's income tax rate of 40%, its pre-tax multiple would be 6X [calculated as 10 x (1-40%)]. Recall that the 6X multiple was adopted when valuing the shares of Company X pursuant to the multiple of EBIT methodology.

To summarize, it generally is appropriate to first develop the discount rate, and then to derive the capitalization rate by deducting long-term growth from the discount rate. The after-tax multiple is the inverse of the capitalization rate, which can be converted to a pretax basis if desired.

One of the most critical issues to address when calculating capitalization rates (and resultant valuation multiples) is the determination of the growth figure. Most businesses are able to generate long-term growth that at least covers the rate of inflation (although this is not always the case). A more contentious issue is the rate of real growth (i.e., growth in excess of inflation) that a business will experience. In theory, the real growth rate adopted represents the return that a business is able to generate in excess of its cost of capital over the long term. This is a technical point, but one that is important to understand. Simply because a business experiences growth does not necessarily mean that it is able to create value for its shareholders. Value is created only where a business can generate a return on its invested capital that exceeds its cost of capital. In a competitive market place, such opportunities normally are limited over the long term. Hence, the real growth figure deducted when calculating the capitalization rate often is nil, or a relatively small amount (say 1% to 2%). It is unusual to expect that a company will be able to demonstrate a sustained rate of real growth over the long term in excess of the real rate of growth in the national gross domestic product.

3) Discount Rate Determination

In the context of a business valuation involving a privately-held company, discount rates (and resultant capitalization rates and valuation multiples) normally are expressed as a "weighted average cost of capital" ("WACC"). WACC represents the blended after-tax cost of a company's financing from both debt and equity sources. Regardless of the extent to which a company uses debt financing in its existing capital structure (if at all), in the context of a business valuation it is necessary to consider the level of debt financing that would be considered "appropriate" for a given business over the long term. This is a subjective exercise. However, a reasonable estimate of capital structure normally can be obtained by considering factors such as the level and quality of a company's underlying net assets, the stability of its cash flows, the industry in which it operates, current and prospective interest rates, and so on. The attractive feature of the WACC calculation is that it is not overly sensitive to changes in capital structure assumptions within a reasonable range.

A WACC discount rate is a function of three basic elements, being the:

- nominal unlevered return on equity;
- debt to total capital ratio (i.e., capital structure); and
- income tax rate.

In most cases, the income tax rate is known or can be reasonably estimated. Therefore, the two variables that must be subjectively determined are the nominal unlevered return on equity, and the debt to total capital ratio.

The nominal unlevered return on equity reflects the rate of return required by a purchaser in order to place capital at risk in a given business in light of its operating risks, but before consideration of financial risk. That is, the unlevered return on equity reflects the risks inherent in the operations of the business itself, such as the risks relating to loss of customers, change in competitive landscape, increases in the cost of labour and materials, and so on. These operating risks are distinct from financial risk, which is related to the use of debt in lieu of equity in order to finance the business. Recall from the discussion under "Valuation Methodologies" that the "enterprise value" of a business (i.e., the total value of its operations) typically does not depend on how the business actually is financed.

The nominal unlevered return on equity often is determined pursuant to a "build-up" methodology. Pursuant to this approach, the starting point normally is the yield on long-term "risk-free" securities, such as long-term government of Canada bonds. An equity risk premium is then added to the risk free rate in order to reflect the higher level of risk associated with an equity investment in general, as compared to a risk free security. The determination of the equity risk premium is subjective, but premiums in the order of 4% to 7% are not uncommon. Finally, where appropriate, an adjustment (either upward or downward) is made to reflect fact-specific industry and company risks, where such risks are not reflected in the general equity risk premium.

Returning to the example of Company X, assume that the yield on long-term government bonds at the valuation date is 6%, and that an equity risk premium of 5% is considered appropriate. Further assume that an additional risk premium of 4% for Company X is considered appropriate, based on its relative size, the nature of its operations and the industry in which it competes. It follows that the nominal unlevered return on equity for Company X would be calculated as 15% (being 6% + 5% + 4%). Note that this is a nominal rate of return, including an inflation factor, which is embedded in the yield on the long-term government bonds.

The debt to total capital ratio addresses the extent to which the operations of a business can be financed by debt in lieu of equity. Debt financing is attractive because the cost of debt typically is less than the cost of equity financing, and because interest expense normally is deductible for income tax purposes. The determination of the debt to total capital ratio is subjective, but should reflect the "normal" long-term debt capacity of a business, based on factors such as the stability of the business' cash flows, the nature and quantum of its underlying assets, the industry in which it operates, and so on.

With the nominal unlevered return on equity ("ROE") and the debt to total capital ratio determined, and with knowledge of the income tax rate, the WACC discount rate can be calculated with the following "simplified" formula:

WACC = nominal unlevered ROE × [1 – (tax rate x debt to total capital)]

To illustrate the application of the WACC formula, assume that the nominal unlevered return on equity for Company X is estimated at 15% (as previously calculated pursuant to the "build-up" approach). Further assume that a normalized debt to total capital ratio for Company X is estimated at 30%, and that Company X has an income tax rate of 40%. Based on these assumptions, the WACC discount rate for Company X would be determined as follows:

15% × [1 – (40% x 30%)] = 13.2% (rounded to 13%).

Recall that the 13% discount rate was the rate used to determine the value of the shares of Company X pursuant to the discounted cash flow methodology, and was the base used for calculating Company X's capitalization rate and valuation multiple.

As noted above, the WACC calculation is not overly sensitive to minor changes in the debt to total capital assumption. For example, if we assume a debt to total capital ratio for Company X of 35% (instead of 30%), with no change in its nominal unlevered return on equity (15%) or income tax rate (40%), Company X's WACC discount rate would decline to 12.9% (using the simplified formula). This represents a difference of only 0.3% from the 13.2% previously determined. Accordingly, counsel generally should not expend a large amount of time and effort arguing the assumed debt to total capital ratio where it is not believed to have a significant impact on the overall determination of value.

As an alternative to a "build up" methodology to develop rates of return, many corporate acquirers adopt so-called "hurdle rates" that are used to assess investment opportunities. These hurdle rates may be expressed as a return on equity or a WACC. In today's environment, ROE hurdle rates in the order of 12% to 15% are not uncommon, which generally translate into WACC hurdle rates (discount rates) in the order of 10% to 15% (depending on the capital structure and income tax rate assumptions). This range of after-tax rates of return is consistent with those sometimes adopted by the courts.[12]

Corporate hurdle rates may be adjusted (upward or downward) to reflect the fact-specific circumstances of a particular acquisition opportunity. When assessing a corporate acquirer's hurdle rate, it is important to understand what it represents (i.e. a ROE or a WACC), and the assumptions inherently embedded therein (with respect to inflation, capital structure, and so on).

4) Litigious Issues in Rates of Return and Valuation Multiples

Rates of return and valuation multiples frequently are a principal source of contention in litigation. They often are challenged on the basis of their subjectivity (including possible perceived bias) or on the basis of their technical determination.

There is no doubt that the determination of rates of return and valuation multiples used in the valuation of a privately-held business inherently is subjective. However, the issue is whether or not the rates adopted are reasonable. In this regard, in the context of a notional valuation, it is important for the valuation expert to take into account all of the material factors (both positive and negative) that likely have an influence on the rates of return, and to assess these factors in an objective manner.

Counsel can gain some insight into whether or not the valuation expert considered certain important factors by examining the "scope of review" section of a valuation report. The scope of review section sets out the information base that was relied upon, and the individuals with whom the valuation expert held discussions regarding the business. In a notional valuation, it often is helpful for a valuation expert to obtain information from sources outside of the company (such as industry reports or third party industry experts). Independent sources of information often lend greater credibility to the analysis conducted and the valuation conclusions that are reached. In some cases, counsel might successfully challenge the valuation expert's rate of return selection on the basis that the scope of review was inadequate to afford the valuation expert a sound understanding of the risks and opportunities facing the business at the valuation date.

Technical errors in the determination and application of rates of return and valuation multiples are not uncommon in valuation reports. While a detailed explanation of the types of deficiencies that sometimes occur is

---

12 See, for example, *R.G. Mersereau v. MNR*, [1977] C.T.C. 2412, 77 D.T.C. 290 (T.R.B.).

beyond the scope of this chapter, counsel should be aware some of the more common technical errors, which include:

- internal inconsistency between the discount rate and the cash flows to which the rate is applied. For example:
  - the inflation assumptions embedded in the discount rate should be consistent with those used when developing the cash flow projections. Discounting real cash flows (i.e., excluding inflation) by a nominal discount rate (i.e., including inflation) results in an understatement of value, and vice-versa, and
  - where a discount rate or capitalization rate is expressed as a WACC, the cost and risks associated with debt financing are embedded in the rate of return. Therefore, the cash flows (or earnings) to which the rate of return is applied should exclude debt servicing costs.

  Counsel might be able to establish whether these types of technical errors exist in a valuation report based on a careful reading of the valuation methodology and related assumptions, and employing the principles set out in this chapter;
- commingling the valuation multiple used pursuant to a multiple of EBIT or multiple of EBIT-DA methodology, and the earnings base to which the multiple is applied. For example, multiples of EBIT sometimes are erroneously applied to EBIT-DA, resulting in an overstatement of value, and vice-versa. Once again, counsel might be able to ascertain that such errors exist based on a careful reading of the valuation report;
- misapplication of the growth rate used to calculate the capitalization rate. Recall that the growth rate is deducted from the discount rate in order to determine the capitalization rate. The growth rate adopted should be the long-term sustainable rate of growth, which normally is comprised of inflation and in some cases a small amount of real growth (say, 1% to 2% over inflation). High rates of assumed real long-term growth usually are suspect, and can result in overstated value conclusions. Accordingly, where long-term real growth rates are high (say, more than 3% above inflation), counsel should consider the basis by which such an optimistic assumption can successfully be challenged. In some cases, counsel might assist the court in understanding the impact that high assumed long-term growth rates have on the valuation conclusions by preparing alternate "sensitivity analysis" calculations; and
- reliance on comparable transactions, or so-called comparable public companies to develop rates of return and valuation multiples of privately-held businesses. As previously discussed, comparable transactions may incorporate an element of synergies and strategic advantage, or

may include a significant non-cash component. These things may inflate the multiple (or reduce the rate of return) beyond what is appropriate for a privately-held company that is valued on an intrinsic basis. Alternatively, public equity market multiples are influenced by factors such as differences in liquidity and the availability of information. While comparable company multiples and public equity market comparables can sometimes be used as a test of reasonableness, these methodologies seldom are appropriate as a primary basis for developing rates of return and valuation multiples. Where a valuation report places significant weight on the valuation multiples observed in "comparable" companies and transactions, counsel often can successfully challenge the methodology itself, and challenge each "comparable" on the basis of differences between it and the subject private company in terms of business size, markets served, circumstances (in the case of an open market transaction) and so on.

Finally, in some cases rates of return are developed using the "Capital Asset Pricing Model" ("CAPM"). CAPM is sometimes used by stock market analysts and by portfolio managers as a tool for analyzing publicly traded equity securities, and the model often serves reasonably well for that purpose. However, CAPM generally cannot be meaningfully applied to develop rates of return for privately-held businesses. This is principally because CAPM makes certain underlying assumptions that may be relevant to a portfolio of liquid public-held equity securities but that are not appropriate when analyzing a stand-alone privately-held business. For example, CAPM assumes that "non-systematic" (i.e., company-specific) risk is eliminated based on the assumption that an investor holds a diversified portfolio of securities. Clearly non-systematic risk is not eliminated when valuing a particular privately-held company for income tax (or other) purposes. When reviewing a valuation report that relies on CAPM to develop rates of return, counsel should consult one of the reference sources noted at the beginning of this chapter to obtain a list of deficiencies in the utilization of CAPM in the context of valuing a privately-held business en bloc.

5) Conclusions — Rates of Return

To summarize, rates of return that are used in the context of a business valuation exercise normally are expressed as a WACC. It is important that the underlying components of the WACC (particularly the unlevered return on equity and the debt to total capital ratio) are reasonable and supportable in the circumstances. It also is important to ensure that rates of return are applied in a manner that is internally consistent. Finally, as previously illustrated under "Valuation Methodologies," rates of return and the cash flows (or earnings) to which they are applied are inter-related. The value of a business cannot be altered by changing either of these variables in isolation. Counsel might successfully challenge the rates of return or valuation multiples adopted by the valuation expert either on the basis of the expert's lack of understanding of the risks and opportunities facing the business at the valuation date (mainly through an assessment of the scope of review set out in the valuation report), or on the basis of various technical deficiencies as explained herein.

E. MINORITY DISCOUNTS

1) Overview

Up to this point, the discussion has been on the valuation of the shares of a privately-held company viewed "en bloc." However, in many cases, the issue at hand is an interest in a privately-held business that represents less than 100% of its voting shares.

Where a person holds a controlling interest in a privately-held business (generally defined as an interest in excess of 50% of the voting shares), in most cases, the fair market value of that controlling interest is calculated as its pro-rata portion of the en bloc fair market value. This is because a controlling shareholder typically is in a position to elect the majority of the board of directors, thereby controlling decisions that influence the strategic direction of the company, the quantum of dividend and bonus distributions, the timing of sale or liquidation of the business, and so on.

For example, assume that the en bloc fair market value of Company X is estimated at $4 million (determined pursuant to the discounted cash flow methodology, as previously illustrated) and that there are 1 million common shares issued and outstanding. Further assume that there are two shareholders of Company X, one that holds 75% of the shares and the other that holds 25%. The pro-rata value of each share in Company X is $4 per share. In most cases, the fair market value of the interest held by the 75% shareholder of Company X would be estimated at $3 million, being its pro-rata portion of en bloc fair market value.

The value of a minority interest, on the other hand, must reflect the fact that a minority shareholder does not enjoy the same rights and privileges as a controlling shareholder. Further detracting from the value of a minority interest is the fact that in most privately-held companies a less readily available market exists for a minority shareholding than for a controlling interest. As a result, a minority shareholder may be exposed to one or both of:

- a discount for the inability to unilaterally control the company (i.e., a "discount for non-control"); and
- a discount for the absence of a ready market in which to sell the minority interest (i.e., a "discount for illiquidity").

Discounts for non-control and discounts for illiquidity are inter-related, since a non-controlling position in a privately-held business generally is less marketable than a controlling interest. Therefore, these two discounts often are combined into an all-inclusive "minority discount."

Extending the example above, the fair market value of the interest held by the 25% shareholder of Company X may not be its pro-rata value of $1 million. Rather, depending on the circumstances, the fair market value of that minority interest may be considerably less.

2) Determining Minority Discounts

The determination of a minority discount (or alternatively a discount for non-control and a discount for illiquidity) inherently is subjective. A reasonable determination of a minority discount requires a thorough and objective assessment of the fact-specific circumstances surrounding a particular minority shareholding. In addition, developing a meaningful minority discount requires an understanding of the basis by which "en bloc" fair market value was determined.

The quantification of a minority discount normally should begin with an assessment of the provisions set out in a company's articles of incorporation and in its shareholders agreement (where one exists). In many cases, these documents specifically address the valuation of a minority interest in the company. It is not uncommon for a shareholders agreement to specify that a minority shareholder is entitled to receive "fair value" for his or her shares under certain circumstances. "Fair value" generally is defined as a pro-rata portion of en bloc fair market value without the application of a minority discount.

However, in many situations, no shareholders agreement exists. Further, even if a shareholders agreement does exist, it often is vague or silent on important parameters regarding the valuation of a minority shareholding. In such cases, the quantification of a minority discount normally should consider factors such as the:

- size of the shareholding, both in relative and absolute terms. In most cases, a larger discount is applied to a minority interest in a company where there is one controlling shareholder, as opposed to a company in which no one individual (or group of related individuals) has control;
- relevant provisions of the federal or provincial legislation under which the company was incorporated;
- relationships among the shareholders. Where such relationships are favourable, it normally serves to reduce the quantum of discount;
- the minority shareholder's level of involvement in the company. A minority shareholder that is actively involved in a company generally is in a better position vis-à-vis his or her influence on the direction of the business, as contrasted with a passive shareholder with a similar percentage interest in the business; and
- historic and prospective distributions from a company in terms of dividends, shareholder bonuses, and so on.

In arriving at the fair market value of a particular shareholding, consideration must also be given to the restrictions, if any, placed on the transfer of the shares in question. Such restrictions typically are found in the incorporating documents or shareholders agreement, if one exists.

Where minority shareholding interests are valued for income tax purposes, the guidelines for group and family control set out by the CRA should be considered. CRA Information Circular 89-3 entitled "Policy Statement on Business Equity Valuations" includes a discussion as to the considerations to be made when assessing whether group and family control exist.

According to the CRA, group control is deemed to exist where shareholders voting shares aggregating more than 50% of the votes cast at a general meeting of shareholders can demonstrate a pattern of acting in concert with respect to their shareholdings, and that they are restricted in their right to vote and sell their shares independently. To satisfy the CRA, such evidence could be contained in the Articles of Incorporation, the by-laws, or in a shareholders agreement. Experience to date suggests the CRA primarily looks to consistent application of group control (or the lack thereof) at relevant valuation dates.

When referring to the valuation of an individual minority shareholding in a corporation collectively controlled by individuals with a familial relationship, the term "family control" often is used. CRA generally has accepted a premise that, barring family disputes, family members who collectively control may be presumed to act in concert to exercise some control over the economic direction and the liquidity of their investment. The rationale which underlies this theory is that related shareholders who hold in the aggregate more than 50% of the voting shares are in a position to realize proceeds not less than the ratable value of their respective shareholdings by acting in concert to sell a control shareholding. Information Circular 89-3 also includes discussion as to the considerations to be made in assessing whether family control exists.

3) Litigious Elements of Minority Discounts

Minority discounts (or discounts for non-control and discounts for illiquidity) are highly subjective. Furthermore, minority discounts applied for income tax purposes often have been in the range of 20% to 40% of pro-rata fair market value.[13] Therefore, minority discounts can have a significant influence on the final determination of the fair market value of a particular minority shareholding.

The quantum of minority discounts (or even whether a minority discount should be applied at all) in any fact-specific situation usually is the subject of considerable debate. In addition to their inherent level of subjectivity, counsel sometimes can successfully challenge the basis by which minority discounts were developed in terms of technical misapplication stemming from the following:

- a lack of understanding of the basis by which en bloc fair market value was determined. Discounts are "relative" concepts. As such, it is important for the valuation expert to demonstrate that consideration was given to the methodology and assumptions underlying the determination of en bloc fair market value in order to develop a meaningful discount from pro-rata value;
- inconsistent application of minority discounts at different points in time. A change in the quantum of discount in respect of a particular shareholding should be supported by a demonstrable change in relevant factors affecting such a discount at different points in time (e.g., a change in the relationship among the shareholders). Counsel should compare valuation reports prepared for the subject company at different dates to determine if such inconsistencies do exist; and
- double counting. Where a minority discount is derived based on a discount for non-control and a discount for illiquidity, the factors giving rise to each discount sometimes are double counted, which may result in an overstatement of the combined minority discount. Counsel can

13 See, for example, *Krafve v. MNR*, [1984] C.T.C. 2021, 84 D.T.C. 1002 (T.C.C.).

often ascertain if this is the case through a careful reading of the valuation report.

In some cases, minority discounts are calculated based on the inverse of so-called "control premiums" (or "premiums for control"). As briefly discussed under "Rates of Return and Valuation Multiples," some individuals in the valuation field believe that shares of publicly held companies trade in the public equity markets at prices that reflect a minority discount. When a third party purchaser acquires a publicly-held company, the price paid usually exceeds the market capitalization of the public company prior to the transaction. The "premium" that is paid sometimes is assumed to arise from the elimination of the minority discount embedded in the market capitalization of the public company. Premiums for control in the order of 40% are not uncommon, although they tend to fall within a wide range. Based on the assumption that the premium for control represents the elimination of a minority discount, the minority discount would be calculated in the order of 29% (being [1 - [1 / (1 + 40%)]).

This approach to determining a minority discount normally is flawed. It inherently assumes that the premium paid in an open market transaction is entirely due to the elimination of an inherent minority discount embedded in the market price of the shares of the acquired public company prior to the transaction. The existence of minority discounts for public company shares is debatable, particularly for public companies with a large public share float. Rather, in most cases, some or all of a "control premium" more likely is attributable to post-acquisition synergies anticipated by the purchaser, and/or the fact that the form of payment included non-cash terms (e.g., a share for share exchange), with a cash equivalent amount less than its face value. The existence of synergies or non-cash deal terms serves to inflate the premium that is paid to consummate the transaction. As previously noted, these things are inconsistent with fair market value determined on an intrinsic basis. Hence, where a minority discount is developed based on the inverse of an assumed "premium for control," counsel might successfully argue that it may be significantly overstated.

4) Conclusions — Minority Discounts

Minority discounts are highly subjective, and their quantification is dependent on fact specific circumstances. A meaningful conclusion as to the quantum of discount for a given minority interest generally requires consideration of the relevant provisions of a shareholders agreement and incorporation documents, as well as the relationship among the shareholders of the company. Discounts are relative concepts, and hence an understanding of the basis by which en bloc fair market value was determined is fundamental to a supportable minority discount conclusion. Minority discounts developed on the basis of the assumed elimination of a "premium for control" often are successfully challenged on the basis of the inherent questionable assumptions in that methodology.

F. CONCLUSIONS

Determining the fair market value of the shares of a privately-held business is a subjective exercise. A reasonable conclusion requires a thorough and objective assessment of the pertinent factors, combined with an appropriate valuation methodology and plausible rates of return, properly applied.

When faced with a situation that requires that the fair market value of a privately-held business interest be determined, counsel should consider whether circumstances warrant consideration of so-called "special purchasers," which might have a significant impact on the value conclusion. Unless qualified to the contrary, the definition of fair market value in Canada contemplates the possibility that special purchasers may exist, although the quantification of a special purchaser premium might be highly speculative.

Counsel should also be cognizant of the inherent challenges that arise where a valuation is prepared as of a specific date that has long since past. In such cases, valuation experts sometimes must contend with the difficulties of limited information and the possible influence of hindsight, each of which may impair the credibility of the valuation conclusions.

Another challenge that sometimes arises, particularly in the valuation of smaller privately-held companies, has to do with the form of goodwill. Specifically, in some businesses the owner-manager's knowledge, skills and personal relationships have a substantial influence on its operating results. Where the goodwill element of the business' value is believed to be attributable to "individual goodwill," that portion of goodwill forms a part of fair market value. However, the valuation expert must take into account the risks associated with individual goodwill, which should be reflected in the value conclusion. Conversely, that portion of the goodwill element of the business that is believed to be attributable to "personal goodwill" represents "value to owner," and it is not a component of fair market value. The distinction between individual goodwill and personal goodwill often is subjective, and in some cases the valuation expert's conclusions can be successfully challenged by counsel, depending on the nature and extent of the work that was undertaken to substantiate the goodwill conclusions.

There are numerous valuation methodologies that sometimes are used to determine the fair market value of a privately-held business that is a going concern. These include the capitalization of earnings, capitalization of discretionary cash flow, multiple of EBIT or EBIT-DA, discounted cash flow, comparable public companies, comparable transactions, and adjusted net book value methodologies. Valuation methodologies based on cash flows, such as the capitalization of discretionary cash flow methodology and the discounted cash flow methodology, generally are preferred. The mechanics of the capitalization of discretionary cash flow methodology involve estimating the after-tax unlevered cash flow that a business prospectively is expected to generate on an annual basis, and which can be withdrawn as a return on capital, without compromising the ability of the business to continue generating indicated revenue and profitability levels over the long term. Estimated maintainable discretionary cash flow is divided by a rate of return to determine capitalized cash flow. Redundant assets are then added to determine the "enterprise value" of the business. Interest bearing debt and equivalent amounts are then deducted to determine the value of the shares of the business, viewed "en bloc."

The discounted cash flow valuation methodology is conceptually similar to the capitalization of discretionary cash flow valuation methodology, except that the discounted cash flow methodology involves forecasting prospective discretionary cash flows for a number of years, and then estimating the "terminal value" of the business. Fundamental to any valuation conclusions derived pursuant to the discounted cash flow methodology is a forecast developed based on assumptions that are both reasonable and internally consistent. Valuation conclusions arrived at based on the discounted cash flow methodology can be unrealistic where the forecast has not sufficiently considered all of the costs associated with growth, which normally include incremental operating costs as well as incremental capital spending and working capital requirements.

Valuation conclusions developed based on the multiple of EBIT or EBIT-DA methodology are sometimes flawed because these methodologies do not explicitly consider important value drivers such as capital expenditure requirements and income taxes. The comparable public companies methodology is deficient in many respects. In particular, the notion that meaningful value conclusions can be drawn by comparing public equity market trading prices of companies that may be significantly different in terms of size, product offerings and so on, to a subject privately-held company normally is flawed. Similarly, the comparable transactions methodology also usually suffers from the shortcomings associated with the quality of the selected comparables, and in most cases is hampered by the absence of essential information regarding the terms of the transactions and the expectations of the parties involved, both of which may have had a significant influence on the observed price that was paid. For these reasons, application of the multiple of EBIT or EBIT-DA, comparable public companies, and comparable transactions methodologies generally is limited to providing a test on the value conclusions derived pursuant to the capitalization of discretionary cash flow methodology or the discounted cash flow methodology.

In the context of a business valuation, the rate of return adopted normally is a weighted average cost of capital, which comprises both a return on equity and debt financing. The WACC rate of return is a function of the required unlevered return on equity given the operating risks of the business, a debt to total capital ratio that is considered appropriate, and the income tax rate.

Rates of return and valuation multiples frequently are a source of contention in income tax litigation because of their subjectivity. They sometimes are effectively challenged on the basis that the valuation expert did not have an adequate understanding of the operations of the business and the industry in which it competes in order to make an informed and objective determination of appropriate rates of return. The scope of review section of the valuation report provides some insight into the depth of analysis undertaken by the valuation expert. In addition, the determination of rates of return and valuation multiples can be technically complex. As a result, their determination sometimes suffers from technical deficiencies, which often are in the form of internal inconsistencies between the assumptions underlying the rates of return and the assumptions underlying the earnings or cash flow base to which the rates are applied. Counsel should closely scrutinize the explicit and implicit assumptions used by valuation experts when developing their rates of return and valuation conclusions.

Finally, when determining the fair market value of a non-controlling interest in a privately-held company, the issue of a minority discount often must be addressed. Minority discounts are influenced by the level of liquidity and the degree of control (or non-control) associated with a particular business interests. Minority discounts are subjective and they can fall within a wide range, depending on the fact-specific circumstances. Consequently, they can have a significant impact on the fair market value of non-controlling interests in privately-held companies. Discounts are relative concepts, and so fundamental to forming a reasonable estimate of an appropriate minority discount is an understanding of the basis by which "en bloc" fair market value was determined. A defensible estimate of the quantum of minority discount also necessitates that the valuation expert carefully consider all of the material pertinent facts that influence the legal rights attaching to a particular equity interest, as well as the relationships among the shareholders. Where the valuation expert has not sufficiently considered these factors, the minority discount conclusion might successfully be challenged.

In the end, effective litigation of a business valuation report and its conclusions requires an understanding of the challenges faced by the valuation expert in a particular valuation assignment, the technical aspects of the methodology(ies) employed and the rates of return adopted, and an understanding of the underlying assumptions on which the conclusions are premised. It also requires a careful reading of the valuation report, and particular scrutiny of the scope of the valuation expert's work and the assumptions that underlie the value conclusions.

Chapter Sixteen

Valuing Computer Software, Brands, and other Intellectual Property: Concepts, Complexities, and Controversies*

James L. Horvath and Steven A. Hacker

A. INTRODUCTION

During the last twenty years, the business community has devoted ever-greater attention to investing in, accumulating, managing and protecting "knowledge assets" or intellectual property ("IP"). These intangible assets are among the most strategic and most coveted assets of many companies and are often the most significant driver of competitive advantage and business growth. Also, unlike plant and equipment, IP can be moved fairly easily from country to country and thus often figures prominently in tax minimization plans. US Federal Reserve Board Chairman Alan Greenspan recently commented: "In recent decades . . . the fraction of the total output of our economy that is essentially conceptual rather than physical has been

* The Authors wish to thank our colleagues John Anderson, CA, PhD, Richard K. Ellsworth, PE, ASA, CFA, D. Alan Jones FCBV, Zareer Pavri, CA, CBV, ASA, and Jeremy Webster, CA, CBV, ASA for their review and suggestions for this paper. Case research was assisted by Laurie A. Smith and Kerry Blair of Deloitte's Tax Information Services group.

rising. This trend has . . . shifted the emphasis in asset valuation from physical property to intellectual property and to the legal rights that inhere in the latter."[1]

As a result of the heightened emphasis on IP, disputes with the Canada Revenue Agency ("CRA") relate increasingly to the valuation of and transfer pricing surrounding IP. Central to many tax plans and disputes is the valuation of software, trademarks, patents, know-how, and other intangible assets, for example, in connection with non-arm's length transfers or offshore transactions in which the IP is transferred to low tax jurisdictions. The purpose of this paper is to provide practitioners involved with taxation litigation and tax planning an understanding of the concepts, complexities and controversies surrounding the valuation of IP.

Although valuations of technology such as software and other IP are generally based on the same principles and methodologies as those traditionally employed by business valuators in valuing shares, or underlying tangible assets such as real estate, and machinery and equipment, there are several techniques that are unique to IP valuations. Using examples from our experience with hundreds of IP transactions and valuation assignments, this paper illustrates the application of some of these techniques. Also discussed in this paper are a number of complicating factors related to the valuation of IP that present challenges to valuators. For example, while the life expectancy of a building or piece of equipment may be readily estimated based on past experience, the estimated lifespan of IP, which tends to be a critical driver of value, is a much more subjective prediction. The lifespan of technology-based IP depends on, among many factors, technical assessments of the IP, the uncertain demand for new technology, the expected future rate of advancement in the industry, patent life and formal IP protection, the ability of competitors to duplicate the technology and force further innovation, the availability of capital to develop the technology and finance further innovation, and so forth. For IP that is new or under development, there is the question of whether the item will ever be marketable. Unlike real estate or shares in corporations, where there is an abundance of market data on which to base a valuation, there is relatively less publicly available data on transactions involving ownership interests in IP such as software or brand names. In response to these challenges, business valuators must continually build on their personal technical and

---

1 Alan Greenspan, "Market Economies and Rule of Law," presented at the 2003 Financial Markets Conference of the Federal Reserve Bank of Atlanta, Sea Island, Georgia (via satellite) April 4, 2003.

industry knowledge, and must often rely on, and incorporate in their valuations, the findings of technical experts (e.g., software engineers, scientists), and other industry experts and participants.

B. REASONS FOR INTELLECTUAL PROPERTY VALUATIONS

The purpose of a valuation of IP is the development of the asset's fair market value at a specific time for a specific purpose. Although not defined in the Canadian *Income Tax Act* (the "Act"), the generally accepted definition of fair market value is:

> The highest price, expressed in terms of money or money's worth, obtainable in an open and unrestricted market between knowledgeable, informed and prudent parties acting at arm's length, neither party being under any compulsion to transact.[2]

Fair market value as defined above is a notional concept, and differs from the price that may be realized between a buyer and seller of the same asset in an actual open market transaction. This difference may arise from a variety of factors that exist in the real market and do not exist in the notional marketplace contemplated by the aforementioned fair market value definition. These factors may include:

- differing negotiating ability, knowledge or other circumstances of the actual buyer and/or actual seller. Under the definition of fair market value, buyers and sellers are assumed to be fully informed, prudent, under no compulsion to transact, and of equal negotiating ability.
- the structure and consideration of the actual purchase price. The definition of fair market value refers to a price that is in terms of money or money's worth, whereas actual open market transactions often involve non-cash consideration.[3]
- time differences. Market conditions in existence at the notional valuation date may differ from those in existence at the time of comparable open market transactions.
- momentum and public market dynamics.

The specified valuation date is critical in the case of most IP given the dynamic nature of the demand for such assets, and the tendency for com-

---

2 Information Circular IC 89-3, published by the CRA.

3 Examples of non-cash consideration include debt, restricted shares, employment or consulting agreements, and contingency-based price adjustment clauses, among others.

peting technology or subsequent innovations to render it obsolete. Notional valuations of IP must reflect the technological and economic climate, competitive conditions, and future prospects (and related risks) in existence at the valuation date. Given the rate of change of these conditions and prospects, a change in valuation date can significantly impact the valuation of IP. Valuation principles do not generally permit valuators to make reference to hindsight data (i.e., information relevant to the period after the valuation date such as results of further testing, further innovations, industry or economic conditions), although Canadian courts have permitted its use in a limited way, to verify the reasonableness of assumptions made in the valuation analysis.

Valuations of IP may be required in a number of taxation contexts:

1) Income tax planning

- going off shore. Development of value to support terms of planned non-arm's length transactions including purchase and sale price where an asset is being transferred to a non-arm's length taxpayer or non-resident corporate entity (s. 69 of the Act).
- estate planning. Determination of value to support estate freezes and other estate plans involving tax-deferred transfer of assets (e.g., s. 85 of the Act).
- formulating tax planning strategies. In certain circumstances, the tax planning approach to follow may be critically dependent on the value of an IP asset, and tax planning alternatives are formulated or finalized only after the subject asset has been valued, and the amounts of items such as capital gains, deemed dividends, royalties, etc. have been quantified.

2) Income tax compliance

- non-arm's length transactions (s. 69 of the Act).
- deemed dispositions, e.g., upon the death of individual taxpayer (s. 70 of the Act), permanent departure from Canada, or deemed disposition of trust property after 21 years (s. 104(4) of the Act).
- for purposes of establishing Eligible Capital Expenditure ("ECE") pool balances or for Capital Cost Allowance ("CCA") purposes. As a result of certain transactions, valuations of IP may be required. In the case of a limited partnership established to exploit software or other IP, the value of the IP acquired by the limited partnership needs to be valued for CCA purposes. In the case of a corporate acquisition, where the transaction has been structured as an asset acquisition as opposed to a share acqui-

sition, the purchase price of the business must be allocated to its tangible and intangible assets, including IP. A change of corporate status from exempt to taxable (e.g. in the case of a crown corporation being privatized, becoming a publicly traded company) would also require the determination of values for purposes of determining deductions for ECE and CCA.

- for purposes of assessing the reasonableness of CCA or ECE deductions in compliance with s. 67 of the Act, which states that for the purposes of determining income, deductions for outlays and expenses are permitted to the extent that the outlay or expense was reasonable in the circumstances. If a transaction involving the transfer of ownership of IP is deemed to be at arm's length, the value of the IP on which the acquirer bases its subsequent CCA or ECE deductions must be reasonable in the circumstances. Valuations may be used to support or attack the reasonableness of the CCA or ECE deductions.
- transfer pricing, e.g., to support the development of cross-border royalty rates or licence fees.
- determination of value in the case of payment of dividends in kind (s. 52(2) of the Act).
- establishment of value in connection with a charitable donation of an IP asset.
- calculation of value of trust property.
- measurement of stock option benefits in companies where the primary asset is IP (e.g., a biotechnology company or a software development company).

There are numerous other non-tax related reasons for valuing IP including:

- financial reporting of the acquisition of a business. According to current Canadian and US accounting standards, the allocation of the purchase price of an acquired business must be allocated amongst the acquired business' tangible and identifiable intangible assets based on fair value.[4]

---

4 This requirement is set out in Section 1581 of the Canadian Institute of Chartered Accountants Handbook ("CICA 1581"), and in the US Financial Accounting Standards Board statement FAS 141. Under CICA 1581, which deals with business combinations, fair value is defined as the amount of consideration that would be agreed upon in an arm's length transaction between knowledgeable, willing parties who are under no compulsion to act. It should be noted that due to the unique specifications of the aforementioned accounting standards, in some circumstances, fair value calculated for financial statement purposes may not be equal to fair market value calculated for income tax compliance or other purposes.

- commercial litigation (e.g., patent or trademark infringement, copyright infringement such as music, film, and game piracy, breaches of contract, business interruption, family law).
- financing (e.g., in connection with evaluating security for a loan, or determining the amount to loan).
- licensing (i.e., determining the amount of royalty or licence fees to charge to use the IP).
- joint ventures (i.e., calculating the relative share of value contributed to a joint venture by the parties).
- bankruptcy and restructuring.

C. EXAMPLES OF INTELLECTUAL PROPERTY

The following is a listing of some of the intellectual properties that are typically valued for income tax planning and/or compliance purposes:

1) Technology-related Intellectual Property

- computer software.
- patents — i.e., the right to make, use, and sell an invention, design, product, process, etc.
- designs such as circuit layouts.
- chemical formulations.
- industrial designs.
- trade secrets, formulae, processes, recipes, know-how.
- research and development (IP under development).
- life sciences technologies such as biologics, medical devices, therapeutics, diagnostics and systems.
- databases.
- various types of data (e.g., geophysical seismic data used by physicists in oil and gas exploration, satellite images, among others).

2) Marketing-related Intellectual Property ("marketing intangibles")

- trademarks, logos, images, service marks — i.e., words, names or symbols or combination thereof, adopted and used by a manufacturer or merchant to indicate the source of the product or service, and to distinguish it from the product or services of others.
- brands/brand names — i.e., general marketing terms used to refer to a group of complementary assets such as the trademark (or service mark) and its related trade name, formulae, recipes, technological expertise,

and legal registrations (copyright, trademark, etc.). The trademark provides legal protection preventing competitors from using the same or similar mark in a manner that is likely to cause confusion in the minds of the consumer.
- internet domain names.
- packaging designs/labels.

3) Artistic-related Intellectual Property

- copyright.
- musical works, song lyrics.
- literary works.
- plays, operas, ballets.
- films, scripts, etc.
- publishers rights.
- broadcast rights including films, sound broadcasts, television broadcasts and webcasts.

D. VALUE DRIVERS

Among a valuator's first considerations when valuing IP are its qualitative aspects. These are the aspects or factors that influence value, and are referred to as "value drivers." The value of IP is primarily a function of a number of such factors, and a qualitative, and in some cases, technical assessment should be completed before a decision can be made as to which valuation method(s) to utilize.

Value is often a function of the degree to which the item is considered unique. In the case of technology, an example would be technical advancements that result in better or more profitable products, or improvements to productivity that are not otherwise achievable. In the case of marketing intangibles, an example would be a distinctive and appealing brand name or trademark, which helps increase visibility, recognition, admiration and sales for the product or service to which it is attached.

Included in this preliminary assessment of value drivers is consideration of the commercial viability of the asset and whether a notional third party, such as a competitor, would pay to acquire it, or whether the item really only has value to its owner (i.e., non-commercial value).

The following is an outline of some of the key value drivers that should be considered when assessing IP. These value drivers are general, in that they apply to most types of IP. A more detailed discussion of value drivers unique to software and brand names is found later in this paper.

There is a significant degree of judgment involved with evaluating these value drivers, and divergent opinions of value by valuators can usually be traced to their different perceptions of these factors:

- uniqueness or degree of innovation. To what degree does the IP represent an innovation that sets it apart from other IP available at the valuation date? Is it a technical advancement that represents or assists in the producing of a superior or more profitable product? Or in the case of marketing intangibles such as a brand name, does it effectively help set the product apart from an identification point of view? In the case of a trademark or brand name, the valuator may examine market research studies that gauge consumer attitudes and perceptions, to assess the extent to which the IP is distinctive. While a company may believe that its brand name is extremely valuable to its operations, market research surveys might show that the consumer's purchase decision is unrelated to branding and more dependent on other factors, such as convenience, packaging, location, and so forth. In this case, the brand name neither contributes significantly to differentiating the product nor contributes to incremental profits. In the case of a technological item such as software, where innovation is critical to success, the valuator should consider factors such as:
  - product reviews and surveys.
  - orders on hand for the product.
  - nature of competing products.
  - the target industry's appetite for innovation.
  - results of beta testing.[5]

  The valuator may also consider consulting software developers with expertise in the related area for their views on the technical merits of the code, relative to other products available at the valuation date.
- breadth of use. To what extent does the IP have wide applicability to a range of industries or customers? For example, in the case of software used to control manufacturing processes, one would consider whether the software is industry specific (e.g., electronics), or has applicability in a variety of industries (e.g., pharmaceuticals, food, automotive parts assembly). Similarly, for a brand name, value is greatly influenced by the owner's ability to utilize the brand in product extensions (related products or variations with the same brand) or new product introductions.

---

5 Beta testing usually refers to the release of pre-commercialized software or product, on a test basis, to a small group of users, who provide the developer with feedback on the workings of the program or product.

- ease of use or adoption. In the case of technological IP, such as software, how easy is it to implement and integrate in existing operations, and/or with existing software used for other applications.
- status of legal protection. To what extent does the IP enjoy legal protection (e.g., a patent or trademark) or if warranted, the potential to successfully apply for such protection in the future? If a patent has not been applied for, value may reflect the future costs of such an application, assuming a patent is warranted. Value is also influenced by the degree to which the IP can be substituted with something providing the same functionality without the necessity of paying royalties to the originator.
- ownership and other legal rights. Is the ownership of the IP clear? In some cases, IP is developed jointly, i.e., through joint ventures, or collaborations between universities and corporations. Disputes often arise as to who actually owns the technology, i.e., the employee, or the company or institution that did the research and development, or the body that funded the research and development. Value is influenced by the extent to which ownership of the IP is clearly defined.
- life cycle status/remaining life. What is the expected remaining useful life of the IP, and to what extent might the related revenues or cash flows increase or decrease as the item moves through the life cycle? What stage of the life cycle is the IP in (development, early, mature)? In the case of technology under development, what is the likelihood that the innovation will ever be successfully marketed? The estimate of life expectancy usually has a significant impact on the valuation of IP, and given the highly subjective nature of the estimate, is often one of the most controversial aspects of an IP valuation.
- market demand or acceptance. To what extent is there a ready market for the innovation, and to what extent will demand need to be stimulated? In some instances, an innovation is ahead of its time, or is just not something that the public wants or needs, even though the innovation may represent an improvement in quality or function. Market potential for the product is reviewed in order to understand the nature of competition, potential sales, and associated risks. Owners of IP sometimes have a sentimental, non-objective view of it, given the effort and expenditures that may have gone into its development. Fair market value as commonly defined measures commercial value to third parties, in contrast with value perceived by the owner.
- incremental profit margin. To what extent will the IP contribute to increased profitability, or earnings? A patented innovation may result in

a smoother production process but may not contribute to a measurable increase in profit.

- barriers to competition. The dominance of a certain technology or product often represents a barrier to competition and enhances the value of that IP. Although there is nothing preventing personal computer users from installing operating systems other than Microsoft Windows, most users are reluctant to switch because of the lack of software available to run on other operating systems, and the potential lack of compatibility with other computer users. As a result, there are few products competing with Microsoft Windows. Other examples of barriers to technological competition are the potentially high degrees of capital investment, time, and expertise required to develop new technology in a given sector.
- quality of management. IP is not developed and marketed in a vacuum. The success of IP is also a function of the ability of management to attract human and financial capital, its ability to allocate scarce resources, and to build relationships with suppliers and customers. In many cases, technological innovations fail to succeed because of the inability of the hands-on developers to properly and strategically manage the business affairs of the enterprise. However, one must be careful to differentiate between the value of IP and the quality or financial capabilities of management to develop, market, or optimize the value of the IP.

Practice Tip

Not all management is equally skilled:

"Similar to a venture capitalist or other investor, the valuator must carefully evaluate the degree of reliance that can be placed on company management to be able to implement plans and achieve forecasts, and to be continually aware of potentially superior products, activities of global competitors and ever changing market that could potentially adversely impact the IP being valued, even to the point of obsolescence."

– Patrick Coady, CA, CBV

E. TECHNICAL ASSESSMENT

To assess value drivers and risks and to identify a suitable valuation method, it is often prudent to complete a technical assessment. Given the nature of the assets involved in IP valuations, this type of assessment is usually completed by or based on the findings of an expert in the particular field. For example, in valuing software, it may be appropriate to consult with and review the findings of an experienced software developer. A software developer with experience in the relevant industry sector or application can address issues such as

- complexity of the software.
- whether the software and language used is state of the art, unique, innovative, and suitable.
- whether the software actually functions as advertised or specified.
- quality of the documentation.
- whether users have a need for the innovation (for which they will pay).
- useful life of the software.
- the degree of difficulty to enter the target market.
- the time and cost involved in developing a competitive product offering with essentially the same functionality of the software.

It is not unusual to find that software, claimed to be marketable at the valuation date, actually did not function as advertised (despite potentially significant amounts of time and money spent developing the product), or was already obsolete, or on the way to becoming so, or did not even exist at the valuation date. It is also important to review patents — if applicable — in order to understand the level and type of protection provided along with the uniqueness of the patented technology.

In valuing marketing intangibles such as a brand name or trademark, as discussed above, it is important for the valuator to review the findings of related market research (in many cases the owner of the asset has already commissioned such research). Detailed market research will assist the valuator in understanding the history of the asset, consumer perceptions, competitive strength, the extent to which the intangible is supported by advertising or other marketing costs, and the role or importance of the brand name or trademark in the consumer purchase decision.

F. INTELLECTUAL PROPERTY VALUATION METHODOLOGY

There are three recognized and universally accepted approaches to valuing IP:

- the cost approach;
- the income approach; and
- the market approach.

Within each approach are a number of methods. Each method emphasizes different value drivers, and the selection of the appropriate valuation method will depend on various factors and circumstances. The three approaches are introduced below.

1) Cost Approach

The basis for the cost approach is the economic principle of substitution, i.e., the premise that a prudent third-party purchaser would pay no more for the IP than it would cost to replace the asset. Valuators measure two types of cost:

- the reproduction cost, which measures value as the cost to recreate an exact copy of the asset; and
- the replacement cost, which measures value as the cost to recreate the asset's functionality or benefits.

The replacement cost of an IP asset would include the costs necessary to construct a similar asset of equivalent utility (i.e., benefits to owner and/or user) at prices applicable at the time of reconstruction. To the extent that the asset being valued provides less utility than a newly constructed asset, the reproduction or replacement cost is adjusted to reflect appropriate decline in value due to functional and technological obsolescence, and economic obsolescence.

When IP such as software is valued at a date after its original development, it is often the replacement cost that is determined, which reflects the existing know-how and level of technology available at the valuation date, as opposed to that available during the development period. As discussed above, the replacement cost is in contrast to the reproduction cost, i.e., the cost to reproduce an exact copy, using the same techniques and knowledge as was used in the asset's original development. For example, software built five years ago at a cost of $10 million, can in many instances be built today at significantly reduced cost due to the subsequent development of more powerful and efficient software building tools. In some cases, the replacement asset may represent a significant improvement over the subject asset and thus the reproduction cost could overstate value, and valuation adjustments are necessary. The development of cost estimates necessitates knowledge pertaining to the modeling techniques, design standards and the current state of technology for the software.

Whatever the particular cost base used, the cost approach requires analysis and possible inclusion of a number of items, including:

1. labour costs (including costs of benefits, payroll taxes).
2. materials consumed (supplies, equipment, etc.).
3. overheads (rent, administrative costs, licence fees, regulatory compliance costs).
4. profit margin or rate of return on the above costs, based on the premise that the developer of the replacement asset would demand to be

compensated for an extra margin over the costs of labour, materials and overhead (i.e., a developer's profit margin or rate of return).[6] The rate of return should be reflective of the nature of the asset or industry and the related risks.

The use of the cost approach as a primary valuation approach can be controversial in a taxation advocacy context due to — in many cases, widely-differing perspectives of the parties on the IP's functionality, degree of innovation or differentiation, market demand, future prospects, and other value drivers. Depending on the assumptions made in the valuation, the cost approach can yield a significantly lower value than the income or market approaches described below; however, there are many instances where the cost approach is the most applicable technique and provides the best indication of the highest price obtainable in a notional market.[7] For example, a medical discovery or scientific advance may not be considered valuable based on its replacement cost; however, it may be technologically significant enough that products which are based on the IP can generate significant future earnings in the form of royalties, licence fees, and so forth. In this case, an income-based approach should be used. Another example would be software developed for a company for its own use in controlling operations (e.g., logistics software used by a transportation company, or trading software or back office administration software used by a stock brokerage firm). Ownership of the software does not directly generate revenue in the form of licence revenues but instead saves the company money that it would have to pay to purchase or license the software from a third party. In such a case, the highest price obtainable for the software would likely relate to the cost of replacing the software.[8] In one final example, a technology IP may have cost millions to develop (and would probably cost millions to replace or reproduce) but is not saleable in the marketplace because of, for example, the existence of superior competitive products. In this scenario, replacement cost may well overstate value. It is important to note that in some cases, especially for very early stage technology and some software, the cost approach will be the primary method used. The reason

6 The profit margin may not be applicable in those instances where the owner of the IP has its own development personnel who could develop the IP as opposed to acquiring it from a third party.

7 The market contemplated in the definition of fair market value is a notional market.

8 See *CIT Financial Ltd. v. R.*, [Amended Judgment] 2003 TCC544 [*CIT Financial*]. Some of the valuation implications of this case are further discussed below.

for this is that discounted cash flow approaches are subject to a high degree of sensitivity and variation based on small changes in key assumptions, and there is a lack of market data against which to benchmark the IP.

2) Income Approach

Under the income approach, value is based on the present value of expected future earnings, cash flows, cost savings or other benefits associated with use or ownership of the asset. It is important to note that when valuing a specific IP asset, only the net earnings or cash flows (or other such measure of earnings or benefits) related to the subject asset should be considered. Income-based valuations of IP that fail to exclude earnings or cash flows related to tangible assets, other intangible assets, or related to the business enterprise that owns the IP, or that fail to reflect all the costs associated with the earning of cash flows generated by the subject asset, distort value significantly.

There are several income-based valuation methods applicable to IP. Some of the more commonly used methods are described below.

a) Discounted Cash Flow Approach

Under the discounted cash flow approach ("DCF"), the value of IP is established as the present value of projected future after-tax net cash flows (which can be measured as revenues less expenses, expected licence fees or royalties, or costs saved as a result of owning the asset as opposed to licensing it from a third party). The annual after-tax cash flows are discounted using a discount rate that reflects both expected basic investment returns, and the general and specific risks associated with the cash flows (including general economic and industry specific risks), the profitability associated with the IP, the nature of competing products, etc. The discount rate selected depends generally on rates of return from alternative investments of similar type and quality as of the valuation date, as well as asset and industry specific risk factors.[9] The discount rate development process sometimes may involve establishing an applicable range of discount rates for the entire business owning the IP, and the development of underlying discount rates applicable to each class of tangible and intangible assets owned by the business, including the IP. The discount rates determined are based on their respective relative risk and the related market-based rates of return. Given

---

9 Asset and industry specific risk factors are outlined above under the heading Value Drivers.

the degree of valuator judgment involved, the discount rate is often an area of divergence in valuations of the same IP by different valuators.

The cash flows are only projected for the expected remaining life of the IP. If the IP life is indefinite, then, at the time where the cash flows related to the asset are expected to stabilize (or in the case where there is an exit value), the residual value (also known as terminal value) is calculated, based on the capitalized cash flow approach (i.e., dividing the maintainable annual cash flows at that point in time by an appropriate, risk-adjusted capitalization rate).[10] The projected cash flows, and the residual value, if applicable, are discounted at an appropriate risk-adjusted discount rate, and the discounted cash flows are summed, resulting in the fair market value of the asset. The estimation of expected remaining useful life might sometimes be controversial. For example, as IP such as software, trademarks and brands ages and moves closer to becoming obsolete, a business usually invests in upgrades, improvements, alterations, or substitutions. The valuator must consider to what extent the anticipated changes to the IP modify the original asset, and to what extent the changes result in new IP, whose value is distinct from the original asset or merely loosely based on the original IP. As many industries experience rapid technological innovation, core technology and know-how often continue to contribute to cash flows.

In addition to projecting future revenues and expenses, an income-based method should reflect a charge on the capital (tangible and intangible) used in the business to derive cash flows from the IP. Software IP does not usually generate cash flows in isolation but rather relies on other capital assets employed to create the overall cash flow stream. In valuing IP, however, a valuator must isolate the cash flows generated by the IP from cash flows generated by other assets. When valuing the IP using an income-based method, this is achieved by deducting a charge on other capital employed (referred to as contributory assets) from the income or cash flows. The capital charge represents the required rate of return on the contributory asset. Capital assets on which a charge should be applied include monetary assets such as working capital, as well as fixed assets, the assembled and trained workforce, among other tangible and intangible assets. In calculating the rate of return to apply to such assets, consideration is given to the nature of the asset, the rates of return available in the market on other similar assets, and investment risk. For example, for working capital (i.e., cash, accounts receivable, net of accounts payable), given its liquid,

---

10 In some cases, there may be a specified or estimated exit value, which would be discounted to reflect the time value of money related to the specific amount.

short-term nature, an appropriate rate of return would be based on rates available from investment in short-term, low-risk securities, such as short-term loans, or risk-free securities exemplified by government bonds, plus an appropriate risk premium. The rates of return on tangible fixed assets would be higher than those of working capital, given the relatively higher risks involved.[11] Still higher would be the required rates of return charged on the enterprise's intangible assets such as other technology, and its workforce, given the higher risks involved. Of course, in the case of such other intangible assets, in order to apply a capital charge, a value must be established, to which the charge is applied. In the case of an assembled and trained workforce, the value is usually based on its after-tax replacement cost (reflecting staffing costs including advertising, recruitment, relocation, training, reduced productivity during the vacancy, or training or learning period, among others).

Other key assumptions required under the discounted cash flow method are the length of the cash flow projection period (and applicability of a residual or terminal value), level of annual capital investment (and increases to working capital) required to sustain the forecasted net cash flows, future rates of income tax, future inflation, among others. Particular care must be taken to reflect obsolescence, impact of competition, and changes in demand for the IP in the projected future revenues and expenses. Furthermore, the valuator must consider the interrelationship between the discount rate, which is partially a function of the risks of achieving the projected cash flows, and the level of projected cash flows. For example, if the projected cash flows are very optimistic, then the discount rate should reflect the higher degree of risk related to that optimism, suggesting a relatively higher discount rate. Conversely the relative ease of attaining projected cash flows in a more conservative scenario should suggest a relatively lower discount rate.

The following simplified example illustrates the use of the discounted cash flow approach to value IP. For this example, we have assumed that the IP has a five-year limited life. This example could apply to technology, a brand, or other IP. The calculation is based on the following assumptions (all $ amounts represent millions):

1. forecast period (useful life): 5 years.
2. residual value: nil, as the IP is assumed to be obsolete at the end of the forecast period.

---

11 Consideration should be given to also reflecting a return of fixed assets (i.e., depreciation) in the fixed asset contributory charge.

3. after-tax cash flows: assumed to grow by 20% in each of years 2 and 3, and decline by 40% per annum in years 4 and 5. Cash flows are assumed to be received equally throughout the year, which we have modeled by assuming that cash flows are received at the mid-way point of each year.
4. capital expenditures: capital expenditures of $10.0 million, net of tax savings are assumed required in years 2 and 3.
5. after-tax contributory asset charges are included for illustrative purposes, and could relate to a charge for capital such as working capital, fixed assets, work force, customer relationships, etc.
6. IP discount rate: 25%.

	Discounted Cash Flow				
	Year 1 $ millions	Year 2 $ millions	Year 3 $ millions	Year 4 $ millions	Year 5 $ millions
After-tax cash flow	100	120.0	144.0	86.4	51.8
Capital expenditures to maintain IP	0	(10)	(10)	0	0
After-tax contributory charges	(4)	(4.8)	(5.8)	(2.9)	(1.4)
Free cash-flow	96	105.2	128.2	83.5	50.4
Discount rate factor	0.8944	0.71554	0.57243	0.45795	0.366364
Present value (cash flow x discount factor)	85.9	75.3	73.4	38.2	18.5
Fair market value, before tax shield	291.3				

Note that as discussed below, the value of the IP should be increased to reflect the present value of the tax shield related to the present value of future CCA or ECE deductions that a notional purchaser of the IP would realize.

b) Variants of the Discounted Cash Flow Approach

Some variations of the basic discounted cash flow approach, sometimes used in valuing IP under development or start-up stage IP, are termed probability adjusted discounted cash flow approaches. These approaches involve the estimation of future projected cash flows under different scenarios and the application of probability factors relating to the likelihood of the various scenarios or outcomes.

A simple example concerns biotechnology IP under development, in which probabilities are applied to scenarios relating to varying degrees of commercialization success or failure. Generally, such a probability-based approach requires a base case scenario, and then a range of outcomes or variations. The scenarios are assigned probability weightings (i.e., percentages) to reflect the likelihood of attainment of the outcomes (i.e., 60% likely, 20% likely, and so forth). The discounted cash flow value obtained under each scenario is multiplied by the respective probability weighting to arrive at the probability-weighted value. Care must be taken to ensure that the risks explicitly reflected in the scenarios are not again included as risk premiums in the development of the DCF discount rate.

The probability-weighted approach is further defined for IP under development or other uncertain business situations in approaches or models known as the real-options approach or decision tree approach (or in other words, an if/then approach). Under these models, the results of a sequence of probability-weighted possible outcomes are discounted using option models such as the binomial and trinomial approaches. The underlying notion is that at various stages of the development process, management will make decisions to continue to develop, increase or decrease investment, and so forth, based on internal and external occurrences relating to technological, regulatory or financial circumstances. Consider again the biotechnology example, with the uncertain outcome of pre-clinical and clinical testing at various phases in the discovery cycle, as well as the uncertainty of obtaining regulatory approval (e.g., government health and drug bodies, patent bodies), and achieving targeted patient penetration rates. Under the decision tree approach, a simulation, based on a decision tree of possible outcomes is developed (e.g., results of testing — successful or unsuccessful, further investment or discontinue development), and at each stage, possible financial outcomes (e.g., costs, sales, and net cash flows, etc.) are estimated, probabilities assigned, and probability-weighted cash flows then discounted. These probability-based methods are widely used in the pharmaceutical and biotechnology industry and have become the recommended approach for early-stage technology valuations by the American Institute of Certified Public Accountants (AICPA).

i) Capitalized Maintainable Cash Flow/Capitalized Maintainable Earnings Method

The capitalized cash flow or capitalized earnings method involves capitalizing the estimated future after-tax maintainable cash flow or earnings produced by the IP by a multiple, which serves as a measure of the rate of return required by a prospective purchaser of the IP. The rate of return or multiple reflects, among other factors, the risk inherent in achieving the expected level of maintainable cash flow/earnings. As in the case of the discounted cash flow method, annual sustaining capital investment, and income taxes need to be reflected, as well as a charge on other tangible and intangible capital employed in the business enterprise that owns the IP. Furthermore, the inter-relationship between the risk reflected in the capitalization rate and the level of risk reflected in the maintainable earnings and cash flow should be assessed so as to avoid double counting of risk factors. The capitalization rate is calculated as the discount rate minus the projected compound annual growth rate (if any) related to the future earnings. The multiple referred to above is the reciprocal of the capitalization rate (i.e., 1 divided by the capitalization rate).

ii) Relief from Royalty Method

Under what is known as the relief from royalty method, IP is valued based on the present value of the avoided expenditures that would be incurred if the asset had to be licensed from an arm's length party at a market-based licence rate. In other words, this method considers the hypothetical royalty or licence expense (net of related income tax) that is not paid to an independent party for the use of the IP, by virtue of the fact that the owner owns the subject asset. The present value of the future stream of after-tax cash savings is calculated using a risk-adjusted capitalization rate, if a constant annual savings is projected, or a discount rate, if the future projected annual savings vary from year to year.

The licence rates used in the relief from royalty method are generally estimated based on published market data with respect to rates for similar assets published in IP databases, cross-border transfer pricing data, financial statements, and various other financial disclosures. Depending on the comparable royalty data found and the nature of the IP, the estimated royalty rate is applied to the appropriate base (e.g., revenue, units sold, transactions processed, profit), and the related annual after-tax savings are calculated. Notional royalty rates may also be derived using the profit split approach, described below.

The following simplified example illustrates the use of the relief from royalty approach to value IP. For this example, we have assumed that the IP has an indefinite life, and that the related revenue (i.e., avoided royalties) is constant. Accordingly, we have capitalized the net after-tax avoided royalty revenue. The example could be modified to reflect periodically changing royalty rates and/or cash flows, in which case a discounted cash flow analysis, as opposed to capitalized cash flow analysis would be used. The calculation is based on the following assumptions (all $ amounts represent millions):

1. annual maintainable revenue related to the IP: $100.
2. comparable IP royalty rate: 5% of revenue earned from the use of the IP.
3. tax rate: 40%.
4. capitalization rate: 20%.

Relief from royalty example

		$ millions
Annual maintainable revenue	A	$ 100
Royalty rate	B	5%
Royalties avoided	C = A x B	5
Less: income taxes	D = C x 40%	-2
Net royalties avoided	E = C - D	3
Capitalization rate	F	20%
Multiple (inverse of capitalization rate)	G = 1/F	5
Capitalized royalties avoided equals fair market value of IP, beforeconsideration of ECE tax shield	H = E x G	15

Note that as discussed below, the value of the IP should be increased to reflect the present value of the tax shield related to the present value of future CCA or ECE deductions that a notional purchaser of the IP would realize.

The identification of similar assets and/or comparable royalty rates is often a significant challenge in the application of this method. A number of qualitative and quantitative factors are analyzed in the selection of licence or royalty rates, including the profit margin contributed by the IP, and the relative comparability of value drivers, such as those discussed elsewhere in this paper. When evaluating comparable royalty data for use in this method, consideration should be given to the attributes of the licensing arrangement including, among other attributes:

- the term.
- renewal options.
- minimum royalty payments.
- lump sum payments.
- exclusivity.
- marketing support such as advertising to be borne by the parties.
- degree of value to be added by the licensee.
- restrictions on use.
- geographic jurisdiction.

The relief from royalty method is sometimes referred to as a market-based method due to the usage of market-based royalty or licence rates in its application.

Practice Tip

Avoid Stacking Royalty Rates When Valuing IP Portfolios

"In many instances, the relief from royalty method is applied to establish the value of IP portfolios. The initial inclination is to value the IP portfolio on an individual asset basis and then summing the individual results to conclude a value for the portfolio. This approach may lead to a cumulative royalty payment that does not reflect the economic attributes of the IP portfolio. In extreme cases, the stacking of royalty rates one on top of the other leads to royalty payments greater than the profitability attributable to the business operations. Consequently, the valuation process considers the economic influences driving business performance when developing the worth of IP portfolios."

– Richard K. Ellsworth, PE, ASA, CFA

Although the relief from royalty method for valuing IP has enjoyed wide acceptance for many years, the method was criticized by the United States Court of Appeals for the Second Circuit: *Nestle Holdings, Inc. v. Commissioner of Internal Revenue,*[12] an appeal of a United States Tax Court decision.[13] The case involved the calculation of a capital gain relating to the non-arm's length sale of some US and Canadian trademarks, trade names, patents and technology owned by Carnation Company, a subsidiary of Nestle Holdings, Inc. The valuation of the IP was one of the issues argued. The Tax Court adopted the valuation submitted by the Commissioner of Internal Revenue's expert, which was based on the relief from royalty approach. The Second Circuit commented on this approach: "Underlying this methodology is the view that the only value a purchaser of a mark receives is relief from paying a royalty for its use." The taxpayer's expert also made use of the relief from royalty approach (as well as three other approaches, including the profit split method,[14] which was the expert's primary method). The Appeal Court, as discussed below, rejected the application of the relief from royalty approach. The Appeal Court doubted that the relief from royalty approach was reasonable, mainly because the method fails to capture the value of all the rights of ownership such as when and where the IP may be used, or benefits in excess of royalty payments that can be derived:

12 *Nestle Holdings, Inc. et. al. v. Commissioner of Internal Revenue,* 152 F.3d 83; 1998 U.S. App. LEXIS 18161; 98-2 U.S. Tax Cas. (CCH) P50,606; 82 A.F.T.R.2d (RIA) 5467.

13 The Tax Court judgment in the case is *Nestle Holdings Inc., et. al. v. Commissioner of Internal Revenue,* Docket No. 21562-90, T.C. Memo 1995-441; 1995 Tax Ct. memo LEXIS 439; 70 T.C.M. (CCH) 682.

14 The profit split method is described below.

> "In our view, the relief from royalty method necessarily undervalues trademarks. The fair market value of a trademark is the price a willing purchaser would have paid a willing seller to buy the mark . . . The relief from royalty method does not accurately estimate the value to a purchaser of a trademark. Royalty models are generally employed to estimate an infringer's profit from its misuse of a patent or trademark . . . Resort to a royalty model may seem appropriate in such cases because it estimates fairly the cost of using a trademark . . . However, use of a royalty model in the case of a sale is not appropriate because it is the fair market value of a trademark, not the cost of its use that is at issue. A relief-from-royalty model fails to capture the value of all of the rights of ownership, such as the power to determine when and where a mark may be used, or moving a mark into or out of product lines. It does not even capture the economic benefit in excess of royalty payments that a licensee generally derives from using a mark. Ownership of a mark is more valuable than a license because ownership carries with it the power and incentive both to put the mark to its most valued use and to increase its value. A licensee cannot put the mark to uses beyond the temporal or other limitations of a license and has no reason to take steps to increase the value of a mark where the increased value will be realized by the owner. The Commissioner's view, therefore, fundamentally misunderstands the nature of trademarks and the reasons why the law provides for exclusive rights of ownership in a mark. Given the shortcomings of the relief-from-royalty methodology, the Tax Court erred when it adopted the Commissioner's trademark valuations. The Tax Court is instructed to examine alternate methods of determining the fair market value of the trademarks in question."[15]

Despite the decision of the Second Circuit in the *Nestle* case, the relief from royalty approach (and other asset valuation approaches based on cost or expense avoidance), when properly applied and supported by closely comparable market data, is widely accepted in the valuation profession as a method for deriving notional fair market values.

We note, however, that in a more recent appeal of a US Tax Court case involving the valuation of a trademark owned by DHL Corporation,[16] although many of the valuations expert witnesses utilized a relief from roy-

---

15 *Nestle*, above note 12 [United States Court of Appeals for the Second Circuit].

16 *DHL Corp. v. Commissioner*, 1998 Tax Ct. Memo, LEXIS 461 (1998)), Appealed (United States Court of Appeals for the Ninth Circuit, 285 F.3d 1210: 2002 U.S. App. LEXIS 6687; 2002-1 U.S. Tax Cas. (CCH) P50,354; 89 A.F.T.R.2d (RIA) 1978; 2002 Cal. Daily Op. Service 3097; 2002 Daily Journal DAR 3787.

alty approach, ultimately the Tax Court determined its own value, which was upheld on appeal. The Tax Court took issue with the experts' valuations partly because it was felt that the valuations included income benefits that were enjoyed by virtue of other intangible assets owned by the company such as its network (i.e., its infrastructure and know-how, etc.), as opposed to its brand or trademark. The Tax Court considered the various expert opinions and measured the trademark value as approximately 50% of the total $300 million intangible value implied by the transaction that was the subject of the case. The Ninth Circuit, in affirming the Tax Court decision, noted that the Tax Court "painted with a broad brush, that is to be expected given the imprecise art of valuing an intangible asset. DHL may dispute the exact figures used by the tax court in reaching its valuation, but DHL fails to demonstrate clear error, either in the Tax Court's methodology or in its final result."[17]

The findings in the *Nestle* and *DHL* cases underline the desirability of comparison and/or reconciliation of values obtained under one approach with value conclusions reached under other approaches. Given the above critique of the relief from royalty method in the *Nestle* case, it would not be unusual for the value obtained under that method to be lower than the values obtained under other approaches such as the DCF approach. Recognition should also be given to the fact that given the characteristics of the subject IP, comparable royalty data may not be sufficiently similar to reasonably apply or to rely on the results of the relief from royalty method. As well, the valuator should demonstrate that the values of individual IP items are consistent with a business entity's overall intangible value, and/or the value contributed to the business entity by other intangibles such as know-how, infrastructure, customer base, trained and assembled workforce, distribution network, general business goodwill, to cite a few.

iii) Profit Split Approach — The 25% Rule

A widely accepted approach to valuing IP is based on the notion that owners and third party users of the IP will typically negotiate to license its use, at royalty rates that will yield an allocation of pre-tax operating profits in a base case range of approximately 20% to 33% to the owner of the IP, and approximately 67% to 80% to the licensee of the IP. The actual allocation of profits reflected in the valuation is a function of the specific attributes and contributory nature of the IP, and the technological, industry, and economic circumstances. The royalty rate derived using this rule, often

17 United States Court of Appeals for the Ninth Circuit, 285 F.3d 1210; 2002 U.S. App. LEXIS 6687, at para. 22.

referred to as the "25% rule" can then be used in the relief from royalty approach to IP valuation. For example, if the expected pre-tax operating profit on $10 million of sales related to the IP are $4 million, an allocation of 25% of the pre-tax operating profits to the licensor, or $1 million would apply, which implies a 10% royalty rate (i.e., $1 million allocated to licensor, divided by $10 million of sales):

		$ millions
IP related sales	A	$10
Pre-tax operating profit	B	$4
Allocation of 25% to licensor	C = B x 25%	1
Implied royalty rate	D = C/A	10%

This approach is a notional guide, and the actual licensing arrangements may be more complex (e.g., sliding scales, fixed fee portions, percentages of profits as opposed to sales, etc.).

Alternatively the 25% rule can be applied to expected future cash flows or earnings associated with the IP, in order to allocate a portion of the future cash flows or earnings to the ownership of the IP as opposed to other business attributes/assets. After reflecting the deduction of other expenses, taxes, and contributory charges on other tangible and intangible assets, the allocated future cash flows/earnings are then discounted or capitalized using a suitable discount or capitalization rate.

As with any valuation benchmark, the percentage to be applied in a given situation can only be derived after a sufficient qualitative analysis, and recognizing differences in industries, technologies, products, profitability, risks, availability of alternative products, and other circumstances. The rule of thumb profit-split allocation range is flexible, and in certain circumstances, a significantly different allocation might be appropriate between licensees and licensors, depending on the nature of the IP, the specific industry etc.

Although this rule arguably represents only a rule of thumb, factual analysis of actual licensing deals supports both the allocation concept and the quantum of the allocation. In an article by Robert Goldscheider,[18], the results of an empirical study of average operating profits and median roy-

18 R. Goldscheider, J. Jarosz & C. Mulhern, "Use of the 25% Rule in Valuing IP," Les Nouvelles, (December 2002) page 123.

alty rates for a number of industries lent support to the 25% rule. A survey of licensing executives published by Stephen A. Degnan and Corwin Horton[19] found that approximately 25% of licensing organizations used the 25% rule as a starting point in negotiations, and that approximately 50% of the organizations used some sort of profit sharing analysis (like the 25% rule) in calculating royalties. Moreover, the rule has been cited in tax court cases, civil court cases involving IP infringements, and is referred to in the establishment of licence rates for cross-border transfer pricing purposes. The Goldscheider paper refers to numerous US court cases in which the 25% rule is cited,[20] as well as some arguments that have been put forth by other authorities rejecting the validity and usefulness of the 25% rule.

The importance of comparability (of industry, product) in the profit split method was underlined in the *Nestle* case heard in the US Tax Court, which found that the royalty data on which the taxpayer's expert's trademark profit split calculations depended were not sufficiently comparable to the circumstances at hand (i.e., food product trademarks) and criticized the expert's reliance on case law, as opposed to independent analysis. According to the Tax Court judgment in *Nestle*,[21], the royalty rates referred to in the profit split method were determined

> under specific factual circumstances in other cases . . . contact lens manufacturing intangibles, . . . airplane technology-manufacturing intangibles, chemical manufacturing intangibles, not on comparable profit split agreements or any substantial objective evidence. We have serious reservations about using the results of other cases as the basis for expert testimony. An expert is useful if and because he or she brings independent evidence to the Court. A survey of opinions, by contrast, suggests that the witness is simply relying on "what the traffic will bear." Any new opinion based on factual evidence is likely to change the average — which thus is not a reliable indicator of value in other cases. Value should be based on the market, not on the case law. See *Estate of Pillsbury v. Commissioner*, T.C. Memo. 1992-425.[22]

---

19 S. A. Dregnan & C. Horton, "A Survey of Licensed Royalties," Les Nouvelles (June 1997), page 92, cited in Goldscheider, page 127.

20 For example, *Standard Manufacturing Co. Inc. and DBP, Ltd. v. United States*, 42 Fed. Cl. 748 (1999, U.S. Claims LEXIS 11); *Ajinomoto Co., Inc. v. Archer-Daniels-Midland Co.*, No. 95-218-SLR, 1998 U.S. Dist. LEXIS 3383, at 052 n.46 (D.Del. March 13, 1998); and others listed at footnote 39 of Goldscheider.

21 T.C. Memo 1995-441, 1995 Tax Ct. Memo LEXIS 439, 70 T.C.M. (CCH) 682.

22 *Nestle*, above note 12 at 35.

Additionally the Court noted that the taxpayer claimed that profit split agreements are widespread in the food industry; yet the agreements relied upon by the taxpayer were dated five years after the valuation date; and the respondent's experts indicated that royalties based on profit splits were not widespread in the industry. Moreover, the Court found that the taxpayer cited agreements or examples in articles that were not demonstrated as comparable to the trademark portfolio of Carnation (food product) trademarks.[23]

A judgment in a significant US court case, *Georgia-Pacific Corp. v. United States Plywood Corporation,*[24] cited by Goldscheider and others, outlines 15 factors influencing the development of a reasonable royalty in relation to a patent infringement dispute. Factors influencing the development of a reasonable royalty rate include:[25]

- rates paid by the licensee for the use of other patents comparable to the subject patent.
- nature and scope of the licence in terms of exclusivity and territorial restrictions.
- the licensor's established policy and marketing program to maintain its patent monopoly by not licensing others to use the invention or by granting licences under special conditions designed to preserve that monopoly.
- the commercial relationship between the licensor and licensee, such as whether they are competitors in the same territory in the same line of business.
- the effect of use of the patent in promoting sales of other products of the licensee, and the existing value of the invention to the licensor as a generator of sales of its non-patented items.
- the duration of the patent, and term of the licence.
- the profitability of the product made under the patent, its commercial success, and popularity.
- the utility and advantages of the patent over old modes or devices, if any.
- the portion of the realizable profit that should be credited to the invention as distinguished from non-patented elements, the manufacturing process, or business risks.

---

23 According to the *Nestle* Tax Court judgment, "one of the agreements cited was for a premium product, while the other was a license agreement for technology, not for the use of a trademark or trade name." *Nestle*, page 35.

24 *Georgia-Pacific Corp. v. U.S. Plywood Corp.*, 318 F. Supp. 1116; 1970 U.S. Dist. LEXIS 11541; 166 U.S.P.Q. (BNA) 235, affirmed 446 F.2d 295 (2d Cir. 1971).

25 *Ibid.*, at para. 7.

- the amount that a prudent licensor and licensee would have agreed upon as a royalty while allowing each to make a reasonable profit.

3) Market Approach

Under the market approach, value is established by comparison to actual transactions involving similar assets, and adjusted for differences in the assets, or transactions. The difficulty in applying this approach relates to the scarcity of reasonably comparable transactions. More data is available for transactions involving shares of companies with significant IP (e.g., software development companies, consumer products companies) than for transactions involving stand-alone intangible assets. Moreover, details of many transactions are either not fully disclosed in financial statements and other filings, or involve significant elements of non-cash consideration such as restricted shares, which make difficult the comparison for purposes of developing fair market value.

Recent changes in the realm of financial accounting standards in North America relating to the reporting of business combinations (i.e., mergers and acquisitions) have resulted in a growing pool of publicly available information on IP asset valuations. New Canadian and American standards[26] require that companies acquiring the assets or shares of other companies must allocate the purchase price amongst the fair value of all identifiable tangible and intangible assets (including various forms of IP). The valuation information is contained in the notes to the financial statements. The new standards thus provide some valuation data that is market-related, however it should be noted that there are limitations to the applicability of the disclosed valuations:

- the disclosed values are allocations of prices paid for entire businesses, and are established (usually) by valuators in accordance with the requirements of the accounting standards, as opposed to being the product of direct negotiations between buyers and sellers for the individual intangible asset.
- in some cases, application of the accounting standards may establish fair value that is not equivalent to the value that would be calculated for other purposes, or under other definitions of value. The fair market

26 In Canada, the Canadian Institute of Chartered Accountants (CICA) introduced CICA 1581, while in the United States, the Financial Accounting Standards Board (FASB) instituted FAS 141 to deal with the disclosure of the allocation of the purchase price on business combinations. The new standards became effective beginning in 2002 for public companies and beginning in 2003 for private companies.

value of a business entity's customer relationships may be significant to its operations and future profitability. However, for purposes of the accounting standards governing business combinations, one must consider whether the asset results from contractual or other legal rights, or whether the asset is capable of being separated from the acquired enterprise. If neither of these criteria are satisfied, the customer relationships would not be required to be separately reported on the financial statements.
- there are the usual concerns about comparability of the IP, especially given the lack of information disclosed about the intangible assets acquired on a business combination.

The purchase price allocation disclosure of intangible asset valuations of comparable companies however, can sometimes provide the valuator with useful benchmark information with which to measure the reasonability of conclusions reached using other methods. For example, valuation metrics such as IP value divided by sales or earnings, or IP value as a percentage of total intangible value can sometimes be derived from financial statements and compared with those derived for the particular asset being valued.

Some of the key markets that a valuator should consider when valuing technology-based IP include:

- the Venture Capital market and the pre-money and post-money valuations implied by comparable transactions. This is highly applicable to software and biotechnology valuations where there are thousands of transactions annually that are tracked, analyzed and categorized by information sources such as VentureOne.
- the licensing market and the total implied value of licensing transactions is a very important source of market data when estimating the value of pre-market biotechnologies. Sources such as Recombinant Capital have extensive, searchable databases summarizing comparable transactions.
- the implied technology values from stock market capitalizations are also very helpful in testing the reasonableness of a value conclusion. The implied technology valuation is determined by subtracting the net tangible asset value from the market capitalization. In most cases the majority of the value is in the intangible value.

a) Income Taxes and Tax Shield

IP valuation calculations based on costs avoided (e.g., relief from royalty), profit split, or capitalized or discounted cash flow techniques are done on the basis of cash flows net of taxes payable.

Valuations of stand alone assets such as IP that are earnings based should also reflect a tax-related component of value: the present value of the future tax savings ("tax shield") related to the ability to deduct (i.e., amortize) in future years, the capital cost of the asset for income tax purposes (i.e., CCA or ECE deduction). The inclusion of the tax shield in the valuation makes the calculations circular: the value of the tax shield is a function of the value of the subject asset, and the value of the subject asset in its turn is a function of the value of the tax shield, and so forth.

The variables in the formula for calculating the present value of the tax shield are:

- the value of the IP.
- the rate of return.
- the tax rate.
- the tax deduction rate (e.g., CCA rate, or ECE deduction rate).

The present value formula for CCA classes in which the declining balance method[27] is used, is as follows:

$$\frac{\text{Asset Value x Income Tax Rate} \times \text{CCA Rate}}{\text{Rate of Return} + \text{CCA Rate}}$$

For CCA classes in which only 50% of the acquisition cost is reflected in the calculation of CCA in the year of acquisition, the present value formula is as follows:

$$\frac{\text{Asset Value x Income Tax Rate x CCA Rate}}{\text{Rate of Return} + \text{CCA Rate}} \times 1 - \frac{\text{Rate of Return}}{\text{2x } (1 + \text{Rate of Return})}$$

b) Valuation Synthesis

Once the valuation calculations under the various suitable methods have been completed, the valuator takes a step back, analyzes the results, weighs the merits of the various methods for the given circumstances and recon-

27 Declining balance method refers to the method of amortization whereby each year's CCA or ECE deduction is based on a specified percentage of the unamortized balance for the specific asset class.

ciles the results obtained. The valuator considers which method and result to give the greatest weight, and the degree to which variances between the results obtained under the various methods can be accepted and/or whether further calculations and analysis is necessary. Only then can the final range of values for the IP be established.

G. VALUING SOFTWARE

Software valuations have been at the centre of many tax planning related transactions in recent years. The principles and approaches relating to valuing other IP are relevant to software valuations. However, the unique technical attributes of software and the way in which it is developed enable the valuator to use some special techniques.

As discussed above, there are three approaches to establishing fair market value of IP such as software:

- the cost approach.
- the income approach.
- the market approach.

The following discusses software-specific value drivers and illustrates several software valuation methods typically used by valuators, and companies dealing in software.

1) Software Value Drivers

In addition to the general IP value drivers discussed above, the following drivers, among others, can significantly influence the valuation of software:

- technology. Given the rapid rate of advancement in software, assessments of the innovation level, ease of modification and updating, remaining useful life or degree of obsolescence, and replacement cost are critical. For example, is the software written in an up-to-date, widely used language? Or is there an optimal replacement for the software that is more useful? These types of considerations must also be tempered with the fact that effectively functioning software (i.e., that which clearly meets the business purpose) does not necessarily become less valuable merely because it is not written in the most contemporary programming language.
- richness of functionality. The value of software is very dependent on the level of functionality it provides to the user, and in the case of software produced for commercialization, the level of functionality relative to

competing products. As well, software that is easy to use, maintainable, efficient and widely applicable will command a higher value than a complicated or cumbersome product.

- adaptability. Robust software that can be easily scaled to handle broader business structures and be readily interfaced with other software applications will inherently command higher valuations.
- documentation. The valuator considers the extent and quality of the documentation aimed at both programmers and users (e.g., the quality of the help utility, along with the adequacy of user and developer manuals); and
- other value drivers relevant to software produced for commercialization include quality of user support service, reputation of the vendor in the user community, size of the installed base, nature and market share of competitive products, among others.

2) Replacement Cost Methods

An asset's value is generally established as the present value of the future income or cash flows related to ownership. However, sometimes the value of software is appropriately calculated by replacement cost methods:

- software under development, where future success/outcome is not reasonably ascertainable (although in some circumstances, the speculative value may be higher or lower than the value determined under replacement cost methods).
- single purpose software developed for internal use in the operation or management of the developer's business (e.g., various types of enterprise management systems), rather than for sale to third parties.
- software that other developers can relatively easily replicate (i.e., in terms of its functionality and utility), in which case a notional purchaser would pay no more for the software than the cost to develop similar software. The cost approach would not typically be applicable in the case of an innovative and complex program, the functionality of which is in demand and not readily duplicated by others. The cost approach may apply, however, under certain circumstances, to software that is not strongly differentiated from competing products, such as point of sale software, bookkeeping software, enterprise resource planning (ERP) software, and other management software.
- software of a poor quality, software for which there is little or very questionable market demand, software that is not particularly innovative, and aging software that may be nearing obsolescence. In some cases, the fair market value could be significantly less than the replacement cost.

Moreover, software's replacement cost can also be used to assess the reasonableness of the valuation conclusion reached under other approaches. When completing software valuations, the present authors often estimate the replacement cost, or at least consider the historical cost in selecting our primary valuation approach, or in verifying the reasonability of the conclusion reached under our primary valuation approach.

3) Time Adjusted Historical Cost Method

One of the most objective ways to measure reproduction cost of software is to establish the actual historical development costs, and adjust the costs to the valuation date to reflect inflation. Costs to accumulate include programmer personnel costs (including the allocations of costs of items such as benefits, payroll taxes, overhead, and a profit element, and excluding time spent by staff on maintenance and other such tasks not related to development), hardware, and software acquired for purposes of developing the code. The costs are then time adjusted to the valuation date through an indexing process.

The foremost obstacle to applying this method is that in many cases, historical records of development costs are unavailable, not suitably documented, or co-mingled with operations, maintenance costs, and other software development projects. In addition, the replacement cost for the software may be lower than the reproduction cost. The valuator (likely with the assistance of a technical software expert) should consider the extent to which certain elements of the program's functionality would be achieved differently (and developed quicker) as at the valuation date. Moreover, the valuator must assess the need to adjust for software development technology and know-how in existence at the valuation date, in order to reflect innovations in the software development process, and improvements in developer competencies that could result in a quicker replacement (as opposed to reproduction) of the subject software.

4) Software Development Cost Models

In situations where software development cost records are unavailable or not useful, valuators may utilize software development cost models. These are sophisticated models created by software developers to estimate production time, costs and resources required to develop software. These models are principally used by project managers in the software development process. Although not specifically designed for use in valuations, the models can help valuators in estimating development cost and in assessing program complexity and functionality. We will discuss two such models in this paper: COCOMO II, and Function Point Analysis. The models yield estimates of the number of person hours required to write the code, which can then be used by the software valuator to estimate the development cost.

a) COCOMO II

COCOMO II is an acronym for the Constructive Cost Model version II. It is a program, which measures development effort based on program size, which in turn is measured by the number of statement lines of source code. A statement line of code is defined as a non-blank, non-comment line of source code. Program complexity is then established through rigorous consideration of a number of factors and development attributes discussed below including various product attributes, platform attributes, personnel attributes, and project attributes.

Using COCOMO II in a software valuation context would essentially involve determining the number of statement lines of code (i.e., not including blank or commentary lines of code), analyzing the extent to which some lines of code are merely variations of existing code (adapted code[28]), and considering various factors or attributes that contribute to the development project's overall required effort. According to user manuals, the COCOMO II model classifies these factors into four user categories:

1. product attributes, which relate to the constraints and requirements placed upon the product to be developed, including the required software reliability, database size, and complexity.
2. platform attributes, which refer to the limitations placed upon development effort by the hardware and operating system used to run the project, including platform volatility, execution time constraint, and main storage constraint.
3. personnel attributes, which relate to the level of skills possessed by the development team, including analyst capabilities, programmer capabilities, applications experience, platform experience, language and tool experience, and personnel continuity.
4. project attributes, meaning the constraints and conditions under which the project development takes place; specifically, the use of software tools in the development, and the extent to which the software is developed on a multi-site basis.

---

28 COCOMO II considers adapted code in its calculations through the use of a number of factors to measure the effort required to meet the objectives including the percent of design modified, percent of code modified, the percent of integration required for modified software, to name a few.

Each of the foregoing factors is ranked using a specific rating scale, with up to six ratings per factor, and with detailed criteria. Each rating has a corresponding numeric value based upon the factor and the degree to which the factor can influence development productivity. For example, a rating of less than 1 indicates a factor that can decrease the schedule and effort, while a rating of greater than 1 is for a factor that extends the schedule or effort. A rating equal to 1 is neutral in terms of its effect on schedule and effort to develop. Using the ratings, and considering the required development schedule, the COCOMO II software calculates an overall Effort Adjustment Factor ("EAF"), from which it then calculates a range of development scenarios for the application, expressed in terms of person-months to complete the development. The replacement cost for the program can then be calculated by multiplying the number of person-months by the appropriate labour rates, which take into account all relevant costs including benefits, overheads, and a suitable profit element, if applicable. This cost includes the software development costs but does not reflect the value of time that may be spent by other members of the organization in terms of specifying the requirements, or providing the development team with technical information about the required application.

The COCOMO II methodology (and other lines of code counting methods), although widely used for planning and managing software development projects, has not been unanimously accepted for developing fair market value of such custom software. For example, Barnaby has pointed out that the use of different coding styles for a routine may result in a program of differing line counts, yet can achieve the same objective, and run at about the same processing speed.[29] Under the COCOMO II methodology, one code would be valued higher than the other, but not be intrinsically worth more. Barnaby also criticizes some of the COCOMO cost adjustment factors to support his contention that "COCOMO does not directly assign value for optimization and efficiency. Indirectly, it assigns optimized, efficient code a lower value even though such software costs more."[30] As discussed below, some of the concerns about the use of COCOMO II for software valuation, raised by Barnaby and others, are reduced through the use of function point analysis.[31]

---

29 P.G. Barnaby, "Re-Evaluation" (January 1993) Valuation 175.

30 *Ibid.*, at 175.

31 As discussed above, valuation practice recommends that conclusions should be tested/supported by reference to at least one alternate valuation method. Differences between conclusions reached under various methods should be reconciled.

b) Function Point Analysis

Function Point Analysis was developed by Allan J. Albrecht, of International Business Machines (IBM), in the 1970's. The methodology gained acceptance among software engineers, and in 1986 the International Function Point User Group[32] was established.

Function points measure the size of a program's functionality from an outside user's (i.e. a person's, or an external system's) perspective. Function point analysis is relevant to measuring value because it measures the functionality delivered by the software in satisfying user requirements. Function Point Analysis is considered by many to be superior to methods that measure the effort to create software by counting lines of source code (e.g., COCOMO II), because function points measure the degree of functionality in a program in a manner that is independent of the language in which that program is written. The number of lines of source code required to achieve a certain degree of functionality varies depending on the programming language used. From a Function Point Analysis perspective, the development effort to create a program that has 200 function points is considered comparable regardless, of the programming language in which it is written.

As discussed below, Function Point Analysis can be used in software valuation to estimate the replacement cost, by determining the number of function points in an application, and applying a standard productivity measure or delivery rate (i.e., number of developer hours per function point, times a suitable labour rate). Function Point Analysis would typically be done at the outset of a development project, in order to communicate the users' needs to the development team, and to formulate a time and cost budget. In a valuation setting however, the number of function points may be calculated based on an analysis of the existing code (i.e., "back-calculated" or "Backfire Conversion"), discussed below.

In the function point analysis model, with its users' perspective, an application is measured with reference to Data Functions, which address the data requirements of an end user, and Transactional Functions, which

32 The International Function Point Users Group (IFPUG) is a non-profit professional organization of software developers. Its stated mission (according to its internet site: www.ifpug.org) is to be a recognized leader in promoting and encouraging the effective management of application software development and maintenance activities through the use of Function Point Analysis and other software measurement techniques. IFPUG maintains the "Function Point Counting Practices Manual," which it refers to as "the recognized industry standard for FPA." IFPUG's activities include education, training and professional certification.

address the end user's need to access data. The functions considered in Function Point Analysis are as follows:

Data Functions:

- Internal logical files — files (i.e. data) that are managed and manipulated by the user.
- External interface files — files that are referred to but not maintained by the user. This data exists outside the application in question.

Transactional Functions:

- External Inputs — relates to the users' ability to maintain internal logical files through the ability to add, change and delete the data (i.e. the ability of the user to manipulate data that is sourced from outside the application in question).
- External Outputs — relates to the users' ability to produce output using data that is maintained (internal logical files) and data that is referenced (external interface files). The output produced or displayed is known as an External Output in Function Point Analysis. External outputs can also be used by other applications.
- External Inquires — relates to the users' ability to select and display specific data from files.

Function Point Analysis also addresses functional complexity, using a different rating system for each of the aforementioned five functional components. All of the functional components of an application are analyzed and the number of function points is calculated, reflecting the functional complexity ratings. The resulting count of function points is referred to as an Unadjusted Function Point count, which is then multiplied by a second adjustment factor called the Value Adjustment Factor, which is comprised of a subset of 14 factors or questions. The 14 factors relate to characteristics of the software and its development such as the nature of data communications, installation ease, operational ease, reusability of code, to name a few. Each characteristic is rated on a scale of zero to five, reflecting the degree of influence the particular factor has on the system. The Value Adjustment Factor is calculated using a formula, which uses as an input, the result of the evaluation of the aforementioned 14 characteristics. The total number of function points is calculated as the number of Unadjusted Function Points times the Value Adjustment Factor.

Records of actual function point delivery rates (i.e. number of hours required to produce a function point) for a variety of project types are maintained in a database by the International Software Benchmarking Standards Group. This database contains information on the nature, size and development effort of a variety of software development projects.

The valuation obtained under Function Point Analysis can be checked using the so-called Backfire Conversion or Reverse Engineering method.[33] Backfire Conversion or Reverse Engineering involves the calculation of function points based on the number of lines of source code, and a conversion factor (i.e. number of lines of code per function point). For example for every 40 lines of statement line of code, it may hypothetically be estimated that 1 function point is contained. The number of function points so obtained is converted into effort to reproduce using industry benchmarks for function point productivity (i.e. the number of function points produced per person month), to which is applied development labour costs. For example, software with 20,000 statement lines of code would be estimated to have 500 function points before application of the Valuation Adjustment Factor (i.e. 20,000 statement lines of code divided by 40), which, using an assumed productivity factor of 5 function points per person month, would take 100 person months to develop. This variation of Function Point Analysis is generally used as a check of other methods, since the number of function points is determined by means of a conversion formula as opposed to direct technical analysis of the software.

5) Earnings or Cash Flow Methods

Software produced for purposes of resale (licensing) to users is typically valued using some or all of the following methods, among others, which are illustrated elsewhere in this paper:

- discounted cash flow.
- relief from royalty.
- profit split.

H. VALUING TRADEMARKS AND BRANDS

We have previously defined a trademark or brand name (which we will refer to as brands). Brands can have great significance to consumers. The function of a brand is to indicate to the consumer the sources from which

33 The limitations of relying on line counting based methods are discussed by IFPUG on its website, www.ifpug.org. It should be noted that the primary objective of Function Point Analysis (FPA) and IFPUG relates to the managing the development of new software, as opposed to analysis of already developed software for valuation purposes. As noted below, Backfire or Reverse Engineering is generally used as a check of other methods.

goods and services originate. A high level of public recognition of a brand can result in a high degree of buyer acceptance. The consumer identifies the particular product characteristics with the brand, and this association can help sell the product. When the product's reputation has been established in conjunction with the use of the brand, the marketability of the product is often greatly enhanced. Well-established and powerful brands such as Coca-Cola, Microsoft, GE, McDonald's, Toyota/Lexus, Sony, and Intel, serve to enhance future revenue prospects of a company and will thus possess value to their owners. The importance of brands and trademarks is well-documented and supported by the findings of market research into the consumer decision-making process. An existing brand or trademark that has won consumer recognition has value because it allows the owner to avoid or reduce expenditures on advertising. Given their potentially significant value, brands are frequently the subject of income tax planning and related non-arm's length transactions.

Marketing intangibles such as brands are also valued using one or more of the three basic valuation approaches:

- the cost approach.
- the income approach.
- the market approach.

The following discusses value drivers that are specific to trademarks and brands and illustrates the valuation methods typically used by valuators.

1) Brand Value Drivers

In addition to the general IP value drivers discussed above, the following key factors, among others, are critically assessed in the valuation of brands:

- *consumer recognition*. A fundamental factor in trademark or corporate brand values is the degree of consumer recognition. This provides competitive advantage, facilitates sales of branded products or services and can increase profitability. The significant cost of developing consumer recognition and awareness is a significant barrier to introducing and developing new products and services in many industries.
- *age/longevity*. A trademark or corporate brand with an established history is more likely to retain consumer recognition in the future. Some trademarks or brands span generations whereas others may have a short lifespan.
- *market share*. A larger market share generally leads to greater and more enduring recognition and profitability.

- *leveragability or potential for expansion or exploitation*. Because new products are costly to introduce, a trademark or corporate brand that can be used for brand or product extensions[34] is often more valuable than a trademark or corporate brand associated with a single product.
- *profitability*. The value of most business assets or segments is related to their profitability or contribution to profitability. Familiar trademarks or corporate brands can contribute to profitability by delivering higher profit margins for the underlying product (e.g., through higher prices and/or lower advertising and other marketing costs).
- *advertising*. Highly advertised and promoted trademarks or corporate brands are more likely to continue to develop increasing consumer recognition and develop longevity.
- *means of promoting*. The value of a brand or trademark will be influenced by the extent to which there are numerous means available to promote the name.
- *protection*. The value of a trademark or corporate brand is also related to the degree to which its exclusivity is protected through registration and defended against infringement. A more distinctive trademark or corporate brand is easier to protect and less subjective to confusion with competitive products.
- *geographic appeal/use*. The appeal and extent of international recognition or potential use, influences the value of a trademark or corporate brand.
- *associations*. The extent to which the name or brand is associated with a distinguished person, event or location influences the brand's value.

2) Brand Valuation Methods

The methods most typically applied in the valuation of brands are the relief from royalty and profit split methods discussed above. The relief from royalty method is most frequently employed, largely because of the abundance of available market-derived data with respect to licences of comparable brands or products.

The market comparable method is also employed, where market data on transactions involving brands, or brand-driven businesses is available. For example, food companies commonly sell brands, including all of the relevant IP such as recipes, know-how, trademarks, package design, along with the related tangible assets such as a manufacturing facility (although in some cases, the actual manufacturing and packaging may be out-

34 Such as situations where a brand can be used for a family of related products, or to introduce new related products.

sourced). In such transactions, it is often the IP that is driving the transaction price (as the manufacturing facility is essentially a commodity whose value can be readily established), and useful IP valuation metrics for comparison can be derived.

The replacement cost approach is often used to value relatively new brands, but is difficult to apply to established trademarks or brands, because of the lack of accumulated historical cost information relating to the IP's development. In many cases, the brands are significantly old, and historical costs to develop the IP have not been maintained. In some cases, however, companies have tracked or estimated costs to re-brand a product (for example, in the case of the acquisition of, or merger with a competitor). Such costs would include logo design, packaging design, signage, development of advertising, legal registrations, uniforms, among others.

In analyzing the historical expenditures for purposes of the replacement cost approach, one should consider that a portion of the marketing expenditures may relate to current sales and brand maintenance with the remainder, if any, relating to increasing brand value. As well, although there is likely a correlation between marketing expenditures and the value of marketing-related intangibles, the correlation is not necessarily one-to-one. In some unusual cases, the expenditures may create negative values, while in other cases the increase in value may be greater than the marketing costs incurred. Marketing-related expenditures often have two components: current transaction value and ongoing cash-flow producing value. The current transaction value portion relates to producing current sales and the remainder relates to building the value of the marketing intangible. Since the foregoing portions are usually entwined, it is often difficult to segregate that portion of the expenditure which resulted in increasing the value of the marketing intangibles.

The contributory nature of other assets of a business must also be kept in mind. The success of a consumer products company, such as Procter & Gamble, is in part due to its many strong brands and also to its research and product development activities and related research and development workforce.

I. TAX SHELTERS

Income tax shelters involving limited partnerships acquiring interests in computer software or other IP have often been controversial from a valuation perspective. Typically, the limited partnership acquires the IP, and the investors deduct the capital cost, based on the acquisition cost. The reasonableness of the CCA or ECE deduction (in other words, the acquisition cost) is sometimes challenged by the CRA, and valuators have frequently addressed the value of the IP acquired, either at the investment stage or as part of the tax litigation process.

In many tax shelters, the IP is paid for with a small share of cash, and a relatively large share of debt payable to the vendor, the repayment of which is tied to the profits earned by the IP. In some cases, there is an ongoing contractual relationship between the vendor and the limited partnership to use or commercially exploit the IP. The terms of the relationship may not be market-based. Valuations of IP that are on an earnings or cash flow basis should reflect market terms rather than non-market based arrangements between vendor and purchaser. In other words, the valuator should value the IP directly, regardless of the debt repayment or IP usage terms that the shelter structure might entail. This is especially important when parties do not act at arm's length, and the acquisition price can be increased to provide an attractive outcome to both the vendor and the limited partnership.

For example, in *McCoy v. The Queen*,[35] involving a software limited partnership tax shelter,[36] the court found that the software vendor and the limited partnership were at arm's length (and hence did not reassess the taxpayer under s. 69 of the Act), but, referring to s. 67 of the Act, the court found that the CCA claim based on the software valuation reflected by the limited partnership investors was unreasonable. The court decided that the value of the software acquired by the limited partnership was less than the purchase price, and that the value of the promissory notes (approximately two-thirds of the total purchase price) given by the limited partners, were worth less than their face value. The decision of the court in *CIT Financial Ltd. v. Her Majesty The Queen*,[37] a case involving a non-arm's length transfer of software, discussed below, has some similarity to *McCoy*, and included the court's critique of an expert's valuation of software which was based on non-market leasing terms.

---

35 *McCoy v. The Queen*, 2003 D.T.C. 660 (T.C.C.).

36 Jim Horvath, a co-author of this paper, provided expert testimony in the Tax Court of Canada on behalf of the Crown in *McCoy*.

37 *CIT Financial*, above note 8, at para. 60.

J. TAX COURT OF CANADA CASES INVOLVING VALUATION OF SOFTWARE AND OTHER INTELLECTUAL PROPERTY

Several Tax Court of Canada judgments have referred to valuation of software and other IP. The following discussion highlights some of the valuation issues identified in the judgments of some notable cases.

1) *Petro-Canada v. Her Majesty the Queen*[38]

This case related to a deduction in respect of Canadian exploration expense, and referred in part to the valuation of seismic data used for oil and gas exploration.[39] The case illustrates the importance of taking into consideration market transactions when valuing IP. It also highlights that a valuation methodology that determines value-to-owner[40] as opposed to fair market value is inadmissible. Finally, it highlights the issue of the reliance by expert witnesses on the expertise of others, in the formation of the expert's judgment or opinion.

The Tax Court judgment noted that the parties wanted the price paid for the seismic data to be as high as they could justify.[41] The Tax Court's written decision noted that the concept of value reflected by the taxpayer was one of value-to-owner, and that the taxpayer's methodology for valuing the seismic data did not reflect market transactions or negotiations that would typically take place between buyers and sellers:

> The concept is clearly one of value to the owner, which does not depend on, or even take into account, actual sales in the market, or the negotiation that takes place between buyers and sellers. That this methodology has no validity in the search for fair market value is demonstrated by the evidence led by the Respondent of certain sales of seismic data, negotiated at arm's length in the market place. . . . The selling prices cannot all be

---

38 *Petro-Canada v. Her Majesty the Queen*, 2003 D.T.C. 94 [T.C.C.], aff'd, 2004 D.T.C. 6329 [F.C.A.]. The appeal did not disturb the Tax Court decision regarding valuation.

39 Seismic data is a geophysical record of the results of controlled explosions on or under the ground. It may be used to assist in the search for oil and gas resources.

40 Value-to-owner is not necessarily equivalent to fair market value. Value-to-owner refers to the value of an asset to a particular investor. Value-to-owner can be greater than fair market value, with the excess due to taking into account additional earnings or other economic advantage enjoyed by or perceived by the owner of the asset, which would not be transferable to another investor (i.e., has no commercial value). In many cases, the excess of value-to-owner over fair market value relates to personal goodwill or sentimental value.

41 *Petro-Canada* [T.C.C.], at para. 85.

> established precisely, as in some cases, a share of future revenues from the data for some period was to go to the vendor. However, these sales all were clearly made at a small fraction of Mr. Curts' opinion of value. In the one instance where the entire selling price was in cash, Mr. Curts appraised the data at $2,946,860; the previous day it had sold, at arm's length, for $163,907. An appraisal at eighteen times the consideration given in a contemporaneous arm's length sale is startling enough; even more startling was Mr. Curts' evidence that, had he known of the sale, it would not have affected his opinion of fair market value.[42]

A second valuation was criticized by the Tax Court for the same reasons at paragraph 95 of *Petro-Canada* (i.e., the valuation was "a computation of value-to-owner, arrived at without regard for what actually happens in the market").[43] The findings on value were upheld in the Federal Court of Appeal.[44]

In another Tax Court of Canada case dealing in part with the valuation of seismic data, *Global Communications Ltd. v. R.*,[45], the importance of actual market transaction evidence was highlighted: "Obviously, Global's appraisers were not prepared to look at the price paid for seismic data on the open market. According to the Minister's uncontradicted evidence, seismic data trades at about 10% of the value at which it is appraised. In my opinion, appraisals which ignore cash transactions are simply self-serving opinions designed to inflate the value of seismic data and, therefore, must be rejected for tax purposes."[46]

In evaluating the evidence of the Respondent's valuator in *Petro-Canada*, the court noted that the valuator made frequent references to both factual material that had "been provided to him by 'consultants,' and also to matters of judgment as to which he had sought opinions from those 'consultants,' and then adopted their judgments as his own."[47] With regard to the "consultants," it was noted that, "[w]hatever the level of their expertise might be, they were not at the trial, they did not give evidence, and counsel for the Appellant had no opportunity to cross-examine them."[48] The judgment continued with a discussion acknowledging that experts may

42 *Ibid.* at paras. 90-91.
43 *Ibid.* at para. 95.
44 *Petro-Canada*, [F.C.A.], at para. 48.
45 *Global Communications Ltd. v. R.*, 99 D.T.C. 5377 [T.C.C.].
46 *Ibid.*, at paras. 37–38.
47 *Petro-Canada*, [T.C.C.], at para. 103.
48 *Ibid.*

consult other sources in forming their own opinions, but cannot reiterate or over-rely on such third party opinions:

> Opinion witnesses, at least in civil proceedings, have a certain latitude to base their opinions upon information that they have gathered outside the courtroom, and which is not formally proved. It becomes part of the general body of knowledge that contributes to the expertise of the witness.[49] No such latitude is available in respect of matters of judgment or opinion, however. The reason that certain witnesses may express opinions is because they possess knowledge and expertise, acquired through study and experience, that will assist the Court. They may consult recognized texts and reference materials in formulating and in defending their opinions, but they may not simply reiterate the opinions of others, with or without attribution. The opinion evidence of [the CRA valuator] in this case is tainted by his wholesale adoption of the advice of those he consulted, not simply as to facts of transactions, but as to matters which are primarily matters of judgment, such as the establishment of a copy price, and the appropriate levels of discount to be applied to large volume sales. However, I know nothing of the qualifications of these consultants, I have had no opportunity to assess their competence, and, most importantly, they have not been subject to cross-examination. In my view, their opinions pervade the evidence of [the CRA valuator] to such an extent, and so inextricably, as to destroy any probative value that it might otherwise have.[50]

2) *Peter M. Brown v. Her Majesty The Queen*[51]

This case involved the appeal of income tax assessments related to losses from a partnership. The partnership investment was a limited partnership, that had acquired 11 computer game programs for resale. The valuation of the computer software was a central issue to the case.

Rip, T.C.J. found that the partnership's acquisition of the software was not on an arm's length basis, and considered the evidence of expert witnesses about the value of the software. This evidence included two valuations using a discounted cash flow approach to value, and a third valuation by a software developer, using a replacement cost approach. Rip, T.C.J.

---

49 *Petro-Canada* [T.C.C.] cited *City of Saint John v. Irving Oil Co. Ltd.*, [1996] S.C.R. 581 at 592. Note that the published judgment incorrectly cited the year of this case. The correct citation is *City of Saint John v. Irving Oil Co. Ltd.* , [1966] S.C.R. 581 at 592.

50 *Petro-Canada* [T.C.C.], at para. 104.

51 *Brown v. R.*, 2001 D.T.C. 1094 [T.C.C.], aff'd, 2003 D.T.C. 5298 [F.C.A.]. The appeal did not disturb the Tax Court decision regarding valuation.

determined that the price paid for the programs by the limited partnership was greater than fair market value but did not fix a value. However, the judgment contained some valuation commentary, including a review of the relevant value drivers, approval of the discounted cash flow approach to valuing commercial software, and discussion of the reasonableness of the revenue projections and discount rates reflected in the respective valuation expert testimony. The judgment cited some technical errors in the valuations, including misinterpretations of projected sales data, and an incorrect assumption made by one of the technical experts regarding the language used to write the code. The appellant's projections were found to be overly optimistic and with no substantial foundation. Given the type of software being valued, Rip, T.C.J. disagreed with the inclusion of a residual value beyond the three-year projection period. Of general significance to software and other IP valuations, the judgment cited the need to reflect the cash flows on an after-tax basis (i.e., to reduce discretionary cash flows by the related income taxes).[52]

After Rip, T.C.J. released his judgment, counsel for both parties sought direction on the value of the software. A series of conference calls took place, during which the parties resolved the outstanding valuation issues. One of the issues not resolved during the conference calls, and subsequently considered by the court based on correspondence to the court from the parties, involved the method of calculating the present value of the CCA tax shield related to the software. The specific issues involved the appropriate rate of return or discount rate to use (i.e., the same discount rate as used to calculate the present value of the cash flows generated from sales of the software, or a lower or risk-free rate), and the timing of the realization of the tax benefits of deducting CCA.

The appellant's expert's testimony reflected a tax shield discount rate of 20%, while the respondent reflected 31% (the midpoint of the range of discount rates used to value the software itself). During the subsequent discussions, the appellant's expert argued for a discount rate reflecting the (lower) risk-free rate of return of 7.28%, on the basis that the benefit to be derived from reducing the taxes payable is virtually certain, whereas the value of the software business cash flow is more risky. Rip, T.C.J. in rejecting the appellant's argument, concluded that the appellant's position was that,

> even if the software does not generate any revenues, the Partners would still have realized the tax shield by deducting CCA against their other income. This approach assumes a purchaser has income from other sources against

52 *Brown [T.C.C.], at Ibid.*, at para. 143.

> which to apply CCA . . . I am only interested in the value of the engines, without regard to any potential purchaser's tax situation . . . For example, to consider the personal tax situation of the appellant and the other Partners, assumes that they are special purchasers. But I had been advised earlier that this was not so . . . The tax aspects of the transaction to any individual taxpayer should not influence the value of the engines; the taxes payable by any one purchaser is not intrinsic to the asset itself . . . In my view, to consider the tax implications to different potential purchasers in valuing the engines would distort value.[53]

The timing of the recognition of the CCA tax benefits was also argued. The reasons for directions rejected the use of timing that would be available to an individual taxpayer (as opposed to a corporation). As with the discount rate issue, Rip, T.C.J. rejected a treatment that would be consistent with a specific individual taxpayer, and appears to have accepted that the CCA benefits would be realized 50% one year after the valuation date (i.e., one year after December 1993), and 50% two years after the valuation date.

3) *CIT Financial Ltd. v. Her Majesty The Queen*[54]

The Amended Reasons For Judgment by Bowman, A.C.J. in this case contains reference to several of the methods and concepts discussed in this paper. The case dealt with a number of issues involving the General Anti-Avoidance Rule ("GAAR") and the valuation of software under s. 69 of the Act, and the question of reasonableness under s. 67. The software in question was custom operations software used by a steel-manufacturing corporation resident in New Zealand ("BHP"). The software was internal use software, as opposed to commercial software from which license income would be derived. The facts of the case involved a complex series of transactions in 1993 with non-arm's length and arm's length parties (including the ultimate acquirer, Commcorp) involving a number of layers of leases and licence agreements. The taxpayer valued the software at $33 million, while the Crown's expert valued the software in a range of $12 million to $18 million.

Bowman, A.C.J. noted the difficulty in finding market evidence for such unique software, and further noted that ". . . any company that wanted to install a computer system to run its steel mill would find it easier and

53 *Peter M. Brown and Her Majesty The Queen*, February 21, 2002, Docket 97-3264-IT-G, Directions and Reasons for Directions, at paras. 11-19.

54 Above note 8.

cheaper to develop its own system and then try to adapt it. The more precisely tailored it is to BHP's business and hence the greater its commercial value to BHP, the less useful or valuable it will be to another user."[55] The court accepted the use of replacement cost under the circumstances, i.e., that no market for the software had been identified, but that the IP helped BHP to carry on business.

One of the taxpayer's valuation experts used several replacement cost methods, including Function Point Analysis, cost of development time, and lines of code. The expert concluded on replacement cost, but added a further amount of approximately $2 million, to reflect the competitive advantage that the use of the software gives to BHP. The court rejected this adjustment: "If you are determining replacement cost you do so by the best method you can. You do not add to the replacement cost that you have determined some arbitrary percentage based on an unrelated factor having to do with how good the product is."[56]

The Crown's expert[57] provided a critique of the taxpayer's valuation reports and a recalculation of the taxpayer's expert's valuation, based on several adjustments, which suggested that the replacement cost of the software was overvalued. Some of the noteworthy adjustments made related to:

- inappropriate inclusion of significant implementation and training time as a component of replacement cost.
- overstated daily labour rate.
- double counting of overhead costs relating to management and administrative time.
- double counting of software development time in respect of 'general purpose code' for certain applications.
- inclusion of the aforementioned $2 million premium for competitive advantage.

The court accepted the conclusions of the Crown's expert, and after making some adjustments, determined the value of the software to be $13.1 million, under s. 69 of the Act.

The court also commented on another expert report prepared for the taxpayer, which concluded that the value of the software was $34 million. The taxpayer's expert report appears to have valued the software based on the lease between two of the parties involved in the series of transactions.

---

55 *CIT Financial LtdIbid..*, at para. 36.

56 *Ibid.*, at para. 46.

57 Mr. Howard Johnson, whose article "The Litigious Elements of Business Valuation" is found in this volume.

Bowman, A.C.J. and the Crown's expert noted the weakness of the approach. Bowman, A.C.J. noted that the taxpayer's report did not value the software, "It values the lease based on the rentals which are themselves too high. If you start from a value of $33 million, base your rents on that figure knowing that the money is going to come back to where it started it is not surprising if you end up with a value for the lease that is equal to $33 million. If they had started with a figure of $100 million and based the rentals on that amount they could have determined the discounted cash flow to be $100 million and therefore the value of the software with the lease to be that amount.[58] We referred to this case, and the need to value the IP directly, based on market terms, above under the heading Tax Shelters.

The Crown's expert also commented on several aspects of the taxpayer's expert report. He pointed out that the discount rate adopted of 8.64% was close to the risk-free rate of return, and was not a reasonable rate of return by which to determine the fair market value of the software, and was not market-based, given the risks involved in software. Bowman, A.C.J. agreed, noting: "It is in my view artificial to base a valuation on the discounted cash flow under a lease where the rentals are themselves based upon an excessive valuation and in which it makes no difference what the rentals are because they substantially come back in one form or another to where they started."[59] These comments are especially significant given the non-arm's length nature of many of the participants in the series of transactions.

K. CONCLUSION

The heightened emphasis by the business community on IP and the current rapid rate of evolution of technology are a fact of life in today's economy. As a result, valuations of IP figure prominently in tax plans and disputes. The valuation of IP, although based on the same principles and methodologies as those used in valuing shareholding interests or tangible assets, often involves the application of special approaches and methods discussed in this paper, including:

- relief from royalty.
- profit split.
- capitalized maintainable cash flow/capitalized maintainable earnings.
- discounted cash flow.

---

58 *CIT Financial*, above note 8 at paras. 58–59.

59 *Ibid.*, at para. 60.

- probability-based earnings methods.
- market approaches such as venture capital approach and licensing approach.
- excess earnings.
- selling-price differential method.
- time adjusted historical replacement cost method.
- software development cost models (COCOMO II and Function Point Analysis).

Given the nature of IP, the assessment of value drivers (such as those outlined in this paper) is critical, and is often the source of dispute between valuators, taxpayers, and the CRA. Valuators often must incorporate in their assessment of value drivers, the findings and technical expertise of experts in the particular field (e.g., software development, market research, biotechnology, etc.).

In this paper, we have further illustrated the concepts, complexities and controversies surrounding IP valuations with references to relevant taxation cases. The courts have grappled with a variety of aspects of IP including valuation, and have relied to some extent on the expertise of valuators and other experts. The cases cited in this paper show how the experts and the courts have evaluated IP value drivers, and selected and applied the most appropriate IP valuation methods, in particularly controversial circumstances.

L. REFERENCES

Anson, W., "Identify, Value, Leverage Your Intellectual Assets", (March 1998) Les Nouvelles.

Cole, S.R., & Anhang, J., "Valuations and Software Tax Shelters", (July 1995) 1:1 Business Valuation Digest 13.

Ellsworth, R.K., "Identifying the Economic Value of Trade Marks", in Managing Intellectual Property Trade Mark Yearbook 1998, April 1998, pages 16–20.

Goldscheider, R., Jarosz, J., & Mulhern, C., "Use of the 25 Per Cent Rule in Valuing IP", (December 2002) Les Nouvelles, 123.

Heller, R. "An Introduction to Function Point Analysis", (November/December 1995) CrossTalk — The Journal Of Defense Software Engineering.

Horvath, J.L. & Canham, P.J., "Bits, bytes and bucks", (August 1998) CA Magazine, 65–68.

Horvath, J.L., "Strategies for Valuing Intellectual Property for Tax Purposes", 2000 Infonex, 4th Annual Taxation of Intellectual Property, pages 7.1–7.42.

Kellogg, D. & Charnes, J.M., "Real-Options Valuation for a Biotechnology Company", (May/June 2000) Financial Analysts Journal, 76.

Reilly, R.F., & Garland, P.J., "Valuation of Data Processing Intangible Assets", 1997 7:2 Business Valuation Digest, 18.

Reilly, R.F., & Schweihs, R.P., *Valuing Intangible Assets*, (New York: McGraw-Hill, 1998).

Robak, E., "Lessons from *Nestle v. Comm'r*: Second Circuit Rejects Popular Trademark Valuation Method", (Summer 1999) Journal of Corporate Taxation, 135.

Webster, J., "Valuation of Biotechnology Companies and Their Assets — Stage of Clinical Development is Most Important", 2002 21:4 Business Valuation Review.

Werner, Dr. M., "Real Option Valuation", (2001) Journal of Business Valuation 137.

Part Two: Taxation

Chapter Seventeen

Interest Deductibility, the Reasonable Expectation of Profit Test, and the Supreme Court of Canada: From *Bronfman Trust* and *Moldowan* to *Singleton*, *Ludmer*, *Stewart*, and *Walls*

David G. Duff

A. INTRODUCTION

Until the 1970s, Canadian courts affirmed a narrow approach to the application of tax legislation, according to which these statutes were interpreted in a strict and literal manner and tax consequences were based on the legal character of transactions and arrangements irrespective of their commercial or economic substance and the absence of any non-tax purpose for their existence.[1] Characterized by one Canadian writer as the two "pillars of tax planning,"[2] these judicially-established norms of literalism and formal-

1 The leading example of this approach is *C.I.R. v. Duke of Westminster*, [1936] A.C. 1 (H.L.).

2 Douglas J. Sherbaniuk, "Tax Avoidance — Recent Developments, in *Report of the Proceedings of the Twenty-First Tax Conference*, 1968 Conference Report (Toronto: Canadian Tax Foundation, 1969) 430–42 at 430.

ism were highly conducive to tax avoidance. They also account for much of the length and complexity of Canadian tax legislation, which has been drafted and amended in order to anticipate and respond to restrictive interpretations by the courts and taxpayer efforts to avoid tax burdens that might otherwise apply.[3]

From the late-1970s to the early 1990s, the Supreme Court of Canada adopted a much broader approach to tax statutes, favouring a more purposive method of statutory interpretation,[4] endorsing a more substantive approach to the application of tax rules having regard to "commercial and economic realities, rather than juristic classification of form,"[5] and suggesting that tax-motivated transactions could fail to achieve their intended results where they contradict the "object and spirit" of a relevant statutory provision or the provision itself requires a business purpose.[6] Leading examples of this broader approach include the Court's decisions in *Bronfman Trust* and *Moldowan*, which addressed respectively the deductibility of interest expenses and the concept of a reasonable expectation of profit.

In the past decade, the Supreme Court of Canada has returned to the narrow approach of earlier tax jurisprudence, restoring a version of literalist interpretation in the form of a "plain meaning" rule,[7] reasserting the for-

---

3 See, e.g., S. W. Bowman, "Interpretation of Tax Legislation: The Evolution of Purposive Analysis" (1995) 43: 5 Canadian Tax Journal 1167–89 at 1183–84.

4 See especially the rejection of strict construction in *Stubart Investments Ltd. v. The Queen*, [1984] C.T.C. 294; 84 D.T.C. 6305 (S.C.C.); and *The Queen v. Golden*, [1986] 1 C.T.C. 274, 86 D.T.C. 6138 (S.C.C.). For other leading decisions during this period in which the Court emphasized the purpose of the applicable statutory provision, see *Moldowan v. The Queen*, [1977] C.T.C. 310, 77 D.T.C. 5213 (S.C.C.) [*Moldowan*]; *The Queen v. Savage*, [1983] C.T.C. 393, 83 D.T.C. 5409 (S.C.C.); *The Queen v. Bronfman Trust*, [1987] 1 C.T.C. 117, 87 D.T.C. 5059 (S.C.C.) [*Bronfman Trust*]; and *The Queen v. McClurg*, [1991] 1 C.T.C. 169, 91 D.T.C. 5001 (S.C.C.) [*McClurg*]. For a detailed analysis of different approaches to the interpretation of tax legislation, see D. G. Duff, "Interpreting the *Income Tax Act* — Part 1: Interpretive Doctrines" (1999) 47: 3 Canadian Tax Journal 464-533, and "Interpreting the *Income Tax Act* — Part 2: Toward a Pragmatic Approach" (1999) 47: 4 Canadian Tax Journal 741–98.

5 *Bronfman Trust*, above note 4 at para. 40. See also *McClurg*, above note 4 at para. 46.

6 *Stubart*, above note 4 at para. 65.

7 See, e.g., *Antosko v. The Queen*, [1994] 2 C.T.C. 25, 94 D.T.C. 6314 (S.C.C.) at para. 29 (suggesting that the context and purpose of a provision "cannot alter" its interpretation "where the words of the statute are clear and plain"); *Friesen v. The Queen*, [1995] 2 C.T.C. 369, 95 D.T.C. 5551 (S.C.C.) at para. 16 ("the plain meaning of the relevant sections of the *Income Tax Act* is to prevail unless the transaction is a sham"); *65302 British Columbia Ltd. v. Canada*, [2000] 1 C.T.C. 57, 99 D.T.C. 5799 (S.C.C.) at para. 51 ("in applying the principles of interpretation to the Act, attention must be paid to the fact that the Act is one of the most detailed, complex, and comprehensive statutes in our legislative inventory and courts should be reluctant to embrace unexpressed

malist principle that tax consequences should turn on the legal form of transactions irrespective of their commercial or economic reality,[8] and reaffirming the traditional adage that taxpayers may take advantage of tax rules even where their sole purpose is to avoid tax.[9] The culmination of the current Court's return to a narrow approach is its judgments on interest deductibility in *Singleton* and *Ludmer* and on the reasonable expectation of profit test in *Stewart* and *Walls.* In October 2003, the federal Department of Finance released draft legislation designed to limit the effect of these decisions.[10]

This article traces the change in the Supreme Court of Canada's approach to tax legislation by examining the criteria for interest deductibility set out in *Bronfman Trust, Singleton* and *Ludmer,* and the role of the reasonable expectation of profit test in *Moldowan, Stewart* and *Walls.* Section B reviews the cases on interest deductibility, contrasting the substantive approach employed in *Bronfman Trust* and various post-*Bronfman Trust* decisions with the formalist approach adopted in *Singleton* and *Ludmer.*

---

notions of policy or principle in the guise of statutory interpretation"); and *Ludmer v. M.N.R.*, [2002] 1 C.T.C. 95, 2001 D.T.C. 5505 (S.C.C.) [*Ludmer*] at para. 64 ("where the provision at issue is clear and unambiguous, the court's duty is to simply apply its terms to the transaction at issue"). For critical commentaries on this interpretive approach, see B.J. Arnold, "Statutory Interpretation: Some Thoughts on Plain Meaning" in *Report of the Proceedings of the Fiftieth Tax Conference,* 1998 Conference Report (Toronto: Canadian Tax Foundation, 1999), 6:1-36; and Duff, "Interpreting the *Income Tax Act* — Part 2" above note 4 at 769–79.

8 See, e.g., *Shell Canada Limited v. The Queen,* [1999] 4 C.T.C. 313, 99 D.T.C. 5669 (S.C.C.) at para. 39 *per* McLachlin C.J.C. ("absent a specific provision of the Act to the contrary or a finding that they are a sham, the taxpayer's legal relationships must be respected in tax cases"); and *Singleton v. The Queen,* [2002] 1 C.T.C. 121, 2001 D.T.C. 5533 (S.C.C.) [*Singleton*] at para. 31 (rejecting any search for the "economic realities of the situation").

9 See, e.g., *Neuman v. The Queen,* [1998] 3 C.T.C. 177, 98 D.T.C. 6297 (S.C.C.) at para. 39 ("a transaction should not be disregarded for tax purposes because it has no independent or *bona fide* purpose" and that "taxpayers can arrange their affairs in a particular way for the sole purpose of deliberately availing themselves of tax reduction devices in the *ITA*"; *Duha Printers (Western) Ltd. v. The Queen,* [1998] 3 C.T.C. 303, 98 D.T.C. 6334, (S.C.C.) at para. 87 ("no 'business purpose' is required for a transaction to be considered valid under the *Income Tax Act,* and that a taxpayer is entitled to take advantage of the Act even where a transaction is motivated solely by the minimization of tax"); *The Queen v. Walls,* [2002] 3 C.T.C. 421, 2002 D.T.C. 6960 (S.C.C.) [*Walls*] at para. 22 ("a tax motivation does not affect the validity of transactions for tax purposes"); and *Stewart v. The Queen,* [2002] 3 C.T.C. 439, 2002 D.T.C. 6969 (S.C.C.) [*Stewart*] at para. 65 ("a tax motivation does not affect the validity of transactions for tax purposes").

10 See Department of Finance, *News Release 2003-055* (October 31, 2003).

Section C considers the reasonable expectation of profit test, contrasting the broad formulation in *Moldowan* and subsequent Federal Court of Appeal decisions with the much narrower interpretation adopted in *Stewart* and *Walls*. Section D offers concluding remarks, considering the reasons for and implications of the Court's current approach, and the draft legislation released by the Department of Finance.

B. INTEREST DEDUCTIBILITY: FROM *BRONFMAN TRUST* TO *SINGLETON* AND *LUDMER*

According to subparagraph 20(1)(c)(i) of the federal *Income Tax Act* ("the *Act*"),[11] taxpayers may deduct "an amount paid in the year or payable in respect of the year . . . pursuant to a legal obligation to pay interest on . . . borrowed money used for the purpose of earning income from a business or property . . . ." In the application of this provision, the most contested issue is whether borrowed money has been "used for the purpose of earning income from a business or property." In *Bronfman Trust*, the Supreme Court of Canada interpreted these words in a substantive sense, having regard to the "true commercial and practical nature of the taxpayer's transactions"[12] — an approach that subsequent decisions relied upon both to allow the deduction of interest expenses in some cases and to disallow the deduction in others. In *Singleton* and *Ludmer*, the Court rejected this substantive interpretation, adopting instead a decidedly formalist approach strikingly at odds with the decision in *Bronfman Trust*.

1) *Bronfman Trust*

In *Bronfman Trust*, the taxpayer was a personal trust established by Samuel Bronfman for the benefit of his daughter, Phyllis, and her children. For each of the 1970, 1971 and 1972 taxation years, the trust sought to deduct interest expenses on borrowed funds which it used to finance capital allocations to Phyllis. On the basis that the money was used to pay capital allocations to Phyllis and not "for the purpose of earning income from a business or property," the Minister disallowed the deduction. On appeal the taxpayer argued that the borrowed funds were used *indirectly* for the purpose of earning income since they allowed the trust to "retain income-producing investments until the time was ripe to dispose of them."[13] The revenue authori-

11 R.S.C. 1985, c. 1 (5th Supp.) [as amended].

12 *Bronfman Trust*, above note 4 at para. 39.

13 *Ibid.* at para. 9.

ties also argued that the deduction should be allowed on the basis that "[t]he end result of the transactions . . . was the same as if the trustees had sold assets to pay the allocations and then borrowed money to replace them, in which case . . . the interest would have been deductible."[14]

Writing for a unanimous Court, Dickson C.J.C. rejected both arguments. With respect to the first, he reasoned, since both the text of subparagraph 20(1)(c)(i) and the presumed purpose of the provision to encourage the accumulation of income-producing capital distinguish between eligible and ineligible uses of borrowed funds,[15] it follows that "borrowing money for an ineligible direct purpose ought not to entitle a taxpayer to deduct interest payments."[16] Furthermore, he explained, "[e]ven if there are exceptional circumstances in which, on a real appreciation of the taxpayer's transactions, it might be appropriate to allow the taxpayer to deduct interest on funds borrowed for an ineligible use because of an indirect effect on the taxpayer's income-earning-capacity,"[17] these circumstances were not

---

14 *Ibid.*

15 *Ibid.* at para. 23.

16 *Ibid.* at para. 41. See also *ibid.* at para. 42, concluding that the text and purpose of the provision "precludes the allowance of a deduction for interest paid on borrowed funds which indirectly preserve income-earning property but which are not directly 'used for the purpose of earning income from . . . property'." In support of this conclusion, the Court pointed both to "the weight of judicial authority" and to "the consequences of the interpretation sought by the Trust" which it considered "cannot have been intended by Parliament." *Ibid.* at para. 31. With respect to judicial authority, the Court relied principally on the Supreme Court of Canada's earlier decision in *Canada Safeway Ltd. v. M.N.R.*, [1957] C.T.C. 335, 57 D.T.C. 1239 (S.C.C.), which rejected the taxpayer's argument that borrowed funds used to purchase shares in a related corporation were used to earn income indirectly by giving it control over a wholesale supplier (the direct use to earn dividend income being an ineligible use at the time as inter-corporate dividends were tax exempt) on the basis (at para. 15) that: "What is aimed at by the section is an employment of the borrowed funds immediately within the company's business and not one that effects its purpose in such an indirect and remote manner." With respect to the consequences of the Trust's interpretation, the Court concluded that it would allow a deduction "for borrowings by any taxpayer who owned income-producing assets" regardless of the use to which the funds were put — a result that would be unfair to less wealthy taxpayers and would "make a mockery of the statutory requirement that, for interest payments to be deductible, borrowed money must be used for circumscribed income-earning purposes." *Bronfman Trust*, above note 4, at para. 31.

17 *Ibid.* at para. 43, referring to the decision in *Trans-Prairie Pipelines Ltd. v. M.N.R.*, [1970] C.T.C. 537, 70 D.T.C. 6351 (Ex. Ct.), in which the Court allowed a deduction for interest on borrowed money used to redeem preferred shares on the basis (at para. 12) that the funds "as a practical matter of business common sense, went to fill the hole left by redemption of the . . . preferred [shares]."

present on the facts of the case since the taxpayer had not established that its "bona fide purpose in using the funds was to earn income."[18] Indeed, he observed:

> . . . the assets which were preserved for a brief period of time yielded a return which grossly fell short of the interest costs on the borrowed money. . . . The taxpayer cannot point to any reasonable expectation that the income yield from the Trust's investment portfolio as a whole, or indeed from any single asset, would exceed the interest payable on a like amount of debt.[19]

Nor could the fact that the use of the borrowed fund may have prevented capital losses assist the taxpayer, he added, since the deduction is "limited to use of borrowed money for the purpose of earning *income*."[20]

With respect to the taxpayer's second argument, that the interest would have been deductible had the trustees "sold assets to pay the allocations and then borrowed money to replace them,"[21] Dickson C.J.C. began by noting that "[i]t would be a sufficient answer to this submission to point to the principle that the courts must deal with what the taxpayer actually did, and not what he might have done."[22] In any event, he continued, even if the trust had sold assets to pay the capital allocations and borrowed funds to repurchase the assets, it was not clear that the deduction would have been allowed. On the contrary, he suggested, dismissing the hypothetical transactions as "the epitome of formalism":

> If . . . the trust has sold a particular income-producing asset, made the capital allocation to the beneficiary and repurchased the same asset, all within a brief interval of time, the courts might well consider the sale and repurchase to constitute a formality or a sham designed to conceal the essence of the transaction, namely that money was borrowed and used to fund a capital allocation to the beneficiary.[23]

---

18 *Bronfman Trust*, above note 4, at para. 43.

19 *Ibid.*

20 *Ibid.* [emphasis in original].

21 *Ibid.* at para. 9.

22 *Ibid.* at para. 44.

23 *Ibid.*, referring to *Zwaig v. M.N.R.*, [1974] C.T.C. 2172 (T.R.B.), in which the taxpayer sold securities, used the proceeds to purchase a life insurance policy, and then borrowed on the policy to repurchase the securities. According to the Court in *Bronfman Trust*, above note 4, at para. 44: "The Tax Review Board rightly disallowed the deduction sought for interest payments, notwithstanding that the form of the taxpayer's transactions created an aura of compliance with the requirements of the interest deduction provision."

As a result, the deduction was disallowed.

For the purposes of this article, the specific decision in *Bronfman Trust* is of less importance than the manner in which it was reached. In addition to its initial responses to each of the taxpayer's arguments — that the use of the borrowed funds must be direct and that the hypothetical transactions were not in fact carried out — the Court provided more substantive reasons for disallowing the deduction based on "a real appreciation of the taxpayer's transactions"[24] and "the essence"[25] of the hypothetical transactions. With respect to the taxpayer's first argument, Dickson C.J.C. concluded, the difference between the substantial interest expenses incurred by the trust and the limited yield on the trust's assets suggested that the real or *bona fide* purpose for which it used the borrowed funds was to make capital allocations to the beneficiary, not to earn income by preserving trust assets. With respect to the second argument, he maintained, the "true commercial and practical nature" of the hypothetical transactions suggested that their real or essential purpose would have been to pay capital allocations to the beneficiary, notwithstanding that the direct use of the borrowed funds would have been to repurchase income-producing assets.[26]

More generally, the Court emphasized, in the application of tax statutes, the rejection of strict construction has been accompanied by a "trend . . . towards attempting to ascertain the true commercial and practical nature of the taxpayer's transactions" — "a movement away from tests based on the form of transactions and towards tests based on what Lord Pearce has referred to as a 'common sense appreciation of the guiding features' of the events in question: *B.P. Australia Ltd. v. Commissioner of Taxation of Australia*, [1966] A.C. 224 (P.C.)."[27] Welcoming this trend as "laudable . . . provided that it is consistent with the text and purposes of the taxation statute,"[28] the judgment thus endorsed a substantive approach to

24 *Ibid.* para. 43.

25 *Ibid.* para. 44.

26 The Court's use of the word "sham" in the passage quoted in the text is unfortunate and at odds with its traditional definition for the purposes of Canadian income tax law, based on the following definition from *Snook v. London West Riding Investments, Ltd.*, [1967] 1 All E.R. 518 at 528 (C.A.) *per* Lord Diplock: "acts done or documents executed by parties to the 'sham' which are intended by them to give to third parties or to the court the appearance of creating between the parties legal rights and obligations different from the actual legal rights and obligations (if any) which the parties intend to create."

27 *Ibid.* at para. 39.

28 *Ibid.* at para. 40.

the application of tax rules as well as a more purposive method of statutory interpretation. Finally, the Court observed:

> Assessment of taxpayers' transactions with an eye to commercial and economic realities, rather than juristic classification of form, may help to avoid the inequity of tax liability being dependent upon the taxpayer's sophistication at manipulating a sequence of events to achieve a patina of compliance with the apparent prerequisites of a tax deduction.[29]

As a result, the decision suggested, attention to the "commercial and economic realities" of a taxpayer's transactions could help to promote tax equity and prevent tax avoidance.

2) Post-*Bronfman Trust* Cases

In the decade after *Bronfman Trust*, courts relied on its substantive approach to the application of subparagraph 20(1)(c)(i) on several occasions, both to allow the deduction of interest expenses in some cases and to disallow the deduction in others. In *Grenier v. M.N.R.*,[30] for example, where the taxpayer used borrowed funds to purchase a residence after selling a former residence against which he had borrowed $66,000 to invest in a business which he continued to carry on, the Court looked to "the economic context of the transactions" in order to conclude that the taxpayer could deduct the interest expense incurred on $66,000 of the new loan.[31] According to Lamarre-Proulx T.C.J.:

> When the taxpayer sold his first house, he received $110,000 cash less $66,000. Why did he not receive the full amount of $110,000? This was because part of the amount had been lent for the financial support of his business . . . . When the time came to purchase his other house, he did not have the full $110,000 in hand, again because the money was used in the business. The reason he mortgaged his second home by $66,000 and more is that he did not have the $66,000 he had lent to the business . . . . He had to pay off the first loan secured by a hypothec on his house, because he sold the house. However, when he bought another house, he had to borrow money to make up for the decrease in his assets brought about by the loan to his business, or in other terms, to fill the hole left in

29 *Ibid.*

30 [1992] 1 C.T.C. 2703, 92 D.T.C. 1678 (T.C.C.), aff'd. [1998] 3 C.T.C. 243, 98 D.T.C. 6439 (F.C.T.D.).

31 *Ibid*, [1992] 1 C.T.C. 2703, 92 D.T.C. 1678 (T.C.C.) at para. 15.

> his assets by the money he had lent to his business and that was still being used to earn income.[32]

Ineligible under the direct use test initially suggested in *Bronfman Trust*, the interest expenses were deductible only by adopting a broad view of the purpose for which the borrowed funds were used, having regard to the "commercial and economic realities" of the transactions at issue.

In *Robitaille v. The Queen*,[33] on the other hand, where the taxpayer withdrew $100,000 from a partnership of which he was a member in order to purchase a home, borrowed $100,000 on the security of the home the next day, and contributed these funds to the partnership a day later, the Court disallowed the deduction of interest expenses incurred on the loan on the basis that "the focus must be had not on the direct and immediate result of the use to which the funds were put but rather, in a real and practical manner, on the ultimate economic objectives sought by the transactions."[34] According to Dussault T.C.J.:

> Applying the reasoning of Dickson C.J. [in *Bronfman Trust*] to the facts of the instant case, I consider that the analysis of the "true commercial and practical nature" of the transactions carried out by the appellant leads to the conclusion that their ultimate purpose was the purchase . . . of his residence, not investment in the law firm in which he is one of the partners. Investment in the law firm already existed and the purpose of the loans was only to reimburse money withdrawn and used for personal purposes a few days earlier in 1985.[35]

Eligible under the direct use test initially suggested in *Bronfman Trust*, the interest expenses were non-deductible when "the ultimate economic objectives" and "true commercial and practical nature" of the taxpayer's transactions were taken into account.

Similarly, in *Mark Resources Inc. v. The Queen*,[36] where the taxpayer used borrowed funds to capitalize a U.S. subsidiary with accumulated business losses, which invested the funds at a lower interest rate than that payable on the loan, distributing the resulting interest income to the taxpayer in the form of dividends that were deductible in computing the taxpayer's taxable income, the Court looked beyond the immediate use of the

---

32 *Ibid.*
33 [1997] 3 C.T.C. 3031, 97 D.T.C. 1286 (T.C.C.).
34 *Ibid.* at para. 16.
35 *Ibid.* at para. 21.
36 [1993] 2 C.T.C. 2259, 93 D.T.C. 1004 (T.C.C.).

borrowed funds to their ultimate economic objective in order to disallow the deduction of interest expenses on the loan. Rejecting the taxpayer's argument that the borrowed funds were used by the taxpayer to earn dividend income from its U.S. subsidiary, the Court held that the "overriding ultimate economic purpose for which the borrowed funds were used" was to enable the taxpayer to, in effect, import the losses of its U.S. subsidiary to be deducted in computing the taxpayer's income.[37] According to Bowman T.C.J.:

> The direct and immediate use [of the borrowed funds] was the injection of capital into a subsidiary with the necessary and intended consequence that the subsidiary should earn interest income from term deposits from which it could pay dividends. The earning of dividend income cannot, however, in my opinion, be said to be the real purpose of the use of the borrowed funds . . . . That purpose — and it is a practical and real one, and in no way remote, fanciful or indirect — is the importation of the losses from the U.S. . . . Here the immediate step of investing in a subsidiary that in accordance with the scheme must necessarily pay dividends was not the real purpose of the use of the funds. The earning of interest income by [the US subsidiary] and the payment by it of dividends to [the taxpayer] were integral but subservient and incidental steps to the real objective that lay behind the implementation of the plan. The amount of dividends, albeit deductible in computing taxable income, and based upon the interest from the term deposits, was less than the interest paid . . . . It is true that the overall economic result, if all of the elements of the plan work, is a net gain to the appellant, but this type of gain is not from the production of income but from a reduction of taxes otherwise payable in Canada.[38]

Here too, therefore, an emphasis on the real purpose for which the borrowed funds were used and the economic and commercial realities of the transactions suggested that the deduction should be disallowed.[39]

---

37 *Ibid.* at para. 39.

38 *Ibid.* at para. 45.

39 For a similar result, involving a much more complicated series of transactions designed to transfer accumulated tax losses among companies that were unrelated before the series of transactions commenced, see *Canwest Broadcasting Limited v. The Queen*, [1995] 2 C.T.C. 2780, 96 D.T.C. 1375 (T.C.C.).

3) *Singleton*

The facts in *Singleton* were much like those in *Robitaille*. The taxpayer, a partner in a law firm in which he had invested capital of at least $300,000, engaged in a number of transactions on October 27, 1988 — borrowing $298,750, contributing these funds to his capital account in the partnership, and withdrawing $300,000 from this account in order to purchase a house for personal use. Relying on the substantive approach set out in *Bronfman Trust*, the Minister disallowed the deduction of interest expenses on the basis that the taxpayer's real economic purpose in using the borrowed money was not to invest in the partnership but to buy the house. The Tax Court of Canada upheld the assessment on the basis that the borrowed money was as a "matter of economic reality" used to purchase the house, not to earn income from the partnership.[40] A majority of the Federal Court of Appeal allowed the taxpayer's appeal on the grounds that the direct use of the borrowed funds was to refinance the taxpayer's capital account in the firm, that the transactions must be considered separately, and that taxpayers are entitled to arrange their affairs solely to reduce taxes otherwise payable.[41] The Minister appealed.

At the Supreme Court of Canada, a majority of the Court dismissed the appeal, allowing the taxpayer to deduct the interest expenses. Citing the Court's prior decision in *Shell Canada Ltd. v. The Queen*,[42] Major J. (Gonthier, Iacobucci, Binnie and Arbour JJ. concurring) began by rejecting the substantive approach adopted in *Bronfman Trust* and other cases involving the deductibility of interest expenses, emphasizing instead that the Court "must simply apply s. 20(1)(c)(i) rather than search for the economic reali-

---

40 *Singleton v. The Queen*, [1996] 3 C.T.C. 2873, 96 D.T.C. 1850 (T.C.C.).

41 *Singleton v. The Queen*, [1999] 3 C.T.C. 446, 99 D.T.C. 5362 (F.C.A.).

42 Above note 8, at para. 39 [*Shell Canada*]: ". . . this Court has never held that the economic realities of a situation can be used to recharacterize a taxpayer's *bona fide* relationships. To the contrary, we have held that, absent a specific provision of the Act to the contrary or a finding that they are a sham, the taxpayer's legal relationships must be respected in tax cases . . . ." See also *ibid.* at para 40: ". . . it is well established in this Court's tax jurisprudence that a searching inquiry for either the 'economic realities' of a particular transaction or the general object and spirit of the provision at issue can never supplant a court's duty to apply an unambiguous provision of the Act to a taxpayer's transaction. Where the provision at issue is clear and unambiguous, its terms must simply be applied." For a critical examination of this decision, see D. G. Duff, "Weak-Currency Borrowings and the General Anti-Avoidance Rule in Canada: From *Shell Canada to Canadian Pacific*" (2001) 55:6 Bulletin for International Fiscal Documentation 233–40.

ties of the transaction."[43] As a result, he continued, the Court should assess the various transactions carried out by the taxpayer independently of one another "[i]n order to give effect to the legal relationships" that they created.[44] So also should it look to the direct use to which the borrowed funds were put, without regard to any other purpose that might have been achieved.[45] On this basis, Major J. concluded, regardless of the order in which the transactions had occurred, the borrowed funds had been used to refinance the taxpayer's capital account in the partnership[46] — an income-earning purpose that qualifies as "a direct, eligible use within the meaning of s. 20(1)(c)(i) of the Act."[47] Dissenting, LeBel J. (Bastarache J. concurring) insisted that the statutory language in subparagraph 20(1)(c)(i) itself suggests a broader inquiry into the economic realities of the transactions,[48] on the basis of which it followed that the borrowed funds were in fact used to finance the purchase of the taxpayer's residence.[49]

Although the current author is inclined to agree with the dissent,[50] the crucial point for this article is not the merits of each decision, but the manner in which each was reached and the distinction between the majority's

---

43 *Singleton*, above note 8, at para. 31. See also *ibid.* at paras. 41–42, dismissing Dickson C.J.C.'s response to the hypothetical transaction contemplated in *Bronfman Trust* as *obiter dicta* and "more musing than jurisprudence."

44 *Ibid.* at para. 34.

45 *Ibid.* at para. 39: "If a direct link can be drawn between the borrowed money and an eligible use, then the money was used for the purpose of earning income from a business or property." See also para. 26, referring to the Supreme Court of Canada decisions in *Bronfman Trust* and *Shell Canada*, and para. 34, adopting Rothstein J.A.'s conclusion in *Singleton*, above note 41, at para. 54, that "Treating the borrowed funds as used for financing the purchase of the home, ignores what the appellant actually did, i.e. use the borrowed funds to replace the funds required for his capital account in the firm."

46 *Singleton*, above note 8, at paras. 32–34.

47 *Ibid.* at para. 43.

48 *Ibid.* at para. 53: "it is not at all clear that the statutory language itself requires us to consider two transactions in isolation from one another."

49 *Ibid.* at para. 87.

50 As the dissenting opinion rightly observes, the application of subparagraph 20(1)(c)(i) depends on the manner in which a court interprets the requirement that borrowed funds be used for the purpose of earning income. Having regard to economic realities for this purpose is not only compatible with the language of the provision but better suited than the formalist approach to the scheme and purposes of the Act and the likely intentions of Parliament to limit deductions to circumstances in which taxpayers incur expenses for the genuine purpose of earning income. Nor does a reference to economic reality involve a re-characterization of legal relationships, which instead constitute the framework for a more searching inquiry into the taxpayer's true economic purpose in using borrowed funds.

approach and the Court's earlier judgment in *Bronfman Trust*. While the dissenting judgment favours a broad contextual approach to the interpretation of the *Act*,[51] the majority relies on a presumed "plain meaning" to conclude that courts "must simply apply s. 20(1)(c)(i) rather than search for the economic realities of the transaction."[52] More importantly, whereas the dissent follows the substantive approach endorsed in *Bronfman Trust* by looking at the economic realities of the transactions,[53] the majority's conclusion that the taxpayer's "transactions must be viewed independently" in order to "give effect to the legal relationships" affirms the very "epitome of formalism" that the Court explicitly rejected in *Bronfman Trust*.[54] In each respect, it is impossible to reconcile the majority judgment in *Singleton* with the Court's prior decision in *Bronfman Trust*.

4) *Ludmer*

In *Ludmer*, as in *Singleton*, the taxpayers carried out a number of transactions the purpose of which, in part at least, was to reduce tax through the deduction of interest expenses. Between September 1977 and June 1979, the taxpayers borrowed approximately $6.5 million which was used to acquire shares in two offshore companies, the declared goals of which were to accumulate earnings for reinvestment, the activities of which involved investing in Canadian and U.S. withholding-tax-exempt debt securities or fixed-income securities, and the investments in which were structured to avoid the *Act*'s Foreign Accrual Property Income ("FAPI") rules as they then read.[55] When the FAPI rules were amended in 1984, the taxpayers disposed of their shares, realizing capital gains of $9.24 million.[56] Over the eight

---

51 *Singleton*, above note 8, at paras. 59–68.

52 *Ibid.* at para. 31. As suggested by my comments in note 50, it is not clear that the formalistic interpretation adopted by the majority in *Singleton* represents a more obvious or "plain" reading of the statutory language in subparagraph 20(1)(c)(i) than the substantive approach favoured in *Bronfman Trust*. For critical evaluations of the plain meaning approach more generally, see Arnold, "Statutory Interpretation: Some Thoughts on Plain Meaning" above note 7; and Duff, "Interpreting the *Income Tax Act* — Part 2" above note 4, at 769–79.

53 *Ibid.* at paras. 54–58 and 70–87.

54 See above text accompanying note 23. To repeat the argument in note 50 above, the substantive approach does not disregard or re-characterize valid legal relationships that taxpayers may have established, but relies upon these legal relationships to answer a deeper question regarding the taxpayer's true economic purpose in using borrowed funds.

55 See the account of these facts in *Ludmer*, above note 7, at paras. 4-12.

56 *Ibid.* at paras. 17–18.

years during which they held the shares, they had received approximately $600,000 in dividends and incurred interest expenses of $6 million.[57]

In 1986 and 1987, the Minister reassessed the taxpayers in respect of their 1981 to 1985 taxation years, disallowing the deduction of interest expenses incurred during these years on the basis that the borrowed funds were used not for the purpose of earning income from a business or property as required by subparagraph 20(1)(c)(i), but to defer taxes and convert income into capital gains.[58] The assessment was upheld by the Tax Court of Canada,[59] by the Federal Court Trial Division,[60] and again by a majority of the Federal Court of Appeal.[61] The taxpayer appealed to the Supreme Court of Canada.

In a unanimous decision, the Court allowed the taxpayer's appeal, concluding that the borrowed funds had indeed been used for the purpose of earning income within the meaning of the *Act*. This conclusion, which is strikingly at odds with the Court's express views in *Bronfman Trust*,[62] turns on its interpretation of the income-earning purpose requirement and the word "income" in subparagraph 20(1)(c)(i).

Beginning with the income-earning purpose requirement, the Minister had relied on the Court's judgment in *Bronfman Trust* to contend that taxpayers must have a "*bona fide* purpose" in using borrowed funds to earn income from a business or property in order to qualify for the interest deduction under subparagraph 20(1)(c)(i). As the offshore companies paid little in the way of dividends, operating under a declared policy whereby they accumulated earnings for reinvestment, the Minister reasoned, the taxpayers' real purpose in using the borrowed funds was not to earn income from a business or property, but "to defer taxes and convert income into capital gains."[63]

Writing for the Court, Iacobucci J. (Gonthier, Major, Bastarache, Binnie, Arbour and LeBel JJ., concurring) rejected the Minister's argument for six reasons. First, he declared, since "Dickson C.J.'s suggestion [in *Bronfman Trust*] that a *bona fide* purpose test should apply was made as a passing comment and did not result from an analysis of the text of the provision" it should not be regarded as "a rule of law."[64] Second, he contin-

57 *Ibid.* at para. 18.
58 *Ibid.* at para. 19.
59 [1993] 2 C.T.C. 2492, 93 D.T.C. 1274 (T.C.C.).
60 [1998] 2 C.T.C. 104, 98 D.T.C. 6045 (F.C.T.D.).
61 [1999] 3 C.T.C. 601, 99 D.T.C. 5153 (F.C.A.).
62 See text accompanying notes 19–20 and accompanying text.
63 *Ludmer*, above note 7, at para. 19.
64 *Ibid.* at para. 49.

ued, "[a]part from the use of the definite article 'the' [in subparagraph 20(1)(c)(i) to refer to the taxpayer's purpose in using the borrowed funds], . . . nothing in the text of the provision indicates that the requisite purpose must be the exclusive, primary or dominant purpose, or that multiple purposes are to be somehow ranked in importance in order to determine the taxpayer's 'real' purpose."[65] On the contrary, he suggested, "it is perfectly consistent with the language of s. 20(1)(c)(i) that a taxpayer who uses borrowed money to make an investment for more than one purpose may be entitled to deduct interest charges provided that one of those purposes is to earn income."[66] Consequently, he continued, reading such a test into subparagraph 20(1)(c)(i) would involve inappropriate "judicial innovation and rule making" by requiring "a rewriting of the provision to introduce a concept of degree, exclusivity, or primacy in the taxpayer's purposes."[67] Moreover, he added, a *bona fide* purpose test would force courts to consider the "economic realities" of the investments at issue, causing them "to stray from the express terms of s. 20(1)(c)(i) and supplement the provision with extraneous policy concerns that are said to form part of its purpose."[68] Finally, he insisted, "the application of any such test is impractical in the context of investments in securities" and "would open the door to many reassessments and in each case impose on taxpayers a tremendous burden to justify that their real or dominant purpose was to earn income."[69] As a result, he concluded, "a taxpayer's ancillary purpose may be . . . equally capable of providing the requisite purpose for interest deductibility in comparison with any more important or significant primary purpose."[70]

With respect to the meaning of the word "income" in subparagraph 20(1)(c)(i), the Minister had argued that it should be understood as profit or net income, after deducting interest expenses, rather than gross income irrespective of the interest expenses incurred. On this basis, it followed, since the expected and actual interest expenses greatly exceeded expected and actual dividend income, the interest deduction should be disallowed even under the ancillary purpose test adopted by the Court.

---

65 *Ibid.* at para. 50.

66 *Ibid.*

67 *Ibid.* at para. 53.

68 *Ibid.* at para. 64.

69 *Ibid.* at para. 53.

70 *Ibid.* at para. 51. See also *ibid.* at para. 54, adding that courts should "go about identifying whether the requisite purpose of earning income is present" by asking "whether, considering all the circumstances, the taxpayer had a reasonable expectation of income at the time the investment is made."

Rejecting this argument, Iacobucci J. advanced six reasons why the word "income" in subparagraph 20(1)(c)(i) should be understood as gross income rather than net income. First, he began, "[t]he *Income Tax Act* does not define the term 'income,'" referring to "net income" "taxable income" and "income from different sources," but neither identifying nor describing "the legal characteristics of 'income'."[71] Second, he declared, neither the "plain meaning of s. 20(1)(c)(i)" nor "the text of the Act" supports "an interpretation of 'income' as the equivalent of 'profit' or 'net income'."[72] In any event, he maintained, "[s]uch an approach would be too subjective and certainty is to be preferred in the area of tax law."[73] Fourth, he reasoned, the explicit exclusion from the deduction in subparagraph 20(1)(c)(i) of interest on borrowed money used to acquire property the income from which is tax-exempt makes it "clear that 'income' in s. 20(1)(c)(i) refers to income generally, that is an amount that would come into income for taxation purposes, not just net income."[74] Fifth, he continued, as "amendments to the Act that would have restricted interest deductibility to circumstances where borrowed money is used for the purpose of making a profit were proposed [in 1981 and 1991] but never enacted," his opinion was "bolstered . . . by . . . other evidence of Parliamentary intention."[75] Finally, he added, reading "income" in subparagraph 20(1)(c)(i) as gross income rather than net income "is more consistent with the objective the interest deductibility provision . . . to create an incentive to accumulate . . . income producing capital [that] creates wealth and increases the income tax base."[76] As a result, he concluded, "where a taxpayer uses borrowed money for a purpose yielding a reasonable expectation of [gross] income from business or property . . . , the interest charges incurred will fall within the ambit of s. 20(1)(c)(i) and

71 *Ibid.* at para. 57.

72 *Ibid.* at para. 59, adding: "Nowhere in the language of the provision is a quantitative test suggested. Nor is there any support in the text of the Act for an interpretation of 'income' that involves a judicial assessment of the sufficiency of income."

73 *Ibid.*

74 *Ibid.* at para. 61.

75 *Ibid.* at para. 62, adding: "If Parliament had intended interest to be deductible only in circumstances where borrowed money was used for the purpose of earning 'net income,' it could have expressly said so."

76 *Ibid.* at para. 63, adding that: "It is clearly sufficient for the purpose of the provision that an investor have a reasonable expectation of gross income . . . when investing borrowed money. In contrast, the incentive would be much less effective if the investor bore the additional burden of establishing a reasonable expectation of net income or profit."

77 *Ibid.* at para. 65.

are deductible."[77] Consequently, it followed, the taxpayers could deduct the interest expenses that they had incurred on the borrowed funds.

As the primary aim of this article is to document the Supreme Court of Canada's return to the narrow approach of earlier tax jurisprudence, this is not the place to engage in a detailed critique of the decision in *Ludmer*. That said, one might question the Court's failure to seriously consider the role of the definite article "the" in subparagraph 20(1)(c)(i)[78] its failure to attend to the phrase "income from a business or property" which is defined in net terms in subsection 9(1) as "the taxpayer's profit from that business or property,"[79] and its odd conclusion that permitting the deduction of interest expenses vastly in excess of any income that can reasonably be expected to be earned from the use of borrowed funds somehow serves the purpose of the interest deduction to "create an incentive to accumulate . . . *income producing* capital [that] creates wealth and *increases the income tax base*."[80]

As important as the actual decision in *Ludmer*, however, is the Court's clear rejection of the broad and substantive approach favoured in *Bronfman Trust*. With respect to statutory interpretation, for example, the Court consistently relies on the presumed "plain meaning" of subparagraph 20(1)(c)(i),[81] notwithstanding that it initially affirms the words-in-total-context approach

---

78 See text accompanying note 66. Although Iacobucci J. acknowledges that the use of the definite article "the" might suggest that "the requisite purpose must be the exclusive, primary or dominant purpose," he dismisses this possibility as "hardly conclusive of the issue before us," concluding on this basis that affirmation of a *bona fide* purpose test would require "a rewriting of the provision." *Ludmer*, above note 7, at paras. 50 and 53. At the same time, the Court adopts an ancillary purpose test which effectively rewrites subparagraph 20(1)(c)(i) to require only that "a" purpose for which the borrowed money is used must be to earn income.

79 While the *Act* does use the word "income" in the sense of gross income as well as net income, the specific phrase "income from a business or property" generally denotes the net sense of the word, as confirmed by subsection 9(1). That subparagraph 20(1)(c)(i) specifically excludes the deduction of interest on "borrowed money used to acquire property the income from which would be exempt . . ." supports this interpretation by using a different verbal formulation.

80 *Ludmer*, above note 7, at para. 65 [emphasis added]. In practice, of course, tax arbitrage transactions like those carried out by the taxpayers in *Ludmer decrease* the tax base by generating fully deductible interest expenses in current years and partly taxable capital gains in subsequent years.

81 See, e.g., *ibid.* at para. 50 (referring to the "purpose" test) and para. 59 (referring to the meaning of the word "income"). See also *ibid.* at para. 64 (rejecting any reference to "economic realities" on the basis that "where the provision at issue is clear and unambiguous, the court's duty is to simply apply its terms to the transaction at issue"). As the comments in the previous paragraph suggest, the meaning of a statutory text is rarely as "plain" as the advocates of this interpretive approach often suppose.

reflected in Driedger's "modern rule."[82] On this basis, it adopts a decidedly formalistic approach to the statutory requirements for interest deductibility, concluding that taxpayers may deduct interest expenses on borrowed funds whenever they have a "reasonable expectation" of at least some revenue at the time when the borrowed funds are invested.[83] Whether this rule accords with the text and purpose of subparagraph 20(1)(c)(i) is, as the previous paragraph suggests, doubtful. That it directly contradicts the substantive approach favoured in *Bronfman Trust* is certain.

C. THE REASONABLE EXPECTATION OF PROFIT TEST: FROM *MOLDOWAN* TO *STEWART* AND *WALLS*

While the deduction of interest expenses is governed by a specific statutory provision, the reasonable expectation of profit (REOP) test is a judicial creation. Though the words "reasonable expectation of profit" appear in the statutory definition of "personal or living expenses" in subsection 248(1) of the Act, the deduction of which in computing a taxpayer's income from a business or property is prohibited by paragraph 18(1)(h), the use of the test relates to the characterization of a business or property as a source of income losses from which may be deducted in computing a taxpayer's aggregate net income under paragraph 3(d). In *Moldowan*, the Supreme Court of Canada adopted a broad understanding of the REOP test as a general requirement for the characterization of a business as a source of income. In subsequent decisions, the Federal Court of Appeal affirmed the test's general application to the characterization of a business or property as a source of income,[84] embracing the REOP test as a general rule aimed at preventing "inappropriate tax avoidance" such as the deduction of losses resulting from a hobby or other personal endeavour.[85] In *Stewart* and *Walls*,

82 *Ibid.* at paras. 36-37. For a detailed discussion of the words-in-total-context approach, see Duff, "Interpreting the *Income Tax Act* — Part 1" above note 4, at 518–32, and Duff, "Interpreting the *Income Tax Act* — Part 2" above note 4, at 779-87. For an account of the various interpretive elements that enter into the words-in-total-context approach, see D. G. Duff, *Canadian Income Tax Law*, (Toronto: Emond-Montgomery in association with the Canadian Tax Foundation, 2003) at 74–95.

83 *Ludmer*, above note 7, at para. 54.

84 See *Landry v. Canada*, [1995] 2 C.T.C. 3, 94 D.T.C. 6624 (F.C.A.) at para. 5; *Tonn v. Canada*, [1996] 1 C.T.C. 205, 96 D.T.C. 6001 (F.C.A.) at paras. 36–37; and *Mastri v. The Queen*, [1997] 3 C.T.C. 234, 97 D.T.C. 5420 (F.C.A.) at para. 9.

85 *Tonn v. Canada*, above note 84, at para. 41. See also *ibid.* at para. 46, characterizing the REOP test as "a useful tool by which the tax-inappropriateness of an activity may be reasonably inferred when other, more direct forms of evidence are lacking."

the Court rejected this broad formulation of the REOP test, narrowing the scope of its application to circumstances in which the taxpayer engages in an activity having an identifiable "personal element."

1) *Moldowan*

In *Moldowan*, the taxpayer was a Vancouver businessman who sought to deduct losses from farming operations of approximately $21,000 in computing his aggregate net income for each of his 1968 and 1969 taxation years. Applying the restricted farm loss provision in then subsection 13(1) of the 1952 *Income Tax Act* [now subsection 31(1) of the *Act*], the Minister limited the deductions to $5,000 for each year. On appeal to the Supreme Court of Canada, the sole question was whether the taxpayer's "chief source of income" for the taxation years at issue was farming or "a combination of farming and some other source of income."[86] If answered in the affirmative, the provision would not apply and the deductions would not be limited; if answered in the negative, the provision would apply and the deductions would be limited to $5,000 for each taxation year.

Writing for the Court, Dickson J. (as he then was) identified two paradoxes in the provision that required statutory interpretation. On the one hand, he observed, if a farming loss incurred in a taxpayer's taxation year were to preclude farming from being the taxpayer's chief source of income for that year, the restriction would always apply.[87] On the other hand, he explained, if the "combination of farming and some other source of income" were understood as the "simple addition of two sources of income," the restriction would never apply since "a taxpayer could combine his farming loss with his most important other source of income, thereby constituting his chief source."[88] In either event, the words limiting the restriction to cases in which the taxpayer's chief source of income "is neither farming nor a combination of farming and some other source of income" would be rendered meaningless.

Rejecting the taxpayer's argument that the provision was indeed meaningless,[89] Dickson J. began by addressing the meaning of the words "source of income."[90] Affirming that a taxpayer must have "a profit or a rea-

86 *Moldowan*, above note 4, at para. 8.

87 *Ibid.* at para. 10.

88 *Ibid.* at para. 15.

89 *Ibid.* at para. 3, responding that: "We must endeavour to construe the language of Parliament. It is not an impossible task."

90 *Ibid.* at para. 10: "the only way in which the section can have meaning is to place emphasis on the words 'source of income'."

sonable expectation of profit" in order to have a business source of income,[91] he concluded that a taxpayer's "chief source" of income is "decidedly not a pure quantum measurement" but depends on "the taxpayer's reasonable expectation of income from his various revenue sources and his ordinary mode and habit of work."[92] On this basis, it followed, a taxpayer whose chief source of income is farming can reasonably expect to rely on farming "to provide the bulk of income" and "the centre of work routine,"[93] while a taxpayer whose chief source of income is "a combination of farming and some other source of income" looks to farming as a "major preoccupation" while also having "other pecuniary interests . . . such as income from investments, or income from a sideline employment or business."[94] As a result, Dickson J. held, the *ITA* "envisages three classes of farmers": (1) those who look to farming for their livelihoods, who are free from the statutory limit on the deduction of farming losses; (2) those who do not look to farming or farming and a subordinate source of income for their livelihoods, but carry on farming as a sideline business, who are subject to the statutory limit; and (3) those who carry on farming activities as a hobby, for whom losses are "not deductible in any amount."[95] Concluding that the taxpayer fell into the second of these categories, the Court upheld the Minister's assessment.

For the purposes of this article, the significance of the Supreme Court of Canada decision in *Moldowan* lies not in its interpretation of the restricted farm loss provision, but in its interpretive approach and its understanding of a business as a source of income. Rejecting a literal interpretation of a taxpayer's "chief source of income" as "a pure quantum measurement,"[96] Dickson J. adopted a substantive approach to the characterization of a business source and a chief source of income, emphasizing the commercial and economic realities of a taxpayer's activities rather than purely formal characteristics. For an activity to qualify as a business source of income, therefore, he held that there must be objective evidence of business activity in the form of actual profitability or a reasonable expectation of profit.[97] Similarly, he concluded, characterization as a taxpayer's "chief source of

---

91 *Ibid.* at para. 11, citing *Dorfman v. M.N.R.*, [1972] C.T.C. 151, 72 D.T.C. 6131 (F.C.T.D.).
92 *Moldowan*, above note 4, at para. 13.
93 *Ibid.* at para. 15.
94 *Ibid.* at para. 17.
95 *Ibid.* at para. 16.
96 *Ibid.* at para. 13.
97 *Ibid.* at para. 11. See also para. 12, characterizing the REOP test as "an objective determination to be made from all of the facts."

income" turns on objectively determinable economic criteria such as "the taxpayer's reasonable expectation of income from his various revenue sources and his ordinary mode and habit of work."[98] As the result, as the Federal Court of Appeal subsequently suggested, the REOP test can be viewed as "an early harbinger of the modern approach to tax statutes."[99]

2) Post-*Moldowan* Cases

In the years after *Moldowan*, the revenue authorities relied on the REOP test to disallow the deduction of losses on numerous occasions — mostly in cases involving a personal element in which the activity engaged in by the taxpayer could be characterized as a hobby or other personal endeavour, but also in other cases involving ostensibly commercial activities.[100] In a number of cases decided in the mid-1990s, the Federal Court of Appeal affirmed the REOP test's broad application to the characterization of a business or property as a source of income,[101] upholding the use of the test to disallow the deduction of losses on several occasions,[102] but rejecting its application on others.[103] The most important of these decisions is *Tonn v. Canada*.[104]

In *Tonn*, the taxpayer purchased a vacant residential property in August 1989 for $245,000 with the stated purpose of earning rental income, financing the purchase by assuming an existing mortgage on the property of $168,000, mortgaging his own principal residence for $50,000, and borrowing the remainder interest-free. When revenues did not increase as anticipated and expenses were higher than forecasted, the taxpayer experienced losses in each of the taxation years 1989, 1990 and 1991. Although the operation became profitable in 1992 after the taxpayer discharged the mortgage on his principal residence and the interest-free loan was convert-

---

98 *Ibid.* at para. 13.

99 *Tonn v. Canada*, above note 84, at para. 40.

100 For an extensive review of these cases, see *Tonn v. Canada*, above note 84, at paras. 47–60. See also the discussion of cases in S. Silver, "Great Expectations: Are They Reasonable?" in *Real Estate Transactions: Tax Planning for the Second Half of the 1990s*, 1995 Corporate Management Tax Conference (Toronto: Canadian Tax Foundation, 1996) 6:1-21; and J.R. Owen, "The Reasonable Expectation of Profit Test: Is There a Better Approach?" (1996) 44:4 Can. Tax J. 979–1015.

101 See *Landry v. Canada*, above note 84, at para. 5; *Tonn v. Canada*, above note 84, at paras. 36–37; and *Mastri v. The Queen*, above note 84, at para. 9.

102 *Landry v. Canada*, above note 84; *Hugill v. Canada*, [1995] 2 C.T.C. 16, 95 D.T.C. 5311 (F.C.A.); *Poetker v. M.N.R.*, [1996] 1 C.T.C. 202, 95 D.T.C. 5614 (F.C.A.); and *Mastri v. The Queen*, above note 84.

103 See, e.g., *Tonn v. Canada*, above note 84.

104 Above note 84 [*Tonn*].

ed into an equity interest, the Minister disallowed the deduction of rental losses in computing the taxpayer's income for each of the taxation years 1989, 1990 and 1991. The assessment was upheld by the Tax Court of Canada,[105] but reversed by the Federal Court of Appeal on the grounds that the activity was "purely commercial" involving no element of personal satisfaction,[106] that the taxpayer was not a sophisticated investor who could be expected to foresee that a profit was unlikely,[107] and that the enterprise should have been given more time to become profitable.[108]

For the purposes of this article, the specific decision in *Tonn* is of less importance than the Court's understanding of the REOP test, specifically its origins, its purpose, and its scope. With respect to its origins, the Court concluded, the test derived not merely from the statutory definition of "personal or living expenses" in subsection 248(1) of the Act, but also from "the principles and purposes of the Act" which generally oppose "inappropriate tax avoidance."[109] With respect to its purpose, the Court held, the REOP test was "ideally suited to situations where a taxpayer is attempting to avoid tax liability by inappropriate structuring of his or her affairs."[110] As a result, it followed, the scope of the test should extend not only to cases in which a taxpayer attempts to deduct "the costs of what are essentially hobby or personal expenses,"[111] but also to other circumstances in which taxpayers engage in tax-motivated transactions contrary to the purposes of the Act.[112]

---

105 *Tonn v. Canada*, [1995] 2 C.T.C. 2979 (T.C.C.).

106 *Tonn*, above note 84, at para. 70.

107 *Ibid.* at paras. 71–72.

108 *Ibid.* at paras. 73–74.

109 *Ibid.* at paras. 40–41. See also *ibid.* at para. 41, emphasizing that "the Act's fundamental purposes are not easily construed as contemplating such tax avoidance."

110 *Ibid.* at para. 42. See also *ibid.* at para. 46, characterizing the test as "a useful tool by which the tax-inappropriateness of an activity may be reasonably inferred when other, more direct forms of evidence are lacking."

111 *Ibid.* at para. 41.

112 See, e.g., *ibid.* at para. 42, citing *Moloney v. Canada*, 1992] 2 C.T.C. 227, 92 D.T.C. 6570 (F.C.A.), in which the Court disallowed the deduction of expenses incurred to obtain a tax refund. A better example, perhaps, is *Quebec (Deputy Minister of Revenue) v. Lipson*, [1979] C.T.C. 247 (S.C.C.), in which the taxpayer sought to deduct losses arising from a rental arrangement through which the taxpayer and others sought to extract rental losses from a corporation in which they had invested. Although the losses were incurred in the context of a commercial transaction, the Court disallowed the deduction on the basis that they did not result from a genuine business operation but from a "disadvantageous contract" providing no reasonable expectation of profit. See also *Tonn*, above note 84, at para. 53, emphasizing that the REOP test has "a role" to play even in "situations where the taxpayer's motive for the activity lacks any element of personal benefit, and where the activity cannot be classified as a hobby." Nonethe-

Like the Supreme Court of Canada judgments in *Bronfman Trust* and *Moldowan*, therefore, the Federal Court of Appeal decision in *Tonn* adopted a broad approach to the interpretation of the Act and a substantive approach to the application of the statutory and judicial rules, having regard to commercial and economic realities and the inequity of "inappropriate tax avoidance."[113]

3) *Stewart*

As in *Tonn*, the taxpayer in *Stewart* incurred repeated rental losses on residential properties the acquisition of which had been financed almost entirely with borrowed funds. Unlike *Tonn*, however, where an unsophisticated investor in a vacant residential property both anticipated and realized a profit after three years, the taxpayer in *Stewart* was "an experienced real estate investor" who acquired four condominium units in 1986 as part of a syndicated real estate development which promised a turnkey operation and management and projected negative cash flow and rental losses for a ten year period.[114] Although losses were anticipated, the actual experience was worse than projected, causing the taxpayer to reduce the extent of debt financing beginning in 1991 and obtain new management in 1995 and 1996. When the taxpayer claimed rental losses of $27,814 in 1990, $18,673 in 1991 and $12,306 in 1992, most of which resulted from the deduction of interest expenses on money borrowed to acquire the units, the Minister disallowed the deduction on the basis that the taxpayer had no reasonable expectation of profit.

The assessment was upheld by the Tax Court of Canada,[115] which concluded that the investments "held out no expectation of profit from rental income," but were structured "to use rental losses to offset other income and realize a gain at the end of the day from the expected appreciation in the value of the property."[116] The Federal Court of Appeal affirmed this deci-

---

less, the Court concluded, "when the circumstances do not admit of any suspicion that a business loss was made for a personal or non-business motive, the test should be applied sparingly and with a latitude favouring the taxpayer, whose business judgment may have been less than competent." *Ibid.* at para. 46. See also *ibid.* at para. 61, emphasizing that the "primary use" of the REOP test is "the prevention of inappropriate reductions in tax," not "as a vehicle for the wholesale judicial second-guessing of business judgments."

113 *Ibid.* at para. 41.

114 *Stewart*, above note 9, at paras. 7–9.

115 *Stewart v. The Queen*, [1998] 3 C.T.C. 2662, 98 D.T.C. 1600 (T.C.C.).

116 *Ibid.* at para. 20.

sion,[117] rejecting the taxpayer's argument that the REOP test "has no application unless the particular activity or property has an element of personal use,"[118] and accepting the Tax Court's conclusion that "the expectation from the acquisition and holding of the property was a capital gain from its disposition at the end of the projected holding period and not profit from the rental of the property."[119] The taxpayer appealed.

In a unanimous judgment, the Supreme Court of Canada allowed the taxpayer's appeal. Writing for the Court, Iacobucci and Bastarache JJ. began by reviewing the origins of the REOP test in *Moldowan* and pre-*Moldowan* cases,[120] and the application of the test in several post-*Moldowan* cases.[121] On this basis, they concluded, "[t]he only coherent message . . . is that the proper role of 'reasonable expectation of profit' is in need of clarification."[122] The rest of the decision identifies various problems with the REOP test,[123] outlines the Court's recommended approach to the characterization of a source of income,[124] and applies this approach to the facts of the case.[125]

With respect to the test itself, Iacobucci and Bastarache JJ. offered several reasons why a reasonable expectation of profit should not be viewed as a general test for the existence of a business or property as a source of income. First, they reasoned, since "Dickson J.'s *obiter* comments"[126] in *Moldowan* cited an earlier case in which the concept of a reasonable expectation of profit was employed to extend the concept of a source to circumstances in which there is no net income,[127] it followed that the test should be understood as a sufficient condition for a source of income, not a necessary requirement for a business or property source.[128] Second, they

117 *Stewart v. The Queen*, [2000] 2 C.T.C. 244, 2000 D.T.C. 6163 (F.C.A.).

118 *Ibid.* at para. 7. According to Rothstein J.A.: "We do not think *Moldowan* is necessarily so limited. The *Moldowan* principle is that in order to have a source of income, the taxpayer must have a profit or a reasonable expectation of profit. No subsequent Supreme Court authority has altered the *Moldowan* principle."

119 *Ibid.* at para. 10.

120 *Stewart*, above note 9, at paras. 21–25.

121 *Ibid.* at paras. 26–34.

122 *Ibid.* at para. 34.

123 *Ibid.* at paras. 35–47.

124 *Ibid.* at paras. 48–60.

125 *Ibid.* at paras. 61–69.

126 *Ibid.* at para. 36.

127 *Dorfman v. M.N.R.* [1972] C.T.C. 151 (F.C.T.D.).

128 *Stewart*, above note 9, at paras. 36–37, citing B.S. Nichols, "Chants and Ritual Incantations: Rethinking the Reasonable Expectation of Profit Test," in *Report of the Proceedings of the Forty-Eighth Tax Conference*, 1996 Conference Report (Toronto: Canadian Tax Foundation, 1997) 28:1 at 28:4-5; and Silver, "Great Expectations: Are They Reasonable?" above note 100, at 6:6-7.

observed, "equating the term 'business' with the phrase, 'reasonable expectation of profit' does not accord with the traditional common law definition of business, which is that "anything which occupies the time and attention and labour of a man for the purpose of profit is a business."[129] Third, they suggested, both the *Moldowan* decision and subsequent cases make it unclear whether the test was intended as "a broadly applicable source test" or "simply [to] distinguish . . . between mere hobbies and *bona fide* businesses."[130] Fourth, they continued, "the limited use of the phrase, 'reasonable expectation of profit'" in the definition of "personal or living expenses" in subsection 248(1) of the Act "does not support its use as a stand-alone source test."[131] As a result, they added, "the only way" to accept the REOP concept as a general source test "is to adopt an interpretive rule of law which is independent of the provisions of the Act" — an approach that would cross the line between legitimate judicial interpretation and inappropriate judicial rule-making.[132] Finally, they concluded, "even if one were to accept the use of the REOP test as a legitimate source of income standard, there are numerous practical difficulties which arise in its application that suggest that the test is ill-suited for the purpose"[133] — such as uncertainty as to what the test means by "profit,"[134] a tendency for the test to encourage retrospective application,[135] and significant variation in the application of the test according to the manner in which a venture is capitalized.[136] For all these reasons, the Court concluded, the REOP test "should

---

129 *Stewart*, above note 9, at para. 38, citing *Smith v. Anderson* (1880), 15 Ch. D. 247 (C.A.) at 258; and *Terminal Dock and Warehouse Co. v. M.N.R.*, [1968] 2 Ex.. C.R. 78, aff'd 68 D.T.C. 5316 (S.C.C.).

130 *Stewart*, above note 9, at para. 39, observing that "in the same paragraph where Dickson J. equates a business with a reasonable expectation of profit, he states '[i]f the taxpayer in operating his farm is merely indulging in a hobby, with no reasonable expectation of profit, he is disentitled to claim any deduction at all in respect of expenses incurred'."

131 *Ibid.* at para. 41.

132 *Ibid.* at para. 42. See also para. 43, citing the Court's earlier statement in *Candarel Ltd. v. Canada*, [1998] 1 S.C.R. 147, at para. 41, that "[t]he law of income tax is sufficiently complicated without unhelpful judicial incursions into the realm of lawmaking."

133 *Stewart*, above note 9, at para. 43.

134 *Ibid.* at para. 44, questioning "whether the capacity for profit should be determined after taking into account depreciation and, if so, whether capital cost allowance or accounting depreciation should be used," as well as "how much expected profit [is] required, in what time frame, and whether the amount of expected profit should vary with the risk of the venture."

135 *Ibid.* at para. 45.

136 *Ibid.* at para. 46.

not be accepted as the test to determine whether a taxpayer's activities constitute a source of income."[137]

Turning to the Court's recommended approach to the characterization of a source of income, Iacobucci and Bastarache JJ. began by stating that this determination "must be grounded in the words and scheme of the Act."[138] On this basis, they concluded, "the issue of whether or not a taxpayer has a source of income is to be determined by looking at the commerciality of the activity in question."[139] More specifically, they emphasized, "[w]here the nature of an activity is clearly commercial, . . . a source of income by definition exists, and there is no need to take the inquiry any further."[140] In contrast, they held, "[w]here the activity could be classified as a personal pursuit, then it must be determined whether or not the activity is being carried on in a sufficiently commercial manner to constitute a source of income."[141] For this purpose only, they declared, could the courts rely on the concept of a reasonable expectation of profit — not as a "conclusive" test to assess commerciality but as one "factor" among others.[142]

Returning to the facts of the case, the Court had no difficulty concluding that the taxpayer was engaged in a commercial activity, as a result of which the rental units were characterized as a source of income. According to Iacobucci and Bastarache JJ.:

> In our view, a property rental activity which lacks any element of personal use or benefit to the taxpayer is clearly a commercial activity. . . . As a result, the appellant satisfies the test for a source of income.[143]

Nor did it matter that the investments were, as the Tax Court had concluded, structured "to use rental losses to offset other income and realize a gain at the end of the day from the expected appreciation in the value of the property,"[144] because:

---

137 *Ibid.* at para. 47.

138 *Ibid.* at para. 48.

139 *Ibid.* at para. 60.

140 *Ibid.* at para. 54, adding that "[s]uch endeavours necessarily involve the pursuit of profit." See also *ibid.* at para. 60: "Where the activity contains no personal element and is clearly commercial, no further inquiry is necessary."

141 *Ibid.* at para. 60. See also *ibid.* at para. 53, emphasizing that the Court's source test "will only require analysis in situations where there is some personal or hobby element to the activity in question."

142 *Ibid.* at para. 55.

143 *Ibid.* at para. 62.

144 *Stewart v. The Queen*, above note 115, at para. 20.

> [I]n our view, the motivation of capital gains accords with the ordinary business person's understanding of "pursuit of profit," and may be taken into account in determining whether the taxpayer's activity is commercial in nature.[145]

Consequently, the Court concluded, REOP test did not apply, and the taxpayer was allowed to deduct the rental losses for each of the taxation years at issue.[146]

As explained in the introduction to this chapter, the primary purpose of this analysis is not to criticize recent Supreme Court of Canada decisions but to contrast the broad and substantive approach to tax law that the Court employed from the late 1970s to the early 1990s with the literal and formalistic approach adopted in more recent tax jurisprudence. Nonetheless, one might reasonably challenge the Court's characterization of Dickson J.'s comments in *Moldowan* as *obiter*,[147] its conclusion that Dickson J. regarded the REOP test as a necessary condition for the existence of a business source of income,[148] its view that a general REOP test is incompatible with the traditional common law definition of a business,[149] and its odd conclusion that a source concept that is ostensibly "grounded in the words and scheme of the Act" should recognize the pursuit of capital gains in assessing the existence of a business or a property as a source of *income*.[150]

---

145 *Stewart*, above note 9 at para. 68.

146 *Ibid.* at para. 69.

147 *Ibid.* at para. 36. As the discussion of *Moldowan* earlier in this article suggests, the Court's understanding of a "source of income" was essential to its disposition of the case. See above notes 89–95 and accompanying text.

148 *Ibid.* at paras. 36–37. As Dickson J.'s actual words were that a taxpayer must have "a profit or a reasonable expectation of profit" in order to have a business source of income, it is clear that he did not regard a reasonable expectation as a necessary condition for every business. See above note 91 and accompanying text. Where an activity incurs a loss, however, Dickson J.'s formulation suggests that a reasonable expectation of profit is necessary for the activity to be characterized as a business.

149 *Stewart*, above note 9, at para. 38. As the Federal Court of Appeal suggested in *Tonn*, the REOP test does not contradict the common law definition of a business, but merely adds to the requirement of a subjective profit-making purpose an objective reasonable expectation of profit requirement in order to assess this subjective purpose "when other, more direct forms of evidence are lacking." See above note 110.

150 Emphasis added. See above notes 138 and 145 and accompanying text. As section 3 and the rest of Division B of Part I of the *ITA* make clear, the scheme of the Act distinguishes between a business or a property as a source of income or loss and a capital gain or loss from the disposition of property. See also subsection 9(3), which specifies, for the purposes of the Act, that "'income from a property' does not include any capital gains from the disposition of that property and 'loss from a property' does not include any capital loss from the disposition of that property."

For the purpose of this chapter, however, it is more important to contrast the understanding of the source concept and the REOP test in *Moldowan* and subsequent Federal Court of Appeal decisions with the approach adopted in *Stewart*. Whereas the former decisions affirmed a substantive approach to the characterization of a business or property as a source of income, emphasizing commercial and economic realities by requiring objective evidence of a subjective pursuit of profit in the form of actual profitability or a reasonable expectation of profit,[151] *Stewart* adopted a formalistic and categorical approach to the determination of a source of income by distinguishing "clearly commercial" activities from those with a "personal or hobby element" and regarding the concept of a reasonable expectation of profit as merely one factor to asses the commerciality of an activity.[152] The difference in judicial approaches is striking.

4) *Walls*

In *Walls*, the taxpayers invested in a limited partnership which had acquired a "mini-warehouse" under an agreement that was clearly structured to generate substantial tax losses that investors could use to offset other income.[153] At trial,[154] Pinard J. concluded that the partnership "was set up as a tax shelter, with the intention that the operation of the storage park would give rise to large initial losses in order to provide the limited partners with tax claims,"[155] and that "the only financial advantage that could reasonably have been expected by a purchaser of a limited partnership unit in this arrangement would have been by way of tax refunds as a result of claiming the inevitable losses from the arrangement."[156] On this basis, he disallowed the deduction of the taxpayers' share of the partnership losses on the basis that the investments had no reasonable expectation of profit and the losses lacked a source within the meaning of the *Act*. On appeal,[157] the Federal Court of Appeal reversed this decision on the grounds that the

151 See above, notes 96–99 and accompanying text.

152 See above, notes 139–41 and accompanying text.

153 For the purposes of this analysis, the details of the arrangement are not essential. In general, however, they involved a highly leveraged purchase at what may have been an exaggerated value, interest charges computed at a rate of 24 percent per annum, as well as substantial annual management and service fees. See *Walls*, above note 9, at paras. 2–4.

154 *Wallsv. Canada,* [1996] 2 C.T.C. 14, 96 D.T.C. 6142 (F.C.T.D.).

155 *Ibid.* at para. 17.

156 *Ibid.* at para. 19.

157 *Walls v. Canada*, [2000] 1 C.T.C. 324, 2000 D.T.C. 6025 (F.C.A.).

investment involved no "personal element" and that the taxpayers had purchased "an ongoing commercial business."[158] On appeal to the Supreme Court of Canada, the only issue was whether the storage park operation was a source of income for the purposes of the *Act*.[159]

Writing for a unanimous Court, Iacobucci and Bastarache JJ. had no difficulty concluding that the operation was a source of income the losses from which could be offset against other income. Relying on their concurrent judgment in *Stewart*, they began by commenting that the storage park was "self-evident[ly] . . . commercial in nature," and that "there was no evidence of any element of personal use or benefit in the operation."[160] As a result, it followed, the issue of a reasonable expectation of profit "does not arise for consideration."[161] Nor did it matter that the taxpayers "were clearly motivated by tax considerations" when they acquired their interests in the partnership, since "it is a well-established proposition that a tax motivation does not affect the validity of transaction for tax purposes."[162] For these reasons, the Court dismissed the appeal.[163]

The *Walls* decision adds little to the Court's concurrent judgment in *Stewart*, other than the simple confirmation that the Court's recommended approach to the characterization of a source of income applies notwithstanding any tax motivation on the part of taxpayers engaging in the relevant activity. In this respect, however, the case marks a further departure from the broad understanding of the REOP test in *Moldowan* and subsequent Federal Court of Appeal decisions, which the Court in *Tonn* considered "ideally suited to situations in which a taxpayer is attempting to avoid tax liability by inappropriate structuring of his or her affairs."[164] Emphasizing that courts "should not be quick to embellish provisions [in the *Act*] in response to tax avoidance concerns,"[165] the Court's approach in *Walls* could not differ more.

---

158 *Ibid.* at para. 1.

159 *Walls*, above note 9, at para. 18.

160 *Ibid.* at para. 20.

161 *Ibid.*

162 *Ibid.* at para. 22, citing among other decisions *Shell Canada*, above note 8; and *Antosko*, above note 7.

163 *Ibid.* at para. 23.

164 *Tonn*, above note 84, at para. 42.

165 *Walls*, above note 9 at para. 22.

D. CONCLUSION

The Supreme Court of Canada judgments in *Singleton*, *Ludmer*, *Stewart* and *Walls* represent the culmination of a return to the literalism and formalism that characterized Canadian tax jurisprudence until the 1970s. While the Court adopted a more purposive and substantive approach to tax statutes from the late 1970s to the early 1990s, this trend has been reversed over the past decade. As the differing approaches to the deduction of interest expenses and the REOP test make clear, the Court has rejected the broad and substantive approach of *Bronfman Trust* and *Moldowan*, adopting a modern version of strict construction in the form of a "plain meaning" rule and a formalist approach to the characterization of a taxpayer's transactions and activities.

Since different approaches to tax statutes reflect different underlying values, it is impossible to conclude that one or the other approach is "wrong" in any legal sense. While the substantive approach to interest deductibility and the REOP test reflects concerns about tax avoidance and tax equity,[166] the narrow approach adopted in recent Supreme Court of Canada tax decisions reflects concerns about the simplicity and predictability of tax rules and the appropriate roles of the courts and the legislature.[167] How one weights these different values is apt to shape one's preferred approach to tax statutes.

That said, one might question the extent to which the Court's current approach promotes enduring simplicity and certainty and truly defers to the supremacy of Parliament. On the contrary, as the decisions in *Singleton*, *Ludmer*, *Stewart* and *Walls* suggest, the Court seems willing not only to engage in considerable judicial innovation and rule-making but also to disregard both the words and the scheme of the Act in order to reverse earlier judgments with which it disagrees. As illustrated by the draft legislation released by the Department of Finance, moreover, a return to the literalism and formalism of earlier tax jurisprudence is apt to increase the complexity of Canadian income tax law by compelling Parliament to amend the *Act*

---

166 See, e.g., *Bronfman Trust*, above note 4, at para. 40, cited above at text accompanying note 29; and *Tonn*, above note 84, at paras. 4041, cited above at note 109 and accompanying text.

167 See, e.g., *Ludmer*, above note 7, at para. 53, emphasizing that "in matters of tax law, a court should always be reluctant to engage in judicial innovation and rule making"; and *ibid.* at para. 39, commenting that because the Act has "many specific anti-avoidance provisions . . . courts should not be quick to embellish the provisions of the Act in response to concerns about tax avoidance when it is open to Parliament to be precise and specific with respect to any mischief to be prevented."

in order to prevent the tax avoidance arrangements that this judicial approach facilitates.

Turning to the draft legislation, finally, it is clearly designed to limit the effect of *Stewart* and *Walls* by declaring in proposed subsection 3.1(1) that:

> A taxpayer has a loss for a taxation year from a source that is a business or property only if, in the year, it is reasonable to expect that the taxpayer will realize a cumulative profit from that business or property for the period in which the taxpayer has carried on, and can reasonably be expected to carry on, that business or has held, and can reasonably be expected to hold, that property,

by stipulating in proposed subsection 3.1(2) that "[f]or the purpose of subsection (1), profit is determined without reference to capital gains or capital losses," and by amending subsection 9(3) to read "[i]n this Act, income or loss from a business or property does not include any capital gain or capital loss." As these decisions left open the use of a reasonable expectation of profit concept to distinguish between commercial activities and hobbies or personal endeavours, the aim of this provision is presumably to prevent tax shelter arrangements like those in *Walls*, where the economic advantage to the taxpayer results from the deduction of tax losses rather than the return on the investment, as well as transactions like those in *Ludmer* and *Stewart*, where the investment is structured to produce net income losses (typically from the deduction of interest expenses) and subsequent capital gains.

While one can sympathize with the purpose of the draft legislation to prevent these tax-motivated transactions, the solution seems unduly harsh, as the disallowed losses should properly be added to the capital cost of the business or property in order to compute subsequent capital gains or losses. As the key structural feature of the ITA that allows these transactions is the mismatch between currently deductible interest expenses and deferred and partly taxable capital gains, perhaps it is time to revisit the idea of capitalization rules for interest expenses incurred to earn capital gains.[168]

---

168 See the discussion in B.J. Arnold and T. Edgar, "Deductibility of Interest Expense" (1995) 43:5 Can Tax. J. 1216-44 at 1237–44.

Chapter Eighteen

GAAR and the Supreme Court of Canada: The Road to Nowhere

Daniel Sandler*

The general anti-avoidance rule in section 245 of the *Income Tax Act*[1] (affectionately known as GAAR) has been on the statute books for over 15 years. It has been the subject of approximately twenty court cases, eight of which have been decided by the Federal Court of Appeal.[2] The Supreme Court of

---

* I am grateful to Tim Edgar for his comments.

1 R.S.C. 1985, c. 1 (5th Supp.), as amended (herein referred to as "the Act"). Unless otherwise stated, statutory references in this chapter are to the Act.

2 The eight cases decided by the Federal Court of Appeal are: *OSFC Holdings Ltd. v. The Queen*, 2001 D.T.C. 5471, [2001] 4 C.T.C. 82 [*OSFC*]; *Canadian Pacific Ltd. v. The Queen*, 2002 D.T.C. 6472 [*CP*]; *Duncan v. The Queen*, 2002 D.T.C. 7172, [2002] 4 C.T.C. 1 [*Duncan*]; *Produits Forestiers Donohue Inc. v. The Queen*, 2002 D.T.C. 7512 [*Donohue*]; *Jabin Investments Ltd. v. The Queen*, 2003 D.T.C. 5027, [2003] 2 C.T.C. 25 [*Jabin*]; *Mathew et al. v. The Queen*, 2003 D.T.C. 5644, [2004] 1 C.T.C. 115 [*Mathew*]; *The Queen v. Imperial Oil Limited*, 2004 D.T.C. 6044, [2004] 2 C.T.C. 190 [*Imperial Oil*]; and *The Queen v. Canada Trustco Mortgage Company*, 2004 D.T.C. 6119 [*Canada Trustco*].

A ninth case decided by the Federal Court of Appeal, *S.T.B. Holdings Ltd. v. The Queen*, 2002 D.T.C. 7450, [2003] 1 C.T.C. 36 [*S.T.B.*], concerned a preliminary issue: whether subsection 245(7) of the Act requires that reference to GAAR be made on the face of the notice of assessment or reassessment [the court held that it did not, concluding that subsection 245(7) was applicable only to third parties seeking tax relief following a reassessment of another taxpayer under GAAR].

There are also a number of GAAR cases currently on appeal to the Federal Court of Appeal.

Canada recently granted leave in its first two GAAR cases.[3] This paper considers the judicial attitude to GAAR, specifically the approach that the Supreme Court of Canada will likely take in a GAAR case. In my view, the judicial attitude to GAAR is tied very much to the judicial attitude to tax avoidance generally and there appears to be little consensus among judges about the role, if any, of the judiciary in combating tax avoidance. Without giving too much away at the outset, the comments of Iacobucci and Bastarache, JJ. in the recent decision of *Stewart v. The Queen*[4] speak volumes about the approach that the Supreme Court of Canada will likely take to GAAR: there is "a distinction between judicial interpretation and judicial rule-making" and tax law "is sufficiently complicated without unhelpful judicial incursions into the realm of lawmaking."[5] These remarks seem to reflect the view of the Supreme Court of Canada regarding the judiciary's role in tax avoidance cases, which has been made abundantly clear in recent years: the court should not be quick to embellish provisions of the Act in response to concerns about tax avoidance; it is Parliament's job to be "precise and specific with respect to any mischief to be prevented."[6] And to conclude this train of thought, GAAR is hardly a model of precision or specificity.

A. "AND YOU MAY ASK YOURSELF — WELL . . . HOW DID I GET HERE?"[7]

Beginning with the 1984 decision in *Stubart Investments Ltd. v. The Queen,*[8] and more particularly in the past decade, the Supreme Court of Canada has emasculated virtually all judicial anti-avoidance doctrines, to the point where little remains beyond sham and legally ineffective transactions, both of

3 Leave to appeal was granted to the taxpayers in *Mathew*, [2003] S.C.C.A. No. 538 (June 24, 2004) and to the Crown in *Canada Trustco*, [2004] S.C.C.A. No. 157 (June 24, 2004). Previously, the Supreme Court of Canada denied leave to appeal (without reasons) in two substantive GAAR cases: *OSFC*, [2001] S.C.C.A. No. 522 (June 20, 2002) and *Duncan*, [2002] S.C.C.A. No. 386 (March 20, 2003) The Supreme Court of Canada also denied leave (without reasons) in *S.T.B.*, [2002] S.C.C.A. No. 513 (March 27, 2003).

4 2002 D.T.C. 6969, [2002] 3 C.T.C. 439 (S.C.C.) [*Stewart*].

5 *Ibid.*, at paras. 42–43.

6 *Ludco Enterprises Ltd. et al. v. The Queen*, 2001 D.T.C. 5505, [2002] 1 C.T.C. 95 (S.C.C.) [*Ludco*], at para. 39.

7 Talking Heads, "Once in a Lifetime," from the album, *Once in a Lifetime* (1984).

8 84 D.T.C. 6305, [1984] C.T.C. 294 (S.C.C.) [*Stubart*].

which are narrow in scope and easily avoided with proper planning.[9] At the same time, the Supreme Court has also undermined the scope of a number of more general statutory provisions that could play a roll in minimizing "abusive" tax avoidance, particularly the limitations on interest deduction in paragraph 20(1)(c) and the general expense limitation in section 67. The remainder of this section considers the demise of the various judicial doctrines and these two statutory provisions as effective anti-avoidance tools.

1) A General Business Purpose Test

In *Stubart*, the Supreme Court of Canada firmly rejected a general business purpose test for Canada. While rejecting a business purpose test, Estey, J. indicated that the "modern approach" to statutory interpretation applied to the Act (as it did to all other statutes in Canada) and that the "object and spirit" test that he espoused in that case would "reduce the attraction of elaborate and intricate tax avoidance plans, and reduce the rewards to those best able to afford the services of the tax technicians."[10]

2) The "Object and Spirit" Test

GAAR was introduced in the aftermath of *Stubart*,[11] suggesting that Parliament did not share Estey, J.'s view of the object and spirit test as an effec-

9 Sham is more closely tied to tax evasion than to tax avoidance. According to the Supreme Court of Canada in *Stubart* (at para. 50), sham is limited to its classic definition, from *Snook v. London & West Riding Investments Ltd.*, [1967] 2 Q.B. 786 at 802 (C.A.): "acts done or documents executed by the parties . . . which are intended by them to give to third parties or to the court the appearance of creating between the parties legal rights and obligations different from the actual legal rights and obligations (if any) which the parties intend to create." In essence, a sham involves an element of deceit on the part of the taxpayer. Even aggressive tax planning, properly structured, is not designed to deceive.

A legally ineffective transaction is a technically defective transaction: the taxpayer missed some essential legal formality when carrying out the transactions or the transactions were not carried out on a timely basis. Again, the doctrine is narrow in scope. Provided that the taxpayers create legally binding transactions and dot their "i"s and cross their "t"s, it is highly unlikely that the planning will be considered legally ineffective. How technically defective the transactions must be before the doctrine applies remains unclear. For example, in *Continental Bank of Canada v. The Queen*, 98 D.T.C. 6505, [1998] 4 C.T.C. 119 (S.C.C.) [*Continental Bank*], the fact that the bank was precluded from investing in a partnership under section 174(2)(i) of the *Bank Act* did not preclude the Supreme Court of Canada from concluding that a partnership existed.

10 *Stubart*, at para. 56.

11 See, generally, Brian J. Arnold and James R. Wilson, "The General Anti-Avoidance Rule — Part 1" (1988) 36: 4 Canadian Tax Journal 829 at 837–41.

tive anti-avoidance doctrine. Certainly taxpayers and their advisers became increasingly aggressive in the transactions that they undertook following *Stubart*. And indeed, the approach of the Supreme Court of Canada to tax avoidance cases (in pre-GAAR fact situations) in the 15-plus years since the introduction of GAAR has confirmed Parliament's misgivings. Despite the consistent reference to Driedger's principles of statutory interpretation in virtually every Supreme Court of Canada tax decision since *Stubart*, the court, particularly in the past decade, has indicated that the object and purpose of a provision is irrelevant where the meaning of the provision is "plain" or "clear and unambiguous." Unfortunately, this rationale has moved the judicial debate away from the purpose of statutory provisions to whether their meaning is plain. The Supreme Court of Canada decisions in *Friesen v. The Queen*[12] and *Singleton v. The Queen*[13] are classic examples. In both cases, the difference between the majority and dissenting opinions turned in part on whether the statutory provisions in issue had a plain meaning. As an independent judicial anti-avoidance principle — indeed, as a general principle of statutory interpretation — the "object and spirit" approach of Estey, J. has proved ineffective.

3) Economic Substance

"Economic substance" as a judicial doctrine is pretty much dead. The Supreme Court of Canada made that abundantly clear by in *Shell Canada Ltd. v. The Queen*.[14] There, McLachlin J. indicated:

> This court has repeatedly held that courts must be sensitive to the economic realities of a particular transaction, rather than being bound to what first appears to be its legal form. . . . But there are at least two caveats to this rule. First, this Court has never held that the economic realities of a situation can be used to recharacterize a taxpayer's *bona fide* legal relationships. To the contrary, we have held that, absent a specific provision of the Act to the contrary or a finding that they are a sham, a taxpayer's legal relationships must be respected in tax cases. Recharacterization is only permissible if the label attached by the taxpayer to the particular transaction does not properly reflect its actual legal effect. . . . Second, it is well-established in this Court's tax jurisprudence that a searching inquiry for either the "economic realities" of a particular transaction or the

12 95 D.T.C. 5551, [1995] 2 C.T.C. 369 (S.C.C.) [*Friesen*].

13 2001 D.T.C. 5533, [2002] 1 C.T.C. 121 (S.C.C.) [*Singleton*].

14 99 D.T.C. 5669, [1999] 4 C.T.C. 313 (S.C.C.) [*Shell*].

> general object and spirit of the provision at issue can never supplant a court's duty to apply an unambiguous provision of the Act to the taxpayer's transaction. Where the provision at issue is clear and unambiguous, its terms must simply be applied.[15]

Despite the Court's suggestion that these limitations are caveats to a general principle that economic realities must be considered, the limitations amount to a wholesale rejection of the principle. In effect, absent a sham, the legal substance of the transaction as documented by the taxpayer governs and there is no role for economic realities.[16]

4) Attacking Partnerships, a Common Vehicle Used in Aggressive Tax Planning Arrangements

In tax avoidance schemes involving partnerships, an argument often raised by the Minister is that no legally effective partnership was created because the essential ingredients of a partnership — a business carried on in common with a view to profit — did not exist. The effectiveness of this argument has been whittled away by the Supreme Court of Canada, as evidenced by cases such as *Continental Bank, Spire Freezers Ltd. v. The Queen*[17] and *Backman v. The Queen*.[18] First, the short length of time that a partnership is in existence is not a determinative issue. Second, it does not appear to take much to constitute a "business," and the receipt of passive income may be considered sufficient. And third is the court's interpretation of a "view to profit." Both *Spire Freezers* and *Backman* involved Canadians buying into US partnerships for the obvious purpose of accessing significant accrued but unrealized losses. In both cases, window dressing was

---

15 *Ibid.*, at paras. 39–40. As is discussed further below, the notion of a "clear and unambiguous" meaning has found its way into the GAAR lexicon.

16 Not all judges at the Supreme Court necessarily subscribe to this view. For example, LeBel J., in his dissent in *Singleton*, disagreed as to the scope of the caveats, although in doing so he defined *bona fide* legal relationships as something more than valid legal relationships that were not a sham. LeBel J. stated at para. 71, "Whether or not such a series of transactions constitutes a sham, they clearly do not constitute a set of *bona fide* legal relations. It is an undisputed finding of fact that the respondent funnelled money through his law firm simply to secure a tax advantage; his borrowing was not made with the *bona fide* purpose of generating income from his business." LeBel, J. seems to be resurrecting a business purpose test in order to evaluate a taxpayer's *bona fides* — at least in the context of the interest deduction under paragraph 20(1)(c) — notwithstanding that a general business purpose test was rejected in *Stubart*.

17 2001 D.T.C. 5158, [2001] 2 C.T.C. 40 (S.C.C.) [*Spire Freezers*].

18 2001 D.T.C. 5149, [2001] 2 C.T.C. 11 (S.C.C.) [*Backman*].

added in an attempt to support the legitimacy of the partnership structure, specifically the requirement that the partnership be carrying on a business with a view to profit. The window dressing in both cases was the acquisition of other income-producing property. In *Spire Freezers*, the window dressing was considered sufficient; in *Backman*, it was not. In my view, the notion of a "view to profit" or, more generally, a reasonable expectation of profit, requires *ex ante* evidence that over the life of the particular business or investment or at least over its reasonably projected future, it would be "in the black" on a net basis.[19] Otherwise, what is the point of going into business or making the investment (other than for tax purposes)? If, using reasonable criteria, it would be impossible for the business or investment to demonstrate overall profitability, the business is not carried on or the investment was not made with a view to profit. *Spire Freezers* and *Backman* proved me wrong. As Iacobucci and Bastarache JJ. stated in *Backman*: ". . . where a partnership is formed with the predominant motive of acquiring a tax loss, it is not necessary to show an intention to profit by the amount necessary to recoup the acquired losses or produce a net gain."[20] All that is necessary is to demonstrate that in future years there is expected to be an annual profit, even if it would be impossible to ever recoup the initial loss.[21]

5) Reasonable Expectation of Profit

Given the conclusions in *Spire Freezers* and *Backman*, it is not surprising that in the Supreme Court of Canada's latest foray into the anti-avoidance arena, it virtually eliminated the doctrine of "reasonable expectation of profit" (REOP). Before the Supreme Court of Canada released their judgments in *Stewart* and *Walls v. The Queen*,[22] I speculated that the decisions

19 Interestingly, that is the test adopted in proposed section 3.1, except that subsection 3.1(1) requires an annual reevaluation of expectations. See below, notes 31–33 and accompanying text.

20 *Backman*, at para. 24.

21 If that is the case, had the taxpayers in *Backman* bought a number of government bonds with the extra $5,000 invested rather than a one percent interest in an oil and gas property that flooded shortly after purchase and never showed a profit, the result in the case may well have been different.

22 2002 D.T.C. 6960, [2002] 3 C.T.C. 421 [*Walls*]. Both cases involved real estate tax shelters that generated significant losses that the taxpayers deducted against other sources of income. In *Stewart*, the taxpayer acquired four Reemark condominiums, each for $1,000 down and the balance fully financed. In *Walls*, the taxpayers were limited partners in a partnership that acquired a mini-warehouse. The partnership's purchase price was almost double what the vendor paid for the property a few months earlier and the price was completely financed (except for $1) with a high interest, vendor

were in little doubt: REOP, as a threshold test for determining whether a source of income exists in a pure commercial setting, was dead.[23] On May 23, 2002, the Supreme Court of Canada released the obituary. The decisions themselves are not surprising. REOP was built on a shaky foundation. Its source, the Supreme Court of Canada decision in *Moldowan v. The Queen*,[24] involved the application of the restricted farm loss provisions. That the taxpayer's activities in *Moldowan* constituted a business was not in dispute. However, Dickson J.'s obiter comment that "in order to have a 'source of income' the taxpayer must have a profit or a reasonable expectation of profit"[25] laid the cornerstone for one of the most important weapons in the anti-avoidance arsenal of the Canada Revenue Agency ("CRA"): deny the deductibility of losses because no source of income exists. But REOP went beyond tax avoidance, permitting the CRA to successfully reassess with hindsight commercial transactions with no tax avoidance element. It was used to deny losses from a law practice in *Landry v. The Queen*[26] and from a restaurant business in *Sirois v. The Queen*.[27] REOP should never have gained the prominence that it did.

Iacobucci and Bastarache JJ., writing for the Supreme Court of Canada in both *Stewart* and *Walls*, suggested a two-stage approach to the source question: 1) Is the activity undertaken in pursuit of profit, or is it a personal endeavour?; 2) If it is not a personal endeavour, is the source of income a business or property?[28] The first stage determines whether a source of income exists; if a source does exist, the second stage categorizes it. The Supreme Court of Canada concluded that in a pure commercial setting —

---

take-back loan. In *Stewart*, the taxpayer was reassessed solely on REOP. In *Walls*, the taxpayers were reassessed on a number of grounds including REOP, but the trial judge found for the Crown based on REOP and therefore did not deal with the other grounds for assessment (which challenged as excessive the purchase price paid by the partnership and the interest rate on the loan): 96 D.T.C. 6142 (F.C.T.D.). The taxpayers' appeals to the Federal Court of Appeal were allowed on the basis that REOP was inapplicable and the matter was referred back to the trial judge to reconsider the other grounds: 2000 D.T.C. 6025 (F.C.A.).

23 I made the prediction in my talk at the Department of Justice lunchtime seminar on February 7, 2002, upon which this chapter is based.

24 77 D.T.C. 5213, [1977] C.T.C. 310 (S.C.C.) [*Moldowan*].

25 *Ibid.*, at para. 11.

26 94 D.T.C. 6624, [1995] 2 C.T.C. 3 (F.C.A.).

27 88 D.T.C. 1114, [1988] 1 C.T.C. 2147 (T.C.C.).

28 Both cases concerned only the first stage. No comments were made on the second stage (characterizing the source) apart from the suggestion in *Stewart* (at para. 51) that "business income is generally distinguished from property income on the basis that a business requires an additional level of taxpayer activity."

i.e., one with no personal element — there is undoubtedly a source of income and REOP has no role to play. However, in situations that involve some personal or hobby element, it is necessary to determine whether "the venture is undertaken in a sufficiently commercial manner" to constitute a source of income.[29] In making this determination, REOP is one consideration. REOP has been successfully used as a basis to deny losses in a number of cases since *Stewart* and *Walls*, but in all cases there was an initial finding that there was some personal or hobby element in the activity under review.[30]

On October 31, 2003, the Minister of Finance released draft legislation that establishes a statutory REOP test.[31] Proposed subsection 3.1(1) will deny a taxpayer's loss for a taxation year from a business or property unless "in the year, it is reasonable to expect that the taxpayer will realize a cumulative profit from that business or property" over the entire period that the taxpayer can "reasonably be expected" to carry on the business or hold the property. Subsection 3.1(2) specifically excludes capital gains and capital losses from the determination of cumulative profit for this purpose. The proposals have come under significant criticism from both business and tax professionals.[32] As an anti-avoidance provision, proposed section 3.1 goes well beyond what is warranted.[33]

---

29 *Stewart*, at para. 52.

30 See, e.g., *Durber v. The Queen*, [2002] 4 C.T.C. 2192 (T.C.C.) (rental property with personal element); *Johnson v. The Queen*, [2003] 3 C.T.C. 2185 (T.C.C.) (interest in racehorse considered a hobby).

31 Canada, Department of Finance, "Proposed Amendments to the *Income Tax Act* Related to the Deductibility of Interest and Other Expenses Related to a Source," annex to Release no. 2003-055, October 31, 2003.

32 See, for example, Sandra Rubin, "Proposed Tax Changes 'Draconian'," National Post, March 10, 2004. See also, CICA-CBA Joint Committee on Taxation, "Submission on the October 31, 2003 Draft Proposals Regarding the Deductibility of Interest and Other Expenses," February 19, 2004, available from the Canadian Tax Foundation Website, http://www.ctf.ca/whatsnew/jointcommittee.asp.

33 For a short critique of the proposals, see Daniel Sandler, "REOP Resurrected — This Year's Hallowe'en Trick," *Tax Topics* No. 1653 (Toronto: CCH Canadian, November 13, 2003), 1. For a more comprehensive examination of the jurisprudence leading to the proposals, see David Duff's contribution to this book, "Interest Deductibility, the Reasonable Expectation of Profit Test, and the Supreme Court of Canada: From *Bronfman Trust* and *Moldowan* to *Singleton, Ludmer, Stewart* and *Walls*."

6) Limiting the Anti-Avoidance Utility of Statutory Provisions — Paragraph 20(1)(c) and Section 67

a) Interest Expense: Paragraph 20(1)(c)

Tax shelters, by their very nature, are designed to create tax losses that taxpayers can use to reduce other sources of income and therefore reduce their tax liability. In many tax shelters, it is an interest deduction under paragraph 20(1)(c) that generates the loss. Take the interest expense out and most tax shelters would show a profit. Thus, the denial or reduction of the interest expense in a tax shelter would be tantamount to denying the loss.

i) Paragraph 20(1)(c): A Statutory Business Purpose Test?

Despite the rejection in *Stubart* of a general business purpose test in Canada, other cases, particularly *Mark Resources Inc. v. The Queen*[34] and *Canwest Broadcasting Ltd. v. The Queen*,[35] suggested that an insufficient business purpose can undermine a taxpayer's claim for interest deductibility in paragraph 20(1)(c). In these cases, the interest expense was denied on the basis that the "true purpose," the "economic purpose," the "overall economic result" or the "only purpose" of the transactions in issue was to transfer losses — in *Mark Resources* between related companies but across an international border; in *Canwest* between unrelated companies. Based on these cases, it is arguable that paragraph 18(1)(a), which denies the deduction of outlays or expenses except to the extent that they are incurred "for the purpose of gaining or producing income" from a business or property, contains a business purpose test applicable to all expenses.

The more recent decision in *Novopharm Limited v. The Queen*,[36] which considered an elaborate scheme to transfer losses between unrelated companies through the use of the interest deduction under paragraph 20(1)(c), provides an interesting study of this issue. At the trial level, Bowie T.C.J. dismissed the taxpayer's appeal on the basis that the transactions undertaken had no purpose other than to transfer tax losses and therefore did not meet the requirement for interest deductibility under paragraph 20(1)(c). This decision came as a surprise to many tax practitioners who believed that *Mark Resources* and *Canwest* were effectively overruled by *Shell*, and if not, then certainly by *Ludco* and *Singleton*. Both *Ludco* and *Singleton* suggest

---

34 93 D.T.C. 1004, [1993] 2 C.T.C. 2259 (T.C.C.).

35 96 D.T.C. 1375, [1995] 2 C.T.C. 2780 (T.C.C.).

36 2003 D.T.C. 5195 (F.C.A.) (affirming 2002 D.T.C. 1307, [2002] 1 C.T.C. 2872 (T.C.C.)) [*Novopharm*]. Application for leave to appeal to the Supreme Court of Canada dismissed without reasons, [2003] S.C.C.A. 201.

that the requisite business purpose under paragraph 20(1)(c) is met provided that one of the purposes of the taxpayer is to earn income. Iacobucci J. suggested in *Ludco* that a test that introduced a concept of degree, such as dominant purpose, "would open the door to many reassessments and in each case would impose on taxpayers a tremendous burden to justify that their real or dominant purpose was to earn income" and that such a test would be "impractical in the context of investments in securities."[37] In dismissing the taxpayer's appeal in *Novopharm*, the Federal Court of Appeal did not rely on paragraph 20(1)(c); in fact, the court concluded, based on *Singleton*, that paragraph 20(1)(c) would permit the interest expense because the direct use of the borrowed money was to purchase common shares of a corporation. Rather, the court dismissed the taxpayer's appeal under former subsection 245(1), which denied deductions that unduly or artificially reduced income.[38]

ii) Paragraph 20(1)(c): The Meaning of Income

In order for interest to be deductible under paragraph 20(1)(c), the borrowed money has to be "used for the purpose of earning income from a business or property." In *Ludco*, Iacobucci J. concluded that "income" in this context is a gross concept — any amount that "comes into income for taxation purposes" is income. The facts of *Ludco* are relatively straightforward. Taxpayers resident in Canada borrowed substantial funds in order to purchase shares of foreign corporations.[39] These shares paid nominal dividends, which the taxpayers included in income. The taxpayers deducted the interest expense, giving rise to substantial losses.[40] Ultimately, when the taxpayers disposed of the shares, the resulting gain was reported as a capital gain. The CRA denied the interest expense on the basis that it was not incurred for the purpose of earning income from a business or property, but rather to defer taxes and convert income into capital gains.

In permitting the deduction, Iacobucci, J. indicated that if Parliament intended that interest should only be deductible where borrowed money

---

37 *Ludco*, at para. 53.

38 In applying former subsection 245(1), the court followed the approach enunciated in its earlier decision in *Fording Coal Ltd. v. The Queen*, 95 D.T.C. 5672, [1996] 1 C.T.C. 230. The fact that the Federal Court of Appeal relied exclusively on a repealed statutory provision may have contributed to the Supreme Court of Canada's refusal to give the taxpayer leave to appeal the case.

39 The shareholdings in the offshore companies were structured to avoid the foreign accrual property income (FAPI) rules in section 95 and predated the introduction of the off-shore investment entity provisions in section 94.1.

40 Over the eight years that the shares were owned, the taxpayers received approximately $600,000 in dividends and deducted approximately $6 million of interest.

was used for the purpose of earning "net income," Parliament could have expressly said so. In fact, the term "net income" is not found anywhere in the Act except for references to a "net income stabilization account" (NISA), created under the net income stabilization program of the *Farm Income Protection Act*.[41] Moreover, the term "income" is not found unmodified in paragraph 20(1)(c). Rather, the phrase "income from a business or property" is used and that phrase is defined explicitly in section 9 as "profit." To suggest otherwise is not only disingenuous, but also raises other interpretative problems. Take, for example, the rental property rules in regulation 1100(11). Under these provisions, a taxpayer is not permitted to claim capital cost allowance (CCA) to the extent that it exceeds "his income for the year from renting or leasing a rental property . . ." Does this now mean that provided that the CCA does not exceed gross rental income, it is deductible notwithstanding any other expenses (e.g., interest) incurred by the taxpayer? If so, it makes a mockery of the provision.

iii) Paragraph 20(1)(c): Tracing Requirements

Courts have accepted for a long time that it is the current, direct use of the borrowed money that is relevant under paragraph 20(1)(c). It is a highly formalistic approach and it can cut both ways. *Bronfman Trust v. The Queen*[42] and *Attaie v. The Queen*[43] are examples of this rule operating against the taxpayer; *Singleton* is simply the converse situation. In the two former cases, the court denied the interest expense because the direct use of the borrowed money was not for an income-earning purpose, even though the borrowed funds were indirectly used to preserve income-producing assets. In *Singleton*, the taxpayer, a lawyer in a professional partnership, withdrew his capital from the partnership in order to finance the purchase of a principal residence (registered in his wife's name) and then borrowed money in order to replace the partnership capital (with a mortgage on the house provided as security for the loan). His interest expense deduction was denied and the taxpayer appealed. At trial, the taxpayer was unsuccessful. Bowman, T.C.J. concluded that "even if one accepts the legal validity of the steps that were taken and also treats the obvious tax motivation as irrelevant, one is still left with the inescapable factual determination

---

41 "Net income" is used in the definition of "net accounting income" in proposed subsection 94.1(1), in the draft foreign investment entity rules, the most recent version of which was released on October 30, 2003 (effective, January 1, 2003). This provision would be a first in the Act to use the term "net income" otherwise than in reference to a NISA.

42 87 D.T.C. 5059, [1987] 1 C.T.C. 117 (S.C.C.) [*Bronfman Trust*].

43 90 D.T.C. 6413, [1990] 2 C.T.C. 157 (F.C.A.).

that the true economic purpose for which the borrowed money was used was the purchase of a house, not the enhancement of the firm's income earning potential by a contribution of capital."[44] The taxpayer successfully appealed to the Federal Court of Appeal and the Crown's appeal to the Supreme Court of Canada was dismissed. For the majority of the Supreme Court, the matter was made simple by its earlier decision in *Shell*. Economic realities are irrelevant in the absence of a sham. The question simply is whether the current, direct use of the borrowed money was for the purpose of earning income from a business or property. When the issue is phrased in this manner, the clear answer is yes. In fact, given the decision in *Shell*, it is unclear why the Minister bothered to appeal *Singleton* at all.[45]

Ludco also appears to relax the direct tracing requirement espoused in other decisions. As *Singleton* affirmed, it is the direct, current use of the borrowed money that is relevant in determining whether interest is incurred for the purpose of earning income from a business or property. In *Ludco*, the shares in the foreign corporations were acquired between 1977 and 1979. However, in 1983, the taxpayer transferred the shares and other assets to a wholly-owned subsidiary under section 85 in exchange for both share and non-share consideration. The total value of the assets transferred was approximately $12.7 million, of which the shares of the foreign companies were worth $8,645,715. The taxpayer's debt attributable to those shares was $4,800,000. Based on the tracing principle, the current use of the borrowed money was no longer the shares of the foreign corporations, but rather the consideration received for these shares on the rollover. The non-share consideration received by the taxpayer amounted to $7,985,000, of which $7,380,000 represented two non-interest bearing promissory notes. The taxpayer also received an interest-bearing note (face amount $605,000) plus preferred shares with a fixed dividend and an aggregate redemption/retraction amount of $4,700,000. Thus, the total value of consideration received that was income-producing was $5,305,000. On this basis, the Crown argued that since only approximately five-twelfths of the

---

44 *Singleton*, [1996] 3 C.T.C. 2873, 96 D.T.C. 1850 (T.C.C.), at para. 17.

45 The Crown relied on Dickson, C.J.'s *obiter* comment in *Bronfman Trust* that even if the taxpayer trust had properly structured its transactions — i.e., sold some of its investments in order to make a distribution to beneficiaries and then borrowed money in order to replace the investments — "courts might well consider the sale and repurchase to constitute a formality or a sham designed to conceal the essence of the transaction, namely that money was borrowed and used to fund a capital allocation to the beneficiary." According to Major, J. in *Singleton* (at para. 42), the Crown "has over-stated the importance of this statement," that it "was more musing than jurisprudence."

consideration was income-producing, only five-twelfths of the interest should continue to be deductible. Iacobucci, J. disagreed. Referring to the Supreme Court of Canada's earlier decision in *Tennant v. The Queen*,[46] he stated that tracing requires merely "a link" between the original and current use of the borrowed money. According to Iacobucci J., this is a more flexible approach than specific tracing.[47] He concluded that the borrowed money could still be traced to income-earning assets since the value of the income earning assets received as consideration exceeded the amount of the borrowed money. In other words, if the consideration received is both non-income producing and income-producing and is commingled, provided that the value of the income-producing consideration exceeds the amount of the original loan, the interest remains deductible. There are a number of problems with his conclusions. First, the election form under section 85 specifically requires the taxpayer to indicate the consideration received for each asset (or class of assets) transferred and presumably those election forms would have been introduced into evidence at the trial level. The shares of the foreign company were worth $8.6 million; the income-producing consideration amounted to only $5.305 million. So, even if all of the income-producing consideration was allocated to these assets (which I doubt — because that would have triggered a capital gain), it is difficult to suggest that all of the interest remains deductible. In effect, in order to achieve Iacobucci, J.'s results, there must be some form of ordering of the consideration that is linked to the loan, first to income-earning assets and second to non-income earning assets. This flies in the face of accepted practice and raises more general concerns. Suppose a taxpayer borrows $100 to buy $100 worth of common shares. The shares increase in value to $200 and the taxpayer sells the shares. The taxpayer uses $100 of the proceeds to invest in other shares and $100 on a nice dinner (with no business element). I would have thought interest on only $50 of the original loan remains deductible because only one-half of the proceeds were invested in income-producing assets. However, based on Iacobucci, J.'s reasoning in *Ludco*, interest on the full $100 loan should remain deductible because the entire loan can be linked (as opposed to traced) to another income-producing asset.[48]

---

46 96 D.T.C. 6121, [1996] 1 C.T.C. 290 (S.C.C.).

47 *Ludco*, at para. 76.

48 If the taxpayer had used the $100 remaining after the nice dinner to repay the loan and then borrowed another $100 to make the new investment, then interest on the entire $100 loan would be deductible. Perhaps that is the rationale underlying Iacobucci, J.'s more relaxed approach to tracing. However, numerous cases have indi-

b) The General Expense Limitation: Section 67

In neither *Stewart* nor *Walls* did the Minister challenge the quantum of the deductions claimed by the taxpayers under section 67. While section 67 is most often applied to reduce non-arm's length expenses (for example, salaries paid to family members), it has been applied to reduce unreasonably large expenses without any personal element.[49] Indeed, in *Tonn v. The Queen*,[50] Linden, J.A. suggested that section 67 was a more appropriate basis than REOP to challenge the reasonableness of a taxpayer's deductions in a *bona fide* business setting. Now that REOP is dead, it is possible that the CRA will use section 67 more often to challenge expenses in commercial settings. However, given McLachin, J.'s comments in *Shell* on reasonableness in the context of paragraph 20(1)(c) — i.e., that if the rate of interest charged is an arm's length rate, the amount of interest paid is reasonable[51] — it is doubtful that section 67 has any utility to expenses paid in arm's length scenarios.

I would sum up to this point by suggesting that the weapons in the CRA's arsenal that can be used to attack abusive tax avoidance transactions that technically comply with all statutory provisions in the Act are now essentially non-existent — other than GAAR.

B. WHERE DO WE GAAR FROM HERE?

In order for GAAR to apply, a court must address two basic questions: 1) was there an "avoidance transaction" as defined in subsection 245(3) (which includes a determination of whether there was a "tax benefit," as defined in subsection 245(1))?; 2) if so, did the transaction result in a misuse of the provisions of the Act or an abuse of the Act as a whole? This section considers two of the most contentious elements of GAAR for which we are awaiting guidance from the Supreme Court of Canada: paragraph 245(3)(b) and subsection 245(4).

---

cated that the court must determine the tax result based on what the taxpayer actually did, not what the taxpayer might have done: see, e.g., *Bronfman Trust*, at para. 53; *Attaie*, at para. 25. The CRA now appears to accept Iacobucci, J.'s position and allow interest on the full $100 loan to remain deductible: Ted Citrome, "Interest: Where Now, For How Long, What Next?" (2003) 14: 1 Taxation Law 8 at 10, clarifying the position in a February 21, 2003 technical interpretation, doc. no. 2003-0181585.

49 See, e.g., *No. 511 v. MNR*, 58 D.T.C. 307 (T.A.B.), in which advertising expenses exceeding one-half of the business's net income were considered unreasonably high.

50 96 D.T.C. 6001, [1996] 1 C.T.C. 205 (F.C.A.).

51 *Shell*, at para. 34.

Before turning to these provisions, it is worth emphasizing — as the courts have continually emphasized[52] and indeed the Department of Finance commented when the GAAR legislation was first released[53] — that GAAR is a provision of last resort. As Bowman, T.C.J. commented in *Jabs Construction*,

> Section 245 is an extreme sanction. It should not be used routinely every time the Minister gets upset just because a taxpayer structures a transaction in a tax effective way, or does not structure it in a manner that maximizes the tax.[54]

Likewise the CRA must be selective about which cases it wants to pursue to court under GAAR. If GAAR is used as a basis for reassessment too often, as in the case of the boy who cried "wolf," the courts may not listen.

1) Avoidance Transaction in a Series of Transactions — Paragraph 245(3)(b)

Paragraph 245(3)(b) is not a model of clarity. It provides that a transaction is an avoidance transaction if it is part of a series of transactions that gives rise to a tax benefit, unless the transaction was entered into for *bona fide* purposes other than to obtain the tax benefit. Given the fact that in most sophisticated tax planning schemes, the tax benefit will arise from a combination of transactions rather than a single transaction, paragraph 245(3)(b) will come into play much more often than paragraph 245(3)(a).

a) What Constitutes a Series?

The meaning of "series of transactions" in the context of paragraph 245(3)(b) was considered in *OSFC*, in which conflicting views were expressed in the majority decision, written by Rothstein, J.A., and the concurring opinion of Létourneau, J.A. The case involved a series of transactions structured by the liquidator for Standard Trust Company ("Standard") in order to maximize the value in a prospective asset sale of a mortgage

---

52 *CIT Financial Ltd. v. The Queen*, 2003 D.T.C. 1138, [2004] 1 C.T.C. 2232 (T.C.C.), at para. 66; *Loyens v. The Queen*, 2003 D.T.C. 355, [2003] 3 C.T.C. 2381 (T.C.C.) [*Loyens*], at para. 119; *S.T.B.*, at para. 26; *Rousseau-Houle v. The Queen*, 2001 D.T.C. 250 (T.C.C.) [*Rousseau-Houle*], at para. 26; *Geransky v. The Queen*, 2001 D.T.C. 243, [2001] 2 C.T.C. 2147 (T.C.C.) [*Geransky*], at para. 25; *Jabs Construction Ltd. v. The Queen*, 99 D.T.C. 729, [1999] 3 C.T.C. 2556 (T.C.C.) [*Jabs Construction*], at para. 45.

53 Canada, Department of Finance, *Explanatory Notes to Legislation Relating to Income Tax (Bill C-139)*, June 30, 1988, 313.

54 *Jabs Construction*, at para. 48.

portfolio that was "pregnant" with substantial accrued losses. Specifically, certain transactions were undertaken by Standard in order to give a purchaser of the portfolio the benefit of the losses for which Standard had no use. In order to package the mortgage portfolio, the following three steps were undertaken: 1) Standard incorporated a wholly-owned subsidiary; 2) Standard and the subsidiary formed a partnership (STIL II); 3) Standard transferred the mortgage portfolio to STIL II in exchange for a 99 percent partnership interest. This transfer did not trigger any loss as a consequence of subsection 18(13) of the Act (as it then read).[55] All that was left for Standard to do was to find a buyer for its partnership interest before the end of the partnership's taxation year (at which point the losses would have crystallized from either the sale of mortgages or the write-down of the partnership's inventory at its year-end and the resultant business loss would be allocated to its partners, of which the buyer of Standard's partnership interest would be allocated 99 percent). The three transactions to package the mortgage portfolio were undertaken in October 1992 and the partnership year-end was fixed at September 30. That essentially gave the liquidator approximately 11 months to find a buyer interested in the mortgage portfolio and its approximately $52 million of accrued losses before those losses would have to be recognized. There was no purchaser "in the wings" in October 1992. Standard's liquidator started a marketing campaign shortly after the three transactions were undertaken and entered into intense negotiations with the taxpayer between January and May 1993; the taxpayer ultimately entered into an agreement of purchase and sale of Standard's interest in the STIL II partnership on May 31, 1993 and closed the purchase on June 29, 2003. The consideration paid comprised three elements:

1. $17.5 million ($3 million cash and a $14.5 million promissory note);

---

55 Subsection 18(13) is one of a number of "superficial loss" rules contained in the Act. In essence, it provided that where a money-lender realized a loss on a transfer of certain property (including loans) to a person or partnership that does not deal at arm's length with the money-lender, the money-lender's loss is deemed to be nil and the loss is added to the cost of the property to the recipient. In this case, where the mortgage portfolio had an aggregate cost to Standard of approximately $85 million and a fair market value of $33 million, subsection 18(13) denied the loss of $52 million to Standard and added it to the cost of the portfolio to the partnership (which, in the absence of subsection 18(13), would have been $33 million). As a consequence of amendments originally announced in 1995, subsections 18(13) and (15) now essentially hold the loss in abeyance in the hands of the transferor (rather than the transferee) in such circumstances and the transferor (rather than the transferee) recognizes the loss when the transferee disposes of the property in an arm's length transaction.

2. an "earn-out" based on any actual proceeds of sale of the mortgage portfolio in excess of $17.5 million; and
3. an amount, up to $5 million, payable to Standard for the tax losses, contingent on the partners being successful in deducting the losses from their other income.

Not having a use for all $52 million in losses to which it would become entitled, the taxpayer syndicated its 99 percent interest in STIL II by transferring it to another partnership (SRMP) in July 2003. The taxpayer retained a 24 percent interest in SRMP after selling the remaining interests to other investors. On September 30, 1993, STIL II reported a loss of $52.6 million, of which 99 percent was allocated to SRMP. On SRMP's year-end, one month later,[56] SRMP reported a loss of $52.2 million, of which $12.6 million (24 percent) was allocated to the taxpayer. The CRA denied the taxpayer's loss under GAAR. The taxpayer's appeal was dismissed at trial and the taxpayer appealed to the Federal Court of Appeal.[57]

The taxpayer did not deny that the transactions gave rise to a tax benefit, but argued that none of the transactions was an avoidance transaction for three reasons: first, its acquisition of the STIL II partnership interest was primarily for a business purpose — to acquire a portfolio of distressed mortgages and use its expertise to dispose of them for optimum proceeds; second, that the first three transactions did not give rise to any tax benefit to Standard and therefore could not have been undertaken to obtain a tax benefit; and third, that even if any of the Standard transactions gave rise to a tax benefit, the transaction by which the taxpayer acquired its interest in STIL II was not part of the same series of transactions.

Both the majority and concurring opinions suggested three possible meanings of the phrase "series of transactions":

- the "step-transaction" doctrine, adopted in a series of House of Lords cases in the 1980s, under which transactions are considered part of the

---

56 The staggered year-end essentially gave the taxpayer an additional month to find other taxpayers interested in the syndication.

57 The companion case to *OSFC*, *Mathew*, concerns the reassessment of the remaining partners of the SRMP partnership. Their appeal was dismissed by both the Tax Court and the Federal Court of Appeal and is currently on appeal to the Supreme Court of Canada. In that case, the taxpayers appealed not only on the merits of the case, but also on the basis that GAAR was impermissably vague, and therefore of no force and effect as being contrary to the substantive requirements of the Rule of Law and pursuant to section 52 of the *Constitution Act, 1982*, for violation of section 7 of the *Canadian Charter of Rights and Freedoms*.

same series if they are "pre-ordained" — that is, "there was no practical likelihood that the preplanned events would not have taken place in the order ordained;"[58]

- the "mutual interdependence test," under which two or more transactions are considered part of a series "if the transactions are so interdependent that the legal relations created by one transaction would be meaningless without a completion of the series;"[59] and
- the "end results test," under which "purportedly separate transactions will be amalgamated as a single transaction when it appears that they were really component parts of a single transaction intended from the outset to be taken for the purpose of reaching the ultimate result."[60]

The majority of the court concluded that the first approach applied in Canada, citing comments of David Dodge (then Senior Assistant Deputy Minister of Finance) that Parliament intended to adopt the step transaction doctrine in the formulation of GAAR.[61] Based on this approach, Rothstein, J.A. had "no difficulty" concluding that the three transactions undertaken in October 1992 were a series of transactions;[62] however, he concluded that the fourth transaction, the sale of the partnership interest to the taxpayer, was not part of the common law series because the buyer was not identified at the time that the first three transactions took place and because the taxpayer ultimately became the buyer only after lengthy and "difficult" negotiations. The majority therefore had to consider the application of subsection 248(10), which deems a series of transactions to include "any related transactions or events completed in contemplation of the series." Létourneau, J.A., on the other hand, was prepared to apply any of the three common law interpretations of series and concluded that under any of these interpretations, all four transactions would be considered part of the same series; therefore, in his view, it was not necessary to resort to subsection 248(10). There can be little doubt that the fourth transaction would be considered part of the same series if the mutual interdependence test or the end results test applied. However, based on the UK jurisprudence

58 *Craven v. White*, [1989] A.C. 459 at 514 (H.L.).

59 *OSFC*, at para. 21.

60 *Ibid.*

61 *OSFC*, at paras. 23–24, relying on David A. Dodge, "A New and More Coherent Approach to Tax Avoidance" (1988) 34: 1 Canadian Tax Journal 1 at 15.

62 *OSFC*, at para. 25.

relied on by the court, the sale of the STIL II partnership interest to the taxpayer could not be said to be "preordained" in October 1992.[63]

Whatever the common law notion of series of transactions (and its breadth), subsection 248(10) clearly expands the transactions included in a series for Canadian tax purposes. Subsection 248(10) is a deeming provision and a deeming provision "artificially imports into a word or an expres-

---

63 Certainly a sale of the mortgage portfolio prior to September 30, 1993 was critical for the first three transactions to serve any purpose (i.e., to increase the sale proceeds that Standard could realize because the purchase price would include some amount for the losses to the purchaser). However, the UK concept of a "series" requires that "all essential features of the subsequent transaction or transactions [must be] determined by persons who have the firm intention and ability to implement them" and that "there must be no practical likelihood that the subsequent transaction or transactions will not take place": *OSFC*, at para. 24, adopting Vern Krishna's interpretation of the House of Lords' decisions in *Tax Avoidance: The General Anti-Avoidance Rule* (Toronto: Carswell, 1990) at 69, quoted in *OSFC*, at para. 20. Michael Hiltz, one of the directors in the Rulings Directorate of the CRA also suggested that series had a narrow meaning: a subsequent transaction would be included in a series "only if, at the time the preliminary transaction was carried out, all important elements of the subsequent transaction are settled, and the subsequent transaction is eventually carried out." (Michael J. Hiltz, "Section 245 of the *Income Tax Act*" in *Report of the Proceedings of the Fortieth Tax Conference*, 1988 Conference Report (Toronto: Canadian Tax Foundation, 1989) 7:1 at 7:7). These comments certainly reflect the consensus of the majority of the House of Lords in the trilogy of cases decided in the summer of 1988, *Craven v. White*, *Baylis v. Gregory*, and *IRC v. Bowater Property Developments Ltd.*, all reported in [1988] S.T.C. 476 (H.L.).

Although beyond the scope of this chapter, the reasoning of the House of Lords in tax avoidance cases has evolved since 1988. In the most recent decision, *Macniven v. Westmoreland Investments Ltd.* , [2001] S.T.C. 237 (H.L.) [*Westmoreland*], the House of Lords suggested (per Lord Hoffmann at para. 49) that the step transaction or composite transaction doctrine was not "a principle of construction," but rather "a statement of the consequences of giving a commercial construction to a fiscal concept." Thus, according to the court, the step transaction doctrine is applicable only if the statutory language to be interpreted refers to a commercial concept rather than a juristic or legal concept. *Westmoreland*, for example, concerned a circular, pre-ordained series of transactions undertaken between a shareholder (a tax-exempt pension fund) and its wholly-owned corporation (the taxpayer), which had no assets and substantial indebtedness to its shareholder. The transactions were undertaken solely for the purpose of converting the corporation's accrued (nondeductible) interest liability to its shareholder into paid (deductible) interest in order to generate a substantial loss in the corporation. This loss would have some value to a purchaser of the corporation's shares and therefore increase the sale price that the shares could command. The House of Lords concluded that the concept of "payment" of interest, as used in the tax legislation, is a legal concept and does not have a commercial meaning. Accordingly, since the legal effect of the taxpayer's transactions was to pay the interest, the circularity of the transactions and the fact that they were preordained and carried out solely or mainly in order to obtain a reduction in tax liability was irrelevant.

sion an additional meaning which they would not otherwise convey besides the ordinary meaning."[64] In addition, the statute enacting GAAR in 1988 included a "grandfather" provision specifically pertaining to subsection 248(10): GAAR was not applicable to "transactions that are part of a series of transactions, determined without reference to subsection 248(10) . . . , commencing before [September 13, 1988] and completed before 1989."[65] If subsection 248(10) was not supposed to expand the common law meaning of series, this grandfather provision would be irrelevant.

The more difficult question, to which some authoritative guidance from the Supreme Court of Canada would be welcome, is to what extent does subsection 248(10) expand the notion of a series. In contrast to Rothstein, J.A.'s narrow interpretation of a common law series, he provides an expansive interpretation to subsection 248(10), concluding that a transaction will be considered part of a series if it has "some connection" to the common law series and if the parties "knew of the common law series, such that it could be said that they took it into account when deciding to complete the transaction."[66] Since the preamble to the purchase agreement pursuant to which the taxpayer acquired the STIL II partnership interest specifically referred to the creation of STIL II and the transfer of the mortgage portfolio to it, the taxpayer clearly knew of the earlier series of transactions and took it into account when completing the purchase of the partnership interest.

This interpretation of subsection 248(10) is, in my view, too broad. The impact of this interpretation on other provisions of the Act in which a series of transactions is contemplated, such as the exceptions to the application of subsection 55(2) set out in paragraph 55(3)(a), is problematic.[67] In

---

64 *R. v. Verrette*, [1978] 2 S.C.R. 838 at 845, cited with approval by Rothstein, J.A. in *OSFC*, at para. 33.

65 S.C. 1988, c. 55, s. 185(2)(a).

66 *OSFC*, at para. 36.

67 Consider, for example, a taxpayer (Mr. X) who is the sole shareholder of a Canadian-controlled private corporation (Opco) that carries on an active business in Canada but does not meet the definition of "small business corporation" in subsection 248(1) due to the value of its non-active business assets. Mr. X undertakes a series of transactions in order to "purify" Opco of its non-active business assets so that the shares of the corporation can qualify for the capital gains exemption in subsection 110.6(2.1). Mr. X may "crystallize" the exemption through a further corporate reorganization in which he disposes of the shares of Opco and elects into a capital gain under subsection 85(1). The series of transactions through which the non-active business assets are removed gives rise to a number of inter-corporate deemed dividends that, but for paragraph 55(3)(a), would be subject to subsection 55(2). In a technical interpretation provided by the CRA's Rulings Directorate on June 30, 1989, document no. 5-7939,

my view, the more appropriate approach to the notion of a "series of transactions" as contemplated by subsection 248(10) is that suggested by Bowie, T.C.J. in *Granite Bay Charters Ltd. v. The Queen*,[68] a case concerning paragraph 55(3)(a):

> it is relevant to consider proximity in time, as well as purpose and result. . . . while care must be taken not to cast too wide a net, it is also important to give the legislation a construction that will permit it to achieve its anti-avoidance purpose.[69]

This guidance is equally appropriate in the context of GAAR. Even based on this narrower interpretation, the sale of the STIL II partnership interest to the taxpayer, if not considered part of the common law series that commenced in October 1992, should certainly be included in the series as a consequence of subsection 248(10).[70]

---

the directorate commented on such a hypothetical situation in which Mr. X had no intention of selling the shares at the time of the purification. The directorate commented that "if as hypothesized Mr. X has no intention at the time of the Reorganization of ever selling the Opco Shares, the Deemed Dividends and an eventual sale of the Opco Shares would generally not be part of the same series of transactions. It is in our view unlikely that such a situation would occur, however, since in most situations a shareholder who causes a reorganization to be carried out for the purpose of causing shares to qualify as QSBC shares does so in order that a deduction under subsection 110.6(2.1) of the Act will be available to him upon a disposition of the shares. In such cases the shareholder would have some intention at the time of the reorganization of eventually selling the shares." This broad interpretation of series of transactions, as modified by subsection 248(10), is consistent with Rothstein, J.A.'s interpretation in *OSFC*, but, in my view, is beyond the appropriate scope of a series of transactions.

68 2001 D.T.C. 615, [2001] 3 C.T.C. 2516 (T.C.C.) [*Granite Bay*]. *Granite Bay* is currently on appeal to the Federal Court of Appeal.

69 *Ibid.*, at para. 8.

70 This assumes that a transaction or event occurring *after* the common law series can be considered to have been "completed in contemplation of the series." Brian S. Nichols suggests that the words "in contemplation" in subsection 248(10) means "(a) *before* the series and (b) in anticipation or expectation of the series" [emphasis in the original]: see Brian S. Nichols, "GAAR and More" in *2002 Ontario Tax Conference Report*, 1:1 at 1:13. John Tiley also seems to suggest that subsection 248(10) refers to transactions completed before the series: see John Tiley, "Series of Transaction" in *Report of Proceedings of the Fortieth Tax Conference*, 1988 Conference Report (Toronto: Canadian Tax Foundation, 1989), 8:1 at 8:4-5. Even if subsection 248(10) included in a common law series of transactions only previously completed transactions, the response in OSFC would be that the common law series was the sale of the STIL II partnership interest to the taxpayer on May 31, 1993 and that the transactions occurring in October 1992 were related transactions completed in contemplation of the series. One concern in this respect is whether the common law series to which the

b) Parsing the Series

Once the breadth of the series is clear, the proper application of paragraph 245(3)(b) must be considered. Paragraph 245(3)(b) states that if a series of transactions gives rise to the tax benefit, then each transaction in the series must be reviewed in order to determine whether it was undertaken primarily for a *bona fide* purpose other than to obtain a tax benefit. Thus the entire series is considered in determining whether there is a tax benefit and if so, then the primary purpose of each transaction in the series must be separately reviewed. The trial decision in *CP* was clearly wrong to suggest that if the entire series primarily had a *bona fide* purpose, then each step in the series must have that same *bona fide* purpose.[71] That was certainly not the purport of paragraph 245(3)(b) nor does it follow from its words, however ambiguous they are. The proper application of paragraph 245(3)(b) can be discerned from its placement in the GAAR provision, particularly the interaction among subsections 245(2), (3) and (4).

Subsection 245(2) is the operative provision in GAAR. Under subsection 245(2), where there has been an avoidance transaction, the tax consequences to a person shall be determined in order to deny a tax benefit that results from the transaction or from a series of transactions that includes the transaction. Subsection 245(4) denies the application of subsection 245(2) where it may reasonably be considered that the transaction (i.e., not the series of transactions) does not result in a misuse of the provisions of the Act or an abuse of the Act as a whole. Thus, for example, it is possible that the primary purpose of a series of transactions as a whole is *bona fide* (e.g., an arm's length sale of an asset) but that steps have been inserted in the series exclusively in order to obtain a tax benefit. That was the original genesis of the step transaction doctrine in the United Kingdom,[72] upon which the "series" concept in paragraph 245(3)(b) was based.

---

related transaction is added can be a single transaction (i.e., the sale of the partnership interest), so that series contemplated by subsection 248(10) means that transaction together with related transactions. Tiley (at 8:5), suggests that it should, "otherwise, the provision will not work as the draftsmen hope (which may be different from what the legislators are taken in law to intend)."

71 2000 D.T.C. 2428, [2001] 1 C.T.C. 2190 (T.C.C.). There, Bonner, T.C.J. suggested (at para. 15) that "[n]o transaction forming part of the series can be viewed as having been arranged for a purpose which differs from the overall purpose of the series." The decision of Bowman, T.C.J. in *Geransky* may be criticized on the same basis.

72 The oft-cited conditions for the application of the step transaction doctrine are taken from Lord Brightman in *Furniss v. Dawson*, [1984] A.C. 474 at 527:

> First, there must be a pre-ordained series of transactions; or, if one likes, one single composite transaction. This composite transaction may or may not include the

In *OSFC*, the transactions undertaken in October 1992 were clearly avoidance transactions: the primary purpose, indeed the sole purpose, of the three transactions then undertaken was to package the mortgage portfolio in such a way that an arm's length purchaser could benefit from the accrued losses inherent in the portfolio. In this respect, they were no different from the transactions undertaken in *Furniss v. Dawson*, apart from the issue as to which taxpayer (the purchaser, as in *OSFC*, or the vendor, as in *Furniss v. Dawson*) has its tax liability reduced as a consequence of the tax benefit. Although no tax benefit arose directly from the first three transactions in *OSFC*, they formed part of a larger series (i.e., the series that included the sale of the partnership interest to the taxpayer) that gave rise to a tax benefit. There is no requirement under GAAR that the taxpayer who ultimately derives the tax benefit from the series of transactions must have participated in each avoidance transaction in the series. Thus, even if the primary purpose of the sale of the STIL II partnership interest to the taxpayer was a *bona fide* non-tax purpose,[73] GAAR could still apply to the taxpayer, subject to the application of subsection 245(4).

In considering the interpretation of paragraph 245(3)(b), the decision in *OSFC* should be contrasted with the Federal Court of Appeal decision in *CP*. In *CP*, a Canadian taxpayer required money for its business carried on

---

> achievement of a legitimate commercial (i.e., business) end. . . . Secondly, there must be steps inserted which have no commercial (business) purpose apart from the avoidance of a liability to tax — not "no business effect." If these two ingredients exist, the inserted steps are disregarded for fiscal purposes. The court must then look at the end result. Precisely how the end result will be taxed will depend on the terms of the taxing statute sought to be applied.

See further, above, note 63, for more recent consideration of the step transaction doctrine by the House of Lords.

73 In his concurring opinion, Létourneau, J.A. agreed that each transaction in the series must be separately reviewed to determine whether it is an avoidance transaction; however, in his judgment, nothing turned on whether the arm's length sale was itself an avoidance transaction because the first three transactions clearly were avoidance transactions and were not saved by subsection 245(4). Rothstein, J.A., on the other hand, suggested (at para. 48) that "it is normally necessary to analyse the primary purpose of all the relevant transactions" because "subsection 245(4) involves assessing whether an avoidance transaction would result in a misuse or an abuse of the provisions of the Act" and "[i]t may be that some avoidance transactions in a series would not result in a misuse or abuse. Therefore, it is necessary to review all of the relevant transactions to determine which ones are avoidance transactions, in order for the analysis under subsection 245(4) to be complete." Based on the relative economic (i.e., after-tax) value of the accrued losses compared to the income and gains that could be realized from the ultimate sale of the mortgage portfolio, Rothstein, J.A. concluded that sale of the STIL II partnership interest was also an avoidance transaction.

in Canada. Rather than simply borrowing Canadian dollars, the taxpayer undertook an aggressive weak currency loan transaction in order to maximize its current interest expense and thereby reduce its Canadian tax liability. The taxpayer borrowed Australian dollars rather than Canadian dollars because the interest rate charged on Australian dollar loans was substantially higher than that charged on Canadian dollar loans. The taxpayer immediately converted the proceeds of the loan to Japanese yen and then from Japanese yen to Canadian dollars. The taxpayer entered into a series of forward contracts under a master swap agreement in order to cover its obligations in both Japanese yen and Australian dollars. As a consequence, the taxpayer significantly increased its interest expense over the term of the loan while realizing a capital gain on the loan's maturity based on the reduced value of the Australian dollar at that time. There is no doubt that the transactions gave rise to a tax benefit to the taxpayer. However, the Federal Court of Appeal concluded that there was no avoidance transaction because the tax benefit arose from the loan denominated in Australian dollars and the primary purpose of the loan was to raise capital for business purposes; it was not possible, as the Crown argued, to segregate the currency of the loan from the loan itself.

I agree with the court that in considering the original Australian dollar loan on its own, it is difficult to conclude that its primary purpose was something other than a *bona fide* business purpose. I also agree that you cannot parse the loan into two transactions, one being the loan and another being the currency of the loan. However, even on a narrow reading of paragraph 245(3)(b), the "extra juice" added to the transactions by interposing Japanese yen between the Australian dollar loan and the Canadian dollars used in the business had no purpose other than to increase the tax benefit to the taxpayer. Perhaps the Crown did not raise this argument,[74] but I cannot see how the interposed steps involving Japanese yen could be viewed as anything other than avoidance transactions under paragraph 245(3)(b).[75] Assuming that the Japanese yen transactions were avoidance transactions (and further assuming that such transactions constituted a misuse or abuse), the question then arises as to which tax benefits subsection 245(2) would deny: all of the tax benefits derived from the series, including from the Australian dollar denominated loan, or only the "extra

74 In the pre-GAAR *Shell* decision, which also involved a weak currency loan, the taxpayer did not interpose another strong currency between the weak currency New Zealand dollar loan and the US dollars used in the business.

75 Whether or not they would be considered a misuse of provisions of the Act or an abuse of the Act as a whole is another matter.

juice" obtained from inserting the Japanese yen transactions. The wording of subsection 245(2) appears to support either interpretation.[76] Perhaps the tax benefit of the impugned step or steps in the transaction would be denied without denying the tax benefit from the entire series if the impugned step or steps are not "integral" to the entire series — in other words, if the impugned steps can be ignored without undermining the entire series. If so, then even if the Crown could successfully impugn the Japanese yen transactions, the much larger benefit from the Australian dollar loan would remain. Thus, while it might be accepted as a general maxim in the tax community that "pigs get fat; hogs get slaughtered," a hog subject to GAAR may suffer only a surgical tummy-tuck in the right circumstances.

More generally though, if the court were to take a broader view of the "transaction" that the taxpayer undertook — to consider the loan and master forward swap arrangements as a single composite transaction — an argument could be made that the primary purpose of the composite transaction as structured was to achieve a tax benefit.[77] That does not necessarily mean that the result in *CP* is wrong. However, it would at least move the debate to whether there was a misuse of the interest deductibility rules or an abuse of the Act as a whole; that is, to a consideration of subsection 245(4) rather than subsection 245(3). In my view, the more appropriate approach to subsection 245(3) is that taken by Miller, T.C.J. in *Canada Trustco Mortgage Company v. The Queen*: "[t]he emphasis should shift from the tax benefit and avoidance transaction argument, where the threshold is not particularly high, to the misuse argument, where I believe the GAAR emphasis should, in this particular case, be placed."[78] While Miller, T.C.J. acknowledged that the transactions in issue in that case[79] provided a profitable investment in a

---

76 Nichols, above note 70 at 1:7, suggests that one tainted transaction that generates a small tax benefit can taint an entire series that generates a much larger tax benefit.

77 In this respect, it is debatable whether the court would have to weigh the economic benefits of the weak currency loan versus the business use of the loan itself, as Rothstein, J.A. suggests in OSFC. Based on Rothstein, J.A.'s analysis, the interest rate on the weak currency would have to be more than double the rate on the actual currency needed for business purposes in order to successfully argue that the primary purpose of the weak currency loan structure was to generate a tax benefit.

78 2003 D.T.C. 587 [*Canada Trustco* (T.C.C.)], at para. 55. Unfortunately, Miller, T.C.J. went on to suggest that "GAAR can be viewed as an endorsement of avoidance transactions, an endorsement of the grand old Duke, except for those transactions that clear the considerably higher abuse and misuse hurdle." The Federal Court of Appeal dismissed the Crown's appeal in brief reasons delivered from the bench (above, note 2) and the case is currently on appeal to the Supreme Court of Canada.

79 The taxpayer was the purchaser/lender in a purchase and lease-back arrangement. The taxpayer borrowed a substantial portion of the purchase price on a limited

commercial context, this finding did not outweigh the primary purpose of obtaining a tax benefit: "the tax benefit drove the deal."[80] Similarly, it could be argued that while there was a business purpose for the Australian dollar loan in *CP*, the tax benefit drove the deal, specifically the manner in which the deal was structured. However, given the unwillingness of the Supreme Court in pre-GAAR cases to weigh into a purposive analysis of statutory provisions, it is unlikely that the court will set such a low threshold for subsection 245(3). To the extent that they can, I suspect that the Supreme Court of Canada will resolve cases under subsection 245(3) (i.e., in favour of the taxpayer) rather than having to resort to subsection 245(4).

The consequences of a higher threshold under subsection 245(3) remain clear. For example, while weak currency loans are now dealt with under specific anti-avoidance legislation,[81] a lot of aggressive planning remains available through the use of creative financial instruments for businesses in need of capital. As Iacobucci, J. pointed out in *Ludco*, a test of degree — i.e., whether the primary purpose of a transaction is for *bona fide* non-tax purposes — will be "impractical in the context of investments in securities."[82] That same test of degree is applicable in determining whether there has been an avoidance transaction under GAAR in situations in which there are both tax and non-tax purposes for a transaction. Consequently, more highly technical and perhaps overreaching specific anti-avoidance legislation can be expected, for example in the government's ongoing review of the interest deductibility rules and proposed section 3.1.

2) Misuse or Abuse — Subsection 245(4)

The highly formalistic or plain meaning approach to statutory interpretation that the Supreme Court of Canada has adopted in numerous decisions since *Stubart* suggests that they may take a similar approach to the application of GAAR, particularly subsection 245(4). Various GAAR cases decided by the Tax Court and Federal Court suggest a restrictive interpretation of subsection 245(4). First, GAAR apparently did not apply to a misuse or abuse of regulations because they are not part of the Act;[83] however, the March 2004 federal budget introduced a provision, applicable retroactive-

---

recourse basis and the lease payments were prepaid to the purchaser to effectively cover the principal amount owing under its debt.

80 *Canada Trustco* (T.C.C.), at para. 57.

81 Section 20.3, added in the 2000 federal budget.

82 *Ludco*, at para. 53.

83 *Rousseau-Houle; Fredette v. The Queen*, 2001 D.T.C. 621, [2001] 3 C.T.C. 2468 (T.C.C.).

ly from the time that GAAR was introduced, specifically providing that "for greater certainty," GAAR applies to a misuse of the provisions of the Act, the regulations, the Income Tax Application Rules or any tax treaty, or an abuse having regard to those provisions read as a whole.[84] Second, it is not possible to misuse a provision if its application has been avoided.[85] Third, and most importantly, in most cases it will be extremely difficult to satisfy a court that there is a misuse of provisions of the Act (assuming certain provisions have been "used" in an inappropriate manner) or an abuse of the Act as a whole (e.g., where more specific anti-avoidance measures have been avoided), based on the test established by Rothstein, J.A. in *OSFC*. His test is certainly in keeping — to the point of adopting similar terminology — with the Supreme Court's views on statutory interpretation in tax cases and will likely be endorsed by the Supreme Court when they finally hear a GAAR case.

In *OSFC*, Rothstein, J.A. proposed a two-stage analytical process for applying subsection 245(4) and this process has been adopted in all subsequent GAAR cases in which the provision was in issue: 1. identify the relevant policy of the provisions or the Act as a whole; and 2. assess whether the avoidance transaction constitutes a misuse or abuse having regard to the identified policy.[86] This process is not unreasonable. However, Rothstein, J.A.'s comments on the application of this process are reminiscent of the "plain meaning" approach that the Supreme Court of Canada has taken in pre-GAAR tax avoidance cases (to the point of adopting a similar mantra, albeit in a different context):

> Ascertaining the relevant policy is a question of interpretation. As such it is ultimately the duty of the Court to make this determination. There is no onus to be satisfied by either party at this stage of the analysis. However, from a practical perspective, the Minister should do more than simply recite the words of subsection 245(4), and allege that there has been misuse or abuse. The Minister should set out the policy with reference to the provisions of the Act or extrinsic aids upon which he relies. Otherwise he places the taxpayer and the Court in the difficult position of trying to

84 Canada, Department of Finance, *The Budget Plan, 2004*, Notice of Ways and Means Motion to Amend the *Income Tax Act*, paragraph (18). See the proposed amendments to subsection 245(4) in Canada, Department of Finance, "Legislative Proposals, Draft Regulations and Explanatory Notes Relating to Income Tax," September 2004, subsection 36(1).

85 *Jabin.*

86 *OSFC*, at para. 67.

guess the relevant policy at issue. Trying to ascertain the policy of a specific provision or of an Act as a whole, in the case of an Act as complex as the *Income Tax Act*, is a difficult exercise, particularly when the transaction in question conforms to the letter of the Act. Therefore, the Court requires the assistance of the parties to enable it to reach a correct conclusion. Nonetheless, with or without that assistance, the Court must attempt to determine the relevant policy.

. . . This is not an exercise of trying to divine Parliament's intention by using a purposive analysis where the words in a statute are ambiguous. Rather, it is an invoking of a policy to override the words that Parliament has used. I think, therefore, that to deny a tax benefit where there has been a strict compliance with the Act, on the grounds that the avoidance transaction constitutes a misuse or abuse, requires that the relevant policy be clear and unambiguous. The Court will proceed cautiously in carrying out the unusual duty imposed upon it under subsection 245(4). The Court must be confident that although the words used by Parliament allow the avoidance transaction, the policy of relevant provisions or the Act as a whole is sufficiently clear that the Court may safely conclude that the use made of the provision or provisions by the taxpayer constituted a misuse or abuse.

In answer to the argument that such an approach will make the GAAR difficult to apply, I would say that where the policy is clear, it will not be difficult to apply. Where the policy is ambiguous, it should be difficult to apply. This is because subsection 245(4) cannot be viewed as an abdication by Parliament of its role as lawmaker in favour of the subjective judgment of the Court or particular judges. In enacting subsection 245(4), Parliament has placed the duty on the Court to ascertain *Parliament's* policy, as the basis for denying a tax benefit from a transaction that otherwise would meet the requirements of the statute. Where Parliament has not been clear and unambiguous as to its intended policy, the Court cannot make a finding of misuse or abuse, and compliance with the statute must govern.[87]

In pre-GAAR cases, "[w]here the provision in issue is *clear and unambiguous*, its terms must simply be applied" regardless of the "object and spirit" of the provision or the "economic realities" of the transaction.[88] Now, in the context of GAAR, we find the same terminology used to frame the test in subsection 245(4): unless the court can determine that the relevant policy underlying a scheme in the act is "clear and unambiguous" and has

87 *Ibid.*, at paras. 68–70 [emphasis in original].
88 Above, note 15 [emphasis added].

been misused or abused, GAAR does not apply. Whereas courts, and particularly the Supreme Court of Canada, have been quite willing to find that the meaning of a provision of the Act is clear and unambiguous, making reference to its "object and spirit" irrelevant, I suspect that it will be a rare case indeed in which a court will find that the underlying policy of a provision or series of provisions is not only clear and unambiguous but also that such policy contradicts the apparently clear words of the Act.[89]

In *Imperial Oil*, the Federal Court of Appeal succinctly describes the impact of subsection 245(4) (at paras. 39–40):

> While the Act does not expressly provide that the policy must be "clear and unambiguous", this is implicit in the language of subsection 245(4) . . . Thus, if the scheme may reasonably be considered not to result directly or indirect in a misuse or an abuse, GAAR does not apply: *in effect, the taxpayer is given the benefit of any doubt. Consequently, for GAAR to apply it must be clear that the provisions of the Act are being misused or the Act as a whole is being abused. It is not enough that a court might reasonably consider them to be misused or abused.* [emphasis added]

With respect, it should be "enough" that a court reasonably considers the provisions of the Act or the Act as a whole to be misused or abused. A "clear and unambiguous" test is not implicit in the language of subsection 245(4); the test is one of "reasonableness" and it seems to me that the function of the court *is* to be the arbiter of reasonableness. The court should not to shirk its responsibility by placing a virtually impossible burden on the Crown to establish that all tax legislation has a "clear and unambiguous" policy.[90]

---

89 In *OSFC*, Rothstein, J.A. refers to a "clear and unambiguous" policy in both paragraphs 69 and 70. However, he states in paragraph 69 that the policy must be "sufficiently clear" for the court to conclude that there has been a misuse or abuse.

90 As David Duff states in his comment on the *OSFC* decision, "While legislators should make the policy of tax legislation as clear as possible through careful drafting and explanatory materials, and the revenue authorities should bear the burden of establishing that avoidance transactions contradict the relevant policies of specific provisions or the [Act] as a whole, it is not obvious that a general anti-avoidance rule should apply only when these policies are clear and unambiguous — particularly since the misuse and abuse test comes into play only after a transaction is determined to be an avoidance transaction. For this reason, instead of providing that the GAAR does not apply where the transaction can reasonably be considered not to result in a misuse or abuse, the burden in Sec. 245(4) might be explicitly shifted to the revenue authorities and relaxed by amending the provision to state that the GAAR does not apply unless it may reasonably be considered that the transaction results in a misuse or abuse." David Duff, "Judicial Application of the General Anti-Avoidance Rule in Canada: *OSFC Holdings Ltd. v. The Queen*" (2003) 57: 3 Bulletin for International Fiscal Documentation 278 at 288.

The difficulties in applying subsection 245(4), thus interpreted, are illustrated by the majority and concurring judgments in *OSFC* as well as various Federal Court and Tax Court cases since *OSFC*.

In *OSFC*, Rothstein, J.A., for the majority, concluded that the transactions undertaken did not constitute a misuse of subsection 18(13) (as it then read) but that they did constitute an abuse of the Act as a whole. In contrast, Létourneau, J.A. concluded that the transactions constituted both a misuse of subsection 18(13) and an abuse of the Act as a whole. In determining whether there had been a misuse of subsection 18(13), Rothstein, J.A. took a highly technical approach. First, subsection 18(13) was limited only to non-arm's length transfers and the provision specifically maintained the existence of an accrued loss to be recognized by the transferee in a subsequent arm's length disposition. Second, subsection 18(13) specifically contemplated transfers to a non-arm's length partnership and the partnership rules therefore applied in the context of subsequent transfers. Third, the partnership rules recognize that a partner's share of the partnership's income or loss is determined at the partnership's year-end regardless of when the partner entered the partnership. Finally, nothing in subsection 18(13) or the partnership rules precluded the sale of a partnership interest prior to the partnership's year end. "No extrinsic aid to interpretation provides a contrary indication."[91] In contrast, Rothstein, J.A., following a detailed review of legislative scheme dealing with corporate non-capital losses and a review of certain commentators on the legislative scheme, had "no difficulty concluding that the general policy of the *Income Tax Act* is against the trading of non-capital losses by corporations, subject to specific limited exceptions."[92] While Rothstein, J.A. was unwilling to find a policy against the transfer of losses between partners, the transactions undertaken resulted in a transfer of losses between corporations through the mechanism of subsection 18(13) and the partnership rules and was therefore an abuse of the Act as a whole. It seems paradoxical to suggest that the use of a specific statutory provision in order to accomplish something that is an abuse of the Act as a whole is not, at the same time, a misuse of the specific provision. Perhaps Létourneau, J.A. saw this paradox. To him (as to the trial judge), "[s]ubsection 18(13) was not intended to be used

---

91 *OSFC*, at para. 81. In fact, the only extrinsic aid Rothstein, J.A. referred to was the 1988 technical notes to subsection 18(13), which simply reiterated the manner in which the provision applied. Perhaps there were no extrinsic aids that spoke to the policy of the provision.

92 *OSFC*, at para. 98.

by a corporation to increase the adjusted cost base of a related corporation or partnership for the purpose of selling its losses to an arm's length corporation."[93]

Duncan involved a scheme in the genre of *Spire Freezers* and *Backman*. In *Duncan*, Canadian taxpayers acquired 98 percent of an existing US partnership ("Klink") in December 1991;[94] the remaining two percent was retained by the original US partners. Klink owned an old mainframe computer with an original cost of more than $4 million and a fair market value of approximately US$7,000; the computer had over time been fully depreciated for US tax and accounting purposes. On December 20, 1991, Klink transferred the computer to a newly formed Canadian limited partnership ("ILP") in exchange for a 50 percent interest in ILP; on the transfer, Klink's partnership capital in ILP was credited with $50,000. As a result of the sale, the Canadian partners took the position that for Canadian tax purposes, Klink recognized a terminal loss in its fiscal period ending December 31, 1991 in excess of $4 million (i.e., the cost of the computer, which had never been depreciated for Canadian tax purposes, less its proceeds of disposition (the value of the partnership interest in ILP received as consideration)) pursuant to subsection 20(16) of the Act; the resultant substantial net loss was allocated to Klink's partners. The CRA denied the use of the loss to the Canadian partners on two bases: that Klink was no longer a subsisting partnership after the Canadian partners acquired their interests or, in the alternative, that GAAR applied to deny the loss. At trial, Bowie, T.C.J. concluded that partners of Klink no longer carried on a business in common with a view to profit after the Canadian partners joined the partnership because the Canadian partners had nothing to do with the remaining US partners (no commonality) and that there was no foreseeable profit from the operations.[95] Alternatively he held that GAAR applied.

On appeal, Noël, J.A., writing the unanimous decision of the court, held that Bowie, T.C.J.'s conclusion on the partnership issue was wrong in law, citing the decisions of the Supreme Court of Canada in *Spire Freezers, Buckman, Stewart* and *Walls* (all released after the trial court's decision in *Duncan*). However, Noël, J.A. concluded that GAAR did apply to deny the loss. There was little doubt that the transactions undertaken constituted avoid-

93 *Ibid.*, at para. 134.

94 In fact, a Canadian promoter acquired the entire 98 percent interest for $51,500 and then syndicated the deal by selling approximately 93.5 percent of the interests in Klink to a number of other Canadian taxpayers for an aggregate of $320,000.

95 2001 D.T.C. 96, [2001] 2 C.T.C. 2284 (T.C.C.).

ance transactions.[96] The primary issue was whether the transactions constituted a misuse of the CCA provisions or an abuse of the Act as a whole. In concluding that the CCA provisions were misused, Noël, J.A. found that the underlying policy of the CCA provisions, or their "object and the spirit,"

> is to provide for the recognition of money spent to acquire qualifying assets to the extent that they are consumed in the income earning process under the Act.[97]

Noël, J.A. further indicated that although the CCA provisions, particularly the determination of the undepreciated capital cost of the computer, "give rise to no ambiguity,"[98] their application by the appellants "exploited what can only be seen as an obvious loophole" and created a result "which was both anomalous and unintended when regard is had to their reason for being."[99] Noël, J.A. concluded that the provisions were misused and GAAR was properly applied to deny the tax benefits. In contrast to *OSFC*, Noël, J.A. reached these conclusions without reference to any extrinsic aids, although he "placed particular emphasis"[100] on Rothstein, J.A.'s comments in paragraph 69 of *OSFC* that the relevant policy must be "clear and unambiguous." In Noël, J.A.'s view, "this very particular threshold has been met in this instance."[101]

In *Donohue*, the taxpayer invested over $62 million for a 50 percent interest in a corporation (DMI) in order to finance the construction of and improvements to various pulp and paper mills in Quebec. Following the collapse in the price of wood pulp, the taxpayer's investment in DMI became worthless. In cooperation with the other 50 percent shareholder, the taxpayer undertook a series of transactions in order to retain the bulk of the assets held by DMI (through another company owned by the taxpayer and the other shareholder) but sell the shares of DMI for a nominal amount in order to recognize a business investment loss. The CRA denied the loss under GAAR. The taxpayer's appeal to the Tax Court of Canada was

96 At trial, two of the Canadian investors in Klink gave evidence that the acquisition of their interests in Klink was motivated by business opportunities for use of the computer in Eastern Europe. The trial judge did not believe their evidence and Noël, J.A., while acknowledging that this finding was the privilege of the trial judge, indicated (at para. 35) that it was amply supported by the evidence.

97 *Duncan*, at para. 44.

98 *Ibid.*, at para. 49. Accordingly, in the absence of GAAR, the court would not have found in favour of the Minister.

99 *Ibid.*, at paras. 45 and 51.

100 *Ibid.*, at para. 52.

101 *Ibid.*, at para. 53.

successful, and the Crown's appeal to the Federal Court of Appeal was dismissed. Both courts dismissed the Crown's argument that there was an underlying policy in the Act denying a loss at the shareholder level when the assets that generated that loss are retained within the same corporate group. According to Noël, J.A., writing for a unanimous Federal Court of Appeal:

> Under corporate law, a business corporation's property belongs to the corporation and not the shareholders. The Act recognizes this legal reality, as it recognizes the effects of private law. The entire system of taxation of corporations and their shareholders is conceived in terms of this legal reality. This is what explains, as the trial judge notes, that a gain or loss may be realized at the same time by a shareholder in respect of his shares and by the corporation in respect of its own property (reasons, paragraph 76). There is no principle that would allow the effect of these transactions to be consolidated by matching them. The principle underlying the Act, if there is one, is contrary to the one invoked by the Minister.[102]

In reaching this conclusion, Noël, J.A. did not refer to any specific extrinsic material, although he did consider various provisions of the Act cited by the Minister to support his position. According to Noël, J.A., none of these provisions were applicable in the instant case and furthermore, the winding-up provisions of the Act applicable other than in the case of a 90 percent-owned subsidiary, support the opposite result. It is difficult to fault the decision of the courts in *Donohue*. Indeed, one wonders why the Minister pursued the case at all.

In *Imperial Oil*, the taxpayer entered into a series of transactions that reduced its capital tax liability under Part I.3 of the Act. Shortly before its year end, the taxpayer made three short-term (approximately 30-day) loans from its accumulated cash to wholly-owned subsidiaries of banks with the loans guaranteed in each case by the parent bank. The taxpayer claimed that the loans, totaling $500 million, formed part of its investment allowance, thus reducing its taxable capital subject to capital tax. While such loans would have formed part of the taxable capital of the borrowers if they had been outstanding at the year-end of the borrowers (and therefore would not have resulted in any tax "leakage"), the loans were made and repaid during each borrower's taxation year (ending June 30) while straddling the year-end (December 31) of the taxpayer. The Minister disallowed $346.8 million of the $500 million loans as an investment allowance

102 *Donohue*, at para. 18.

under GAAR.[103] The Tax Court allowed the taxpayer's appeal and the Crown's appeal was dismissed by the Federal Court of Appeal. The Federal Court of Appeal did not consider the taxpayer's alternative argument that the transactions undertaken were avoidance transactions;[104] it focused on the misuse or abuse issue. On this point, the court suggested (at paras. 78–80):

> . . . It is difficult to characterize this transaction as either aggressive or adventuresome.
>
> No doubt Imperial took advantage of a loophole in the statutory scheme, namely the failure to deal with the consequences of different corporate years. But, as we have already indicated, that cannot in and of itself amount to a "misuse" of the statutory provisions. Indeed, it must have been perfectly foreseeable to Parliament that large corporations would make short term loans to other large corporations which spanned the end of the lender's financial year, but not the borrower's, so that both corporations would escape the [large corporation tax] on the amount of the loans.
>
> The scheme established by Parliament thus virtually invited the use of different corporate fiscal year ends as the basis for the calculation of taxable capital. . . .

It is surprising the amount of foresight that courts are ready to attribute to Parliament when they draft statutory provisions. While Parliament clearly intended to avoid "double taxation" of large corporations through the investment allowance mechanism, surely it did not intend to permit the sort of double non-taxation that the loophole in the provisions provided in these circumstances, in the same way that it did not intend to create a loophole in the stop-loss rules through the use of subsection 18(13). While the tax planning in *OSFC* has been explicitly curtailed through amendments to subsection 18(13), the planning in *Imperial Oil* remains available.

Before concluding this discussion of subsection 245(4), it is worth considering some recent decisions of the Tax Court, particularly the manner in which they have applied Rothstein, J.A.'s two-stage process under subsection 245(4). *Hill v. The Queen*[105] was released after *OSFC* but before *Dun-*

103 The Minister allowed the remainder on the basis that it would have been invested in securities, such as commercial paper, that would have been eligible as an investment allowance in any event.

104 However, the court indicated that one of the reasons why the loans did not constitute a misuse or abuse was that "the loan was an ordinary commercial transaction, with no artificial elements, undertaken for both tax and non-tax purposes." Surely, that is relevant only to the issue of characterizing the loans as avoidance transactions.

105 2002 D.T.C. 1749 (T.C.C.) [*Hill*].

can. In *Hill*, the Minister challenged a particular loan structure, under the terms of which interest that could not be paid in a particular year (because it was payable only out of certain cash flows) could, at the request of the borrower, be advanced to the borrower as additional principal. The taxpayer argued that interest payable on such additional principal (whether paid or not) was deductible under paragraph 20(1)(c). The Minister contended that such interest was compound interest (i.e., interest payable on interest) and was deductible only when paid under paragraph 20(1)(d) or, in the alternative, that GAAR denied the deduction of these additional payments. Miller, T.C.J. readily concluded that the transactions — the conversion of unpaid interest into further advances of principal — were avoidance transactions, but that they did not constitute a misuse of paragraphs 20(1)(c) or (d) or an abuse of the Act as a whole. After referring to Rothstein, J.A.'s comments in paragraphs 68 through 70 of *OSFC* and considering the Minister's written submissions as to the underlying policy rationale for distinguishing between simple interest and compound interest, Miller, T.C.J. concluded:

> I can glean no identifiable policy from this argument. It is simply a reiteration of what the Act itself says, that is, simple interest can be deducted on a paid or payable basis and compound interest must be paid to be deductible. That is not an underlying policy statement, that is a summary of the legislation. I was not referred by the Respondent to any materials that would assist me in understanding why the government permitted the deduction of simple interest on a payable basis and only permits the deduction of compound interest on a paid basis. What is the policy? It is not my role to speculate; it is the Respondent's role to explain to me the clear and unambiguous policy. He has not done so. I am therefore unable to find that there has been a misuse or abuse as contemplated by subsection 245(4) of the Act. Consequently, subsection 245(2) does not apply to the Appellant's avoidance transactions.
>
> The Appellant has most deliberately relied on the sanctity of legal relationships, not to be impugned by the economic realities of a situation, in achieving his goal. I am satisfied that indeed the law supports his position, and while GAAR may be the ultimate weapon for the government to undo such legal relationships, in this instance the application of GAAR is simply ineffective.[106]

---

106 *Ibid.*, at paras. 62–63.

Miller, T.C.J. appears to place a higher burden on the Minister than that suggested by Rothstein, J.A. in *OSFC* — an onus, perhaps — to explain to the court the clear and unambiguous policy of the Act and to support that position through extrinsic materials. It will be extremely difficult for the Minister to provide such guidance to the court, particularly when the transactions deal with older statutory provisions or, in the case of newer provisions (particularly highly detailed provisions), the guidance published by the Department of Finance (primarily through technical notes) does little more than restate the statutory provisions.

In *Loyens*, Campbell, T.C.J. sought to clarify the apparent diverse views of Rothstein, J.A. in *OSFC* and Noël, J.A. in *Duncan* as to the necessity of extrinsic evidence supporting a particular policy position. In *Loyens*, the taxpayers undertook a two-step transaction in order to transfer land inventory with an accrued gain into a corporation that they controlled so that the corporation's losses could shelter the gain (reported on income account) arising on an arm's length disposition of the land inventory. A direct transfer of the land inventory to the corporation could not have been undertaken on a rollover basis (paragraph 85(1.1)(f)), so the taxpayers transferred the land inventory to a partnership on a rollover basis under subsection 97(2) and then transferred their partnership interests to the corporation on a rollover basis under subsection 85(1). The Minister reassessed the transactions as a direct sale of land inventory by the individuals rather than by their corporation. In applying GAAR, the Minister argued that the transactions constituted a misuse of the rollover provisions in subsections 97(2) and 85(1) and an abuse of the Act as a whole.

In considering the policy underlying subsections 97(2) and 85(1), and specifically the prohibition against transfers of land inventory under subsection 85(1), Campbell, T.C.J. suggested that the Crown "has an obligation to refer to materials that might have assisted me in formulating a policy behind these provisions" where the policy behind them is not clear and unambiguous.[107] In some respects, Campbell, T.C.J.'s comments are reminiscent of the linguistic gymnastics emanating from the Supreme Court of Canada in its attempts to rationalize its application of the "modern approach" to statutory interpretation in cases such as *Antosko et al. v. The Queen*[108] and *Friesen* with *Stubart* and *Corporation Notre-Dame de Bon-Secours v. Québec*.[109] For example, Cory, J. commented in *The Queen v. Alberta Treasuries Branches and T-D Bank*:

107 *Loyens*, at para. 100.
108 94 D.T.C. 6314, [1994] 2 C.T.C. 25 (S.C.C.).
109 95 D.T.C. 5017, [1995] 1 C.T.C. 241 (S.C.C.).

> Thus, when there is neither any doubt as to the meaning of the legislation nor any ambiguity in its application to the facts then the statutory provision must be applied regardless of its object or purpose. I recognize that agile legal minds could probably find an ambiguity in as simple a request as "close the door please" and most certainly in even the shortest and clearest of the ten commandments. ... Even if the ambiguity were not apparent, it is significant that in order to determine the clear and plain meaning of the statute it is always appropriate to consider the "scheme of the Act, the object of the Act, and the intention of Parliament."[110]

In *Loyens*, the Minister proffered no evidence concerning the policy underlying the prohibition on transfers of land inventory under subsection 85(1). The taxpayer, on the other hand, provided the court with commentary on the prohibition in commercial tax texts, which suggested that it was intended to prevent a real estate trader from converting an income gain on a sale of land inventory into a capital gain on a share sale. This aspect of the court's conclusion is sound, although it is interesting to note that the court will consider commercial tax commentary (as opposed to government commentary) for the policy underlying statutory provisions.

The Minister further argued in *Loyens* that the taxpayer's transactions constituted an abuse of the Act as a whole. The Minister relied on *OSFC* for the proposition that profit trading was prohibited under the Act. This aspect of the Crown's argument and the manner in which the court dealt with it are problematic. In my view, *OSFC* stands for the proposition that the Act prohibits arm's length, inter-corporate loss *trading* (as opposed to loss *transfers*). There is certainly no prohibition in the Act against non-arm's length, inter-corporate loss trading (or non-arm's length profit and loss consolidation). *Loyens* concerned a non-arm's length situation: two brothers seeking to consolidate a profit which would otherwise be realized at the personal level with losses previously realized by their wholly-owned corporation. There is certainly no prohibition in the Act against an individual transferring a property with an accrued gain to a related corporation in order to use corporate level losses to shelter the gain on the sale of the property. As the court correctly noted, the Minister's information circular

---

110 96 D.T.C. 6245, [1996] 1 C.T.C. 395 (S.C.C.), at para. 15. On the other hand, Major, J., in dissent, suggested (at para. 100) that "the traditional Canadian jurisprudence [requires] that the words of a taxing statute are to [be] read strictly for their plain and ordinary meaning and that only if there is a true ambiguity is the intention of Parliament to be considered" [emphasis added].

on GAAR specifically countenances such transactions.[111] That is exactly what occurred in this case. However, in rejecting the Crown's argument, Campbell, T.C.J. concluded "that the general rule against loss trading has no equivalent rule when it comes to profit trading."[112] This blanket statement suggests that *OSFC* is limited strictly to inter-corporate loss transfers and that arm's length profit transfers or "profit trading" — such as that undertaken in *Duha Printers (Western) Ltd. v. The Queen*,[113] in which a profitable company transferred profits to an arm's length loss company in order to shelter those profits with the transferee's losses — would not be caught by GAAR. Surely if any pre-GAAR fact situation warrants the application of GAAR, it is the fact situation in *Duha*. *Loyens* throws that into some doubt. With respect, the Crown should never have pursued the argument that the transactions constituted an abuse of the Act as a whole; when it lost the misuse argument, that should have ended the matter.

Beyond the relatively few legislative schemes where the Minister has successfully argued subsection 245(4) — the anti-surplus stripping provisions;[114] the CCA provisions;[115] and the provisions governing corporate loss transfers[116] — it may be difficult to find a "clear and unambiguous" policy for a number of reasons. First, the Act is not a true income tax in the eco-

111 Information Circular IC 88-2, "General Anti-Avoidance Rule — Section 245 of the *Income Tax Act*," October 21, 1988, paragraph 9.

112 *Loyens*, at para. 114.

113 98 D.T.C. 6334, [1998] 3 C.T.C. 303 (S.C.C.) [*Duha*].

114 *McNichol et al v. The Queen*, 97 D.T.C. 111, [1997] 2 C.T.C. 2088 (T.C.C.); *RMM Canadian Limited v. The Queen*, 97 D.T.C. 302, [1998] 1 C.T.C. 2300 (T.C.C.) [*RMM Canadian*]; *Nadeau v. The Queen*, 99 D.T.C. 324, [1999] 3 C.T.C. 2235 (T.C.C.); and *Geransky* (all decided prior to the Federal Court of Appeal decision in *OSFC*) all dealt with various types of "surplus stripping" transactions, and the discussion of subsection 245(4) in these cases was limited to such circumstances. In none of these cases did the courts undertake a detailed examination of the scheme of the Act applicable to corporate distributions and the underlying rationale for the distinction between capital gains and dividends. Typical of the approach of the courts in these cases is *RMM Canadian*, in which Bowman, T.C.J. stated in obiter (i.e. he decided the case on other grounds) (at page 313):

> . . . the *Income Tax Act*, read as a whole, envisages that a distribution of corporate surplus to shareholders is to be taxed as a payment of dividends. A form of transaction that is otherwise devoid of any commercial objective, and that has as its real purpose the extraction of corporate surplus and the avoidance of the ordinary consequences of such a distribution, is an abuse of the Act as a whole.

115 *Duncan*. Although, the Minister was not successful in challenging a leveraged purchase and lease-back arrangement in *Canada Trustco*, (currently on appeal to the Supreme Court of Canada) where the purchased assets benefited from a high rate of CCA.

116 *OSFC*.

nomic sense of that term. The technical tax provisions — the tax base in particular — have inherent in them a number of significant departures from the economist's notion of income. For example, the concept of a source of income; the realization basis for capital gains; the differing treatment of dividends versus capital gains or interest versus dividends are all endemic in our income tax system and it may often be difficult to determine whether there is a clear policy rationale underlying these provisions. Furthermore, the Act contains within it an entire separate code of non-income tax provisions, commonly referred to as tax expenditures. These are not technical tax provisions — they are government spending provisions — and a number of aggressive tax avoidance structures are designed to take advantage of these provisions. However, it is sometimes difficult to distinguish between the technical tax and tax expenditure provisions and even if one can clearly conclude that a provision is one or the other, it will be difficult to discern a "clear and unambiguous" policy underlying the provision. However, I would prefer to see judges face these issues, enter this debate, rather than side-stepping it entirely through a restrictive view of their role as interpreters of the statute.[117]

C. "SAME AS IT EVER WAS . . ."[118]

Like Elvis, the Duke of Westminister seems to be alive and well and living somewhere in Canada notwithstanding the introduction of GAAR. The Supreme Court of Canada's views on the judiciary's role toward tax avoidance have been made abundantly clear in recent years: the court should not be quick to embellish provisions of the Act in response to concerns about tax avoidance; it is Parliament's job to be "precise and specific with respect to any mischief to be prevented."[119] Clearly, the Supreme Court views judicial innovation as undesirable and it is unlikely that GAAR will be employed by the Supreme Court as a tool of judicial innovation. However, if the Supreme Court of Canada is serious that there is no room for "judicial rule-making" in tax cases, then it ought to abolish one of the longest

117 Neil Brooks goes further, suggesting that it is the responsibility of judges "to give a meaning to the statutory language that will lead to the most sensible tax policy result in the particular case." Rather than "attempting to divine legislative meaning, intent or purpose, [judges] instead should act as pragmatic tax analysts." Neil Brooks, "The Responsibility of Judges in Interpreting Tax Legislation" in Graeme S. Cooper, ed., *Tax Avoidance and the Rule of Law* (Amsterdam: IBFD, 1997), 93 at 94.

118 Above, note 7.

119 Above, note 6.

standing judicial rules, the *Duke of Westminister*.[120] After all, where is the legislative basis for the proposition that a taxpayer is free to arrange his or her affairs in order to minimize tax? Clearly, courts can and should take a more purposive approach to the interpretation of the Act without being accused of judicial rule-making.

The current attitude of the Supreme Court of Canada has encouraged an active and aggressive tax avoidance industry notwithstanding GAAR. Their attitude to tax avoidance has inevitably resulted in more complex legislation and more specific anti-avoidance rules. Hardly a satisfactory result. The approach that the Supreme Court of Canada ultimately takes in its first two GAAR cases, *Mathew* and *Canada Trustco*, can have a profound impact in this respect.

120 *I.R.C. v. Duke of Westminister*, [1936] A.C. 1 (HL).

Chapter Nineteen

Competent Authority as a Dispute Resolution Tool

Sandra M. Goldberg and Gary L. Zed

A. INTRODUCTION

This chapter will examine the Competent Authority legal framework and administrative procedures in Canada as they relate to tax dispute resolution.

The Canadian tax treaty network is impressive, and Canada remains a leading country in both the number of its tax treaties and the maturity of its administrative procedures for resolving treaty disputes. Canada's first comprehensive tax treaty was signed with the United States in 1942. As of the end of June, 2004, Canada had 83 tax treaties in force, 6 treaties pending ratification, and 19 treaties under negotiation or renegotiation. The majority of treaties negotiated by Canada are structured following the OECD model tax convention. The model treaty, as amended, sets the standard and serves as the foundation for treaty negotiations by Canadian officials.

The pressure continues for industrial countries to adopt pro-growth tax policies that will attract foreign investments. Advancements in technology and reduction in communication and transportation costs have boosted international investment flows and increased economic integration. At the same time, the tax administrations of many countries have historically benefited, or more correctly, profited, from cooperative endeavours made possible by the mutual agreement procedures ("MAP") and exchange of information articles that are common to all tax treaties. This is particularly true between two or more countries that derive additional benefits from mature treaty relationships and membership in various multilateral tax administration alignments, such as the Pacific Area Tax Administrators ("PATA"), the Group of Four ("G-4"), the OECD, as well as other less familiar forums. PATA is made up of Australia, Canada, Japan, and the United States, and by and large limits the scope of its activities to administration issues only. The G-4 (France, Germany, the United Kingdom, and the United States) and the OECD, on the other hand, engage in a broad range of cooperative efforts that include both tax policy and administration.

The cooperation of countries linked by tax treaties is complicated by various abiding circumstances: political and domestic pressures facing revenue administrations to raise additional dollars to combat deficits[1]; global companies trying to stick handle their way through tax regimes lacking in transparency and predictability; and worst, the lack of effective dispute resolution mechanisms by some members of the global treaty community.

B. COMPETENT AUTHORITY

1) General

"Competent Authority" as part of a discussion on "tax advocacy" may, at first glance, seem somewhat unnatural; however, in the context of international dispute resolution, competent authority as a tool of first resort is more and more commonplace and quickly becoming top of mind in developing and managing tax disputes with revenue administrations around the world.

The Competent Authority function in Canada is split between the International Tax Directorate ("ITD") and the Policy and Legislation Directorate of the Canada Revenue Agency ("CRA").[2] In ITD, the Director of the Competent Authority Services Division serves as Competent Authority to resolve specific dispute cases of double taxation or taxation not in accordance with a tax treaty. The Director of the Legislative Policy Division of the Policy and Planning Branch is the Competent Authority for issues involving interpre-

1 See, for example, recent reports of the Auditor General, such as the *2002 Report of the Auditor General of Canada* – December – Chapter 4 – "Canada Customs and Revenue Agency Taxing International Transactions of Canadian Residents," c. 4, December 2002; *2001 Report of the Auditor General of Canada* "Canada Customs and Revenue Agency – International Tax Administration: Non-Residents Subject to Canadian Income Tax," c. 7, December 2001. As well, in the United States, the U.S. Senate Finance Committee leaders in a letter of December 23, 2003 asked Internal Revenue Service Commissioner Mark Everson to determine whether multinational corporations that secure special advance pricing agreements are paying their fair share of U.S. taxes.

2 A December 12, 2003 announcement stated that the Canada Customs and Revenue Agency (CCRA) be split into two agencies, the Customs Branch would join a new Border Services Agency and the remainder of the CCRA would be renamed the Canada Revenue Agency.

tation, nondiscrimination, treaty shopping, double non-taxation issues, and general issues concerning the application of tax treaties where specific taxpayers are not involved. It is noted that the divide between the two functions is increasingly blurred given the significant cooperation between these two functions and utilization of specialist resources.

The day-to-day operations of key Competent Authority programs are carried out by the ITD of the CRA. The Competent Authority program as administered by the ITD plays a critical role in fostering international compliance with tax laws as well as dispute resolution. Over the years, the CRA has sought to increase cooperation with many foreign tax authorities in improving the mechanisms for resolving disputes under tax treaties. For Canada, cooperation and reciprocity have been the cornerstones to building fruitful relationships with its treaty partners. Traditionally, the Competent Authority activities carried out by the ITD, more commonly known as the "Competent Authority" function, have been those tied to the double taxation program. However, the full range of key Competent Authority activities under the responsibility of the ITD includes:

- double taxation program;
- exchange of information program; and
- Advance Pricing Arrangement ("APA") program.

The Canadian Competent Authority process is a well-established program that will be subject to both challenges and opportunities in the coming years. For example, transfer pricing and other international transactions in Canada continue to be at the forefront of the audit issues facing taxpayers, and it is these very issues that are making their way at an unprecedented pace before the Competent Authority for resolution. These issues result from an array of sometimes inconsistent and evolving domestic rules and interpretations. Thus, multinational enterprises ("MNEs") are forced to operate in an environment that creates numerous pitfalls and risks of (economic) double taxation but can also create beneficial anomalies that the astute can exploit.

2) Legislative Framework

The legal basis for the above-noted programs is contained in articles 9, 25, and 26 of the OECD model treaty, along with their counterparts in Canada's tax treaty network.[3] Model provisions 9 and 25 are key to the world of

3 The OECD is currently undertaking a study of the effectiveness of the Mutual Agreement Procedures and will make recommendations for improvements to be included in the model treaty and commentaries.

international taxation – in particular, transfer pricing and the mutual agreement procedures. The authority for carrying out the administrative aspects of these provisions is vested in the "competent authorities" of the contracting states. With respect to Canada's treaties, the Competent Authority is the Minister of National Revenue, who can delegate his or her powers.

These Model provisions provide as follows:[4]

Article 9

ASSOCIATED ENTERPRISES

1. Where
   a) an enterprise of a Contracting State participates directly or indirectly in the management, control or capital of an enterprise of the other Contracting State, or
   b) the same persons participate directly or indirectly in the management, control or capital of an enterprise of a Contracting State and an enterprise of the other Contracting State,

   and in either case conditions are made or imposed between the two enterprises in their commercial or financial relations which differ from those which would be made between independent enterprises, then any profits which would, but for those conditions, have accrued to one of the enterprises, but, by reason of those conditions, have not so accrued, may be included in the profits of that enterprise and taxed accordingly.
2. Where a Contracting State includes in the profits of an enterprise of that State — and taxes accordingly — profits on which an enterprise of the other Contracting State has been charged to tax in that other State and the profits so included are profits which would have accrued to the enterprise of the first-mentioned State if the conditions made between the two enterprises had been those which would have been made between independent enterprises, then that other State shall make an appropriate adjustment to the amount of the tax charged therein on those profits. In determining such adjustment, due regard shall be had to the other provisions of this Convention and the competent authorities of the Contracting States shall if necessary consult each other.

---

4 The counterpart provisions for the Canada-US Treaty are contained in Appendix 1.

Article 25

MUTUAL AGREEMENT PROCEDURE

1. Where a person considers that the actions of one or both of the Contracting States result or will result for him in taxation not in accordance with the provisions of this Convention, he may, irrespective of the remedies provided by the domestic law of those States, present his case to the competent authority of the Contracting State of which he is a resident or, if his case comes under paragraph 1 of Article 24, to that of the Contracting State of which he is a national. The case must be presented within three years from the first notification of the action resulting in taxation not in accordance with the provisions of the Convention.
2. The competent authority shall endeavour, if the objection appears to it to be justified and if it is not itself able to arrive at a satisfactory solution, to resolve the case by mutual agreement with the competent authority of the other Contracting State, with a view to the avoidance of taxation, which is not in accordance with the Convention. Any agreement reached shall be implemented notwithstanding any time limits in the domestic law of the Contracting States.
3. The competent authorities of the Contracting States shall endeavour to resolve by mutual agreement any difficulties or doubts arising as to the interpretation or application of the Convention. They may also consult together for the elimination of double taxation in cases not provided for in the Convention.
4. The competent authorities of the Contracting States may communicate with each other directly, including through a joint commission consisting of themselves or their representatives, for the purpose of reaching an agreement in the sense of the preceding paragraphs.

In general terms, the associated enterprises article (generally article 9 of a tax treaty) provides the authority to a contracting state to adjust the profit or income of an enterprise where that profit or income does not reflect the amount that should have accrued if dealings were between independent enterprises. Article 25 creates a MAP whereby taxpayers can apply to the Competent Authority of their state of residence for relief from taxation not in accordance with the convention – usually double taxation. The MAP also provides the authority for the APA program. Article 26, the exchange of information article, provides the mechanism for the exchange of information between treaty countries. A more detailed discussion follows below.

3) Taxpayer Cases

a) Trends

The double taxation program continues to experience exponential growth. From 1995 to 2004,[5] the inventory of cases increased by more than 300 per cent; the number of new cases accepted into the system increased by more than 400 per cent; and the number of closed cases has increased by 500 per cent. In the fiscal period ending March 31, 2004, the CRA maintained a record pace, closing 234 cases. Traditionally approximately 80–85 per cent of the Canadian MAP work involves the United States, and thus many of the comments contained herein and the policies of the CRA are reflective of that relationship. However, whether a trend or not, it is interesting to note that in the last two years, the per centage of cases not involving the United States has more than doubled, having gone from about 15 per cent of the inventory in 2002 to more than 33 per cent of the inventory now. Arguably there is a heightened level of concern for both the Canadian Competent Authority and Canadian-based MNEs as they venture into relatively new double taxation territory. As developing countries get on the "competent authority bandwagon", MNEs will be subject to less transparency and predictability as these treaty partners go to the negotiating table with little experience or procedures in resolving double taxation cases. On the one hand, this will raise concerns around the ability to seek certainty on both process and results. On the other hand, it creates an opportunity for the MNE to advocate its position more than what might otherwise be the norm.

There has been recognition of the need to improve service relating to the MAP program and to provide taxpayers with timely, complete assistance, and guidance. The CRA has undertaken a number of initiatives in the last few years to find ways of shortening the process, including the recently released Draft Information Circular IC 71-17R5, Competent Authority Process,[6] commented on in detail below. While still in draft, we expect considerable changes from the first draft as a result of the consultation process that has taken place and the further internal review now in progress.

Table 1 below illustrates the statistics relating to competent authority requests workload by March 31 fiscal years ending March 31, 1996 through March 31, 2004. Table 2 below illustrates the statistics relating to the APA program for fiscal periods ending March 31, 1999 and March 31, 2004.[7]

---

5 The Canadian fiscal year ends on March 31.

6 Online at http://www.cra-arc.gc.ca/tax/nonresidents/draftic-README.html.

7 The significant increase for "new cases" and "closed cases" for fiscal years ending 2002–2004 reflects a new approach for counting workload statistics. These years

Table 1: Competent Authority Requests, by March 31 Fiscal Year-Ends

Fiscal Year Ending	Opening Inventory	New Cases	Closed Cases	Closing Inventory
1996	61	55	42	74
1997	74	85	46	113
1998	113	80	50	143
1999	143	77	70	150
2000	150	85	74	161
2001	161	70	81	149
2002	149	162	123	188
2003	188	195	193	190
2004	190	239	234	195

Table 2: APA Programs — Statistics, by March 31 Fiscal Year-Ends

Fiscal Year Ending	Opening Inventory	Accepted	Completed	Closing Inventory	Pre-Filing Meetings	Withdrawn/ Revoked
1999	29	1	5	25	3	3
2000	25	10	5	30	20	3
2001	30	10	11	29	3	2
2002	29	13	5	37	14	0
2003	37	15	15	37	20	1
2004	37	17	17	37	23	3

As shown in Table 1, the CRA's APA Program enjoyed its best year yet in 2004. During this period there were a significant number of APA pre-filing meetings and acceptances as well as a record number of completions.

b) Framework

As noted above, the framework for the double taxation program is contained in articles 9 and 25 of the OECD model tax treaty, along with their counterparts in Canada's tax treaty network. Article 9, the associated enterprises article, provides the authority to a contracting state to adjust the profit or income of an enterprise where that profit or income does not reflect the amount that would have accrued if dealings had been between independent enterprises. This relates to what is commonly known as transfer pricing. The Canadian domestic rules for transfer pricing are set out in section 247 of the *Income Tax Act* ("the Act").[8] Further administrative guidance as to the CRA's application of the transfer pricing rules is found in IC 87-2R.

include "requests" many of which would ultimately not require action or be considered part of the "traditional" double taxation workload.

8 Section 247 of the *Income Tax Act* is reproduced in Apeendix 2.

Article 25 creates a dispute resolution procedure, known as the Mutual Agreement Procedure or MAP, whereby taxpayers can apply to the Competent Authority of their state of residence for relief from taxation not in accordance with the convention — usually, double taxation resulting from a transfer pricing adjustment by a revenue authority. Where a taxpayer is faced with a potential double taxation situation and wants to seek Competent Authority assistance, a notice of objection should also be filed as a protective measure to preserve the right to the appeals process in the event that the taxpayer is not satisfied with the settlement reached by the competent authorities.[9] It is also advised to file timely waivers to keep taxation years open to allow adjustments to be made following a competent authority settlement.[10]

There are situations where a taxpayer may be asked to waive appeal rights. This can arise where a taxpayer agrees to a settlement with the auditor and as part of that settlement agreement, the taxpayer is granted the right to repatriate to Canada the amount at issue in the proposed assessment in exchange for relief from a withholding tax under Part XIII of the Act relating to a deemed dividend paid to a non-resident.[11] It is important to note that although the CRA's repatriation policy asks for a waiver of appeal rights, the right to seek relief from double tax under the MAP cannot be denied.

c) Timeframes

The chart in appendix 3 to this chapter was developed as a tool to assist both the CRA and taxpayers with articles 9 and 25.[12] In order to make effective use of tax treaties in resolving disputes, it is critical to take note of the wording of the particular tax treaty at issue. Although Canada generally follows the OECD model tax treaty, each treaty, by virtue of the fact that it is a negotiated document between two states, has its own nuances. The chart highlights some of the key issues to take note of in articles 9 and 25, such as the different time limits for notification or presentation of a case to Competent Authority. Missing these time limits can jeopardize a taxpayer's right to take advantage of the dispute resolution capabilities available under the MAP.

Article 9(1) of the OECD Model grants tax authorities of a Contracting State (State A) the right to adjust the profits of an enterprise if it is their

---

9 See Competent Authority process below for normal procedures as defined in Draft IC 71-17R5.

10 Pursuant to subparagraph 152(4)(a)(ii) of the Act, a taxpayer must have filed with the Minister a waiver in a prescribed form (Form T2029) within the normal reassessment period for the taxpayer in respect of the year.

11 CRA TPM-02: Repatriation of funds by Non-residents – Part XIII Assessments.

12 Revised and current to August, 2004.

view that as a result of a special relationship with an enterprise in another State (State B), the true taxable profits are not properly reflected in State A.[13] It is interesting to note that although the OECD model does not provide a time limit within which adjustments to profits may be made under article 9, most of Canada 's treaties provide for a time limit, being the lesser of the time limit under domestic law and six years. In the vast majority of Canada's treaties, these time limits relate solely to the initial adjustment or reassessment by State A under article 9(1). Several treaties, however, have time limits that also apply to the correlative adjustment that can be provided by State B in article 9(2).[14] Article 9(2) provides an ability for State B to provide a corresponding adjustment to the accounts of the associated enterprise in its State to relieve the double taxation resulting from the upward adjustment to the profits of the associated enterprise in State A. Double taxation results when profits that have already been subject to tax in State B are again subject to tax by the upward adjustment in State A.

Canada clearly favours having a correlative relief provision in its treaties, similar to article 9(2) of the OECD model. The absence of this provision though should not hamper the availability of relief from double taxation under the MAP article. Article 9(2) of the OECD model provides that where a contracting state includes in the profits of an enterprise of that state — and taxes accordingly — profits on which an enterprise of the other contracting state has been charged to tax in that other state as a result of a transfer-pricing adjustment, "then that other State shall make an appropriate adjustment to the amount of the tax charged therein on those profits."

Where time limits to raise adjustments are provided, many of Canada's treaties contain an anti-abuse clause, which provides that the time limits will not apply where there has been fraud, willful default, or neglect. This type of clause acts as a counterbalance to prevent taxpayers from manipulating the time limits to raise an adjustment. Since article 9 of the OECD model does not contain any such time limits, this anti-abuse provision is not needed in the model. From a Canadian domestic perspective, paragraph 152(4)(a) of the Act contains similar rules as an exception to the Minister's obligation to assess or reassess within the "normal reassessment period," as defined in subsection 152(3.1).

---

13 Guidelines for the application of Article 9 are contained in *Transfer Pricing Guidelines for Multinational Enterprises and Tax Administrations*. This report was originally approved by the Council of the OECD on June 27, 1995 and is updated regularly.

14 See by way of example the treaties with Australia, Bulgaria, New Zealand, Sweden, and the United States.

Where adjustments are raised by State A under article 9(1), State B would not normally grant a correlative adjustment under article 9(2) without having the competent authorities engaged to discuss the case. The normal procedure would be for the associated enterprise subject to economic double taxation to present the case to the competent authority of its state of residence under the MAP article of the relevant treaty, that is article 25 of the OECD model or its equivalent. The standard Canadian time frame to present a case to the Competent Authority under the MAP article of the treaty is two years from the first notification of an action resulting in taxation not in accordance with the convention. For a Canadian resident, this would normally mean that Competent Authority assistance must be sought within two years from a notice of assessment that gives rise to double taxation.

Article 25(2) of the OECD model allows countries to make adjustments to implement a Competent Authority settlement, "notwithstanding any time limits in the domestic law of the Contracting States." Canada and several other countries have reserved the right to take a different approach on this sentence, preferring to offer more certainty to taxpayers and tax administrators through time limits to make adjustments. The time limit is either five or six years and is often accompanied by an anti-abuse provision similar to the one mentioned above in article 9 waiving the time limits in cases of fraud, willful default, or neglect.

C. COMPETENT AUTHORITY PROCESS FOR DISPUTE CASES

1) General

In addition to the legal framework for the Competent Authority and its interaction with domestic law as outlined above, the CRA sets out guidance regarding obtaining assistance from the Canadian Competent Authority in Income Tax Information Circular IC 71-17.

The CRA recently devoted considerable time and energy to updating the last version of IC 71-17R4, dated May 12, 1995. A draft of IC 71-17R5 has been distributed for consultation and will be the focus of the discussion below. There will be further additions and refinements to the draft IC so readers will need to be governed by any further pronouncements by the CRA.

This latest revision of the IC provides much more guidance to taxpayers than has been publicly available in the past. The Competent Authority procedures and practices are now described in much greater detail. Particular emphasis is given to special procedures available under the Canada-U.S. tax treaty relating to requests to defer: capital gains arising from reorganizations, taxes arising on death and taxes relating to S. Corporations. For the first time, template agreement letters relating to these special procedures are attached as appendices to the IC.

2) Taxes and Issues Covered

Each specific treaty contains a definition of the taxes covered by that convention. For Canada, the taxes covered are normally all taxes imposed under the Act. As for the issues covered, generally, Competent Authority assistance may be requested relating to any issue that may result in double taxation or taxation not in accordance with the convention. The draft IC provides many examples of taxation that may warrant a request for assistance to the Canadian Competent Authority. These include:

- a person considered to be a resident of Canada under Canadian law is also considered to be a resident of a treaty country under that country's domestic law, and each country asserts that the taxpayer is a resident of their jurisdiction for the purposes of the convention. If unresolved, the taxpayer could be subject to tax on the same income in both countries (double taxation). A request to the Canadian Competent Authority will be necessary to initiate negotiations between the competent authorities regarding the proper application of the tiebreaker rules contained in the residency article of the convention.
- a taxpayer in a treaty country is subject to additional tax because of a transfer pricing adjustment to the price of goods or services transferred to or from a related party in Canada. The Canadian taxpayer may request that the Canadian Competent Authority allow a corresponding deduction in Canada to prevent economic double taxation.
- a branch of a Canadian resident taxpayer operating in a treaty country is subject to additional tax because of an adjustment by the treaty country of the income allocated to the branch. The taxpayer can request that the Canadian Competent Authority allow an increased foreign tax credit in Canada to prevent double taxation.
- a Canadian taxpayer subject to tax in Canada on worldwide income, including income from carrying on a business in a treaty country, is taxed in the treaty country on the business income earned in the treaty country despite not having a permanent establishment (PE) in that country under the convention.
- tax is withheld by a treaty country on a payment to a Canadian resident at a rate in excess of the rate stated in the convention.

- the convention specifies that a different time be allowed for refunds or other relieving procedures than is allowed under the domestic law of Canada or the treaty country, a Canadian taxpayer may request that the Canadian Competent Authority allow, or assert with the other Competent Authority the taxpayer's right to, the applicable relief despite the domestic time limitation.
- there is uncertainty whether an item of income in the other jurisdiction is covered by the treaty.[15]

3) Making an Application under the Dispute Resolution Mechanism

The Competent Authority process normally begins when a request is made to the Competent Authority under the MAP article of a particular treaty. Normally a taxpayer makes requests to the Competent Authority of its country of residence. Assume, for example, that the CRA issues a reassessment on X Co., a Canadian resident corporation, increasing the income of X Co in Canada by reducing the transfer price that X Co. pays to Y Co., its U.S. parent, for raw materials. Unless Y Co.'s U.S. income is decreased accordingly, double taxation will result.

X. Co. could pursue the appeals process to resolve the dispute with the CRA but this will not address the double taxation issue unless the reassessment is vacated in its entirety. Where a tax treaty is available as a method of dispute resolution, it is usually less expensive, less adversarial, less time consuming and more effective than the appeals process. In this case, X. Co. would likely choose to obtain relief from double taxation by making a request to the Canadian Competent Authority under Article XXVI of the Canada-U.S. tax treaty (the MAP article). The preferred procedure would be for Y Co. to make a similar request to the U.S. Competent Authority. As noted above, in Canada, the Competent Authority function relating to the resolution of cases involving specific taxpayers is carried out by the Director, Competent Authority Services Division, International Tax Directorate.

The general rule is that a taxpayer applies for relief by applying to the Competent Authority of the Contracting State of residence. The term "resident" for the purposes of a convention is normally defined in article 4 of the relevant convention. In article IV of the Canada-U.S. convention, for example, the term "resident" of a Contracting State means:

---

15 Draft Information Circular IC 71-17R5, "Requests for Competent Authority Consideration Under Mutual Agreement Procedures in Income Tax Conventions," at para. 4.

> any person that, under the laws of that State, is liable to tax therein by reason of that person's domicile, residence, citizenship, place of management, place of incorporation or any other criterion of a similar nature . . .

One exception to this general rule is found in the related persons article of the Canada-U.S. treaty. That article allows a Contracting State to adjust the income, loss or tax payable of a "person" related to a person in the other Contracting State. Thus, for example, a company resident in a third state, such as France, with a PE in Canada and related to a company resident in the United States could face double taxation and be entitled to Competent Authority relief under article IX of the Canada-U.S. treaty.

4) Timing for Raising Disputes to Competent Authority for Resolution

A taxpayer need not wait until a formal reassessment has been issued to request Competent Authority assistance. The standard wording of the MAP article states that a request can be made when the actions of one of the treaty partners "result, or will result, in taxation not in accordance with the convention."[16] This has been interpreted to mean that a request can be made on the basis of a written proposal letter.

As discussed above, most of Canada's tax treaties specify a time limit within which a case must be presented to the Competent Authority. The standard time limit in the majority of Canada's tax treaties is two years from the first notification of an action resulting in taxation not in accordance with the treaty. This standard wording follows the wording of article 25(1) of the OECD model, except that the OECD model provides for a three-year time limit.

Paragraph 18 of the OECD Commentary provides that the starting point of the time limit should be interpreted in the way most favourable to the taxpayer. Thus, if there have been a combination of decisions or actions by the revenue authority resulting in taxation not in accordance with the convention, the time limit will begin to run from the first notification of the most recent decision or action.

It is imperative to check the wording of each relevant treaty to ensure that the specified time limit is not missed. Missing the time limit will usually result in not having access to Competent Authority assistance. Many countries, including Canada, have a policy of including time limits in their

---

16 Model Tax Convention on Income and on Capital (Paris: OECD) (looseleaf), published in 1992 and amended in 1994, 1997, 2000 and 2003, Article 25, at para. 1.

double taxation treaties so as to not keep issues open indefinitely (see Appendix 3).

The time limit applicable to the Canada-U.S. treaty does not follow the standard OECD wording described above. Where the OECD language requires cases to be "presented" within a certain time, the Canada-US treaty speaks of "notification" to the Competent Authority within six years from the end of the taxable year to which an adjustment relates. Paragraph 3 of Article IX of the Canada-U.S. treaty contains the rules relating to time limits for cases involving related persons. In a typical Canada-U.S. transfer pricing case, if the IRS makes an adjustment to the 2002 income of Y. Co., for example, Canada will make a corresponding adjustment to the income of X. Co. to alleviate double taxation notwithstanding domestic time limitations[17] if the following two conditions are met:

- Canada agrees with the adjustment made by the United States; and
- the Canadian Competent Authority has received notification of the adjustment within six years of the end of Y. Co.'s 2002 taxable year.

If timely notification is not provided to the Canadian Competent Authority, the competent authorities have the ability to agree to consider the case provided it is not statute-barred domestically.[18] Contrary to the former wording of the treaty, applicable to the 1985–1995 taxation years, there is now no obligation on the country raising the adjustment to withdraw it if notification was not timely.[19]

5) Unilateral Relief

The wording of the MAP article in most treaties suggests that unilateral relief should always be considered as a first step once an application for Competent Authority assistance has been presented.[20] It is only where the Competent Authority to which the case has been presented is not able to arrive at a satisfactory solution on its own that it is obligated to endeavour to resolve the case by mutual agreement with the other Competent Authority. Unilateral relief is not common but has occurred from time to time in certain situations, for example, where the Competent Authority does not believe there is sufficient back-up in the audit file to support the reassessment. At odds with this perspective are the recent statements by officials of

---

17 Domestic time limitations are set out in ss. 152(4) of the Act.

18 Canada-U.S. Treaty, Art. IX (3).

19 See former wording to Art. IX (3)(b).

20 For example, see paragraph 1 of Art. XXVI of the Canada-U.S. Treaty.

the CRA to suggest that competent authority case officers would develop the necessary evidence in certain cases where the field audit work is insufficient to support the adjustment. The draft IC71-17R5 also contains statements to the effect that Competent Authority officers have the ability to request information that was not requested at audit or was requested and not provided.[21]

6) Role of Appeals

The Appeals Branch of the CRA does not play a direct role in the Competent Authority process in Canada. Unlike the United States, Canada has decided against implementing a formal simultaneous appeals process whereby a taxpayer can request Appeals to work in conjunction with the Competent Authority by taking a first look at a case and provide Competent Authority with a starting point from which to negotiate with the other Competent Authority.

In Canada, a taxpayer in need of dispute resolution must initially choose whether to pursue a remedy through domestic appeals or through the Competent Authority. Where the dispute involves a transaction with a non-treaty country, then domestic appeals will be the only option. Where a treaty is available, the majority of taxpayers choose to pursue relief through the Competent Authority process. The reason for this is that through the Competent Authority process, most taxpayers will obtain relief from double taxation or taxation not in accordance with a convention. In the appeals process, taxpayers may or may not obtain full relief. If full relief is not obtained, there is a strong likelihood that some double taxation will remain.

The interaction between the Appeals Branch and the Competent Authority in Canada is one area that has been the subject of much recent debate and discussion.[22] These discussions lead to new policy directions outlined in draft IC71-17R5. There is little doubt that this is one area that will change again before the final version of the IC is issued. Based upon the public statements by the CRA, the interim policy as set out in the draft IC is in effect until further changes are announced. Previously taxpayers were advised to protect their appeal rights by filing a Notice of Objection with the Appeals Branch and requesting that the Notice of Objection be held in abeyance pending the Competent Authority resolution. Taxpayers were cautioned that if they proceeded down a road with Appeals that led to an

21 See draft IC71-17R5, at para. 27.

22 See comments made by Jim Gauvreau, Director, CRA Competent Authority Services Division, at the meeting of the Canadian Branch of the International Fiscal Association held in Toronto in May 2003.

Appeals "settlement," their rights to have the matter dealt with in the Competent Authority process would be jeopardized. The administrative interpretation of the term "Appeals settlement" by the Canadian Competent Authority included any decision by Appeals, such as a decision to vary, confirm, or vacate, even if this decision was not with the taxpayer's concurrence.

There is a proposal to modify this policy in draft IC71-17R5. According to the draft, a taxpayer could pursue an issue first with Appeals and if double taxation or taxation not in accordance with the convention remains following an Appeals Branch decision, the taxpayer could submit the issue to the Competent Authority at that time.[23] For example, a Canadian taxpayer faced with a transfer pricing assessment that gives rise to double taxation with a U.S. affiliate can file a Notice of Objection with Appeals and meet with Appeals to discuss the file. If Appeals subsequently varies the assessment (with or without the taxpayer's concurrence), the taxpayer is still free to make an application to the Canadian Competent Authority for relief from the remaining double taxation. This would not have been possible under the former policy.

Remaining unchanged is the fundamental principle that the CRA will not allow two independent procedures (the Competent Authority process and either the Appeals process or court action) to continue simultaneously. If a taxpayer proceeds with either an Appeals process or a court action on a matter that is under Competent Authority consideration, the Competent Authority process will be suspended. It is recommended that taxpayers always file a Notice of Objection within the statutory time period to keep their options open. If the taxpayer pursues the Competent Authority route and does not obtain full relief or is not happy with the Competent Authority settlement, appeal rights will still be available as long as a timely Notice of Objection had been filed and held in abeyance pending the outcome of the Competent Authority discussions.[24]

7) Prefiling and Postfiling Conference

The discussions and negotiations between competent authorities to resolve cases take place without the presence of taxpayers or their advisors. The reason for this is to protect the treaty secrecy that surrounds these discussions and also to allow frank, open discussions, recognizing that Competent Authority settlements are not precedent setting. The Canadian

23 Draft Information Circular IC 71-17R5, "Requests for Competent Authority Consideration Under Mutual Agreement Procedures in Income Tax Conventions," at para. 30.

24 Of course, the appeal rights will not be available if earlier waived as part of a repatriation agreement as discussed above.

procedures, unlike the US, do not include a reference to prefiling and post-filing conferences. However, it is possible to arrange telephone or face-to-face meetings or conferences with Competent Authority staff to discuss cases. This is especially important where there are difficult facts or issues involved that can easily be clarified through discussions.

8) Information Required

There is no prescribed form for making a request to the Competent Authority. The style and format of Competent Authority requests will vary greatly but the CRA does require certain basic information, as set out in draft IC 71-17R5:

1) the name, address, and social insurance number, or corporation identification and business number, of the Canadian taxpayer;
2) the name of the foreign tax administration involved, the treaty article(s) which the taxpayer asserts is not being correctly applied by Canada or the other country, and the taxpayer's interpretation of the application of the article;
3) the name, address, and, if possible, the identification number of any foreign taxpayer involved;
4) the relationship between the Canadian taxpayer and any related foreign taxpayers involved (applicants should also keep the Competent Authority informed of any changes in these relationships that occur after the request has been filed.);
5) the taxation years or periods involved;
6) the TSO or Taxation Centre that has made or is proposing to make the adjustment, if applicable;
7) a summary of the facts and an analysis of the issues for which Competent Authority assistance is requested, including any specific issues raised by the foreign tax administration or CRA affecting the Canadian taxpayer and the related amounts (in both Canadian and foreign currency), each supported by calculations;
8) a copy of the Competent Authority request and all the documents filed, or to be filed, with the relevant foreign Competent Authority, including copies of any correspondence from the other tax administration, and copies of any briefs, objections, etc., submitted in response to the action or proposed action of the other tax administration (if such copies are in a foreign language, an English or French translation must be supplied);
9) a statement whether the taxpayer or a predecessor has made a prior request to the Canadian Competent Authority on the same or a related issue;

10) for each taxpayer involved in the request, a schedule of the statute-barred dates in each jurisdiction (domestic time limits) in respect of all years for which relief is sought;
11) a statement whether the taxpayer has filed a notice of objection or a notice of appeal in Canada;
12) where the request for Competent Authority assistance involves issues that are currently or were previously considered as part of an Advance Pricing Arrangement (APA) in Canada or in similar proceedings in the foreign country, a statement to this effect;
13) if consent has not already been provided for a person to act as an authorized representative, a completed Form T1013 Authorizing or Canceling a Representative;
14) any other relevant facts; and
15) any possible bases on which to resolve the issues.

Because there is no prescribed form, the above information can be provided in as brief or lengthy format as necessary, depending on the complexity of the case. If the taxpayer's view is that the assessment position is incorrect or that facts have been misconstrued, it is in the taxpayer's interest to take the time to set this out in a detailed submission to the Competent Authority. A thorough CA submission will save the competent authorities time in preparing their position paper and will have far greater chance of shaping the case toward the taxpayer's viewpoint.

9) Protective Measures

Certain protective measures must be taken in all cases in order to protect and leave open all avenues of dispute resolution. There are three different issues to consider. First, ensure that the time limits for presenting a case to the Competent Authority or notifying the Competent Authority according to the relevant treaty are respected.[25] Second, ensure that a Notice of Objection is filed with the Appeals Branch to protect the right to appeal.[26] Third, ensure that taxation years do not become statute-barred under domestic law. In Canada, the filing of a waiver within the normal reassessment period will allow the Canadian Competent Authority to provide relief despite the expiration of the domestic time limitation.[27]

25 See Chart in Appendix 3.

26 Information Circular IC 98-1R, "Collections Policies", September 15, 2000.

27 Subsections 152 (4) and (5) of the Act. The definition of "normal reassessment period" is set out at section 152 (3.1) of the Act.

10) Denial of Requests

One of the more controversial areas of the proposed draft IC will undoubtedly be the sections discussing circumstances where the Competent Authority can deny a request for relief. One of these paragraphs deals with so-called "Uncooperative Taxpayers."[28] The CRA is taking a tough stance and has now stated that a taxpayer's failure to cooperate with the Canadian Competent Authority during any part of the Competent Authority process may lead to the denial of a request. In principle, it is understandable that taxpayers should be cooperative for the Competent Authority process to function properly. The difficulty is in determining when a taxpayer is not being cooperative as opposed to information truly not being available, or where requests for information are so broad or unreasonable that not supplying all information requested could be perceived by the CRA as not being cooperative. If information is simply not available because of abnormal passage of time, key people leaving positions or a change in control, for example, then one should question whether taxpayers should suffer double taxation as a result.

There are other provisions of the revised circular that limit the availability of relief in certain cases. One such provision is new and states that cases will not be negotiated by the Canadian Competent Authority where the primary position of a CRA reassessment was made under anti-avoidance sections of the Act, including the Income Tax Regulations.[29] It is somewhat unclear what this means for the taxpayer faced with such a reassessment. The IC does not say that such requests will automatically be denied but instead it states that "if it is determined that there is taxation not in accordance with the convention," the Canadian Competent Authority will "limit itself to forwarding the case to the other Competent Authority for any relief that the foreign Competent Authority may provide at its discretion."[30] This provision could push taxpayers to take their cases to Appeals rather than competent authority. Limiting the availability of competent authority relief in an administrative document such as an IC rather than in the convention itself, could be viewed as being contrary to the object and spirit of the convention, that is, to avoid double taxation. Also noted in the IC is a long-stand-

---

28 Draft Information Circular IC 71-17R5, "Requests for Competent Authority Consideration Under Mutual Agreement Procedures in Income Tax Conventions," at para. 27.

29 This would apply, for example, to reassessments made under sections 17, 94, 212.1, 245, 246, or paragraph 247(2)(b) of the Act or subsection 5907(5.1) of the Income Tax Regulations. It is interesting to note that paragraph 247 (2)(a), dealing with "regular" transfer pricing adjustments is also an anti-avoidance provision but is not one of the listed provisions.

30 Above note 21, at para. 38.

ing position regarding imputed interest in thin capitalization cases. Canada will continue to limit the deductibility of interest in these situations under paragraph 20(1)(c) and subsection 18(4) of the Act. Relief from any double taxation that may arise from these issues for U.S. residents will be possible only in the United States at the discretion of its Competent Authority.

The CRA will notify the taxpayer within 30 days of making a request whether it has been accepted or declined. Reasons will be provided where a request has been declined.[31] There are no formal appeal rights available from denial of requests for Competent Authority assistance.

11) Competent Authority Services Division Case Management

The day-to-day management of a competent authority file begins once a taxpayer sends a request to the Canadian Competent Authority for assistance. The request is logged into the system and assigned to one of the groups. The manager of that group then assigns the file to a lead analyst. The lead analyst prepares all correspondence and is the sole point of contact for the taxpayer (or representative), the foreign Competent Authority, the local CRA Tax Services Office, and Appeals. A position paper is prepared by the lead analyst based on the audit working papers, the taxpayers submission and subsequent discussions with the TSO auditor.

If the Canadian adjustment has merit, the lead analyst will normally propose in the Canadian position paper, that full relief be granted by the foreign Competent Authority. If there are aspects to the adjustment that lack merit, the lead analyst may state in the position paper that part (or all) of the adjustment will be withdrawn and full relief is being requested for the remaining portion. The lead analyst will remain in contact with the foreign Competent Authority analyst assigned to the file to determine case timelines as well as to determine whether the case may be resolved over the phone. If face-to-face negotiations are required, the points of contention will usually be discussed over the phone beforehand so that both parties are prepared to discuss and resolve the file. If necessary, the group manager may intervene in negotiations if necessary to bring the negotiations back on track. After the two competent authorities have reached a resolution, the lead analyst asks the Canadian taxpayer whether it wishes to accept or reject the Competent Authority resolution. Based on this response, closing letters are then issued to the taxpayer, the TSO, and Appeals.[32]

---

31 *Ibid.* at para. 19.

32 For CRA Service Standard – Appeals, see http://www.ccra-adrc.gc.ca/agency/annual/2002-2003/performance-e/schd_srv_stnd.html

The general flow of a Competent Authority case from start to finish is set out in the chart below.

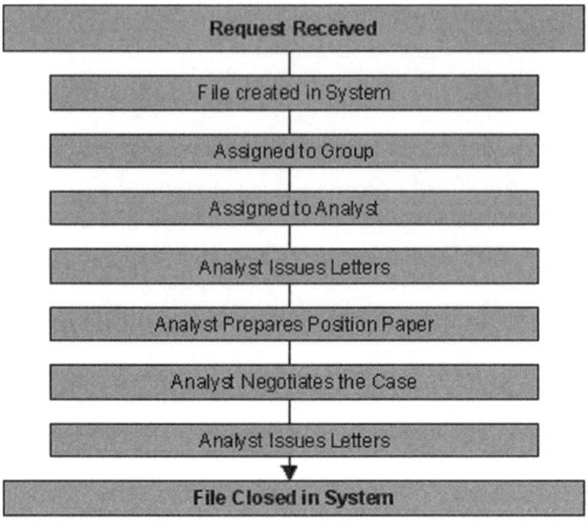

Taxpayers are free to withdraw a MAP request at any stage. Withdrawals are exceptional but this could change given the new draft policies on choosing appeals versus Competent Authority.

D. EFFECT ON DOMESTIC TAX PROVISIONS AND PROCEEDINGS

An application for Competent Authority assistance does not stop the clock domestically on assessments, the legal requirement to pay tax liabilities, or the related interest. The normal collection rules continue to apply. The rules under the collection provisions of the Act provide that the CA may not commence collection action until 90 days after the date of a taxpayer's assessment or reassessment. If a taxpayer files a Notice of Objection or appeals to the Tax Court of Canada, the CRA must further defer collection until 90 days after the objection or appeal is decided.

These collection restrictions do not apply to "large corporations," as defined under subsection 225.1(8) of the Act. Large corporations are required to pay one-half of an assessed amount at the time of assessment. The collection restrictions also do not apply to tax, interest, and penalties assessed on payments made to non-residents that are subject to withholding under Part XIII, or section 116 (dispositions of property) of the Act.

1) Court Proceedings

The position of the CRA is that it will not vary a decision of a court. In the event that a matter is decided by a court before a Competent Authority application is made, the Canadian Competent Authority will present the case to the other Competent Authority but will not vary from the court decision. It will be up the other Competent Authority to grant unilateral relief if it so chooses.

2) Interest on Deficiencies and Refunds and Penalties

Canada's income tax treaties cover taxes as defined in the "taxes covered" article but the treaties do not extend to interest or penalties. Therefore, the Canadian Competent Authority does not have the delegated authority under Canada's treaties, or under the Act, to waive or negotiate any portion of interest or penalties resulting from reassessments or adjustments that are the subject of a request for Competent Authority assistance. Domestically, requests for interest relief under subsection 220(3.1) of the Act should be directed to the fairness officials of the relevant TSO. It is the practice of the Canadian Competent Authority to recommend not waiving interest for reassessments involving Competent Authority agreements. However, in certain cases, such as where there has been inordinate delay in negotiating a settlement, it may be appropriate to seek interest relief.

Interest on tax assessments will continue to run pending the resolution of a Competent Authority case. This issue is one of the main irritants to taxpayers during the Competent Authority process. Although average time frames to resolve cases have been declining, it is not unusual to have Competent Authority cases outstanding for two to three years. This means that in many cases, the interest costs often become the most significant part of the final liability for the taxpayer. Although most treaty partners will pay interest to their taxpayers on refunds arising as a result of a Competent Authority settlement, interest costs are not always neutralized because of different treatment of interest in different jurisdictions. For many taxpayers, the interest costs often are one of the most important factors in deciding on a dispute resolution strategy. There are many considerations in assessing whether to proceed first to Appeals or Competent Authority. The impact of interest costs certainly are one of the critical considerations.

Penalties, for example the application of the Canadian transfer pricing penalty, are a compliance issue not covered by the MAP article of a convention. Therefore, the Canadian Competent Authority will not negotiate the amount or applicability of a penalty with a foreign tax administration. Likewise the Canadian Competent Authority will not challenge the position of foreign tax administrations with respect to the application of their penalties. However, where the CRA has proposed to reassess or has reassessed a transfer pricing penalty and the competent authorities negotiate a change to the amount of the transfer pricing income or capital adjustments, the CRA will adjust the amount of the Canadian transfer pricing penalty accordingly.

3) Repatriation of Funds after a Reallocation

Where a transfer pricing adjustment is made under section 247 of the Act, in addition to being disallowed as a deduction to the Canadian payer, the amount of the adjustment may also be subject to withholding tax under Part XIII as a deemed dividend paid to a non-resident. However, at the audit stage, the CRA may enter into a repatriation agreement to grant relief for the Part XIII tax if the Canadian taxpayer agrees in writing to the proposed transfer pricing adjustments, provides a waiver of appeal rights, and agrees to repatriate funds from the non-resident equivalent to the amount of the transfer pricing adjustment. The CRA has published a policy on repatriation that can be found on their web site.[33]

Under a repatriation agreement, the repatriation of funds can be accomplished by offsetting the Canadian company's intercompany liability to the non-resident in the year of the transfer pricing adjustment or by creating or adjusting a shareholder's loan account for the year of the adjustment. If a shareholder's loan is used, repayment of the loan must be made within 180 days of concluding the repatriation agreement with the CRA. Use of a shareholder's loan will result in interest charges on the outstanding Part XIII tax from the year of the adjustment until the shareholder's loan is repaid. The repatriation may be subject to audit verification.

A repatriation agreement reached at the audit stage will not preclude a request by the taxpayer for Competent Authority assistance. Where a taxpayer proceeds to request Competent Authority assistance after concluding a repatriation agreement, the Canadian Competent Authority will amend the repatriation agreement for any change made to the amount of the transfer pricing adjustment as a result of the Competent Authority process. Where a taxpayer proceeds to request Competent Authority assistance without having concluded a repatriation agreement at the audit stage, the Canadian Competent Authority may conclude a repatriation agreement with the taxpayer.

---

33 For more information on repatriation, see Repatriation of funds by Non-residents — Part XIII Assessments at http://www.ccra-adrc.gc.ca/tax/nonresidents/business/repat-e.html.

E. OTHER UNIQUE FEATURES

1) Application in Provinces and Territories

The provinces and territories are not bound by Canadian income tax treaties. However, any Competent Authority settlements will apply automatically for the "agreeing provinces" because those provinces use the same taxable income as is used for federal tax. The "agreeing provinces" are Newfoundland and Labrador, Prince Edward Island, Nova Scotia, New Brunswick, Manitoba, Saskatchewan, British Columbia, and the Yukon, Northwest and Nunavut territories for individuals and corporations, and Ontario and Alberta for individuals.

In the case of non-agreeing provinces, that is, Quebec for individual taxpayers, and Quebec, Ontario, and Alberta for corporations, Canada's tax treaties are formally recognized to varying degrees in their tax legislation. These provincial tax administrations have also historically accepted Competent Authority settlements, although there is no obligation for them to do so.

If a waiver has been filed under subsection 152(4) of the Act, the waiver is also valid for purposes of the Ontario *Corporation Tax Act*. In the case of Alberta and Quebec, however, a waiver should be filed in accordance with the relevant provincial legislation.[34] If a waiver is not filed, provincial legislation in the three non-agreeing provinces automatically keep returns open for 12 months following the date of reassessment under the ITA.

2) Mandatory Use of MAP to Protect Availability of Canadian Foreign Tax Credit

The Canadian position regarding what is referred to as "self-help" is set out in draft IC71-17R5.[35] Taxpayers are warned that they should not make claims for corresponding adjustments or foreign tax credits for foreign tax administration adjustments either when filing their current Canadian income tax returns or by filing amended income tax returns, without first seeking assistance from the Canadian Competent Authority. The intention certainly is for taxpayers to obtain a corresponding adjustment through the Competent Authority process. If taxpayers request corresponding adjustments or increased foreign tax credits from a local TSO or Taxation Centre, the procedure states that such cases will be referred to the Competent Authority Services Division in Ottawa. Fail-

---

34 *Alberta Corporate Tax Act*, subsection 43(1); *Quebec Taxation Act*, subsection 1010(2).

35 Draft Information Circular IC 71-17R5, "Requests for Competent Authority Consideration Under Mutual Agreement Procedures in Income Tax Conventions," at para.21.

ure to seek Competent Authority assistance or an attempt to bypass the Competent Authority process does not automatically result in double taxation but the IC cautions that this may be the result or that there may be delays.

This policy is supported by subsection 247(10) of the Act that provides that downward adjustments to transfer prices can only be made at the discretion of the Minister of National Revenue. The goal of this provision is also to guide cases to Competent Authority for resolution where appropriate.

F. RESOLVING DISPUTES BEFORE THEY HAPPEN: ADVANCE PRICING AGREEMENT PROGRAM

One of the main pillars to the CRA's international compliance strategy and for that matter, its proactive approach in managing and resolving disputes prospectively, is the Advance Pricing Arrangements (APA) program, recently celebrating its 10th anniversary, having originated in 1993.

The APA Program is a service provided by the CRA to help taxpayers resolve transfer pricing disputes that may arise in the future through a proactive approach that gives tax certainty to all stakeholders. The APA process is different from an audit. The focus of an APA is on future tax years rather than past tax years. An APA requires mutual cooperation and a free flow of information to achieve its goal.

An APA is an arrangement between a taxpayer and a tax administration that confirms the appropriate transfer pricing methodology to establish an arm's length price for transactions between related parties. An APA can be "unilateral" that is between a Canadian taxpayer and the CRA or bilateral, that is between the CRA and another treaty partner as to the same transfer pricing treatment for certain transactions.[36] In a climate where transfer pricing audits are becoming more frequent and often more adversarial, an APA can offer a better and more cost effective dispute resolution environment for certain MNEs.

There are many benefits offered by the APA program, including:

- certainty, usually in more than one jurisdiction;
- avoiding difficult and costly audits;
- penalty proofing;
- a cooperative process;
- skilled and experienced staff;

36 There is also an ability to request a multilateral APA which would include three or more tax administrations all agreeing to the same transfer pricing treatment for certain transactions.

- satisfying Canadian transfer pricing documentation rules; and
- renewal options after expiration of the term of the arrangement.

An APA may not necessarily be the right dispute resolution mechanism for all situations. This determination is dependent upon the nature of transactions, the relevant treaty partner and the level of cooperation among all parties involved.

Canada's Information Circular 94-4R, Advance Pricing Arrangements, released March 16, 2001, contains guidance, policy, and direction on the CRA's APA program. It provides an excellent guide to the APA process and provides necessary information to allow a taxpayer to first determine whether to seek an APA and how to proceed through the process from prefiling meeting to preparation of submission to resolution.

The Competent Authority Services Division of the ITD has the responsibility for the day-to-day operations of the APA program. The APA program has recently enjoyed its best year since its inception.

1) Circular Contents

The circular outlines the 10 stages of the APA process:

1) prefiling meetings;
2) APA request;
3) acceptance letter;
4) APA submission;
5) preliminary review of the APA submission and establishment of a case plan;
6) review, analysis and evaluation;
7) negotiation;
8) agreement;
9) post-settlement meeting; and
10) APA compliance.

Certain aspects of this list will be discussed in more detail below. The circular also confirms that the APA program is broad enough to deal with issues other than the application of Canada's rules governing transactions between a Canadian resident and a non-resident-related entity. The CRA may also consider the attribution of income to a PE for APA purposes, which could be an area of significant growth for the APA program as the OECD and its member countries struggle to deal with the proper attribution of income to PE. To date, however, we have seen limited, if any, PE cases brought before the APA program which no doubt stems, in part, from the IRS' view that PE cases would not be considered for APAs.

The circular discusses in some detail the notion of rollbacks and the fact that such decisions in fact rest with the relevant TSO.[37] A rollback involves rolling back the results reached for the prospective APA years to open audit years. As a practical matter, rollbacks are for the most part the norm and taxpayers have come to expect that rollbacks, barring any unforeseen situations or fundamental changes from the APA years versus the back years, would be included as part of the APA-Competent Authority process. The number of years to be covered by a rollback is always a question of fact and circumstances but two to three years would not be considered unusual. If the taxpayer requests retroactive application of an APA to years that are not statute-barred at the time of the request, waivers may need to be filed to ensure that those years do not become statute-barred before the conclusion of the APA. Once an APA has been concluded, it is necessary for the tax administrations involved to implement the necessary domestic adjustments to reflect the agreed-to transfer pricing methodology ("TPM"). If any of the retroactive years are beyond the statute of limitations and no waivers have been filed, depending on the wording of the relevant tax treaty, the CRA may not be able to issue reassessments for those years.

This problem should not arise with the true APA years since an APA by its very nature should deal with taxation years that are prospective and perhaps the few years intervening between the submission of the APA request and the conclusion of the APA. It is unlikely that those years would be close to being statute-barred in Canada (seven years for transactions with related nonresidents).

2) Prefiling Meetings

The prefiling meeting is a critical first step to understanding the rules for entering into an APA. Not only does it allow both the CRA and the taxpayer to determine the suitability of the taxpayer for an APA, this informal meeting hopefully sets a tone for what should be an amicable and cooperative process. Since relatively few taxpayers are familiar with the APA program, this meeting represents the first real opportunity for all participants to meet with each other to discuss the taxpayer's business, the transactions sought to be covered, the years to be covered, the proposed TPMs and the types of information that may be required.

---

37 See the CRA's APA Program Report, at page 7: the TSO auditor plays an additional role when the taxpayer seeks an APA with a rollback to previous tax years. Authority over the previous tax years rests with the TSO auditor, who must gain a level of comfort with applying the TPM in these years. Due to their participation in the APA review, TSO auditors are receptive to a rollback when it is requested as part of the initial APA submission.

The circular provides clear language for both the timing for a prefiling meeting and the information that must be available for that meeting. One should assume that failing to have a prefiling meeting within 180 days of the end of a particular taxation year would knock that year out of the APA system. Of course, that year could still qualify for rollback treatment, but this requires consultation with the TSO and others as described above.

The type of information to be provided for the prefiling meeting includes an overview of the organizational structure of the multinational corporation, the parties and transaction flows to be covered, the transfer pricing and audit history and the TPMs contemplated and their impact on taxable income. The CRA states that it "must" have this information in its possession two weeks before the meeting. This ensures that the prefiling meeting will be productive, and will permit the CRA to determine early on the suitability of an APA in the circumstances described.

3) Processing an APA Request

In keeping with its commitment to set forth benchmarks and service standards, the CRA has set a goal of sending the taxpayer a letter usually within 45 days after receiving the APA request. The CRA expresses a strong preference for bilateral or multilateral APAs, that is involving at least one other country in the negotiations, but will entertain requests for unilateral APAs provided the CRA is satisfied with the taxpayer's explanation as to its reasons for not pursuing a bilateral or multilateral arrangement. In such circumstances, it is noted that the CRA, through its treaty exchange of information powers, has the authority to share such information relating to a unilateral APA with the relevant treaty partner.

With respect to "user charges," the CRA continues to adopt a flexible fee guide tied to forecasted costs for travel and accommodation and does not adopt a guide similar to other treaty countries where the amount is essentially predetermined and fixed. It would not be surprising to find a standardized approach to fees in the future.

In the past, there was a tendency on the part of the CRA to accept most requests for APAs. To date, we have not yet observed a change in the environment on the CRA's criteria in accepting an APA. However, the CRA is taking more "policy" stances in some areas and signaling to the taxpayer community its preferences and dislikes. Thus, the nature of the transactions will ultimately determine the "acceptability" of the taxpayer into the APA program.

4) APA Submission Content

Items to include in an APA submission will undoubtedly depend upon the nature, scope, and complexity of the covered transactions. The precise information requirements will depend on the facts and circumstances of each case.

The circular sets time frames for receiving final information, which will improve the timeliness in the program and ensure that all participants are playing with the same set of information.

Any analysis for APA purposes cannot take place without considering the application of Information Circular 87-2R, International Transfer Pricing and the OECD Guidelines. In the discussion relating to the proposed TPM, the taxpayer is required to show the effect on the covered transactions by applying it consistently to the three previous years, or the most recent business cycle if appropriate, and to the time period covered by the APA, to the extent practicable. When such an analysis deviates from what was otherwise reported, the taxpayer would be expected to explain the rationale for choosing the proposed TPM over another one.

5) Use, Disclosure, and Protection of Information

One of the concerns often raised by taxpayers when considering whether to pursue an APA relates to the breadth of information they will need to disclose and the protections that will apply to what is often confidential business or trade secret information. It is now clear that APA information is no better or worse than any other information obtained by the CRA for the purpose of the administration or enforcement of the Act. As a result (and similar to information gathered on audit), all of the rules on the use, disclosure and protection of that information contained in s. 241 of the Act and the relevant tax treaty apply. This means that information provided during the course of an APA could potentially be used for the purposes of an audit of another taxpayer, to the extent this would be allowed under section 241. The CRA continues to be criticized for its use of so called "secret comparables" as an audit tool. The CRA is aware of the damage that would be done to the APA program if confidential taxpayer information was misused or disclosed to competitors and, as a result, does take the confidentiality of APA information seriously.

6) Renewal

Renewing an APA can be relatively routine, following to a great degree the process in place for an original application. One would expect the process to be quicker since the renewal process would be merely updating the existing information that the CRA has on hand. Taxpayers should remember, however, that the CRA wishes to have requests for renewal normally at least nine months before the end of the existing APA's terms.

The time and effort for an APA renewal will depend, in large part, on whether there have been material changes to the facts and circumstances since the original APA was negotiated.

G. COMPARISON OF DISPUTE RESOLUTION MECHANISMS

A taxpayer faced with a transfer pricing dispute must determine the best forum or mechanism in the particular circumstances for dispute resolution. The various options are set out below with key advantages and disadvantages of each.

Option 1: Appeals

Advantages	Disadvantages
Taxpayer involvement in procedure	Timeliness
Impact of draft IC — can still go back to CA as long as no concurrence with Appeals	No certainty of relief Costs
	Public procedure
	Court often more swayed by domestic rather than treaty rules
	Unilateral relief only
	Competent authority will not deviate from undesirable court result

Option 2: Double Tax

Advantages	Disadvantages
Competent authorities "shall endeavour" to resolve this type of case — taxation not in accordance with the Treaty	Taxpayer not involved in negotiations Will be presented a result to accept or reject Not precedent setting
Appeal option open if no acceptable competent authority resolution	
Resolves issue for both sides of the border	
Possibility of adding other back years	
Less costly than litigation	
Ability to manage the Process	

Option 3: Integrated Solution – CA/APAs

Advantages	Disadvantages
Provides certainty for the future — also could resolve all prior open years with Rollback	Information and documentation requirements
Takes case out of audit	Need for flexibility in result
Taxpayer more involved than with double tax case — open, co-operative process	
Can utilize documentation and work already done as basis for an APA Submission	
Renewed strength of Canadian APA program	
Penalty protection	

H. ARBITRATION

The MAP has been an extremely successful vehicle for the elimination of economic double taxation. Historically, the Canadian Competent Authority has enjoyed a highly successful double taxation program under the MAP. For example, from 1990 to the present, the Canadian Competent Authority has resolved well in excess of 1000 double taxation cases (not including APAs). It is noteworthy that, to date, while there are difficult cases currently before the revenue administration, the Canadian Competent Authority has had only a handful of cases for which it has been unable to successfully negotiate a reasonable resolution.

A number of Canada's tax treaties include an arbitration clause. For example, Article XXVI (6) of the Canada-U.S. treaty, added by the third protocol, provides for a voluntary arbitration procedure for the competent authorities to resolve issues not otherwise resolvable pursuant to the provisions of Article XXVI.[38]

To date, none of Canada's tax treaty arbitration provisions has been implemented. Given its successful track record with the traditional MAP process, the arbitration process, if implemented, will likely be restricted to exceptional cases. The Competent Authority process remains a strong favoured dispute resolution tool. Arguably, with the implementation of the new processes under the draft IC 71-17R5, the Competent Authority process will be further reinforced as the mechanism of choice in Canada.

The suggestion that arbitration be adopted as an alternative but complementary vehicle to the MAP has been made frequently in the recent past.[39]

---

38 See the technical explanation to Article XXVI of the Canada-U.S. tax treaty.

39 See OECD document, "Cross Border Tax Treaty Dispute Resolution: Country Profiles and Draft Progress Report."

It is an idea worth pursuing, because the MAP does not function particularly well in a relatively small number of aberrantly large-dollar or politically sensitive cases. It should be available to resolve cases that cannot be resolved at Competent Authority. In addition, the availability of a mandatory alternative would serve the threshold purpose of putting pressure on the competent authorities to resolve cases more quickly.

It is apparent that the increasing level of international tax controversy, including the spread of inconsistent documentation and penalty regimes mandates a more efficient and effective dispute process and the lack of such an improved and streamlined process, will make arbitration an attractive alternative. However, before Canada migrates to a complementary but mandatory vehicle for arbitration, several significant issues must be resolved, not least among which are questions of sovereignty and design of the "rules of engagement" with its treaty partners.

I. INFORMATION GATHERING IN THE CA DISPUTE RESOLUTION PROCESS

1) Secrecy and Confidentiality in Competent Authority Proceedings

The confidentiality of information provided by taxpayers to the CRA is protected by s. 241 of the Act and the provisions of the relevant treaty. All exchange of information articles contain a secrecy provision that generally states that any information exchanged shall be treated as secret in the same manner as any tax information is treated in the requesting state and shall not be disclosed to any persons other than those concerned or involved with the assessment or collection of the taxes to which the treaty applies. This secrecy clause serves as the basis for mutual trust and reciprocity and fosters an environment of cooperation between countries. While not specifically listed in the treaty as an exemption, the concept of reciprocity is central to all international treaties.

To ensure the confidentiality of taxpayer affairs, steps must be taken to prevent protected information from being disclosed or misused. Protective measures vary from country to country. In Canada, information obtained from another treaty partner could constitute "taxpayer information" as defined in subsection 241(10) of the Act or "confidential information" as defined in section 295(1) of the *Excise Tax Act* (*ETA*). This type of information is subject to comprehensive rules relating to access, use, and disclosure. For example, pursuant to ss. 241(4) of the Act, disclosure of "taxpayer information" is permitted in certain situations that are non-tax-related. However, if some of the "taxpayer information" proposed to be disclosed is from a treaty partner, the stricter secrecy rules of the treaty govern. These rules limit the use and disclosure of such information to purposes relating to the taxes covered by the treaty. Thus, depending on the wording of a particular treaty, the disclosure of that information for a non-tax, non-treaty purpose would be prohibited since the implementing legislation to all of Canada's tax treaties contains a clause stating that the treaty overrides domestic law to the extent of any inconsistency.[40]

In the course of the government-to-government discussions between competent authorities, confidential taxpayer information will be exchanged, either verbally or in writing such as position papers, for example. Pursuant to the standard exchange of information article found in all of Canada's tax treaties, any such information exchanged is treated as secret and subject to the confidentiality rules of the country receiving the information. Taxpayers are not entitled to copies of position papers or other information exchanged between competent authorities. One exception to this would be information that is considered to be the taxpayer's information, such as bank statements.

J. CONCLUSION

The role and function of Competent Authority as a key tool for international tax dispute resolution is a far more strategic business issue than in the past. Used appropriately, competent authority can be both the beginning and end game in any taxpayers' audit dispute. Not considering competent authority can result in real economic double taxation with taxpayers being left with no solution to overcoming the asymmetrical tax regimes that exist between countries. As well, and ironically at odds with traditional dispute mechanisms, competent authority can be invoked proactively. Thus it has the interesting capacity to act as a "pre-emptive strike" to difficult audit controversy, preventing disputes before they even arise.

The global tax issues facing MNEs have caused an unprecedented level of tax disputes around the world. The audit attention on foreign controlled corporations, the need for governments to protect their revenue base and the fear of the unknown in the emerging economies of developing nations has put competent authority on the "map" as a destination point for most MNEs. Unfortunately, the climate is mixed: the more developed countries

---

40 *Canada-United States Tax Convention Act*, 1984, subsection 3(2).

having transparent rules and processes; the less developed countries lacking transparency and predictability. Fortunately, Canada continues to be a model revenue administration and continues to work closely with all willing administrations around the world to improve processes and procedures for competent authority.

APPENDIX 1

Article IX

Related persons

1. Where a person in a Contracting State and a person in the other Contracting State are related and where the arrangements between them differ from those which would be made between unrelated persons, each State may adjust the amount of the income, loss or tax payable to reflect the income, deductions, credits or allowances which would, but for those arrangements, have been taken into account in computing such income, loss or tax.

2. For the purposes of this Article, a person shall be deemed to be related to another person if either person participates directly or indirectly in the management or control of the other, or if any third person or persons participate directly or indirectly in the management or control of both.

3. Where an adjustment is made or to be made by a Contracting State in accordance with paragraph 1, the other Contracting State shall (notwithstanding any time or procedural limitations in the domestic law of that other State) make a corresponding adjustment to the income, loss or tax of the related person in that other State if:

(a) it agrees with the first-mentioned adjustment; and
(b) within six years from the end of the taxable year to which the first-mentioned adjustment relates, the competent authority of the other State has been notified of the first-mentioned adjustment. The competent authorities, however, may agree to consider cases where the corresponding adjustment would not otherwise be barred by any time or procedural limitations in the other State, even if the notification is not made within the six-year period.

4. In the event that the notification referred to in paragraph 3 is not given within the time period referred to therein, and the competent authorities have not agreed to otherwise consider the case in accordance with paragraph 3(b), the competent authority of the Contracting State which has made or is to make the first-mentioned adjustment may provide relief from double taxation where appropriate.

5. The provisions of paragraphs 3 and 4 shall not apply in the case of fraud, willful default or neglect or gross negligence.

Article XXVI

Mutual Agreement Procedure

1. Where a person considers that the actions of one or both of the Contracting States result or will result for him in taxation not in accordance with the provisions of this Convention, he may, irrespective of the remedies provided by the domestic law of those States, present his case in writing to the competent authority of the Contracting State of which he is a resident or, if he is a resident of neither Contracting State, of which he is a national.

2. The competent authority of the Contracting State to which the case has been presented shall endeavor, if the objection appears to it to be justified and if it is not itself able to arrive at a satisfactory solution, to resolve the case by mutual agreement with the competent authority of the other Contracting State, with a view to the avoidance of taxation which is not in accordance with the Convention. Except where the provisions of Article IX (Related Persons) apply, any agreement reached shall be implemented notwithstanding any time or other procedural limitations in the domestic law of the Contracting States, provided that the competent authority of the other Contracting State has received notification that such a case exists within six years from the end of the taxable year to which the case relates.

3. The competent authorities of the Contracting States shall endeavor to resolve by mutual agreement any difficulties or doubts arising as to the interpretation or application of the Convention. In particular, the competent authorities of the Contracting States may agree:

(a) to the same attribution of profits to a resident of a Contracting State and its permanent establishment situated in the other Contracting State;
(b) to the same allocation of income, deductions, credits or allowances between persons;
(c) to the same determination of the source, and the same characterization, of particular items of income;
(d) to a common meaning of any term used in the Convention;
(e) to the elimination of double taxation with respect to income distributed by an estate or trust;
(f) to the elimination of double taxation with respect to a partnership;
(g) to provide relief from double taxation resulting from the application of the estate tax imposed by the United States or the Canadian tax as

a result of a distribution or disposition of property by a trust that is a qualified domestic trust within the meaning of s. 2056A of the Internal Revenue Code, or is described in s. 70(6) of the Income Tax Act or is treated as such under paragraph 5 of Article XXIX B (Taxes Imposed by Reason of Death), in cases where no relief is otherwise available; or

(h) to increases in any dollar amounts referred to in the Convention to reflect monetary or economic developments.

They may also consult together for the elimination of double taxation in cases not provided for in the Convention.

4. Each of the Contracting States will endeavor to collect on behalf of the other Contracting State such amounts as may be necessary to ensure that relief granted by the Convention from taxation imposed by that other State does not enure to the benefit of persons not entitled thereto. However, nothing in this paragraph shall be construed as imposing on either of the Contracting States the obligation to carry out administrative measures of a different nature from those used in the collection of its own tax or which would be contrary to its public policy (ordre public).

5. The competent authorities of the Contracting States may communicate with each other directly for the purpose of reaching an agreement in the sense of the preceding paragraphs.

If any difficulty or doubt arising as to the interpretation or application of the Convention cannot be resolved by the competent authorities pursuant to the preceding paragraphs of this Article, the case may, if both competent authorities and the taxpayer agree, be submitted for arbitration, provided that the taxpayer agrees in writing to be bound by the decision of the arbitration board. The decision of the arbitration board in a particular case shall be binding on both States with respect to that case. The procedures shall be established in an exchange of notes between

APPENDIX 2

(1) Definitions

The definitions in this subsection apply in this section.

"arm's length allocation"

"arm's length allocation" means, in respect of a transaction, an allocation of profit or loss that would have occurred between the participants in the transaction if they had been dealing at arm's length with each other.

"arm's length transfer price"

"arm's length transfer price" means, in respect of a transaction, an amount that would have been a transfer price in respect of the transaction if the participants in the transaction had been dealing at arm's length with each other.

"documentation-due date"

"documentation-due date" for a taxation year or fiscal period of a person or partnership means

(a) in the case of a person, the person's filing-due date for the year; or

(b) in the case of a partnership, the day on or before which a return is required by section 229 of the Income Tax Regulations to be filed in respect of the period or would be required to be so filed if that section applied to the partnership.

"qualifying cost contribution arrangement"

"qualifying cost contribution arrangement" means an arrangement under which reasonable efforts are made by the participants in the arrangement to establish a basis for contributing to, and to contribute on that basis to, the cost of producing, developing or acquiring any property, or acquiring or performing any services, in proportion to the benefits which each participant is reasonably expected to derive from the property or services, as the case may be, as a result of the arrangement.

"tax benefit"

"tax benefit" means a reduction, avoidance or deferral of tax or other amount payable under this Act or an increase in a refund of tax or other amount under this Act.

"transaction"

"transaction" includes an arrangement or event.

"transfer price"

"transfer price" means, in respect of a transaction, an amount paid or payable or an amount received or receivable, as the case may be, by a participant in the transaction as a price, a rental, a royalty, a premium or other payment for, or for the use, production or reproduction of, property or as consideration for services (including services provided as an employee and the insurance or reinsurance of risks) as part of the transaction.

"transfer pricing capital adjustment"

"transfer pricing capital adjustment" of a taxpayer for a taxation year means the total of

(a) all amounts each of which is
  (i) 1/2 of the amount, if any, by which the adjusted cost base to the taxpayer of a capital property (other than a depreciable property) is reduced in the year because of an adjustment made under subsection (2),
  (ii) 3/4 of the amount, if any, by which the adjusted cost base to the taxpayer of an eligible capital expenditure of the taxpayer in respect of a business is reduced in the year because of an adjustment made under subsection (2), or
  (iii) the amount, if any, by which the capital cost to the taxpayer of a depreciable property is reduced in the year because of an adjustment made under subsection (2); and
(b) all amounts each of which is that proportion of the total of
  (i) 1/2 of the amount, if any, by which the adjusted cost base to a partnership of a capital property (other than a depreciable property) is reduced in a fiscal period that ends in the year because of an adjustment made under subsection (2),
  (ii) 3/4 of the amount, if any, by which the adjusted cost base to a partnership of an eligible capital expenditure of the partnership in respect of a business is reduced in a fiscal period that ends in the year because of an adjustment made under subsection (2), and
  (iii) the amount, if any, by which the capital cost to a partnership of a depreciable property is reduced in the period because of an adjustment made under subsection (2),

  that

  (iv) the taxpayer's share of the income or loss of the partnership for the period

  is of

  (v) the income or loss of the partnership for the period,

and where the income and loss of the partnership are nil for the period, the income of the partnership for the period is deemed to be $1,000,000 for the purpose of determining a taxpayer's share of the partnership's income for the purpose of this definition.

"transfer pricing capital setoff adjustment"

"transfer pricing capital setoff adjustment" of a taxpayer for a taxation year means the amount, if any, that would be the taxpayer's transfer pricing capital adjustment for the year if the references, in the definition "transfer pricing capital adjustment", to "reduced" were read as "increased".

"transfer pricing income adjustment"

"transfer pricing income adjustment" of a taxpayer for a taxation year means the total of all amounts each of which is the amount, if any, by which an adjustment made under subsection (2) (other than an adjustment included in determining a transfer pricing capital adjustment of the taxpayer for a taxation year) would result in an increase in the taxpayer's income for the year or a decrease in a loss of the taxpayer for the year from a source if that adjustment were the only adjustment made under subsection (2).

"transfer pricing income setoff adjustment"

"transfer pricing income setoff adjustment" of a taxpayer for a taxation year means the total of all amounts each of which is the amount, if any, by which an adjustment made under subsection (2) (other than an adjustment included in determining a transfer pricing capital setoff adjustment of the taxpayer for a taxation year) would result in a decrease in the taxpayer's income for the year or an increase in a loss of the taxpayer for the year from a source if that adjustment were the only adjustment made under subsection (2).

(2) Transfer pricing adjustment

Where a taxpayer or a partnership and a non-resident person with whom the taxpayer or the partnership, or a member of the partnership, does not deal at arm's length (or a partnership of which the non-resident person is a member) are participants in a transaction or a series of transactions and

(a) the terms or conditions made or imposed, in respect of the transaction or series, between any of the participants in the transaction or series differ from those that would have been made between persons dealing at arm's length, or

(b) the transaction or series

(i) would not have been entered into between persons dealing at arm's length, and

(ii) can reasonably be considered not to have been entered into primarily for bona fide purposes other than to obtain a tax benefit,

any amounts that, but for this section and section 245, would be determined for the purposes of this Act in respect of the taxpayer or the partnership for a taxation year or fiscal period shall be adjusted (in this section referred to as an "adjustment") to the quantum or nature of the amounts that would have been determined if,

(c) where only paragraph (a) applies, the terms and conditions made or imposed, in respect of the transaction or series, between the participants in the transaction or series had been those that would have been made between persons dealing at arm's length, or

(d) where paragraph (b) applies, the transaction or series entered into between the participants had been the transaction or series that would have been entered into between persons dealing at arm's length, under terms and conditions that would have been made between persons dealing at arm's length.

(3) Penalty

A taxpayer (other than a taxpayer all of whose taxable income for the year is exempt from tax under Part I) is liable to a penalty for a taxation year equal to 10% of the amount determined under paragraph (a) in respect of the taxpayer for the year, where

(a) the amount, if any, by which

(i) the total of

(A) the taxpayer's transfer pricing capital adjustment for the year, and

(B) the taxpayer's transfer pricing income adjustment for the year

exceeds the total of

(ii) the total of all amounts each of which is the portion of the taxpayer's transfer pricing capital adjustment or transfer pricing income adjustment for the year that can reasonably be considered to relate to a particular transaction, where

(A) the transaction is a qualifying cost contribution arrangement in which the taxpayer or a partnership of which the taxpayer is a member is a participant, or

(B) in any other case, the taxpayer or a partnership of which the taxpayer is a member made reasonable efforts to determine arm's length transfer prices or arm's length allocations in respect of the transaction, and to use those prices or allocations for the purposes of this Act, and

(iii) the total of all amounts, each of which is the portion of the taxpayer's transfer pricing capital setoff adjustment or transfer pricing income setoff adjustment for the year that can reasonably be considered to relate to a particular transaction, where

(A) the transaction is a qualifying cost contribution arrangement in which the taxpayer or a partnership of which the taxpayer is a member is a participant, or

(B) in any other case, the taxpayer or a partnership of which the taxpayer is a member made reasonable efforts to determine arm's length transfer prices or arm's length allocations in respect of the transaction, and to use those prices or allocations for the purposes of this Act,

is greater than

(b) the lesser of

(i) 10% of the amount that would be the taxpayer's gross revenue for the year if this Act were read without reference to subsection (2), subsections 69(1) and (1.2) and section 245, and

(ii) $5,000,000.

(4) Contemporaneous documentation

For the purposes of subsection (3) and the definition "qualifying cost contribution arrangement" in subsection (1), a taxpayer or a partnership is deemed not to have made reasonable efforts to determine and use arm's length transfer prices or arm's length allocations in respect of a transaction or not to have participated in a transaction that is a qualifying cost contribution arrangement, unless the taxpayer or the partnership, as the case may be,

(a) makes or obtains, on or before the taxpayer's or partnership's documentation-due date for the taxation year or fiscal period, as the case may be, in which the transaction is entered into, records or documents that provide a description that is complete and accurate in all material respects of

(i) the property or services to which the transaction relates,

(ii) the terms and conditions of the transaction and their relationship, if any, to the terms and conditions of each other transaction entered into between the participants in the transaction,

(iii) the identity of the participants in the transaction and their relationship to each other at the time the transaction was entered into,

(iv) the functions performed, the property used or contributed and the risks assumed, in respect of the transaction, by the participants in the transaction,

(v) the data and methods considered and the analysis performed to determine the transfer prices or the allocations of profits or losses or contributions to costs, as the case may be, in respect of the transaction, and

(vi) the assumptions, strategies and policies, if any, that influenced the determination of the transfer prices or the allocations of profits or losses or contributions to costs, as the case may be, in respect of the transaction;

(b) for each subsequent taxation year or fiscal period, if any, in which the transaction continues, makes or obtains, on or before the taxpayer's or partnership's documentation-due date for that year or period, as the case may be, records or documents that completely and accurately describe each material change in the year or period to the matters referred to in any of subparagraphs (a)(i) to (vi) in respect of the transaction; and

(c) provides the records or documents described in paragraphs (a) and (b) to the Minister within 3 months after service, made personally or by registered or certified mail, of a written request therefor.

(5) Partner's gross revenue

For the purpose of subparagraph (3)(b)(i), where a taxpayer is a member of a partnership in a taxation year, the taxpayer's gross revenue for the year as a member of the partnership from any activities carried on by means of the partnership is deemed to be that proportion of the amount that would be the partnership's gross revenue from the activities if it were a taxpayer (to the extent that amount does not include amounts received or receivable from other partnerships of which the taxpayer is a member in the year), for a fiscal period of the partnership that ends in the year, that

(a) the taxpayer's share of the income or loss of the partnership from its activities for the period

is of

(b) the income or loss of the partnership from its activities for the period,

and where the income and loss of the partnership from its activities are nil for the period, the income of the partnership from its activities for the period is deemed to be $1,000,000 for the purpose of determining a taxpayer's share of the partnership's income from its activities for the purpose of this subsection.

(6) Deemed member of partnership

For the purposes of this section, where a person is a member of a partnership that is a member of another partnership,

(a) the person is deemed to be a member of the other partnership; and
(b) the person's share of the income or loss of the other partnership is deemed to be equal to the amount of that income or loss to which the person is directly or indirectly entitled.

(7) Exclusion for loans to certain controlled foreign affiliates

Where, in a taxation year of a corporation resident in Canada, a non-resident person owes an amount to the corporation, the non-resident person is a controlled foreign affiliate of the corporation for the purpose of section 17 throughout the period in the year during which the amount is owing and it is established that the amount owing is an amount owing described in paragraph 17(8)(a) or (b), subsection (2) does not apply to adjust the amount of interest paid, payable or accruing in the year on the amount owing.

(8) Provisions not applicable

Where subsection (2) would, if this Act were read without reference to sections 67 and 68 and subsections 69(1) and (1.2), apply to adjust an amount under this Act, sections 67 and 68 and subsections 69(1) and (1.2) shall not apply to determine the amount if subsection (2) is applied to adjust the amount.

(9) Anti-avoidance

For the purposes of determining a taxpayer's gross revenue under subparagraph (3)(b)(i) and subsection (5), a transaction or series of transactions is deemed not to have occurred, if one of the purposes of the transaction or series was to increase the taxpayer's gross revenue for the purpose of subsection (3).

(10) No adjustment unless appropriate

An adjustment (other than an adjustment that results in or increases a transfer pricing capital adjustment or a transfer pricing income adjustment of a taxpayer for a taxation year) shall not be made under subsection (2) unless, in the opinion of the Minister, the circumstances are such that it would be appropriate that the adjustment be made.

(11) Provisions applicable to Part

Sections 152, 158, 159, 162 to 167 and Division J of Part I apply to this Part, with such modifications as the circumstances require.

APPENDIX 3

The following chart is current as of August 31, 2004 and was developed to provide a quick reference guide for both the CRA and taxpayers with articles 9 and 25. The chart is separated into four sections:

Section one, "Treaty partner and year of coming into force", begins with the OECD model, then lists alphabetically the names of the countries with which Canada has a tax treaty and notes significant dates. The first date mentioned in the column with the Treaty partner name is that of the coming into force date, or the date of signature if the treaty is not yet in force. The second date is the date at which the relevant provisions of the treaty have effect.

Section two, "Article 9: Associated Enterprises," provides:

- Time limits to raise an article 9(1) adjustment;
- Availability of article 9(2) correlative adjustment by the treaty partner; and
- Consequences of fraud, willful default, or neglect.

Section three, "Article 25: Mutual Agreement Procedure," provides:

- Time limits to present the case to the Competent Authority; and
- Time limits to raise adjustment.

Section four, "Comments," notes other items of interest, such as the presence of an arbitration clause and about which treaties are under renegotiation.

Treaty partner and year of coming into force	Article 9: Associated Enterprises			Article 25: Mutual Agreement Procedure		Comments
Country 1st date: entry into force date or date of signature if not yet in force 2nd date: date from which relevant provisions have effect	Time limit to raise 9(1) adjustment	Availability of 9(2) correlative adjustment by treaty partner	Consequences of fraud, willful default or neglect	Time limit to present case to competent authority	Time limit to raise adjustment	Comments
1. OECD Model Adopted by OECD on April 11, 1977, and updated to Jan. 2003	No time limit	Art. 9(2) Standard wording: "the other State shall make an appropriate adjustment to the amount of the tax charged therein"	Not covered	Art. 25(1) 3 years from the first notification of the action resulting in taxation not in accordance with the provisions of the convention	No time limit	Notification for art. 25(1) is explained in paragraphs 17 and 18 of the OECD commentary. For Canada, "first notification" would be the notice of assessment. Canada has entered a reservation on the 3-year time period stating that it is too long. Any agreement reached shall be implemented notwithstanding any time limits in the domestic law of the contracting state.
2. Algeria Dec. 26, 2000 Jan. 1, 2000	Art. 9(3) Lesser of domestic law time limits and 5 years	Art. 9(2) Standard wording	Art. 9(4) Correlative adjustment not available No time limit to raise 9(1) adjustment	Art. 25(1) 2 years from the first notification	No time limit	Art. 25(4): The competent authorities can exchange oral opinions through a Commission consisting of their representatives.
3. Argentina Dec. 30, 1994 Jan. 1, 1995	Art. 9(3) Lesser of domestic law time limits	Art. 9(2) Standard wording	Art. 9(4) Correlative adjustment not available No time limit to	Art. 25(1) 2 years from the first notification	Art. 25(3) Lesser of domestic law and 5 years No time limit if	Note different time limits in art. 9 and art. 25 (6 years vs. 5 years).

	and 6 years		raise 9(1) adjustment		fraud, willful default or neglect	
4. Armenia						Negotiations completed. Procedures for obtaining government approval of Convention underway in both countries.
5. Australia April 29, 1981 Jan. 1, 1976 **a) Protocol** Dec. 18, 2002 Jan. 1, 2003	No time limit	Art. 9(3) Standard wording, subject to art. 9(4) time limit Art. 9(4) Time limit of 6 years	Not covered	No time limit	No time limit	Art. 9(2): If the competent authority does not have sufficient information to determine profits to be attributed to the enterprise, it may apply the tax laws of its state to that enterprise, provided that the law is applied in accordance with the principles of art. 9 (also contained in art. 7 and in Canada's treaties with Papua New Guinea and New Zealand).
6. Austria Feb. 17, 1981 Jan. 1, 1980	No time limit	Not covered	Not covered	Art. XXV(1) 2 years from the first notification	No time limit	Art. XXV(3): Provides that the competent authorities may consult together to endeavor to agree to the same attribution of profits for PE situation and to the same allocation of income for art. 9 situation.
7. Azerbaijan						Negotiations completed. Procedures for obtaining government approval of Convention underway in both countries.
8. Bangladesh Jan. 18, 1985 Jan. 1, 1982	Art. 9(3) Lesser of domestic law time limits and 5 years	Art. 9(2) Standard wording	Art. 9(4) Correlative adjustment not available No time limit to raise 9(1) adjustment	Art. 24(1) 2 years from the first notification	Art. 24(3) Lesser of domestic law and 5 years No time limit if fraud, willful default or neglect.	Art. 24(4): Provides that the competent authorities may consult together to endeavor to agree to the same attribution of profits for PE situation and to the same allocation of income for art. 9 situation.

Treaty partner and year of coming into force	**Article 9: Associated Enterprises**			**Article 25: Mutual Agreement Procedure**		**Comments**
Country 1st date: entry into force date or date of signature if not yet in force 2nd date: date from which relevant provisions have effect	Time limit to raise 9(1) adjustment	Availability of 9(2) correlative adjustment by treaty partner	Consequences of fraud, willful default or neglect	Time limit to present case to competent authority	Time limit to raise adjustment	Comments
9. Barbados Dec. 22, 1980 Jan. 1, 1976	Art. IX(3) Lesser of domestic law time limits and 5 years	Art. IX(2) Standard wording	Art. IX(3) No time limit to raise 9(1) adjustment	Art. XXVII(1) 2 years from the first notification	Art. XXVII(3) Lesser of domestic law and 5 years No time limit if fraud, willful default or neglect	Art. XXVII(4): Provides that the competent authorities may consult together to endeavor to agree to the same attribution of profits for PE situation and to the same allocation of income for art. 9 situation. This treaty is under renegotiation. Discussions were held in December 1997 and November 1998 relating to possible changes to the existing treaty.
10. Belgium 11. Aug. 12, 1976 Jan. 1, 1976	No time limit	Not covered	Not covered	Art. XXV(I) 2 years from the first notification	No time limit	This convention remains applicable until the entry into force of the new treaty (see below).
12. Belgium Signed May 23, 2002 Implemented by Bill S-2 on December	Art. 9(3) Lesser of domestic law time limits and 6 years	Art. 9(1) The "other State shall make such an adjustment *as it considers appropriate* to the amount of tax	Art. 9(4) Correlative adjustment not available No time limit to raise 9(1) adjustment	Art. 25(1) 2 years from the first notification	No time limit	Procedures for obtaining government approval underway in Belgium. Once in force, the new convention will replace the existing convention, which entered into force on August 12, 1976.

12, 2002		charged therein"	Omits "neglect"			
Republic of Bolivia						Negotiations for this treaty began June 23, 2003.
13. Brazil Dec. 23, 1985 Jan. 1, 1986	No time limit	Not covered	Not covered	No time limit	No time limit	
14. Bulgaria Oct. 25, 2001 Jan. 1, 2002	Art. 9(3) Lesser of domestic law time limits and 5 years	Art. 9(2) Standard wording subject to Art. 9(3) time limit	Art. 9(4) Correlative adjustment not available No time limit to raise 9(1) adjustment	Art. 25(1) 2 years from the first notification	Art. 25(3) Lesser of domestic law and 5 years No time limit if fraud, willful default or neglect	
Cameroon June 16, 1988 Jan. 1, 1988	No time limit	Not covered	Not covered	Art. 22(1) 2 years from the first notification	No time limit	
Chile Oct. 28, 1999 Jan. 1, 2000	Art. 9(3) Lesser of domestic law time limits and 5 years	Art. 9(2) The "other State shall, *if* it *agrees*, make an appropriate adjustment to the amount."	Art. 9(4) Correlative adjustment not available No time limit to raise 9(1) adjustment	No time limit	No time limit	Art. 25(5): Arbitration clause: if both competent authorities agree, difficulties or doubts relating to the application or interpretation of the Convention may be submitted for arbitration.
People's Republic of China Dec. 29, 1986 Jan. 1, 1987	No time limit	Not covered	Not covered	Not time limit	No time limit	This treaty is under renegotiation. Negotiations were held the third week of March 2002 in Ottawa. Date for further discussion of issues not as yet determined.

Treaty partner and year of coming into force	**Article 9: Associated Enterprises**			**Article 25: Mutual Agreement Procedure**		**Comments**
Country 1st date: entry into force date or date of signature if not yet in force 2nd date: date from which relevant provisions have effect	Time limit to raise 9(1) adjustment	Availability of 9(2) correlative adjustment by treaty partner	Consequences of fraud, willful default or neglect	Time limit to present case to competent authority	Time limit to raise adjustment	Comments
Columbia						This treaty is under negotiation. Last round of negotiations took place in Ottawa in March 1999. No date has been set as yet for the next round of negotiations.
Republic of Costa Rica						Negotiations for this treaty began June 2, 2003.
Croatia Nov. 23, 1999 Jan. 1, 2000	No time limit	Not covered	Not covered	Art. 25(1) 2 years from the first notification	No time limit	
Republic of Cuba						Negotiations for this treaty began May 26, 2003.
Cyprus Sept. 3, 1985 Jan. 1, 1985	Art. 9(3) Lesser of domestic law time limits and 5 years	Art. 9(2) Standard wording	Art. 9(4) Correlative adjustment not available No time limit to raise 9(1) adjustment	Art. 26(1) 2 years from the first notification	Art. 26(3) Lesser of domestic law and 5 years No time limit if fraud, willful default or neglect	Art. 26(4): Provides that the competent authorities may consult together to endeavor to agree to the same attribution of profits for PE situation and to the same allocation of income for art. 9 situation.

Czech Republic and Slovakia July 22, 1992 Aug. 1, 1992	Art. 9(3) Lesser of domestic law time limits and 5 years	Art. 9(2) Standard wording	Art. 9(4) Correlative adjustment not available No time limit to raise 9(1) adjustment	Art. 25(1) 2 years from the first notification	Art. 25(3) Lesser of domestic law and 5 years No time limit if fraud, willful default or neglect	The treaty with the former Czechoslovakia is considered to be in force, effective Jan. 1, 1993, with both the Czech Republic and Slovakia. With respect to the Czech Republic, this treaty remained applicable until the entering into force of the new Czech Republic Treaty (see below). With respect to the Slovak Republic, this treaty remained applicable for taxation years beginning before Jan. 1, 2002.
Czech Republic May 28, 2002 Jan. 1, 2003	Art. 9(3) Lesser of domestic law time limits and 5 years	Art. 9(2) Standard wording	Art. 9(4) Correlative adjustment not available No time limit to raise 9(1) adjustment	Art. 24(1) 2 years from the first notification	Art. 24(3) Lesser of domestic law and 5 years No time limit if fraud, willful default or neglect	This Convention replaces, as far as relations between Canada and the Czech Republic are concerned, the tax treaty that entered into force on Jan. 1, 1993 between Canada and Czechoslovakia. However, provisions of the former convention remained applicable for taxation year beginning prior to Jan. 1, 2003.
Denmark March 2, 1998 Jan. 1, 1999	Art. 9(3) Lesser of domestic law time limits and 6 years	Art. 9(2) Standard wording	Art. 9(4) Correlative adjustment not available No time limit to raise 9(1) adjustment	No time limit	Art. 25(3) Lesser of domestic law and 6 years No time limit if fraud, willful default or neglect	The 1955 Agreement will cease to have effect as the provisions of the new Convention enter into force but, if greater relief is provided under any provision of the 1955 Agreement than under the new Convention, those provisions will continue to have effect for taxation years ending on or before December 31, 1999 (art. 31(3) and (4)).
Dominican Republic Sept. 23, 1977	Art. IX(3) Lesser of domestic law time limits	Art. IX(2) Standard wording	Art. IX(3) No time limit to raise 9(1) adjust-	Art. XXV(1) 2 years from the first notification	Art. XXV(3) Lesser of domestic law and 5 years	Art. XXV(4): Provides that the competent authorities may consult together to endeavor to agree to the same attribution of profits for PE situation and to

Treaty partner and year of coming into force	Article 9: Associated Enterprises			Article 25: Mutual Agreement Procedure		Comments
Country 1st date: entry into force date or date of signature if not yet in force 2nd date: date from which relevant provisions have effect	Time limit to raise 9(1) adjustment	Availability of 9(2) correlative adjustment by treaty partner	Consequences of fraud, willful default or neglect	Time limit to present case to competent authority	Time limit to raise adjustment	Comments
Jan. 1, 1977	and 5 years		ment		No time limit if fraud, willful default or neglect	the same allocation of income for art. 9 situation.
Ecuador Dec. 20, 2001 Jan. 1, 2002	Art. 9(3) Lesser of domestic law time limits and 5 years	Art. 9(2) Standard wording	Art. 9(4) Correlative adjustment not available No time limit to raise 9(1) adjustment	Art. 24(1) 2 years from the first notification	Art. 24(3) Lesser of domestic law and 5 years No time limit if fraud, willful default or neglect	Art. 24(5): If the competent authorities and the taxpayer agree, an unresolved case may be submitted for arbitration provided the taxpayer agrees in writing to be bound by the decision of the arbitration board. In such a case, the decision shall be binding on both States.
Egypt Oct. 2, 1984 Jan. 1, 1985	Art. 9(3) Lesser of domestic law time limits and 5 years	Art. 9(2) Standard wording	Art. 9(4) Correlative adjustment not available No time limit to raise 9(1) adjustment	Art. 24(1) 2 years from the first notification	Art. 24(3) Lesser of domestic law and 5 years No time limit if fraud, willful default or neglect	This treaty is under renegotiation. Negotiations completed in August 1998. Egyptian authorities have since requested that negotiations be re-opened. Date for a further round of negotiations as yet to be determined.
Estonia Dec. 28, 1995 Jan. 1, 1996	Art. 9(3) Lesser of domestic law time limits	Art. 9(2) Standard wording	Art. 9(4) Correlative adjustment not available	Art. 25(1) 2 years from the notification	Art. 25(3) Lesser of domestic law and 5 years	

	and 5 years		No time limit to raise 9(1) adjustment		No time limit if fraud, willful default or neglect	
Finland Aug. 20, 1992 Jan. 1, 1993	Art. 9(3) 6 years	Art. 9(2) The "other State shall make an appropriate adjustment to the amount of tax *where that other State considers the adjustment justified.*"	Art. 9(4) Correlative adjustment not available No time limit to raise 9(1) adjustment	Art. 24(1) 2 years from the first notification	Art. 24(3) 6 years No time limit if fraud, willful default or neglect	Art. 24(5): Provides that the competent authorities may consult together to endeavor to agree to the same attribution of profits for PE situation and to the same allocation of income for art. 9 situation. This treaty is under renegotiation.
France July 29, 1976 Jan. 1, 1976 **Second protocol** Sept. 1, 1998 Sept. 1, 1998	No time limit	Not covered	Not covered	Art. XXV 2 years from the first notification	No time limit	The second protocol eliminated: the correlative relief provisions of art. IX(2), the time limits for making adjustments in art. IX(3) and art. XXV(3), which provided a time limit to make adjustments. An arbitration clause was added in art. XXV(5): If the competent authorities agree, difficulties or doubts relating to the application or interpretation of the Convention may be submitted to an arbitration commission whose decisions will have force of law. This procedure has not yet been put into place through exchange of diplomatic notes.
Gabon Signed Nov. 14, 2002. Will be implemented by Bill.	No time limit	Not covered	Not covered	Art. XXV 2 years from the first notification	No time limit	Procedures for obtaining government approval underway in both countries

Treaty partner and year of coming into force	**Article 9: Associated Enterprises**			**Article 25: Mutual Agreement Procedure**		**Comments**
Country 1st date: entry into force date or date of signature if not yet in force 2nd date: date from which relevant provisions have effect	Time limit to raise 9(1) adjustment	Availability of 9(2) correlative adjustment by treaty partner	Consequences of fraud, willful default or neglect	Time limit to present case to competent authority	Time limit to raise adjustment	Comments
16. Germany Sept. 23, 1983 Jan. 1, 1983	No time limit	Not covered	Not covered	No time limit	No time limit	Art. 25(4): Provides that the competent authorities may consult together to endeavor to agree to the same attribution of profits for PE situations and to the same allocation of income for art. 9 situations. This convention remained applicable until the entry into force of the new treaty (see below).
17. Germany March 28, 2002 Jan. 1, 2001	No time limit	Not covered	Not covered	Art. 25(1) 2 years from the first notification	No time limit	This Convention replaces the tax treaty between Canada and Germany that entered into force on September 23, 1983. Art. 25(4): Provides that the competent authorities may consult together to endeavor to agree to the same attribution of profits for PE situation and to the same allocation of income for art. 9 situation. Art. 25(6): If both competent authorities agree, an unresolved case may be submitted to an arbitration commission. In such a case, the decision shall be bind-

						ing.
18. Greece						This treaty is under negotiation. Last round of negotiations took place in Athens in May 2001.
Guyana May 4, 1987 Jan. 1, 1987	No time limit	Not covered	Not covered	No time limit	No time limit	
Hungary Oct. 1, 1994 Jan. 1, 1995	Art. 9(3) Lesser of domestic law time limits and 5 years	Art. 9(2) Standard wording	Art. 9(4) Correlative adjustment not available No time limit to raise 9(1) adjustment	Art. 25(1) 2 years from the first notification	Art. 25(3) Lesser of domestic law and 5 years No time limit if fraud, willful default or neglect	
Iceland Jan. 30, 1998 Jan. 1, 1999	Art. 9(3) Lesser of domestic law time limits and 6 years	Art. 9(2) Standard wording	Art. 9(4) Correlative adjustment not available No time limit to raise 9(1) adjustment	Art. 25(1) 2 years from the first notification	Art. 25(3) Lesser of domestic law and 6 years No time limit if fraud, willful default or neglect	Art. 25(6): Arbitration clause: If the competent authorities and the taxpayer agree, difficulties or doubts relating to the application or interpretation of the Convention may be submitted for arbitration, provided that the taxpayer agrees in writing to be bound by decision of the arbitration board. The decisions will be binding on both States. Procedures to be established in an exchange of notes between the Contracting States.
India May 6, 1997 Jan. 1, 1998	Art. 9(3) Lesser of domestic law time limits	Art. 9(2) Standard wording	Art. 9(4) Correlative adjustment not available	Art. 25(1) 2 years from the first notification	Art. 25 No time limit	

Treaty partner and year of coming into force	Article 9: Associated Enterprises			Article 25: Mutual Agreement Procedure		Comments
Country 1st date: entry into force date or date of signature if not yet in force 2nd date: date from which relevant provisions have effect	Time limit to raise 9(1) adjustment	Availability of 9(2) correlative adjustment by treaty partner	Consequences of fraud, willful default or neglect	Time limit to present case to competent authority	Time limit to raise adjustment	Comments
	and 5 years		No time limit to raise 9(1) adjustment			
Indonesia Dec. 23, 1980 Jan. 1, 1980 **a) Second protocol** Dec. 31, 1998 Jan. 1, 1999	Art. 9(2) Lesser of domestic law time limits and 5 years	Not covered	Art. 9(2) No time limit to raise 9(1) adjustment	Art. 24(1) 2 years from the first notification	Art. 24(3) Lesser of domestic law and 5 years No time limit if fraud, willful default or neglect	The second protocol dated April 15, 1998, changed the numbering of certain articles of the treaty, including art. 25, which is now art. 24. Art. 24(4): Provides that the competent authorities may consult together to endeavor to agree to the same attribution of profits for PE situation and to the same allocation of income for art. 9 situation.
Ireland Dec. 6, 1967 Jan. 1, 1968	No time limit	Not covered	Not covered	No mutual agreement procedure	No mutual agreement procedure	No mutual agreement procedure is set out. Art. XV(2) provides that the taxation authorities may communicate to give effect to the Convention or resolve difficulties or doubts. The existing Agreement between the Government of Canada and the Government of Ireland for the avoidance of double taxation and the prevention of

						fiscal evasion with respect to taxes on income signed at Ottawa on November 23, 1966, shall cease to have effect from the dates on which the new Convention becomes effective.
Ireland A new Convention was signed on Oct. 8th, 2003. Will be implemented by Bill	Art. 9(3) Lesser of domestic law time limits and 6 years	Art. 9(2) Standard wording	Art. 9(4) Correlative adjustment not available No time limit to raise 9(1) adjustment	Art. 25(1) 2 years from the first notification	Art. 25(3) Lesser of domestic law and 6 years No time limit if fraud, willful default or neglect	Procedures for obtaining government approval underway in both countries. Once in force, the new convention will replace the existing convention, which entered into force on Dec. 6, 1967.
Israel July 27, 1976 Jan. 1, 1976	Art. IX(3) Lesser of domestic law time limits and 5 years	Art. IX(2) Standard wording	Art. IX(3) No time limit to raise 9(1) adjustment	Art. XXV(1) 2 years from the first notification	Art. XXV(3) Lesser of domestic law and 5 years No time limit if fraud, willful default or neglect	Art. XXV(4): Provides that the competent authorities may consult together to endeavor to agree to the same attribution of profits for PE situation and to the same allocation of income for art. 9 situation.
Italy Dec. 24, 1980 Jan. 1, 1980	No time limit	Not covered	Not covered	Art. XXIII(1) 2 years from the first notification Case may be presented irrespective of the remedies provided by national laws	No time limit	Art. XXIII: It is understood that the term "irrespective of the remedies provided by the national laws" means, in the case of Italy, that the introduction of a mutual agreement procedure does not represent an alternative to the national legal procedures to which, in all cases, recourse must first be had when the conflict relates to an application of Italian taxes, which is not in accordance with the Convention (Protocol of Understanding, paragraph (h). signed Nov.

Treaty partner and year of coming into force	Article 9: Associated Enterprises			Article 25: Mutual Agreement Procedure		Comments
Country 1st date: entry into force date or date of signature if not yet in force 2nd date: date from which relevant provisions have effect	Time limit to raise 9(1) adjustment	Availability of 9(2) correlative adjustment by treaty partner	Consequences of fraud, willful default or neglect	Time limit to present case to competent authority	Time limit to raise adjustment	Comments
						17, 1977). This convention remains applicable until the entry into force of the new treaty (see below).
Italy Signed June 3, 2002 Implemented by Bill S-2 on December 12, 2002	Art. 9(3) Lesser of domestic law time limits and 6 years	Art. 9(2) Standard wording	Art. 9(4) Correlative adjustment not available No time limit to raise 9(1) adjustment	Art. 24(1) 2 years from the first notification Case may be presented irrespective of the remedies provided by national laws	No time limit	Art. 24(4): The competent authorities can exchange views through a Commission consisting of their representatives. Art. 24(5): If the competent authorities and the taxpayer agree, difficulties or doubts relating to the application or interpretation of the Convention may be submitted for arbitration, provided that the taxpayer agrees in writing to be bound by the decisions of the arbitration board. The decisions will be binding on both States. The procedure shall be established by an exchange of notes between the Contracting States. Procedures for obtaining government approval underway in Italy. Once in force, the new convention will replace

						the existing convention, which entered into force on December 24, 1980. Provisions of the former convention remain applicable until provisions of this convention take effect.
Ivory Coast Dec. 19, 1985 Jan. 1, 1986	Art. 9(3) Lesser of domestic law time limits and 5 years	Art. 9(2) Standard wording	Art. 9(4) Correlative adjustment not available No time limit to raise 9(1) adjustment	Art. 23(1) 2 years from the first notification	No time limit	
Jamaica April 2, 1981 Jan. 1, 1977	Art. IX(3) Lesser of domestic law time limits and 5 years	Art. IX(2) Standard wording	Art. IX(4) No time limit to raise 9(1) adjustment	Art. XXV(1) 2 years from the first notification	Art. XXV(3) Lesser of domestic law and 5 years Art. XXV(4) No time limit if fraud, willful default or neglect	
Japan Nov. 14, 1987 Jan. 1, 1988 **b) Second Protocol** Dec. 14, 2000 Jan. 1, 2001	No time limit Art. 9(3) *Second Protocol* 7 year time limit	Not covered Art. 9(2) *Second Protocol* Standard wording	Not covered Art. 9(4) *Second Protocol* Correlative adjustment not available No time limit to raise 9(1) adjustment Omits "neglect"	Art. 23(1) 2 years from the first notification	No time limit	

Treaty partner and year of coming into force	Article 9: Associated Enterprises			Article 25: Mutual Agreement Procedure		Comments
Country 1st date: entry into force date or date of signature if not yet in force 2nd date: date from which relevant provisions have effect	Time limit to raise 9(1) adjustment	Availability of 9(2) correlative adjustment by treaty partner	Consequences of fraud, willful default or neglect	Time limit to present case to competent authority	Time limit to raise adjustment	Comments
Jordan Dec. 24, 2000 Jan. 1, 2001	Art. 9(3) Lesser of domestic law time limits and 5 years	Art. 9(2) Standard wording	Art. 9(4) Correlative adjustment not available No time limit to raise 9(1) adjustment Omits "neglect"	Art. 23(1) 2 years from the first notification	Art. 23(3) Lesser of domestic law and 5 years No time limit if fraud or willful default Omits "neglect	
Kazakhstan March 30, 1998 Jan. 1, 1996	No time limit	Art. 9(2) The "other State may make an appropriate adjustment to the amount of tax"	Not covered	Art. 25(1) 2 years from the first notification	No time limit	Art. 25(5): Arbitration clause: If the competent authorities and the taxpayer agree, difficulties or doubts relating to the application or interpretation of the Convention may be submitted for arbitration, provided that the taxpayer agrees in writing to be bound by the decisions of the arbitration board. The decisions will be binding on both States. No yet in effect.
Kenya Jan. 8, 1987	Art. IX(3) Lesser of domestic law time limits	Art. IX(2) Standard wording	Art. IX(3) No time limit to raise	Art. XXVI(1) 2 years from the	Art. XXVI(3) Lesser of domes-	

Jan. 1, 1987	and 5 years		IX(1) adjustment	first notification	tic law and 5 years No time limit if fraud, willful default or neglect	
Republic of Korea Dec. 19, 1980 Jan. 1, 1980	Art. 9(2) Lesser of domestic law time limits and 5 years	Not covered	Art. 9(2) No time limit to raise 9(1) adjustment	Art. 22(1) 2 years from the first notification	Art. 22(3) Lesser of domestic law and 5 years No time limit if fraud, willful default or neglect	
Kuwait Aug. 26, 2003 Jan. 1, 2003	Art. 9(3) Lesser of domestic law time limits and 5 years	Art. 9(2) Standard wording	Art. 9(4) Correlative adjustment not available No time limit to raise 9(1) adjustment	Art. 25(1) 2 years from the first notification	No time limit Failure to respect 6-year notification rules could result in double taxation if domestic statute is not open. Unilateral relief is available.	
Kyrgyzstan Dec. 4, 2000 Feb. 1, 2001	Art. 9(3) Lesser of domestic law time limits and 5 years	Art. 9(2) Standard wording	Art. 9(4) Correlative adjustment not available No time limit to raise 9(1) adjustment	Art. 25(1) 2 years from the first notification	Art. 25(3) Lesser of domestic law and 5 years No time limit if fraud, willful default or neglect	
Latvia Dec. 12, 1995	Art. 9(3) Lesser of domes-	Art. 9(2)	Art.9(4) Correlative adjust-	Art. 25(1) 2 years from the	Art. 25(3) Lesser of domes-	

Treaty partner and year of coming into force	Article 9: Associated Enterprises			Article 25: Mutual Agreement Procedure		Comments
Country 1st date: entry into force date or date of signature if not yet in force 2nd date: date from which relevant provisions have effect	Time limit to raise 9(1) adjustment	Availability of 9(2) correlative adjustment by treaty partner	Consequences of fraud, willful default or neglect	Time limit to present case to competent authority	Time limit to raise adjustment	Comments
Jan. 1, 1996	tic law time limits and 5 years	Standard wording	ment not available No time limit to raise 9(1) adjustment	first notification	tic law and 5 years No time limit if fraud, willful default or neglect	
Lebanon Signed Dec. 29, 1998. Will be implemented by Bill S-3	No time limit	Art. 9(2) Standard wording subject to domestic law time limits	Art. 9(3) Correlative adjustment not available	Art. 24(1) 2 years from the first notification	No time limit	
Lithuania Dec. 12, 1997 Jan. 1, 1998	Art. 9(3) Lesser of domestic law time limits and 5 years	Art. 9(2) Standard wording	Art. 9(4) Correlative adjustment not available No time limit to raise 9(1) adjustment	Art. 25(1) 2 years from the first notification	Art. 25(3) Lesser of domestic law and 5 years No time limit if fraud, willful default or neglect	
Luxembourg July 8, 1991 July 8, 1991	No time limit	Not covered	Not covered	Art. 25 2 years from the first notification	No time limit	This Convention remains applicable until the entering into force of the new treaty on Jan. 1, 2000 (see below).

Luxembourg Oct. 17, 2000 Jan. 1, 2001	Art. 9(3) Lesser of domestic law time limits and 5 years	Art. 9(2) Standard wording	Art. 9(4) Correlative adjustment not available No time limit to raise 9(1) adjustment Omits "neglect"	Art. 25(1) 2 years from the first notification	No time limit	Art. 25(4): Provides that the competent authorities may consult together to endeavor to agree to the same attribution of profits for PE situation and to the same allocation of income for art. 9 situation. Reference to consulting to endeavor to avoid double taxation in the case of an estate or trust.
Malaysia Dec. 18, 1980 Jan. 1, 1980	No time limit	Not covered	Not covered	Art. XXVI(1) 2 years from the first notification	No time limit	
Malta May 20, 1987 Jan. 1, 1987	Art. 9(3) Lesser of domestic law time limits and 5 years	Art. 9(2) Standard wording	Art. 9(4) Correlative adjustment not available No time limit to raise 9(1) adjustment	Art. 25(1) 2 years from the first notification	Art. 25(3) Lesser of domestic law and 5 years No time limit if fraud, willful default or neglect	Art. 25(4): Provides that the competent authorities may consult together to endeavor to agree to the same attribution of profits for PE situation and to the same allocation of income for art. 9 situation.
Mauritius						This treaty is under negotiation. Second round of negotiations, scheduled to take place in Ottawa in October 2000, was postponed at the request of Mauritius due to elections in that country. New date has not been fixed.
Mexico May 11, 1992 Jan. 1, 1992	Art. 9(3) Lesser of domestic law time limits and 5 years	Art. 9(2) The "other State shall make an appropriate adjustment to the amount of tax	Art. 9(4) Correlative adjustment not available No time limit to	Art. 24(1) 2 years from the first notification	Art. 24(3) Lesser of domestic law and 5 years No time limit if	This treaty is under renegotiation. The negotiation of a new treaty substantially completed. Date for further discussion of outstanding issues not as yet determined.

Treaty partner and year of coming into force	Article 9: Associated Enterprises			Article 25: Mutual Agreement Procedure		Comments
Country 1st date: entry into force date or date of signature if not yet in force 2nd date: date from which relevant provisions have effect	Time limit to raise 9(1) adjustment	Availability of 9(2) correlative adjustment by treaty partner	Consequences of fraud, willful default or neglect	Time limit to present case to competent authority	Time limit to raise adjustment	Comments
		charged *where it agrees with the inclusion*"	raise 9(1) adjustment		fraud, willful default or neglect	
Moldova Dec. 13, 2002 Jan. 1, 2003	Art. 9(3) Lesser of domestic law time limits and 5 years	Art. 9(2) Standard wording	Art. 9(4) Correlative adjustment not available No time limit to raise 9(1) adjustment	Art. 24(1) 2 years from the first notification	Art. 24(3) Lesser of domestic law and 5 years No time limit if fraud, willful default or neglect	Art. 24(6): If the competent authorities and the taxpayer agree, difficulties or doubts relating to the application or interpretation of the Convention may be submitted for arbitration, provided that the taxpayer agrees in writing to be bound by the decisions of the arbitration board. The decisions will be binding on both States. The procedure shall be established by an exchange of notes between the Contracting States. With respect to the 9(2) correlative adjustment, the Protocol of Understandings provides that it is understood that the other Contracting State is only required to make the appropriate adjustment to the extent it considers that the adjustment made in the first-mentioned State is justified both in principle and in

						amount.
Mongolia Dec. 20, 2002 Jan. 1, 2003	No time limit	Not covered	Not covered	Art. 25(1) 2 years from the first notification	No time limit	Art. 25(5): If the competent authorities and the taxpayer agree, difficulties or doubts relating to the application or interpretation of the Convention may be submitted for arbitration, provided that the taxpayer agrees in writing to be bound by the decisions of the arbitration board. The decisions will be binding on both States. The procedure shall be established by an exchange of notes between the Contracting States.
Morocco Nov. 9, 1978 Jan. 1, 1978	No time limit	Not covered	Not covered	Art. XXIV(1) 2 years from the first notification	No time limit	
Netherlands Aug. 21, 1987 Jan. 1, 1987	Art. 9(3) Lesser of domestic law time limits and 6 years	Art. 9(2) Standard wording	Art. 9(3) No time limit to raise 9(1) adjustment Omits "neglect"	Art. 25(1) 2 years from the first notification	Art. 25(3) Lesser of domestic law and 6 years No time limit if fraud or willful default Omits "neglect"	Art. 25(5): Arbitration clause: If the competent authorities agree, any difficulty or doubt as to the application or interpretation of the Convention may be submitted for arbitration. Procedures not yet established. Added by 1993 protocol.
New Zealand May 29, 1981 Jan. 1, 1976	No time limit	Art. 9(3) Standard wording, subject to the provisions of paragraph 4	Not covered	No time limit	No time limit	Art. 9(2): If the competent authority does not have sufficient information to determine profits to be attributed to the enterprise, it may apply the tax laws of its State to that enterprise, provided that the law is applied in accordance with the principles of art. 9 (also con-

Treaty partner and year of coming into force	**Article 9: Associated Enterprises**			**Article 25: Mutual Agreement Procedure**		**Comments**
Country 1st date: entry into force date or date of signature if not yet in force 2nd date: date from which relevant provisions have effect	Time limit to raise 9(1) adjustment	Availability of 9(2) correlative adjustment by treaty partner	Consequences of fraud, willful default or neglect	Time limit to present case to competent authority	Time limit to raise adjustment	Comments
		Art. 9(4) Time limit of 6 years				tained in art. 7 and in Canada's treaties with Papua New Guinea and Australia). Art. 22(3): Provides that the competent authorities may consult together to endeavor to agree to the same attribution of profits for PE situation and to the same allocation of income for art. 9 situation.
Nigeria Nov. 16, 1999 Jan. 1, 2000	Art. 9(3) Lesser of domestic law time limits and 6 years	Art. 9(2) Standard wording	Art. 9(4) Correlative adjustment not available No time limit to raise 9(1) adjustment	Art. 25(1) 2 years from the first notification	No time limit	
19. Norway Aug. 24, 1967 1966 taxation year	No time limit	Not covered	Not covered	No time limit	No time limit	This convention remained applicable until the entry into force of the new treaty (see below).
20. Norway Dec. 19, 2002	No time limit	Not covered	Not covered	Art. 26(1)2 years from the first noti-	No time limit	The new convention replaces the existing convention, which entered into force on August 24, 1967. Provisions of

Jan. 1, 2003				fication		the former convention remain applicable until provisions of this convention take effect.
21. Oman						This treaty is under negotiation. Negotiations completed. Procedures for obtaining government approval of Convention underway in both countries.
Pakistan Dec. 15, 1977 Jan. 1, 1977	No time limit	Not covered	Not covered	Art. XXIV(1) 2 years from the first notification	No time limit	
Papua New Guinea Dec. 21, 1989 Jan. 1, 1990	Art. 9(4) Lesser of domestic law time limits and 6 years	Art. 9(3) Standard wording	Art. 9(5) Correlative adjustment not available No time limit to raise 9(1) adjustment	Art. 24(1) 2 years from the first notification	Art. 24(3) Lesser of domestic law and 6 years No time limit if fraud, willful default or neglect	Art. 9(2): If the competent authority does not have sufficient information to determine profits to be attributed to the enterprise, it may apply the tax laws of its State to that enterprise, provided that the law is applied in accordance with the principles of art. 9 (also contained in art. 7 and in Canada's treaties with Australia and New Zealand).
Peru Feb. 17, 2003 Jan. 1, 2004	Art. 9(3) Lesser of domestic law time limits and 5 years.	Art. 9(2) Standard wording. Paragraph 2 of Protocol provides that for art. 9(2), the State being asked to make the adjustment to income is required to do so only to the extent it considers that the adjustment made in	Art. 9(4) Correlative adjustment not available No time limit to raise 9(1) adjustment	Art. 25(1) 2 years from the first notification	Art. 25(3) Lesser of domestic law and 5 years No time limit if fraud, willful default or neglect	Art. 25(6): If the competent authorities and the taxpayer agree, an unresolved case may be submitted for arbitration provided the taxpayer agrees in writing to be bound by the decision of the arbitration board. In such a case, the decision shall be binding on both States.

Treaty partner and year of coming into force	Article 9: Associated Enterprises			Article 25: Mutual Agreement Procedure		Comments
Country 1st date: entry into force date or date of signature if not yet in force 2nd date: date from which relevant provisions have effect	Time limit to raise 9(1) adjustment	Availability of 9(2) correlative adjustment by treaty partner	Consequences of fraud, willful default or neglect	Time limit to present case to competent authority	Time limit to raise adjustment	Comments
		the other State is justified both in principle and in amount.				
Philippines Dec. 21, 1977 Jan. 1, 1977	Art. IX(3) Lesser of domestic law time limits and 5 years	Art. IX(2) Standard wording	Art. IX(3) No time limit to raise 9(1) adjustment	Art. XXIV(1) 2 years from the first modification	Art. XXIV(3) Lesser of domestic law and 5 years No time limit if fraud, willful default or neglect	Art. XXIV(4): Provides that the competent authorities may consult together to endeavor to agree to the same attribution of profits for PE situation and to the same allocation of income for art. 9 situation.
Poland Nov. 30, 1989 Jan. 1, 1989	Art. 9(3) Lesser of domestic law time limits and 5 years	Art. 9(2) Standard wording	Art. 9(4) Correlative adjustment not available No time limit to raise 9(1) adjustment	Art. 25(1) 2 years from the first notification	Art. 25(3) Lesser of domestic law and 5 years No time limit if fraud, willful default or neglect	Art. 25(4): Provides that the competent authorities may consult together to endeavor to agree to the same attribution of profits for PE situation and to the same allocation of income for art. 9 situation.
Portugal Oct. 24, 2001	Art. 9(3) Lesser of domes-	Art. 9(2) Standard wording	Art. 9(4) Correlative adjust-	Art. 24(1) 2 years from the	No time limit	With reference to Article 9, paragraph 2, it is understood that the State being asked to make the adjustment to in-

Jan. 1, 2002	tic law time limits and 5 years		ment not available No time limit to raise 9(1) adjustment	first notification		come is required to do it only if it considers that the adjustment made in the other Contracting State is justified in principle and in its amount (paragraph 6 of protocol, concluded at same time as signature of Convention).
Romania Dec. 29, 1980 Jan. 1, 1978	Art. 9(3) Lesser of domestic law time limits and 5 years	Art. 9(2) Standard wording	Art.9(3) No time limit to raise 9(1) adjustment	Art. 24(1) 2 years from the first notification	Art. 24(3) Lesser of domestic law and 5 years No time limit if fraud, willful default or neglect	This treaty is under renegotiation. Negotiations completed. Procedures for obtaining government approval of Convention underway in both countries.
Russia May 5, 1997 Jan. 1, 1998	Art. 9(3) 5 years	Art. 9(2) Standard wording	Art. 9(3) Correlative adjustment not available No time limit to raise 9(1) adjustment Omits "neglect"	Art. 25(1) 2 years from the first notification	No time limit	
Saint Lucia						This treaty is under negotiation. Opening round of negotiations held in Castries in December 1997. No date has been set as yet for the next round of negotiations.
Senegal Oct. 7, 2003 Jan. 1, 2004	Art. 9(3) Lesser of domestic law time limits and 5 years.	Art. 9(2) Standard wording	Art. 9(4) Correlative adjustment not available No time limit to	Art. 24(1) 2 years from the first notification	No time limit	Art. 24(3): Provides that the competent authorities may consult together to endeavor to agree to the same attribution of profits for PE situation and to the same allocation of income for art. 9

Treaty partner and year of coming into force	Article 9: Associated Enterprises			Article 25: Mutual Agreement Procedure		Comments
Country 1st date: entry into force date or date of signature if not yet in force 2nd date: date from which relevant provisions have effect	Time limit to raise 9(1) adjustment	Availability of 9(2) correlative adjustment by treaty partner	Consequences of fraud, willful default or neglect	Time limit to present case to competent authority	Time limit to raise adjustment	Comments
			raise 9(1) adjustment			situation. Art. 24(5): The competent authorities can exchange views through a Commission consisting of their representatives.
Serbia and Montenegro						Negotiations for this treaty will begin the first week of March 2004 in Belgrade.
22. Singapore Sept. 23, 1977 Jan. 1, 1977	No time limit	Not covered	Not covered	Art. XXIV(1) 2 years from the first notification	Not time limit	
Slovak Republic Dec. 20, 2001 Jan. 1, 2002	Art. 9(3) Lesser of domestic law time limits and 6 years.	Art. 9(2) Standard wording	Art. 9(4) Correlative adjustment not available No time limit to raise 9(1) adjustment	Art. 25(1) 2 years from the first notification	Art. 25(3) Lesser of domestic law and 6 years No time limit if fraud, willful default or neglect	This Convention replaces, as far as relations between Canada and the Slovak Republic are concerned, the tax treaty that entered into force on Jan. 1, 1993 between Canada and Czechoslovakia. However, provisions of the former Convention remain applicable for taxation years beginning before Jan. 1, 2002.

Slovenia Aug. 12, 2002 Jan. 1, 2003	Art. 9(3) Lesser of domestic law time limits and 6 years.	Art. 9(2) Standard wording	Art. 9(4) Correlative adjustment not available No time limit to raise 9(1) adjustment	Art. 25(1) 2 years from the first notification	No time limit	
South Africa April 30, 1997 July 1, 1997	Art. 9(3) Lesser of domestic law time limits and 5 years	Art. 9(2) Standard wording	Art. 9(4) Correlative adjustment not available No time limit to raise 9(1) adjustment	Art. 24(1) 2 years from the first notification	Art. 24(3) Lesser of domestic law and 5 years No time limit if fraud, willful default or neglect	Art. 24(6): Arbitration clause: If the competent authorities agree, difficulties or doubts relating to the application or interpretation of the Convention may be submitted to an arbitration commission whose decisions will be binding on the competent authorities. Procedures to be determined by competent authorities.
23. Spain Dec. 26, 1980 Jan. 1, 1980	Art. IX(3) Lesser of domestic law time limits and 5 years	Art. IX(2) Standard wording	Art. IX No time limit to raise 9(1) adjustment (see para. 1 of Nov. 1976 protocol)	Art. XXV(1) 2 years from the first notification	No time limit	Art. XXV(3): Provides that the competent authorities may consult together to endeavor to agree to the same attribution of profits for PE situation and to the same allocation of income for art. 9 situation.
Sri Lanka June 9, 1986 Jan. 1, 1986	Art. 9(3) Lesser of domestic law time limits and 6 years	Art. 9(2) Standard wording	Art. 9(4) Correlative adjustment not available No time limit to raise 9(1) adjustment	Art. 25(1) 2 years from the first notification	Art. 25(3) Lesser of domestic law and 6 years No time limit if fraud, willful default or neglect	
Sweden Dec. 23, 1997	No time limit	Art. 9(2) Standard wording	Not covered	No time limit	No time limit	

Treaty partner and year of coming into force	Article 9: Associated Enterprises			Article 25: Mutual Agreement Procedure		Comments
Country 1st date: entry into force date or date of signature if not yet in force 2nd date: date from which relevant provisions have effect	Time limit to raise 9(1) adjustment	Availability of 9(2) correlative adjustment by treaty partner	Consequences of fraud, willful default or neglect	Time limit to present case to competent authority	Time limit to raise adjustment	Comments
Jan. 1, 1998		Art. 9(2) Time limit: domestic law				
Switzerland April 21, 1998 Jan. 1, 1998	Art. 9(3) Lesser of domestic law time limits and 5 years	Art. 9(2) "the competent authorities of the Contracting States may consult together with a view to reach an agreement on the adjustments of income in both Contracting States"	Art. 9(3) No time limit to raise 9(1) adjustment Omits "neglect"	Art. 24(1) 2 years from the first notification	Art. 24(3) Lesser of domestic law and 5 years No time limit if fraud or willful default Omits "neglect"	Art. 24(4): Provides that the competent authorities may consult together to endeavor to agree to the same attribution of profits for PE situation and to the same allocation of income for art. 9 situation.
Tanzania Aug. 29, 1997 Jan. 1, 1998	Art. 9(3) Lesser of domestic law time limits and 5 years	Art. 9(2) Standard wording	Art. 9(4) Correlative adjustment not available No time limit to raise 9(1) adjustment	Art. 26(1) 2 years from the first notification	Art. 26(3) Lesser of domestic law and 5 years No time limit if fraud, willful default or neglect	Art. 26(6): Competent authorities may develop bilateral and unilateral procedures, conditions, methods and techniques to implement the mutual agreement procedure (see also Canada's treaty with Zimbabwe, UN model tax convention).

Thailand July 16, 1985 Jan. 1, 1985	Art. 9(3) Lesser of domestic law time limits and 6 years	Art. 9(2) Standard wording	Art. 9(4) Correlative adjustment not available No time limit to raise 9(1) adjustment	Art. 24(1) 2 years from the first notification	No time limit	Art. 9(4): Fraud, willful default and neglect includes a case where an enterprise has not filed a return within the time limit specified in the laws of the State of which it is a resident. Art. 24(3): Provides that the competent authorities may consult together to endeavor to agree to the same attribution of profits for PE situation and to the same allocation of income for art. 9 situation.
Trinidad and Tobago Feb. 8, 1996 Jan. 1, 1996	Art. 9(3) Lesser of domestic law time limits and 6 years	Art. 9(2) Standard wording	Art. 9(4) Correlative adjustment not available No time limit to raise 9(1) adjustment	Art. 24(1) 2 years from the first notification	Art. 24(3) Lesser of domestic law and 6 years No time limit if fraud, willful default or neglect	
Turkey						This treaty is under negotiation. Negotiations completed. Procedures for obtaining government approval of Convention underway in both countries.
Tunisia Dec. 4, 1984 Jan. 1, 1985	Art. IX(3) Lesser of domestic law time limits and 5 years	Art. IX(2) Standard wording	Art. IX(3) No time limit to raise IX(1) adjustment	Art. XXIV(1) 2 years from the first notification	Art. XXIV(3) Lesser of domestic law and 5 years No time limit if fraud, willful default or neglect	Art. XXIV(4): Provides that the competent authorities may consult together to endeavor to agree to the same attribution of profits for PE situation and to the same allocation of income for art. IX situation.
Ukraine	Art. 9(3)	Art. 9(2)	Art. 9(4)	Art. 25(1)	Art. 25(3)	From the date of entry into force, the Canada-USSR treaty shall, as between

Treaty partner and year of coming into force	**Article 9: Associated Enterprises**			**Article 25: Mutual Agreement Procedure**		**Comments**
Country 1st date: entry into force date or date of signature if not yet in force 2nd date: date from which relevant provisions have effect	Time limit to raise 9(1) adjustment	Availability of 9(2) correlative adjustment by treaty partner	Consequences of fraud, willful default or neglect	Time limit to present case to competent authority	Time limit to raise adjustment	Comments
April 29, 1997 Jan. 1, 1998	Lesser of domestic law time limits and 5 years	The "other State shall, *where it agrees with the inclusion,* make an appropriate adjustment to the amount of tax."	Correlative adjustment not available No time limit to raise 9(1) adjustment	2 years from the first notification	Lesser of domestic law and 5 years No time limit if fraud, willful default or neglect	Canada and the Ukraine, terminate.
United Arab Emirates Signed June 9, 2002 Implemented by Bill S-2 on December 12, 2002	Art. 9(3) Lesser of domestic law time limits and 5 years	Art. 9(2) Standard wording	Art. 9(4) Correlative adjustment not available No time limit to raise 9(1) adjustment	Art. 26(1) 2 years from the first notification	Art. 26(3) Lesser of domestic law and 5 years No time limit if fraud, willful default or neglect	Procedures for obtaining government approval underway in the United Arab Emirates.
United Kingdom Dec. 18, 1980 1976 and subsequent taxation years *Third protocol* Signed on May 7,	Art. 9(3) Lesser of domestic law time limits and 6 years (in Canada) or the chargeable period (in the UK)	Art. 9(2) Standard wording	Art. 9(4) Correlative adjustment not available No time limit to raise 9(1) adjustment Adds "gross negli-	No time limit	No time limit	Art. 23(3): Provides that the competent authorities may consult together to endeavor to agree to the same attribution of profits for PE situation and to the same allocation of income for art. 9 situation. Art. 9(3): For the purposes of this article, competent authority must receive

2003. Will be implemented by Bill			gence" for Canadian purposes Adds "fraudulent conduct" for UK purposes			notification within 6 years (or chargeable period) from the end of the taxable year to which the adjustment (or proposed adjustment) relates
United States Aug. 16, 1984 Jan. 1, 1985 *Third protocol* Nov. 9, 1995 Jan. 1, 1996 *Fourth protocol* Dec. 16, 1997 Jan. 1, 1996	Currently no time limit For the 1985–95 taxation years, under the 3rd protocol, art. IX(1) adjustment not permitted to the extent that • it would give rise to double taxation and • there was no notification to the competent authority of the other contracting state within six years or, failing which, the taxpayer was not notified of the proposed adjustment within 5½ years.	Art. IX(3) The other State "shall make a corresponding adjustment, notwithstanding any time of procedural limits if: • it agrees with adjustment and it has been notified within 6 years," • competent authorities can agree to consider late notification cases where correlative adjustment is not statute-barred Art. IX(4) Unilateral relief available if proper notification not received or if competent authorities have not agreed to consider as a late notification case	Art IX(5) Correlative adjustment not available State who made or proposed the first adjustment will not provide unilateral relief under art. IX(4) Adds "gross negligence"	Art. XXVI No time limit to present case. Except where art. IX applies, agreements can be implemented, notwithstanding any time or procedural limitations, if competent authority receives notification within 6 years from the end of the taxable year to which the case relates	No time limit Failure to respect 6-year notification rules could result in double taxation if domestic statute is not open. Unilateral relief is available.	Art. IX(2): For the purposes of this Article, a person shall be deemed to be related to another person if either person participates directly of indirectly in the management or control of the other, or if any third person or persons participate directly or indirectly in the management or control of both. Art. XXVI(6): Arbitration clause: If the competent authorities and the taxpayer agree, any difficulty or doubt as to the application or interpretation of the Convention may be submitted for arbitration, provided that the taxpayer agrees in writing to be bound by its decisions. The decisions will be binding on both States. Not yet activated through exchange of notes. This treaty is under renegotiation. Last round of meetings held in Washington in July 2001.

Treaty partner and year of coming into force	Article 9: Associated Enterprises			Article 25: Mutual Agreement Procedure		Comments
Country 1st date: entry into force date or date of signature if not yet in force 2nd date: date from which relevant provisions have effect	Time limit to raise 9(1) adjustment	Availability of 9(2) correlative adjustment by treaty partner	Consequences of fraud, willful default or neglect	Time limit to present case to competent authority	Time limit to raise adjustment	Comments
April 29, 1997 Jan. 1, 1998	Lesser of domestic law time limits and 5 years	The "other State shall, *where it agrees with the inclusion,* make an appropriate adjustment to the amount of tax."	Correlative adjustment not available No time limit to raise 9(1) adjustment	2 years from the first notification	Lesser of domestic law and 5 years No time limit if fraud, willful default or neglect	Canada and the Ukraine, terminate.
United Arab Emirates Signed June 9, 2002 Implemented by Bill S-2 on December 12, 2002	Art. 9(3) Lesser of domestic law time limits and 5 years	Art. 9(2) Standard wording	Art. 9(4) Correlative adjustment not available No time limit to raise 9(1) adjustment	Art. 26(1) 2 years from the first notification	Art. 26(3) Lesser of domestic law and 5 years No time limit if fraud, willful default or neglect	Procedures for obtaining government approval underway in the United Arab Emirates.
United Kingdom Dec. 18, 1980 1976 and subsequent taxation years *Third protocol* Signed on May 7,	Art. 9(3) Lesser of domestic law time limits and 6 years (in Canada) or the chargeable period (in the UK)	Art. 9(2) Standard wording	Art. 9(4) Correlative adjustment not available No time limit to raise 9(1) adjustment Adds "gross negli-	No time limit	No time limit	Art. 23(3): Provides that the competent authorities may consult together to endeavor to agree to the same attribution of profits for PE situation and to the same allocation of income for art. 9 situation. Art. 9(3): For the purposes of this article, competent authority must receive

Social Republic of Vietnam Dec. 16, 1998 Jan. 1, 1999	Art. 9(3) Lesser of domestic law time limits and 5 years	Art. 9(2) Standard wording	Art. 9(4) Correlative adjustment not available No time limit to raise 9(1) adjustment	Art. 24(1) 2 years from the first notification	Art. 24(3) Lesser of domestic law and 5 years No time limit if fraud, willful default or neglect	
Zambia Dec. 28, 1989 Jan. 1, 1989	Art. IX(3) Lesser of domestic law time limits and 6 years	Art. IX(2) Standard wording	Art. IX(3) No time limit to raise IX(1) adjustment	Art. XXIV(1) 2 years from the first notification	Art. XXIV(3) Lesser of domestic law and 6 years No time limit if fraud, willful default or neglect	Art. XXIV(4): Provides that the competent authorities may consult together to endeavor to agree to the same attribution of profits for PE situation and to the same allocation of income for art. IX situation. Oral exchange through Commission.
Zimbabwe Dec. 15, 1994 Jan. 1, 1995	Art 9(3) Time limits in domestic law	Art. 9(2) Standard wording	Art. 9(4) Correlative adjustment not available No time limit to raise 9(1) adjustment	Art. 26(1) 2 years from the first notification in Canada 3 years in Zimbabwe	Art. 26(3) Lesser of domestic law and 5 years No time limit if fraud, willful default or neglect	Art. 9(3): Provides for a time limit according to domestic law while art. 26(3) provides for a time limit that is the lesser of the time limits in domestic law and 5 years. Art. 26(6): Competent authorities may develop bilateral and unilateral procedures, conditions, methods and techniques to implement the mutual agreement procedure (see also Canada's treaty with Tanzania, UN model tax convention).

Chapter Twenty

Tax Litigation in the New Economy

Arthur J. Cockfield

A. INTRODUCTION

This chapter surveys a number of emerging litigation concerns within the new economy. Three main factors are driving these concerns: (a) the increase in the sale or exchange of intangible goods and services; (b) the rise of e-commerce and the increased reliance on computers and computer networks to enable commercial activity; and (c) an increase in cross-border economic activity by individuals and small to medium-sized firms.

The chapter initially focuses on valuation issues for software tax shelters and the judicial response thus far to these developments. Next, the chapter discusses recent changes to the OECD model tax treaty that permit countries to tax profits attributable to computer servers as well as some of the initial policy views on this development. The chapter then reviews the difficulties that tax authorities encounter when they strive to audit out-of-state individuals and firms that do not maintain any physical presence within Canada: the discussion references developments surrounding European Union VATs, the Canadian GST, and offshore credit card accounts.

Most of the matters under scrutiny within this chapter have not yet attracted judicial attention. As such, the analysis is meant to highlight the relevant policy issues that tax advocates could integrate within their arguments to assist with protecting client interests. The chapter concludes by noting that the CRA should increase information exchanges with foreign tax authorities in order to effectively audit "information arbitrage" strategies by taxpayers that take advantage of recent developments that make it harder to align economic income with financial income which is subject to taxation.

B. SOFTWARE TAX SHELTER LITIGATION

An interesting example of an emerging tax litigation concern surrounds the use of cross-border software tax shelters, which place a few new interesting twists on traditional shelter activity. This section reviews a recent Tax Court and Federal Court of Appeal decision where the CRA challenged the valuation of intangible assets within a software tax shelter.[1]

1) The *Brown* Case

The story begins when Peter Brown, CEO of a Toronto stock brokerage firm, is approached by one of his clients with an investment opportunity. The client — described as the "godfather" of software joint ventures — told Mr. Brown of a potential investment in a Canadian partnership (registered as a tax shelter under the *Income Tax Act*) that planned to purchase video game engines from American Softworks Corporation (ASC), a U.S.-based company. Mr. Brown jumped at the deal and purchased 80 units in the partnership for $800,000: $140,000 of the purchase price consisted of equity and the remainder consisted of a promissory note. The partnership and ASC were non-arm's length parties that carried on the business of selling computer games in a joint venture.

In 1993 and 1994, ASC was unprofitable — partly due to large capital cost allowances that amortized the total value of the computer engines within these two years — and Mr. Brown deducted his share of the losses (which amounted to roughly $1 million) from his other sources of income. In 1995, the company became profitable and Mr. Brown included a portion of the company's income within his own gross income (and deducted interest charges for amounts paid to finance his investment, which gave him a net loss of roughly $4,000).

The CRA assessed Mr. Brown and denied his deductions for losses associated with ASC as well as any interest deductions.

In many ways, the facts of the case resemble the structure of many 'old economy' tax shelters such as the low income housing shelters that were popular in the 1980s. Under these older models, high income individuals would buy units in a limited partnership which would in turn purchase low

---

1 See *Brown v. The Queen*, 2002 D.T.C. 1094 (additional reasons at 2002 D.T.C. 1385 and 2002 D.T.C. 1925 (T.C.C.), aff'd 2003 D.T.C. 5298 (F.C.A).

income housing. The depreciation charged against the housing along with expenditures to upgrade the property for eventual sale all but guaranteed that the project would lose money in the short term, enabling the investor to offset her share of the losses against other sources of income.

The *Brown* software shelter seems to differ from these traditional shelters in terms of the complexity of the structure, the fact that the investor was effectively purchasing an investment in an intangible asset rather than a tangible asset and the fact that the venture took place on an international basis.

For the most part, the Tax Court upheld the Minister's reassessment and Brown appealed to the Federal Court of Appeal. Brown alleged the Tax Court had erred by finding that the partnership and ASC were non-arm's length parties and that he was a limited partner. The subsequent analysis, however, deals only with Brown's contention that the Tax Court erred by holding that the fair market value of the software was below the purchase price.

2) Valuation of Intangibles and Expert Witnesses

Intangible goods and services often make up a significant component of the value added to economic activity by firms within the new economy. These goods and services are often difficult to value due to their uniqueness and the uncertainty surrounding their potential economic return. Furthermore, intangible goods and services are so-called information goods when they are rendered into digital format, as occurs with respect to all software programs and all digital e-commerce goods and services.[2] These information goods share two main characteristics that increase valuation uncertainty in many circumstances: information goods have often high fixed costs of production (e.g., the initial outlays to pay game developers to develop the game engine) and low or nil costs of reproduction and distribution (e.g., the cost of copying a game engine and transmitting it over a computer network to a third party).[3]

One of the main issues that the trial judge scrutinized was how to properly value the eleven software game engines that were transferred from ASC to the Canadian partnership. Game engines are the shell of a video game computer program that can be filled in later with specific attributes for the game. For example, a game engine could be a computer program that enables players to walk around the game landscape and shoot

---

2 For a discussion of the tax treatment of software payments, see C.A. Brown, "The Canadian Income Tax Treatment of Computer Software Payments" (1994) 42:3 Cdn. Tax J. 593.

3 For discussion, see A.J. Cockfield, "The Law and Economics of Digital Taxation" (2002) 56 Bulletin for International Fiscal Documentation 606.

enemies: this type of engine is sometimes referred to as a "first person shooter" because it gives the gamer the perspective that he is moving through the game world. Later on, other computer programmers can add additional code to create a fully-formed computer game.

ASC maintained that the games were worth US$8,170,000. This is the amount the partnership added to the capital cost of its Class 12 assets. The Minister reassessed on the basis that the fair market value of the programs was US$275,000. There was clearly a significant difference in the valuation estimates, leading to a battle of the experts during the trial.

Five expert witnesses testified to the value of the programs. The Minister's and Brown's experts used the discounted cash flow ("DCF") method to get a present value of the cash flow from programs. In order to come up with a valuation estimate, the DCF requires: (a) an estimate of future cash flows; (b) a discount rate to be used to find the present value of the future receipts; and (c) a salvage value, if any.[4]

The trial judge agreed that the DCF method is the best valuation technique although he recognized that the choice of discount rate is inherently "subjective." Further, estimating future cash flows could be similarly problematic. According to the trial judge, factors that determine future cash flow would include: (1) whether engines will actually be completed; (2) whether finished games will generate demand for sequels; (3) whether 16 bit platform (for which engines can be used) become obsolete and when; (4) the demand for completed games, which depends on specific gaming genres; (5) whether completed games should be valued individually or as a group; (6) the history and position of ASC with respect to sales and game developers' success rates; (7) the fact that a game might become a bestseller could be taken into account; and (8) the impact of licensing agreements with game distributors like Sega and Nintendo and geographic sales area permitted under the license (e.g., worldwide vs. North American sales only). As a result, the trial judge pointed out there is great deal of uncertainty surrounding the ultimate economic potential of a completed game.

In determining the best estimate of the expected cash flows, the trial judge noted: "The question that ought to be asked is what are the average game sales that ASC could expect to produce from each engine, having regard to market conditions." It is therefore appropriate to look to ASC's

---

4 For discussion, see W.A. Klein & J.C. Coffee, Jr., *Business Organization and Finance: Legal and Economic Principles* (New York: Foundation Press, 2000), at chapter 5. Also see the chapters by Howard E. Johnson, "The Litigious Elements of Business Valuation" and James L. Horvath and Steven Hacker, "Valuing Computer Software and Other Intellectual Property: Concepts, Complexities and Controversies" in this book.

past sales performance where the company had only lukewarm success as none of its previous game titles sold more than 50,000 units and its total annual sales represented only two-tenths of one percent of the total market share. The trial judge ultimately decided that the game engines should be valued at CAD$4,128,000 in comparison to the acquisition cost of US$8,170,000.

The Federal Court of Appeal ultimately accepted the trial judge's view on valuation, noting that Brown had "not shown [a] palpable and overriding error on the part of the Tax Court Judge in respect of the valuation."[5] As a result, the court dismissed Brown's appeal on the valuation issue.

3) Lessons from *Brown*

The *Brown* case suggests a number of lessons with respect to the valuation of intangible assets. First, experts should present figures as reasonable valuations while recognizing the uncertainty within the scheme. The trial judge found much of the expert testimony to be unsatisfactory, suggesting the Crown and taxpayer witnesses made a number of errors. For example, one of the taxpayer's experts based his valuation estimate by looking at games that ASC and the partnership never purchased.

Other experts based their revenue projections on speculative evidence while portraying these estimates as concrete facts. As finance theorists often state, financial analysis is part art and part science: the seemingly objective aspects of certain valuation techniques in fact involve a number of assumptions based on conjecture or a "feeling" for past performance measures.[6] This uncertainty can be assessed through sensitivity analysis where the valuators can test different assumptions concerning, for example, expected sales or different hurdle rates. Other commentators have suggested that the DCF model should be modified when dealing with highly uncertain high technology products: probability-weighted scenarios with different possible outcomes, for example, can be used to address this uncertainty.[7]

---

5 The Federal Court of Appeal rejected the taxpayer's argument that a lower standard of deference is applicable to the assessment of expert evidence by a trial judge on the basis of a recent Supreme Court ruling. See *Housen v. Nikolaisen*, [2002] 2 S.C.R. 235.

6 See, e.g., R.T. McDermott, *Legal Aspects of Corporate Finance* (New York: LEXIS Publishing, 2000).

7 For discussion, see L. Racette, "Valuation Issues in High-Tech Businesses," in *2000 Canadian Tax Foundation Conference Report* (Toronto: Canadian Tax Foundation, 2000).

Second, judges should only accept the most reasonable valuation technique under the DCF approach. As the Delaware courts (the most influential courts in the United States with respect to corporate law developments) have recognized, the DCF method has a built-in protection within the business world as managers will often be held accountable for their estimates: the market will punish the use of faulty assumptions or exaggerated claims.[8] But the litigation process does not present similar protections and litigators may be tempted to offer unreasonable estimates using the DCF method perhaps with the hope that the trier of fact will come to some middle position. These unreasonable approaches should be rejected, as the trial judge recognized.

One aspect of the trial judge's decision, however, may give pause to their south-of-the-border brethren. The trial judge in *Brown* came up with his own valuation after taking into account evidence and methodologies presented by each side. A Delaware Court's Chancellor, however, has written: "Subparts of the DCF model used here are not interchangeable. With certain exception, each expert's model is a complex, interwoven whole, no part of which can be removed from that model and substituted into the alternative model."[9] In the Chancellor's view, if it is understood that the court will or is likely to accept the whole of one expert witnesses' testimony, then the parties will be given an incentive to conform their valuation estimates to reasonable standards. This approach might prove useful to provide incentives for the Minister and taxpayers to generate reasonable valuations instead of extreme views of either side as occurred in *Brown*.

Third, the parties should test their valuation assumptions through comparison to prices for similar products. Intangible assets tend to be unique and it is often difficult to find comparable assets to estimate prices, creating problems under the traditional approach to international transfer pricing that seeks out comparable transactions on a case-by-case basis to obtain an objective arm's length price.[10] Nevertheless, it is sometimes possible to locate a roughly similar asset where the marketplace has determined a price.

In *Brown*, the parties could have presented evidence of the price of other game engines. For example, the game engine for Quake III, one of

---

8 Delaware courts accept only most reasonable testimony. See *Cede v. Technicolor*, 1990 D. Ch. LEXIS 259 (Oct. 19, 1990).

9 *Ibid.* at 17.

10 For discussion, see A.J. Cockfield, "Balancing National Interests in the Taxation of Electronic Commerce Business Profits" (1999) 74 Tul. L. Rev, 133, 195–98 (hereafter "Balancing National Interests").

the most successful and popular engines in the world, sells for $250,000 plus a royalty fee in 2003.[11] Brown maintained that the eleven game engines purchased by the partnership in 1993, a time when video game sales were much lower than today, should equal US$8,170,000 or roughly $743,000 per game: this figure seems grossly out of line with the fair market value of game engines like Quake III with proven track records. Further, the trial court's view that the games should be valued at CAD$4,128,000 (or roughly CAD$375,000 per game) seems to be on the high end when compared to the fair market value of the Quake III game engine.[12] In contrast, the Quake III price arguably bolsters the Minister's initial assessment that the game engines were worth a total of $275,000 (or roughly $25,000 per game). The Minister's assessment was likely more in line with the true value of the game engines, as they would in all probability not obtain anything near the sales level of a game based on the successful Quake III model.

C. ATTRIBUTING PROFITS ATTRIBUTABLE TO COMPUTER EQUIPMENT

1) The New Computer Server Rule

Within the new economy, businesses are increasingly turning to computers and computer networks to accomplish traditional economic activities.[13] Consider the purchase of music by consumers. Traditionally a Canadian consumer would have to go to a local store to buy his latest album or CD. Assuming the store was owned by a foreign company located in a non-tax treaty partner country, the store would be taxed as a Canadian tax resident under the "carrying on business in Canada" test set out within the *Income Tax Act*.[14] Alternatively, assume the store was owned by a foreign company located in a tax treaty partner country, the store would still be taxed as Canadian tax resident because the store constitutes a "permanent establishment" under tax treaties, which generally entitles Canada to tax any profits attributable to the store's activities.

---

11 See D. Kushner, "Prepare to Meet Thy Doom" (2003) 11.05 Wired 150, 160.

12 This amount takes into account the present value of the tax shield for Brown's investment, which equalled CAD$1,231,000.

13 For a comprehensive discussion of issues relating to the taxation of international e-commerce, see J. Li, *International Taxation in the Age of Electronic Commerce: A Comparative Study* (Toronto: Canadian Tax Foundation, 2003).

14 See, e.g., s.253 of the *Income Tax Act*.

But now assume that the foreign business does not own any stores located in Canada. Rather the foreign company sells digital music in the form of MP3 files (i.e., compressed digital music files) through its commercial web site directly to Canadian consumers.[15] Consumers can visit Internet web sites and download digital music directly to their computer hard drives.

If this foreign company is located in a tax treaty partner, should the web site constitute a permanent establishment in Canada? Should any computer equipment within Canada be considered to be a permanent establishment?

After several years of considering this issue, the OECD amended its Commentary to the OECD model tax treaty in January 2003 to deal with these issues.[16] Under these changes, on the one hand, web sites in and of themselves will not constitute permanent establishments. On the other hand, certain forms of computer equipment such as computer servers may constitute permanent establishments in certain circumstances. A computer server is a computer that has been networked to the Internet: there are tens of millions of computer servers that make up an important component of the Internet's infrastructure. Servers now constitute a permanent establishment under the OECD model tax treaty if (a) the server performs integral aspects of a cross-border function, and (b) the nonresident firm owns or leases the server within the source country.

The Commentary offers an example of a retail server/permanent establishment that displays a web page, takes a customer's order, processes payment and transmits a digital good or service to the end consumer. Under these circumstances, the server will now constitute a permanent establishment entitling the source country to tax profits attributable to the server.[17]

---

15 The Internet is essentially a "network of networks" where a common communications protocol (TCP/IP) permits information to be broken down into packets and exchanged among computers connected to the network. See *ACLU v. Reno*, 929 F. Supp. 824, 830 (E.D. Pa. 1996).

16 See Organization for Econ. Co-operation and Dev., *Model Tax Convention on Income and on Capital* (Paris; OECD, 2003) (hereiafter OECD model tax treaty), commentary on art. 5 at par. 42.1 to 42.10.

17 In other works, I have argued that servers should never constitute PEs, mainly as a result of the fact that the location of a server need not have any geographic connection to activities that add value and create income. Servers and the software functions within a server form part of the hardware and software infrastructure of the Internet and can be shifted outside of the country where an e-commerce firm is based or where software products are developed as well as outside of the source country where e-commerce goods and services are purchased. Two main deficiencies of the new rule have been identified: (a) server/PEs will not effectively allocate taxing jurisdiction and revenues to source countries, and (b) server/PEs offer tax planning opportunities for

Note also that the presence or absence of any human intermediary is not determinative of the issue: even if no person is present in the foreign country to service, maintain or modify the software within the server, a permanent establishment may nevertheless be constituted.

For example, in a recent German court ruling, the issue was whether a German GmbH (a private limited company), whose main business was to provide its customers information prepared and presented by an affiliate company, had a permanent establishment in Switzerland through an unstaffed server located there.[18] The server stored text information that Swiss customers were able to retrieve electronically for a fee. The court disagreed with the German tax authorities' position that the German company did not have a permanent establishment in Switzerland. The court held that the customers' ability to electronically retrieve information from the server for a fee constituted an integral aspect of the business. Therefore, the server performed the core business of the enterprise and constituted a permanent establishment. Taxes attributable to the profits generated by the server were exempt from German taxation pursuant to the German-Swiss tax treaty.

2) Profit Attribution Issues

Profit attribution will likely become a source of controversy in this area, and the OECD has issued a draft report on the topic of server profit attribution as part of its broader efforts to reach consensus on the application of profit attribution in the context of transfer prices.[19] Auditing these e-commerce businesses is also complicated by the fact that records are typically only maintained in electronic form, the records may be encrypted for security purposes, and records maintained by traditional business intermediaries may be absent.[20] Moreover, enforcement of any tax liability may also present

---

multinational firms to shift income outside of residence countries. See A.J. Cockfield, "Transforming the Internet into a Taxable Forum: A Case Study in E-Commerce Taxation" (2001) 85 Minn. L. Rev. 1171; A. J. Cockfield, "Should We Really Tax Profits From Computer Servers?" (2000) 21 Tax Notes Int'l 2407.

18 Decision of the Tax Court Schleswig-Holstein, Sept. 6, 2001, IStR 2002, 134. The case was under appeal at this writing. The facts from this case were taken from an unofficial English translation located at http://www.itaa.org/taxfinance/tthabstract.cfm?ID=856 (last accessed May 2004).

19 For discussion, see A. J. Cockfield, "Through the Looking Glass: Computer Servers and E-Commerce Profit Attribution" (2002) 25 Tax Notes Int'l 269. See also OECD, *Discussion Draft on the Attribution of Profits to Permanent Establishments (PES): Part II (Banks)* (2003).

20 See A. J. Cockfield, "Tax Compliance Issues for U.S. Companies with International Electronic Commerce Transactions" (2000) 20 Tax Notes Int'l 223.

challenges because there may be no physical assets to seize to satisfy the judgment for back taxes as the foreign business may only maintain servers.

Under traditional tax laws, tax treaty partners are only permitted to tax profits attributable to a permanent establishment. For example, a French retail branch of a United States-based retail chain will only be obligated to pay the French government tax on any profits that are attributable to the branch, such as the profits derived from all sales from the French retail outlet to French consumers. In February 2001, the OECD issued a draft paper that discusses how taxpayers should attribute profits to their computer servers in the context of Internet retailing (assuming a permanent establishment is found to exist).[21]

Because the transfers take place among related parties, the price paid or charged for goods or services may not correspond to fair market value. Tax laws try to ensure that the transfers among related parties in different countries are measured on an objective basis: in other words, these tax authorities develop transfer pricing laws to force taxpayers to sell their goods and services to related parties at market prices (so-called "arm's length" prices) for tax purposes.[22] Otherwise, a multinational firm can manipulate its transfer prices in such a way as to shift profits to a relatively lower-taxed jurisdiction.

The draft applies a two-step process for determining the appropriate amount of profit attribution.

Step One employs a functional and factual analysis to determine which of the identified activities can be associated with the computer server and to what extent. The functional analysis asks what risks are being assumed by the permanent establishment in the course of its operations and how the permanent establishment uses its assets. A Web server, in the context of an online retailing operation, that takes a customer's orders, processes payment, and delivers a digital product to the end consumer is compared with a traditional retailer. A traditional retailer makes a number of deci-

21 OECD Technical Advisory Group on Monitoring the Application of Existing Treaty Norms for the Taxtion of Business Profits, *Attribution of Profits to a Permanent Establishment involved in Electronic Commerce Transactions* (2001).

22 See s. 247 of the *Income Tax Act*. In *Ford v. Ontario Municipal Employees Retirement Board*, [2004] O.J. No. 191 (S.C.), an Ontario court held that the transfer pricing policy between Ford U.S. and its subsidiary Ford Canada was unfair and prejudicial to the interests of minority shareholders of Ford Canada. Importantly, the court held that it may not be sufficient for transfer pricing methods to merely comply with Canadian tax legislation, but that the chosen method must also be fair to minority shareholders because transfer pricing methods affect a firm's profitability, which is ultimately reflected in the firm's share values.

sions involving functions, such as ordering and maintaining inventory and negotiating terms with suppliers. In contrast, the OECD draft report notes that a Web server lacks this type of decision-making ability and, accordingly, is not the same as a full-function retail outlet.

Further, the risks assumed by the Web server are scrutinized because profit-making activities are generally associated with the assumption of different forms of risk (for example, an investor who buys shares in a public company assumes greater risk and hence expects a potentially greater return in comparison to an investor who buys an asset with minimal risk, such as a government bond with a fixed return). The OECD report concludes that the Web server's primary function is to provide support services for the retailing activities of the firm and that the server operations provide very little operational risk (for example, credit risk, technological risk and marketing risk).

Step Two determines the amount of profits attributable to the computer server by looking to see what appropriate return would be earned by a distinct enterprise providing the same transaction. For example, a Web server is said to generally employ assets used or developed by the head office, and thus the server would have to compensate the head office for this use. As a service provider, the Web server is only entitled to be compensated by fees, but should not be entitled to a percentage of the profits derived from Internet sales. By tightening up the profit attribution rules, the OECD has presumably hoped that abusive tax planning will be limited.

It may, however, be the case that taxpayers will employ strategies to try to shift profits to low tax jurisdictions. Consider an example involving Company A, a Canadian manufacturer of automobile components. Company A is based in Toronto and contracts out the manufacture of auto components to firms based in Mexico and Malaysia. These components are ultimately transported to Company A's manufacturing facilities in Oshawa, Ontario for final assembly and sale to automobile manufacturers.

Company A is networked via an extranet (i.e., a part of the Internet that is secured from access by the general public) to its suppliers and customers in order to enhance efficiencies surrounding the timing of the delivery of the auto components (e.g., Company A wants its suppliers to supply the engine components "just-in-time" for the final assembly of the automobile's engine in Oshawa). The payment for each auto component is conducted through the use of electronic agents: in other words, the payment for each component occurs automatically via the extranet through the workings of software code.[23] Finally, this same extranet extends to the deal-

23 Recent legal reform efforts in many countries generally accept that so-called electronic agents (i.e., software programs) can create legally binding contracts. See, e.g., Uni-

ers that order cars from Company A and these orders are similarly handled in an automated fashion by electronic agents.

Company A may be able to lower its overall tax burden by setting up a global sales and distribution center in a low or nil tax jurisdiction then shifting income attributable to its global sales to this jurisdiction. Company A can set up a foreign corporation to own its computer servers to defer tax liability and can additionally hire employees to maintain or service the server in the foreign country. Under traditional tax principles, the profit attributable to the corporation or the permanent establishment should be identical (because the permanent establishment is treated as a fictional separate legal entity under transfer pricing rules), but Company A may still try to use the existence of the corporation and its employees to bolster its argument that profits should be attributed to the country where the server is based.

The order of a new car from Company A by a car manufacturer, the negotiation of the price for the supply and the completion of the order can now all be accomplished through the use of electronic agents based on the automated functioning of computer code. Company A can still deduct payments for the auto components from its foreign suppliers. Furthermore, Company A can ensure that the foreign-based servers perform integral aspects of the cross-border sales and distribution function to Company A's customers so that at least a portion of this income can be attributable to the low or nil tax jurisdiction. If the server is owned by a corporation located in a treaty partner country then any active business profits generated by the server will come out of the taxpayer's exempt surplus account and will be effectively exempt from Canadian taxation.

Computer code within Company A's foreign-based servers can accomplish other overhead-related functions related to the global sale of Company A's products, including accounting, finance, intellectual property rights management or other functions. For example, the foreign-based servers can process Company A's payroll or maintain ownership rights to intellectual property produced by Company A in order to potentially isolate income produced by this property within the foreign corporation. Royalty payments could generate income in the low tax jurisdiction and offsetting deductions to lower income in high tax jurisdictions. It remains unclear how the proposed OECD transfer pricing rules will deal with these sorts of strategies.

---

form Law Conference of Canada, *Uniform Electronic Commerce Act* (1999). Canadian courts have upheld the validity of so-called click-wrap agreements between consumers and web sites. See, e.g., *Rudder v. Microsoft*, [1999] O.J. 3778 (S.C.J.).

3) Different Views on Server/Permanent Establishments

This new rule may raise enforcement concerns for tax authorities and possibly compliance concerns for taxpayers. Different national tax authorities have taken different perspectives on the server/permanent establishment issue. For example, the U.S. initially came out in a Department of Treasury report against server/permanent establishments.[24] The U.S., however, later changed its view and agreed with the OECD's view that servers could constitute permanent establishments in certain circumstances. United Kingdom tax authorities have suggested that they will not follow the new rule because, in their view, servers should not be used to create a nexus for international income tax purposes. On the other hand, Spain and Portugal dissented from the OECD view on the grounds that web sites should be treated as permanent establishments, presumably in the hope that more revenues would be allocated to these net e-commerce importing nations through a broader view of nexus for e-commerce purposes. An expert tax group appointed by the Indian government has also suggested that modifications to the permanent establishment rule will not suffice to protect source-based tax erosion.[25]

The Canadian government and the CRA have taken a cautious stance on the issue up to this point. For example, in 1998 Revenue Canada (as it was then) refused to take a position when a U.S. company asked about the tax implications of storing proprietary information on a Canadian-based server.[26] Further, two Canadian government reports published in 1998 suggested that a server might in fact constitute a PE under certain circumstances.[27] As of March 2004, the CRA had prepared but not released a draft Interpretation Bulletin on server/permanent establishments so its views on the topic remain unknown.

Finally, it is worth mentioning that that the 2003 changes to the OECD model tax treaty commentary on permanent establishments also indicate

---

24 See Office of Tax Policy, U.S. Department of the Treasury, *Selected Tax Policy Implications of Global Electronic Commerce* (Washington, D.C.: Dept. of Treasury, 1996).

25 See Ministry of Finance, India, *Report of the High Powered Committee on E-Commerce and Taxation* 11-12 (2001), available at http://www.laws4india.com/indiantaxlaws/notification/ecomcontent.asp.

26 See Revenue Canada, Internal Memo 981646 (Aug. 31, 1998).

27 See *Electronic Commerce and Canada's Tax: A Report to the Minister of National Revenue Administration from the Minister's Advisory Committee on Electronic Commerce* (April 1998); *Electronic Commerce and Canada's Tax Administration: A Response to the Advisory Committee's Report on Electronic Commerce by the Minister of National Revenue* 21 (September 1998).

that a permanent establishment will be created if, in the course of providing consulting or other services to a client, the foreign taxpayer or its employees use the client's premises for an extended period of time. This position was expressly rejected by the Federal Court of Appeal several years ago in *Dudney*.[28] The new changes to the OECD model tax treaty provide support for the CRA's position in *Dudney* and elsewhere that the permanent establishment concept is flexible and can be broadly interpreted to capture sustained economic activities conducted by non-resident taxpayers within Canada.[29]

D. AUDITING OUT-OF-STATE BUSINESSES AND INDIVIDUALS

1) GST and VAT Enforcement on Cross-border Sales

The last part discussed certain issues surrounding the income taxation of e-commerce goods and services. This part will turn to consumption tax issues through a discussion of recent developments in the legal regime that surrounds European Union VATs and Canada's Goods and Services Tax (GST).

a) Enforcing the EU VAT

All of the European Union (EU) countries impose a value-added tax (VAT) on the sale of most goods and services at rates varying between 15 and 25 percent. Businesses within the EU must typically register for VAT purposes and charge, assess and collect the VAT on these sales; the business intermediary hence plays a critical role in the effective enforcement of the tax. With respect to international transactions, the EU member states generally impose their VATs on the importation of most goods and services. VATs are generally imposed at the border by customs agents when tangible goods are imported from outside of the European Union.

The sale of intangible goods or services can prove more troublesome. For example, consider a hypothetical online retailer based in Ottawa called

---

28 See *Dudney v. The Queen*, 2000 D.T.C 6169 (F.C.A.). In this case, the Crown argued that the term "fixed base" (with respect to an independent contractor) should have a wider interpretation than the term "permanent establishment." The Crown also argued that the use by Mr. Dudney of premises made available to him by a Canadian client was a fixed base of Mr. Dudney in Canada. The Federal Court of Appeal rejected both arguments.

29 For discussion on the development of a permanent establishment fiction to capture above threshold sales into source countries, see A.J. Cockfield, "Reforming the Permanent Establishment Principle through a Quantitative Economic Presence Test" (2003) 38 Cdn. Bus. L.J. 400.

"CanuckDVD.com" that sells a digital movie to a consumer in Spain. CanuckDVD.com is located outside of the EU and therefore is not subject to registration obligations. The Spanish consumer is required to self-assess the VAT owed, but consumer self-assessment on all foreign sales is not a realistic option. Business-to-business sales where the EU-based business is subject to self-assessment obligations is, however, a workable option. In fact, it will be difficult or impossible for the EU to collect the VAT on this consumer transaction unless it subjects CanuckDVD.com to registration obligations.

As a result, the EU has passed a Directive, effective July 1 2003, to force companies like CanuckDVD.com to charge and collect the Spanish VAT (at a 25 percent rate!) and then remit the tax payment to European Union tax authorities.[30] Under the new Directive, all non-EU suppliers of digital goods and services to EU resident consumers must register and be subject to all VAT obligations.

Companies are concerned that they may have to incur significant compliance costs to comply with the new Directive. It also remains unclear how the EU will enforce its new law because there are not any international agreements that govern cross-border sales and consumption taxes. For example, all of Canada's tax treaties focus on income and capital taxes (although non-discrimination treatment is extended to the GST in some Canadian tax treaties). Despite an absence of any effective enforcement mechanism, certain large companies such as Time Warner Inc. have indicated that they will strive to comply with the new European rules. Other companies may try to set up tax strategies to insulate themselves from the EU VAT obligations.[31]

b) Changes to Canadian GST Rules

In contrast to the EU efforts, the CRA announced a much less ambitious plan for changes to the legal regime that governs the GST. Under the *Excise*

---

30 European Council, Council Regulation 792/2002 amending temporarily Regulation (EEC) 218/92 on administrative cooperation in the field of indirect taxation (VAT) as regards additional measures regarding electronic commerce (May 7, 2002); European Council, Directive amending Directive 77/388/EEC as regards the value-added tax arrangements applicable to certain electronically supplied services and radio and television broadcasting services (Feb. 12, 2002). The most recent Directive modified an earlier Directive that indicated registration would only apply if the non-European Union supplier had sales to European Union consumers in excess of 100,000 Euros.

31 A potential strategy could involve setting up a separate subsidiary for international online sales, as U.S. companies sometimes do to avoid paying state and local sales and use taxes on out-of-state sales. See A.J. Cockfield, "Walmart.com: A Case Study in Entity Isolation" (2002) 25 State Tax Notes 633.

Tax Act, a non-resident (other than a small supplier) that is carrying on business in Canada and which makes taxable supplies in Canada is required to register for GST purposes and must charge, collect and remit GST payments to the Canadian government. A facts and circumstances test is used to determine whether a business is being carried on in Canada. In 2002, the CRA issued Technical Information Bulletin B-090 "GST/HST and Electronic Commerce" to provide administrative guidance with respect to the CRA's policies for companies that buy and sell digital goods and services.[32] The CRA adopted a "place of operations" approach be used to determine whether the non-resident business should register for GST purposes. Under this approach, taxpayers and Canadian tax authorities would scrutinize a number of factors — none of them predominant — to determine whether the requisite threshold test has been met. These factors include:

1. the place where agents or employees of the non-resident are located;
2. the place of delivery;
3. the place of payment;
4. the place where purchases are made;
5. the place where the service is performed; and
6. the place from which transactions are solicited.

The list of factors provided was said to be non-exhaustive and new factors may become relevant in the future. There are a number of problems with these rule changes. Bulletin B-090 indicates that it is unlikely that a non-resident online retailer that sells digital goods and services would be considered to be carrying on business in Canada if it merely sells goods and services to Canadian consumers without any significant physical presence within Canada. An example is provided of a U.S.-based online retailer that supplies downloadable audio files to Canadian consumers. The example indicates that the web site is maintained on a server based in the United States, advertisements are directed to the Canadian market and the

---

32 See Canada Customs and Revenue Agency (CCRA), Excise and GST/HST Rulings, Policy and Legislation, "GST/HST and Electronic Commerce: A discussion paper for public comment on the administration of the Goods and Services Tax/Harmonized Sales Tax in an Electronic Commerce Environment," November 2001; CCRA, Technical Information Bulletin B-090, "GST/HST and Electronic Commerce," July 2002. For a critique of CRA current and proposed policy, see A.J. Cockfield, "Canada's GST E-commerce Policy (or How to Catch the Big Fish)," (2002) 3 Internet and E-commerce Law in Canada 1 ; J. Li, "Consumption Taxation of Electronic Commerce: Problems, Policy Implications and Proposals for Reform" (2003) 38 Cdn. Bus. L. J. 425.

place of contract is in Canada. Under this fact pattern, the CRA maintains that the non-resident company would not be considered to be carrying on a business in Canada.

The GST rules will thus likely be unsuccessful at subjecting foreign businesses to GST registration obligations and could potentially lead to significant revenue losses in the long run as foreign firms sell GST-free digital goods and services into Canada. Further, Canadian businesses will remain at a competitive disadvantage vis à vis foreign firms because the Canadian companies will have to charge and assess the GST on domestic sales in contrast to their foreign competitors. In other cases, the CRA may argue that a foreign firm should be subject to GST registration obligations as the firm's activities within Canada meet the multi-factoral test. This could lead to legal squabbles as the foreign firm insists that its activities do not meet the elements of the test.

2) Offshore Credit Card Accounts

Another worrisome trend that has been identified by Canadian regulators involves the increased usage by Canadians of offshore accounts to evade taxes. In 2001, Canadians invested an estimated $44.6 billion in tax haven countries, which represents a staggering 891 percent increase from 1988.[33] One of the factors that led to a greater use of offshore havens to evade taxes is the proliferation of Web pages that discuss the ease of setting up an offshore bank account or holding company along with step-by-step instructions on how to transfer amounts offshore. One review of Web sites promoting offshore tax havens revealed that over eighty percent of the sites promoted illegal tax evasion.[34]

There are three general approaches available to the CRA to combat this problem. First, the CRA could use the litigation process to try to find the identity of the account holders. Similarly, the IRS has targeted United States residents who employ offshore tax havens to hide funds and income from the government by launching one of the largest audit investigations in the history of the organization.[35] The U.S. government estimates that approximately three trillion dollars in assets are currently hidden away in

33 See K. Howlett & P. Waldie, "Lure of Tax Havens Proving Irresistible," *The Globe and Mail*, June 9, 2003, B1.

34 See D. L. Lupi-Sher, "The U.S. IRS's Fight Against Abusive Offshore Trusts" (2000) 21 Tax Notes Int'l 176 at 177.

35 For discussion, see A. J. Cockfield, "Designing Tax Policy for the Digital Biosphere: How the Internet is Changing Tax Laws" (2002) 34 Conn. L. Rev. 333 at 345–46.

tax havens, protected from outside scrutiny by bank secrecy laws within the tax havens.[36] In order to discover the identity of the suspected account holders, the IRS served several thousand John Doe summonses on credit card companies that have affiliate companies based in tax havens. According to the IRS, the litigation has resulted in the identification of many account holders resulting in the development of "hundreds of cases for civil audits or potential criminal investigation."[37]

Second, the Canadian government could encourage greater disclosure of assets held offshore. Previously, the government mandated disclosure of foreign assets in excess of $100,000 as part of the taxpayer self-assessment process. A more effective approach could involve focusing efforts to secure heightened disclosure from the business intermediaries that enable offshore tax strategies. For example, the Office of the Superintendent of Financial Institutions, a federal regulator of Canada's banks, has announced plans for new rules that require Canadian banks to know the names of the individual holders of bank accounts, and not just the name of the business entity that opened the account.[38]

In a related development, the Investment Dealers Association of Canada will require its members to verify the identity of foreign account holders: this development was largely driven by the perceived need for heightened financial information to counter money laundering efforts as well as terrorist financing.[39] This development could help to curtail illegal tax evasion as a 2001 survey of Canada's investment dealers found that Canadian brokerage firms were operating 13,000 offshore accounts for their clients in 23 countries that had been blacklisted by the OECD as part of the efforts to constrain harmful international tax competition.[40]

Third, the Canadian government could offer an amnesty to taxpayers that would insulate these taxpayers from criminal and civil penalties as long as the funds were fully disclosed and taxed. Beginning in January 2003, the IRS offered such an amnesty through its Offshore Voluntary

---

36 See Associated Press & Scripps Howard News Serv., "IRS Not Battling Tax Scams, Senators Told," San Diego Union-Trib., Apr. 6, 2001, A-17, LEXIS, News Library, Sdvt File (reporting an estimate by IRS Commissioner Charles Rossotti).

37 See IRS Chronology on Credit Cards and John Doe Summons, available at http://www.irs.gov/newsroom/ (accessed May 2003).

38 See Editorial Board, "The Offshore Accounts Where Criminals Pay" *The Globe and Mail*, June 16, 2003, A16.

39 See Bloomberg News, "IDA Sets New Policy for Offshore Accounts" *The Globe and Mail*, June 23, 2003, B3.

40 See Editorial Board, "The Offshore Accounts Where Criminals Pay" *The Globe and Mail*, June 16, 2003, A16.

Compliance Initiative although it is unclear whether this approach proved to be successful. In any event, the amnesty would likely prove to be unsuccessful unless the Canadian government simultaneously attacked the problem through litigation that would create a fear among the account holders that their identity could be discovered and they could be subject to serious criminal and civil sanctions.

E. CONCLUSION

The issues identified within this chapter show how traditional tax laws can at times be thwarted by the growing ease to conduct cross-border economic activity coupled with the proliferation of intangible goods and services (which include all digital e-commerce goods and services). Moreover, companies may have to spend more resources to deal with compliance uncertainty and increasingly complex international filings. Perhaps the clearest example of the challenges presented by the new economy surrounds the increased usage of offshore accounts where tax haven bank secrecy laws typically prevent foreign tax authorities from accessing information concerning their own taxpayer's worldwide income. This activity is clearly tax evasion as it involves purposeful non-disclosure of income by Canadian taxpayers: offshore information concerning income simply never reaches Canadian tax authorities, creating a form of "information gap."

Other information gaps appear when the increase in hard-to-value intangible goods and services is accompanied by expanded international sales, making it more difficult for tax authorities to properly align economic income with financial income that is subject to taxation within their jurisdictions. Taxpayers appear to be increasingly employing what might be called 'information arbitrage' strategies to take advantage of the gaps in the system. An increased sharing of information among national tax authorities along with joint audits, reciprocal enforcement of tax liabilities and so on would likely deter many of these efforts. Non-tax developments such as efforts to constrain money laundering or combat terrorism have encouraged greater sharing of financial information although it is unclear whether tax authorities have or will benefit from these developments.

Chapter Twenty-One

Principles for Assessing Aboriginal Income and Commodity Tax in Canada

J. Milan Legris

A. INTRODUCTION

It would be the rare aboriginal person[1] whose affairs do not demand a sound understanding and appreciation of the current income and commodity tax principles. Moreover, since the initiatives of aboriginal persons, aboriginal-owned businesses and aboriginal communities wield increasing economic influence in Canada, the opportunities for lawyers and other professionals to assist in these endeavours cannot be overlooked.

The purpose of this paper is to discuss the current aboriginal income and commodity tax principles. I will do so by examining the income tax treatment in Canada of an aboriginal person's employment, business and investment income. In this examination, I will canvass both the statutory framework and the reported tax cases to reveal the approach and principles developed by the courts. I will then discuss and review the commodity tax issues and cases applicable to aboriginal persons. The goal of my analysis is to assist aboriginal persons, professional advisors and the assessing authorities in understanding these principles. Furthermore, I suggest pos-

1 The term "aboriginal peoples of Canada" is defined in ss. 35(2) of the *Constitution Act, 1982* as including "the Indian, Inuit and Métis peoples of Canada."

sible amendments or clarification of the applicable statutes and case law in this area.

B. INCOME AND COMMODITY TAX PRINCIPLES

The implications of the *Constitution Act, 1867*, and *1982*,[2] the *Indian Act*[3] and applicable treaties represent a prerequisite before examining the governing provisions of the *Income Tax Act*,[4] the *Excise Tax Act*[5] and the case law.

1) *Constitution Act, 1867*

Section 91.24 gives the Parliament of Canada exclusive authority in relation to: "Indians, and Lands reserved for the Indians." Parliament has exercised its authority under this section by enacting the *Indian Act*.

2) *Indian Act*

It is my intention to focus this discussion primarily on the exemption from taxation of an "Indian"[6] laid out in s. 87 of the *Indian Act*, and give less attention to its application to a "band."[7] This analysis will reveal that the tax exemption:

- is restricted to an Indian's "personal property" that is "situated on a reserve";
- is limited to those aboriginal persons who qualify as "Indians"; and
- has been given a narrowed or restricted interpretation by the courts.

The courts have done so by developing a "connecting factors" test to determine whether income is situate on-reserve (or applying the *situs* test in the case of commodity taxes). It will be shown that with respect to investment income, the application of the "connecting factors" test has virtually elimi-

---

2 *Constitution Act, 1867*, enacted by the *Constitution Act, 1982*.

3 *Indian Act*, R.S.C. 1985, c. I-5. The appendix to the paper contains the text of the relevant sections of the *Indian Act*.

4 *Income Tax Act (Canada)*, R.S.C. 1985 (5th Supp.), c.1, as amended, and hereinafter referred to as the "*ITA*."

5 *Excise Tax Act*, R.S.C. 1985, c. E-15, as amended, and hereinafter referred to as the "*ETA*."

6 I have chosen to use the term *Indian* in this discussion, because significant reference in this paper is made to statutory enactments where this term continues to exist. As unfortunate as this may be in light of modern aboriginal and Canadian societal circumstances, I recognize for the reader, aboriginal persons and all Canadians generally, that the preferred term to be used or in reference thereto, would or should be; "Native" or "Native person(s)."

nated the exemption, unless, as suggested, careful planning is made or the *Indian Act* is amended.

a) Who is an Indian?

The first question arising from the foregoing exemption is who is an "Indian"? In subsection 2(1) of the *Indian Act*, "Indian" is defined to mean "a person who pursuant to this Act is registered as an Indian or is entitled to be registered as an Indian." Historically speaking, the right to be registered[8] as Indians existed for those band members who were Indians, the descendants of Indian males and their wives. Until the *Indian Act* was amended in 1985,[9] Indian native women who married non-Indian men were not entitled to be registered as an Indian. Any children from such marriages were also denied Indian status.

Non-status Indians, Métis, and Inuit who are resident in Canada are taxed just as other Canadian resident persons.[10] The Supreme Court of

---

7 I acknowledge that the preferred term of use or reference by aboriginal persons would or should be in this case, "First Nation."

8 The registration of Indians is dealt with in sections 5 to 7 of the *Indian Act*.

9 *Ibid.* s. 7(2) and (3).

10 While s. 35(2) of the *Constitution Act, 1982* includes Inuit in the definition of "Indian," this inclusive definition does not apply for purposes of the *Indian Act*. Therefore, Inuit do not qualify as "Indians" for purposes of the exemption from taxation in the *Indian Act*. It should also be noted that the term "Métis" describes persons who are a mixture of Indian and European descent, and Métis are also included in s. 35(2) of the *Constitution Act*. Again, however, since Métis are not included in the definition of Indian in the *Indian Act*, they too do not qualify for the tax exempt treatment afforded the "property" of Indians as described in s. 87 of the *Indian Act*. The unanimous decision of the Supreme Court of Canada in *R. v. Powley*, [2003] 2 S.C.R. 207 is very important to the Métis (as rights holders but not in terms of their identity) in Canada. In *Powley*, the Supreme Court of Canada noted that: 1) the Métis were included in ss. 35(2) of the *Constitution Act* to protect as "rights" the historically important practices of Métis that remain important to Métis today to their contemporary communities; 2) Métis in ss. 35(2) does not include all persons who are a mixture of Indian and European descent, and although the Court did not comprehensively define the Métis, it offered guidance that they are distinct Métis persons who also developed particular customs, a way of life and collective identity, which is separate from their Indian, Inuit or European ancestors; 3) established a 10 part test that defines Métis rights in s. 35(2); 4) provided three factors to identify Métis rights-holders, and 5) directed that identifying Métis rights holders is an "urgent priority," which undertaking is not insurmountable and Métis constitutional rights should not be denied by exaggerating any difficulties in doing so, as well as suggesting it is an unjustified infringement of Métis rights when recognition and affirmation (and priority equal to First Nations) of Métis rights is not contained in legislated programs.

Likewise, non-status Indians — those not registered or eligible to be registered as an Indian under the *Indian Act* — do not qualify for the tax-exempt treatment for

Canada confirmed this statement in *Nowegijick v. The Queen*, stating: "Indians are citizens and, in affairs of life not governed by the treaties or the Indian Act, they are subject to all of the responsibilities, including payment of taxes, of other Canadian citizens."[11]

The courts have also held that a corporation or a non-profit corporation cannot satisfy the definition of "Indian" in s. 87 — even if all members or shareholders are Indians or bands, and its head office and all assets are located and all its business is conducted on a reserve.[12]

The same position was also reflected in the interpretation of s. 87 of the *Indian Act* by then Revenue Canada, Taxation[13] in former Interpretation Bulletin IT-62 dated August 18, 1972 and titled "Indians." Paragraph 6(d) of former IT-62 stated:

> a corporation cannot meet the definition of "Indian" in the *Indian Act* and its income is not exempted from tax by these provisions, even where its only shareholder are Indians, its head office and physical assets are on a reserve and all of its business is carried out there.[14]

Interpretation Bulletin IT-62 was cancelled by Special Release IT-397RSR dated July 15, 1995. Special Release IT-397RSR (i.e., paragraph 2 thereof), reflected the recent jurisprudence from the Supreme Court of Canada in *Williams*[15] — and its "connecting factors" test, and amendments to the *Indian Act* — the 1985 amendments to ss. 7(2) and (3) dealing with

---

property of an Indian otherwise available under s. 87 of the *Indian Act*. Readers seeking a more comprehensive treatment and discussion of this topic should consult chapter 3 "Who are the Aboriginal People of Canada?," chapter 5 "Aboriginality: Legal Foundations, Past Trends, Future Prospects," and chapter 13 "Towards and Understanding Métis Aboriginal Rights: Reflections on the Reasoning in *R. v. Powley*," in J.E. Magnet & D.A. Dorey, *Aboriginal Rights Litigation* (Toronto: LexisNexis Butterworths, 2004).

11 *Nowegijick v. The Queen*, [1983] 1 S.C.R. 29 at 36.

12 *Kinookimaw Beach Association v. R.* (1979), 6 W.W.R. 84 (Sask. C.A.); *Kostyshyn v. West Region Tribal Council Inc.* (1994), 1 C.N.L.R. 94 (Fed. T.D.).

13 Revenue Canada, Taxation became an Agency known as the "Canada Customs and Revenue Agency" or "CCRA" in November 1999. Although still responsible to Parliament through the Minister of National Revenue as an Agency, the CCRA was able to offer wider services and enter agreements with the provincial governments. In December 2003, the CCRA changed its name and is now known as the "Canada Revenue Agency" (CRA).

14 Interpretation Bulletin IT-62 "Indians" dated August 18, 1972 was cancelled by Special Release IT-397RSR dated July 15, 1995.

15 Below note 37.

and rectifying the earlier denial of registration entitlement as Indians of Indian-born women who married non-Indian men and of their children.[16]

Consequently, whether a corporation wholly owned by aboriginal persons is resident on or off-reserve, the corporation cannot benefit (as it does not come within the definition of "Indian") from the tax exemption in s. 87 of the *Indian Act*. However, it should be pointed out that in certain situations, such a corporation may be able to rely on paragraph 149.1(1)(d) of the *ITA* which is an exemption from income tax for non-profit corporations, or perhaps in the case of a band, rely on the exemption from income tax in paragraph 149(1)(d) of the *ITA*, where the corporation is owned 90 percent by a municipality. While the Tax Court of Canada ("Tax Court") found in *Otineka*[17] that these corporations were exempt from tax under paragraph 149(1)(d) of the *ITA* because the corporations were wholly owned by bands (and the bands qualified as municipalities by reason of their by-law powers exercised and services provided to band members), the CRA has responded to the decision by taking a stricter interpretation of how it will apply the decision in *Otineka* to other Indian band business enterprises. Furthermore, in light of the *Otineka* decision and to clarify the circumstances in which a corporation will be entitled to the tax exemption in paragraph 149(1)(d) of the *ITA* (i.e., to more accurately reflect the intent or tax policy behind this exemption for municipal corporations), the Department of Finance amended the operation of paragraph 149(1)(d) — by introducing new paragraph 149(1)(d.5) to the *ITA*. New paragraph 149(1)(d.5) narrows the availability of the municipal corporation exemption — by adding a further requirement that (on top of the 90 percent municipality ownership test) the municipal corporation must also earn at least 90 percent of its income within its boundaries (i.e., on the reserve).

It is also clear that a court cannot "lift the corporate veil" to find that lands or property are held by a corporation in trust for its shareholders for purposes of the s. 87 exemption.[18] It remains to be determined whether the s. 87 exemption will be viewed by the courts as available in the circumstances where there is a true agency (or a trust relationship) existing at law between a corporation or other person for an Indian(s).

---

16 Above notes 9 and 14. Special Release IT-397RSR also updated IT-397R (originally issued February 23, 1990 and titled "Amounts Excluded from Income - Statutory Exemptions and Certain Service or RCMP Pensions, Allowances and Compensation").

17 *Otineka Development Corporation Ltd. v. The Queen*, [1994] 1 C.T.C. 2424 (T.C.C.).

18 Above note 11, and the decisions in *Nedco Ltd. v. Clark*, [1973] 6 W.W.R. 425 (Sask. C.A.), *British Columbia (Assessor of Area #25 Northwest/Prince Rupert) v. N & V Johnson Services Ltd.* (1990), 73 D.L.R. (4th) 170; [1991] 1 W.W.R. 527; 49 B.C.L.R. (2d) 173; [1991] 1 C.N.L.R. 90; 1 M.P.L.R. (2d) 170 (B.C.C.A.).

b) Section 83 of the *Indian Act*

The preamble to ss. 87(1) stipulates that the exemption from taxation is subject to s. 83. The particular emphasis on s. 83 ensures that a council of a band may make money by-laws for its purposes.

c) What constitutes a "tax"?

By definition, the operation of s. 87 of the *Indian Act* necessitates that there must be a "tax," from which the exemption is sought to be applied. Accordingly, it may be of assistance briefly to consider what constitutes a "tax."

A "tax" is perhaps best defined as a mandatory contribution imposed upon individuals, business entities or property, the primary purpose of which is to fund government initiatives, programs or operations.[19]

It is also important to bear in mind the character of a tax because there is the ever evolving and increasing delivery of government services or facilities that are now being offered or better yet financed, by looking to the consumers (of the service/user of the facility) to pay a fee in connection therewith. Such amounts or user fees are typically characterized or described as a "levy(ies)," "assessments" or "contributions." As a result, there is a possibility that the imposition of such existing or future charges[20] may not necessarily qualify as a "tax," and may therefore fall outside the exemption in s. 87 of the *Indian Act*.

---

19 The following principles were reiterated by the Supreme Court of Canada in its decision in *Re Eurig Estate*, [1998] 2 S.C.R. 565, 1 C.T.C. 284 (S.C.C.) that a "tax" is:
1. enforceable by law,
2. imposed under the authority of the legislature,
3. levied by a public body, and
4. intended for a public purpose.

See also the Supreme Court of Canada's earlier decision in *Lawson v. Interior Tree Fruit and Vegetable Committee of Direction*, [1931] S.C.R. 357. However, it should be noted that a tax can also be an instrument to direct change associated with other economic, social or political initiatives of a government.

20 In those cases that have considered whether a charge or fee qualifies as a tax, the following principles have emerged: 1) mandatory fees used to finance a legislated marketing program are a "fee for service" and not a tax (see *Agricultural Products Marketing v. The Queen*, [1978] 2 S.C.R. 1198), and 2) mandatory fees imposed on distributors and used for a compensation fund for customers for losses or damages are not a tax (see *Massey-Ferguson v. Saskatchewan*, [1981] 2 S.C.R. 413.). Accordingly, it is suggested that where the collected fees do not go to a consolidated fund that is charged with satisfying compensatory claims, and the persons obliged to pay or collect such funds or the beneficiaries are limited to those participating in the activity or endeavour — a public purpose would be absent, and the fees do not have the character of a tax. The *Eurig* case is also important for the Supreme Court of Canada's comments on the distinction between a levy and a tax, and it is suggested that readers refer to this decision for its particular discussion on that matter.

d) Section 87 Exempt Property and Paragraph 81(1)(a) of the *ITA*

Lastly, our discussion of s. 87 considers tax exempt property of Indians. The property of an Indian (or band) that is exempt from tax is either:

1) an interest in reserve or surrendered land, or
2) personal property situated on a reserve.

The terms "reserve" and "surrendered land" are both defined in ss. 2(1) of the *Indian Act*.[21] In considering the definition of "reserve," it is found to include the term "designated lands"[22] which itself is defined in ss. 2(1) of the *Indian Act*. Surrendered and designated lands are important to the initiatives of aboriginal persons and First Nations for furthering future economic activity and development. In order for aboriginal persons and First Nations to benefit from economic mainstream activity and development, it is necessary to consider and be aware of the protection (security) for third party participants involved with or pursuing such economic activity alone or in conjunction with aboriginal persons or First Nations — i.e., development agreements, financing and security in such lands. This is currently evidenced by commercial business and other leasing activities — strip malls, plazas, marinas and the construction and operation of medical, educational, industrial and other processing facilities, of aboriginal persons and First Nations on such surrendered or designated lands.

I note also the deeming provisions of s. 90 of the *Indian Act*, which clarifies the property of an Indian that is "situated on a reserve."[23] Apart

---

21 Above note 3. "Reserve" (a) means a tract of land, the legal title to which is vested in Her Majesty, that has been set apart by Her Majesty for the use and benefit of a band, and (b) except in subsection 18(2), ss. 20 to 25, 28, 36 to 38, 42, 44, 46, 48 to 51, 58 to 60 and the regulations made under any of those provisions, includes designated lands. "Surrendered lands" means a reserve or part of a reserve or any interest therein, the legal title to which remains vested in Her Majesty, that has been released or surrendered by the band for whose use and benefit it was set apart. Readers seeking a more thorough analysis of what constitutes and how a "reserve" may be created (i.e. a fact specific but by no means an exclusive or single process) are referred to a paper titled "Current Tax Issues Affecting First Nations," M.J. Flatters, in *Report of Proceedings of the Fifty-Fourth Tax Conference* (Toronto: Canadian Tax Foundation, 2002), and the reported decisions in *Sterriah et al v. The Queen* (2002), D.T.C. 7079 (S.C.C.), *sub nom. Ross River Dena Council Band v. Canada* (1999), 182 D.L.R. (4th) 116 (Y.T.C.A.); rev'g [1998] 3 C.N.L.R. 284 (Y.T.S.C.) and *Jeddore v. The Queen* (2001) D.T.C. 1058 (T.C.C.).

22 *Ibid*. "Designated lands" means a tract of land or any interest therein, the legal title to which remains vested in Her Majesty and in which the band for whose use and benefit it was set apart as a reserve has, otherwise than absolutely, released or surrendered its rights or interests, whether before or after the coming into force of this definition.

23 See paragraphs 90(1)(a) and (b) of the *Indian Act*, the specific provisions of which are set out in the appendix to this paper.

from considering the deeming rule in s. 90,[24] much of the tax jurisprudence involving aboriginal persons has been concerned to decide what is meant by the phrase "situated on a reserve." The pertinent jurisprudence has fallen in areas including both income tax and involving income from employment — *Williams*,[25] investment income — *Recalma*,[26] business income — *Southwind*,[27] and commodity taxes such as the Goods and Services Tax ("GST") (imposed under Part IX of the *ETA*), excise tax and provincial retail sales tax — *Francis*[28] and *Union of N.B. Indians.*[29]. Another matter to note is the practical result of the s. 87 exemption of an Indian's income from taxation. In this regard, the Tax Court has held a spouse must take into consideration the exempt income (under this provision) of a spouse, in calculating spousal deductions.[30]

Before reviewing the jurisprudence, it is also worth setting out the following "exempting" provision in paragraph 81(1)(a) of the *ITA*:

> 81. (1) **Amounts not included in income** — There shall not be included in computing the income of a taxpayer for a taxation year,
>
> > (a) **statutory exemptions [including Indians]** — an amount that is declared to be exempt from income tax by any other enactment of Parliament, other than an amount received or receivable by an individual that is exempt by virtue of a provision contained in a tax convention or agreement with another country that has the force of law in Canada; . . .[31]

The importance of this *ITA* provision may be subject to differing views. In one sense, it may be seen as not necessary, in light of the term "notwithstanding" being used in ss. 87(1) of the *Indian Act*. Therefore, reliance on paragraph 81(1)(a) of the *ITA* could be seen as unnecessary. However, to others it may offer added comfort to the ss. 87(1) exemption. At the same time, it should be noted that the term "notwithstanding" has been used

---

24 In *Greyeyes v. The Queen*, [1978] C.T.C. 91 (F.C.T.D.) the court held that federal government scholarship money paid to an Indian to attend post-secondary schooling off-reserve was not taxable by reason of both s. 87 and paragraph 90(1)(b) of the *Indian Act*. The scholarship money was personal property and deemed situate on-reserve and was therefore entitled to the exemption from taxation.

25 Below note 37.

26 Below note 61.

27 Below note 71.

28 Below note 75.

29 Below note 76.

30 *Sinclair v. Minister of National Revenue*, [1991] 2 C.T.C. 2167 (T.C.C.).

31 Above note 4.

more sparingly in the 1985 revisions to s. 87 of the *Indian Act*.[32] Specifically, the term "notwithstanding" is now only used in ss. 87(1) and not in ss. 87(2) or (3) of the *Indian Act*. On the other hand, prior to the 1985 revisions, it was also used in the exemptions from taxation in ss. 87(2) (i.e., dealing with an Indian or bands ownership, occupation, possession or use of property) and in ss. 87(3) (i.e., dealing with succession duty, inheritance tax or estate duty . . . on the death of any Indian in respect of any property . . .). What affect this drafting or change in the use of the word "notwithstanding" (or lack thereof) will have on future taxation issues raised by aboriginal taxpayers, the CRA or court decisions, remains to be seen.

e) Jurisprudence[33]

The 1983 Supreme Court of Canada decision in *Nowegijick*[34] was and remains a landmark tax case for Canadian aboriginals. It is Canada's leading case for expounding the principle that "income or wages" are a debt or chose in action, and as a form of personal property,[35], are eligible for the s.87 exemption if the location of the debt is on a reserve. The taxpayer in *Nowegijick* was a status[36] Indian who worked as an employee of a corporation (Gull Bay Development Corporation) owned and operated by the Gull Bay First Nation (a band under the *Indian Act*). While the corporation's registered office was on reserve as were the office operations, the taxpayer worked off-reserve, although he resided and was paid by cheque on-reserve. In establishing the location of the taxpayer's personal property (i.e., on-reserve), the court applied the test of where the employee could enforce payment — against the employer and at its residence and therefore held the "location of the debtor" was the test to be applied.

The Supreme Court of Canada's subsequent decision in *Williams*[37] cast further doubt on the exemption from taxation that aboriginal persons enjoyed. In this case, the court stated the location of the debtor was now only one factor to be considered in deciding whether the income of an abo-

---

32 Above notes 3, 9, and 16.

33 Readers seeking a comprehensive review of the case law applicable to Canadian aboriginals more generally are referred to S. Imai, *The 2004 Annotated Indian Act and Aboriginal Constitutional Provisions* (Toronto: Carswell, 2004).

34 Above note 11.

35 The importance of this decision by the Supreme Court of Canada in finding income was personal property is in contrast to previous court decisions holding "taxable income" was not personal property. In this regard, readers are referred to those decisions in *R. v. National Indian Brotherhood*, [1978] C.T.C. 680 (F.C.T.D.) and *Snow v. The Queen*, [1979] C.T.C. 227 (F.C.A.).

36 Above note 10.

37 *Williams v. Canada*, [1992] 1 S.C.R. 877, 90 D.L.R. (4th) 129.

riginal person was exempt from taxation under s. 87. The issue in *Williams* was the taxation of unemployment insurance benefits[38] paid to a status Indian resident on-reserve and paid in connection with previous employment with a logging company that was also situate on-reserve. While there was no question the benefits were paid by the federal government (or Crown), the Supreme Court of Canada stated that:

- it is necessary to look at the connecting factors which are relevant (sufficient) in order to determine whether the income in question was located on-reserve, and
- the same factors have to be analyzed and the appropriate weight given to them in examining the location of the property, and in light of the purpose of the s. 87 exemption, the type of property in issue as well as the nature of the taxation of that particular property.

In *Williams*, the Supreme Court of Canada noted the following connecting factors: 1) the debtor's (i.e., payor's) residence; 2) the residence of the individual receiving the benefits; 3) the place where the benefit payments are made; and 4) the location of the employment income which gave rise to eligibility for the benefit payments. The effect of the *Williams* decision was to cast uncertainty on the exemption from taxation as understood in the years following *Nowegijick*. As a result, aboriginal persons and their advisors have less assurance — albeit with a "connecting (and weighted) factors" test that is applied to the particular facts of each case, and giving due consideration to the purpose of the exemption, the type of property and its taxation.

It is equally important to observe the Court in *Williams* reflecting on its earlier decision in *Mitchell*. Particular attention should be given to the Court's statements in *Williams* that:

- the s. 87 exemption is to be applied bearing in mind its "purpose," and
- while sections of the *Indian Act* are of a preservative intent and nature for Indian property on-reserve (i.e., from taxation and seizure), the same

38 The *Williams* decision and the tax-exempt treatment of employment insurance benefits of an Indian is confirmed in the views of the CRA and discussed in VIEWS document 2003-0012284. Similarly, in the view of the CRA pension income and Canada Pension Plan benefits may also be exempt if the employment income to which it is related was exempt — see VIEWS document 2002-0148995. It should also be noted that while financial assistance for (re)training offered under the *Department of Human Resources Development Act* or a prescribed program is taxable as income, the recipient may be eligible for deduction under paragraph 110(1)(g) of the *ITA* where the assistance qualifies as tuition.

> provisions are not meant to provide a general economic benefit to aboriginal persons and particularly to those involved in the economic mainstream off-reserve.[39]

For example, the Court noted that the s. 87 exemption is not intended to rectify any economic disadvantage felt by Indians, but rather to offer protection to Indian-held property on-reserve. Furthermore, this protection of Indian property on-reserve was evident in *Williams*, where the court also commented that later taxation of future payments or benefits (i.e., the unemployment payment benefits) would erode the entitlements(s) of Indians and as Indians on-reserve.

In response to *Williams*, the CRA (then the CCRA) issued Special Release IT-397RSR described above.[40] Again, paragraph 2 of IT-397RSR reflects the CRA's interpretation of s. 87 of the *Indian Act* in light of recent tax jurisprudence, the amendments to the *Indian Act* in 1985, and guidelines issued by the CCRA in June 1994 concerning the exemption from taxation for employment and other income of Indians. In the last 10 years, there have also been a number of reported tax decisions involving aboriginal persons and whether their employment income is situate "on-reserve." A review of these decisions,[41] will be helpful in understanding how the courts are or are likely to be considering the "connecting factors" and purpose test formulated in *Williams* which may be summarized as follows:

1. the residence of the employer (in employment income cases) or the business enterprise (in business income cases) as well as the location of the operational activity of the employer or business enterprise, and whether it has close connections with a reserve;
2. the residence of the employee and any other workers in a business;
3. the place of work performance by employees or other workers in a business and whether the place of work has a close connection with a reserve;

---

39 Below note 79, and the discussion that "economic or commercial mainstream" reflects on enterprise activities "benefiting an individual," in comparison to being "integral to reserve life," which offers benefits or opportunity to the whole reserve community.

40 Above note 14.

41 Readers are also referred to papers (nos. 30-34) reviewing the case law which has developed on interpreting s. 87 of the *Indian Act* (and its historical background) presented at the 2001 National Tax Conference of the Canadian Tax Foundation in *Report of Proceedings of the Fifty-Third Tax Conference* (Toronto: Canadian Tax Foundation, 2001).

4. the place of payment or remittance of remuneration; and
5. any "special or strong circumstances."

"Special or strong circumstances" include i) the manner in which the business is carried on; ii) whether the business improves conditions for aboriginal persons and particularly on-reserve (rather than in the commercial mainstream off-reserve); and iii) the flexibility that may be available to aboriginal persons in planning or arranging their affairs and understanding that the courts have ultimately to analyze the tax treatment afforded Indians and the manner they have arranged their affairs.

i) *Employment income cases*

(a) Decisions of the Federal Court of Appeal

- In *Desnomie*,[42] there were insufficient connecting factors to situate the taxpayer's employment income on-reserve, when as an employee of an aboriginal-owned corporation, he lived and worked off-reserve (his employer was also located off-reserve and provided services to off-reserve students). The decision is also notable for its rejection of the "necessity" argument and its suggestion that the s. 87 tax exemption applies to an Indian's personal property on his or her own reserve.
- In *Bell*,[43] no tax exemption was available for aboriginal persons employed by a commercial fishing company. However, the decision is notable for its statements that the connecting factor "benefit to native community" is not free standing but rather a way to evaluate the "nature of employment" factor; and for taxpayers to ensure that their undertakings are effective and completed in order to gain the desired result and benefits (i.e., while it is purposeful to locate an employer's office or business enterprise on-reserve to gain tax advantages, facts must also exist that support this as being legally effective — for example, the business will be found to reside where it really is managed and carried on from and ideally this is on-reserve). However, in light of the *Williams* case, evidence of additional connecting factors, not just the registered office or mind and management of a company being on-reserve, will likely also be necessary to find a company is located on-reserve.
- In *Shilling*,[44] the tax exemption was not available to an employee who lived and worked off-reserve, for an on-reserve sole proprietor, where the

---

42 *Desnomie v. The Queen* (2000), D.T.C. 6250 (F.C.A.).

43 *Bell et al. v. The Queen* (2000), D.T.C. 6365 (F.C.A.).

44 *The Queen v. Shilling*, [2001] 3 C.T.C. 181, D.T.C. 5420 (F.C.A.), rev'g (1999) 3 C.T.C. 415, D.T.C. 5441 (F.C.T.D.).

employee's services were engaged by an off-reserve Native health centre. The decision is also notable for: 1) giving the connecting factor of "on-reserve employer" less weight (absent other evidence) than the employee's location and nature of employment (in the commercial mainstream as opposed to integral to the life of the reserve) in finding her income was "off-reserve"; 2) reiterating the suggestion that the s. 87 tax exemption applies to an Indian's personal property situated on his or her own reserve; and 3) reiterating that the purpose of this exemption is to preserve Indian property on-reserve and not necessarily provide a general economic benefit to aboriginal persons as discussed in *Williams*[45] since the off-reserve services of Ms. Shilling were provided to both on and off-reserve Natives.

- In *Monias*,[46] the tax exemption was not available because the Federal Court of Appeal held the income of the taxpayers was situated off-reserve. This decision reversed the Tax Court's ruling, which found the income situated on-reserve. The Federal Court of Appeal noted that the taxpayers did not live on-reserve, and although the work and employer was closely connected to and benefited Indians living on-reserve in Northern Manitoba, that was not enough to situate the taxpayer's employment on-reserve. The Tax Court mentioned that special circumstances were important to its finding the employment was situated on-reserve. These include: 1) the "necessity" that the nature of the work had to be performed off-reserve and hence the residence of the taxpayers also had to be off-reserve, was nonetheless directed and had as its main purpose the provision of benefits to Indians on-reserve; 2) the special circumstances were not diminished by the fact the employer was off-reserve, but the employer was also by necessity located off-reserve and conducted meetings off-reserve in the circumstances; and 3) the nature of the services and employment was not commercial mainstream. On the other hand, the Federal Court of Appeal pointed out that the employer did not bring economic benefits to persons on-reserve, since its meetings and administrative operations were (by necessity) off-reserve. In contrast to its other decisions, in *Monias*, the Federal Court of Appeal discounted the necessity, nature and purpose of employment arguments; it also discounted the fact that the employer was off-reserve.

---

45 Above note 37.

46 *R. v. Monias*, [2001] 3 C.T.C. 244, D.T.C. 5450 (F.C.A.), rev'g [1999] 4 C.T.C. 2354, D.T.C. 1021 (T.C.C.).

- In *Folster*,[47] the taxpayer's income was found to be situate on-reserve and thus eligible for the s. 87 tax exemption. It appears the "connecting factors" test was appropriately applied to find the income on-reserve, where the taxpayer resided, while the employer was situated just off the reserve; yet the majority of its patients were on-reserve. Both the taxpayer's residence and perhaps more so her employment as an administrator at the hospital integrated her with the reserve community. Of the original seven appellants involved in this case, three alone were successful in their appeals at the Tax Court[48] as the income was deemed under s. 90 of the *Indian Act* to be situated on-reserve. In *Folster* and *Poker*, the Tax Court found the taxpayers' earnings to be situate on-reserve. In the Federal Court Trial Division, the Tax Court's decision in Poker was upheld; but in Folster's case the connecting factors were insufficient to find that the income was situated on-reserve. Ms. Folster was successful in her appeal to the Federal Court of Appeal, which found that her income was property of an Indian on-reserve.
- In *Amos*,[49] the taxpayer's income was situated on-reserve (where he resided), and the tax exemption applied. His employment was with a commercial pulp mill located slightly off-reserve. Yet, the Court noted this business enterprise was on reserve land surrendered for the specific purpose of leasing it to the mill, subject to the overriding condition that it was to provide employment for persons resident on the reserve.
- In *Kakfwi*,[50] the tax exemption did not apply to the employment income of a chief of a band paid by the federal government under a funding program. While the Tax Court found the funding program agreement came within paragraph 90(1)(b) of the *Indian Act*, the Federal Court of Appeal disagreed. The Federal Court of Appeal held the agreement fell outside paragraph 90(1)(b) because it was neither a treaty or attached to a treaty. Although the parties disputed whether the band office was located on-reserve, the case had proceeded on the basis that it was off-reserve. In light of the Federal Court of Appeal's decision, the issue remained of whether the band office was situated on a reserve and this was remitted

---

47 *Folster v. Minister of National Revenue* (1997), D.T.C. 5315 (F.C.A.), (*sub nom. Clarke v. M.N.R.*), 184 D.L.R. (4th) 314 (F.C.A.); and *Poker v. M.N.R.* (1994), D.T.C. 6658 (F.C.T.D.). In *Poker*, the taxpayer worked at a school adjacent to the reserve that was part of the reserve school system).

48 *Clarke, Poker , Clarke, Wilson, Paupanekis, Albert and Folster v. M.N.R.*, [1992] 2 C.T.C. 2743, 92 D.T.C. 2267 (T.C.C.).

49 *Amos et al v. The Queen* (1999), D.T.C. 5333 (F.C.A.).

50 *The Queen v. Kakfwi* (1999), D.T.C. 5639 (F.C.A.).

back to the Tax Court. Chief Krakow would not have to pay income tax if it was found the band office was on-reserve.

(b) Decisions of the Tax Court of Canada

- In *Naponse*,[51] the tax exemption was unavailable, although the taxpayer resided on-reserve. The taxpayer's employment at Cambrian College in Sudbury, Ontario, although the program trained aboriginal students — living both on and off-reserve — in child care, was more closely linked with the commercial mainstream than with benefiting reserve communities.
- In *Odjig*,[52] another "teaching" case decided by the Tax Court and similar to *Naponse*, the tax exemption was not available. In *Odjig*, the taxpayer resided on-reserve and taught native studies and Ojibway language in an off-reserve high school on Manitoulin Island in Ontario. Even though the majority of Mr. Odjig's students were aboriginals who resided on-reserve, the special circumstances did not enable the Court to find that his employment income was situated on-reserve.
- In *Boissoneau*,[53] the tax exemption was unavailable to the taxpayer, an employee of the Department of Indian and Northern Affairs in Hull, Quebec, who resided off-reserve. The Tax Court found that the City of Hull in the Province of Quebec is not a reserve as defined in the *Indian Act*.
- In *McNab*,[54] the tax exemption was available to the employment income of the taxpayer who lived and worked — both by necessity — on and off-reserve. The nature and primary purpose of the work was to benefit Indians on-reserve and therefore recognized as important connecting factors to the taxpayer's eligibility for the s. 87 tax exemption.
- In *Brant*,[55] the tax exemption was unavailable to the taxpayer, who while residing on-reserve, worked off-reserve as an audit officer for Revenue Canada (now known as the CRA). Those connecting factors pointing to the off-reserve location of the employment income — the source of income as well as the payor and its source of revenues, and the site of work — outweighed the taxpayer's residence and receipt of the income on-reserve.
- In *McRae*,[56] the tax exemption was unavailable to the taxpayer who lived on-reserve and worked off-reserve for a non-Indian corporation. The tax-

---

51 *Naponse v. The Queen* (2001), D.T.C. 414 (T.C.C.).
52 *Odjig v. The Queen* (2001), D.T.C. 419 (T.C.C.).
53 *Boissoneau v. The Queen* (2001), D.T.C. 3729 (T.C.C.).
54 *McNab v. The Queen*, [1992] 2 C.T.C. 2547 (T.C.C.).
55 *Brant v. Minister of National Revenue* (1992), D.T.C. 2274 (T.C.C.).
56 *McRae v. The Queen* (1998), D.T.C. 3400 (T.C.C.).

payer's duties were carried out off-reserve, and the remuneration was earned in the commercial mainstream; there was no connection of the business enterprise to a band or reserve.

- In *Adams*,[57] the tax exemption was unavailable to the taxpayer who lived in an Indian Affairs Subdivision[58] (while the Subdivision's purpose was to house Indians, it did not formally qualify as a reserve), worked as a band secretary in the band office (off-reserve) and was paid by the federal government in the same program considered in *Kakfwi*. The employment income was not exempt, as it was not situated on-reserve and was not deemed to be situated on-reserve under paragraph 90(1)(b) of the *Indian Act*. Although the band received the government program funding, the taxpayer was paid by reason of the employment relationship with the band. In addition, while the work benefited band members, not all members resided on-reserve and connection to the reserve appeared more tenuous, although the band had to relocate from its reserve when a residential school was closed.

Most tax cases that I have just described deal with employment income. Some additional cases concern the issue of vacation, holidays and sick leave time. Two decisions of the Tax Court warrant particular attention, *Horn*[59] and *Laine*.[60] Neither taxpayer was successful with respect to the tax exemption for employment income associated with the specific time or portion thereof spent on-reserve. In *Horn*, the taxpayer was an employee of the Department of Indian and Northern Affairs who worked and lived off-reserve in Ottawa, and the site of her work was off-reserve. Therefore, her holiday and sick leave remained off-reserve. The same conclusion held in *Laine* for vacation and sick days spent on-reserve.

---

57 *Adams v. The Queen* (2000), D.T.C. 1627 (T.C.C.).

58 An Indian Affairs Subdivision is Federal Crown land or land acquired by Canada for the purpose of providing band housing, offices and other facilities where the reserve(s) set aside by Canada for the band are not developed or are less accessible. In this case, the Indian Affairs Subdivision included Federal Crown land and land acquired from the Province of Alberta to provide band housing, offices and a nursing station. Acquiring municipal lots for Indian housing is not a common occurrence, and the land acquired in this case is to be re-transferred to the Province of Alberta when it is no longer required for Indian housing. A "reserve" above note 21, are lands set apart by Her Majesty (by Order-in-Council) for the use and benefit of a band. Since the Indian Affairs Subdivision in Adams was not so designated, it did not qualify as a reserve under the *Indian Act*.

59 *Horn v. Minister of National Revenue*, [1989] 1 C.T.C. 2208 (T.C.C.).

60 *Laine v. Minister of National Revenue*, [1990] 2 C.T.C. 2025 (T.C.C.).

The foregoing discussion suggests that a status Indian who resides on-reserve and either works on-reserve or with an employer situate on-reserve will likely have his or her employment income exempt from taxation under s. 87 of the *Indian Act.* The employment income of a status Indian who fails to fulfill these conditions may well be liable to taxation. As for vacation and sick leave time, if the employment to which it is related is off-reserve then the vacation and sick leave is situate off-reserve as well. An Indian is not able to change the tax character of his or her vacation or sick leave from off-reserve to on-reserve and therefore qualify it for exemption by residing on-reserve during any time period of vacation or sick leave.

ii) Investment income cases

The leading case dealing with the taxation of an aboriginal person's investment income is *Recalma.*[61] This 1998 decision by the Federal Court of Appeal considers the "connecting factors" test in determining what is meant by the phrase "property situate on a reserve" in s. 87 of the *Indian Act.* A significant amount of the family's wealth was invested in various financial instruments through a branch of the Bank of Montreal situated on the Squamish Indian Reserve in British Columbia. The Federal Court of Appeal gave greatest weight to: 1) the residence of the issuers of the securities or financial instruments (i.e., the head offices of the corporations offering Bankers' Acceptances and the offices of the managers of mutual funds); and 2) the location of the same issuers' income-generating operations and their property — which was remote from the reserve. The Court gave less weight to: 1) the taxpayer's residence; 2) the source of the taxpayer's capital giving rise to the financial instruments purchased; and 3) the place where the financial instruments were purchased and held, and income received thereon and in turn spent. The Federal Court of Appeal's judgment shows the importance of the location where the taxpayer's capital was invested to earn its return. This analysis suggests that where an aboriginal person (lender) structures his or her investments as a loan to another aboriginal person for use in on-reserve business or activities, the lender's investment income from this loan may now be exempt from tax since it would likely be viewed as situated on-reserve.

- In *Hill,*[62] the taxpayer's investment income from a term deposit made at a bank branch on-reserve was not exempt from taxation. Although the taxpayer resided and worked on-reserve, the Tax Court found, consistent

61 *Recalma et al v. The Queen,* (1998) D.T.C. 6238 (F.C.A.).

62 *Hill v. The Queen* (1999), D.T.C. 3504 (T.C.C.).

with *Recalma*, that the interest income on the term deposit arose from the bank's investments off-reserve.

- In *Bennett*,[63] the taxpayer (a lawyer who resided and worked off-reserve) claimed that her income from withdrawals from a registered retirement savings plan (RRSP) and retirement income fund (RIF) from a term deposit made at a bank branch on-reserve, was exempt from taxation. The Tax Court found that the income from the withdrawals was not situated on-reserve under *Recalma*, and that the financial instruments here were distinct from a bank account. These financial instruments resembled more closely investments in the commercial mainstream off-reserve. It is also important to note the taxpayer had claimed a deduction from income for the contributions to the RRSP at the bank branch on-reserve. For the Court to have held otherwise would have been tantamount to the taxpayer in this case of "having her cake and eating it too" — taking a deduction from income and enjoying the resulting tax savings on making the contribution to the RRSP and later not being subject to or paying tax on the withdrawals from the RRSP and RIF.
- In *Sero*,[64] as in the companion case of *Frazer*,[65] the taxpayers were registered band members associated with the Six Nations of the Grand River Reserve No. 40 — south of Brantford, Ontario. In *Sero*, the Tax Court held that there were no connecting factors to the reserve other than deposits with an on-reserve branch of the Royal Bank of Canada Therefore, applying *Recalma* and finding the income generating activities of the bank were situated off-reserve, the Court found Ms Sero's investment income also to be situated off-reserve. In *Frazer*, a wider variety of investment instruments were on deposit with a Royal Bank of Canada branch on-reserve. However, in *Frazer*, the taxpayer was resident on-reserve, accumulated the capital amounts from his business operated on-reserve and deposited in an on-reserve bank branch the capital amounts he accumulated from his business. On appeal, the Federal Court of Appeal dismissed both taxpayers' appeals,[66] noting in particular that: 1) six of the bank's 1,000 branches were situated on reserves; 2) although the deposits were called "First Nations Term Investments" (for what appears to be marketing purposes of the bank), they were available to aboriginal and non-aboriginal clients of the bank; 3) the source of the income earned by the taxpayers was in the commercial mainstream; and

63 *Bennett v. The Queen* (1999), D.T.C. 938 (T.C.C.).

64 *Sero v. R.*, (2001) D.T.C. 575, [2001] 3 C.T.C. 2224 (T.C.C.).

65 *Frazer v. R.*, (2001) D.T.C. 575, [2001] 3 C.T.C. 2224 (T.C.C.).

66 *Ibid.*, (2004), D.T.C. 6037 (F.C.A.).

4) ss. 461(4) of the *Bank Act* was not intended to remove the application of the connecting factors test (or expand its application beyond that Act), and this test prevailed against the *Bank Act* deeming rule. In *Frazer*, although the investments resulted from on-reserve income earning activities, there was no other connection of investments to the reserve (i.e., the income derived from his investments was off-reserve). The bank also provided little connection to the reserve, since the number of branches on-reserve were few and more significantly the bank's revenue and income generating operations were off-reserve. Leave to appeal to the Supreme Court of Canada is to be sought in *Sero* and *Frazer*.[67]

- In *Lewin*,[68] the taxpayer's interest income from certificates of deposit obtained at a credit union located on-reserve was liable to taxation. While the Tax Court noted that the taxpayer resided off-reserve, it mattered more that the interest paid the taxpayer resulted from the reinvestment of the money in the off-reserve economy. The flow of the interest income through the credit union, which had its business on-reserve, did not make the interest income exempt from taxation. The result in *Lewin* suggests that the tax exemption may be available if a financial institution and the investments it offers to aboriginal persons and First Nations are structured differently. For example, the creation of a credit union on-reserve and with its purpose and objective to accumulate deposits for (re)-investment(s) directly into aboriginal activities or enterprises on-reserve would:
  - assist, improve and advance aboriginal persons, band and community initiatives, and
  - provide the strongest argument that the income from the same investment is now exempt from taxation.

Based on recent case law developments, a status Indian's passive investment income will probably be exempt from taxation under s. 87 of the *Indian Act* only when the investment income is situate on-reserve and therefore

67 M. O'Brien, "Current Cases 'Investment Income and Indian Reserves: The Disconnecting Factor'" (2004) 52:2, Canadian Tax Journal 543 for a discussion of the Federal Court of Appeal's decision in the cases of *Sero* and *Frazer*. See also M. O'Brien, "Income Tax, Investment Income, and the *Indian Act*: Getting Back on Track," 50:5 Canadian Tax Journal 1570 on the s. 87 exemption in relation to the investment income of Indians and offering insight into a revised approach to determining whether their investment income is situate on-reserve.

68 *Lewin v. R.* (2001), D.T.C. 479, [2001] 2 C.T.C. 2560 (T.C.C.). On appeal, (2002), D.T.C. 7582, [2003] 3 C.T.C. 151 (F.C.A.), the Federal Court of Appeal summarily dismissed the taxpayer's appeal and the Supreme Court of Canada subsequently denied leave to appeal in an unreported decision, June 19, 2003 (S.C.C.).

such investment income must be shown to have an Indian character — related to investments and earnings derived from that investment activity on reserve. However, an investment or bank account situate on-reserve is insufficient unless the investment and the return it generates is convincingly connected with the life of the reserve. This implication from the various judgments is difficult to reconcile with the realities of modern Canadian commerce and Canadian tax principles. Today, commerce dictates the (barrier) free flow of investible capital in Canada and throughout the world. In my view, the courts have also either ignored or confused the on-reserve investment of aboriginal persons (and that their legal entitlement to the income is on-reserve) with the off-reserve location of the payor's income earning business activity.

Based on my opinion, it appears the courts have applied the connecting factors test from the aboriginal employment income cases too restrictively in the aboriginal investment income cases. As a result, the tax exemption is no longer or seldom available for investment income of aboriginal persons. In my view, this approach would tend to support to the arguments that:

- Courts have legislated in this tax area, otherwise the exclusive legislative jurisdiction of the Parliament of Canada; and
- a parochial approach to earning (reserve or more Indian character) investment income is being dictated to aboriginal persons if they wish to (re)-access the tax exemption for their investment income and this antique notion has no place in Canada's modern economy.

The "connecting factor" test arguably formulates a tracing principle, which looks beyond the site where the Indians' entitlement to investment income arises to examine the location where the bank's source of income (which income is in turn paid on an Indian's account or investment with the bank) is located or derived. It is also noted that most analysis of the income tax exemption applying to an Indian's investment income often ends with a result that is opposite to or can be contrasted with, the result that the Indian's bank account or other investment would be exempt from seizure[69] (i.e., real or personal property of an Indian or band situate on a reserve) under subsection 89(1) of the *Indian Act*. The Parliament of Canada should address

69 *Young v. Wolf Lake Band* (1999), 164 F.T.R. 123 (F.C.T.D.); *Sturgeon Lake Indian Band v. Tomporowski Architectural Group Ltd.* (1991), 95 Sask. R. 302 (Q.B.); *Webtech Controls Inc. v. Crosslake Band of Indians*, [1991] 3 C.N.L.R. 182 (Man. Q.B.); *Vincent v. Quebec*, [1995] 3 C.N.L.R. 204 (Que. C.A.).

this potentially conflicting result when it corrects this imbalance and expands legislatively the tax exemption for investment income of aboriginals.

iii) Business income (enterprise) cases

Aboriginal persons and other Canadian taxpayers, are entitled to enter, structure and carry on business relations and enterprises i.e., to create relationships and legal rights. In these relationships, there may be no other purpose than to access the tax advantages available to them — for aboriginals the exemption under s. 87[70] of the *Indian Act* and for other Canadian taxpayers the tax favourable provisions in the *ITA*. Business relations and enterprises might include carrying on business as a sole proprietorship, partnership or through a corporation. As for a business conducted as a sole proprietorship, the "connecting factors" test from *Williams* is applicable to establish whether its income is situate on-reserve.

A leading case is *Southwind*,[71] which dealt with a status Indian living on-reserve and operating a logging business as a sole proprietorship. The decision in *Southwind* emphasized that the business was not integral to the life of the reserve, but rather in the commercial mainstream. The taxpayer's logging business services were provided exclusively to a non-Indian business that was situated off-reserve. Both the Tax Court and the Federal Court of Appeal found the taxpayer's income from the sole proprietorship was not situated on-reserve. Two connecting factors pointed strongly to this conclusion: 1) the location where the taxpayer performed the (logging) business services; and 2) the location of his only customer. In effect, both courts found that the taxpayer had entered the non-aboriginal commercial mainstream and he was not participating in a business that was integral to reserve life.

Since a partnership[72] is not a legal entity itself, but rather is representative of and by its partners, the considerations I have examined in relation to the taxation of a sole proprietorship will apply to the taxation of the partners of a partnership. Accordingly, and in light of the post-*Williams* jurisprudence, aboriginal persons engaged in a partnership business enterprise should carefully consider the application of the "connecting factors" test to ensure the partnership business, and hence the income allocable to its partners is situate on-reserve. Likewise, even if a corporation belongs to

---

70 Above note 44.

71 *Southwind v. R.*, [1998] 1 C.T.C. 265 (F.C.A.).

72 *Partnerships Act*, R.S.O. 1990, c. P.5, s. 2. The 3 important components of a partnership are: 1) two or more persons, 2) carrying on business in common, and 3) with a view to profit.

a partnership that has its income situated on-reserve and hence the corporation's income allocation is situated on-reserve, the corporation's partnership income will not be exempt from income taxation.

3) Commodity Tax(es) and Custom Duties

In enacting the Goods and Services Tax ("GST") effective January 1, 1991, the federal sales tax was repealed which imposed a sales tax of between 9 and 13.5 percent on the price of goods produced or manufactured in Canada, imported into Canada or sold in Canada by a manufacturer or licensed wholesalers.[73] The s. 87 exemption did not apply to the indirect sales tax imposed on the supplier rather than the end consumer who was an Indian (i.e., before the GST took effect).

Although aboriginal persons are not expressly exempt from the GST, aboriginals can rely on s. 87 of the *Indian Act* to exempt its application to their personal property that is situate on-reserve. This conclusion is also supported by the position outlined in the federal Department of Finance's Technical Paper,[74] which provided that the *Indian Act* exemption from taxation would be available by administrative practice in the case of the GST — although ss. 87(2) lacks the word "notwithstanding." Likewise, the CRA's Interpretation Bulletin B-039, in dealing with Indians' exemption from the GST confirms the exemption from GST for personal property that is situated on-reserve. The relieving statements made by the CRA in B-039 may also make the s. 87 exemption more widely available to other aboriginal entities.

The central issue in consumption or sales taxes (i.e., provincial sales taxes) is the location of the tangible property at the time of taxation. As outlined in the longstanding Supreme Court of Canada decision in *Francis*,[75] reaffirmed by the same court in — *Union of N.B. Indians v. N.B. (Minister of Finance)*,[76] the point of sale is important to the imposition of a sales tax. While the Supreme Court of Canada decision in *Union of N.B. Indians* rejected the application of "paramount location" test,[77] since in a sales con-

---

73 R.C. Strother & R.A. Brown, "Taxation of Aboriginal People in Canada," in *Report of Proceedings of the Forty-second Tax Conference* (Toronto: Canadian Tax Foundation, 1990).

74 Canada, Department of Finance, *Goods and Services Tax: Technical Paper*, (Ottawa, August 1989).

75 *Francis v. The Queen*, [1956] S.C.R. 618.

76 *Union of N.B. Indians v. N.B. (Minister of Finance)*, [1998] 1 S.C.R. 1161.

77 The paramount location test provides that the situs of tangible property is determined where its "pattern of use and safekeeping" suggests it is usually located, but this test does not and cannot otherwise apply in a sale of tangible property since the purchaser has not yet established a pattern of use and safekeeping for the same property. This

text a person's pattern of use or safekeeping does not yet exist, it also offered the Supreme Court of Canada's insight on how its decision was beneficial to Indians on-reserve. The benefits included:

- the point of sales test means the purchase of goods and services on-reserve by Indians living off-reserve is tax exempt;
- the incentive is there for Indians to establish on-reserve businesses and thereby improve their employment and economy; and
- offering aboriginal governments the ability to raise tax revenue for band purposes by taxing the income of the on-reserve businesses.

Therefore, if the sale to an aboriginal person is off-reserve, liability will likely exist for payment of the sales tax.

As noted above, *Francis* is a longstanding decision. *Francis* is also a leading case with respect to custom duties and the exemption from taxation in s. 87 of the *Indian Act*. In *Francis,* the taxpayer was an Indian who imported household appliances into Canada on the Akwesasne Reserve. Mr. Francis had to pay customs duties when he imported the appliances into Canada, since the custom duties fell outside the s. 87 exemption. In *Francis,* the Supreme Court of Canada held that the customs duty was imposed immediately on importation of goods into Canada and goods were not relieved from taxation by the fact they were simultaneously (on importation) on-reserve. In *Francis,* the Supreme Court of Canada also denied that the Jay Treaty of 1794[78] exempted the imported appliances from customs duties on the ground that the Treaty had not been incorporated into the laws of Canada.

More recently, the Supreme Court of Canada reexamined the issue of aboriginals' obligation to pay custom duties in *Mitchell v. Minister of National Revenue.*[79] Grand Chief Michael Mitchell of the Akwesasne Mohawk First Nation argued that by reason of the *Constitution Act, 1982* and the Jay Treaty, he was exempt from custom duties on imported goods that were given to other aboriginal communities. The earlier decisions by the Federal Court (Trial and Appeal) confirmed that the Jay Treaty would not be a

---

test is obviously more relevant and applicable in determining the situs of tangible property for purposes of s. 89 of the *Indian Act.*

78 Treaty of Amity, Commerce and Navigation, between His Britannic Majesty and the United States of America, 19 November 1794. It should not be overlooked that many treaties sought to be applied predate the introduction of an income tax in Canada by the *Income War Tax Act.*

79 *Mitchell v. Minister of National Revenue,* [2001] 1 S.C.R. 911, [2002] 3 C.T.C. 359 (S.C.C.).

treaty coming within subsection 35(1) of the *Constitution Act, 1982* and therefore offered no benefit. However, both Federal Courts did acknowledge an existing aboriginal right[80] to the Mohawk people of Akwesasne to cross the border between Canada and the United States and an accompanying right to import goods for personal and community use into Canada without custom duties. The Supreme Court of Canada overturned both lower court decisions, noting in particular:

- that there was insufficient evidence to find the aboriginal right asserted; and
- that this asserted right could not exist for purposes of subsection 35(1) of the *Constitution Act, 1982* because of Canada's sovereign right to control its borders.

The Supreme Court of Canada's decision in *Mitchell* suggests that there is no such aboriginal right,[81] and that s. 87 does not exempt Indians from the application of legislation of wider impact, including the *Customs Act*.[82]

4) Treaties

Consideration of treaty benefits impacting the taxation of, or offering special treatment for the taxation of aboriginal persons, involves consideration of Treaty 8 and s. 88 of the *Indian Act*.

a) Treaty 8

Treaty 8 does not offer a specific written exemption from taxation for those persons entitled to its benefits. However, the commissioner's report[83] on Treaty 8 indicates that the Indians received assurances that "the Treaty would not lead to any forced interference with their mode of life, that it did not open the way to the imposition of any tax, and that there was no fear of enforced military service." This reference to the commissioner's report is also commented on in the first *Mitchell*[84] case where the Supreme Court of

80 In order to come within ss. 35(1) of the *Constitution Act, 1982* as an aboriginal right, an activity must be shown to be a practice, custom or tradition integral to the aboriginal community which asserts the right.

81 Above note 79, and particularly the Chief Justice not commenting on whether such a right is incompatible with Canada's sovereignty, while other justices of this Court discussed and concluded the right was incompatible with Canada's sovereignty.

82 *Customs Act*, R.S.C. 1985 (2nd Supp.), c. 1.

83 David Laird, Chief Commissioner and Treaty 8 negotiator, Treaty 8 (Queen's Printer, 1899).

84 *Mitchell v. Peguis Indian Band*, [1990] 2 S.C.R. 85, (1990), 71 D.L.R. (4th) 193 (S.C.C.). It should also be noted that the Supreme Court of Canada in *Nowegijick*, above note 11, confirmed that in interpreting or construing treaties, statutes and other "instruments"

Canada suggested that the Indians entitled to Treaty 8's benefits were promised an exemption from taxation of same. While the recent decision in *Benoit*[85] by the Supreme Court of Canada was disappointing for the Treaty 8 beneficiaries, it is also important for offering no additional insight by this Court on the interpretation and meaning of Treaty 8. Since the Supreme Court of Canada denied leave to appeal, the decision of the Federal Court of Appeal has determined this issue in Canada.

The *Benoit* case may also have represented the best argument by aboriginal persons that the broader language in treaties may nonetheless provide an exemption from other forms of taxation (i.e., including income tax, sales tax and property tax). However, the *Benoit* case appears to have put to rest the arguments for the broad tax exemption advanced by the Treaty 8 beneficiaries. Mr. Benoit was a truck driver and operator of heavy equipment who lived off-reserve in Fort McMurray, Alberta, any yet Treaty 8 affects in excess of 30,000 aboriginal persons (Cree and Dene) who then resided in Saskatchewan, Alberta, British Columbia and the Northwest Territories.

The various decisions[86] in *Benoit* are notable for the differing views on whether there is a treaty right to tax exemption established by Treaty 8. The decisions in this case can be summarized as follows:

- the Federal Court (Trial Division), held that Treaty 8 included a right to exemption from tax that was protected by subsection 35(1) of the *Constitution Act, 1982* and included all forms of taxation (including the GST) regardless of the location of the Treaty 8 beneficiaries' property.
- the Federal Court of Appeal disagreed with the trial Judge's decision, concluding that "the respondents did not establish that the aboriginal signatories of Treaty 8 understood that the Treaty Commissioners had made a promise exempting them from taxation at any time for any reason."
- the Supreme Court of Canada denied Mr. Benoit leave to appeal, giving no reasons for its decision.

---

affecting Indians, a "liberal approach" is proper and where there is doubt with an expression it should be resolved in the Indians favour. This would also seem to accord with earlier decisions where less emphasis should be placed on the technical meanings but rather in keeping with the manner in which the Indians would naturally have understood them at that time.

85 *Benoit v. The Queen*, April 29, 2004, (2004) CarswellNat 1209 (S.C.C.). Leave to appeal to the Supreme Court of Canada denied without reasons.

86 *Ibid.*, (2002) D.T.C 6869, [2002] 4 C.T.C. 295 (F.C.T.D.), rev'd (2003) D.T.C. 5366, 228 D.L.R. (4th) 1 (F.C.A.).

The application for leave to appeal to the Supreme Court of Canada raised three questions. First, did the aboriginal signatories of Treaty 8 understand that the Treaty Commissioners had promised that they would not have tax imposed upon them at any time or for any reason? Second, what role does evidence of the parties' subjective understanding play in determining common intention? Third, is there a different and higher standard of proof for claimants in aboriginal and treaty rights cases? The Federal Court of Appeal decision answered only the first question. In my opinion, the Supreme Court of Canada may still support the Federal Court of Appeal's view on the first question. With respect to the second and third questions we have to take a "wait and see" approach.

Before leaving this discussion on treaties, I would like to point out that as a result of a 1998 treaty[87] reached between the federal government and Indians in the Yukon Territory, Indians in the Yukon are no longer entitled to the tax exemption in s. 87 of the *Indian Act*. The Umbrella Final Agreement ("UFA") affected the taxation status of the Yukon First Nations after December 31, 1998, and therefore, s. 87 of the *Indian Act* will not apply to the personal property situated on a reserve in the Yukon of an Indian, Yukon First Nation; or the personal property situated on a reserve outside the Yukon of an Indian person resident in the Yukon or a Yukon First Nation or Band. The UFA also anticipates the negotiation of self-governing agreements with Yukon First Nations, which will also permit those Yukon First Nations to levy an income tax.[88]

b) Section 88 of the *Indian Act*

Section 88 of the *Indian Act* provides that (subject to treaties and other federal laws) provincial laws of general application apply to Indians in the province, except where there is an inconsistency or cover a matter already provided for in the *Indian Act*.

While the meaning of s. 88 is not necessarily obvious, a consideration of the case law dealing with s. 88 will reveal the interpretation the Supreme Court of Canada has given s. 88. While s. 88 does not expressly provide for

---

87 See the Umbrella Final Agreement as discussed in the CRA VIEWS documents 9821446 and 9806857.

88 Readers seeking a more complete discussion and understanding of the taxation authority and agreements of First Nations governments are referred to the article by M.J. Flatters and the publication *Aboriginal Rights Litigation*, described in notes 21 and 10 respectively. Readers should also note that effective July 1, 2004 the First Nations Goods and Services Tax (FNGST) replaced the GST for eight First Nations situated in the Yukon Territory. Further details of the FNGST can be found in the CRA's publication RC4365 "First Nations Goods & Services Tax."

provincial laws to apply to Indian reserve lands, the Supreme Court of Canada stated in *Dick*,[89] that laws of a province do apply to Indians:

- provided the laws do not tread on the exclusive federal jurisdiction in s. 91.24 of the *Constitution Act, 1867* or are inconsistent with other federal legislation;
- by incorporating into federal law through the operation of s. 88 provincial laws of general application;[90] and
- are subject to treaties and other s. 88 exceptions.

Consequently, it is my view the Supreme Court of Canada has recognized the importance and given a modern interpretation to the operation and application of s. 88. Although provincial laws of general application will apply to Indians, it is also possible that aboriginal persons can rely on s. 88 to limit the operation of provincial taxing statutes.[91]

---

89 *Dick v. R., (sub nom. R. v. Tenale)* [1985] 2 S.C.R. 309, [1986] 1 W.W.R. 1, 23 D.L.R. (4th) 33. There are many decisions dealing with s. 88, but Dick undoubtedly the leading case on the interpretation of this provision.

90 *Delgamuukw v. B.C.*, [1997] 3 S.C.R. 1010, 153 D.L.R. (4th) 193 where the Supreme Court of Canada also confirmed that provincial laws may not extinguish aboriginal rights. See also *R. v. Sioui*, [1990] S.C.R. 1025, 70 D.L.R. (4th) 427 in which the Supreme Court of Canada emphasized that s. 88 protects Indians from the laws of a province that may try to derogate from treaty-protected rights.

91 The majority of tax cases dealing with s. 88 involve the claim to tax exemption by reason of a treaty between an Indian's First Nation and the Crown, and are advanced on the basis that either: 1) the tax to be levied has as its objective the raising of revenues associated with items otherwise promised to the Indian beneficiaries of the treaty, or 2) the tax to be imposed is contrary to the oral assurances made to treaty Indians that no taxes would be levied against them. The case of *R. v. Johnston* (1966), 56 D.L.R. (2d) 749; 56 W.W.R. 565 (Sask. C.A.) involved a hospitalization tax imposed by the province and with the revenue being raised applied to the financing of provincial hospitals. In Johnston it was argued that as a beneficiary (i.e. band member) who's band was a signatory to Treaty 6, the treaty exempted him from the hospitalization tax. However, while the court found the treaty could come within s. 88 of the *Indian Act*, the court also found the treaty did not offer an exemption from tax. This was based upon the court's interpretation of the treaty (i.e. the plain meaning of its provisions) — the actual wording which required on the part of the Crown: "That a medicine chest shall be kept at the house of each Indian agent for the use and benefit of the Indians at the direction of such agent . . . That in the event hereafter of the Indians comprised within this treaty being overtaken by any pestilence or by a general famine, the Queen . . . will grant to the Indians assistance of such character and to such extent . . . shall deem necessary and sufficient to relieve the Indians from the calamity that shall have befallen them." in the event of pestilence or general famine. While *Johnston* was decided before the Supreme Court of Canada decision *Nowegijick* and its liberalization of the interpretation to be applied in the construction of Indian treaties, the recent decisions in *Benoit* and specifically the recent dismissal of leave to appeal

C. CONCLUSION

The aim of this paper is to distill the principles of aboriginal income and commodity taxation. In doing so, we have identified for the reader the legislative framework and case law. Most of my analysis has been to show that the issue is whether income or the sale of property is situate on a reserve to be exempt from income or commodity taxes.

At the same time as I reviewed the results of cases dealing with the exemption in s. 87 of the *Indian Act*, I also identified issues and uncertainty arising from the decisions. The resolution of these issues and uncertainty for Parliament is not in my view burdensome or insurmountable.

Parliament should pursue legislative amendments to the *Indian Act* or the *Income Tax Act*. In my view, the exemption in s. 87 of the *Indian Act* is unsatisfactory in modern society and the burgeoning aboriginal and Canadian economies. This observation is reflected in the analysis that only persons who qualify as an "Indian" under the *Indian Act* are eligible for the exemption and only personal property of an Indian "situate on a reserve" is exempt from taxation. Furthermore, the case law reflects a narrowed interpretation of the availability of the exemption and with a "connecting factors" that I submit is not as widely applicable or relevant to aboriginals' investment income as the courts suggest.

The Supreme Court of Canada has expounded tests in its recent decision in *Powley* to determine who is a Métis. In doing so, this Court examined the significant historical and cultural background the Métis and offered directions to resolve the same issue. I submit that Parliament can take full advantage of *Powley*'s lead and take legislative action to not only to modernize the definition of who is an "Indian," but also to offer a more comprehensive definition of the circumstances where the personal property of an Indian is to be situated on a reserve for taxation purposes. It would be expected this second amendment would be congruent with the same principle in the case of an Indian's property that is exempt from seizure.

The antique notions and problems arising therefrom that I have identified and surveyed — in the legislation and case law — should not be neglected by Parliament. The effort in this paper has been to assist in this direction and make the technical aspects of the principles revealed easier to understand.

---

by the Supreme Court of Canada offer no additional insight by the courts on the second possible argument to be advanced under s. 88 that the tax to be imposed is contrary to the oral assurances made to treaty Indians that no taxes would be levied against them.

APPENDIX

Indian Act (excerpts)

2. (1) In this Act, . . .

"reserve"

(a) means a tract of land, the legal title to which is vested in Her Majesty, that has been set apart by Her Majesty for the use and benefit of a band, and

(b) except in subsection 18(2), sections 20 to 25, 28, 36 to 38, 42, 44, 46, 48 to 51, 58 to 60 and the regulations made under any of those provisions, includes *designated lands*; . . .

"designated lands" means a tract of land or any interest therein the legal title to which remains vested in Her Majesty and in which the band for whose use and benefit it was set apart as a reserve has, otherwise than absolutely, released or surrendered its rights or interests, whether before or after the coming into force of this definition, . . .

"surrendered lands" means a reserve or part of a reserve or any interest therein, the legal title to which remains vested in Her Majesty, that has been released or surrendered by the band for whose use and benefit it was set apart; . . . "

. . .

83. (1) Without prejudice to the powers conferred by section 81, the council of a band may, subject to the approval of the Minister, make by-laws for any or all of the following purposes, namely,

(a) subject to subsections (2) and (3), taxation for local purposes of land, or interests in land, in the reserve, including rights to occupy, possess or use land in the reserve;

(a.1) the licensing of businesses, callings, trades and occupations;

. . .

(f) the raising of money from band members to support band projects; and

(g) with respect to any matter arising out of or ancillary to the exercise of powers under this section.

. . .

(3) A by-law made under paragraph (1)(a) must provide an appeal procedure in respect of assessments made for the purposes of taxation under that paragraph.

. . .

87. (1) Notwithstanding any other Act of Parliament or any Act of the legislature of a province, but *subject to section 83*, the following property is exempt from taxation, namely,
(a) the interest of an *Indian* or a band in reserve lands or surrendered lands; and
(b) the personal property of an *Indian* or a band situated on a reserve.

(2) No *Indian* or band is subject to taxation in respect of the ownership, occupation, possession or use of any property mentioned in paragraph (1)(a) or (b) or is otherwise subject to taxation in respect of any such property.

(3) No succession duty, inheritance tax or estate duty is payable on the death of any Indian in respect of any property mentioned in paragraphs (1)(a) or (b) or the succession thereto if the property passes to an *Indian*, nor shall any such property be taken into account in determining the duty payable under the Dominion Succession Duty Act, chapter 89 of the Revised Statutes of Canada, 1952, or the tax payable under the Estate Tax Act, chapter E-9 of the Revised Statutes of Canada, 1970, on or in respect of other property passing to an *Indian*.

88. Subject to the terms of any treaty and any other Act of Parliament, all laws of general application from time to time in force in any province are applicable to and in respect of Indians in the province, except to the extent that those laws are inconsistent with this Act or any order, rule, regulation or by-law made thereunder, and except to the extent that those laws make provision for any matter for which provision is made by or under this Act."

. . .

90. (1) For the purposes of sections 87 and 89, personal property that was
(a) purchased by Her Majesty with Indian moneys or moneys appropriated by Parliament for the use and benefit of Indians or bands, or
(b) given to Indians or to a band under a treaty or agreement between a band and Her Majesty,

shall *be deemed always to be situated on a reserve* [emphasis added].

Chapter Twenty-Two

GST General Principles

Blake M. Murray and Sean Aylward

A. OVERVIEW

The goods and services tax (the "GST") is a value added tax (VAT) applied on final consumption and is generally similar to the European value added tax ("VAT"). Like the VAT, the GST is a multi-stage sales tax collected at each stage in the supply process and provides an offsetting credit for taxes paid on business inputs by most firms.

The GST was enacted as Part IX of the *Excise Tax Act* (Canada) (the "*ETA*") and came into effect on January 1, 1991. The requirement to collect GST will depend on the status and activities of the supplier and the nature of the goods or services to be provided. The provision of goods and services (referred to as supply) is classified as either a taxable supply, zero-rated supply or exempt supply.

GST at the rate of seven percent applies on the value of the consideration paid or payable by the purchaser of a taxable supply of property or of services made in Canada. An additional tax known as the harmonized sales tax ("HST") at the rate of eight percent applies on the value of the consideration where a supply is made in New Brunswick, Nova Scotia and Newfoundland. In the case of taxable supplies made in Canada, although legal liability is imposed on the purchaser, the GST generally is required to be collected by the vendor (registrant) as an agent of the Crown. GST also applies to all imported goods and is payable by the importer at the time of importation at seven percent of the duty paid value of the goods. In addition, GST and HST may apply on a self-assessment basis to the importation of intangible personal property or a service that is not used in a commercial activity. Virtually every transaction is brought within the potential ambit of GST. "Tax is the rule, exemption the exception." Relief from tax is extended to supplies which are made or deemed to have been made outside Canada, zero-rated supplies, exempt supplies and certain other limited situations (such as on the sale of a business and under the group relief provisions). Certain goods and services, such as exports, are completely relieved from tax as "zero-rated" supplies. Other goods and services defined as "exempt supplies" such as financial services, and used residential housing are not taxable to the recipient, but the supplier is not entitled to recover the GST it paid on its inputs for these supplies.

Each of these concepts is now discussed in greater detail.

B. TAXABLE SUPPLIES

The basic charging provision for the GST is found in s. 165 of the *ETA*. Section 165 provides that every recipient of a "taxable supply" . . . "made in Canada" is required to pay tax in respect of the supply equal to seven percent[1] of the value of the consideration for the supply. Section 221 of the *ETA* in turn provides that every person who makes a taxable supply in Canada is required, as agent of the Crown, to collect tax payable by the recipient.

Taken together, these provisions operate to impose on every supplier an obligation to collect and on every purchaser an obligation to pay GST in respect of the consideration for "taxable supplies" made in Canada.

The vast majority of supplies made in Canada are "taxable supplies." A supply is determined to be a "taxable supply" under the *ETA* if it is:

(i) a "supply";
(ii) "made in Canada"; and
(iii) made in the course of a "commercial activity."

These statutory provisions underpinning the imposition of GST are is considered below.

---

1 "Zero-rated" supplies are taxable supplies which are taxed at the rate of 0 percent. Consequently, while the recipient is not liable to pay tax on the consideration for such supplies, the supplier is able to recover all GST paid on inputs through the input tax credit mechanism.

1) What Is A Supply?

A fundamental issue in the application of GST is the determination of whether there has a been a "supply." The term "supply" is broadly defined in s. 123(1) of the *ETA* as follows:

> . . . the provision of property or a service in any manner, including sale, transfer, barter, exchange, licence, rental, lease, gift or disposition.

The terms "property" and "service" are also defined in s. 123(1) of the *ETA*[2] and establish the GST as a tax of broad application.[3]

In practice, there may be considerable doubt as to whether a particular transaction involves a single supply or a compound or multiple supply. Where a transaction is determined to be a single supply, it will often be the case that both taxable and non-taxable components are present. If the supply is determined to be a single or compound supply,[4] the non-taxable component may be subsumed in the taxable characterization of the single supply or vice-versa. For example, one of the earlier decisions in this area involved a question as to whether in the (zero-rated) sale of livestock the (taxable) sales commission was included as part of a single supply or was properly subject to tax as a separate supply.[5]

Related to the single/multiple supply issue are several provisions of the *ETA* which provide that even where multiple supplies are identified the supplier may treat the "incidental" supply as forming part of the principal supply where the two are offered together for a "single consideration."[6]

Issues also arise as to whether supplies of a partner are undertaken in the course of a partnership's activity (in which case a partner is not required to collect GST), or whether such activities are undertaken in the

---

2 As illustrated in *Avenue Business Campuses Ltd. v. Canada*, [2001] G.S.T.C. 125 (T.C.C.) (supply of books (property) and instruction (service)).

3 "Property" is defined in s. 123(1) of the *ETA* as follows: "property means any property, whether real or personal, moveable or immoveable, tangible or intangible, corporeal or incorporeal, and includes a right or interest of any kind, a share and chose-in-action, but does not include money."

"Service" is defined in s. 123(1) of the *ETA* as follows: "a service means anything other than (a) property; (b) money; and (c) anything that is supplied to an employer by a person who is or agrees to become an employee of the employer in the course of or in relation to the office or employment of that person."

4 A "compound supply" is also frequently referred to as a "composite supply."

5 *O.A. Brown Ltd. v. Canada*, [1995] G.S.T.C. 40 (T.C.C.).

6 See ss. 138 and 139 of the *ETA*.

course of the partner's own activities (in which case GST is collectable by the partner from the partnership).[7]

2) Place Of Supply

The place of supply rules are set out in s. 142 of the *ETA*.

Subsection 142(1) of the *ETA* provides that there is a supply "made in Canada" in the case of tangible personal property delivered or made available in Canada; real property located in Canada; a service performed in whole or in part in Canada; or, in the case of intangible person property, such property relates to real property or tangible person property situated in Canada or to a service to be performed in Canada. Conversely, ss. 142(2) provides that the supply is made "outside of Canada" in the case of tangible personal property delivered or made available outside of Canada; real property located outside of Canada; a service performed wholly outside of Canada[8]; or, in the case of intangible personal property, such property relates to real property or tangible personal property situated outside of Canada or to a service to be performed outside of Canada.

Some doubt has arisen concerning the meaning of "delivered or made available" in or outside of Canada as that term is used in paragraphs 142(1)(a) and 142(2)(a) of the *ETA*. The relevant sale of goods legislation for each province (and the *Civil Code* in Quebec) generally provide that delivery includes delivery to a common carrier for delivery to the recipient. Thus, goods shipped by a vendor with a destination outside Canada are normally considered supplied outside of Canada and not subject to GST. However, several cases have reached an opposite conclusion.[9]

An exception to the place of supply rules in s. 142 of the *ETA* is established in respect of certain taxable supplies made by non-residents of Canada. Pursuant to s. 143 of the *ETA*, any supply made by a non-resident of Canada who does not "carry on business" in Canada and is not "registered"

---

7 See s. 272.1 of the *ETA* which sets out specific rules governing activities of partners and partnerships.

8 Note that in the GST context for a service to be deemed to be "made outside of Canada," it must be *wholly* performed outside of Canada. The Canada Revenue Agency takes the position that if any part of a service, even a potentially *de minimis* portion, is performed "in Canada," the entire service is deemed to be made in Canada.

9 See *ADV Ltd. v. Canada*, [1997] G.S.T.C. 60 (T.C.C.), [1998] G.S.T.C. 64 (F.C.A.) (goods delivered by U.S. supplier to courier in U.S. for delivery to Canada Post constituted a supply made in Canada); *Toyota Tsusho America, Inc. v. Canada*, [1997] G.S.T.C. 83 (T.C.C.) (goods delivered by U.S. supplier FOB Canada but cleared through customs by Canadian customer constituted supply made in Canada).

for GST purposes is deemed to be a supply "made outside of Canada." Through this deeming provision, as a practical matter, non-residents who do not carry on business in Canada are excluded from the obligation to collect tax and do not voluntarily register to collect tax because their supplies are deemed not to be "made in Canada" and consequently fall outside the charging provision in s. 165 and the collection provisions in s. 221 of the *ETA*. However, should such non-resident chose to register[10] for GST purposes, it will lose the benefit of this deeming provision and become obligated to collect the GST on the consideration for taxable supplies made in Canada.

3) Commercial Activity

The concept of a "commercial activity" is another fundamental concept of the GST. It governs both the determination of what supplies are taxable as well as the eligibility of a purchaser to claim an input tax credit in respect of its receipt of a taxable supply.[11]

Subsection 123(1) of the *ETA* defines a "commercial activity" as follows:

> A "commercial activity" of a person means
> (a) a business carried on by the person (other than a business carried on without a reasonable expectation of profit by an individual, a personal trust or a partnership, all of the members of which are individuals), except to the extent to which the business involves the making of exempt supplies by the person,
> (b) an adventure or concern of the person in the nature of trade (other than an adventure or concern engaged in without a reasonable expectation of profit by an individual, a personal trust or a partnership, all of the members of which are individuals), except to the extent to which the adventure or concern involves the making of exempt supplies by the person, and
> (c) the making of a supply (other than an exempt supply) by the person of real property of the person, including anything done by the person in the course of or in connection with the making of the supply.

A commercial activity is therefore generally any business activity including an adventure in the nature of trade or a supply of real property. It does not

10 A non-resident may choose to register in order to be eligible to recover the GST if he or she pays on supplies of goods or services to it.

11 See *Miller v. Canada*, [2002] G.S.T.C. 93 (T.C.C.) (recipient satisfied reasonable expectation of profit test and therapeutic horse riding business was found to be commercial activity).

include any employment activity or a supply that is defined to be an "exempt supply."

In the result, a "supply" "made in Canada" in the course of a "commercial activity" is a "taxable supply" on which GST applies equal to seven percent of the consideration "paid" or "payable" by the recipient. As is explained below, exempt supplies fall outside the definition of taxable supplies because they are not made in the course of a commercial activity.

4) Zero-Rated Supplies

Zero-rated supplies consist of a defined list of supplies set out in Schedule VI of the *ETA* on which tax is notionally charged at a rate of zero. In all other respects, zero-rated supplies are treated exactly the same as taxable supplies. That is to say, the supplier of a zero-rated supply may recover all GST paid on inputs to the supply by claiming input tax credits notwithstanding that no tax is collectible on its sales.

The zero-rated supplies listed in Schedule VI of the *ETA* generally include goods and services that which for public policy reasons are to be completely relieved from tax. These include: agricultural products; basic groceries; medical devices; exports; prescription drugs; and transportation services.

Perhaps the most important of the zero-rated supplies are exports. The GST zero-rates most Canadian exports of goods and certain services supplied in Canada. Under s. 1 of Part V of Schedule VI of the *ETA*, exports of tangible personal property which are purchased in Canada by a recipient who intends to export the property are treated as zero-rated. As well, most services performed in Canada where the recipient is a non-resident may be treated as zero-rated, subject to certain exceptions such as where the service is "in respect of" real property or tangible personal property situated in Canada.[12] Hence, in most cases Canadian exports should enter the international market free from tax.

The determination of what properly constitutes a zero-rated service has been the subject of extensive litigation. In particular, zero rated exports and zero-rated basic groceries have been areas of the *ETA* which have produced a substantial volume of cases relating to definitional provisions and documentary requirements.[13]

---

12 See ss. 7 and 23 of Part V of Schedule VI of the *ETA*.

13 See *Uranus Auto Sales Inc. v. R*,. [2002] G.S.T.C. 39 (T.C.C.) in which export documentation requirements were considered.

a) Drop Shipments

In addition to the relief which is afforded non-resident purchasers under the zero-rated export rules, s. 179 of the *ETA* sets out the so-called "drop shipment rules" which allow an unregistered non-resident person to acquire in Canada goods, or services in respect of goods, on a tax-free basis, provided the goods are ultimately exported or are retained in Canada exclusively for consumption, use or supply in the course of a commercial activity of a registrant. Supplies qualifying for relief under s. 179 are technically not "zero-rated"; instead, they are deemed to have been made outside Canada.

5) Exempt Supplies

No liability to pay or collect GST will arise on an "exempt" supply. Unlike taxable and zero-rated supplies, however, a person making exempt supplies is not entitled to claim input tax credits for the GST paid on purchases used by it in or related to the provision of exempt supplies. In effect, an exempt supplier is treated as the final consumer of the goods or services it purchases and must bear the full cost of GST. Supplies which are designated as exempt supplies are set out in Schedule V of the *ETA* and include: child and personal care services; financial services; educational services, including public and private elementary or secondary school programs, school bussing, college and university programs as well as vocational courses and school meal plans; health care services, including health care services provided under provincial medicare, institutional health care services such as nursing homes, nursing, dentistry and other specified services such as psychology, physiotherapy and occupational therapy; certain real property supplies, including the supply of used residential housing, residential but not commercial rentals, and vacant land held by individuals that has not been used in the course of a business; legal aid services; and supplies by charities and public sector bodies.

Considerable litigation has occurred regarding the definition of an exempt "financial service" as that term is defined in ss. 123(1) of the *ETA*. Such services are broadly defined in ss. 123(1) of the *ETA* to include most transactions involving "financial instruments," such as debt securities, equity securities, insurance policies, options, and guarantees. In particular, the definition of financial service includes a service of "arranging for" defined financial services and the scope of the arranging for definition has been litigated in several cases.[14] Other exempt supplies which

14 See *Locator of Missing Heirs Inc. v. Canada*, [1995] G.S.T.C. 63 (T.C.C.), aff'd [1997] G.S.T.C. 16 (F.C.A.) (finding heirs and advising them of property to which they were entitled was not "arranging for" a financial service).

have attracted significant litigation include real property and health care services.[15]

The scheme of the *ETA* places considerable responsibility on the supplier to determine whether a particular supply is a taxable supply on which GST should be collected or whether the supply may fall into one of the exceptions which relieve the purchaser of an obligation to pay tax. For this reason much of the litigation which surrounds the operation of the GST involves suppliers, not because of a failure to pay tax, as in an income tax context, but rather due to a failure, often inadvertent, of a supplier to collect tax.[16]

6) Input Tax Credits

Pursuant to s. 169 of the *ETA*, registrants generally may deduct from taxes collected on taxable supplies in a specific reporting period a credit (the input tax credit) for the GST paid or payable in the period in respect of any property (including capital property) or services purchased by the registrant "to the extent" it is for "consumption, use or supply" in the registrant's commercial activity. The effect of the input tax credit is to remove any GST from the cost of business inputs relating to taxable supplies. Thus, in conceptual terms, the tax is fully borne by consumers at the final point of sale and businesses merely collect, rather than pay, GST. In practice, of course, the economic burden may be wholly or partially shifted back to the supplier in the form of lower prices.

There is no requirement to match revenues that are earned with costs that are incurred (i.e., the input tax credit becomes available immediately without regard to when the taxable supply to which it relates is made). The difference between the tax collected by the registrant on sales and the input tax credits on purchases for a particular reporting period is "net tax." Where the net tax is in the negative (input tax credits exceed GST collected), it is refunded to the registrant.

Related to the operation of s. 169 of the *ETA* is s. 141 of the *ETA* which provides that where "substantially all" of the consumption or use of property or a service by a person is in the course of the person's commercial activities, all of the consumption or use of the property is deemed to be in

15 See *Riverfront Medical Evaluations Ltd. v. Canada*, [2001] G.S.T.C. 80 (T.C.C.), aff'd [2002] G.S.T.C. 110 (F.C.A.) (supply of independent medical reports to legal and insurance company clients was exempt supply).

16 See *Vanex Truck Service Ltd. v. Canada*, [2001] G.S.T.C. 70 (F.C.A.) (corporation found to be liable for GST that it failed to collect on taxable supply to truckers).

commercial activities. Since the Canada Revenue Agency's ("CRA") view is that "substantially all" means 90 percent or more, the effect of s. 141 is essentially that 90 percent use in a commercial activity is effectively deemed to be 100 percent use.

It should be noted that persons who are determined to be "financial institutions" pursuant to s. 149 of the *ETA* are not entitled to rely on the benefit of the "substantially all" rule in s. 141 of the *ETA* and are instead required to fully allocate inputs between use in a commercial activity or non-commercial activity. Generally speaking, s. 149 provides that various entities such as banks, insurers, brokers, etc. are "listed financial institutions." Other entities that are not listed financial institutions but which have both over $10,000,000 in financial income and over ten percent of their revenues from financial income, are treated as *de minimis* financial institutions to which the more stringent input tax credit entitlement rules also apply.

In the case of an acquisition of personal capital property, s. 199(2) of the *ETA* establishes a higher threshold than that described above for non-capital property and requires that the property be used "primarily" (i.e., greater than 50 percent)[17] in a commercial activity in order to obtain an input tax credit. If capital personal property is not used primarily in a commercial activity no input tax credit is allowed. In effect, therefore, for capital personal property, the *ETA* establishes an all-or-nothing rule instead of the pro-rata approach which generally governs non-capital property, services and real property.

By far the most highly contentious area of dispute in the GST to date has been in relation to the recovery of input tax credits under s. 169 of the *ETA*. A GST registrant may recover GST paid "to the extent" a good or service is for consumption, use or supply in the course of a "commercial activity." In practice, issues have often come up as to whether a recipient's "consumption, use or supply" has occurred in the course of a "commercial activity." For example, did the business have a reasonable expectation of profit; was the apportionment between commercial and exempt uses reasonable; was the documentary evidence required in order to claim a credit sufficient; was the supply, in relation to which expenses were incurred, exempt (e.g., the defence of a hostile take-over bid by a corporation[18])?

---

17 See *Navaho Inn v. Canada*, [1995] G.S.T.C. 21 (T.C.C.) (property was found to be acquired for use primarily in the making of exempt supplies, so it was not included in determining an input tax credit).

18 See *BJ Services Co. v. Canada*, [2002] G.S.T.C. 124 (T.C.C.) [*BJ Services*] (fees paid to takeover advisors were expended in the course of a commercial activity).

Other issues arise in connection with whether a person is properly entitled to claim an input tax credit. For example, a number of cases have dealt with agency in the GST context. Was a registrant purchasing as principal and thereby entitled to an input tax credit or was the person merely a purchasing agent; likewise, was the vendor acting as principal or as agent and if so who was required to remit tax?

Partnerships have also created difficulties in the GST context. Unlike the case in an income tax analysis, a partnership is considered for GST purposes to be a separate person. In concept, therefore, tax paid on goods and services acquired by a partnership is properly creditable to the partnership. In practice, however, issues arise as to whether a credit is attributable to the partner, independent of the partnership's activities.[19]

7) Imported Goods

Sections 212–216 of the *ETA* deal with the application of GST to goods imported into Canada. Unlike the supply of goods or services "made in Canada" (where tax is collected by the supplier), GST on imported goods is collected by Canada Customs at the same time as customs duties are payable on an importation.

In general, the laws of customs set out under the *Customs Act* apply to the importation process for the purposes of the GST. The "importer of record" for the purposes of the *Customs Act* is required to pay Canada Customs an amount equal to seven percent of the value of the goods as determined under the *Customs Act*. A serious concern had been identified by many practitioners regarding the proper entitlement of an importer under the *Customs Act* to claim an input tax credit in respect of GST paid on importations. Section 169 of the *ETA* provides for an input tax credit to be claimed by a person who imported goods for the purpose of consumption, use or supply in the course of that person's commercial activities. In practice however this test proved difficult to align with commercial norms. If, for example, the vendor who had supplied goods outside of Canada imported the goods instead of the recipient, a problem arose because the vendor was neither the consumer user of the goods in Canada nor someone who imported the goods for the purposes of supplying them, since the goods would have already been supplied outside Canada. While the Canadian recipient was intended to be in the position of claiming an input tax credit

19 See s. 272.1 of the *ETA* which establishes special rules for supplies involving partnerships.

in respect of the importation of the goods, in many cases the recipient did not meet the conditions for doing so under s. 169. Consequently, many import transactions gave rise to non-recoverable GST.[20]

To address this problem the *ETA* has been proposed to be amended effective October 3, 2003 to provide that an input tax credit will be available to the "constructive importer" of goods regardless of whether such constructive importer acted as the importer of record under the *Customs Act* and was liable to pay GST.[21] A "constructive importer" will be defined as essentially the last person to whom a supply of goods is made outside of Canada before their release from customs. The new provisions provide however that where the importer of record is other than the constructive importer, the constructive importer will be required to obtain from the importer of record copies of the relevant customs documentation substantiating the payment of GST.

8) Imported Services And Intangible Property

Sections 217–220 of the *ETA* set out rules governing the importation into Canada of services and intangible personal property (e.g., intellectual property rights). To summarize, its purpose is to require persons to self-assess and remit GST on the importation of services or intangible property received from outside Canada where such supplies are for use in Canada otherwise than exclusively in the course of a commercial activity of the Canadian recipient.[22]

For GST registrants who are engaged exclusively in a commercial activity these provisions will be of little or no importance because no tax is triggered in respect of a service or intangible property acquired for use in a commercial activity. These sections act in effect as an anti-avoidance regime to ensure that persons not entitled to claim an input tax credit (e.g., consumers or persons engaged in exempt activities) do not realize any tax advantage by sourcing the acquisition of services or intangibles outside of Canada where the supply would not be subject to GST by the vendor.

---

20 See *Clear Customs Brokers Ltd. v. Canada*, [1996] G.S.T.C. 46 (T.C.C.) (customs broker paid, as agent, GST on goods being imported, was not reimbursed by customer, and was found to be ineligible for input tax credit).

21 See Notice of Ways and Means Motion of October 3, 2003 which proposes to add s. 178.8 to the *ETA* with effect from October 3, 2003.

22 See *BJ Services*, above note 18.

9) Registration and Remittance Requirements

Every person who is engaged in a commercial activity and who makes taxable supplies is required to register with the Canada Customs and Excise. In addition, there are a number of special registration requirements when non-residents have branches in Canada, carry on business in Canada or solicit orders for books or magazines in Canada.

Registrants are required to file returns and pay GST on a monthly, quarterly, or yearly basis, depending on their total yearly taxable sales: over $6 million, monthly filing; $6 million or less, quarterly filing; and under $500,000, annual filing.

However, a registrant can elect to file monthly. Such an election would be valuable to any registrant in a net refund position. Corporations that have distinct divisions or branches are permitted to apply for authority to file a separate return for each branch.

Businesses are required to remit GST on taxable supplies in the month following the reporting period in which tax liability arose. The liability to pay GST generally arises on the earlier of the day consideration is paid or becomes due. Consideration becomes due the earlier of (1) the day the supplier first issues an invoice or would have done so but for an undue delay, or (2) the day a recipient is required to pay a supplier pursuant to an agreement in writing.

Thus, a business is entitled to claim an input tax credit for GST paid or payable by it and will be responsible for remitting GST paid or payable by its customers. Consequently, those businesses with lengthy receivables may face a cash flow disadvantage as tax may be required to be remitted on accounts not yet paid. Conversely, those firms that have not paid accounts bearing GST may nevertheless claim an input tax credit once an invoice has been issued to them, and thus they will enjoy a cash flow advantage.

10) Non-Residents

For persons who are non-residents of Canada and do not "carry on business" in Canada, purchase goods for delivery in Canada, or ship goods to Canada, the GST has little direct effect.

Non-residents generally must charge and collect GST only if they are engaged in a commercial activity in Canada and such activity includes the non-resident "carrying on business" in Canada or receiving income from commercial real property located in Canada. Non-residents who charge admission for performances or seminars produced in Canada are also required to charge and collect tax. In all of these cases, registration is required.

In addition, non-residents who solicit orders in Canada for magazines, books, or periodicals for supply by mail or courier are deemed to carry on business in Canada and are therefore required to register and collect GST.

Special rules apply to branches of foreign persons operating in Canada. The *ETA* provides that a person with a permanent establishment in Canada will be a resident in Canada with respect to activities carried on by that establishment in Canada. A business with a Canadian branch will be required to register for GST and collect tax on supplies made through the permanent establishment.

Non-residents without a permanent establishment in Canada will be required to post security with the Minister of National Revenue for their collection and remittance obligations. Also, all non-resident persons carrying on business in Canada will be required to maintain books and records sufficient to determine their GST liabilities.

11) GST Elections and Special Cases

There are a number of relieving provisions under the *ETA* which are intended to provide either cash flow and/or compliance relief to GST registrants. Several of the more significant of these provisions are discussed below.

a) Acquisition Or Start-Up Of A Business

The acquisition of assets required to establish a business in Canada gives rise to a myriad of GST taxable supplies (e.g., capital property, inventory and real property).

In most cases, the new business will be eligible for an input tax credit on tax payable on these assets provided the purchaser has become a GST registrant before such input tax credit is claimed.

Notwithstanding that GST may ultimately be recoverable by a purchaser of a business, the cash flow impact can often be significant, particularly where financing is not available to cover tax costs. To alleviate this problem the *ETA* provides that where a person is acquiring "all or substantially all" of the assets of a "business" or "part" of a business of the vendor, the parties may elect to transfer the assets on a tax-free basis pursuant to s. 167(1) of the *ETA*.

In practice the determination of what constitutes a business or part of a business has proven to be very complex. Numerous cases have examined this point and it is likely that the scope of relief under s. 167(1) will remain a continuing source of complexity in the GST field.[23]

---

23 See *Comeau (R.) v. Canada*, [1996] G.S.T.C. 3 (T.C.C.) (sale of trailer and loader was not sale of business) and *Low Cost Furniture Ltd. v. Canada*, [1997] G.S.T.C. 77 (T.C.C.)

b) Group Relief

Section 156 of the *ETA* provides that two "closely-related" corporations or partnerships of corporations may elect to treat every taxable supply made between the electing parties (other than a supply of real property by way of sale) to be GST-free. The effect of the election eliminates intercompany cash flow burdens and relieves the necessary accounting compliance that would occur if the particular supplies were subject to tax. The election under s. 156 must be made in prescribed form but is not required to be filed with the CRA, rather simply kept in the registrant's files.

The determination of a qualifying "closely-related" corporation or partnership is set out in ss. 128 and 156(1.1) of the *ETA* respectively. Generally the closely-related threshold is determined by reference to whether there is a 90 percent or greater common ownership interest between the electing parties either directly or indirectly.

Section 150 of the *ETA* provides a similar election to relieve GST on the provision of supplies "by way of lease, license or a service" made between closely-related companies, one of which is a "listed financial institution" as that term is defined in s. 149 of the *ETA*.

c) Joint Ventures

For the purposes of the GST, persons who are party to a joint venture are generally required to account for GST on purchases and sales on an independent (fractional) basis notwithstanding that the joint venturers may have delegated administrative control of the joint venture to a co-venturer who is acting as the operator.

Section 273 of the *ETA* provides an election whereby the co-venturers can agree to designate a particular venturer as the "operator" and allow the operator to account for GST payable and collectible on behalf of the joint venture on a consolidated basis.[24] This election thereby relieves all co-venturers other than the operator of the requirement to separately account for GST.

Like the s. 156 election, an election under s. 273 is required to be completed in prescribed form but need not be filed with the CRA.

d) Sales Agency

Subsection 177(1.1) of the *ETA* provides for an election in cases where an agent makes a supply on behalf of a principal who is required to collect

---

(transfer of remaining inventory, filing cabinet, and fax machine did not constitute substantially all of the property reasonably regarded as necessary for the recipient to be capable of carrying on the business or part as a business).

24 See *Westcan Malting Ltd. v. Canada*, [1998] G.S.T.C. 34 (T.C.C.) (joint utilities program found not to be a joint venture).

GST in respect of the supply. In this case the principal and the agent may jointly elect to have the agent report and remit GST as if it were collectible by the agent. In addition, s. 177(1.11) of the *ETA* further provides that in circumstances where a person acts merely as a "billing agent" but not an agent at law for the purposes of making a supply on behalf of a principal, the billing agent will be deemed to have acted as agent of the principal in making the supply and thereby be permitted to enter into the election under s. 177(1.1).

This election may be particularly useful in circumstances where a mass marketer or other person is acting as a sales agent on behalf multiple clients and the sales agent is the party invoicing and collecting proceeds on behalf of its principals (who would otherwise be required to have fractional amounts of GST returned to them for remittance and reporting in their own returns).

e) Sale Of Real Property To Registered Purchasers

Subsection 221(2) of the *ETA* provides that a supplier who makes a taxable supply of real property by way of sale is not required to collect GST from the recipient where the recipient is registered under the *ETA* or where the supplier is a non-resident of Canada.

This exception to the normal tax collection obligation of a supplier is often a very significant cash flow advantage for commercial parties where payment of the tax by the purchaser on closing would result in significant financing costs pending recovery of the tax through the input tax credit system.

Subsection 221(2) operates based on the status of the parties and does not require an election to be made in order to give effect to the tax relief.

12) GST Objections And Appeals

Upon receipt of a registrant's return, the Minister of National Revenue may assess the return and reassess or make an additional assessment of tax, net tax, penalty, interest or another specified amount. If an application for a rebate is made under s. 215.1 or Division VI of the *ETA*, the Minister is required to consider the application and assess the amount of the rebate, if any, payable to the applicant. After making an assessment, the Minister must send a notice of assessment to the person assessed. The limitation periods applicable to such Ministerial assessments are set out in s. 298 of the *ETA*.[25]

---

25 See *Edible What Candy Corp. v. Canada*, [2002] G.S.T.C. 33 (T.C.C.) (corporation found to have made misrepresentation attributable to neglect, so subject to reassessment beyond normal period of time).

A person who disagrees with the Minister's assessment can object to it by filing a notice of objection with the Minster within ninety days after the day the notice of assessment is sent to the person. In order to be valid, a notice of objection must reasonably describe the issue(s) to be decided, specify the relief sought and provide the facts and reasons relied on. The requirements and procedural steps with respect to objections are set out in s. 301 of the *ETA* and anyone contemplating an objection should review the provisions carefully.[26] Particular attention should be directed to determining whether one meets the criteria of a "specified person" under s. 301(1). A specified person is subject to more stringent rules with respect to the objection and appeal procedures than one who is not a specified person.

Unlike the *Income Tax Act* (Canada) (the "*ITA*"), under which temporary relief against collection by the Minister is provided for taxpayers other than large corporations,[27] the *ETA* does not restrict the Minister's ability to collect disputed amounts while an objection is active. The Minister is permitted to begin collection proceedings once an assessment has been made under the *ETA*; however, s. 315(3) of the *ETA* provides the Minister with the discretion to postpone collection action against a person.

Upon receipt of a notice of objection, the Minister must reconsider the assessment and vacate or confirm the assessment or make a reassessment. The Minister is required to send notice of any decision to the person who objected.

If the Minister issues a notice of reassessment or an additional assessment or confirms the assessment, and the person remains dissatisfied, an appeal may be made to the Tax Court of Canada. This is accomplished by filing a notice of appeal with the Tax Court within ninety days after the day notice of the Minister's action was sent to the person. A person is also permitted to appeal to the Tax Court if: the assessment was made under Part IX, Division VIII, subdivision d of the *ETA*; 180 days have elapsed since the filing of the notice of objection; and the Minister has not notified the person that the Minister has vacated or confirmed the assessment or has reassessed. A person can waive the Minister's reconsideration of the assessment at the objection stage so that the objecting person can proceed to the Tax Court quickly. Subsection 301(4) of the *ETA* provides that if a person objecting so requests, the Minister may confirm the assessment without reconsideration. Anyone considering an appeal to the Tax Court of Canada should carefully review ss. 301 to 312 of the *ETA*.

---

26 See *Szczerba v. Canada*, [2000] G.S.T.C. 79 (T.C.C.) (applicant missed deadline to file application for extension of time to file objection).

27 Subsection 225.1(2), *ITA*.

Section 12 of the *Tax Court of Canada Act*, R.S.C. 1985, c. T-2, as amended, provides that the Court has exclusive original jurisdiction to hear and determine references and appeals to the Court on matters arising under Part IX of the *ETA*. Generally, an appeal in the Tax Court may be heard under either an informal or general procedure of the *Tax Court of Canada Rules*. There are significant differences between the two forms of procedure, one of which being that only the general procedure rules make provision for pre-trial discovery. A comparison between the two is beyond the scope of this paper.

A person appealing under Part IX of the *ETA* may elect in the notice of appeal, or within ninety days from which the reply to the notice of appeal was served (with opportunity for an extension), to proceed under the *Tax Court of Canada Rules of Procedure Respecting the Excise Tax Act (Informal Procedure)*. No monetary limits are prescribed for such an election. If no election is made, the appeal will automatically proceed under the *Tax Court of Canada Rules (General Procedure)*.

The Tax Court of Canada may dispose of the appeal by dismissing it or by allowing it and ordering that the assessment be vacated or that the assessment be referred back to the Minister for reconsideration or reassessment. If satisfaction is not achieved, an appeal from the Tax Court's decision to the Federal Court of Appeal may be pursued.

C. HARMONIZED SALES TAX

On April 1, 1997 the provinces of Nova Scotia, New Brunswick and Newfoundland repealed their respective provincial retail sales tax statutes and agreed to participate in the harmonized sales tax ("HST") with the Government of Canada. The HST is enacted under the *ETA* and operates to impose the collection and payment of an eight percent HST in addition to the seven percent GST, resulting in a combined tax rate of fifteen percent in these provinces. The eight percent provincial HST component is in turn transferred by the Federal Government to the participating provinces. As a result, in the participating provinces, both federal and provincial consumption tax are imposed under the *ETA* with collection and enforcement being administered by the CRA.

Special rules have been established under Schedule X of the *ETA* to determine the place of supply of goods or services made either in or outside a participating province and thereby determining the application of either seven percent or fifteen percent tax.

To date, no other provinces have agreed to relinquish their respective retail sales tax systems in favour of the HST, although speculation as to a particular province potentially joining the harmonized regime often arises from time to time.

Most closely associated with the federal GST system is the Province of Quebec which adopted a value-added tax system in 1992 under the *Act Respecting Quebec Sales Tax* ("QST"). The scheme of this Quebec statute is substantially similar to the GST although subject to several material differences.[28] As well, at the time Quebec implemented the *Act Respecting Quebec Sales Tax*, it was also agreed between the federal and Quebec governments that Revenue Quebec would administer both the QST and the GST for persons resident in Quebec or companies headquartered there.

D. CONCLUSION

Although the GST was designed to be a universal tax applied at a single rate with an absolute minimum number of tax exemptions or preferences, it nevertheless remains loaded with complexities that will inevitably require the intervention of lawyers and the courts. As someone observed of the outset of the GST system "it's a simple tax but a complicated world." No doubt those words will ring true in the years to come.

---

28 For example, the QST does not allow input tax credits to be claimed in respect of most road vehicles, electricity, gas, steam and other combustibles, telecommunications or meals and entertainment.

Chapter Twenty-Three

Challenges for Indirect Tax in the New Economy in Canada: A Prediction of Tax Litigation Issues*

Jim Vincze and Craig Robertson

A. INTRODUCTION

It has been said that there is nothing new under the sun. Accordingly, the advent of the new economy, and specifically Internet commerce, probably does not create fundamentally new issues for Indirect Tax (commonly referred to as "consumption taxes" or "sales taxes"). Instead, the new economy only accentuates, in different and sometimes more acute ways, a number of the pressure points already existing in the Indirect Tax regimes.[1] For our purposes, the "new economy" includes e-commerce in particular,

* The authors wish to express their appreciation to Jason Riche and Maria Scullion for their significant effort in the research and writing of this chapter.

1 See for example: "Tax Litigation in the New Economy" by Arthur J. Cockfield in Chapter 20. See also: Organization for Economic Cooperation and Development, Consumption Tax TAG, "Implementation Issues for Taxation of Electronic Commerce," issued June 30, 2003 ("2003 Consumption Tax TAG Report"); Canada Revenue Agency, "Response by the Honourable John Manley to the General Recommendations in the April 30, 1998 Report of the Minister's Advisory Committee on Electronic Commerce" (September 1998).

but more broadly the whole range of business activity that is based on information technology, whether or not in an e-commerce environment.

Most readers will be familiar with the income tax applications and issues respecting the new economy, but may have less involvement and appreciation of the Indirect Tax world. Our primary objective, therefore, is to sensitize the reader to those differences, and the issues and concerns that arise.

There is a large body of material already written about tax, including Indirect Tax, from the economic, tax policy and tax administrative perspectives from the e-Commerce perspective.[2] As this book is directed primarily to a readership interested in tax litigation, rather than policy and administration, we will limit our scope to identifying issues that, in our view, are likely to become the subject of tax litigation either before the Tax Court of Canada for Goods and Services Tax ("GST")[3] or before the provincial courts for provincial sales tax although, in fact, to date, there is little Canadian case law directly on point. We intentionally restrain ourselves from entering into the tax policy debate as to what should be the legislative policy responses.

The issues we believe will likely give rise to litigation are:

- the authority of Canada, and the provinces, to oblige non-resident businesses to collect GST and provincial sales taxes. This will include a discussion on the concept of "carrying on business" and the legislative initiatives of Quebec, British Columbia and Manitoba to impose vendor obligations on businesses beyond the "carrying on business" test. In this context, considerations of constitutional capacity arise.
- characterization of supplies for GST alternatively as tangible personal property ("TPP," i.e., "goods") *versus* services *versus* intangible personal property ("IPP") *versus* telecommunication services, which can be very material to the application of the GST.

---

2 See for example: A. J. Cockfield, "The Law and Economics of Digital Taxation: Challenges to Traditional Tax Laws and Principles," in Centre for Innovation Law and Policy Working Paper (2002); A. J. Cockfield, "Canada's GST E-Commerce Policy (or How to Catch the Big Fish)," (2002) 3 Internet and E-Commerce Law In Canada 1 ("Cockfield, How to Catch the Big Fish"); J. Li, "Consumption Taxation of Electronic Commerce: Problems, Policy Implications and Proposals for Reform," (2003) 38 Canadian Business Law Journal 425 ("Li, Consumption Taxation").

3 Provided for under Part IX of the *Excise Tax Act*, R.S.C. 1985, c. E-15 ("*ETA*") including in particular Schedules V through X. Technically, there is no mention anywhere in the *ETA* to the "goods and services tax," which is only a popular acronym, perhaps adopted from the name given to the New Zealand tax, and intended perhaps as well to distinguish the Canadian tax from the "value-added taxes" ("VAT") that are common in Europe.

- parallel, but different concerns regarding the characterization of sales of electronic and digital products as TPP, taxable services or taxable telecommunication services for purposes of bringing them within the scope of provincial retail sales taxes ("RST").

The Department of Finance is responsible for developing GST policy and legislative amendments and has not proposed significant amendments to the GST legislation in response to the development of e-commerce.[4] The response of the Canada Revenue Agency[5] (the "CRA") that administers the *ETA*, has been to develop its administrative response based on the existing GST legislation, rather than on the basis of possible legislative alternatives. Accordingly, it can be said that *de facto* the formal responses have been the CRA's specific rulings as well as its publication of Technical Interpretation Bulletin B-090, GST/HST and Electronic Commerce ("TIB B-090").[6]

From an administrative policy perspective as well, CRA officials have indicated that they generally concur in the consensus expressed in the reports generated by the Organization for Economic Cooperation and Development ("OECD") relating to electronic commerce.[7] Specifically, the

---

4 The amendments to *ETA* ss. 278 and 278.1 relating to electronic bank remittances and electronic filing of returns, and to *ETA* s. 286 relating to retention of electronic records also can be seen as isolated legislative responses. By contrast, the European Union ("EU") members have enacted a legislative initiative to require foreign businesses, effective July 2003, to register for and collect VAT based on their provision of electronic sales to EU customers, regardless of their place of business. See: Council Directive 2002/38/EC, May 7, 2002, amending Directive 77/388/EEC, Official Journal L128, 15/15/2002 P. 0041-0044.

5 Formerly, the Canada Customs and Revenue Agency. On December 12, 2003, the Canada Customs and Revenue Agency became the "Canada Revenue Agency" although at the time of writing, an Act of Parliament had not yet legislated the change. In addition, effective December 12, 2003 the customs program, which was formerly part of the Canada Customs and Revenue Agency, became the new Canada Border Services Agency which is part of the Department of Public Safety and Emergency Preparedness.

6 The CRA preceded TIB B-090 with a discussion paper released November 2001: "GST/HST and Electronic Commerce — A discussion paper for public comment on the administration of the Goods and Services Tax/Harmonized Sales Tax in a electronic commerce environment" ("Discussion Paper"). TIB B-090 substantially confirmed the positions the CRA had set out in the Discussion Paper.

7 In particular, see: OECD, "Consumption Tax Aspects of Electronic Commerce," A Report from Working Party No. 9 on Consumption Taxes to the Committee on Fiscal Affairs February 2001; OECD, "Tax Treaty Characterization Issues Arising from E-Commerce," Report to Working Party No. 1 of the OECD Committee on Fiscal Affairs, February 1, 2001 ("2001 Tax Treaty Characterization Paper"); OECD, "Report by the Technology Technical Advisory Group," December 2000; and OECD, "Clarification on the Application of the Permanent Establishment Definition in E-Commerce: Changes to the Commentary on the Model Tax Convention on Article 5," December 22, 2000.

CRA has followed the position, agreed to at the OECD meeting in Ottawa in 1998, that a supply of digitized products would not be treated as a supply of goods.[8] This is to be expected given that the GST legislation expressly distinguishes between supplies of TPP, IPP and services.

The provinces have not participated directly at the broader policy level in the international consultations, and have not made general policy-based public announcements in response to e-commerce. Furthermore, with few exceptions that will be discussed further,[9] they have not proposed significant amendments to their provincial sales tax legislation to address the expansion of the new economy or e-Commerce specifically.

B. "INDIRECT TAXES" IN THE CANADIAN CONTEXT:[10] AN OVERVIEW

In one sense, "consumption taxes," or "Indirect Taxes," can be described as those taxes that are not taxes on income. In different jurisdictions, these will include sales taxes, various stamp taxes, excise and customs duties and levies and so forth. In this chapter, we will limit our discussion to the federal GST that is imposed uniformly across Canada, and to the RSTs that are imposed at the level of the provinces.

A starting truism is that consumption taxes differ from income taxes in that their purpose is to tax consumption — and that the consumer, not the supplier (who parallels the person generating the income), is the person on whom the tax is intended to fall. Furthermore, in theory, it should

---

8 OECD, "Electronic Commerce: A Discussion Paper on Taxation Issues," (September 17, 1998) ("1998 Ottawa Paper"). Also, see OECD web site at www.oecd.org/daf/fa/e_com/e_com.htm.

9 See the discussion below of British Columbia's and Manitoba's amendments to impose retail sales tax ("RST") registration and collection obligations on out-of-province businesses regardless of whether they carry on business in those provinces. Amendments to expand the RST base to include computer programs effectively constitutes a legislative response to the evolution of the electronic-based economy. As will be discussed later, these initiatives were not intended as responses to the development of e-commerce, but rather solely to the growth of importance of the software sector.

10 For a general, but more detailed, review of the commodity tax administrative environment in Canada, see: Li, Consumption Taxation, above note 2; J. Vincze & C. Robertson, " GST and PST in the Digital Environment — The Canadian Commodity Tax Perspective," (2001) 5:4 Sales and Use Tax 287; J. Vincze & C. Robertson, "The Canadian Commodity Tax Perspective — Part II," (2001) 6:2 Sales and Use Tax 315; and J. Vincze & C. Robertson, "Revised E-Commerce — The Canadian Commodity Tax Perspective — A Further Update," (2003) 7:1 Sales and Use Tax 354.

only be consumption in Canada or in the province that is taxed in Canada or the province respectively.[11]

Although not entirely unique, the Canadian situation is different from most other countries, notably most European Union countries and the United States, in that there exist separate, concurrent and structurally different sales tax regimes at the federal and the provincial levels, creating a veritable matrix through which businesses have to work, and that require different and sometimes contrasting interpretational methods. For example, the key concept for GST is the "supply," whereas for RST, generally, the key concept is the "sale."[12] As a result, "supply analysis" and characterization of products as services, IPP or TPP, whether there is a "single supply" of multiple components that must be characterized as a service, IPP or TPP, or characterized as separate supplies and each component then separately characterized, is key to GST interpretation.[13] It has been far less accepted in the RST context where the tendency often continues to be to look at discrete components of a product to determine whether RST

---

11 See for example: 1998 Ottawa Paper, above note 8; and 2003 Consumption Tax TAG Report, above note 1.

12 Under *ETA* s. 165, GST applies to "supplies" made in Canada. The term "supply" is defined broadly in ss. 123(1) as follows:

> "supply" means, subject to sections 133 and 134, the provision of property or a service in any manner, including sale, transfer, barter, exchange, licence, rental, lease, gift or disposition;

By contrast, each of the provincial RST Acts impose RST on a "sale" within the province. See for example the combination of the charging section for Ontario RST in s. 2(1) of the *Retail Sales Tax Act*, R.S.O. 1990, c. R.31 (the "Ontario Act") with the definitions of "purchaser" and "sale" in s. 1(1) of that legislation. In particular:

> "sale" is defined, in part as follows:
> (a) any transfer of title or possession, exchange, barter, lease or rental, conditional or otherwise, including a sale on credit or where the price is payable by instalments, or any other contract whereby at a price or other consideration a person delivers to another person tangible personal property[.]

See also for example the definition of "sale" in British Columbia's *Social Service Tax Act*, R.S.B.C. 1996, c. 431, s. 1 (the "BC Act").

13 A discussion of GST "supply analysis" is beyond the scope of this chapter. For an excellent discussion, see, for example: M. Matthews, "Single versus Multiple Supplies," (1999) Commodity Tax Symposium Papers (CICA's Virtual Professional Library). See also the CRA's Policy Statements P-077R2, Single and Multiple Supplies and P-159R1, Meaning of the Phrase "Reasonably Regarded as Incidental" [related to *ETA* s. 138, "incidental supplies"] and P-160 — "Meaning of the Phrase "Where A Particular Property or Service is Supplied Together With any Other Property or Service" [relating to s. 138 — "incidental supplies"].

applies, and moreover apply RST even if an RST-taxable component is only secondary in importance or value.[14]

1) The Federal GST

The GST that applies at the federal level is a multi-stage, Value-Added Tax ("VAT") style tax, the rules for which will generally be familiar to persons having experience with the VATs of European Union countries or the Goods and Services Tax of New Zealand and Australia.

The GST applies broadly at the uniform rate of 7 percent to most supplies of TPP and real property, as well as to IPP and to services made in Canada. Certain supplies of property and services are "exempt" from GST, and other classes are "zero-rated" — i.e., taxable at the rate of zero percent. Businesses that make GST-taxable supplies are entitled to claim "input tax credits" ("ITCs") to recover the GST that they are required to pay on inputs acquired to make GST-taxable supplies. Businesses cannot, however, claim ITCs to the extent of inputs that do not relate to making GST-taxable supplies, such as GST-exempt supplies of financial services, educational or health care services. The GST is a real cost to these businesses.

Registrant suppliers are required to collect the GST. GST is also payable at Customs on the importation of most goods, and individuals and businesses that do not qualify for full ITCs are technically required to self-assess on the importation of certain services and IP such as downloaded software or digitized entertainment products.

---

14 See later section on "characterization" of software and the "bundling" rules for software.

The contrast between GST and RST is frequently revealed in the context of online information products, which often contain components of software that the provider allows the subscriber to download and use to allow access to the database and execute manipulation of the data to achieve the objectives of the product — say, online data search. In the GST world, the question would usually be whether the software is merely a facilitating component rather than the essence of what the subscriber desires to acquire. By contrast, RST administrators have tended, although less so recently, to take the position that the software component should be identified and taxed, regardless of its ancillary nature. In fact, "bundling" rules may render the entire product taxable, unless the software component represents less than a specified value of the package, or the value of the components is separately identified and invoiced. Like all generalizations, however, there are exceptions to the foregoing. See for example: Ontario's Guide 651 — Internet Related Services, where Ontario agrees that access to an online encyclopedia is a right to access to information, and not a taxable computer service. The matter can, however, be different if there is an identifiable charge for the software components.

In the three "harmonized provinces,"[15] the Harmonized Sales Tax ("HST") applies at the rate of 15 percent, representing the seven percent federal component and a further eight percent provincial component, replacing the RST that formerly applied in those provinces. The HST is an extension of the GST provided under the *ETA*, and is administered by the CRA under the *ETA*. The federal government then makes a transfer of the provincial component to the Harmonized provinces according to a revenue sharing formula established outside the *ETA*.

Two fundamental conceptual and technical underpinnings of the GST regime that deserve being highlighted because they will emerge repeatedly throughout this chapter are:

- "supply analysis"; and
- the "place of supply" rules.

As already noted,[16] determining the characterization of a supply, i.e., what is being supplied, is always the essential first step to determining how the GST applies to a specific transaction. For GST purposes, the supply can be one of TPP, IP, real property or services (including telecommunication services as a specific subset).

Although all supplies are, generally, subject to tax (subject to specific certain exemptions such as for "financial services"), the characterization of the supply as a service, real property, TPP or IPP will have very important implications for the application of the "zero-rating" rules, and for the place of supply rules.[17] These place of supply rules differ depending on the characterization of the supply as TPP, for which the place of supply will generally be the place of delivery; IPP for which the place of supply is determined by where the IPP may be used; and services, for which the place of supply will generally be where the service is actually performed.

Moreover, one significant way in which the Canadian GST legislation contrasts with both income tax legislation and the VAT legislation of other jurisdictions, notably Europe, is the treatment of supplies of IPP as being

---

15 New Brunswick, Newfoundland and Labrador, and Nova Scotia. The term "Harmonized Sales Tax" ("HST"), like the "GST," is not officially sanctioned in Part IX of the *ETA*. Rather, the HST is merely the additional tax raised under the *ETA* attributable to supplies in or into, or consumption within, the Harmonized Provinces.

16 Above note 13.

17 Primarily in *ETA* ss. 142 and 143, and s. 143.1 for telecommunication services. Elaborate HST place-of-supply rules for HST are set out in Schedule IX. Determining the characterization of a supply may also be relevant in order to ascertain the manner in which tax is collected as well as determining the timing of liability for tax. See TIB B-090.

a supply of property rather than as a supply of services (as is the case in many VAT jurisdictions).

2) The Provincial Sales Tax Regimes

Quebec imposes the Quebec Sales Tax ("QST"),[18] which parallels in most regards the mechanics of the GST and the HST. Accordingly, the difficulties and complexities that arise in applying the "place-of-supply" rules for HST, apply also to the QST. The QST is administered by the Ministère du Revenu du Québec. QST applies at a nominal rate of 7.5 percent, but on the consideration for a supply after application of the GST, creating an effective QST rate of 8.025 percent.

The other five provinces of Canada[19] (excluding Alberta), impose RST that applies to sales of goods (i.e., TPP), and a limited number of services, notably telecommunication services. Although IPP does not generally come within the scope of the RST, these provinces, in response to the development of the information-based economy, have moved to bring a broad range of software and software-related services within the scope of their RST regime. As we will see, this creates difficulties in describing the nature of the IPP and "new economy services" that should be swept into the range of those taxes. Given the high value of those new products — notably software solutions and other information products — the stakes can be high, with businesses seeking to avoid the additional RST burden, and sales tax authorities seeking to bring the potential new revenue sources into the RST net. This will be discussed in a later section.

Unlike the GST, all purchasers — businesses and individual consumers — bear the economic burden of the RST, as the RST regimes do not have a mechanism that allows recovery of the tax on business inputs such as exists under the ITC mechanism in VAT-style taxes. Accordingly, inherent in the RST regimes is an element of multiple incidence of tax — or "tax on tax" as suppliers must build the RST into their cost base and then charge RST on the final price if they produce RST-taxable goods or servic-

---

18 Title I of *An Act Respecting the Québec Sales Tax*, R.S.Q. c. T-0.1 (the "Quebec Act"). See also *An Act Respecting the Ministère du Revenu*, R.S.Q. 1977, c. M-31.

19 British Columbia under the BC Act (7.5%); Saskatchewan (7% effective April 1, 2004) under *The Provincial Sales Tax Act*, 2000, c. P-34.1 (the "Saskatchewan Act"); Manitoba (7%) under *The Retail Sales Tax Act*, R.S.M. 1987, c. R130 (the "Manitoba Act"); Ontario under the Ontario Act (8%); and Prince Edward Island (10% on the GST-included price) under the Revenue Tax Act, 1988, R.S.P.E.I. 1988, c. R-14 (the "PEI Act"). The aforementioned are the generally applicable RST rates: different rates apply to specific taxable property or services in some cases.

es. Specific conditional and unconditional exemptions do exist that are either product-specific or purchaser-specific: for example, equipment and materials for use by a manufacturer to produce TPP is conditionally exempt, which reduces the multiple incidence of RST that would otherwise occur where the final product would also be RST-taxable.

Vendors that carry on business in a province, and that have a regular and significant presence there, will be required to obtain a vendor licence or permit, and to collect and remit RST on their taxable sales.

Where the vendor fails to collect, however, or where a consumer brings goods into a province, the purchaser is also under a legal obligation to self-assess provincial RST, and QST in some cases. The provinces that impose RST place a high priority in their audit programs to monitoring businesses' self-assessment of RST.

The provinces' jurisdiction to impose sales tax and to enforce their sales tax legislation is constitutionally restricted within their provincial borders. For this reason, they have limited ability to deal with the "virtual" and electronic nature of e-commerce transactions that may involve participants that are both inside and outside the province.

3) Taxation Of Imported Goods And Services

GST applies on all GST-taxable goods declared at Canada Customs on their release from Customs into Canada, with the exception of limited classes of "non-taxable importations" defined under Schedule VII to the *ETA*.

Canada Customs does not collect GST on importations of services and IPP. Instead, individuals and businesses that are not entitled to claim full ITCs to recover GST on their inputs purchased in Canada are required to self-assess the GST/HST on "imported taxable supplies" of services and IPP.

The Federal Government has entered into agreements with all of the provinces that impose RST or QST[20] to collect the provincial tax on "consumer goods," which generally are goods imported by individuals and not for use in business.

Accordingly, the mechanisms for collection of tax on importation will generally ensure that individual Canadian consumers will be required to pay both GST and QST or RST on imported goods, other than on small-value importations. As Canada Customs does not collect tax on business inputs, or on IPP (including software), however, the provinces are required

20 The agreements do not apply to Alberta which does not impose a retail sales tax, or to Prince Edward Island which does not have a border touching on a foreign country.

to rely on the self-assessment requirements in their legislation for these imports, which are less effective in the case of individuals.

The requirement, therefore, applies to businesses such as financial institutions, e.g., banks who make GST-exempt supplies of "financial services," but it also applies to individuals who download electronic products from the Internet. The CRA is relatively confident about its ability to enforce businesses' obligation to self-assess through its established audit process; but far less so in the case of individuals, who are both ignorant of, but also largely indifferent toward, any obligation to self- assess GST and far too numerous for the CRA to have an effective enforcement process.

4) The Canadian Constitutional Framework

A fact that distinguishes the Canadian sales tax reality from the income tax reality is the absence of international treaties that apply to sales taxes[21] and there are no International Competent Authority arrangements to which Canada is a party. Accordingly, when there is over-reaching of the GST according to its technical terms, or where the Canadian GST and VAT of another jurisdiction (or the sales and use tax of a U.S. state) overlap, there is no treaty that resolves this. Under the *Constitution Act, 1867*,[22] the federal Parliament has competence, under clause 91(3), with respect to

> [T]he raising of Money by any Mode or System of Taxation.

In addition, there does not appear to be any constitutional restriction or international law restriction on Canada's legal right to impose its GST as broadly as the Parliament of Canada wishes.[23] Accordingly, there is no restriction based on proportionality or degree of consumption in Canada. It is doubtful, of course, that the Fathers of Confederation, or the British Parliament in 1867, would have understood the breadth of this tax reach, given the nature of the economy at that time, and how it has expanded to our time.

By contrast, as will be discussed later, there may be relevant constitutional restrictions on the provincial sales tax authorities whose competence under clause 92(2) is with respect to

---

21 Other than the inclusion of provisions under the income tax treaties requiring Canada to provide administrative assistance and to share tax information that now includes information gathered in the course of administration of the GST. These, of course, do not bind the provinces, nor give them rights to obtain information from jurisdictions outside Canada.

22 (U.K.), 30 & 31 Vict., c. 3, reprinted in R.S.C. 1985, App. II, No. 5.

23 J. Li, *International Taxation in the Age of Electronic Commerce: a Comparative Study* (Toronto: Canadian Tax Foundation, 2003) at 5.

Direct Taxation within the Province in order to the raising of a Revenue for Provincial Purposes.[24]

5) Broad-based Indirect Tax Issues Arising in the New Economy Business Environment

The sales tax authorities have traditionally relied on the supplier or vendor to collect the tax as agent for the government. As already noted, the alternative self-assessment mechanisms generally are viewed as being successful only in business-to-business (commonly referred to as "B2B") transactions, but not effective in business-to-consumer (commonly referred to as "B2C") transactions.

Where a supplier is required to charge GST or RST, the traditional tax point is the transaction viewed from the perspective of the supplier or vendor — the moment when the "supply" (for GST) or the "sale" (for RST) takes place.[25] Moreover, because the vendor/supplier as tax collector can have only limited knowledge of its customer, and particularly as to where and how the customer will use or consume the product or service, there is little attempt to apportion GST or provincial taxes according to actual consumption or use, at least not at the time of the transaction when the supplier/vendor must decide whether or not to collection the tax. Rather, the decision is based generally on place of supply rules, discussed later.

This leads to some interesting GST challenges that become particularly accentuated in the new economy, and in particular:

- when, and how, to enforce the obligation to collect on the supplier/vendor; and
- how to define what has been "consumed" and where that consumption occurred.

The advent and expansion of the new economy, and e-commerce in particular, has created the same issues for sales tax administrators in Canada as in other countries. These include:

- the removal of traditional local intermediaries on whom they can impose the obligation to collect the tax from purchasers ("disintermediation").

---

24 *Atlantic Smoke Shops Ltd. v. Conlon*, [1943] A.C. 536 (P.C.), although clearly establishing that a provincial retail sales tax can be "Direct Taxation within the Province" for purposes of s. 92(2), also points to the territorial limitation on the provinces' taxing competence.

25 See the contrast between the "supply" for GST, and the "sale" for RST discussed earlier.

To illustrate, in the electronic era of rapid and effective telecommunications, a business can provide a wide range of products without having a physical presence at all in Canada. At the time of writing, many Canadian businesses outsource large components of computer software writing and computer software support services to service providers who are located in East Asia and Eastern Europe: the support technician or programmer no longer needs to be located anywhere near the client in the geographic sense. The Canadian GST, on the other hand, relies on the concept of "carrying on business" as the primary factor that triggers the obligation on that service provider to be registered for and collect the GST.

In the current environment of increased outsourcing for IPP services, this is having greater significance. This may well give rise to tax leakage and competitive equity issues in the near future that the Department of Finance will no longer be able to ignore.[26]

- difficulties in determining the correct characterization of transactions to lead to the appropriate taxation of the transaction.

  The development of electronics and telecommunications has led to the development of new products that have transformed what in the past might have been viewed as TPP or services. For example, information research or data processing might in the past have been viewed as services, but may now have become supplies of IPP, such as licenses of software or access to information databases, for example, an online research library.[27] The CRA, in TIB B-090, has stated its view that to be a service there usually would have to be a human involvement in the delivery of the product. In the electronic environment, this often is not the case, and instead the customer has a license to access the database, and hence such products should be viewed as IPP. As earlier noted, the character-

---

26 As noted, businesses that make GST-taxable supplies can claim ITCs to recover GST they pay, so that there is ultimately no GST burden. Nevertheless, the Department of Finance and the CRA have always insisted on the importance of staged collection of GST at each transaction level through the economy, both for the cash flow benefit to the government, and for purposes of GST competitive equity so as not to disadvantage Canadian businesses vis-à-vis foreign-based businesses in procurements by Canadian-based businesses. See for example: Cockfield, How to Catch the Big Fish, above note 2.

27 In the Discussion Paper that preceded TIB B-090, the CRA reviewed the 28 categories of typical e-Commerce transactions identified and discussed in the 2001 Tax Treaty Characterization Paper, note 7 above. Notably, the CRA insisted on the GST characterization of certain categories (e.g., electronic ordering and downloading of digital products; and web subscriptions for downloading digital products) as being in the nature of IPP, not services, whereas the OECD characterized the categories as giving rise to business income versus income from property.

ization as IPP rather than services leads to different and more stringent place-of-supply and zero-rating rules: the supply of IPP by a Canadian supplier to a non-resident will be deemed "made in Canada" unless the IPP cannot be used in Canada at all. Even if supplied to a non-resident, it will only be zero-rated if the IPP can be classified as "intellectual property" — a narrow subset of IPP,[28] whereas a broader range of zero-rating opportunities would likely exist if the supply were a "service."

Although the distinction that the CRA draws between "services" and IPP is clearly supported in some degree by the GST legislation, the CRA's enthusiasm in TIB B-090 has created problems for Canadian businesses attempting to market to non-residents in the electronic environment, and creates traps for the unwary, which may well eventually lead to contentious GST assessments.

Furthermore, like the offshore software support services example, the geographical location of these products is no longer geographically constrained, as will be seen in the discussion immediately following;

- difficulties in determining whether suppliers have a "presence" in Canada to be required to be registered for and to collect the tax. See the later discussion of "carrying on business"; and
- apportionment of consumption to Canada or the province, when products such as IPP or services can and often are applied to the purchaser's operation in multiple locations.

To illustrate, international marketing rights relating to the sale of tennis shoes of a particular brand are frequently defined to cover a region: for example, "the Americas," including Canada. Assume that a Mexican business wishes to purchase a Canadian franchise holder's distribution rights in order to develop a market in Central America, because the brand has not been successful in Canada and the Canadian franchise holder is abandoning the brand in Canada.

As already noted, the supply of IPP is deemed made in Canada if it *may* be used in whole *or in part* in Canada. It will only be deemed not a

28 Section 10 of Part V, Schedule VI zero-rates only a subset of intangibles, being "intellectual property" — generally, trademarks, copyright, patents, etc. The Department of Finance has indicated its intention to review, and presumably expand, the scope of section 10. In the meantime, however, the CRA has consistently stated it will not give a broader interpretation of the scope of section 10. See for example question no. 24 at the Annual Meeting of the CRA and the Canadian Bar Association (National Sales and Excise Tax Section, Sales Tax Committee) February 26, 2004.

supply in Canada, and therefore made outside Canada, if the IPP may not be used in Canada.[29]

In the scenario described, the franchise rights may be used in Canada as Canada is part of the territorial range. The express intention of the Mexican assignee not to market in Canada is not relevant — rather, only the theoretical legal right to do so is relevant in order to bring into play the GST place of supply rule. Furthermore, it is an all-or-nothing result: either the supply is made in Canada, or it is made outside Canada. When a Canadian vendor who is registered for GST makes a GST-taxable supply that is made within Canada and that is not zero-rated, the supplier must collect GST.[30] There is no degree of apportionment based on actual connection with or consumption in Canada.

C. THE TEST OF "CARRYING ON BUSINESS"

The scope of the "carrying on business"[31] test is one of the most controversial Canadian issues in the context of the new economy because, broadly speaking, it is the starting point to determine a business' liability to collect and remit the GST, QST and RST, although we will see how Quebec, British Columbia and Manitoba have attempted to expand beyond it.

By contrast, the concept of "permanent establishment" which receives so much attention for income tax purposes, is in the authors' view of only secondary importance for Indirect Tax purposes and will not be discussed in detail.[32]

---

29 *ETA* subparas. 142(1)(c)(i) and 142(2)(c)(i).

30 *ETA* ss. 165(1) and 221(1). A number of supplies to non-residents that would otherwise be GST-taxable supplies may be "zero-rated" under Part V of Schedule VI to the *ETA*. The provisions for zero-rating IPP, however, are quite limited compared to the more generous zero-rating rules applicable to services. TIB B-090 contains a useful discussion generally of the application of the zero-rating rules in the e-commerce environment.

31 A selection of articles on the "carrying on business" test includes: C. M. McDougall, S. E. Jack & D. B. Nixon, "Income Tax Fundamentals in a Global Economy: Old Rules and the New Reality," in *Report of Proceedings of Fifty-Third Tax Conference, 2001 Tax Conference* 27 ("McDougall"); J. Li, "Rethinking Canada's Source Rules in the Age of Electronic Commerce: Part 2," (1999) 47:6 Canadian Tax Journal 1411; J. Li, "Rethinking Canada's Source Rules in the Age of Electronic Commerce," (1999) 47:5 Canadian Tax Journal 1077; C. A. Kryes, "Carrying on Business in Canadian," (1995) 43:5 Canadian Tax Journal 1629; J. Durnford, "The Distinction Between Income from Business and Income from Property, and the Concept of Carrying on Business," (1991) 39:5 Canadian Tax Journal 1131 ("Durnford"); H.H. Stikeman, "Carrying on Business in Canada in Dominion Income Tax Law," (1942) XX Canadian Bar Review 77.

32 See the definition of "permanent establishment" in *ETA* ss. 123(1) for GST purposes. The extended definition of "permanent establishment" in Canada's income tax treaties

ETA ss. 240(1) requires every non-resident person who carries on business in Canada, other than a small supplier,[33] to register for GST/HST purposes if the non-resident person makes a taxable supply in Canada under the place of supply rules referred to earlier. An over-ride rule in *ETA* ss. 143(1) deems a non-resident not to make supplies of TPP, IPP, or services in Canada if it does not carry on business in Canada.[34]

Avoiding the obligation to register for and collect GST is a significant advantage for a foreign-based business, both in the reduction of administrative burden and systems development costs, as well as in pricing relative to Canadian-based businesses, especially in B2C transactions.

In contrast with the body of case law generated for income tax as discussed hereinafter, remarkably little case law has yet arisen for GST or for provincial sales taxes.[35] It is foreseeable, however, that the CRA (and the provinces) will become more assertive in pursuing offshore businesses to force them to be registered and collect the tax, as tax leakage and tax equity concerns become more acute.

---

does not apply for GST.

Under *ETA* ss. 132(1), a non-resident is deemed to be a resident in Canada to the extent of activities carried on through a permanent establishment in Canada. The non-resident, however, will usually have crossed the threshold of "carrying on business" in Canada before crossing the threshold of having a permanent establishment. Nevertheless, having a permanent establishment is not entirely insignificant, and has consequences in particular as to the zero-rated status of supplies made by Canadian suppliers to a foreign-based business.

33 Under *ETA* s. 148, a small supplier, in general terms, is a person whose GST-taxable supplies, worldwide, do not exceed $30,000. For purposes of the threshold, the supplies of associated persons must also be included.

34 *ETA* s. 143.1 and ss. 240(4) contain specific rules to require non-resident publishers to register for GST if they solicit subscriptions for sales of magazines and other "prescribed property" to be sent by mail or courier to an address in Canada. See the later discussion of "solicitation." Customs enforces this obligation in the case of shipments by courier, and Canada Post enforces the obligation in the case of shipment by mail, in either case by delaying the delivery and requiring the subscriber to pay the GST if the publisher has not registered and collected the GST.

35 In the GST situation, prior to the onset of B2C e-commerce, perhaps this was explicable because the CRA was less concerned about forcing businesses to register for GST given that in the B2B context many Canadian-based businesses would claim ITCs and recover the tax; and given the mechanisms for enforcing self-assessment where the business is not entitled to ITCs. In fact, there was a positive benefit to the CRA in non-residents not registering, in terms of reducing the CRA's administrative load of processing non-resident accounts, and in terms of ITCs that were not paid to the non-resident businesses on their GST expenses.

There is no definition of "carrying on business" in the *ETA*, although "business" is defined.[36]

In TIB B-090, the CRA changed its long-standing policy[37] on the criteria it will use to determine whether a person is carrying on business in Canada, and has thereby arguably diverged from the position still taken for income tax purposes.

As the CRA has pointedly noted, the definition for GST expressly excludes a requirement of expectation of profit. It is an open issue the extent to which this reduces the test for carrying on business for GST from what it might be in the income tax context. See in particular the discussion below on solicitation.

The CRA's previous position was that two traditional factors predominated: where the contract is made and the place where the operations from which profits arise take place. Thereafter, consideration would be given to a number of secondary factors which, in theory, were to be accorded less weight. These included the place where delivery of the goods is made, the place where payment is made, the place where the goods in question are manufactured, and the place where bank accounts are maintained. In summary, it was the CRA's position that a non-resident had to have a "significant presence in Canada" in order to be carrying on business in Canada.

The new approach in TIB B-090 emphasizes that a long list of factors should be considered depending upon the nature of the business activity under review, and the particular facts and circumstances of that case. The complete list of factors set out in TIB B-090 is:

- the place where agents or employees of the non-resident are located;
- the place of delivery;
- the place of payment;
- the place where the non-resident makes purchases;
- the place from which transactions are solicited;
- the location of an inventory of goods;

---

36 In *ETA* ss. 123(1), "business" is defined as follows:

> "business" includes a profession, calling, trade, manufacture or undertaking of any kind whatever, whether the activity or undertaking is engaged in for profit, and any activity engaged in on a regular or continuous basis that involves the supply of property by way of lease, licence or similar arrangement, but does not include an office or employment[.]

37 Stated in Policy Statement P-051R- Carrying on Business in Canada and in GST/HST Memorandum 2.5 — Non-Resident Registration, para. 15 et seq. In P-051R, the Agency had already noted the exclusion of the expectation of profit from the definition. [Draft revised policy statemnt P-051RX was released for comment September 8, 2004–ed.]

- the place where the business contracts are made;
- the location of a bank account for the non-resident;
- the place where the non-resident's name and business are listed in a directory;
- the location of a branch or office of the non-resident;
- the place where the contracted service is performed; and
- the place of manufacture or production of the non-resident's product.

The CRA still takes the position that a "significant presence in Canada" is required, but now the facts and circumstances of each case will determine the weight given to each factor; and none of the factors, including place of contract, is *prima facie* to receive priority. "Place of operations" is not even mentioned. The CRA expressly states that the above list is not exhaustive or closed, and that the relative importance of a factor may change as business evolves.

The CRA has announced that it is currently revising Policy Statement P-051R and Memorandum 2.5 in light of its position stated in TIB P-090, so that the factors test will also apply to businesses not engaged in e-commerce.

The CRA's change in position has been controversial. It arguably diverges from and ignores the previous common law, and is too burdensome and subjective to apply. For some, the "place of contract" criterion presented a useful "bright line" that could be objectively determined with some clarity,[38] and potentially adjusted to provide a "safe harbour" to obtain

---

38 See the recent decision of the Canadian International Tribunal in *AAi FosterGrant of Canada Co.v. The Commissioner of the Canada Customs and Revenue Agency*, [2003] 4550 E.T.C. (C.I.T.T.) where the tribunal appears to have applied a "factors" type approach in holding that FosterGrant Canada *was not* carrying on business in Canada, although the company was incorporated under the laws of Nova Scotia and sold goods to consumers and retailers in Canada. For commentary on this case see for example, C. B. Todgham Cherniak, "I Need New Glasses: I Cannot Believe My Eyes!," (2003) XVII GST & Commodity Tax 51. [Reversed F.C.A. July 14, 2004, based on the presence of significant indicators of "carrying on business."]

Additionally, a "factors" type approach could be used to justify an equitable result which may not otherwise be supportable. In that regard, see Durnford's commentary, (note 31 above at 1198–1202), on *Gurd's Products Co. v. R.*, [1985] 2 C.T.C. 85 (F.C.A.) [*Gurd's Products*] concerning the application of such an approach where Urie J. found the taxpayer's behaviour offensive.

See also for example, the decision of the Exchequer Court of Canada in *United Geophysical v. Minister of National Revenue*, [1961] C.T.C. 134 [*United Geophysical*] which suggests that a non-resident provider of intellectual property may be considered to be carrying on business in Canada by virtue of the provision of services in Canada, even where the services in question are ancillary to the provision of the intellectual property and the provision of services is not a significant profit centre for the non-resident. See: N. H. Armstrong, "Exploring the Unique Features of Intellectual Property," in *R & D Credits Today, Innovation Tomorrow, 1999 Corporate Tax Management Tax Conference* 9.

the desired outcome — usually to exclude a foreign-based business from the necessity of registering for and collecting GST.

In our view, however, an examination of the case law supports the CRA's position, if not from a policy or tax-equity perspective, at least from an interpretational perspective.[39]

1) Place where Contract is Concluded

Canadian courts have frequently cited the classic English case where Lord Watson states:

> . . . neither the British nor the foreign merchant can . . . be said to exercise his trade beyond the limits of his own country, so long as all contracts for the sale of their goods and all deliveries to the purchaser are made within these limits.[40]

On that line of authority, Canadian courts have stated that absent evidence to the contrary, the place where an entity's contracts are made determines the place where it carries on business.[41]

Application of the place of contract in the e-commerce environment, however, especially in B2C transactions, leads to surprising results and excessively weights the conclusion toward Canada being the place of contract.

Different rules of offer and acceptance apply depending on whether one applies the classic postal rule or the rules for instantaneous communication. Under the base common law rule for offer and acceptance, where two persons concluded a contract face-to-face, the contract was concluded when the offeror heard the offeree communicate acceptance of the offeror's offer. The postal rule evolved as the first exception to the original rule in response to the development of contractual negotiations between persons who were not face-to-face, and determined that the contract is concluded where the offeree mails the acceptance. The case law indicates that electronically concluded contracts, which are particularly common in the web-based environment, should be treated as a return to the original rule for instantaneous communications, and therefore the contract is made

---

39 We will not participate in the policy debate alluded to by Professor Cockfield who notes some of the competitive issues as well as international relations issues that argue for a legislative solution: see his chapter in this book and Cockfield, How to Catch the Big Fish, above note 2. See also the EU's response, above note 4.

40 *Grainger and Son v. Gough*, [1896] A.C. 325 (H.L.) [*Grainger*].

41 See for example: *Geigy (Canada) Ltd. v. Commissioner, Social Services Tax*, [1969] C.T.C. 79 (B.C.S.C.) [*Geigy*].

when the offeror receives the offeree's acceptance.[42] For parties interested in using the "place of contract" rule as a "safe harbour," thereby keeping a foreign-based supplier outside the scope of Canadian sales tax obligations, it becomes a matter of adjusting the terms of the electronically transmitted contract to ensure that the offshore business is the "offeror" and that the Canadian customer is the offeree. It is clear that this would not always please the CRA, if the result was that GST was not being collected on supplies to consumers in Canada.

On the other hand, a major concern expressed by the industry representatives on the Minister's Technical Advisory Committee on the issue of "carrying on business" was that application of the instantaneous communication rule would deem most web-based suppliers to be carrying on business in Canada, because the most common form of web-based B2C contract resulted in the contract being concluded on the computer of the consumer. It is not always a simple matter to determine whether something constitutes an "offer," which is specific enough to be accepted to create a binding contract, versus a mere "invitation to treat."[43] In the absence of express terms, it is likely, however, that the web-based provider's setting out terms of its products, price and so forth on its website, constitutes an invitation to treat, not an offer to sell. Therefore, when the consumer located in Canada transmits an order over the net, this constitutes an "offer to purchase," which the offshore provider will receive at its offshore server's location. The offshore provider will process and presumably accept the order and send a confirmation back to the customer's terminal located in Canada. As a result, the "place of contract" is usually in Canada.

2) Place of Operations from Which Profit Arise

The Saskatchewan Kings Bench applied the place of operations test as early as 1937 in the *Proctor & Gamble*[44] case. More recently, the test has been

42 The courts have held that a fax is similar to a telex, both of which are simultaneous modes of communication, and that a contract is concluded by a fax communication when the offeror receives the acceptance, not when the acceptance is sent. For a general discussion on acceptance see: G.H.L. Fridman, *The Law of Contract in Canada*, 4th ed. (Toronto: Carswell, 1999) ("Fridman"). For a succinct summary of the law in regards to the different modes of acceptance see McDougall, above note 31.

43 See for example: *Carlill v. Carbolic Smoke Ball Company*, [1892] 2 Q.B. 484, aff'd [1893] 1 Q.B. 256 (C.A.).

44 *Proctor & Gamble Co., Re*, [1937] 3 W.W.R. 680 (Sask. K.B.) [*Proctor & Gamble*]. See also: *Cutlers Guild Ltd. v. R.*, [1981] C.T.C. 115 (F.C.T.D.) [*Cutlers Guild*], where Dubé J. said at para 14:

applied by the Federal Court of Appeal in *London Life Insurance Co. v. Canada*.[45] The test requires that a combination of factors (such as the purchase of materials, the manufacture or production of goods, the location of inventory, the solicitation of orders, delivery and payment) be considered to determine the place of business.[46]

In *London Life*, the court examined whether the company was carrying on business outside Canada in a particular year when it had expanded its insurance operations to Bermuda. Such a finding would enable the company to make a beneficial election under the *Income Tax Act*. Both the Federal Court Trial Division and the Federal Court of Appeal considered that, despite the fact that the insurance contracts had to be concluded in Canada, a number of important functions had to be carried out in Bermuda. Stone, J.A., for the Federal Court of Appeal, stated:

> If the respondent's activities in Bermuda had consisted only of soliciting orders there for acceptance in Canada it might be arguable on the basis of certain utterances in *Grainger* . . . that, to use the phraseology of Lord Herschell, what was done in Bermuda was only "ancillary" to the carrying on of a business in Canada . . . . [I]t remains that other acts of overriding importance and significance had to be done and could only be done in Bermuda. The initial solicitation of business was but one of these.[47]

Some commentators view *London Life* as signaling a shift in judicial thinking that is more all-encompassing[48] and may mean that a taxpayer will be found to be carrying on business in the place where important activities, such as solicitation, in connection with the making of contracts occur, whether or not that is the place of contract.

> Another test emanating from the jurisprudence is "Where do the operations take place from which the profits arise? Soliciting orders in one country may only be ancillary to the exercise of a trade in another country. *F.L. Smidth & Co. v. F. Greenwood* (1922) . . . Certain authorities establish that activities and operations other than contracts for sale constitute the carrying on of a business, specially where these respective activities and operations produce or earn income. While income may be realized through sales, it may not arise entirely from that one activity or operation . . .

See also: *GLS Leasco Inc. v. Minister of National Revenue*, [1986] 2 C.T.C. 2034 (T.C.C.) [*GLS Leasco*]; *Gurd's Products*, above note 38; and *United Geophysical*, above note 38.

In the British context, see for example *F.L. Smidth & Co. v. F. Greenwood* (1922), 8 T.C. 193 (H.L.).

45 [1990] 1 C.T.C. 43 (F.C.A.).

46 *Gurd's Products*, above note 38 and Durnford, above note 31, at 1198–1202.

47 Above note 45, at para 13.

48 McDougall at 27:17-27:18, above note 31 and Durnford at 1196, above note 31.

Has the CRA made a radical change in approach? We would argue no. Although the CRA no longer refers to the "place of operations" test, the operational factors that it lists probably amount to applying the test itself. Furthermore, while the courts have often referred to the predominant role of the place of contract, they immediately thereafter would cite a number of other factors that either supported or discounted the place of contract factor, so that in the final analysis the place of contract does not appear to have been particularly determinative by itself. The courts, moreover, seem to have been cognizant of the evolution of business when deciding what were the relevant factors to the determination of "carrying on business." Arguably, the CRA in TIB B-090 is merely attempting to predict what are the new factors relevant in the evolved electronic environment.

An important issue is the extent to which the factor of solicitation (and for that matter advertising) will constitute a determining factor given that a foreign-based business's ability to promote and market its goods into Canada is one of the hallmarks of the Internet business environment. Solicitation has traditionally been viewed as a preliminary and/or ancillary activity to "carrying on a business."[49] In the expanded web-based marketplace this may no longer be the case, at least for purposes of sales tax and, in our view it is likely that the CRA will rely more frequently on solicitation in Canada when taking the position in rulings or litigation that a foreign based business is carrying on business here.[50]

Finally, the "place of delivery" factor listed in TIB B-090 would be interesting to explore. The concept of "delivery" of course is difficult to apply technically in the context of IPP such as software or other digitized

---

49 See *Grainger*, above note 40 where Lord Watson said that soliciting orders does not constitute carrying on business in a country. See also: *Geigy*, above note 41; *Cutlers Guild*, above note 44; *Proctor & Gamble*, above note 44; and *Sudden Valley Inc.v. R.*, [1976] C.T.C. 775 (F.C.A.), aff'g [1976] C.T.C. 297 (F.C.T.D.).

50 See for example *Great Bear Lake Lodge Ltd. v. Canada*, [1997] G.S.T.C. 35 (T.C.C.), where Sarchuk T.C.J. said the following (at para 8) on the meaning of the term "conducting business" as used in *ETA* s. 252.1 in the context of the non-resident rebate:

> In this day and age when business is conducted and sales are made *inter alia* by telephone, mail order and now even on the Internet, a narrow interpretation of the phrase is inappropriate. *There was continuous and sustained activity in the U.S. by the Appellants to seek out and solicit customers for their lodges. The fact that such solicitation may have taken place by facsimile or by telephone or other method of communication is in my view, irrelevant to a determination of whether or not the Appellants conducted business in the U.S. What we have here are not isolated transactions. The Appellants performed a series of acts in the U.S. occupying their time, attention, and labour, all done for the purpose of profit. That, in my view, is sufficient to bring their endeavours within the meaning of the words "conducts business in the U.S."* [Emphasis added.]

products.[51] Will a combination of solicitation that is tailored to Canadian consumers, plus "delivery" of digitized products to customers' terminals in Canada, draw a business closer to, or across the line of, "carrying on business" in Canada?

It has been noted elsewhere[52] that Canada's reliance on the "carrying on business" standard creates issues of competitive equity and possible tax loss. Nevertheless, in our view, unless and until the Department of Finance decides that a legislative response is required, the CRA is simply exercising the legislative levers that are currently available.

By contrast, other jurisdictions, notably the European Union, have made a different decision. Concerned specifically about the potential revenue loss and distortion of the marketplace that could result from web-based vendors located outside the Community, effective July 2003, foreign-based vendors are required to register for and collect VAT even when they have no physical business connection in the Community.[53]

3) The Provinces

A standard similar to, if not identical to, "carrying on business" applies to determine when vendors are required to collect and remit provincial sales taxes.

For HST purposes, once the business is registered for GST, it is also required to collect the expanded HST on its supplies into the Harmonized provinces, based on the HST "place of supply rules" whether or not it carries on business in a Harmonized province. The ability of the Federal Gov-

---

51 Specific issues arise as in the context of leasing activities, and at the time of writing, the CRA has publicly stated that it is examining whether, and in combination with what other factors, the existence of a leasing portfolio in Canada will constitute carrying on business in Canada for GST purposes. See question 36 at the February 26, 2004 meeting between the CRA and the Sales Tax Committee of the Canadian Bar Association. It is likely that these issues will be reflected in the proposed revisions to Policy Statement P-051R, referred to above at note 37. [Draft revised Policy Statement P-051R2 released for comment September 8, 2004.]The decision of the Tax Court in *GLS Leasco*, above note 44, may provide some support for the CRA's position that specific factors surrounding the business of leasing — location where the portfolio is acquired among others - may lead to a more relaxed standard for "carrying on business." Ironically, in *GLS Leasco*, the U.S.-based leasing company successfully argued that it was carrying on business, against the Minister's argument that it was not. Because leasing is not strictly a "new economy" phenomenon, we have not pursued this issue further.

52 Cockfield, How to Catch the Big Fish, above note 2.

53 For further details see: http://europa.eu.int/comm/taxation_customs/taxation/vatindex_en.htm

ernment to enforce the obligation to collect the additional provincial component of the HST is in fact one of the motivating factors for provinces to agree to "harmonize" with the federal GST.

The QST provisions are "harmonized" with the GST, so that an express "carrying on business" test is included in the QST legislation.[54]

In the RST provinces, the test is probably equivalent to "carrying on business," though not expressly so stated. For example, under the Ontario Act, "vendor" is defined as

> . . . a person who, *in the ordinary course of business*,
> (a) sells or licenses tangible personal property, [or]
> (b) sells or renders a taxable service . . . "[55] [emphasis added]

In recent years, Quebec, British Columbia and Manitoba have legislated expanded collection requirements on businesses who likely would not be "carrying on business" in those provinces.

These provisions may raise constitutional questions as to the provinces' competence. Effective January 1993, the definition of "carrying on business" for QST purposes was expanded to include

> . . . by means of advertising directed at the Québec market, soliciting orders in Québec for the supply by the person of . . . prescribed property . . .[56]

Effective May 15, 1995, and in response to catalogue shopping, a new registration and collection requirement applies to Canadian-based vendors whether or not resident and carrying on business in Canada, who solicit orders for sales of moveable personal property for delivery to "consumers," but not businesses, in Quebec.[57]

British Columbia followed Quebec's example effective April 1, 2000,[58] based again on whether the vendor "solicits persons in British Columbia for orders to purchase tangible personal property, by advertising or any

---

54 Quebec Act s. 407 (obligation to register), paralleling *ETA* s. 240; and s. 23 (non-resident override), paralleling *ETA* s. 143.

55 Subsection 1(1) of the Ontario Act. See also the definition of "vendor" in: s. 1 of the BC Act; ss. 1(1) of the Manitoba Act; para. 3(1)(o) of the Saskatchewan Act; and para 1(1) of the PEI Act.

56 Quebec Act s. 409.

57 Quebec Act s. 409.1.

58 Subsection 93(1.1) of the BC Act requires a non-resident business to obtain a license and collect social services tax where three ingredients exist:
- the vendor solicits sales of TPP to persons in British Columbia;
- orders to purchase originate from locations in British Columbia;
- the vendor causes the TPP to be delivered into British Columbia.

other means." Since "tangible personal property" includes software, this provision is especially relevant for the new economy.[59] The British Columbia requirement is broader than Quebec's in that it applies to both B2B and B2C sales whereas Quebec's requirement applies only to B2C sales.

Finally, effective April 1, 2002, Manitoba joined British Columbia and Quebec in attempting to expand collection requirements on out-of-province vendors, by amending the definition of "vendor"[60] to eliminate the element that a person must make a sale while in the course of a business carried on in the province. There is no requirement written into the Manitoba provision that refers to direct solicitation in the province as exists in British Columbia. Furthermore, Manitoba's provision does not limit itself to the sale of TPP, and would seem to include sales of services, which is an expansion beyond both Quebec and British Columbia.

4) What constitutes "solicitation"?

What constitutes "solicitation" within the province for both Quebec and British Columbia purposes may well prove to be contentious, given that both provinces have made solicitation a key factor in determining whether out-of-province vendors should come within the scope of their legislation. We have already seen as well that "solicitation" is one of the indicators of "carrying on business" included in TIB B-090 for GST purposes. As noted, it is a live question whether solicitation itself could constitute "carrying on business" particularly in light of the seemingly categorical statements in some earlier cases that solicitation may be an "ancillary" and/or perhaps a "preliminary" activity.

From a contractual analysis perspective, we have already seen that solicitation will usually fall short of making an "offer." But, we suggest that something more than mere advertising is required to constitute "solicitation." In *Sudden Valley Inc. v. The Queen*,[61] it was stated that "soliciting orders means that orders must be sought and attempts made to obtain them within the jurisdiction." It may not include "a mere invitation to treat" which is merely an invitation to commence negotiations.[62] Arguably,

---

59 See the definitions of "tangible personal property" and "software" in s. 1 of the BC Act.

60 See the definitions of "retail sale" and "vendor" in ss. 1(1) of the Manitoba Act.

61 Above note 49.

62 See Fridman, above note 42, at 36:

> One situation which has been characterized by the courts as necessarily involving an invitation to treat rather than an offer is the exposure of goods for sale in a shop or other commercial premise, or in a catalogue.

solicitation activities by a seller in the context of the new economy fall somewhere in between an "invitation to treat" and an offer. Many activities of a seller may simply be an "invitation to treat" and may not even amount to "solicitation."[63]

By contrast, British Columbia appears to confuse the distinction in its reach-out provision, which refers to an out-of-province vendor who "*solicits* persons in British Columbia for orders to purchase tangible personal property, *by advertising or any other means.*" Nevertheless, even British Columbia appears to admit that advertising must have some connection with the British Columbia market in order to constitute "soliciting" as illustrated by the following excerpts on "solicitation" from British Columbia's Technical Interpretation Manual:[64]

> *Solicitation via an Internet Web site that is accessible from anywhere in the world would not meet the solicitation criteria as outlined above as there is no decision to enter the BC market.* However, a seller who operates such a Web site and also actively solicits in the province (e.g., sends promotional material into the province or advertises on broadcasts aired in the province), would meet the requirement.
>
> . . .
>
> Placing an advertisement in a BC or a Western edition of a national publication that is distributed in the province generally represents a conscious decision to enter into, and solicit in, the BC market and would meet the criteria. *However, please note that there may be situations where placing an ad in a Western edition may not meet the criteria. For example, if BC is a small, or insignificant part of the seller's market (i.e., their primary market is the three prairie provinces), advertising in a Western edition of a publication may not represent a conscious decision to enter the provincial market.* British Columbia may have been included only because of how the publisher distributes its product. [emphasis added]

---

63 For example, Black's Law Dictionary (7th ed.) defines "solicitation" to mean, among other things:

> The act or an instance of requesting or seeking to obtain something; a request or petition . . . An attempt or effort to gain business . . .

64 See: British Columbia Consumer Taxation Branch Technical Interpretation Manual, R.8. See also: British Columbia Consumer Taxation Branch Bulletin No. 44.

In the GST context, see: RC 4103 — GST/HST Information for Suppliers of Publications, which sets out the CRA's position as to what it considers to be "soliciting orders" for purposes of *ETA* s. 240(3) and s. 143.1. Both the CRA's and British Columbia's position appear to focus on the "intent" of the seller and in particular whether the seller has specifically targeted the British Columbia/Canadian market.

5) The Concept of Nexus

It could be argued that the Manitoba and British Columbia positions merely extend the provinces' grasp over out-of-province vendors in a manner that parallels the U.S. concept of "nexus." Perhaps, the same can be said for the Agency's approach in TIB B-090.

"Nexus" is the measure that has been evolved by the U.S. courts for the degree of contact a business must have with a state before it can be compelled to submit to the use or sales tax laws of that state.[65] The states' capacity is constrained by the "Due Process Clause" and the "Commerce Clause" of the U.S. Constitution, that work in combination to require both a commercial and some degree of physical connection or presence of the out-of-state business with that State.

It is certainly the authors' experience that U.S. state sales and use tax administrators have in the past been much more assertive and insistent in pursuing Canadian businesses who have made sales into the U.S. states, and moreover, have effectively focused resources to compel compliance by

---

65 See: *Quill Corporation. v. North Dakota*, 504 U.S. 298 (1992) [*Quill*]; *Nat'l Geographic v. Cal. Equalization Bd.*, 430 U.S. 551 (1977) [*Nat'l Geographic*]; *Scripto, Inc. v. Carson*, 362 U.S. 207 (1960). A detailed discussion of "nexus" is beyond the scope of this chapter.
The "Due Process" clause provides that:

> No State . . . shall deprive any person of life, liberty or property, without due process of law. (U.S. Const. amend. XIV, s. 1)

In the sales and use tax context, the clause applies to require that there be a minimal connection between the state and an out-of-state business before it is fundamentally fair that the state can impose the burdens of collecting the state's sales tax. That contact threshold, however, appears to be quite low, and may require nothing more than the purposeful exploitation of a state's markets: see *Quill*.
The "Commerce Clause" provides that:

> . . . Congress shall have power . . . to regulate commerce with foreign nations, and among the several states, and with the Indian tribes. (U.S. Const. art. I, s. 8, cl. 3.)

The clause prevents states from unjustifiably discriminating against or putting burdens on the interstate flow of commerce, and in order to avoid infringing on this requirement, there must be "some definitive link, some minimum connection, between a state and the person, property or transaction it seeks to tax." See: *Miller Bros. Co. v. Maryland*, 347 U.S. 340 (1954) 344–45 and *Complete Auto Transit v. Brady*, 430 U.S. 274 (1977). In contrast to the "Due Process" requirement, the "Commerce Clause" test requires some physical connection between the business and the state, albeit that the "slightest connection" has been found to be sufficient: see Cockfield, How to Catch the Big Fish, above at note 2. There appears to be a different — and higher — standard to determine nexus for sales tax as opposed to state franchise or income tax purposes as under the latter standard an economic connection may be sufficient whereas a more physical connection has been held to be necessary before a business can be forced to

out-of-state businesses in a manner that exceeds the efforts of the Canadian provinces.

It is questionable, however, whether the tests in British Columbia or Manitoba in particular purport to require the degree of physical connection with those provinces that the "nexus" test imposes on the U.S. states. Furthermore, given the provinces' authority to raise taxes is limited to "within the province," it is arguable that the reach-out provisions are outside the provincial constitutional capacity, although no doubt the provinces would argue that an economic connection, such as solicitation under British Columbia's provision, is enough. The issue has not been tested to date.

D. INDIRECT TAX ISSUES RELATED TO SOFTWARE

The characterization of computer software for Indirect Tax purposes has been a subject of debate and litigation for over 25 years. This, together with the fact that software expenditures are huge in the new economy, makes software a particularly contentious area. Because RST is largely an unrecoverable business expense, RST issues are particularly contentious, although we will see that there is one contentious point for GST.

Initially, software was not separable from computer hardware, and thus was viewed as part of the "TPP" and subject to sales tax accordingly. As the computer industry expanded and computer functions became more specialized, software became unbundled from hardware and started to become separate commercial commodities, especially applications software. In our day, applications software, such as an Oracle or SAP integrated systems software solution, can have a commercial value equal to or vastly exceeding the value of the hardware system that runs it.[66] Furthermore, software is embedded in many informational and digital products that are now available on the market and over the Internet, as is illustrated by our earlier example of the online research library where a subscriber must enroll and download facilitating software in order to access the database.

The initial point of contention regarding software centred on whether what would otherwise be considered IPP, should be treated for Indirect Tax

comply with sales and use tax requirements: see *Geoffrey, Inc. v. South Carolina*, 313 S.C. 15 (Sup. Ct. No. 23886, 1993) and *Nat'l Geographic*, above.

66 For more background on the history of the Indirect Tax treatment of software, see: A. Wilson, "Computer Software — Becoming More Tangible?," (1992) Commodity Tax Symposium Papers (CICA Virtual Professional Library) and C. Felepchuk & R. Kreklewetz, "Commodity Tax Issues In Managing Intellectual Property and Other Technology Resources (1998) Commodity Tax Symposium (CICA Virtual Professional Library) ("Felepchuk and Kreklewetz").

purposes as TPP. Thinking of computer software as something tangible, such as a car (which is exactly the parallel that some senior RST officials have used in public presentations), seems questionable. Nevertheless, as the software industry evolved and software became more of a "good," and was packaged accordingly on a tape or disk, tax administrators began to view it as TPP, notwithstanding that its intrinsic value is knowledge and the medium is incidental.

Whereas the opposing positions — IPP or TPP — have been heavily litigated in the U.S. courts,[67] there has been much less case law in Canada, and the existing case law is contradictory. On the one hand, in the *Telecheque* case[68] the British Columbia Court of Appeal held that software and franchise rights constituted separate properties in the context of the asset sale of a cheque verification business, and therefore were not subject to RST.

On the other hand, in the *Newfoundland Telephone* case,[69] the Newfoundland Supreme Court Trial Division refused to treat application software embedded in telephone switching systems as being separate from the switches, and therefore concluded that the software was taxable TPP, even though the software was extensively tailored to meet the telephone company's needs to control specialized computerized telephone switching centres. The Court did not accept the possibility that the software at issue might be IPP, on the basis of being intangible knowledge separate from the tangible carrier medium.

Icam Technologies Corporation v. MNR,[70] a decision of the Canadian International Trade Tribunal, appears to be the only decision dealing with

---

67 There is a rich body of U.S. case law (at the state level) concerning the nature of software. Although the earlier cases tended to emphasize the intangible nature of software, the more recent cases have tended to view software as TPP. See: *District of Columbia v. Universal Computer Associates, Inc.*, 465 F.2d 615 (U.S. App. D.C. 1972); *Commerce Union Bank v. Tidwell*, 538 S.W.2d 405 (Tenn. 1976); *Southern Bell v. Department of Revenue*, 366 So.2d 30 (Fla. D.C. App. 1978); *First National Bank of Fort Worth v. Bullock*, 584 S.W. 2d. 548 (Texas Civ. App. 1979); *First National Bank of Springfield v. Department of Revenue*, 421 N.E. 2d 175 (Ill. 1981); and *James v. TRES Computer Systems, Inc.*, 642 S.W. 2d 347 (Mo. 1982).

68 *Continental Commercial Systems Corporation (Telecheque Canada) v. R.*, [1982] 5 W.W.R. 340 (B.C.C.A.), rev'g *Chequecheck Services Ltd. v.* R., [1980] 5014 E.T.C. (B.C.S.C.).

69 *Newfoundland Telephone Company Limited v. A.G. of Newfoundland*, [1992] 5 T.C.T. 4278 (N.S.C.T.D.), referring to *Comptroller of the Treasury v. Equitable Trust Company*, 464 A. 2d 248 (Md. 1983). The decision provides a good overview of both Canadian and U.S. case law and offers some useful counterpoints to some of the conclusions reached in those prior cases.

70 [1991] 4 T.C.T. 3237 (C.I.T.T.).

software under the federal manufacturers sales tax ("FST," which was replaced by the GST). This case dealt with the concept of the "manufacture" of software for FST purposes. Specifically, the taxpayer took the position that it should be able to purchase computer equipment exempt of FST as production equipment, based on the fact that the taxpayer was manufacturing software. The Tribunal held that the exemption was available as Icam was supplying TPP. In reaching this decision, the Tribunal placed great weight on the fact that Icam supplied a physical item, a carrier medium, that was left with the customer; and that the software was priced on a per unit basis, not on an hourly rate.

1) Software and RST

Perhap,s due to the absence of a clear message from the courts, the provinces chose to resolve the (TPP versus IPP) issue by legislation[71] and all provinces' RST legislation now expressly includes software in the RST-taxable base, usually by inclusion within the definition of "TPP."[72] Generally, a distinction is made between "custom" software, i.e., software that was designed and developed (or modified) solely for the exclusive use of a particular person, which is not subject to RST, and other pre-written software which is subject to RST. Although the purest camp would still debate the inequities of such a codification, such a move settles the issue from a

---

71 See the definition of "tangible personal property" in ss. 1(1) of the Ontario Act, the definition of "tangible personal property" in s. 1 of the BC Act, and the definition of "goods" in s. 1 of the PEI Act. Saskatchewan includes "computer services" within the definition of "taxable service": see ss. 3(1) of the Saskatchewan Act. With few exceptions (e.g., custom software is taxable in Saskatchewan) most Canadian jurisdictions have a relatively bright line test to define taxable "canned" software in contrast to exempt "custom" software.

72 British Columbia began taxing software under its Act as early as 1985 and even prior to that by administrative interpretation. British Columbia took the position that its RST applied broadly to licensed as well as other "canned" software. Interestingly, Ontario was the last province to address the taxation of software in legislation, and until 1997 relied on administrative interpretation. Unlike British Columbia, Ontario's position until 1997 was that RST applied to pre-written software if it was made available on disks (or tapes) that were supplied by the vendor and was sold under an assumed, adhesion or shrink-wrapped license agreement. Ontario accepted that any other software variant was not subject to RST. This administrative position caused many software producers to side-step RST by, for example, signing a licence agreement. On the other hand, it also resulted in RST not applying on software solutions that can apply over an enterprise's entire operation, such as an integrated SAP or Oracle implementation. For more discussion of the history and evolution of the taxation of software, see Felepchuk & Kreklewetz, above note 66.

practical point of view.[73] In our view, there is some basis for this approach, if, for example, we draw an analogy between "canned" or "off-the-shelf" software and a music compact disk (CD) purchased at a record store: although there is no doubt that the true value of the CD being purchased resides in the music on the CD, the highly commoditized and mass produced nature of the CD lends itself to a TPP characterization, just as books and vinyl records have always been treated. Conversely, the design and programming of "custom" software is a highly specialized knowledge-based service that is carried out solely for the exclusive use of a particular person.

The practical issue with the distinction between "custom" and other software is in the highly restrictive scope of how the provinces define "custom": essentially, in order for software to be "custom," more than 50 percent of its value must consist of software specifically written or modified at the level of the code itself.[74] In the software industry where even complex software solutions consist of strategic selection and integration of modules of already-written software, the reality is that very little software, including its modification, meets the threshold of half of the code being specifically written or modified. In this regard, the RST rules for "custom software" do not coincide at all with the industry view of "custom." This difference of views has generated significant controversy, at least in Ontario as the new rules since 1997 became better understood, and may yet lead to large assessments of RST where businesses did not collect, or self-assess, RST on software installations. As a matter of legislative interpretation, however, the legislation is relatively clear.

The issue that continues from the historic TPP/IPP debate, that we suggest is not well-settled and will likely resist being clearly settled, is the taxation of services related to software.

As described, RST officials' historic approach to software has been by analogy to other TPP — "the car" earlier referred to. Similarly, their view of what should be taxable services related to taxable software, is by analogy to other RST-taxable services to

> install, assemble, dismantle, adjust, repair or maintain tangible personal property.[75]

---

73 There is, however, still some debate as to what is required to meet the test of "custom" software. Such a test appears to turn on whether original source code is developed.

74 See para. 7(1)(62) of the Ontario Act and s. 14.2(2) of Reg. 1012 pursuant to the Ontario Act; and the definition of "software" in section 1 of the BC Act.

75 Para. 1(1))(c) of the Ontario Act, definition of "taxable service." See also the definition of "taxable service" in section 1 of the BC Act.

The immediate conceptual challenge, becomes drawing a functional parallel between repairing a car, and "install[ing], assembl[ing], dismantl[ing], adjust[ing], [or] repair[ing]" software. [76] In general terms, amongst tax practitioners, the understanding has boiled down to whether the service is "hands on," in which case the service is taxable; or "hands off," in which case the service is not taxable. Given, however, the inherent incorporeal nature of software, when do you put your "hands on" software?

Consider a contract provider of "help desk" services who arguably provides "hands off" consulting-type services when he/she "walks through" a problem with a client over the telephone. However, what happens when the problem cannot be remedied over the telephone and a technician is sent to put his/her "hands on" the client's computer; or when the technician obtains remote access to the client's computer and programs a work-around? In these cases, it would appear that we have a bundled service composed of "hands off" non-taxable services and "hands on" taxable services. Further difficulties arise because of the application of the RST "bundled services" rules.[77]

Moreover, a software vendor typically provides software and related services in the context of an all-encompassing systems solution that generally includes elements of design, consulting and business enterprise systems design, and project management. Once the software is developed, it will be installed, maintained, upgraded, etc. Other support services may include testing, instruction, data management and migration, and help-desk support. Often these services are provided for one "bundled" price. To the extent such service providers do not engage in the very cumbersome process of documenting and unbundling transactions for RST purposes, an RST auditor will often argue that RST applied to the whole invoiced amount.

In an effort to bring some clarity to the scope of taxable software services, and at the same time codify what has been its position since 1997,

---

76 It has been suggested that Ontario fell into taxing such services by deeming non-custom software to be TPP and that the conceptual underpinning of taxing labour was born in a world that did not conceive of software as TPP. See C. Eansor, "Is Ontario going the right direction?," (2002) 10 Commodity Tax News 7.

77 Amendments to Ontario's Regulation 1012 require that RST be collected on the full price of RST-taxable and RST-exempt software and related services where they are not separately invoiced, subject to a 10% *de minimis* exception. British Columbia has had a similar "bundling" rule since 2000: see s. 69.1 of the BC Act together with the definition of "purchase price" and Division 12 of the Social Service Tax Regulation. British Columbia's 2004 Budget released February 17, 2004 proposed changes to the bundling rules. See for example: Ministry of Provincial Revenue Budget Bulletin 2004 and the *Social Service Tax Amendment Act, 2004*, S.B.C. 2004, c. 9.

Ontario has added "configure" and "upgrade" to the earlier list of RST-taxable service activities applicable to a "computer program."[78]

The use of the words "configuration," "modification" and "upgrading" was intended to speak more clearly to the computer software area and the functions of computer software technicians. Whether they do is a question that, in our view, remains to be tested.

The concept of "modification" is one that is fairly well established in the Regulations made to the Ontario Act. But what is "configuration" and does it really encompass the software equivalent of assembly and dismantlement of a car? If the intention is to tax all related labour in respect of software, has Ontario gone far enough with this word? Does the word "upgrade" go so far as to catch services that are more truly consulting in nature? More importantly, do they draw meaningful distinctions between the technical code-related activities that software technicians perform, and the planning and consulting functions that are also a large part of software design and implementation? It is not our intention to "poke holes" in these words, but rather to demonstrate the problems and disputes that can be foreseen that may well lead to litigation.

British Columbia's legislative approach has been different. Unlike Ontario, British Columbia has not revised its definition of "taxable service" to include software-related terms, and as indicated by its interpretative statements that it continues to rely — perhaps with justification — on the wide scope of "taxable services" that already includes "install[ing], assembl[ing], dismantl[ing], repair[ing], adjust[ing], restor[ing], recondition[ing], refinish[ing] or maintain[ing]" TPP.[79]

---

78 See new paragraph (c.1) of the definition of "taxable service," s. 1 of the Ontario Act. By news release dated July 19, 2002 Ontario announced that Regulation 1012 will be revised to reflect the changes in the definition of a "taxable service" as follows:

> "Installation of a computer program" means the work done to load a computer program onto hardware to permit the set-up or operation of the computer program by the user.
>
> "Configuration of a computer program" means the work done to input customer-specific values and parameters with respect to a computer program or hardware.
>
> "Modification of a computer program" means changing the source code of a computer program.
>
> "Upgrading of a computer program" means the work done to remedy problems within a computer program, to provide a standardized enhancement or to provide new features or functionality.

79 See British Columbia Consumer Taxation Branch Bulletin No. 040: "Computer Hardware, Software and Related Services."

Given the Ontario experience, we question whether the British Columbia position is as secure as RST officials may think.

On the other hand, British Columbia has self-imposed limits on the excessively broad potential scope of the general "taxable services" definition, and expressly exempts certain computer software-related services.[80] Specifically, certain services will not be considered "taxable services" regardless of the status of the software as "custom" or otherwise.

Of particular interest are "installation" and "configuration" services that, in certain situations, will be exempt of RST in British Columbia. British Columbia also exempts "configuration" services in respect of non-custom software in certain instances. This is a markedly different approach from Ontario, and will likely create confusion amongst software providers. Of course, any relief that the provinces may choose to offer from the potentially broad application of the RST in the area of software-related services, is most welcome. It is doubtful, however, that clarity has been achieved.

A final RST concern relates to remote access to software. Ontario's position[81] is that ORST will apply if the software is located on a server in Ontario, but not otherwise. For example, if the software is located on a server in another province and is not downloaded into Ontario, the use of such software in Ontario will not attract RST. On the other hand, Ontario's view is that RST will apply on the full fair value of the software program located on the server in Ontario, even though the intention is that the software will be accessed and used from locations outside Ontario.

Ontario's view is not necessarily shared by other provinces. Notably, British Columbia takes the position that its RST will apply to the use of

---

80 Regulation 2.46 under the BC Act prescribes as an "exempt service":

> (j) services respecting the installation, modification or configuration of software if
> (i) the services are provided solely to meet the requirements of a specific person,
> (ii) the services are purchased separately from the purchase or lease of that software, and
> (iii) the cost of the services is greater than the cost of that software;
>
> (k) services respecting the installation, modification or configuration of software if
> (i) the services are provided solely to meet the requirements of a specific person,
> (ii) the purchase or the lease price, as the case may be, is the price for the software, as installed, modified or configured, and
> (iii) the purchase or lease price, as the case may be, is greater than double the price of purchasing or leasing the software without the installation, modification and configuration services.

81 Contrast Ontario Retail Sales Tax Guide 650 and British Columbia Consumer Taxation Branch Bulletin 40.

software by individuals located in British Columbia regardless of the location of the server upon which the software resides.

Neither Ontario's nor British Columbia's position is expressly set out in their respective Acts. This type of conflicting position is unfortunate and only compounds the confusion and risk of litigation where businesses find themselves caught between the conflicting positions of the two provinces. Such situations become more common as software providers more commonly make software available to businesses having multiple locations, using a utility model of centralizing versions of software on a server and providing access to users for a monthly or per-use charge.

2) Software and GST

Unlike the provinces, which, have attempted to define software and related services for the purposes of RST, the *ETA* remains silent for purposes of the GST as to the characterization of software as TPP or IPP. Nor is the issue entirely academic, and there remain at least three areas where it matters:

- for purposes of application of GST at Customs on importation;
- for purposes of the application of the self-assessment provisions on "imported taxable supplies"; and
- for purposes of the zero-rating provisions.[82]

The CRA's interpretation for GST purposes remains unchanged since 1994 and is set out in Technical Information Bulletin B-037R — Imported Computer Software ("TIB B-037R"). Although TIB B-037R deals specifically with the application of GST to software on importation, nevertheless it reflects the CRA's major statement on software in general.[83] In TIB B-037R, the CRA accepts that software should be treated as IPP in most circumstances, and in particular when licenced software is imported into Canada, such that GST only applies on the value of the carrier medium — the computer diskette; or when any software is transmitted into Canada electronically, in which case GST does not apply at all on import. On the other hand,

82 We referred earlier, text and note 28 above, to the limited scope of the zero-rating rule for IPP in section 10 of Part V of Schedule VI, as compared to zero-rating rules for services. The CRA has frequently conceded that software is "intellectual property" that does come within section 10, so generally a Canadian supplier can decide with confidence not to charge GST on supplies of software to non-registered non-residents.

83 TIB B-090 is generally consistent with these characterizations. Also see Customs Memorandum D13-11-6, "Determining Value For Duty of Computer Software" (April 17, 2001).

pre-packaged "canned" software is considered to be TPP, as is custom-designed software that is purchased outright, not pursuant to a license agreement, outside Canada. In these later two cases, GST applies on import on the full value of medium and software.

The CRA's view on custom software that is purchased outright, appears anachronistic, and is likely driven by the influence of Customs administration over the GST administration. Like RST administrators, Customs administrators are goods—focused, and attach considerable importance to the presence of a physical medium. There are, however, significant potential concerns, that could lead to adverse assessments and litigation, if only because of the possibility for confusion and error that it creates.

If "purchased" software is truly TPP for purposes of importation, then the value must be correctly declared for *Customs Act*[84] purposes, or significant penalties can arise for declaration under the Administrative Monetary Penalties System (AMPS) under that legislation. The imposition of AMPS assessments on software importations could well give rise of litigation.

There are significant cash flow implications as the importer must pay GST on the full value, even if it can subsequently claim ITCs. If the software were treated as IPP, an importer engaged in commercial activity would have no self-assessment obligation. Even an importer who is required to self-assess for an "imported taxable supply" (such as a bank described earlier), would self-assess at a later time in its return rather than at the time of import and might be able to claim a partial offsetting ITC.

Finally, there will be situations where the CRA's position will result in potential double-taxation that may lead to litigation.

For example, a non-resident software supplier may develop a complex software package for a Canadian financial institution. Due to the one-off nature of the transaction, the non-resident is not carrying on business in Canada and is not required to register, and does not register for GST. The supplier's technician brings the completed software package to Canada on his/her laptop to install onto the financial institution's computer system, and Customs requires that GST be accounted for at the full value of the software, which the developer owns and for which the developer is the importer of record.

Neither the developer nor the financial institution is concerned at this point, because the developer will pass through the GST cost to the finan-

---

84 R.S.C. 1985, c. 1 (2nd Supp.).

cial institution in the purchase price, and the financial institution does not qualify for ITCs in any case.

The supply by the developer to the financial institution, however, is by lease, not by sale. Although the developer does not charge GST, the license is an "imported taxable supply" to the financial institution who must self-assess on each license payment, resulting in double taxation.

There will, no doubt, emerge other "traps for the unwary" due to the inconsistency of the CRA's position, and the difficulty generally of applying the GST rules to software.

E. INDIRECT TAX ISSUES RELATING TO TELECOMMUNICATION SERVICES

Recent advances in the telecommunications industry are, in many respects, the backbone of the new economy, and the global telecommunications infrastructure has given rise to novel ways to communicate and manage information, spawning many of the novel product offerings discussed earlier in this chapter.

Telecommunication services are subject to GST and RST,[85] as well as to VAT and the sales and use taxes in the United States. The issues relating to telecommunication services, which by now will be familiar to the reader, include the following:

- characterization: whether the supply in question is a telecommunication service;
- since many such services have an inter-jurisdictional nature, which jurisdiction gets to tax it; and
- possibilities of tax leakage — or double-taxation — where foreign based businesses provide telecommunication services into the jurisdiction.

For GST purposes, "telecommunication services" are both the transmission and reception functions; as well as "telecommunications facili-

85 For a more detailed description of the GST and RST applications to the telecommunications sector, see J. Vincze, "The Application of Commodity Taxes to the Telecommunications Industry," (1994) Commodity Tax Symposium (CICA Virtual Professional Library); J. Vincze, "Telecommunications Update, 1996," (1996) Commodity Tax Symposium (CICA Virtual Professional Library); M. Arsenault, "Telecommunications or Not Telecommunications?"(1999) Commodity Tax Symposium (CICA Virtual Professional Library); and F. McFarlane, "Contrasting Ontario/British Columbia Applications," (2000) Commodity Tax Symposium (CICA Virtual Professional Library).

ties," the equipment that facilitates or executes telecommunications.[86] For RST purposes "telecommunication services" include only the transmission and reception functions,[87] although the equipment will generally be RST-taxable TPP under the general rules. Accordingly, the application of the GST telecommunication rules is somewhat broader, but, given that services and TPP are all generally GST-taxable in any case, the real implication is that the application of specific telecommunication services "place-of-supply" and zero-rating rules may come into play in more circumstances.

Although the GST and RST legislative rules for telecommunications are relatively clear, nevertheless their application proves complex and difficult, both because of the highly technical nature of telecommunications

---

86 *ETA* ss. 123(1) defines "telecommunication service" and "telecommunications facility" as follows:

> "telecommunication service" means
> (a) the service of emitting, transmitting or receiving signs, signals, writing, images or sounds or intelligence of any nature by wire, cable, radio, optical or other electromagnetic system, or by any similar technical system, or
> (b) making available for such emission, transmission or reception telecommunications facilities of a person who carries on the business of supplying services referred to in paragraph (a)[.]
>
> "telecommunications facility" means any facility, apparatus or other thing (including any wire, cable, radio, optical or other electromagnetic system, or any similar technical system, or any part thereof) that is used or is capable of being used for telecommunications[.]

87 See ss. 1(1) of the Ontario Act:

> "telecommunication" means any transmission, emission or reception of signs, signals, writing, images or sound or intelligence of any nature by wire, radio, visual or other electromagnetic or laser-based system, but does not include any transmission, emission or reception or class thereof that is prescribed by the Minister to be excluded for the purpose of this paragraph[.]

Inclusions and exclusions from the definition are set out in ss. 5 and 5.1 of Regulation 1012.

See ss. 1(1) of the Saskatchewan Act:

> "telecommunication service" means the right, whether exercised or not, to send or receive one or more telecommunications by means of a transmitter that is ordinarily situated in British Columbia, and includes
> (a) the sending or receiving of a telecommunication by means of a transmitter that is ordinarily situated in British Columbia, and
> (b) a dedicated telecommunication service[.]
>
> "transmitter" means a facility or instrument by which a purchaser of a telecommunication service may send or receive the telecommunications that may be sent or received under that service, and includes a telephone, facsimile machine, modem and television[.]

functions and the fact that the legislation has not kept up with the rapid technical developments in the industry.

There has been much discussion recently around services such as Internet access, data processing and web-based broadcasting ("streaming"), and how the GST and RST telecommunication service rules apply to them. Amongst the RST regimes there has not been a consistent approach. At first blush, these types of services may be thought of as telecommunication services. However, for example, data processing is considered by all of the RST regimes, except Saskatchewan,[88] to be a non-taxable service. Conversely, Internet access is considered taxable in all of the RST regimes except Ontario.

For GST purposes, further inconsistencies arise. Specifically, TIB B-090 states that Internet access, e-mail, voice telephony services, electronic data interchange ("EDI"), and streaming are all considered to be telecommunication services. However, TIB B-090 states that supplies of web hosting and the provision of digitized products would not be considered to be supplies of telecommunication services.

To determine the "place of supply" of a telecommunication service for both GST and RST, generally a "two-out-of-three" rule applies: the service is deemed located in the jurisdiction if any two of the location of the emission, the location of the reception, or the billing location are in the jurisdiction.[89]

Application of the place of supply rules to the more sophisticated forms of telecommunication services can be complex and arduous. Given the complexities and inconsistencies, surprisingly there is no Canadian GST or RST case law on these issues at this point.

A particular issue of great importance for RST is the distinction between making a supply of a telecommunication service versus making a supply of a service or IPP by means of telecommunication. TIB B-090

---

88 Saskatchewan expressly taxes "the processing, input, transformation or other manipulation of data into a form readable by a computer" by inclusion in the definition of "computer services." See paragraph 3(1)(a.1) of the Saskatchewan Act.

89 *ETA* s. 142.1. A "telecommunication service" of a "telecommunications facility" is located in Canada if the whole *or any part* of the facility is located in Canada. A modified form of the two-out-of-three rule is set out in Part VIII of Schedule IX to the *ETA* to determine the place of supply rules for HST purposes. Sections 22.25 to 22.27 of the Quebec Act set out rules that parallel the HST rules in Schedule IX.

For illustrations of the RST rules, see Regulation 1012, p. 5.1 made under the Ontario Act; and the definition of "purchase price" in s. 1(1) of the BC Act. The RST two-out-of three rules generally do not apply for dedicated lines, where typically the provinces allow for a pro-rating of RST based on the distance of the line within the province.

directly identifies and examines this distinction for GST purposes, and notes that in the later situation it is the supplier that is using telecommunications in order to provide its service or IPP product.

Unfortunately, the provincial RST officials are far less accepting of the distinction, notwithstanding that it is clearly established in the case law.[90] This is problematic, and frequently causes disputes as RST auditors threaten to assess vendors for failure to collect RST on a "telecommunication services," whereas the vendor sees the telecommunication service as having been an RST-taxable input into the vendor's providing a non-taxable service or IPP product.

Furthermore, notwithstanding that RST auditors argue that the vendor is providing an RST- taxable product because it includes a pass-through component of the telecommunication services it purchased, they often will not admit that the vendor can purchase the telecommunication services without paying RST "for resale."[91] Generally, they interpret the concept of "purchase for resale" very restrictively to apply only where the service "for resale" is passed through without being further processed or altered in any manner whatsoever.

Sales tax leakage, on the other hand, is also an issue as foreign-based telecommunication service providers expand their operations into Canada and the various provinces. The general rule described earlier that non-resident businesses do not have to collect GST or RST if they do not carry on business in Canada,[92] applies as well for telecommunication services. As suggested earlier, the CRA may well start examining more stringently the operations of these operators, as GST leakage increases. In many cases, the delivery of an enhanced telecommunication service requires that the customer use facilitating equipment provided by the service provider, oftentimes under a lease arrangement. As noted above,[93] the CRA appears to be

---

90 In *Franklin Enterprises Limited v. Province of Nova Scotia* (1981), 45 N.S.R. (2d) 605, the Nova Scotia Supreme Court held that a hotel operator had to pay RST on the soaps and other individually packaged products that it purchased to stock the hotel rooms. The Court rejected the hotel operator's argument that it could purchase those products RST-free "for resale" to its guests. The RST provinces apply this analysis in a broad range of situations.

91 Generally, goods purchased for resale do not attract RST because the provinces can only charge RST to a consumer of the good: otherwise the RST would be an Indirect Tax that is outside the province's constitutional capacity. See: *Cairns Construction Ltd. v. The Government of Saskatchewan*, [1960] S.C.R. 619. The position of the provinces *vis-à-vis* the acquisition of telecommunication services (and services in general) for resale is less than clear and, we suggest, inconsistent across the provinces.

92 *ETA* s. 143. See note 34 above and the corresponding text.

93 See note 51 above.

moving toward the view that the presence in Canada of equipment for lease can be a significant indicator of "carrying on business" here.

Europe's response to the leakage concern was more direct when faced with the so-called "American route." Under the Sixth VAT Directive of the European Union, telecommunication services were originally taxable at the place where the supplier established its business or had a fixed establishment.[94] Accordingly, if a telecommunication company based in the United States provided telecommunication services to a customer, say, in the United Kingdom, the supply would escape VAT. This strategy was, we understand, well received by taxpayers like financial institutions that were unable to recover full VAT. This planning opportunity was closed in 1997 when telecommunication services were brought within the reverse charge (i.e., self assessment) mechanism.

Finally, Canada's GST rule for zero-rating telecommunication services requires comments because of its highly restricted scope. A supply of a telecommunication service will only qualify for GST "zero-rating"

- in the case of a transmission, if it is not emitted and received in Canada;

but more importantly;

- provided the recipient is a non-resident who is not registered for GST; and
- provided the recipient carries on the business of supplying telecommunication services.[95]

The last criterion is unique in the context of the GST "zero-rating" rules. It also imposes a severe competitive constraint on Canadian-based telecommunication service providers, who must charge GST on their services to all other non-residents.

For example, a Canadian-based telecommunication business must charge GST on the supply of a high speed Digital Subscriber Line (DSL) (a telecommunications facility) that a London-based financial institution wishes to acquire to link its Toronto and London offices. There is no appor-

94 Subsection 9(1) of the 1977 Sixth Directive. The "American Route" opportunity was closed by an amendment to the Sixth Directive to include telecommunication services within Article 9(2)(e), thereby requiring business customers to self-assess for such telecommunication services according to the reverse charge procedure. Also note Article 9(3)(b) of the Directive in the context of the provision of telecommunication services by non-EU providers to private consumers.

95 Schedule VI, Part V, s. 22.1 to the *ETA*.

tionment of GST to only the Canadian span of the transmission.[96] The London-based financial institution will also be required to account for UK VAT.[97] Moreover, although the rule itself appears relatively clear in its articulation, nevertheless it is commercially difficult to apply, which in itself may well lead to disputes.

F. CONCLUSION

It would be difficult to predict with certainty what changes and evolutions will occur in the new economy — either the new digitized products, the range of new services, or the telecommunications technology to support and transport them. We can, however, predict without much risk that these evolutions will add to the stresses to the Indirect Tax regimes that we have highlighted earlier: jurisdiction over the business; characterization of products as IPP; and treatment of telecommunications services that are central features of Indirect Tax administration. Perhaps, the federal and provincial ministries of Finance will respond legislatively to cut the Gordian knot if GST, QST and RST leakage becomes too great. But, until that happens it is reasonable to expect the taxing authorities asserting more aggressively positions that protect the tax base as they perceive it, notwithstanding the lack of clarity in certain provisions of their respective legislation. And, we suggest, the issues will become more acute and will result in litigation.

It will be interesting to re-read this chapter in 10 years to see how close to the mark our predictions have come! The jury is not in now!

---

96 The rationale for the restrictive scope might be found in the 1988 Convention of Melbourne, the final act of the World Administrative Telegraph and Telephone Conference that was the forum for discussions on many international telecommunications related issues. The Melbourne Convention proposed that VAT would not apply, at the international level, to telecommunications routing and termination services supplied between telecommunications network operators. Accordingly, the policy seems to recognize that without such an "exemption" telecommunications companies would, in many cases, be subject to unrecoverable taxes from other jurisdictions. The *quid pro quo* for countries giving up VAT on supplies to offshore telecommunication service providers was the broad jurisdiction to tax all other telecommunication services that are connected with the jurisdiction.

97 For a discussion of the U.K. VAT telecommunications rules see N. Purcell, "VAT and the Telecoms Industry — A UK Perspective," (2001) 5 The EC Tax Journal. Also see Article 9 of the Sixth Directive.

Chapter Twenty-Four

Income Taxation of Derivatives*

Lara Friedlander and Andrew Auerbach

A. INTRODUCTION

Derivatives have been the subject of scrutiny by the Canadian tax authorities for many decades; some of the leading cases on futures and forward agreements date back to the 1940s. Even the swap, a type of derivative that has appeared somewhat more recently, received attention from the Canadian tax authorities in the early 1980s. Notwithstanding this relatively long history of derivatives experience, the Canadian tax system generally does not address derivatives as such, relying instead on general taxation principles and on a handful of specific and narrowly applicable provisions. This chapter will provide an overview of the rules governing the taxation of derivatives in Canada, and will then compare the Canadian system with other approaches to the taxation of derivatives from a tax policy perspective.

---

* The authors would like to thank Andrew McGuffin and Daniel MacIntosh, of Osler, Hoskin & Harcourt LLP, for their contributions to this chapter. Much of the substance of this chapter is based on a paper entitled "Fiscalité des produits dérivés" written by Lara Friedlander for a conference entitled "Financement nord-américain dans la turbulence — Partie 1" held by the Association de planification fiscale et financière in 2001, as well as "Taxation of Derivatives: Canada" in S.D. Conlon and V.H. Aquilino, *Principles of Financial Derivatives and International Taxation* (Valhalla, New York: Warren, Gorham & Lamont, 1999), also by Lara Friedlander. The views expressed in this chapter are those of the authors and do not represent the opinions, views, or positions of the Department of Finance (Canada).

B. GENERAL CONSIDERATIONS RELEVANT TO THE FEDERAL INCOME TAXATION OF DERIVATIVES

Derivative instruments, as a category, are not explicitly addressed by the *Income Tax Act* (Canada) (the "Act").[1] Certain provisions of the Act address specific types of derivatives, such as s. 49 of the Act, which governs the treatment of options on capital account. Other provisions of the Act focus on specific aspects of the taxation of derivatives, such as s. 20.3 of the Act, which addresses the deduction of interest on hedged weak currency loans; the postamble to subparagraph 212(1)(b)(vii), which addresses non-resident withholding tax on certain types of participating interest payments; and proposed s. 94.2(9) of the Act, which is the key component of a special taxation regime in respect of "tracked interests" designed to prevent the usage of offshore investments to defer current taxation in Canada. However, in most cases, an analysis of the taxation of derivative instruments relies on the application of more general income tax principles to the particular transaction in question.

1) Nature of a Derivative

For Canadian federal income tax purposes, the nature of a derivative instrument is not necessarily determined by the nature of the reference asset, liability or transaction. For example, the payment by one person to another person under an interest rate swap will not necessarily be considered "interest" under the Act; rather, that payment will be considered interest only if it meets the requirements set out in the case law governing the characterization of a payment as interest.[2]

There are some situations, however, in which the nature of a derivative may be assimilated to the nature of the underlying transaction, asset or liability. For example, in *Echo Bay Mines Ltd. v. Canada*,[3] profits on cash-settled forward sales contracts for silver[4] entered into by a taxpayer who

---

1 R.S.C. 1985, 5th supp. c.1 as amended.

2 An amount is "interest" if (i) it constitutes compensation for the use of borrowed money; (ii) it is calculated with reference to a principal amount and (iii) it accrues daily. See *Reference as to the Validity of Section 6 of the Farm Security Act, 1944 (Saskatchewan)*, [1947] S.C.R. 394, aff'd [1949] A.C. 110 (P.C.); *Re Balaji Apartments and Manufacturer's Life Insurance Co.* (1979), 100 D.L.R. (3rd) 695 (Ont. H.C.J.); *Attorney-General (Ontario) v. Barfried Enterprises Ltd.*, [1963] S.C.R. 570. See also *Sherway Centre Ltd. v. The Queen*, [1998] 2 C.T.C. 343 (F.C.A.). Generally, no funds are considered to be borrowed under a swap. See discussion at Section 4, below.

3 [1992] 2 C.T.C. 182 (F.C.T.D.) [*Echo Bay*].

4 The contracts could have been physically settled but were settled in cash as they became due or were rolled over for new forward contracts.

operated a silver mine were considered to constitute part of the taxpayer's "income for the year from . . . the production in Canada of . . . metals or minerals . . . from mineral resources in Canada operated by him . . . " and therefore the taxpayer's "resource profits" under s. 1204(1) of the regulations to the Act. The Federal Court, Trial Division held that "[a]ctivities reasonably interconnected with marketing the product, undertaken to assure its sale at a satisfactory price, to yield income, and hopefully a profit, are, in my view, activities that form an integral part of production which is to yield income, and resource profits, within Regulation 1204(1)."[5] Cases like *Echo Bay*, however, reflect a statutory expansion of a concept or a creation of a particular type of category of transaction, expense or receipt.[6]

Nevertheless the instances where the nature of a derivative is assimilated to the underlying transaction, asset or liability are relatively rare. Instead, in most instances, the nature of a derivative instrument and the nature of the underlying asset, liability or transaction diverge, giving rise to opportunities and problems for taxpayers.

One of the most common examples of a situation in which derivatives are used to replicate economics without replicating the nature of the underlying transaction, asset or liability for taxation purposes is the "clone fund." Pension funds and certain other tax-exempt entities are subject to a special penalty tax under Part XI of the Act if such an entity owns "foreign property" in excess of a given threshold, currently 30% of all property owned by

---

5 *Ibid.* at 196. "Resource profits" are a component of the calculation of the "resource allowance," for which taxpayers are entitled to a deduction under paragraph 20(1)(v.1) of the Act.

6 Recently the Canada Revenue Agency (the "CRA") issued a statement that could be viewed as an expansion of circumstances when the nature of a derivative may be influenced by the nature of the hedged transaction. In CRA *Document No. 2002-0138617* (August 21, 2002), the CRA considered whether an insurer, who is subject to a very specific and detailed income tax regime for insurance companies, could deduct losses on foreign currency swaps on the basis that the swaps were "used . . . or held by it in the year in the course of . . . carrying on an insurance business in Canada." The swaps hedged foreign currency bonds that were not used or held by the insurer in the course of carrying on an insurance business in Canada. The CRA took the position that, in the absence of additional facts such as the identity of the parties, the circumstances under which the swaps were entered into and the use of the bonds, the swaps should not be considered to be property used or held in the course of carrying on an insurance business in Canada. The CRA referred to the *Shell* decision (described and reviewed below) in support of this position. The CRA stated that "the nature of the underlying asset is an important factor in the determination of whether the contracts were used or held in the insurance business in Canada," but also said that their position was not that "the contracts are not being treated as transactions separate from the underlying bonds."

the taxpayer as measured by reference to the "cost amount" of each property.[7] Units of a mutual fund trust will not be considered to be "foreign property" for a particular month if at no time during the particular month did the cost amount to the trust of all foreign property held by it exceed 30% of the cost amount of all property held by the trust.[8] A multitude of mutual fund trusts have been established such that the units are not foreign property notwithstanding that the trusts mimic investments in foreign property through derivatives such as swaps and cash-settled forwards. These derivatives are typically not considered to be "foreign property" on the basis that they are "intangible property" that is "situated" in Canada.[9]

One example of a problem that has arisen in the past as a result of the divergence between the nature of a derivative and the underlying transaction was hedging transactions entered into by foreign affiliates. A typical fact pattern is set out in *CRA Document No. 9617905*.[10] A controlled foreign affiliate ("FA") of a corporation resident in Canada ("Canco") makes loans to operating controlled foreign affiliates of Canco in various foreign countries. The loans are on income account to FA and are made in a foreign cur-

---

7 Subsection 206(2) of the Act, and particularly paragraph 206(2)(b) of the Act. The threshold is lower in certain circumstances.

8 See paragraphs (i) of the definition of "foreign property" in s. 206(1) and s. 5000(1) of the regulations to the Act.

9 "Foreign property" is defined in s. 206(1) of the Act to include "intangible property . . . situated outside Canada." If the counterparty to a swap or forward contract is a resident of Canada, the CRA will generally take the position that the derivative is situated in Canada. See, for example, *CRA Document No. 2000-004532* (January 1, 2001), under which a cash-settled forward contract linked to the investment returns generated by notional units that were themselves foreign property was considered not to be foreign property. See also *CRA Document No. 0079143* (January 1, 2001). The CRA has recently stated that it will also take into account the place where the derivative was entered into and remains situated when considering whether a derivative is "foreign property." See CRA Document No. 2002-0159065 (January 7, 2003).

Even if such derivatives were considered to be foreign property, the impact of such a characterization would be quite minimal in most cases given that the CRA takes the position that the "cost amount" of such derivatives is the cost of purchasing the derivative, rather than the "notional amount" of the derivative. See CRA Document No. 9609943 (1996), in which the CRA took the position that the "cost amount" of exchange-traded futures contracts and forward currency contracts was equal to the brokerage fees and other costs incidental to entering into the contracts and did not include any amounts in respect of the contract price or amounts paid, if any, as initial or variation margins. See similarly *CRA Document No. 2000-0045323* (January 1, 2001); *CRA Document No. 2001-0076453* (January 1, 2001) and *CRA Document No. 2002-0159065* (January 7, 2003).

10 *CRA Document No. 9617905* (January 16, 1998). See also *CRA Document No. 9729790* (November 21, 1997).

rency. FA enters into swaps with third parties to hedge its foreign currency exposure with respect to the loans. The interest income on the loans is deemed to be included in FA's "active business income" under subparagraph 95(2)(a)(ii), such that the interest income would escape the "foreign accrual property income" rules (which would require current taxation of FA's investment income in Canco's hands) and could eventually be repatriated to Canco free of Canadian tax (as "exempt surplus"). However, the CRA has taken the position that income from the swaps is foreign accrual property income.[11] Subparagraph 95(2)(a)(ii) does not apply to deem the hedging income to be active business income. The Department of Finance has now proposed legislation[12] which would provide that the income or loss on such currency hedges will be considered to be nil.

2) Character of a Derivative

The relevant case law provides that the character (i.e., income or capital) of a derivative instrument can potentially be determined by the character of the reference asset, liability or transaction. A derivative will take its character from an underlying asset, liability or transaction if the derivative is sufficiently linked to the underlying asset, liability or transaction; this concept is sometimes called the "linkage principle." If the derivative is not considered to be a hedge, but instead is considered to be a trading or speculative transaction, the derivative will generally be considered to be on income account regardless of the character of the reference asset, liability or transaction.[13]

Notwithstanding some uncertainty on the point in the past,[14] the linkage principle now appears to be entrenched in Canadian jurisprudence due to the decision of the Supreme Court of Canada in *Shell Canada Ltd. v. The Queen*.[15] Shell, a resident of Canada, required approximately US$100 mil-

11 These statements consider whether the hedging income could be considered to be active business income under subparagraph 95(2)(a)(i).

12 Proposed paragraph 95(2)(g.01).

13 But see discussion of the CRA's administrative concession in *Interpretation Bulletin IT-346R*, at section C(1) below.

14 N. C. Loveland, "Taxation of Currency and Interest Rate Risk Management Strategies and Products," in *Corporate Management Tax Conference 1992* (Toronto: Canadian Tax Foundation, 1992) 11:1 at 11:10; T. Edgar, *The Income Tax Treatment of Financial Instruments: Theory and Practice* (Canadian Tax Paper No. 105) (Toronto: Canadian Tax Foundation, 2000) at 55. Prior to *Shell*, *Salada Foods*, discussed below, was frequently cited as authority for the linkage principle.

15 [1999] 3 S.C.R. 622 [*Shell*]. In *CRA Document No. 2003-0038345* (September 18, 2003) the CRA was asked whether amounts received by a mutual fund trust pursuant to contracts entered into to provide capital protection to itself and its unitholders would

lion for its operations. Rather than borrowing directly in U.S. dollars, Shell borrowed in New Zealand dollars, entering into debentures with an aggregate principal amount of NZ$150 million. At the same time, Shell entered into a forward exchange contract with Sumitomo Bank Ltd. ("Sumitomo"). Under the forward contract, Shell paid Sumitomo the proceeds of the issuance of New Zealand dollar debt (approximately NZ$150 million) and Sumitomo paid to Shell the equivalent amount (measured at then-current exchange rates) in U.S. dollars (approximately US$100 million). Throughout the term of the New Zealand dollar debt, Sumitomo made periodic payments of New Zealand dollars (NZ$11,550,000 each semi-annual period) to Shell sufficient to allow Shell to service its New Zealand dollar debt. In exchange, Shell made periodic payments to Sumitomo in U.S. dollars. The U.S. dollar amounts were determined when the forward contract was entered into on the basis of market forward rates. At the end of the term of the New Zealand debt, Sumitomo paid NZ$150 million to Shell under the forward agreement to allow Shell to repay its New Zealand debt. In exchange, Shell paid approximately US$79.5 million to Sumitomo.

When the final payments under the forward contract were ultimately made, the New Zealand dollar had deteriorated vis-à-vis the U.S. dollar less than expected, and Shell realized a gain of US$21 million.[16] The Supreme Court of Canada made the following statements with respect to the character of the gain:

> The purpose of the Debenture Agreements was to provide Shell with working capital for a five year term. It was a capital debt obligation. Therefore, the foreign exchange gain arising from the fact that the value of the NZ$150 million that Shell returned to the foreign lenders in 1993 was less than the value of the NZ$150 million that Shell borrowed in 1988 was also received on capital account . . .

---

be on income or capital amount. The CRA ruled that, since the payments corresponded to capital losses of the trust, amounts received pursuant to the contract should be a capital receipt giving rise to a taxable capital gain.

16 Shell was required to pay approximately NZ$150 million on the debentures. Under the forward exchange contract with Sumitomo, Shell had contracted to pay approximately US$79.5 million for the NZ$150 million. Because the NZ$150 million was originally an outlay equal to US$100 million, Shell had locked itself into a US$20.5 million gain on the settlement of the debentures. However, the N.Z. dollar depreciated against the U.S. dollar less than expected, and NZ$150 million was actually worth US$81.5 million. Accordingly, Shell had a gain of US$18.5 million on the settlement of the debentures on a stand-alone basis, and another gain of US$2 million on the settlement of the forward agreement.

> Whether a foreign exchange gain arising from a hedging contract should be characterized as being on income or capital account depends on the characterization of the debt obligation to which the hedge relates. As noted, Shell entered into the Forward Exchange Contract in order to hedge with US$ the market risk on the Debenture Agreements, which were denominated in NZ$. Indeed, Shell would not have entered into the Debenture Agreements in the absence of the Foward Exchange Contract. The gain on the Debenture Agreements was characterized as being earned on capital account and so therefore should the gain on the Forward Exchange Contract. . . .
>
> As noted, the proper tax treatment of a foreign exchange gain on both the initial borrowing and any related hedge transaction is to be assessed in light of the characterization of the underlying debt obligation. In this case, for example, the underlying debt obligation recorded in the Debenture Agreements was entered into for the purpose of raising funds for use in Shell's business. Neither it nor the related hedge transaction lose that characteristic simply because they were deliberate and organized.[17]

The Supreme Court of Canada's decision in *Shell* leaves open the question of how closely a derivative and the hedged transaction must be linked in order to import the character of the hedge transaction to the derivative. The link between the New Zealand debt and the forward contract in *Shell* was very strong. The Supreme Court of Canada specifically noted "Shell would not have entered into the Debenture Agreements in the absence of the Forward Exchange Contract."[18]

In *Salada Foods Ltd. v. The Queen*,[19] the taxpayer entered into a forward purchase contract under which it contracted to purchase £500,000 for $1,496,562.50 at a date approximately six months after the taxpayer entered into the contract. On the close of the contract, the taxpayer realized a gain of $186,312. At issue was whether the gain was a capital gain[20] or whether the gain was taxable on the basis that the contract was an adventure in the nature of trade. The taxpayer argued that the forward purchase contract was entered into for the purpose of protecting the value of its investments in its British subsidiaries against an expected devaluation of the British pound. The Court found that:

---

17 *Ibid.* at 654–57.

18 *Ibid.* at 654.

19 [1974] C.T.C. 201 (F.C.T.D.) [*Salada Foods*].

20 If the gain was a capital gain, the gain would not be taxable. Canada did not tax capital gains before 1972; the contract was executed in August 1967.

> there is little or no relationship between the gain received by the plaintiff on its forward sale contract and its actual investment loss occurring as a result of the devaluation of the pound. To that extent then, in my view, the evidence of the witness and the arguments advanced by counsel for the plaintiff in support of the propositions that the gain was offset by the loss in investment and was attributable to capital account and not income tend to be specious and cannot be supported by other evidence nor withstand close scrutiny as to the result achieved by the transaction in question.[21]

The facts upon which the Court relied to reach this conclusion were the following:

- the financial statements recorded the value of the taxpayer's investments in its British subsidiaries as being £532,000, rather than £500,000;
- the value of the investment in the subsidiaries was uncertain; in particular, the value of retained earnings was uncertain given that dividends would have to be declared by the U.K. directors and given that there were strict foreign exchange controls in place in the U.K. at that time; and
- no appraisal of the value of the taxpayer's U.K. subsidiaries had been undertaken.

The Court also noted that the transaction was "acknowledged by the plaintiff to be wholly speculative" in that the taxpayer was speculating that the British pound would be devalued.[22] The fact that the taxpayer stated that the purpose of the transaction was to hedge a potential loss on its capital asset was found not to be relevant and "[h]aving found that the income was from an adventure in the nature of trade on the above authorities, it is immaterial what the motive was that brought the profit into existence and how it was applied thereafter."[23]

Salada has been cited in support of the linkage principle,[24] yet the Trial Division found no linkage in that case and suggested at the end of the decision (arguably in contradiction with the remainder of the decision) that the nature of a forward contract was such that a gain or loss on a forward would always be on income account notwithstanding that the forward con-

---

21 *Ibid.* at 206.

22 *Ibid.* at 208.

23 *Ibid.* at 207.

24 See, for example, R. S. Wilson, "Arbitage Trading," in *2000 Conference Report* (Toronto: Canadian Tax Foundation, 2001) 23:1 at 23:10.

tract may have been hedging a capital asset or liability.[25] This latter point is now moot given the Supreme Court of Canada decision in *Shell*. However, *Salada* could still be cited in the future as support for the position that characterization of a derivative as a hedge may require perfect or near-perfect matching.

Ethicon Sutures Ltd. v. The Queen[26] is a more clear statement of the linkage principle, but also seems to require a very strong link between the two transactions. Here the Court considered whether foreign exchange gains on short-term U.S. dollar deposits were taxable on income or on capital account. There was some evidence that the short-term U.S. dollar deposits were established for the purpose of setting aside U.S. dollars to be distributed as dividends up to the taxpayer's U.S. parent. However, the evidence also established that, although the funds were "earmarked" for this purpose, the funds were also used at times to purchase inventory. Financial statements and other documentation were also inconsistent with the contention that the short-term deposits were to be used for paying dividends. Finally, U.S. dollar short-term deposits continued to exist even after dividend payment dates.

The Court found that the foreign exchange gains were on income account, stating the following:

> The evidence from the appellant's witness that the deposits were primarily earmarked for payment of dividends indicates clearly other intentions . . .
>
> I am satisfied the primary aim of that appellant was to use the funds for payment of dividends, but its secondary option and intention was to have money available from time to time to meet inventory payments.
>
> To be considered capital in nature, the funds must be surplus, must be exclusively for dividend or capital expenditures, i.e. it must be in a firm final dedication, and not enough if "earmarked primarily."[27]

Echo Bay, discussed above, can be considered a "hedging" case. Recall that the issue in this case was whether profits from a cash-settled silver for-

---

25 See D. G. Broadhurst, "Income Tax Treatment of Foreign Exchange Forward Contracts, Swaps and Other Hedging Transactions," in *1989 Conference Report* (Toronto: Canadian Tax Foundation, 1990) 26:1 at 26:8 for further discussion of this case.

26 [1985] 2 C.T.C. 6 (F.C.T.D.) [*Ethicon Sutures*]. The CRA specifically cites *Ethicon Sutures* as authority for the linkage principle in *CRA Document No. 9728215* (February 4, 1998). See also *Atlantic Sugar Refineries v. Minister of National Revenue*, [1949] C.T.C. 196 (S.C.C.), which held that a taxpayer who refined and sold sugar was required to include in business income profits from sugar futures contracts.

27 *Ethicon Sutures*, above note 26, at 11.

ward contract could be considered to be "resource profits." The conclusion that the profits could be so considered was based primarily on the finding that the forwards constituted "hedging." The Court accepted evidence that a "hedge" for GAAP purposes in these circumstances would exist if four criteria were met:

1. The item to be hedged exposes the enterprise to price (or interest rate) risk.
2. The futures contract reduces that exposure and is designated as a hedge.
3. The significant characteristics and expected terms of the anticipated transactions are identified.
4. It is probable that the anticipated transaction will occur.[28]

The court then found that the forwards were indeed "hedges."

> It is my view that the transactions in respect of the forward sales contracts entered into on behalf of the plaintiff constitute "hedging" as that was defined by the plaintiff's expert, Bowles, and accepted by the Court and by counsel . . . it is urged that there was insufficient matching, in respect of quantity of production and time of delivery of product and closing out of the forward sales contracts, between the two parallel sets of transactions, but I note that there is no evidence of correlation or lack of it. Rather, the only evidence is that of Mr. Jenner that the forward sales contracts were hedging, undertaken to assure returns by fixing the price for future production in a fluctuating market, that the sales contracts did not exceed anticipated production, and further the admission of counsel that a number of the forward sales contracts were settled in advance of their date for maturity. Mr. Jenner testified that the estimates upon which the forward sales transactions were based, in total, were close approximations of the actual production carried out. Estimates were being continually revised in order that quantities of silver to be sold forward did not exceed actual production. . . . Exact matching was not feasible from a practical point of view, nor is it required in order to constitute hedging.
>
> I conclude that the price received by the plaintiff for the silver it produced was the sum of receipts from delivery of actual production and from settlement of forward sales contracts. The business of the plaintiff was silver production. In these circumstances where the plaintiff participated in forward sales contracts and settlements, however, as a hedge against price fluctuations in silver, and in which the commodity traded

---

28 *Echo Bay*, above note 3, at 187.

> was silver futures, I do not conclude that the plaintiff was involved in futures speculation for investment purposes.[29]

Echo Bay is virtually alone both in its attempt to define the concept of "hedging" and because of its reliance on GAAP in this respect. However, *Echo Bay* is not unduly cited either in case-law or in administrative pronouncements on more general derivatives questions, and could be considered as having little precedential value outside the "resource profits" definition. Nevertheless, whether a transaction is treated as a hedge for accounting purposes should be very persuasive in determining whether the transaction should be treated as a hedge for tax purposes.[30]

The Department of Finance introduced rules limiting interest deductions in the context of weak currency borrowings such as the one considered in *Shell*. This new legislation, s. 20.3, will be reviewed below, but here it can be noted that s. 20.3(1) contains the following definition of "hedge":

> "hedge" in respect of a debt of a taxpayer that is at any time a weak currency debt means any agreement made by the taxpayer
> (a) that can reasonably be regarded as having been made by the taxpayer primarily to reduce the taxpayer's risk, with respect to payments of principal or interest in respect of the debt, of fluctuations in the value of the weak currency; and
> (b) that is identified by the taxpayer as a hedge in respect of the debt in a designation in prescribed form filed with the Minister on or before the 30th day after the day the taxpayer enters into the agreement.

The technical notes to this legislation state:

> It is contemplated that hedges could be in a variety of legal forms such as forward and futures contracts, options, swaps and long positions in assets denominated in a foreign currency. A hedge need not eliminate all risk associated with foreign currency exposure in a weak currency debt; a contract that serves to reduce risks only partially is included.

Proposed paragraph 95(2)(g.01), which deems certain hedging gains and losses of a foreign affiliate to be nil, as discussed earlier, states as follows:

> Any income, loss, capital gain or capital loss, derived by a foreign affiliate of a taxpayer under or as a result of an agreement that provides for the

29 *Ibid.* at 195-196.

30 See S.D. Porter & K.J.A. Vallillee, "Tax and Accounting Aspects of Treasury Operations," in *2000 Conference Report* (Toronto: Canadian Tax Foundation, 2001) 20:1 at 20:8–9 and 20:26 for more on this point.

purchase, sale or exchange of currency and that can reasonably be considered to have been made by the affiliate to reduce its risk (with respect to any source, any particular income, gain or loss determined in reference to which is deemed by paragraph (g) to be nil) of fluctuations in the value of currency, is, to the extent of the absolute value of the particular income, gain or loss, deemed to be nil . . .

One might cite these provisions in support of the position that perfect matching should not be required for hedge characterization. However, the extent to which these provisions influence the CRA and the courts in determining when a derivative is sufficiently linked to an underlying transaction remains to be seen. Further, note that the bulk of the case law on the linkage principle addresses foreign exchange transactions; that this case law is applicable to other types of hedges is very reasonable but not inevitable.

3) Combination/Bifurcation

Whether a derivative can be combined with another transaction or bifurcated into components is essentially the broader question of whether economic substance can trump legal form for Canadian federal income tax purposes.

a) Combination

The question of whether transactions can be combined for Canadian tax purposes was squarely addressed in *Shell*.

In *Shell*, the Minister argued that the forward agreements and the debentures should be, essentially, collapsed such that Shell should have been considered to have borrowed in U.S. dollars. The Minister then arrived at the amount of the interest deduction by using the market rate of interest applicable to U.S. dollar loans of the U.S. dollar equivalent of the NZ$150 million calculated at the exchange rates prevailing at the time the debentures were issued.[31] This position met with favour at the Federal Court of Appeal but not with the Supreme Court of Canada which rejected this approach, stating:

This Court has repeatedly held that courts must be sensitive to the economic realities of a particular transaction, rather than being bound to

31 This argument is expressed briefly in the judgment of the Supreme Court of Canada, above note 15, at 640, but is expressed in more detail in the decisions of the Tax Court of Canada at [1997] 3 C.T.C. 2238 (T.C.C.) at 2246 and 2250 and the Federal Court of Appeal at [1998] 2 C.T.C. 207 (F.C.A.) at 214 and 227.

> what first appears to be its legal form . . . But there are at least two caveats to this rule. First, this Court has never held that the economic realities of a situation can be used to recharacterize a taxpayer's *bona fide* legal relationships. To the contrary, we have held that, absent a specific provision of the Act to the contrary or a finding that they are a sham, the taxpayer's legal relationships must be respected in tax cases. Recharacterization is only permissible if the label attached by the taxpayer to the particular transaction does not properly reflect its actual legal effect . . .
>
> Second, it is well established in this Court's tax jurisprudence that a searching inquiry for either the "economic realities" of a particular transaction or the general object and spirit of the provision at issue can never supplant a court's duty to apply an unambiguous provision of the Act to a taxpayer's transaction. Where the provision at issue is clear and unambiguous, its terms must simply be applied . . .
>
> It is my respectful view that by paying insufficient attention to these very important principles, the Minister and the Federal Court of Appeal fell into error. First, the Federal Court of Appeal effectively recharacterized for tax purposes Shell's legal relationship with the foreign lenders. Indeed, Linden J.A. held that, when the Forward Exchange Contract between Shell and Sumitomo was considered alongside the Debenture Agreements between Shell and the foreign lenders, "[t]he higher interest rate coupled with the discounted forward rate created a blended payment of interest and principal . . .". With respect, this ignores the actual relationship between Shell and the foreign lenders, a relationship to which Sumitomo was to a party. As between Shell and the foreign lenders, the semi-annual payments were entirely "interest," paid in consideration for the loan NZ$150 million. That characterization cannot be changed by whatever other legal relationships Shell may have concluded with third parties, or indeed by anything that Shell did with the borrowed funds after receiving them from the foreign lenders.[32]

However, in *Hayes et al. v. The Queen*,[33] distinct transactions entered into by separate taxpayers were combined and viewed as one property. In that case several pairs of taxpayers, in most cases a husband and wife, had entered into hedge transactions. One taxpayer would obtain a short position in a stock, while the other would obtain a long position in the same stock in the form of other securities (such as convertible preferred stock or

---

32 *Shell*, above note 15, at 641–42. See an example of the usage of *Shell* by the CRA in the CRA's favour in CRA *Document No. 2000-0001327* (April 11, 2000).

33 2003 D.T.C. 1205 (T.C.C.).

a convertible or exchangeable bond) convertible into that stock or rights to purchase that stock, perhaps with interest bearing securities. Each taxpayer guaranteed the margin account of the other. Dividends or interest received would be used to pay stock borrow fees, leaving a small profit. The fluctuation of the value of the stock would cause one of the legs of the transaction to appreciate and the other to depreciate, leaving the taxpayers with an opportunity to crystallize the loss on one leg of the transaction. Judge Miller found that the stock and the convertible security together were one property, which he called a "convertible hedge." He noted that "property" under the *ITA* is very broadly defined to include "a right of any kind whatever" and went on to state:

> But the right which only arises from the convertible hedge itself, and consequently satisfies me that the convertible hedge is property, is the right to rely on one component of the convertible hedge to satisfy the margin requirements of the other component, whether this be in a single account or through the auspices of a Guarantor's account . . . In summary, the convertible hedge consists of components containing rights; it also, by its very essence, creates a right particular to the convertible hedge alone. The convertible hedge meets the broad *Income Tax Act* definition of property.[34]

As noted, this case is still before the courts and should not be taken as authority on this point, particularly in light of its apparent conflict with *Shell*.[35]

b) Bifurcation

A particular transaction may contain two economic components. For example, a derivative may be embedded in a debt obligation.[36] Generally, Canadian courts do not consider each of these component parts separately in determining the character or nature of an asset, liability or transaction.[37]

This issue was addressed explicitly by the Supreme Court of Canada in *Alberta Natural Gas Company. v. Minister of National Revenue*.[38] In this case,

---

34 *Ibid.* at 1224.

35 The CRA has refused to comment on the treatment of hedged investments while this case is still before the courts: see *CRA Document No. 2003-000137* (October 14, 2003).

36 A relatively straightforward example of this is the convertible or exchangeable debenture, which can be viewed as a debt that has an option to acquire shares embedded within it. See a detailed analysis of this example in the Canadian context in D. H. Watkins, "Equity Exchangeable Debentures and Appreciation Rights," in *1993 Conference Report* (Toronto: Canadian Tax Foundation, 1994) 20:1 at 20:4–8.

37 D. F. Sykora, "The Income Tax Web Surrounding Derivatives," in *1995 Conference Report* (Toronto: Canadian Tax Foundation, 1996) 30:1 at 30:33.

38 [1972] S.C.R. 490 [*Alberta Natural Gas*]. See also *Alberta Gas Trunk Line Co. v. Minister of National Revenue*, [1972] S.C.R. 498.

the taxpayer owned and operated a gas pipeline. The taxpayer was a party to a gas delivery contract that provided that if the taxpayer financed the construction of the pipeline to be used to deliver the gas with securities denominated in U.S. dollars, the gas suppliers would pay for part of the delivery in U.S. dollars (at a 1:1 rate of exchange). The U.S. dollar appreciated in comparison to the Canadian dollar; the issue was whether this foreign exchange gain on the gas delivery contract should be taxed as part of the taxpayer's business income.

The taxpayer argued that the gas delivery contract should be considered to consist of both a delivery contract and a foreign exchange contract. The foreign exchange contract ought to be considered as a hedge of the taxpayer's U.S. dollar denominated securities, in the view of the taxpayer, and therefore the gain should not be considered to be on income account. The Court refused to bifurcate the transaction, stating: "I cannot construe the agreement as being one which provides for payment for the appellant's services in Canadian dollars, coupled with a forward exchange contract for the purchase by the appellant from the shippers of United States dollars."[39]

Minister of National Revenue v. Tip Top Tailors Ltd.[40] is also arguably a bifurcation case. Here, the taxpayer was a clothing manufacturer that purchased cloth from suppliers in the U.K. In January of 1948, the taxpayer anticipated a devaluation of the British pound. Accordingly, the taxpayer arranged for a £250,000 line of credit with the London office of a Canadian bank. For the next one and one-half years, the taxpayer paid for purchases of material out of this line of credit, accumulating a debt with the bank. Upon the devaluation of the British pound in September 1949, the taxpayer paid off its debt to the bank recognizing a foreign exchange gain of approximately $160,000. At issue was the character of the gain.

The Supreme Court of Canada found that the gain was on income account (and therefore taxable) to the taxpayer. Arguably, the agreement to satisfy the debt obligation could have been considered separately from the purchase agreement — the delay in the repayment of the bank debt was not integral to the purchase transaction — the delay was entirely at the option of the taxpayer and was selected by the taxpayer for speculative reasons rather than for reasons relating to the clothing business. Nevertheless, the Court refused to bifurcate the transaction into a forward and a purchase agreement, and took the character of the foreign exchange gain

---

39 *Ibid*, (*Alberta Natural Gas*) at 496–97.

40 [1957] C.T.C. 309 (S.C.C.) [*Tip Top Tailors*].

from what was presumably considered to be the dominant aspect of the transaction, that of a purchase agreement.[41]

In *Netupsky v. The Queen*,[42] the taxpayer wished to refinance a piece of real property. The taxpayer considered borrowing in several different currencies, and ultimately decided on a borrowing in Swiss francs that would be converted into Canadian dollars. When the Swiss loan was repaid several years later, the taxpayer realized a foreign exchange loss. The issue was whether the Swiss loan was "part of the mortgage financing" and therefore on capital account, or whether the Swiss loan and the conversion to Canadian dollars were "two separate and distinct parts to this transaction," in which case the loss on the Swiss loan would be considered to be on income account.[43] The Court noted particularly that the taxpayer dealt frequently in foreign exchange and examined his options carefully when selecting a currency for the loan in question. The Court also found that the Swiss franc loan was secured by a demand promissory note which, in the Court's view, put the Swiss franc loan on current account. The Court also stated that the monthly payments were speculative in that the amount of Canadian dollars required to purchase Swiss funds to make the interest payments varied each month. Accordingly, the Court stated:

> I do not believe that the characterization of the currency loss follows the transaction from which it results to place it on capital account . . . I conclude that there were two separate and distinct transactions as borne out by the evidence with the result being that the appeal is allowed [and the loss was considered to be on income account].[44]

---

41 Justice Rand stated:

> The loan produced working capital used in the course of the company's business; the loan was effected as each payment was made to a seller; but in substance the creation of debt in the bank was merely a substitution of creditor for the actual transactions: no advance was ever made or, so far as the case goes, was ever agreed to be made to the company itself . . . Here there was simply an accumulation of debt as the transactions of the business proceeded . . . The only difference between that course of dealing and the ordinary monthly arrangements with a bank lies in the possibly greater time allowed the outgoings to accumulate. It was a large scale process of overdraft through a substantial period of time which I am quite unable to view as an investment.

(*Ibid.* at 313–14.) See also *D.W.S. Corp. v. Minister of National Revenue*, [1968] C.T.C. 65 (Ex. Ct.).

42 [1992] 2 C.T.C. 2531 (T.C.C.) [*Netupsky*].

43 *Ibid.* at 2533.

44 *Ibid.* at 2534.

Netupsky has been characterized by some as a "linkage" case[45] notwithstanding the absence of linkage found by the Court. However, it is perhaps better seen as a bifurcation case, in which case *Netupsky* could be viewed as, perhaps, the lone example of a Canadian court choosing to bifurcate a transaction into its economic components, albeit through the rather strange method of separating the transaction into two formal components (the loan and the conversion).[46] Alternatively, the Court in *Netupsky* could be seen as having viewed speculation as being the dominant character of the loan notwithstanding that the proceeds of the loan were used to finance a capital property, such that the foreign exchange gain on the loan was viewed as being on income account.

The CRA has also taken the position that an instrument will generally not be bifurcated into its economic components. In *Interpretation Bulletin IT-96R6*,[47] the CRA states the following at paragraph 9 with respect to a security with a conversion feature:

> In the case of a security with a conversion feature which is not severable from the security and cannot be separately traded, no part of the issue price can be allocated to the conversion feature. If the security is converted, the proceeds of disposition cannot be allocated between the conversion feature and the security. Therefore, section 49 does not apply to such a convertible security.[48]

In *CRA Document No. 2000-0062337*,[49] the CRA considered whether an agreement under which a purchaser made a current cash payment for an agreed quantity of resource production could be bifurcated into a sale of production and a loan. The CRA stated that

> . . . the Canadian courts have relied on the legal form of contracts to determine the income tax treatment. The Supreme Court held in *Shell Canada*

45 See P.M. Meredith, "'Linkage' — Characterizing Hedging Profits or Losses" (1993) Corporate Finance 74 at 76.

46 Separating the loan from the conversion such that the character of the loan differs from the character of the foreign exchange gain or loss on the loan directly contradicts a number of cases, including *Shell* (S.C.C.), above note 15; *Ethicon Sutures*, above note 26; *Columbia Records of Canada Ltd. v. Minister of National Revenue*, [1971] C.T.C. 839 (F.C.T.D.); *Eli Lilly and Company (Canada) Limited v. Minister of National Revenue*, [1955] C.T.C. 198 (S.C.C.); *Aluminium Union Ltd. v. Minister of National Revenue*, [1960] C.T.C. 206 (Ex. Ct.); *Neonex International Ltd. v. The Queen*, [1977] C.T.C. 472 (F.C.T.D.).

47 *Interpretation Bulletin IT-96R6*, "Options granted by corporations to acquire shares, bonds or debentures and by trust to acquire trust units" (October 23, 1996).

48 See Watkins, above note 36, at 20:4-8 for further discussion.

49 *CRA Document No. 2000-0062337* (May 31, 2001).

> *Ltd. v. The Queen* . . . and other decisions, that the economic realities of a situation cannot be used to recharacterize a taxpayer's *bona fide* legal relationships. It held that absent a specific provision of the *Income Tax Act* . . . to the contrary or a finding that there is a sham, the taxpayer's legal relationships must be respected in tax cases. Recharacterization is only permissible if the label attached by the taxpayer to the particular transaction does not properly reflect its actual legal effect.

The CRA stated that there was no lender-borrower relationship created between the parties given that the vendor did not have any obligation to repay the funds initially paid by the purchaser. Accordingly, the legal relationships between the parties did not permit a bifurcation of the transaction into its economic components.[50]

4) Timing

A number of timing issues can arise in respect of derivatives. The particular timing issue that will be discussed here relates to matching income and losses as between derivatives and underlying transactions.

A taxpayer entering into an underlying transaction may be required to recognize unrealized income on that transaction; for example, the taxpayer may be required to accrue interest under a special regime for "prescribed debt obligations" found in s. 12(9) of the Act and s. 7000 of the regulations to the Act or may be required to mark-to-market shares or debt obligations under the special mark-to-market regime applicable to financial institutions.[51] Ideally, a taxpayer would want to recognize related expenses and losses on the same basis as accrual or mark-to-market inclusions. However, if the expenses or losses are not yet payable or have not yet been realized, the taxpayer will generally be prohibited from recognizing such expenses or losses on the basis that the liability is contingent.[52]

It may be possible to deduct unrealized losses under s.10(1), which allows a taxpayer to value "inventory" of a business at the end of the year at the lower of the cost of the inventory or its fair market value.[53]

---

50 See discussion under Section 3.5 below as to whether the general anti-avoidance rule can be used to bifurcate a transaction.

51 See ss.142.2 to 142.6 of the Act.

52 Paragraph 18(1)(e). See Wilson, above note 24, at 23:15-17, who argues that due to the decision of the Ontario Court of Appeal in *Canadian Pacific Ltd. v. Ontario (Minister of Revenue)*, [2000] 2 C.T.C. 331 (Ont. C.A.), a liability will not be considered to be contingent merely because its quantum is uncertain.

53 For more discussion on this point, see Edgar, above note 14, at 58–59 and Sykora, above note 37, at 30:23–25. This rule does not apply to a business that is an "adven-

With respect to the recognition of unrealized income, the general principle is that in the absence of specific legislation income is not required to be recognized unless the taxpayer is not restricted as to the use or enjoyment of the amount.[54] Attempts by the CRA to force recognition of income where corresponding losses have been realized but the income has not met with failure in *The Queen v. Friedberg*.[55] Here the taxpayer was a futures trader who bought and sold gold futures contracts. The taxpayer entered into "straddle" transactions closing out the transactions on which he suffered a loss before the end of the taxation year and closing out the transactions on which he would realize a gain in the subsequent taxation year. The Minister argued that the taxpayer ought to be required to recognize the gains and losses on a mark-to-market basis. The Supreme Court of Canada stated:

> On the facts, the respondent reported his losses when they were actually incurred, and his gains when they were actually realized. In our view, the appellant has not demonstrated that there is any error in adopting this approach. While the "marked to market" accounting method proposed by the appellant may better describe the taxpayer's income position for some purposes, we are not satisfied that it can describe income for income tax purposes, nor are we satisfied that a margin account balance is the appropriate measure of realized income for tax purposes. Similarly, while we recognized that the "lower of cost or market" method advocated by the respondent suggests that incurred losses can be deducted in the calculation of income, no unincurred losses were deducted by the respondent on the facts of this case. Accordingly, we need not determine the income tax validity of this implication of the "lower of cost or market" method in this case.[56]

Friedberg may not prohibit the mark-to-market method *per se*.[57] In a technical interpretation,[58] the CRA commented that the "mark-to-market" method was not precluded by *Friedberg* and would be appropriate in the right circumstances. In that case the taxpayer sold products to customers in the United States and so had accounts receivable denominated in U.S. dollars. These accounts receivable were hedged by the sale forward of U.S. dollars.

---

ture in the nature of trade" (a phrase that generally refers to an isolated and speculative transaction).

54 *Robertson v. Minister of National Revenue*, [1944] C.T.C. 75 (Ex. Ct.). See also *Ikea Ltd. v. The Queen*, [1998] 1 S.C.R. 196 at 215–16.

55 [1993] 4 S.C.R. 285 [*Friedberg*].

56 *Ibid.* at 286.

57 See a strong argument to this effect in Wilson, above note 24, at 23:14-15.

58 *CRA Document No. 2002-0160807* (April 16, 2003); see also *CRA Document No. 2003-0019667* (June 27, 2003).

The taxpayer had asked whether the accounts receivable should be translated at the year-end exchange rate or the forward exchange rate on the hedge. The CRA responded by saying that the year-end exchange rate would be appropriate, however, the taxpayer would be entitled to realize gain or loss on the forward currency contracts at the same time on a mark-to-market basis. The CRA stated:

> However, while the CCRA recognizes the realization method of computing income in respect of a financial instrument for a trader in [a]commodity future, it does not mean that the Supreme Court of Canada precluded the use of the "mark-to-market" method (or the margin account balance method) in computing income for income tax purposes. In fact, the Federal Court of Appeal in Friedberg recognized that both accounting experts who testified before the trial judge agreed that the "mark-to-market" method would be a more accurate reflection of the true financial position of the taxpayer, it was only that no legislation required that this method be used. The Supreme Court of Canada in *Canderel* stated that while the "mark-to-market" accounting method proposed by the Minister may better describe the taxpayer's income position for some purposes, it was not satisfied that it can describe income for income tax purposes. However, it did not say that the "mark-to-market" method is not an acceptable method. Therefore, if the taxpayer in this case did not want to use the realization method, it is perfectly legitimate if the method that the taxpayer wanted to use is also acceptable for income tax purposes in that it does not conflict with any provisions of the Act, the case law or the generally accepted business practices.

The absence of a prohibition against the mark-to-market method would be consistent with *Canadian General Electric Company Limited v. Minister of National Revenue*.[59] In this case the taxpayer was in the business of selling electrical machinery and supplies purchased from its U.S. parent and certain other suppliers. In issue was a foreign exchange gain realized in 1952 on the repayment of promissory notes owed by the taxpayer to its U.S. parent. The notes were issued between 1950 and 1952 as payment for supplies purchased by the taxpayer from its U.S. parent. The taxpayer recognized the gain on an amortized basis over the 1950, 1951 and 1952 taxation years using exchange rates prevailing on the last day of each taxation year. Justice Martland held that the taxpayer could indeed recognize the foreign exchange gain on an accrual basis.[60]

59 [1961] C.T.C. 512 (S.C.C.) [*Canadian General Electric*].
60 *Ibid.* at 521.

The CRA has taken the position that foreign exchange gains and losses can be recognized on an accrual basis or a realization basis[61] and that mutual funds can recognize derivative gains and losses on an accrual or realization basis.[62] (Both of these positions are subject to the caveat that the method selected must be used consistently from year to year.) The CRA has recently stated that another type of taxpayer (that was not a mutual fund and that was required under GAAP to mark-to-market equity-linked options) was entitled to use the realization method for gains or losses on equity-linked options provided that it used that method consistently for all its derivatives, but the CRA stated that its position was consistent with its position for mutual funds, which suggests that the accrual method for both gains and losses on derivatives may be acceptable to the CRA in other cases.[63]

5) GAAR

Derivatives, like any other transaction, may be subject to the application of the "general anti-avoidance rule" or "GAAR." The GAAR is found in s. 245 of the Act and is applicable if three requirements are met. First, a "tax benefit" must have resulted, directly or indirectly, from a particular transaction or a series of transactions that includes the particular transaction.[64] A "tax benefit" is defined as "a reduction, avoidance or deferral of tax or other amount payable under this Act or an increase in a refund of tax or other amount under this Act."[65] Second, the particular transaction or series of transactions cannot reasonably be considered to have been undertaken or arranged primarily for *bona fide* purposes other than to obtain the tax benefit.[66] Third, it may reasonably be considered that the transaction would result directly or indirectly in a misuse of the provisions of the Act or in an abuse of the Act having regard to the Act read as a whole.[67]

Although the GAAR has been in force since 1988, it has yet to be considered by the Supreme Court of Canada and has only been considered by the Federal Court of Appeal on a handful of occasions. One of these occa-

---

61 See *CRA Document No. 1991-58* (December, 1991); Interpretation Bulletin IT-95R, para. 8.

62 See *CRA Document No. 2000-0001327* (April 11, 2000) and *CRA Document No. 2003-0184127* (March 24, 2003).

63 *Ibid.*

64 Subsection 245(2) of the Act.

65 Subsection 245(1) of the Act.

66 Subsection 245(3) of the Act.

67 Subsection 245(4) of the Act.

sions was *Canadian Pacific Ltd. v. The Queen.*[68] In this case, the series of transactions was very similar to that considered in *Shell.*[69] The taxpayer was successful at the Tax Court of Canada, which found that: "The transactions which the Respondent says constitute the series were, when viewed objectively, inextricably linked as elements of a process primarily intended to produce the borrowed capital which the Appellant required for business purposes. The capital was produced and it was so used. No transaction forming part of the series can be viewed as having been arranged for a purpose which differs from the overall purpose of the series."[70] At the Federal Court of Appeal, the Minister argued that the designation of the debentures as being in Australian dollars was in itself a "transaction,"[71] the sole purpose of which was to produce a tax benefit. The Federal Court of Appeal rejected the Minister's argument and affirmed the analysis of the Tax Court of Canada. In particular, the Federal Court of Appeal stated that:

> The words of the Act require consideration of a transaction in its entirety and it is not open to the Crown artificially to split off various aspects of it in order to create an avoidance transaction. In the present case, the Australian dollar borrowing was one complete transaction and cannot be separated into two transactions by labelling the designation in Australian dollars as a separate transaction.[72]

In more general terms, the GAAR jurisprudence to date has provided more guidance as to how the GAAR is to be applied. In determining whether there is a tax benefit, for example, a normative or comparative transaction must be identified. This alternative transaction cannot be one which is "theoretically possible but, practically speaking, unlikely in the circumstances."[73] The fact that the person who has organized or arranged the transaction is not the person who obtains the tax benefit is not relevant.[74]

---

68 [2001] 1 C.T.C. 2190 (T.C.C.), aff'd in [2002] 2 C.T.C. 197 (F.C.A.) [*Canadian Pacific*].

69 In fact, the series of transactions in *Canadian Pacific* was different from *Shell* in a variety of ways; most importantly, the series of transactions in *Canadian Pacific* included a forward agreement (purchasing Australian dollars with Japanese yen) and a swap (exchanging Canadian dollars for Japanese yen). Arguably the analysis of these transactions might have been different had the transactions been reviewed in detail; however, both the Tax Court of Canada and the Federal Court of Appeal assumed that the transactions in issue were not materially different from those in *Shell.*

70 *Canadian Pacific* (T.C.C.), above note 68, at paragraph 15.

71 Under s. 245(1), "transaction" is defined to include an arrangement or event.

72 *Canadian Pacific* (F.C.A.), above note 68, at 208.

73 *Canadian Pacific* (T.C.C.), above note 68 at 2196.

74 *OSFC Holdings Ltd. v. The Queen*, [2001] 4 C.T.C. 82 (F.C.A.).

Once the tax benefit has been identified, a court must determine whether the primary purpose of the transaction or series of transactions is to obtain that tax benefit. Here a court may take into account the monetary value of the tax benefit in comparison with the other potential benefits of the transaction, although this comparison is not determinative.[75] Whether and to what extent the transactions were pre-arranged may also be relevant,[76] as well as any alternative transactions that the taxpayer might have entered into to accomplish the same economic objective.[77] If the primary purpose of the transaction or series of transactions was to obtain the tax benefit, the court must then determine whether the transaction or series of transactions may reasonably be considered to have resulted in a misuse of the provisions of the Act or in an abuse of the Act as a whole. At this stage the relevant policy or object and spirit of the Act must be identified, and then the transaction or series of transactions must be measured against that policy or object and spirit in order to determine whether there has been a misuse or abuse. Here the relevant policy or object and spirit can be determined with reference to particular provisions of the Act; reliance on extrinsic aids such as commentary is also permitted.[78] The policy or object and spirit must be clear and unambiguous if GAAR is to be applied.[79]

C. FUTURES AND FORWARD CONTRACTS

1) Physical settlement

There will be no gain or loss for the purchaser on the settlement of a physically-settled forward or future except to the extent that there is a disposition of the consideration (e.g. foreign currency) paid by the purchaser.[80] This result is now codified in section 49.1, which states:

> For greater certainty, where a taxpayer acquires a particular property in satisfaction of an absolute or contingent obligation of a person or partnership to provide the particular property pursuant to a contract or other arrangement one of the main objectives of which was to establish a right, whether

75 *Ibid.*; *Duncan v. The Queen*, [2002] 4 C.T.C. 1 (F.C.A.) [*Duncan*]; *Matthew v. The Queen*, [2003] 1 C.T.C. 2045 (T.C.C.).

76 *OSFC Holdings*, above note 74.

77 *Duncan*, above note 75.

78 *OSFC Holdings*, above note 74; *Loyens et al. v. The Queen*, 2003 D.T.C. 355 (T.C.C.).

79 *OSFC Holdings*, above note 74; *Jabin Investments Ltd. v. The Queen*, [2002] F.C.A. 520 (F.C.A.); *Produits Forestiers Donohue Inc. v. The Queen*, 2002 D.T.C. 7512 (F.C.A.).

80 See, for example, *British South Africa Co. v. Varty*, [1965] 2 All E.R. 395 (H.L.).

absolute or contingent, to the particular property and that right was not under the terms of a trust, partnership agreement, share or debt obligation, the satisfaction of the obligation is not a disposition of that right.

Accordingly, the forward purchase price becomes the cost to the purchaser of the property acquired under a physically-settled forward purchase agreement, and the economic gain or loss in respect of the forward purchase agreement is recognized on the subsequent disposition of the subject matter of the forward contracts. The forward sale price will form proceeds of disposition to the vendor upon physical settlement of the forward.

Gains and losses on forwards and futures should ordinarily be characterized according to the general principles set out above. If the forward or future is a hedge of a capital asset or liability, the gain or loss on the forward or future should also be on capital account; otherwise, the gain or loss on the forward or future is likely to be considered to be a speculative or trading transaction and therefore on income account (recall the forward foreign currency transactions addressed in *Shell*).[81]

The CRA, however, permits a "speculator" to report gains and losses from transactions in commodity futures on capital account so long as such reporting is followed consistently each year.[82] Similar treatment is granted in respect of foreign currency futures.[83] For these purposes, a "speculator" excludes a person who (a) takes futures positions in commodities connected with his or her business as part of their business operations; (b) has access to inside information about the commodity which he or she uses to his or her benefit in one or more such transactions; or (c) is a corporation whose prime or only business activity is trading in futures or commodi-

---

81 Some taxpayers may also be able to guarantee capital treatment due to an irrevocable election available under s. 39(4). A taxpayer who elects under s. 39(4) will be considered to hold and dispose of "Canadian securities" on capital account. A "Canadian security" is, generally, a share of a corporation resident in Canada, a unit of a mutual fund trust or a bond, debenture, bill, note, mortgage, hypothecary claim or similar obligation issued by a person resident in Canada: s. 39(6). See the exceptions to these categories listed in s. 6200 of the regulations to the Act. The election is available to any taxpayer other than a "trader or dealer in securities," certain financial institutions, a corporation whose principal business is the lending of money or the purchasing of debt obligations or a combination thereof and a non-resident: s. 39(5). Mutual fund corporations and mutual fund trusts are, however, always eligible to make the s. 39(4) election.

82 *Interpretation Bulletin IT -346R*, "Commodity Futures and Certain Commodities" (November 20, 1978).

83 *Interpretation Bulletin IT -95R*, "Foreign Exchange Gains and Losses" (December 16, 1980), para. 6.

ties.[84] The CRA's position is particularly welcome given the suggestion made by some that futures contracts might be harder to characterize as hedges given their standardized terms.[85]

As discussed in more detail below in the context of swaps, forwards entered into by a borrower to hedge exposure to currency fluctuations in respect of interest on a debt obligation are generally treated on income account. Income treatment is necessary for an effective hedge of currency risk where interest on the borrowing is deductible for tax purposes. While interest expense is generally considered by the jurisprudence as an outlay of capital,[86] deductible only by virtue of paragraph 20(1)(c) of the Act, the hedging contract linked to such an expense deductible by statute should also give rise to fully includable or deductible gains or losses.

Consider the tax consequences to Party A in the following example. Party A has an outstanding debt obligation under which it owes US$100 in five years at an annual interest rate of 5%. Party A would like to hedge its U.S. dollar obligations by entering into a forward contract with Party B. Because Party A immediately pays out its receipts by way of interest payments and the principal payment on the debt, Party A's net economic cost is its payments under the forward. The forward exchange rates should, theoretically, reflect "interest-rate parity," and so be economically identical.

On the periodic payments, Party A will have a net deduction equal to the amounts paid on the forward agreement. The amounts received on the forward in U.S. dollars will be included under section 9 of the Act but will then be paid by Party A as interest on the underlying debt, which is a payment that is presumably deductible under paragraph 20(1)(c) (subject to new section 20.3, discussed below). Party A is left with a net deduction for payments under the forward under section 9. As the net deduction is in respect of a payment in Canadian dollars, Party A will have no net foreign exchange gain or loss on the periodic payments.

---

84 *Interpretation Bulletin IT -346R*, above note 78, para. 3-6, *Interpretation Bulletin IT - 95R*, Above note 83, at para. 6.

85 *Broadhurst* (1990), above note 25 at 26:8.

86 See e.g., *Canada Safeway Ltd. v. M.N.R.*, [1957] S.C.R. 717; *The Bronfman Trust v. The Queen*, [1987]. 1 S.C.R. 32; and *Shell*, above note 15. The CRA has recently stated that it intends to treat interest expenses incurred by a bank or other moneylender as a current expense deductible under s. 9 of the Act where the borrowed funds are used in the taxpayer's moneylending business. See *Gifford v. The Queen*, 2004 S.C.C. 16, where the Supreme Court of Canada stated that interest expense will be on capital account where the proceeds of the loan add to the financial capital of the borrower (in contrast to loans that are inventory of the borrower).

As noted above, the Supreme Court in *Shell* considered a transaction which included forward contracts hedging currency exposure of interest payments. The Tax Court in *Shell* noted that the taxpayer had reported a single deduction for interest expense equal to its U.S. dollar denominated obligations under the forward. As the Tax Court noted, because the borrowing and the forward were not integrated, the deduction of interest under 20(1)(c) was the Canadian dollar equivalent of the foreign denominated (in *Shell* N.Z. dollars) interest under the borrowing. The net deduction claimed by the taxpayer represented such interest expense, plus or minus income or loss under the forward. While the treatment of the forward hedging the principal repayment was argued at all levels of court in *Shell*, the treatment of the forward contracts hedging interest expense was not argued in *Shell*. Indeed, the (ultimately unsuccessful) argument of the Crown that the transaction should be taxed as a synthetic U.S. dollar borrowing would have rendered treatment of the interest hedge moot.

With respect to the settlement of the debt and the back end of the forward, Party A (or Shell) will have "locked in" a foreign exchange gain (or loss). Party A originally received US$100 million, which it used to purchase CDN$150 million at the spot rate of 1.5. On repayment, Party A is guaranteed to purchase the US$100 million at the price pre-arranged by the parties (say, CDN$140 million). Economically, Party A has locked in its gain (or loss). The gain (or loss) will be spread amongst the forward agreement and the debt depending on the actual exchange rates.

As seen in *Shell*, the gain(s) will be on capital account regardless of how it is (they are) distributed between the forward agreement and the repayment of the debt and notwithstanding that the taxpayer has locked in the total gain. This result has been changed to some extent by the recent enactment of s. 20.3.[87]

---

87 There may be an exception to the matching treatment as between the underlying obligation and the forward. A loss on the portion of a currency forward that hedges the principal amount of an underlying debt obligation may be deductible under paragraph 20(1)(e), which allows certain financing expenses considered to be on capital account to be deducted over five years. In *MacMillan Bloedel Ltd. v. The Queen*, [1990] 1 C.T.C. 468 (F.C.T.D.). the taxpayer was in the forest products business. The taxpayer planned to issue US$70 million in debt. The taxpayer also entered into forward contracts under which the taxpayer sold the U.S. dollars to several parties in exchange for Canadian dollars at predetermined exchange rates. The amount of the debt to be issued and the date of the issuance changed; the terms of the forward agreements were amended to reflect these changes. Ultimately, the sales under the forwards were completed on the same date as the closing of the borrowing transaction. The Canadian dollar depreciated in the few months between the time when the forwards were

Section 20.3 was enacted in 2000 as a result of *Shell*. Very generally, s. 20.3 applies when a taxpayer is obligated under a "weak currency debt." A "weak currency debt" is defined in s. 20.3(1) to be a foreign currency debt of the taxpayer where the debt is in respect of a borrowing or acquisition of property and certain requirements are met. First, very generally, the taxpayer is using funds denominated in another currency (the "final currency") to earn income from a business or property (i.e., the weak currency debt is a type of interim transaction). In somewhat general terms, this refers to a situation in which the taxpayer borrows (this is the borrowing related to the weak currency debt) in the final currency to earn income; the taxpayer borrows money or acquires property to acquire funds in the final currency which are then used to earn income; the taxpayer uses borrowed money or acquires property to settle an obligation denominated in the final currency that was used to earn income or the taxpayer borrows money or acquires property to settle another weak currency debt. Second, the amount of the foreign currency debt in issue has to exceed CDN $500,000. Third, the foreign currency debt must carry an interest rate that is at least two percentage points higher than the interest rate that would have been carried by an equivalent debt in the final currency.[88]

If a debt is a weak currency debt, several consequences result. First, an interest deduction is disallowed to the extent that the interest exceeds the

---

entered into and the time when the forwards were closed out. The taxpayer deducted the loss under subparagraph 20(1)(e)(ii).

The Court found that the loss was indeed deductible under subparagraph 20(1)(e)(ii). The Court's analysis was sparse, providing merely that "[t]he loss on the second transaction was, in my view, an expense incurred in the course of borrowing the U.S. funds . . . Quite apart from accounting techniques or principles, it seems to fall clearly within subparagraph 20(1)(e)(ii)." *Ibid.* at 476. Note that the requirement that the expense be incurred "in the course of borrowing money" (or in the course of an issuance or sale of units or shares, in the course of incurring indebtedness that is an amount payable for property or in the course of a rescheduling or restructuring of a debt obligation) has been interpreted relatively broadly. *See Minister of National Revenue v. Yonge-Eglinton Building Limited.*, [1974] C.T.C. 209 (F.C.A.). The CRA has stated that it considers *MacMillan Bloedel* to be limited to its particular facts. *CRA Document No. 9410620* (May 16, 1994). See *CRA Document No. 2000-0051017* (July 13, 2001), which rejects the application of paragraph 20(1)(e) to swap payments made to hedge a strong currency borrowing.

88 This spread is not measured when the debt is incurred, but rather when the debt is being tested as a weak currency debt. Further rules apply when the interest rate is calculated by way of formula. See definition of "weak currency debt" in s. 20.3(1). In respect of the CDN$500,000 threshold, any debts that can reasonably be regarded as having been incurred or assumed by the taxpayer as part of one series of transactions will be considered together.

amount of interest that would have been payable on an equivalent debt denominated in the final currency.[89] Second, the gain or loss on the extinguishment of the debt will be considered to be on income account and will be included or deducted in computing the taxpayer's income from the business or property to which the debt relates.[90] Third, any interest expense disallowed under section 20.3 will be considered to be an amount paid by the taxpayer to settle or extinguish the debt.[91] If the taxpayer has entered into a "hedge" (see definition above at 2.2) that has been identified properly as such by the taxpayer, the interest paid by the taxpayer on the weak currency debt will be decreased by any gain on the hedge or increased by any loss on the hedge.[92]

a) Cash Settlement

A cash-settled forward or futures contract will be characterized as being on income or capital account in the same way as any other derivative: it will generally be considered to be on income account unless it is considered to be a hedge of a capital asset or liability. The tax treatment of a cash-settled forward or futures contract is similar to that of a swap agreement, described below. If the forward or futures contract is on income account, then payments made under the contract should be deductible in computing income, and payments received under the contract should be included in computing income. If a cash-settled forward or futures contract is on capital account, payments made should be considered to be the cost of a capital asset (or, perhaps more accurately, the costs of disposition of a capital asset) and payments received should be considered to be the proceeds of disposition of a capital asset, such that the net gain (or loss) would be considered to be a capital gain (or loss). It has been suggested that it may be more difficult in some situations to characterize a forward that can be settled in cash only as a hedge.[93]

D. SWAPS

Canadian courts have not yet considered the treatment of a swap and therefore the administrative positions published by the CRA constitute the key authority in this area.

---

89 Paragraph 20.3(2)(a).
90 Paragraph 20.3(2)(b).
91 Paragraph 20.3(2)(c).
92 Subsection 20.3(3).
93 See P. M. Meredith, "Current Problems and Future Directions in Derivatives Taxation" in *1994 Conference Report* (Toronto: Canadian Tax Foundation, 1995) 18:1 at 18:5.

1) Deductions and Inclusions

Most of the CRA's published positions on swaps address interest rate and cross-currency swaps.

a) Interest Rate Swaps

The CRA takes the position that payments made or received under interest rate swaps are deductible or required to be included (as the case may be) on income account under section 9 of the Act.[94] Thus an interest rate swap entered into to swap between fixed and floating interest rates is an effective swap on an after-tax basis to convert the net deduction in respect of a debt obligation carrying fixed deductible interest, for example, to net deduction of a fixed rate.

The CRA has stated that fees payable on interest rate swaps are deductible to the extent that they are reasonable in amount.[95]

b) Currency Swaps

The CRA's position on cross-currency swaps has undergone a somewhat more complicated evolution. The CRA's statements have generally addressed the type of plain vanilla cross-currency swap described above, where one of the taxpayers has entered into the swap for the purpose of hedging a debt obligation. For many years the CRA took the position that the periodic payments made on such a cross-currency swap would be considered to be on income account, and therefore would be fully deductible (if paid) or required to be fully included in income (if received).[96] The gain or loss arising on the lump sum payments at the end of the term of the swap would be considered to match the character of the gain or loss aris-

---

94 See, for example, *CRA Document No. 4M09660* (February 7, 1994) (1993 Round Table, Q. 11); *CRA Document No. 9403868* (March 17, 1994). A number of years ago, the CRA took the position that deductibility of payments made under an interest rate swap depended on the deductibility of interest payment made on the underlying debt obligation being hedged (see, for example, *CRA Document An Audit Perspective of Capital Markets* (April 1991)); 1984 Round Table, Q. 60; *Advance Income Tax Ruling* ATR-4, "Exchange of Interest Rates" (November 29, 1985). The CRA has since changed its position and now takes the position that deductibility of payments under an interest rate swap does not in any way depend on the deductibility of interest on the underlying debt obligation. See *CRA Document No. 4M09660* (February 7, 1994) (1993 Round Table, Q. 11). See also *CRA Document No. 2003-0030597* (October 30, 2003).

95 1984 Round Table, Q. 60. Note that s. 67 disallows a deduction to the extent that an outlay or expense is "unreasonable in the circumstances."

96 1984 Round Table, Q. 60; *CRA Document No. 9204145* (March 10, 1992); *CRA Document No. 2000-0036045* (August 25, 2000).

ing on the repayment of the underlying debt. Assuming that the debt was on capital account, the gain or loss on the lump sum payments under the swap would also be on capital account.[97] The CRA had confirmed following the decision in *Shell* and prior to the July 2001 technical interpretation that its long-standing position as to the treatment of cross-currency swaps remained unchanged.[98]

However, in *CRA Document No. 2000-0051017*,[99] the CRA considered a cross-currency swap under which the taxpayer was entitled to receive a lump sum payment of Japanese yen at the end of the swap term. The CRA stated the following:

> . . . it is our view that the swap payments deducted by XXXXX under section 9 of the Act were, in large part, incurred to acquire a right under contract to purchase Japanese yen at the termination of the swap agreement at a rate, which was much more favorable [*sic*] to XXXXX than the exchange rate the market was predicting at the time the agreement was entered into. The cost of such a right would, in our view, be included in the computation of the gain or loss on a hedge in respect of the principal amount of the loan. Moreover, based on the Supreme Court decision in *Shell*, whether the gain or loss resulting from a hedging contract should be characterized on income or capital account depends on the characterization of the underlying debt obligation to which the hedge relates. Following the reasoning in *Shell*, since the underlying debt obligation to which the hedge relates was a XXXXX-year loan, albeit used to finance working capital, the loss resulting from the hedge should be characterized as being on capital account. The cost incurred to acquire the hedge, in respect of the principal of the loan on capital account, would be a capital expenditure the deduction for which would be denied under paragraph 18(1)(b).[100]

Perhaps unsurprisingly, the CRA has recently returned to its previously long-standing position on currency swaps. In February 2002,[101] the CRA wrote in respect of the July 2001 technical interpretation that the "discussion . . . relating to the possibility of the acquisition of a right should be deleted as we believe the evidence cannot support such an interpretation."

---

97 *Ibid.*

98 *CRA Document No. 2000-0036945* (August 25, 2000).

99 *CRA Document No. 2000-0051017* (July 13, 2001).

100 See Broadhurst, above note 25, at 26:16-17, who foresees this issue.

101 *CRA Document No. 2002-012576* (February 19, 2002).

c) Other Swaps

The CRA has not issued many statements in respect of swaps other than interest rate and cross-currency swaps. In *CRA Document No. 9728125*,[102] the CRA commented more generally on swaps as follows:

> Generally, a swap entails exchanging income flows, for example, exchanging the fixed rate for a variable rate stream or vice versa while not exchanging the security. The payments in your example protect the capital asset of the corporation against an adverse movement in price; in effect, the corporation is purchasing insurance against the asset decreasing in value. In our view, this could be viewed as a type of hedge transaction, and, as noted in the decision in Ethicon Sutures vs The Queen [[1985] 2 C.T.C. 6] (85 DTC 5290), the gain or loss on the costs to hedge the capital asset may depend on the underlying use of the funds. Alternatively, however, if after a review of the documents, the facts show that the arrangement is not a hedge but rather a type of total return or interest rate swap only having reference to an asset, the swap payments may be included in, or deductible from, income pursuant to section 9 of the Act.

The CRA has also stated that swap deductions are subject to paragraph 18(1)(a), which provides that an outlay or expense is not deductible unless it is "made or incurred . . . for the purpose of gaining or producing income from [a] business or property" and that swaps made between related parties may be scrutinized to ensure that the swaps in question were entered into by the parties for the purpose of earning income:

> . . . the key issue that must be resolved is when viewed objectively did XXXXXXXXXX enter into the interest rate swap contracts for the purpose of earning income? Since the swap contracts in question are between related parties it is important to consider whether the terms and conditions of those particular swap contracts are similar or common to the terms and conditions that would otherwise be commercially available in the marketplace. This will require not only an examination of the particular swap contracts in question but a comparison with "normal" commercial terms and conditions. Even if it is determined that XXXXXXXXXX swap contracts have normal commercial terms and conditions it is also fair to question why XXXXXXXXXX would agree to terminate its swap contracts (and incur termination fees) as soon as XXXXXXXXXX started receiving net payments from XXXXXXXXXX (i.e. XXXXXXXXXX swap position is "in-the money"). As noted above, while the determination as to

---

102 *CRA Document No. 9728125* (February 7, 1998).

> whether XXXXXXXXXX entered into the swap contracts for the purpose of earning income remains a question of fact we would seriously question whether this was the case if it can be established that such contracts are consistently terminated by XXXXXXXXXX as soon as they become "in the money". In this regard, while under "normal" circumstances an arm's length party holding an "in the money" position in a swap contract would not agree to terminate the swap contract early, even where they agreed to do so, we would expect that they would receive some form of compensation from the "out of the money" party. Therefore, it is also fair to question the amount of the termination fees charged to XXXXXXXXXX by XXXXXXXXXX. Similarly, while we can understand that a party holding an "out of the money" position in a swap contract (i.e. XXXXXXXX in this case) may want to terminate such a contract early we would again question why the party holding the "in the money" position (i.e., XXXXXXXXXX) would ever agree to pay a termination fee.[103]

The CRA has issued at least one advance income tax ruling in connection with a total return swap. This ruling was issued prior to the time when all advance income tax rulings were published. It appears that the CRA provided rulings to the effect that payments made on the total return leg of the swap (which was the only leg relevant to the analysis as the other leg was paid by a non-resident) were deductible under section 9 and that the deduction was not prohibited by paragraph 18(1)(a) or (b) (which prohibits deductions of expenses on capital account in the absence of a specific provision) of the Act.[104]

2) Withholding Tax

The CRA has also specifically stated that a payment under an interest rate swap is generally not "interest"[105] as there is no debt between the parties,[106] and therefore swap payments would generally not be subject to non-resident withholding tax.[107] For example, where the CRA was asked whether

---

103 *CRA Document No. 9828647* (December 11, 1998). Note also *CRA Document No. 2000-0051017* in this respect.

104 See M.G. Quigley & D.J. Toaze, "Nuts and Bolts of Derivatives," in *Tax Effects of Financial Transactions and Operations* (Toronto: Infonex, 2000) at 25–26 for a discussion of potential issues that can arise with respect to securities lending arrangements in the context of total return swaps.

105 *CRA Document No. 9403868* (March 17, 1994).

106 *CRA Document No. 2000-0051017* (July 13, 2001).

107 *CRA Document No. 2000-0050975* (November 16, 2000); *CRA Document No. 9403868* (March 17, 1994).

principal amounts exchanged under interest rate and currency swaps should be treated as "loans and advances" for purposes of Part I.3 of the Act. The CRA stated that, consistent with their treatment of such amounts for the purposes of Parts I and XIII of the Act, these amounts should not be treated as "loans or advances."[108] The CRA commented, however, that since swaps were increasingly used for purposes other than the hedging of interest rate or exchange rate risks, it was planning a review of its treatment of swaps for taxation purposes.

However, where payments under a swap are not "matched," the CRA takes the position that the swap contains an interest element which would be subject to non-resident withholding tax.[109] In this case, the CRA will consider the swap to be an obligation similar to a bond, debenture, note or mortgage,[110] which could, depending on the facts, allow for the application of a withholding tax exemption.[111] The CRA considers payments to be "matched" if the payments are made on the same date and for the same period.[112]

With respect to the unpublished total return swap ruling referenced above, it appears that this ruling provided that payments made under a total return swap on a total return basis by a resident of Canada to a related non-resident would not be subject to tax under Part XIII of the Act.

Some have suggested that a swap (or, presumably, any derivative) could constitute the provision of a service.[113] Such a characterization could give rise to withholding issues in respect of section 105 of the regulations to the Act, which requires a withholding of 15% of remuneration paid in consideration for services provided in Canada by a non-resident. A "service" characterization could also trigger issues in relation to the service provider "carrying on business in Canada," which would require tax filings and could render the non-resident taxable in Canada.[114] However, it appears that in the unpublished total return swap ruling referenced above, the CRA took the position that the non-resident would not be considered to be carrying on business in

---

108 *CRA Document No. 2003-0027201I7* (February 12, 2004).

109 *CRA Document No. 9809195F* (July 15, 1998) (which actually only states that the payments must be made on the same date); 1984 Round Table, Q. 60; CRA Document No. 9204145 (March 10, 1992); *CRA Document No. April 1991-1* (April 1991).

110 *CRA Document No. 2000-0050975* (November 16, 1992).

111 For example, under clause 212(1)(b)(ii)(C) of the Act.

112 Above note 107.

113 Broadhurst considers this question in the context of reserves under paragraph 12(1)(a). See Broadhurst, above note 25, at 26:20-21.

114 Of course a non-resident may be exempt from taxation of business profits (although not exempt from reporting requirements) under a bilateral income tax treaty.

Canada, including providing services in Canada, solely by virtue of entering into the swap and performing its obligations thereunder.[115]

E. OPTIONS

1) Physically-settled options

a) Capital or Income Account?

With respect to share option transactions, the CRA takes the position that option transactions entered into by the following taxpayers will be on income account: a taxpayer who is participating in the promotion or underwriting of a particular security (to the extent that gains or losses relate to such participation); an officer or employee of a firm that is engaged in the promotion or underwriting of securities (if the gains or losses in question result from the acquisition of securities promoted or underwritten by that firm); a taxpayer who holds himself or herself out to the public as a dealer in securities; a corporation whose prime activity is trading in securities; a money lender; a trader or dealer in securities; an "original lender" and a taxpayer who has used special information not available to the public that would enable the realization of a quick profit.[116]

For all other taxpayers, the CRA presumes the following with respect to share option transactions:

(a) the gain or loss realized by a holder of options is on the same account as the holder's transactions in shares;

(b) the gain or loss realized by a writer of covered options is on the same account as the underlying shares; and

(c) the gain or loss realized by a writer of naked options is normally on income account. However, the Department will accept reporting of gains and losses on capital account provided this practice is followed consistently from year to year.[117]

---

115 See also Quigley & Toaze, above note 104, at 38–40. The CRA has issued several statements considering whether an interest rate cap provided by a bank could be considered to be a "service." In 1990, the CRA stated that an interest rate cap should be considered to be a service (see *CRA Document No. AC567045* (January 29, 1990)). However, two years later the CRA stated that the determination of whether an interest rate cap is a service is a question of fact, and that banks are in a better position to determine whether an interest rate cap is indeed a service (see *CRA Document No. 9005065* (June 2, 1992)).

116 *Interpretation Bulletin IT-479R*, "Transactions in Securities" (February 29, 1984) at paras. 15-17 and 24.

117 *Ibid.* at para. 25.

The CRA does state that the above presumption may not apply in unusual factual situations.[118]

b) Capital Account Treatment

Physically-settled options (both puts and calls)[119] on capital account are the only derivatives the tax treatment of which is explicitly and directly addressed by the Act. The relevant section is s. 49,[120] which deals with both the grantor and the holder of an option.

With respect to the grantor of an option, s. 49(1) provides that the granting of the option (which could be a put or a call) itself is a disposition of a property the adjusted cost base of which to the grantor is nil, thereby triggering a capital gain equal to the premium received. Subsection 49(1) does not apply to the issuance of an option to acquire or dispose of a principal residence, to acquire the shares of the capital stock or bonds or debentures to be issued by the issuer if the issuer is a corporation or to acquire trust units of the issuer if the issuer is a trust.[121]

On the exercise of a call, the disposition of property by the issuer that is deemed by s. 49(1) is reversed: the premium received by the issuer is no longer considered to be the proceeds of disposition of an unspecified capital property on the granting of the option, but rather is considered to be part of the proceeds of disposition of the actual property acquired (along with the strike price received).[122] On the exercise of a put, the disposition deemed by s. 49(1) is also reversed: the premium received by the issuer is no longer considered to be the proceeds of disposition of an unspecified capital property on the granting of the option, but rather is deducted from the cost to the purchaser (the grantor) of the property purchased.[123] These reversals are effected by way of an amendment to the relevant previous tax return.[124]

If the grantor is a corporation that has granted an option to purchase shares, bonds or debentures to be issued by the corporation, the CRA takes the view that any premium from the granting of such an option is general-

118 *Ibid.*

119 These include options that can be physically settled or cash settled at the option of the holder.

120 Section 49 does not explicitly deal with options on capital account only, but is found in the subdivision of the Act that governs the calculation of gains. Accordingly, in the CRA's view, s. 49 applies to only taxpayers who hold or grant an option on capital account. See *Interpretation Bulletin IT-96R6*, above note 47, para. 1.

121 Paragraphs 49(1)(a), (b) and (c).

122 Subsection 49(3).

123 Subsection 49(3.1).

124 Subsection 49(4).

ly tax-free in the hands of the corporation.[125] On the exercise of such an option, the strike price will be part of the paid-up capital of the shares issued (if shares are issued) or part of the corporation's surplus (if bonds or debentures are issued).[126] If such an option expires, the corporation generally will be considered to have disposed of a capital property with an adjusted cost base of nil for an amount equal to the premium paid for the option (i.e., the corporation will be considered to have realized a capital gain equal to the premium paid to the corporation).[127]

From the perspective of the purchaser of an option, on the exercise of a call, the premium paid by the purchaser becomes part of the adjusted cost base to the purchaser of the property purchased.[128] On the exercise of the option the purchaser will not be considered to have disposed of the right to receive the property.[129] If the option is a put, the purchaser of the put will deduct the premium paid by the purchaser from the purchaser's proceeds of disposition. If a call or put expires, the purchaser will generally realize a capital loss equal to the amount of any premium paid to acquire the option.[130]

The CRA has stated that it may apply s. 69, which generally allows the CRA to effectively reprice a disposition between non arm's length parties, if a "non-commercial option" is granted to a non-arm's length party.[131]

c) Income Account Treatment

The CRA's position on options granted or held on income account is set out in *Interpretation Bulletin 479R*.[132] If a call option is held by a purchaser on income account, the premium is added to the cost of the property acquired if the option is exercised. If the option is not exercised, the premium will be a loss and will be deducted from the holder's income on the

---

125 *Interpretation Bulletin IT-96R6*, above note 47, para. 6. The CRA has suggested that paragraph 12(1)(x) could require an income inclusion in respect of the premium in certain circumstances. See *CRA Document No. 9626325* (October 29, 1996).

126 *Ibid.*

127 Subsection 49(2). See s. 49(2.1) for the equivalent rule for options issued by a trust to acquire trust units.

128 Paragraph 49(3)(b); but see the exception in subparagraph 49(3)(b)(i) for stock option benefits.

129 Subsection 49(3); s. 49.1.

130 *Interpretation Bulletin IT-96R6*, above note 47, at paras. 5 and 13. Subparagraph (b)(iv) of the definition of "disposition" in subsection 248(1) provides that the expiry of an option is a disposition.

131 Above note 116, para. 17.

132 *Ibid.* This interpretation bulletin addresses share option transactions only. However, the CRA has stated elsewhere that paragraphs 23 to 32 of this interpretation bulletin describe the CRA's general views on the taxability of option transactions. See *CRA No. 9637505* (January 16, 1997).

expiry of the option.[133] If a put option is held by an option purchaser on income account, on exercise of the option the premium paid is deducted from proceeds of disposition of the underlying property sold. If the option is not exercised, as with an expired call, the cost of acquiring the put is deducted from income in the year the put expires.[134]

With respect to the grantor of a call option to whom the call option is on income account, the CRA takes the position that the premium is to be included in income on exercise or expiry, as applicable.[135] With respect to the grantor of a put option, the premium is to be deducted from the cost of the underlying property if the option is exercised, and is to be included in income if the option expires.[136] Presumably this position is based on the argument that the premium is "unearned" until the option is either exercised or expires, and therefore should not be included in income until that time.[137] This position may also be a confirmation that paragraph 12(1)(a) does not apply to the premium and therefore that the option is not a "service" being delivered by the grantor.[138]

2) Cash-settled options

The tax treatment of cash-settled options must generally be determined by extrapolating from the cases and CRA statements dealing more generally with hedges, reviewed above.

---

133 *Interpretation Bulletin IT-479R*, *ibid.*, para. 28. The CRA states that this position, as well as the positions in paragraphs 29, 31 and 32, applies to exchange-traded options and to options "similar to those transacted on an exchange but which are entered into outside an Exchange." See *ibid.* at para. 26.

134 *Ibid.* at para. 31.

135 *Ibid.* at para. 29.

136 *Ibid.* at para. 32.

137 Edgar, above note 14, at 60. In *CRA Document No. 2003-0184127* (March 24, 2003), the CRA stated that where a taxpayer receives an option premium on income account and is not recording the premium on a mark-to-market basis, the premium received "will be included in income when it is received pursuant to section 9 of the Act, provided that the recipient is absolutely entitled to receive the amount (that is, the amount has the "quality of income" when received, irrespective of whether the option has been exercised)." The CRA continued, stating that the amount paid for the premium would form part of the cost of the inventory of the holder of the option. The CRA stated that this position may cause a lack of symmetry between the grantor and the holder of the option, suggesting that the grantor of the option may be required to include the premium in income upon the granting of the option if the facts could sustain the view that the option premium had the quality of income.

138 See previous discussions of derivatives as "services" at Section 4.2.

As with the other derivatives we have seen, cash-settled options will be considered to be on income account unless they are seen to be a hedge of a capital asset or liability.

If a cash-settled option is on income account to the grantor, the grantor's recognition of the premium should be deferred until exercise or expiry of the option consistent with the CRA's position described above.[139] If the cash-settled option is on income account to the holder of the option, the premium would be deductible to the holder. Consistent with the CRA's position above, such deduction would appear to be upon exercise or expiry. However, it has been suggested that the premium may be deductible immediately[140] or possibly deductible on an amortized basis under s. 18(9).[141] If the option is on income account to the grantor, on the exercise of the option the grantor will likely be required to make a net payment which will be deductible to the grantor. If the option is on income account to the holder, on the exercise of the option the holder will likely be entitled to a net payment which will be included in the holder's income. It may also be possible for the holder and/or the grantor to recognize gain and losses on cash-settled options on an accrual basis.

F. TAX POLICY AND DERIVATIVES

1) Introduction

Derivatives cause us to pose fundamental questions regarding the design of tax legislation. The very fact that the value of a derivative depends on the value of some other asset, in which the owner of the derivative may or may not have a legal interest, differentiates derivatives from more traditional assets around which the Canadian tax rules are based. A swap does not produce a stream of income similar to that of an interest-bearing note or a pre-

---

139 The CRA's position with respect to these options would presumably depend on whether its position in *Interpretation Bulletin IT-479R* with respect to options on income account is an administrative concession or an articulation of its position that the premium is "unearned" and therefore not required to be included under section 9 and, further, not a payment in consideration for the rendering of services in the futures and therefore not required to be included under paragraph 12(1)(a).

140 *Canderel Ltd. v. The Queen*, [1998] 2 C.T.C. 35 (S.C.C.) and *Toronto College Park Ltd. v. The Queen*, [1998] 2 C.T.C. 78 (S.C.C.).

141 Subsection 18(9) requires an amortization of prepaid amounts in respect of services rendered after the end of the year as well as with respect to items such as interest, taxes, rent or royalties in respect of a period after the end of the year. See Quigley & Toaze, above note 104, at 32–33.

ferred share; it may yield a gain on one swap payment date and a loss on another. An option to buy some asset at a fixed price in the future exposes its holder to the potential for gain should the value of the asset rise, but if the value falls, the holder does not suffer.

Derivatives can also combine two or more different economic transactions. Indeed, a small number of relatively simple derivative instruments may be combined in tremendous variety to produce almost any economic position,[142] as was evident in *Shell*. Consider a swap under which one party transfers a significant lump sum to a counterparty in return for periodic payments. The original lump sum may be viewed as a loan embedded in the derivative and, accordingly, portions of the swap payment could be considered interest on that loan. Similarly, a convertible or exchangeable debenture, may be viewed as a debt that has an option to acquire shares embedded within it.[143]

These types of differences, among others, result in a series of questions regarding appropriate treatment for Canadian income tax purposes. Consider a forward contract with an up-front premium paid from one party to the other. How should the premium be taxed? Is it a current income/expense or is it merely a component of the price of the underlying asset? Should it be taken into account now or only when the forward contract is closed out? Should the premium be viewed as a form of financing, as with the swap in the previous example?

The first challenge facing tax legislation designers is to develop rules that will tax derivatives appropriately under traditional tax policy principles. Questions of timing and capital or income treatment, for example, must be determined.

The second, and possibly more pressing, challenge arises from the fact that derivatives can be effective tools in reducing or avoiding tax. For example, a taxpayer who wishes to receive cash proceeds equal to the investment without realizing a capital gain may "monetize" the asset so as to receive the cash proceeds without an actual sale of the underlying asset.[144] As in *Shell*, the taxpayer may wish to borrow in one currency, but be taxed as if

142 See for example, G. May, "Flying on Instruments: Synthetic Investment and the Avoidance of Withholding Tax" (1996) 13 Tax Notes Int'l 1625–35; D. G. Broadhurst, "Derivatives in International Tax Planning," in International Fiscal Association — Canadian Branch, *1997 International Tax Seminar* (Scarborough, Ont.: Carswell, 1998) 85.

143 See above note 36.

144 See, for example, J.L. Rubinger, "Tax Planning Strategies with Equity Derivatives" (2002) 76 Florida Bar J. 45. Convertible and exchangeable debt may also be used to monetize equity positions.

the borrowing were in another currency. This second challenge is particularly difficult in the context of a system of taxation like Canada's which relies on fitting a given instrument into its appropriate category (sometimes labelled a "cubbyhole" system by Tim Edgar and others, as discussed below).

In the remainder of this chapter, we will examine a selection of different approaches to the taxation of derivatives. In particular, we will compare and contrast the current Canadian approach, the American approach and the comprehensive regime advocated by Tim Edgar. Our comparison will focus on one particular example: the weak currency borrowing in *Shell*. We will begin by discussing the attempt by the Minister to apply the GAAR in *Shell* and *Canadian Pacific* and then examine the Canadian legislative response to weak currency borrowing transactions, the manner in which U.S. rules would apply to the same transaction, and then review the comprehensive approach to the taxation of financial instruments suggested by Tim Edgar.

2) The Canadian Approach

As stated at the beginning of this chapter, Canada does not currently have a regime that specifically or comprehensively addresses the taxation of derivatives. Instead, derivatives are subject to (a) more general rules and principles and (b) some extremely specific provisions. As we have seen in the first part of this chapter, where an instrument is an option on capital account, the Act provides for its tax treatment. Otherwise, generally, the tax law relies on general rules regarding timing and character of income, loss or gain.

Shell is a useful example of the application of this approach. The transaction in *Shell* can be reduced to the following elements: a loan of New Zealand dollars; a sale of those New Zealand dollars in exchange for the required U.S. dollars; a forward of U.S. dollars in exchange for New Zealand dollars on the relevant interest payment dates; and finally a forward sale of U.S. dollars in exchange for the New Zealand dollars required to repay the original loan. As set out above, the Canadian regime treats the forward and the borrowing separately, thereby allowing the borrower to claim a high interest deduction notwithstanding that the borrowing has been effectively transferred into a stronger currency. This "cubbyhole" approach does not contemplate the integration of the various elements of the transaction or provide for a tax treatment based on the economic effect of these elements, although the treatment of a hedge necessarily relies on some connection between the different elements.

GAAR allows the Minister to redetermine the tax consequences of an avoidance transaction to deny a tax benefit unless the transaction would not result directly or indirectly in a misuse of the provisions of the Act or an abuse having regard to the provisions of the Act read as a whole. GAAR, therefore, does allow the court to consider a series of transactions and recharacterize the overall treatment in certain cases. While GAAR was not applicable in *Shell*, it was at issue in *Canadian Pacific*. In *Canadian Pacific*, the Minister was not successful in applying GAAR, primarily because the court found that the transaction was not an avoidance transaction. The Tax Court judge had found as a matter of fact that the primary purpose for the Australian dollar borrowing was to acquire capital for business purposes. The primary purpose was not the avoidance of tax. On appeal, the Minister argued that the avoidance transaction was not the borrowing itself, but rather the designation of the debentures as in Australian dollars. As discussed above, the Court responded strongly that a transaction could not be dissected in order to identify an avoidance element, since to do so would allow any transaction that had a tax planning step to be labelled an avoidance transaction:

> The implication of the Crown's argument, if accepted, would have consequences which Parliament did not intend. If this argument was correct, the Crown could allege that the tax planning component of any transaction amounted to an event or arrangement constituting a "separate transaction". Because it was undertaken for purely tax purposes, the "separate transaction" would be an avoidance transaction.[145]

Regarding the question of whether the transactions had resulted in misuse or abuse, the Minister argued that there was an abuse of the provisions of the Act read as a whole because the borrowing was structured so as to result in the deduction of Canadian dollar principal payments, contrary to the policy in the Act prohibiting the deduction of principal in the form of interest. In the view of the court this argument depended upon a recharacterization of the interest payments as capital payments, and recharacterization was something that could only be done under s. 245 once it had been established that there was a misuse or abuse of the Act.

The rejection of both these arguments demonstrates some of the difficulties of applying GAAR to derivatives. For example, *Canadian Pacific* shows that derivatives with two or more economic components may not be addressed by GAAR, as GAAR does not necessarily permit the bifurcation

145 *Canadian Pacific* (F.C.A.), above note 68, at para. 25.

of a transaction into its economic components. Conversely GAAR does not necessarily allow the combination of a derivative and another transaction in order to apply tax consequences to the total transaction. Under GAAR, legal form cannot be entirely disregarded. Further it may be difficult to identify a clear and unambiguous policy in relation to transactions involving derivatives when derivatives are generally not specifically contemplated by the Act.

Depending on GAAR to determine the appropriate tax treatment of derivatives increases the pressure on litigators and judges. Limiting the GAAR to those transactions which are entered into for the primary purpose of avoiding tax and recharacterizing those transactions only where a misuse or abuse of a clear and unambiguous policy is identified, the job of judges and litigators is somewhat more manageable and the prospect of producing a coherent body of law around the GAAR is enhanced. One of the great challenges for a judge is to understand and evaluate a transaction designed and documented by tax professionals who work with the nuances of tax structuring techniques on a daily basis. These techniques, made all the more complex by the proliferation of derivative elements, require a very high level of expertise to manipulate effectively. The complexities at play in both the tax law itself and the transactions that are designed in respect of those laws are a formidable obstacle in ensuing consistent and efficient treatment. A judge of an appeal court, whose caseload may only include a small percentage of tax cases — of which only a small percentage of those are structured tax transactions — may find it extremely difficult to be familiar with the subtleties at play. Even a judge of the Tax Court of Canada may only deal with a few such cases a year. Given this institutional disadvantage, the reliance that may naturally be placed upon litigators, who may themselves find it difficult to master the economics, tax policy and complexity relating to the transactions in issue, particularly in the context of a voluminous and varied case load. Reliance may also increase in respect of expert testimony, where litigators must set out the economic and accounting effects of the transaction as well as attempt to discern a clear and unambiguous policy of the Act.

Balanced against the need for certainty and a desire to streamline the tax system by limiting the universe of transactions subject to recharacterization is a need to prevent taxpayers from using sophisticated tax planning to thwart valid tax policy objectives such as vertical and horizontal equity and neutrality. Whether the GAAR as it stands is a satisfactory compromise between simplicity on the one hand and equity and neutrality on the other is an open question. Furthermore, determining whether it does represent a satisfactory balance is not a simple task since it is not readily apparent how many "undesirable" transactions may be outstanding at any one time and what economic cost these transactions represent to the fisc. While any given transaction might seem an unacceptable affront to tax policy norms, any system must inevitably accept some level of departure from the ideal.

One alternative to GAAR used by the Canadian system is to enact specific anti-avoidance rules once common types of avoidance transactions are identified. The Minister's response to the taxpayers' victories in *Shell* and *Canadian Pacific* was to enact s. 20.3 of the Act, which applies in respect of a debt of a taxpayer which is at any time a "weak currency debt." As discussed above in more detail at Section 3.1, generally, section 20.3 applies where the taxpayer borrows money in a weak currency and uses that money in its business or to satisfy obligations in another currency or to settle a debt of the taxpayer which is itself a "weak currency debt." Section 20.3 also sets a $500,000 *de minimis* amount and only applies where the interest rate in respect of the weak currency exceeds the interest rate on the stronger currency by more than two percentage points.

Section 20.3 is a very limited response to a very specific case. It has no application in the context of a strong currency borrowing, wherein a lender would be able to reduce current income (since the market rate of interest on the strong-currency lending would be lower than on a comparable weak currency lending) and generate a corresponding capital gain on the retirement of the debt. Nevertheless, overall, the provision is targeted and provides a precise remedy. From a judicial perspective, the court's role is merely to determine whether or not, as a factual matter, a given obligation is a weak currency debt. Whether a given series of transactions is subject to s. 20.3 is certainly a much lesser question to answer than whether the transactions in Canadian Pacific should have been subject to GAAR. Unfortunately, the targeted approach to dealing with a given transaction is inherently historical. The process must examine transactions that have already happened and attempt to identify them in the legislation. But what taxpayers were doing then, at some point of time in the past, might be quite different from what those same taxpayers are doing today. Alternatively, the nature of the transactions might be similar, yet their form altered, so that the legislative description of the impugned transaction does not reflect the altered structure. In this regard, derivative instruments may be further resorted to in order to achieve the effect of a given transaction while avoiding being caught by the technical definition contained in the legislation. Indeed, s. 20.3 is an attempt to capture these various permutations and combinations. Unfortunately, such an attempt at comprehensiveness also brings with it complexity and over-breadth.

In addition, s. 20.3 is not retroactive and we would not advocate legislation that did apply to transactions already entered into by the taxpayer. Consequently, taxpayers who wish to reduce their funding costs by some method of tax arbitrage will, going forward, resort to other methods that are available. As a result, section 20.3 will likely never apply to the very taxpayers it was aimed to catch, since those taxpayers are virtually always well-advised by tax counsel. Rather, the section may subsist as a trap for the unwary, despite the *de minimis* provision, which shall diminish in significance over time.

Finally, as taxpayers flock to other sorts of instruments and transactions in response to targeted legislation such as s. 20.3, further legislative action will be required in order to keep pace with financial innovation. The consequence is more complexity in the tax system, without necessarily any payoff in terms of equity or neutrality going forward.

3) The U.S. Foreign Currency Hedging Rules

Under applicable U.S. tax laws, the borrowing which was the subject of the *Shell* decision would have been treated as a "synthetic debt obligation" and taxed as if the taxpayer had borrowed the funds in U.S. dollars directly. The timing, amount, character and source of foreign exchange gains or losses in respect of a foreign exchange transactions are governed by s. 988 of the *Internal Revenue Code* (the "*Code*" or the "*IRC*"). This group of transactions, called "section 988 transactions," are those which involve a "non-functional currency"[146] (the functional currency of a U.S. taxpayer is typically the U.S. dollar, though not always) and include: a disposition of non-functional currency; acquiring or becoming an obligor under a debt instrument denominated in a non-functional currency; accruing a payable, receivable or item of expense or income denominated in a non-functional currency; and entering into or acquiring a forward, futures or option contract or similar financial instrument in a non-functional currency, including a currency swap.[147] Section 988 transactions do not include equity investments denominated in a non-functional currency including all common stock, and, unless provided otherwise in regulations, preferred stock, denominated in non-functional currency, certain non-functional currency transactions entered into by an individual, or certain regulated futures contracts and listed options.

---

146 *IRC*, s. 988(c)(1)(A).

147 *IRC*, s. 988(c)(1)(B).

The foreign currency rules also contain a subset of rules that deal with certain currency risk hedging transactions.[148] Where a s. 988 transaction is a "988 hedging transaction," then all the transactions that are part of the 988 hedging transaction "shall be integrated and treated as a single transaction or otherwise treated consistently."[149] A 988 hedging transaction is any transaction entered into by the taxpayer primarily to manage risk of currency fluctuations with respect to property which is held or to be held by the taxpayer, or to manage risk of currency fluctuations with respect to borrowings made or to be made, or obligations incurred or to be incurred, by the taxpayer, and identified by the Secretary or the taxpayer as being a 988 hedging transaction.[150] The general scheme of the regulations provide that, where a debt instrument and a hedge allow the calculation of a yield to maturity (i.e. the underlying obligation must be fully hedged such that fluctuations in currency cannot effect the value of the amounts owed or received in respect of the underlying obligation) then they together form an integrated economic transaction.[151] In those circumstances they will be treated as a synthetic debt instrument for U.S. federal income tax purposes. The regulations specify the denomination of the synthetic debt instrument, its term and accrual periods, its issue price and its stated redemption price at maturity.[152] Rules are also provided for determining the source of interest income from the synthetic debt instrument.[153]

If the U.S. rules were applied to the transaction in *Shell*, they would deem the transaction to be a synthetic debt instrument created by the integration of the N.Z. dollar debt and the hedge and denominated in U.S. dollars.[154] The term of the synthetic debt instrument would be the period during which the transactions were in effect.[155] The issue price of the synthetic debt instrument would be the issue price of the N.Z. dollar loan translated into U.S. dollars at the spot rate on the date the transactions were entered into.[156] The stated redemption price at maturity would be determined by reference to the amounts to be paid under the hedge to acquire the currency necessary to make the principal payment on the N.Z.

148 Treas. Reg. §1.988-5.
149 *IRC*, s. 988(d)(1).
150 *IRC*, s. 988(d)(2).
151 Treas. Reg. §1.988-5(a)(5).
152 Treas. Reg. §1.988-5(a)(9)(ii).
153 Treas. Reg. §1.988-5(a)(9)(iii).
154 Treas. Reg. §1.988-5(a)(9)(ii)(A).
155 Treas. Reg. §1.988-5(a)(9)(ii)(B).
156 Treas. Reg. §1.988-5(a)(9)(ii)(C).

dollar loan.[157] Consequently, the stated redemption price at maturity for the synthetic debt instrument would be the US$79 million needed to purchase the NZ$150 million upon retirement of the N.Z. dollar debt. As a result, the synthetic debt instrument would be viewed as having been issued at a premium, and under applicable Treasury Regulations, Shell would be required to amortize the amount of the premium against the interest payments,[158] effectively reducing its interest deductions to the rate applicable to a U.S. dollar borrowing. Finally, the issue price of the instrument is adjusted over its term to reflect the portion of the premium that has been disallowed as an interest deduction,[159] reducing (and ultimately eliminating) the gain inherent in the transaction.

The U.S. hedging rules only apply where a hedge and a debt instrument allow for the calculation of a yield to maturity and where the taxpayer identifies the transaction as a qualifying hedging transaction. As a result, there is a sense in which they are elective to the taxpayer, since it is always possible to arrange the transaction such that it is not fully-hedged, and so a yield to maturity cannot be calculated. Alternatively, a taxpayer may simply not identify the transaction as being a qualifying hedging transaction in order to avoid the application of the rules. However, if a taxpayer enters into a qualifying debt instrument and a hedge but fails to comply with one or more of the regulations' requirements, and the Commissioner concludes that the qualifying debt instrument and the hedge are, in substance, a qualified hedging transaction, then the Commissioner may treat the qualifying debt instrument and the hedge as a qualified hedging transaction.[160]

A host of other rules apply to different derivative instruments in varying degrees of complexity. The United States relies on a wide range of detailed legislation apart from the s. 988 transaction rules including straddle rules, wash sale rules, and integrated transactions. Notional principal contracts (e.g. a swap) are subject to specific timing rules[161] that govern the treatment of both periodic as well as non-periodic payments, caps and floors, termination payments and hedged contracts. Hedging is also dealt with generally by separate rules that specify the character and timing of hedging income, gain, deduction of loss[162] and a further, distinct regime

157 Treas. Reg. §1.988-5(a)(9)(ii)(D).
158 Treas. Reg. §1.163-13.
159 Treas. Reg. §1.1275-1(b)(2).
160 Treas. Reg. §1.988-5(a)(8)(iii).
161 Treas. Reg. §1.446-3.
162 Treas. Reg. §1.1221-2.

governs the integration of hedges and debt instruments in certain circumstances.[163] Generally, these rules seek to ensure a clear reflection of income by prescribing timing and character treatment that is consistent with the economics of a taxpayer's situation. In some cases, as with section 988 hedging transactions and the rules under Reg. §1.1275-6, the U.S. tax law goes further in achieving this goal by deeming the existence of a "synthetic" debt instrument comprised of the separate transactions entered into by the taxpayer. The remainder of the rules would then generally apply to this synthetic instrument. Finally, as a backstop to these rules, U.S. courts have recourse to a substance over form approach,[164] and so are not afraid to recharacterize transactions according to economic reality and may also collapse a series of transactions through the application of a step transactions doctrine.[165]

The result is a system of enormous complexity where different regimes sometimes overlap and in other cases particular rules are dispersed throughout various divisions of the *Code* and regulations, in what has been referred to as a "piecemeal" approach.[166]

4) Comprehensive Approaches

Commentators have proposed a variety of recommendations to accommodate the taxation of financial instruments.[167] In general, the solutions focus on eliminating the distinction between the tax treatment of debt as opposed to equity, a factor that creates the incentive for a large amount of tax arbitrage, and move further towards an accrual-based regime.

One of the more well-developed approaches is one developed by Tim Edgar, who outlines a best-case, or "benchmark," system of taxing financial instruments that would tax economic accretion in lieu of a realization-

---

163 Treas. Reg. §1.1275-6.

164 See *Gregory v. Helvering*, 293 U.S. 465 (1935); *Yoc Heating Corp. v. Comr.*, 61 T.C. 168 (1973); Rev. Rul. 79-279, 1979-2 C.B. 125.

165 See, for example, B. Bittker & L. Lokken, *Federal Taxation of Income, Estates and Gifts*, 2d ed. (Boston: Warren, Gorham & Lamont, 1989) at para. 4.3.5.

166 S.D. Conlon & V.H. Aquilino, *Principles of Financial Derivatives and International Taxation* (Valhalla, New York: Warren, Gorham & Lamont, 1999) at section 81.01.

167 G. May, "An Evaluation of Some Financial Instrument Tax Reform Proposals" (2002) 50 Can. Tax J. 218; R. Shuldiner, "A General Approach to the Taxation of Financial Instruments" (1992) 71 Texas Law Rev. 243. N. Cunningham and D.H. Schenk, "Taxation Without Realization: A 'Revolutionary' Approach to Ownership," (1992) 47 Tax Law Rev. 725-814; A. C. Warren, Jr. "Financial Contract Innovation and Income Tax Policy" (1993) 107 Harv. L. Rev. 460.

based, cubby-hole approach.[168] Under such a system, capital gains and losses would be taxed in the same manner as income, thereby eliminating the incentive to transform income into capital gain; all financial instruments would be marked to market, thus forcing taxpayers to realize gains and losses on those instruments on a current basis; and the corporate tax would be eliminated and replaced with a tax at the shareholder level on the accrued gain or loss on the corporation's financial instruments.[169]

Under such a regime, there would be no advantage to structuring equivalent economic positions one way or another: in each case, the tax consequences would be the same. "Financial instruments would be taxed according to their economic substance represented by annual changes in value."[170] However, Edgar assumes that certain practical difficulties would preclude implementation of this approach: valuation of financial instruments that are not actively traded may be difficult; the favourable tax treatment for capital gains versus ordinary income is firmly entrenched in the political landscape; and a tax at the shareholder level would raise liquidity concerns.

Accordingly, Edgar rejects the benchmark approach and endorses a comprehensive accrual regime as a defensible second-best approach. Under this system the crucial distinction to be made by the legislator would be between expected and unexpected gains and losses. What Edgar has in mind is that taxpayers should be taxed on an accrual basis with regard to those gains (or losses) that are inherent in a given transaction. Edgar states:

> A comprehensive accrual regime intended to implement the dictates of "expected-return taxation" should be based on the rigorous identification of expected gains and losses associated with disguised and embedded debt in any financial instrument. Accrual recognition of these gains and losses must be required. Realization-based recognition can be applied to unexpected gains and losses arising on the resolution of a specified bet.[171]

For example, in the *Shell* transaction, the gain inherent in the forward purchase of N.Z. dollars would be an expected gain under such a regime, and so would be taken into account as it accrues over time. In circumstances where a gain (or loss) is not guaranteed to the taxpayer and so is unexpect-

---

168 T. Edgar, above note 14 and idem, "Some Lessons from the Saga of Weak-Currency Borrowings," (2000) 48:1 Can. Tax J. 1.

169 *Ibid.*, "Some Lessons from the Saga of Weak-Currency Borrowings" at 27.

170 *Ibid.* at 27.

171 *Ibid.* at 29.

ed, then the taxpayer would be permitted to be taxed on the traditional realization basis.

Edgar's approach would require, among other things, eliminating the distinction between ordinary income and capital gains, extending accrual accounting to the embedded debt in prepaid and off-market forwards and swaps, applying accrual accounting to actively traded instruments that give rise to selective realization problems. Given that such changes would require significant resources to develop, and more importantly, would be a radical departure from the status quo, it is unlikely that they would be enacted while the current Canadian approach is perceived as being adequate.

5) Conclusion

Much emphasis has been placed on the usage of derivatives for tax avoidance purposes. But derivatives are often used for valid commercial objectives, be they risk management or speculation. The absence of certainty with respect to the tax treatment of derivatives is not helpful to these types of transactions; in this respect, specific rules — whether by way of new legislation or clear and consistent administrative positions — are desirable.

With respect to the usage of derivatives in the context of tax avoidance, the view has been expressed that tax arbitrage itself (or the exploitation of tax asymmetries) is overstated if (i) compared with state sponsored tax preferences and (ii) viewed as a means of reducing double taxes or of utilizing unused tax preferences.[172] In other words, although complex financial instruments that use derivatives to obtain tax advantages might be considered a problem in the abstract, as a practical reality they are less damaging to the tax system than many government initiatives, and, in any event, they work to simply soak up tax advantages that would otherwise lie dormant, like unused RRSP limits. It is not as yet obvious that Canada should expend the resources necessary to develop a more "comprehensive" approach to the taxation of derivatives, at least insofar as they are used to achieve tax avoidance.[173] Part of the criticism of a comprehensive approach is that, as is evident from the U.S. rules, it can never be truly comprehensive, and will invariably require some sort of safety net (as with the step-transaction doctrine) to catch transactions that fall, or can be fit, through the cracks. These are mostly absent in Canada.

The Canadian approach, which relies on the GAAR to the extent that a transaction is entered into for the purpose of tax avoidance, and then upon

---

172 May, above note 167, at 218.

173 *Ibid.* at 219.

targeted legislation where required, has the benefit of overall simplicity when compared to the U.S. approach, though this is mostly a matter of degree rather than substance. The United States has progressively constructed rules and regimes to counter the effects of a variety of problems. In Canada such regimes do not yet exist, but, depending on the effectiveness of targeted rules such as section 20.3 of the Act, these may be seen as a more productive legislative option in the future. Whether that is the right road to follow depends in large part on the cost/benefit of that strategy. Further, as Edgar comments, "a reliance on the courts to address the tax-driven use of synthetics is realistic only in those jurisdictions that have a tradition of robust anti-avoidance doctrines."[174] It is not unlikely that the effect of derivative transactions and other tax products is more acute for the United States than it is here in Canada, but this may change in the future as the North American — and the world — economies become more closely integrated.

174 Above note 14, at 344.

Contributors

Andrew Auerbach is a Tax Policy Officer with the Tax Legislation Division of the Department of Finance (Canada). He holds an LL.B. from Osgoode Hall Law School and the University of Montreal as well as an LL.M. in International Taxation from New York University. Andrew worked in the New York office of Linklaters, where his practice focussed on the US tax law aspects of structured financial products and capital markets transactions. Prior to joining the Department of Finance, he was an associate in the Taxation Department of Osler, Hoskin & Harcourt LLP in Montreal, Quebec, Canada.

Sean C. Aylward is a Partner with Osler, Hoskin & Harcourt LLP. His practice is primarily focused on commodity taxation, customs and related cross-border matters including the GST, HST, federal excise tax and duty, provincial sales tax, tariff classification, origin, customs valuation, penalties and seizures, and NAFTA-related matters. He has appeared before the provincial courts, the Tax Court of Canada, the Federal Court Trial Division, and the Federal Court of Appeal. Sean has spoken on a variety of commodity tax matters for the Canadian Tax Foundation, CICA Commodity Tax Symposium, the Tax Executives Institute, the Canadian Bar Association, and the Canadian Life and Health Insurance Association.

Hon. Donald George Hugh Bowman, B.A., LL.B. is Associate Chief Justice of the Tax Court of Canada. He attended Victoria University, the Ontario College of Education and the Faculty of Law at the University of Toronto. Prior to his call to the Ontario Bar in 1962, Associate Chief Justice Bowman was a teacher in Germany and Ontario, Canada. He joined the Federal Department of Justice, Tax Litigation Section in 1962 and was appointed Director in 1968. He co-founded the Toronto law firm of Stikeman, Elliott, Robarts & Bowman in 1971 and was a partner until his appointment to the bench. He was appointed Queen's Counsel in 1974 and has been a member of the New York Bar since 1982. He was appointed Judge of the Tax Court of Canada in 1991 and Associate Chief Judge in February 2000. He has been the Associate Chief Justice since 2003.

David W. Chodikoff, lawyer, educator, author, musician, and adventure-seeker. He holds a Bachelor of Arts (Specialized Honours) from York University, a Master of Arts and Bachelor of Law degrees from Dalhousie University. David has appeared as Crown Counsel for the Government of Canada before the Ontario Court of Justice, the Superior Court of Justice, the Court of Appeal for Ontario, the Tax Court of Canada, the Federal Court of Canada-Trial Division and the Federal Court of Appeal of Canada. He is an instructor for the National Program for Advocacy Training, Department of Justice (Canada). David has also been an instructor for various components of the Bar Admissions Course of the Law Society of Upper Canada and for the Tax Litigation Skills Certificate Program (2001, 2002 and 2004) of The Advocates' Society. He is a frequent public speaker on the subject of advocacy.

Dr. Arthur Cockfield, H.B.A. (Western), LL.B. (Queen's), JSM, JSD (Stanford), is Associate Professor in the Faculty of Law at Queen's University. Prior to his appointment at Queen's University he practised at Goodmans LLP in Toronto, Canada. He has also taught at the Thomas Jefferson School of Law in San Diego, California. Professor Cockfield's tax publications have appeared in journals in the United States, Canada, Europe, and Asia. He is the author of *NAFTA Tax Law and Policy* (University of Toronto Press, forthcoming 2005), and *Cyberspace Law* (with Raymond Ku and Michelle Farber) (Aspen, 2002). Professor Cockfield has also written a novel entitled *The End*, published by SSI Publishing in 2004.

David G. Duff, B.A. Hons. (Queen's) M.A. (York), LL.B. (Toronto), M.A. (Toronto), LL.M. (Harvard), is Associate Professor at the University of Toronto Faculty of Law, where he teaches and writes in the areas of tax law, tax policy, and distributive justice. He was called to the Bar of Ontario in 1996. Prior to joining the Faculty, Professor Duff was a tax associate at the Toronto office of Stikeman Elliott LLP. Previously, he was a researcher with Ontario Fair Tax Commission, and a tax policy analyst with the Ontario Ministry of Finance. He is the author of a casebook, entitled *Canadian Income Tax Law*, as well as numerous articles on tax law and tax policy.

Harry E. Erlichman is a General Counsel with the Department of Justice (Canada) in Toronto specializing in Income Tax and GST. He has an LL.M. from Osgoode Hall Law School, and is the editor/contributing-author of *Tax Avoidance in Canada: The General Anti-Avoidance Rule.*

Lara Friedlander is an Associate at Osler Hoskin & Harcourt LLP where her practice focuses on corporate finance, financial products and mutual funds. Prior to joining Oslers, she was a member of the tax department of Stikeman Elliott LLP for three years following her call to the Bar of Ontario in 1997. She holds Masters of Law degrees from Columbia University and Osgoode Hall Law School and an LL.B. from the University of Toronto. During the 2002–2003 academic year, Lara was an Assistant Professor at McGill University where she taught taxation and corporate law.

Sandra Goldberg joined the Transfer Pricing and Competent Authority practice at Deloitte in 2001 after a 16-year career as Senior Counsel with the Department of Justice where she advised the Canada Revenue Agency (CRA) on a broad range of international tax matters. Currently, Sandra focuses her practice on transfer pricing, tax treaty issues, the mutual agreement procedures (APAs and double tax), international audit defence matters, including dispute resolution and competent authority proceedings.

Robert Goldstein is Senior Counsel with the Federal Prosecution Service, Department of Justice (Canada). He holds a B.A. and an M.A. from the University of Toronto, and an LL.B. from McGill University. Robert joined the Ontario Regional Office, Department of Justice in March 1990 as a civil litigator and he transferred to the Prosecution Service in 1992. He has conducted trials and appeals in all levels of the Courts of Ontario. Since 1997, Robert has focussed on regulatory and "white-collar" crime, primarily tax and GST fraud, but also money laundering, competition, copyright, bankruptcy, and environmental offences. He has published articles in the *Criminal Law Quarterly* and the *Advocate's Quarterly*, as well as in numerous internal Department of Justice publications. He is a regular lecturer at the Toronto Police College.

Peter H. Griffin is a Partner in the Toronto litigation firm of Lenczner Slaght Royce Smith Griffin LLP. Peter practises in a broad range of areas including commercial, securities, shareholder rights, insolvency, restructuring, professional negligence, life insurance and competition litigation. He is a Director of the Advocates' Society and a Fellow of the American College of Trial Lawyers.

Steven A. Hacker, CA, CBV, MBA, is a Senior Manager with Deloitte's Financial Advisory practice. He has ten years of business valuations, litigation, and transaction advisory experience. He has provided advice to, and prepared reports for clients in connection with mergers and acquisitions, income tax litigation, tax and estate planning, matrimonial property valuations, shareholder and partnership disputes, business interruption litigation and transfer pricing. His intangible asset valuation experience has included valuations of software, brands, asset management agreements, distribution networks, customer contracts, and customer relationships. Steven earned his MBA in 1984, and was qualified as a Chartered Accountant in 1986 and as a Chartered Business Valuator in 1998.

James L. Horvath, CA, FCBV, ASA, B. Math, M.B.A., is a partner at Deloitte specializing in business and securities valuation. Over the last thirty years, he has completed more than 3,000 valuations of businesses, securities, and related intellectual property. Jim has extensive international experience, having worked on valuations, mergers, and acquisitions in over 50 countries. He has testified as an expert witness in court before the Tax Court of Canada, various provincial courts, the Assessment Review Court, and in Arbitration hearings. In addition, he has acted as an arbitrator and sole valuator in resolving valuation-related matters.

Jim holds a B. Math (Double Honours) from the University of Waterloo and an MBA from McMaster University. He is qualified as a member of the Institute of Chartered Accountants of Ontario (CA), a Fellow of the Canadian Institute of Chartered Business Valuators (FCBV), an Accredited Senior Appraiser (ASA) of the American Society of Appraisers, and a Certified Fraud Examiner (CFE) of the Association of Certified Fraud Examiners. Jim is the author of numerous articles dealing with the valuation of businesses, computer software and other intellectual property. He is also the author of *Valuing Professional Practices*, and a contributing author/co-editor of *Commercial Square Foot Building Costs*. He is a frequent speaker on the subject of valuations.

William I. Innes, Counsel, Fraser Milner Casgrain LLP. He has practised in the areas of tax litigation, taxation, and estates and trusts since 1975. His practice includes all aspects of dispute resolution in taxation matters under both federal and provincial legislation, with a special emphasis on appeals under the *Income Tax Act* (Canada). In addition, he acts as counsel in matters of estate and trust law and services as an advisor to large charitable and non-profit institutions on issues of trusts, estates and taxation. He frequently appears as counsel before the Tax Court of Canada, the Federal Court, and the Federal Court of Appeal and has been named one of the top 500 lawyers in Canada by *L'Expert* for the past several years. He has also been named one of the world's leading tax advisors by Mondaq Professional Surveys.

Howard E. Johnson is a Partner at Campbell Valuation Partners Ltd. in Toronto, Canada. He has been involved in business valuations, acquisitions, divestitures, and related assignments throughout North America. Howard holds a B.Comm. from Concordia University, a Graduate degree in Public Accountancy from McGill University, and a Masters degree in Business Administration from McMaster University. Howard is a member of the Institute of Chartered Accountants of Ontario, the Society of Management Accountants of Ontario, the Canadian Institute of Chartered Business Valuators, the American Institute of Certified Public Accountants, and the Association for Investment Management and Research. He is co-author of the *Valuation of Business Interests* (The Canadian Institute of Chartered Accountants, 2001); and a contributing editor of *Canada Valuation Service.*

Hon. John I. Laskin is a Justice of the Court of Appeal for Ontario. Prior to his appointment to the court in 1994, Justice Laskin practised law at Fasken & Calvin, Laskin, Jack & Harris, and Davies, Ward & Beck. He was a member of the Canadian Human Rights Tribunal and served as counsel to several commissions of inquiry. He is a fellow, American College of Trial Lawyers. Justice Laskin has lectured and written extensively on written and oral advocacy and judgment writing. He is an instructor in and co-chair of the annual Judgment Writing Seminar of the Canadian Institute for the Administration of Justice and 2004 Chair of the NJI Appellate Judgment Writing Seminar, 2004. His most recent article, "What Persuades (or What's Going on Inside the Judge's Mind)," appeared in *The Advocates' Society Journal*, Vol. 23, No. 1, June 2004.

J. Milan Legris is Senior Counsel for AIC Ltd. and the Berkshire Group of Companies. Milan was previously the Vice-President of Tax, with the Berkshire Investment Group Inc. and Berkshire Securities Inc. He holds an LL.M. in US Taxation from the University of Miami (Florida), an LL.B. from the University of Ottawa and an H.B.Sc. from the University of Guelph. Milan was called to the bar in 1986 and has practised exclusively in the area of taxation since 1987.

Alan J. Lenczner, Q.C. is a Partner in Lenczner Slaght Royce Smith Griffin LLP, specializing in civil and administrative litigation, with an emphasis on securities and commercial cases. One of Canada's most sought-after trial counsel, Alan regularly appears before a wide variety of courts and tribunals across the country particularly in large and complex litigation matters. He has also appeared before the High Court and the Court of Appeal in England. Alan has taught trial advocacy at the Faculty of Law, University of Toronto and Osgoode Hall Law School, York University and teaches an annual one-week trial advocacy program for the Quebec Bar. Alan holds an M.A. and LL.B. (First Class Hon.) from the University of Toronto. He is a member of the Bars of Ontario, New Brunswick, Nova Scotia and British Columbia. He was appointed Q.C. in 1982. Alan is featured in the *L'Expert/American Lawyer Media Guide to the Top 500 Lawyers in Canada.*

Robert McMechan practises tax dispute resolution, tax litigation and related taxation law providing counsel to individuals and to small, medium and large-sized businesses. He is formerly General Counsel in the Tax Litigation Section of the Department of Justice (Canada) and served for two years as Senior Rulings Officer at Revenue Canada. Robert has been a frequent contributor to the Advocates' Society and the Canadian Tax Foundation programs, and has been a co-author of *Tax Court Practice©* with Gordon Bourgard since 1990. He contributes the Income Tax Administration chapter for the Law Society of Upper Canada Bar Admission Course materials, and is a lecturer, seminar leader, and tutor for the Bar Admission Course on taxation law. He was Chair of the Essentials of Tax Litigation programs for the Law Society in 1994 and 1999, and a member of the Ontario Bar Association Tax Section Executive from 1993 to 2003.

Blake M. Murray is a Senior Partner in the Taxation Department at Osler, Hoskin & Harcourt LLP. He specializes in taxation with a focus on international taxation and transfer pricing, dispute resolution (including litigation), and tax aspects of corporate finance, reorganizations, and merger and acquisitions. In 1989–90, Blake was Senior Counsel to the Standing Committee of the House of Commons on Finance and Economic Affairs with respect to the implementation of the goods and services tax.

L. Ross Oake is the President of Ross Oake & Associates Inc., a company involved in consulting and investigative work for private sector companies, governments, and regulatory agencies. He is formerly a Firm Director with Deloitte. Ross served for 22 years in the Royal Canadian Mounted Police where he specialized in commercial crime investigations. He has worked in numerous jurisdictions worldwide and is recognized as one of the leading commercial crime investigators in Canada, with particular expertise in the securities industry. He has designed and taught courses for the Canadian Police College, the Ontario Securities Commission, the Institute of

Charted Accountants, the Toronto Stock Exchange, and the Investment Dealers Association.

Robert Pardo is the founder and President of The Pardo Corporation, one of the world's leading developers of trading and technical analysis microcomputer software. Beginning with its release of Chartist, in 1983, his firm has continuously updated its software line with such programs as Lightning, Blast, Advanced Chartist, Advanced Trader, and Expert Trader. Bob is also a frequent contributor of articles to such magazines as *Futures, Technical Analysis of Stocks and Commodities,* and *Wall Street Micro Investor.* He is the author of *Design, Testing, and Optimization of Trading Systems.* He has testified as an expert witness before the Tax Court of Canada.

Clifford L. Rand B.A. (Hons.), LL.B. (McGill), LL.M. (Osgoode Hall) is a Partner of Stikeman Elliott LLP, practising income tax litigation. He was a law professor at the University of Windsor from 1984 to 1987. Cliff is the author of *Understanding the Income Tax Act* (Carswell) and has participated in and written papers for a number of conferences on tax matters, including those held by the Canadian Tax Foundation, the Law Society of Upper Canada, CCH, the Canadian Institute, the CGAA, and the Advocates' Society.

M. Craig Robertson, LL.B., M.A. and B.A. (Double Hons.), is a Firm Director with Deloitte. Prior to entering private practice, Craig was Legal Counsel to Revenue Canada where he was member of the GST/HST Policy Review Committee. He advised the Department of Finance on the implementation of the Harmonized Sales Tax, and participated on the Minister of National Revenue's Advisory Committee on the impact of e-commerce for Canada's revenue regimes. He also co-authored with Jim Vincze a series of articles for the Federated Press on the implications of e-commerce for federal and provincial sales taxes. Craig has been a frequent presenter at the Canadian Institute of Chartered Accountants' Commodity Tax Symposium, and has presented on GST issues to the Canadian Bar Association.

Hon. Marshall E. Rothstein, Justice of the Federal Court of Appeal. Prior to his appointment to the bench, Justice Rothstein practised with the Winnipeg firm of Aikins, MacAulay & Thorvaldson. He lectured in transportation law in the Faculty of Law, University of Manitoba for over twenty years and was an adjudicator under the *Manitoba Human Rights Act* and the *Canadian Human Rights Act.* He was appointed Queen's Counsel in 1979. Justice Rothstein was appointed Judge of the Federal Court Trial Division and ex officio member of the Court of Appeal, and appointed Judge of the Court Martial Appeal Court of Canada in 1992, and judicial member of the

Competition Tribunal from 1993–1999. In 1999, Justice Rothstein was appointed as a Judge of the Federal Court of Canada, Appeal Division.

Daniel Sandler is a Professor of Law at the University of Western Ontario and an Associate with Minden Gross Grafstein & Greenstein LLP, specializing in taxation. His practice focuses primarily on tax litigation and he has represented clients in disputes with the Canada Customs and Revenue Agency and the Ontario Ministry of Finance. From 1992–1995, he was a member of the Faculty of Law, University of Cambridge and a Research Fellow for the Institute for Fiscal Studies and the Chartered Institute of Taxation, both in London, England. He has served as a consultant to the Organization for Economic Co-operation and Development (OECD), the Auditor-General of Canada, and the Technical Committee on Business Taxation. He is Editor-in-Chief of *The International Guide to Advance Rulings* and co-editor of *Materials on Canadian Income Tax* (12th ed.).

Alan M. Schwartz is a Partner with Fasken Martineau DuMoulin LLP and is Chair of its National Tax Group. A significant part of his practice includes pleading cases in tax courts at all levels from the Tax Court to the Supreme Court of Canada. Alan has been involved in leading tax cases on the general anti-avoidance rule, the existence of a separate business, partnership reorganizations, asset classification, residence of trusts, and employment benefits. He is also involved in advising on estate planning and trusts. Alan has written numerous articles for the *Canadian Tax Journal, CA Magazine,* and the *Financial Post.* He has lectured at the Canadian Institute of Chartered Accountants In-Depth Tax Course of Corporation Reorganization and on the same topic at Revenue Canada. Alan is rated by the International Tax Review, Chambers, and *L'Expert* as one of the leading tax lawyers in Canada.

Jim Vincze is a Partner with Deloitte where he is the National Service Line Leader for Indirect Tax services. An internationally recognized expert in his field, he has been involved in the development of the sales tax code for Gambia and as a VAT advisor to the Republic of China. He has also served as a GST Advisor to the Canadian Department of Finance (Canada). Jim has written widely on topics related to Indirect Tax and has addressed these topics in speeches to the Canadian Tax Foundation, the Tax Executives Institute, and the Canadian Institute of Chartered Accountants. He was recognized by the International Tax Review (2004) as one of Canada's top six Indirect Tax practitioners. Also under his leadership, the Deloitte Indirect Tax practice was recognized as ranking first in Canada for 2003. Building and expanding the Indirect Tax practice in Canada is his major long-range goal. He holds a Masters degree in Economics.

Edward Yanoshita graduated in 2004 from Osgoode Hall Law School, completing the Taxation Law Stream. In his graduating year, he was the recipient of the Stikeman Elliott/Carswell National Tax Prize and the Osler, Hoskin & Harcourt LLP Research Prize in Corporate/Commercial Law. Edward also holds a B.A.Sc. (Honours) in Mechanical Engineering from the University of Toronto and is a registered Professional Engineer in Ontario. Prior to attending law school, Edward was an industrial equipment supplier and consultant to a diverse range of clients in the petrochemical, automotive, food, pharmaceutical, mining, power generation, oil & gas and public works sectors. He is a Past-President of the Ontario Pollution Control Equipment Association and a former Board member of the Water Environment Association of Ontario. Edward summered and is currently articling with Fasken Martineau DuMoulin LLP in Toronto.

Gary L. Zed is a Partner in the National Transfer Pricing and Competent Authority Group of Deloitte and the Canadian National Director of Deloitte's International Competent Authority Practice. Gary works closely with the firm's Canadian and global transfer pricing practice, as well as with international tax specialists, and is responsible for handling intergovernmental relations, double taxation issues, transfer pricing, and the Mutual Agreement Procedure under tax treaties. Prior to joining Deloitte, he held senior positions with both the Canada Revenue Agency (CRA) and the Department of Justice (Canada). He was the Deputy Director General of the International Tax Directorate at CRA, as well as the Canadian Competent Authority responsible for tax treaty administration. He also served as Director of Transfer Pricing and Competent Authority where he had overall national responsibility for transfer pricing issues and was responsible for directing all international audit matters and the competent authority program.